The Flower Adornment Sutra

An Annotated Translation of the Avataṃsaka Sutra

With a Commentarial Synopsis Of the Flower Adornment Sutra

Volume Two

Chapters 26 – 38

To refrain from doing any manner of evil,
to respectfully perform all varieties of good,
and to purify one's own mind—
This is the teaching of all buddhas.

The Ekottara Āgama Sūtra
(T02 n.125 p.551a 13–14)

A Note on the Proper Care of Dharma Materials

Traditional Buddhist cultures treat books on Dharma as sacred. Hence it is considered disrespectful to place them in a low position, to read them when lying down, or to place them where they might be damaged by food or drink.

The Flower Adornment Sutra

The Great Expansive
Buddha's Flower Adornment Sutra

An Annotated English Translation of the Avataṃsaka Sutra
By Bhikshu Dharmamitra

With a Commentarial Synopsis Of the Flower Adornment Sutra

Volume Two

Kalavinka Press
Seattle, Washington
www.kalavinkapress.org

KALAVINKA PRESS
8603 39TH AVE SW
SEATTLE, WA 98136 USA
(WWW.KALAVINKAPRESS.ORG)

Kalavinka Press is associated with the Kalavinka Dharma Association, a non-profit organized exclusively for religious educational purposes as allowed within the meaning of section 501(c)3 of the Internal RevenueCode. Kalavinka Dharma Association was founded in 1990 and gained formal approval in 2004 by the United States Internal Revenue Service as a 501(c)3 non-profit organization to which all donations are tax deductible.

Donations to KDA are accepted by mail and on the Kalavinka website where numerous free Dharma translations are available.

Kalavinka Buddhist Classics Book 15 / Edition: HY-EO-1022-1.0

This Volume Two ISBN: 978-1-935413-36-3 / LCCN: 2022946845
(Vol. 1 ISBN: 978-1-935413-35-6 / Vol. 3 ISBN: 978-1-935413-37-0)
The Three-Volume Set ISBN: 978-1-935413-34-9

Publisher's Cataloging-in-Publication Data

Names: Dharmamitra, Bhikshu, 1948, translator. | Śikṣānanda, 652 CE, translator.
Title: The Flower Adornment Sutra. An Annotated Translation of the Avataṃsaka Sutra. With a Commentarial Synopsis of the Flower Adornment Sutra.
Other titles: *Mahāvaipulya Buddha Avataṃsaka Sūtra*. English
Description: HY-EO-1022-1.0 | Seattle, Washington : Kalavinka Press, 2022. | Series: Kalavinka Buddhist Classics, Book 15 | Includes bibliographical references. | Summary: "The Flower Adornment Sutra is Bhikshu Dharmamitra's extensively annotated original translation of the *Mahāvaipulya Buddha Avataṃsaka Sūtra* or 'The Great Expansive Buddha's Flower Adornment Sutra' rendered from Tripitaka Master Śikṣānanda's circa 699 CE Sanskrit-to-Chinese 80-fascicle translation as *Da Fangguang Fo Huayan Jing* (大方廣佛華嚴經 / Taisho Vol. 10, no. 279). It consists of 39 chapters that introduce an interpenetrating, infinitely expansive, and majestically grand multiverse of countless buddha worlds while explaining in great detail the cultivation of the bodhisattva path to buddhahood, most notably the ten highest levels of bodhisattva practice known as 'the ten bodhisattva grounds.' To date, this is the first and only complete English translation of the *Avataṃsaka Sutra*."-- Provided by publisher.
Identifiers: LCCN 2022946845 | 3-vol. set ISBN 978-1-935413-34-9 (paperback). This Volume Two ISBN: 978-1-935413-36-3
Subjects: LCSH: Tripiṭaka. Sūtrapiṭaka. Avataṃsakasūtra. | Bodhisattva stages (Mahayana Buddhism)
LC record available at https://lccn.loc.gov/2022946845

Kalavinka Press books are printed on acid-free paper.
Cover and interior designed by Bhikshu Dharmamitra.
Printed in the United States of America

Volume Two Table of Contents

Chapter 26 – The Ten Grounds 871
Chapter 27 – The Ten Samādhis 1057
Chapter 28 – The Ten Superknowledges 1151
Chapter 29 – The Ten Patiences 1165
Chapter 30 – Asaṃkhyeyas 1189
Chapter 31 – Life Spans 1205
Chapter 32 – The Bodhisattva Abodes 1207
Chapter 33 – The Inconceivable Dharmas of the Buddhas 1211
Chapter 34 – The Ocean of Major Marks of the Tathāgata's Ten Bodies 1253
Chapter 35 – Qualities of the Light of the Tathāgata's Secondary Signs 1271
Chapter 36 – The Practices of Samantabhadra 1281
Chapter 37 – The Manifestation of the Tathāgata 1303
Chapter 38 – Transcending the World 1383
Volume Two Endnotes 1589

The Flower Adornment Sutra

Volume Two

The Great Expansive
Buddha's Flower Adornment Sutra

The Mahāvaipulya Buddha Avataṃsaka Sūtra

(Taisho T10, no. 279)

Translated under Imperial Auspices by
Tripiṭaka Master Śikṣānanda from the State of Khotan

English Translation by Bhikshu Dharmamitra

Chapter 26
The Ten Grounds

At that time, the Bhagavat was residing in the Maṇi Jewel Treasury Palace of the Paranirmita Vaśavartin Heaven King, together with an assembly of great bodhisattvas. All of those bodhisattvas had already achieved irreversibility in their progression toward *anuttara-samyak-saṃbodhi*. They had all come to assemble there from the worlds of other regions.

They dwelt in the realm of knowledge possessed by all bodhisattvas. They were tirelessly diligent in entering those places entered by the knowledge of all *tathāgatas*. They were well able to manifest many different sorts of endeavors accomplished by the spiritual superknowledges. They taught and trained all beings and, in doing so, never erred in their timing.

In order to fulfill all of the great vows of the bodhisattva, they remained diligent in the cultivation of all practices, doing so in all worlds, in all kalpas, and in all lands, never desisting even briefly. They had become completely equipped with the bodhisattva's merit and knowledge, the provisions assisting realization of the path, and were never deficient in benefiting beings everywhere. They had achieved the most ultimate perfection in all bodhisattvas' wisdom and skillful means.

They manifested entry into *saṃsāra* as well as nirvāṇa, and yet they still refrained from neglecting their cultivation of the bodhisattva practices. They were skillful in entering all of the bodhisattva's *dhyāna* concentrations, liberations, samādhis, *samāpattis*, spiritual superknowledges, and clear knowledges.[1]

They achieved sovereign mastery in all of their undertakings. They had already garnered all of the freely exercised spiritual powers of the bodhisattva such that, in but a moment, without moving in the slightest, they were all able to go forth to join the assemblies gathered at the *bodhimaṇḍas*[2] of all *tathāgatas* to serve therein as leaders for those congregations, and to request that the buddhas expound the Dharma.

They served there as guardians of the wheel of the right Dharma[3] of all buddhas. With expansively magnanimous minds, they made offerings to and served all buddhas and were always diligent in their cultivation and implementation of all works performed by all bodhisattvas. Their bodies appeared everywhere in all worlds. Their voices reached everywhere throughout the ten directions of the Dharma realm.[4] Their minds and their knowledge were unimpeded. They everywhere saw all bodhisattvas of the three periods of time. They had already entirely cultivated and brought all meritorious qualities to perfect fulfillment. Even in an ineffable[5] number of kalpas, one would still be unable to entirely describe them all. Their names were:[6]

Vajragarbha Bodhisattva;
Jewel Treasury Bodhisattva;
Lotus Blossom Treasury Bodhisattva;
Treasury of Qualities Bodhisattva;
Treasury of Lotus Qualities Bodhisattva;
Solar Treasury Bodhisattva;
Sūrya Treasury Bodhisattva;
Stainless Moon Treasury Bodhisattva;
Treasury of Adornments Manifesting in All Lands Bodhisattva;
Treasury of Vairocana's Knowledge Bodhisattva;[7]
Treasury of Sublime Qualities Bodhisattva;
Treasury of Candana's Qualities Bodhisattva;
Treasury of Floral Qualities Bodhisattva;
Treasury of Kusuma's Qualities Bodhisattva;
Treasury of Utpala's Qualities Bodhisattva;
Treasury of Celestial Qualities Bodhisattva;
Treasury of Merit Bodhisattva;
Treasury of Unimpeded Pure Knowledge Qualities Bodhisattva;[8]
Treasury of Meritorious Qualities Bodhisattva;
Treasury of Nārāyaṇa's Qualities Bodhisattva;
Treasury of Stainlessness Bodhisattva;
Treasury of Defilement Transcendence Bodhisattva;
Treasury of Adornment with All Forms of Eloquence Bodhisattva;
Treasury of the Great Net of Light Rays Bodhisattva;
Treasury of the King of the Pure Light of Awesome Qualities Bodhisattva;
Treasury of the King of Great Qualities' Gold-Adorned Brilliance Bodhisattva;
Treasury of Pure Qualities Adorned with All the Marks Bodhisattva;
Treasury of Adornment with Flaming Vajra Radiance and the Marks of Merit Bodhisattva;
Treasury of Radiant Flames Bodhisattva;

Treasury of Constellation King's Radiance Bodhisattva;
Treasury of Spacious Unimpeded Knowledge Bodhisattva;[9]
Treasury of Unimpeded Sublime Sound Bodhisattva;
Treasury of Dhāraṇī Qualities and Vows Sustaining All Beings Bodhisattva;
Treasury of Oceanic Adornments Bodhisattva;
Treasury of Sumeru-Like Qualities Bodhisattva;
Treasury of All Qualities of Purity Bodhisattva;
Tathāgata Treasury Bodhisattva;
Treasury of Buddha Qualities Bodhisattva; and
Liberation Moon Bodhisattva.

An assembly of bodhisattva-mahāsattvas[10] such as these was present there in countless, measureless, boundless, matchless, innumerable, indescribable, inconceivable, immeasurable, and ineffable numbers.[11] Vajragarbha Bodhisattva served as their head.

At that time, Vajragarbha Bodhisattva, aided by the spiritual power of the Buddha, entered "the bodhisattva's great wisdom light samādhi."[12] After he entered this samādhi, from beyond a number of worlds in each of the ten directions as numerous as the atoms in ten *koṭis*[13] of buddha lands, buddhas as numerous as the atoms in ten *koṭis* of buddha lands, all of them identically named "Vajragarbha," immediately appeared directly before him and uttered these words:

It is good indeed, good indeed, Vajragarbha, that you have become able to enter this bodhisattva's great wisdom light samādhi.

Son of Good Family, these are a number of buddhas from each of the ten directions as numerous as the atoms in ten *koṭis* of buddha lands who have all joined in providing assistance to you here. This is due to the power of the original vows of Vairocana Tathāgata, Worthy of Offerings, of Right and Universal Enlightenment,[14] and because of his awesome spiritual powers. It is also because of your supreme powers of knowledge and because they wish to influence you to describe for all bodhisattvas the inconceivable Dharma light of all buddhas, in particular doing so:

To cause their entry into the grounds of knowledge;
To bring about their gathering together of all roots of goodness;
To enable their skillful selective differentiation of all dharmas of the Buddha;
To bring about their vast knowing of all dharmas;
To enable their skillfulness in the ability to expound on Dharma;
To facilitate their purification of non-discriminating knowledge;
To ensure their non-defilement by any worldly dharma;

To facilitate their purification of roots of world-transcending goodness;
To facilitate their acquisition of the realm of inconceivable knowledge;
To cause their acquisition of the realm of knowledge of those possessed of all-knowledge;
To also cause their acquisition, from beginning to end, of the bodhisattva's ten grounds;
To bring about the reality-accordant explanation of the differentiating aspects of the bodhisattva's ten grounds;
To enable objectively focused mindfulness of all dharmas of the Buddha;
To facilitate their cultivation and differentiation of the dharmas that are free of the contaminants,[15]
To facilitate their skillful adornment through excellence in selection and contemplation employing the light of great wisdom;[16]
To cause their skillful entry into the gate of absolutely definitive knowledge;
To enable them to be fearless in providing sequential expositions wherever they may abide;
To facilitate their acquisition of the light of unimpeded eloquence;
To enable their abiding on the ground of great eloquence with skillful resolve;
To enable their bearing in mind the bodhisattva's resolve without ever forgetting it;
To bring about their ripening of beings in all realms of existence;
And to facilitate their realization of definitive awakening that reaches everywhere.

Son of Good Family, you should eloquently explain the different skillful means dharmas associated with these Dharma gateways, doing so:

To receive the Buddha's spiritual power through being aided by the light of the Tathāgata's knowledge;
To facilitate the purification of one's own roots of goodness;
To everywhere purify the Dharma realm;
To everywhere draw forth beings;
To deeply enter the Dharma body and knowledge body;
To receive the Buddha's consecrating anointing of the crown;
To acquire the most supremely lofty and grand body in the entire world;
To step entirely beyond all worldly paths;

To purify roots of world-transcending goodness;
And in order to completely fulfill the cognition of all-knowledge.

At that time, the buddhas of the ten directions bestowed these things on Vajragarbha Bodhisattva:

They bestowed a body that none could outshine;
They bestowed the skill of unimpeded eloquent expression;
They bestowed skillfully differentiating pure knowledge;
They bestowed the power of skillful remembrance invulnerable to forgetfulness,
They bestowed thoroughly decisive and completely understanding intelligence;[17]
They bestowed awakened knowledge that extends to all places;
They bestowed the freely exercised powers associated with realization of the path;
They bestowed the fearlessnesses of the *tathāgatas*;[18]
They bestowed the Omniscient Ones' eloquence and knowledges[19] that contemplate and distinguish all Dharma gateways;
And they bestowed the adornments of all *tathāgatas'* supremely sublime and utterly perfected body, speech, and mind.

Why did this occur?

Because acquisition of this samādhi dharma entails just such an occurrence;
Because this was generated by his original vows;
Because of his having well purified his resolute intentions;[20]
Because of his having well cleansed the sphere of knowledge;[21]
Because of his having well accumulated the provisions assisting realization of the path;[22]
Because of his having well cultivated and refined whatever he engaged in;
Because his mindfulness made him fit as a vessel able to contain measurelessly many dharmas;[23]
Because of the knowledge that he was possessed of pure resolute faith;[24]
Because of his having acquired the comprehensive retention *dhāraṇīs*[25] in which he was free of errors;
And because of his having been well-sealed by the seal of knowledge of the Dharma realm.[26]

At that time, the buddhas of the ten directions each extended their right hands and rubbed the crown of Vajragarbha Bodhisattva's head. After they had rubbed the top of his head, Vajragarbha Bodhisattva emerged from samādhi and, addressing everyone in that congregation of bodhisattvas, he informed them as follows:

Sons of the Buddha, the vows of the bodhisattva are excellent in their resolve, unmixed, imperceptible, as vast as the Dharma realm itself, and as ultimately far-reaching as empty space. They extend to the very bounds of future time and everywhere throughout all buddha lands. They serve to rescue and protect all beings, are carried out under the protection of all buddhas, and enter into the grounds of knowledge of all buddhas throughout the past, the future, and the present.

Sons of the Buddha, what then are the grounds of knowledge of the bodhisattva-mahāsattvas? Sons of the Buddha, there are ten grounds of knowledge of the bodhisattva-mahāsattvas. All buddhas of the past, the future, and the present have proclaimed them, will proclaim them, and do now proclaim them. In this same way, I too proclaim them here. What then are these ten? They are:[27]

First, the Ground of Joyfulness;
Second, the Ground of Stainlessness;
Third, the Ground of Shining Light;
Fourth, the Ground of Blazing Brilliance;[28]
Fifth, the Difficult-to-Conquer Ground;
Sixth, the Ground of Direct Presence;
Seventh, the Far-Reaching Ground;
Eighth, the Ground of Immovability;
Ninth, the Ground of Excellent Intelligence;[29]
Tenth, the Ground of the Dharma Cloud.

Sons of the Buddha, these ten bodhisattva grounds have been proclaimed by all buddhas of the three periods of time. They have proclaimed them in the past, will proclaim them in the future, and do proclaim them now.

Sons of the Buddha, I have never observed any among all the buddha lands in which the *tathāgata* therein failed to set forth an explanation of these ten grounds. Why is that? These constitute the bodhisattva-mahāsattvas' most supreme path to the realization of bodhi as well as the gateway to the light of the pure Dharma. We refer here to the differentiation and explication of the bodhisattva grounds.

Sons of the Buddha, these stations are inconceivable. We refer here to all bodhisattvas' knowledge as it develops in accordance with their realizations.

Then, having set forth the names of these ten grounds of the bodhisattva, Vajragarbha Bodhisattva fell silent, remained in place, and did not then proceed to present a differentiating explanation of them.

At this time, having heard the names of the bodhisattvas' ten grounds without hearing any attendant explanation of them, that entire congregation of bodhisattvas gazed up at him with thirst-like anticipation as they thought to themselves, "Due to what causes and what conditions does Vajragarbha Bodhisattva merely set forth the names of the bodhisattvas' ten grounds while not then proceeding to explain them?"

Knowing the thoughts in the minds of those in that great assembly, Liberation Moon Bodhisattva then used verses to ask Vajragarbha Bodhisattva:[30]

Why is it that you who are possessed of pure awakening
and are replete with the qualities of mindfulness and knowledge
speak of these supremely sublime grounds, but then,
even with the power to do so, still refrain from explaining them?

All of those here are decisively resolute in all things,
valiantly brave, and entirely free of any timidity.
Why then would one set forth the names of the grounds
and yet still refrain from beginning to expound on them for us?

As for the sublime meanings and import of the grounds,
the members of this congregation all wish to hear them.
Their minds are free of timidity.
Hence they wish you will differentiate and explain these for them.

Those in this congregation are entirely pure,
have abandoned indolence, and are strict in their pristine purity.
They are able to remain solidly unmoving
and are replete with meritorious qualities and wisdom.[31]

After looking at each other, they have all become filled with reverence
and have trained the focus of their gaze up at you.
In this, they are like bees when they bring to mind fine honey or
like one who is thirsty when he longs for the elixir of sweet-dew.

At that time, having heard him say this, the greatly wise and fearless Vajragarbha Bodhisattva, wishing to cause the assembled congregation to feel delighted in mind, spoke verses for the sake of all those sons of the Buddha:

The matter of the bodhisattva's practices on the grounds
is the most supreme of all and is the origin of all buddhas.
To reveal them through a differentiating explanation
is the foremost of all rare and difficult endeavors.

This is extremely subtle and difficult to perceive.
It transcends thought and steps beyond the mind ground.

It produces the domain realized by the Buddha.
Those who hear of it may all be thrown into confusion.

It is those whose minds have a capacity for retention as solid as vajra,
who possess profound faith in the Buddha's supreme knowledge,
and who know the mind ground as devoid of any self
who are then capable of hearing this supreme Dharma.

Like a mural painted in space
and like the appearance of wind in empty space—
The knowledge of the Muni is of this very sort,
for it is very difficult to see using differentiating explanations.

As I call to mind the wisdom of the Buddha,
the most supremely inconceivable of matters,
I see that no one in the world would be able to accept it.
Hence I fall silent and no longer speak.

At that time, having heard him declare this, Liberation Moon Bodhisattva then addressed Vajragarbha Bodhisattva, saying:

O Son of the Buddha, those in this assembly that has gathered together here:

Have well purified their resolute intentions;[32]
Have well cleansed their thoughts;
Have well cultivated all of the practices;
Have well accumulated the provisions for realization of the path,[33]
Have been well able to draw close to hundreds of thousands of *koṭis* of buddhas;
Have perfected countless meritorious qualities and roots of goodness;
Have abandoned delusion;
Have become free of the defilements;
Are possessed of resolute intentions and resolute faith;
And, as they abide in the Buddha's Dharma, do not follow other sorts of teachings.

It would be good indeed, O Son of the Buddha, if, having here received the aid of the Buddha's spiritual powers, you would expound on these matters for their sakes. All of these bodhisattvas are able to achieve realization of such extremely profound stations as these.

At that time, Liberation Moon Bodhisattva, wishing to restate his meaning, spoke verses, saying:

Please speak on what is most conducive to peace and security,
these unsurpassable practices of the bodhisattva,

presenting a differentiating explanation of all of the grounds,
the purification of knowledge, and realization of right enlightenment.

Those in this congregation are free of all defilements,
are entirely bright and pristine in resolve and understanding,
have rendered service to countless buddhas,
and are able to realize the meaning of these grounds.

At that time, Vajragarbha Bodhisattva responded by saying:

O Son of the Buddha, although those within this assembled congregation have well purified their thought, have abandoned delusion and doubts, and within the extremely profound Dharma, do not follow others' teachings, still, there are yet other beings possessed of only inferior understanding who, on hearing of these extremely profound and inconceivable matters, would then generate numerous doubts due to which they would consequently suffer all manner of ruin and torment for a long time. It is because I feel pity for those of this sort that I have therefore fallen silent.

At that time, Vajragarbha Bodhisattva, wishing to once again state his meaning, thereupon spoke these verses:

Although those in this congregation are pure, of vast wisdom,
of extremely deep and brilliant acuity in their selective abilities,
are possessed of minds as immovable as the king of mountains,
and are as invulnerable to overturning as the great oceans—

Still, others, not long-tenured in practice, not yet understanding,
acting in accord with consciousness and thus not with knowledge—
Hearing this, they will raise doubts and fall into wretched destinies.
It is due to pity for those of this sort that I therefore do not speak.

At that time, Liberation Moon Bodhisattva again addressed Vajragarbha Bodhisattva, saying:

O Son of the Buddha, aided by the spiritual powers of the Buddha, please do present here a differentiating exposition of these inconceivable dharmas. These persons will be afforded the protective mindfulness of the *tathāgatas* and will consequently bring forth faith and acceptance.

And how could this be? Whenever an explanation of the ten grounds is set forth, the Dharma of all bodhisattvas is such that they should be afforded the protective mindfulness of the buddhas in this way. Due to having been afforded the protective mindfulness of the buddhas, they will then be able to bring forth heroic valor in cultivating these grounds of knowledge.

And why is this? This is because these constitute what the bodhisattvas practice from the very beginning and utilize in perfecting all dharmas of the buddhas. This is analogous to the circumstance involved in the writing of words wherein everything in the realm of counting and description relies upon the alphabet[34] as its origin and also relies upon the alphabet in the end. There is not even the most minor increment of this that departs from the alphabet.

O Son of the Buddha, all dharmas of the Buddha in every case rely upon the ten grounds as their very origin and also rely upon the ten grounds in the end as they are cultivated and perfected and then culminate in all-knowledge.

Therefore, O Son of the Buddha, please expound on these matters for our sakes. These persons will most certainly be afforded the protection of the *tathāgatas* through which they will be caused to bring forth faith and acceptance.

At that time, Liberation Moon Bodhisattva, wishing to restate his meaning, thereupon spoke these verses:

Good indeed! O Son of the Buddha, please do expound
on the practices taken up in progressing into bodhi's grounds.
Of all of the ten directions' sovereignly masterful Honored Ones,
none fail to hold these roots of knowledge in protective mindfulness.

These bases of establishment in knowledge are also ultimate,
for all the dharmas of the Buddha grow forth directly from them
just as all writing and counting are but expressions of their alphabets.
So too it is with Buddha's Dharma in its reliance on the grounds.

At that time, that entire congregation of great bodhisattvas, simultaneously and with a single united voice, uttered verses to Vajragarbha Bodhisattva, saying:

[May it be that you] of supremely sublime and stainless knowledge
as well as boundless eloquence in differentiation
will expound with profound and exquisite phrases
that correspond to the supreme meaning.

[May you] whose pure practice is maintained with mindfulness,
who have ten powers and have gathered the meritorious qualities
proceed to differentiate their meanings with eloquence
and present the exposition of these most supreme grounds.

With concentration, moral precepts, and accumulated right thought,
as well as transcendence of arrogance and wrong views,
this congregation is entirely free of doubting thoughts
and hence wishes only to hear a skillful proclamation.

We are like the thirsty thinking about cool water,
like the hungry recalling exquisite cuisine,

like the sick calling to mind an especially fine physician,
and like bees craving fine honey.
We are all just like these
in our wishing to hear this sweet-dew Dharma.

Good indeed it would be, you of such vast knowledge.
We only pray that you will expound on the entry into the grounds,
on accomplishment of the ten powers' unimpeded realization,
and on all of the practices of the well-gone ones.

At that time, the Bhagavat emitted from between his eyebrows a pure light known as "the flaming light of bodhisattva powers," a brilliance attended by a retinue of a hundred thousand *asaṃkhyeyas*[35] of light rays. It everywhere illuminated all worlds of the ten directions, having none it failed to entirely pervade. The sufferings of the three wretched destinies then all subsided. It also illuminated the assemblies in attendance on all *tathāgatas*, revealed the inconceivable powers of the buddhas, and also shone upon the bodies of all of the bodhisattvas in all worlds throughout the ten directions who were then being aided by all buddhas in the proclamation of Dharma. After it had done this, it then ascended into space, formed an immense terrace made of a net of light clouds, and then remained there.

At that time, the buddhas of the ten directions all proceeded in this very same manner, emitting a pure light from between their eyebrows wherein that light, its retinue of light rays, and its actions all manifested in just the same manner. In addition, they illuminated this Sahā World, the Buddha, and his great assembly, and then, after shining on the person of Vajragarbha Bodhisattva and his lion throne, those rays ascended up into empty space and formed an immense terrace made of a curtain of light clouds. Then, from within that terrace of light, through the awesome spiritual powers of the buddhas, there then resounded the proclamation of verses, stating:

The buddhas, the equals of the unequaled, are like empty space[36]
in their possession of the ten powers and countless supreme qualities.
They are the most superior of men, supreme in the entire world.
Here they augment the Dharma of the Lion of the Śākya Clan.

Son of the Buddha, you should take on the powers of the buddhas,
open forth the most supreme treasury of this Dharma king,
and employ Buddha's awesome powers to distinguish and explain
the supreme and sublime practices of the grounds' vast knowledge.

Where one is afforded the assistance of the well-gone ones,
one will receive the entry of the Dharma jewel into one's mind.

When one gains sequential fulfillment of the grounds' stainlessness,
he shall then also completely embody a *tathāgata*'s ten powers.

Though residing amidst an ocean's waters or in kalpa-ending fires,
those able to accept this Dharma will certainly be able to hear it.
Wherever someone doubts it or has no faith in it,
he will never be able to hear ideas such as these.

You should expound on the grounds' path of supreme knowledge,
on their entry, abiding, and progressively sequential cultivation,
and on the birth of Dharma knowledge from the domains of practice,
doing so because this will provide benefit to all beings.

At that time, Vajragarbha Bodhisattva surveyed the ten directions and, wishing to enable those in that immense assembly to increase their pure faith, thereupon spoke these verses:

The path of the *tathāgatas,* the great rishis,
is subtle, sublime, and difficult to know.
It is not perceptible through thought nor by abandoning thought.
If one seeks to perceive it in that way, it cannot thereby be realized.
It is without either production or destruction
and is by nature pure and constantly quiescent.

For those who abandon defilement and possess brilliant sagacity,
it is the place in which their knowledge is put into practice.
Its own nature is fundamentally empty, quiescently still,
devoid of duality, and endless.

It brings about liberation from all of the rebirth destinies
and the abiding in a state of uniform identity with nirvāṇa itself.
It has no beginning, has no middle, and has no end.
It cannot be described through words or phrases,
utterly transcends the three periods of time,
and, in character, is comparable to empty space.

The quiescence in which the Buddha courses
cannot be reached through any verbal description.
The practices that are taken up on the grounds are also of this sort,
difficult to describe and difficult for one to be able to accept.

The realm of the Buddha, produced through knowledge,
is not a path accessible through thought or by abandoning thought.
It is not a gate entered by aggregates, sense realms, or sense bases.
It is known by cognition, but not reached by the intellectual mind.

Like the track of a bird through the air,
it is difficult to describe and difficult to show.
In this same manner, the meanings associated with the ten grounds
cannot be entirely fathomed by the mind's intellectual faculty.

Kindness, compassion, and the power of vows
bring forth the practices through which one may enter the grounds
and sequentially realize perfect fulfillment of the mind.
The practices of knowledge are not the domain of mental reflection.

This realm is difficult to perceive.
It can be known but cannot be described.
It is due to the powers of the buddhas that one expounds on them.
You should all receive them in reverence.

Such knowledge-entering practice as this
cannot be completely described even in a *koṭi* of kalpas.
Hence I shall now merely set forth a summarizing explanation
of their genuine meaning, leaving nothing unaddressed.

Attend to this in single-minded reverence as,
aided by the buddhas' powers, I speak
the subtle and sublime voice of the supreme Dharma
in a manner compatible with analogies' phrasings.

The boundless spiritual powers of the buddhas
all arrive here and enter my person.
Of this circumstance so difficult to proclaim,
I shall now describe but a minor measure.

The First Ground

The Joyfulness Ground[37]

Sons of the Buddha, suppose there is a being:

Who has deeply planted roots of goodness;
Who has well cultivated the practices;
Who has well accumulated the provisions facilitating realization of the path;[38]
Who has practiced well the making of offerings to the buddhas;
Who has well accumulated the white dharmas of pristine purity;
Who has been skillfully drawn forth by the good spiritual guide;
Who has well purified his resolute intentions;
Who has established himself in the vast resolve;
Who has developed vast understanding;
And who has brought forth presently manifest kindness and compassion, [having done so]:
For the sake of the quest to acquire the knowledge of the Buddha;
For the sake of gaining the ten powers;
For the sake of realizing the great fearlessnesses;
For the sake of gaining the buddhas' dharma of uniformly equal regard for all;
For the sake of coming to the rescue of all worlds;
For the sake of purifying the great kindness and great compassion;
For the sake of gaining the knowledge that knows everything without exception throughout the ten directions;
For the sake of bringing about the unimpeded purification of all buddha lands;
For the sake of knowing all three periods of time in a single instant; and
For the sake of fearlessly turning the great wheel of Dharma.

Son of the Buddha, the bodhisattva's generation of such resolve:

Takes the great compassion as foremost;
Takes wisdom as its predominant condition;
Is subsumed within skillful means;
Is sustained by the most superior resolute intentions;
[Is aided by] the measureless powers of the Tathāgata;
[Is accompanied by] skillful contemplation and assessment of beings' strength of courage and strength of knowledge;

[Is implemented with] the directly manifested unimpeded knowledge;
Is accordant with spontaneous knowledge;[39]
Is able to take on all dharmas of the Buddha in using wisdom in transformative teaching;
And is as vast as the Dharma realm, as ultimately extensive as empty space, and so enduring as to reach the very end of future time.

Son of the Buddha, when the bodhisattva first brings forth this resolve, he immediately:

Steps beyond the grounds of the common person;
Enters the station of the bodhisattva;
Takes birth into the clan of the *tathāgatas;*
Becomes such that no one can claim his lineage is possessed of any fault;
Leaves behind worldly destinies;
Enters the world-transcending path;
Acquires the bodhisattva dharmas;
Abides in the bodhisattva abodes;
Equally enters the three periods of time;
And becomes definitely bound to realize the unexcelled bodhi in the lineage of the *tathāgatas.*

The bodhisattva who dwells in dharmas such as these is known as one who dwells on the Ground of Joyfulness, this on account of his being imperturbable.

Son of the Buddha, abiding on the Ground of Joyfulness, the bodhisattva is completely endowed with:

Abundant joy;
Abundant pure faith;
Abundant fond delight;
Abundant happiness;
Abundant exultation;
Abundant ebullience;
Abundant valiant fortitude;
Abundant disinclination to disputatiousness;
Abundant harmlessness;
And abundant disinclination to anger.[40]

Son of the Buddha, the bodhisattva dwelling on this Ground of Joyfulness:

Becomes joyful due to calling to mind the buddhas;
Becomes joyful due to calling to mind the Dharma of the buddhas;
Becomes joyful due to calling to mind the bodhisattvas;
Becomes joyful due to calling to mind the conduct practiced by the bodhisattvas;
Becomes joyful due to calling to mind the pure *pāramitās;*
Becomes joyful due to calling to mind the exceptional supremacy of the bodhisattva grounds;
Becomes joyful due to calling to mind the indestructibility of the bodhisattvas;
Becomes joyful due to calling to mind the Tathāgata's teaching of beings;
Becomes joyful due to calling to mind the ability to cause beings to acquire benefit;
And becomes joyful due to calling to mind entry into all *tathāgatas'* knowledge and skillful means.

He also has this thought:

I become joyful due to turning away from and abandoning all worldly states;
I become joyful due to drawing close to all buddhas;
I become joyful due to departing far from the grounds of the common person;
I become joyful due to drawing near to the grounds of wisdom;[41]
I become joyful due to eternally cutting off any vulnerability to entering the wretched destinies;
I become joyful due to serving as a place of refuge for all beings;
I become joyful due to seeing all the *tathāgatas;*
I become joyful due to being born into the domain of the buddhas;
I become joyful due to becoming of the same nature as all bodhisattvas;
And I become joyful due to leaving behind the fear of all circumstances that would cause hair-raising terror.

Why is it that, once this bodhisattva has gained the Ground of Joyfulness, he abandons all forms of fearfulness? In particular, they are:

The fear of failing to survive;
The fear of a bad reputation;
The fear of death;
The fear of rebirth in the wretched destinies;
And the fear of the awesomeness of great assemblies.[42]

He succeeds in forever leaving behind all such forms of fearfulness. And why is this? It is because this bodhisattva has abandoned any perception of a self. Thus he does not even cherish his own body. How much the less might he cherish any provisions or valuables it happens to possess. As a consequence, he is entirely free of any fear of failing to survive.

He does not hope for or seek out offerings from others. Rather, he devotes himself solely to providing for and making gifts to all beings. Consequently he has no fear of a bad reputation.

Because he has abandoned the view that conceives the existence of a self and because he does not perceive any existence of a self, he is therefore entirely free of any fear of death.

He realizes that once he dies, he will definitely not be reborn apart from the buddhas and the bodhisattvas. Consequently he is entirely free of any fear of falling into the wretched destinies.

He thinks, "That to which I aspire is without equal anywhere in the world. How much the less might there be anything superior to it?" Consequently, he is entirely free of any fear of the awesomeness of great assemblies.

Thus it is that the bodhisattva leaves far behind all such circumstances that might otherwise cause fear and hair-raising terror.

Son of the Buddha, this bodhisattva takes the great compassion as foremost. He is possessed of a vast aspiring resolve that no one could obstruct or destroy. Thus he redoubles his diligent cultivation of all roots of goodness, thereby achieving complete success in his aims, in particular doing so:

Through making faith predominant;
Through pure faith;[43]
Through the purity of his resolute faith;[44]
Through the resolute decisiveness of his faith;
Through bringing forth compassionate pity;
Through perfecting the great kindness;
Through remaining free of any tendency to become weary or withdraw from his efforts;
Through being adorned with a sense of shame and dread of blame;
Through perfecting mental pliancy;
Through respectfully according with and venerating the buddhas' teaching dharmas;
Through insatiably cultivating and accumulating roots of goodness day and night;
Through drawing near to good spiritual guides;

Through always cherishing and delighting in the Dharma;
Through insatiably pursuing extensive learning;
Through engaging in right contemplative investigation accordant with the Dharma he has learned;
Through ensuring that his mind remains free of dependent attachments;
Through not indulging any attachment to receiving offerings, becoming renowned, or receiving expressions of reverence from others;
Through not seeking for any life-supporting material possessions;
Through tirelessly bringing forth jewel-like resolve;[45]
Through seeking to reach the ground of all-knowledge;
Through seeking to gain the Tathāgata's powers, fearlessnesses, and dharmas exclusive to the buddhas;
Through seeking proficiency in the *pāramitās* and the other dharmas assisting realization of the path;
Through abandoning all flattery and deceptiveness;
Through being able to practice in accordance with what has been taught;
Through always maintaining adherence to truthful speech;
Through never defiling the house of the *tathāgatas;*
Through never relinquishing the moral precepts of the bodhisattvas;
Through bringing forth a resolve to gain all-knowledge that is as unshakable as the king of mountains;
Through never relinquishing his endeavors in service to anyone in the world while still perfecting the world-transcending path;
Through insatiably accumulating those dharmas that comprise the factors assisting realization of bodhi;
And through always striving to gain ever more superior realization of the most supremely excellent path.

Son of the Buddha, the bodhisattva who completely develops such dharmas for purification of the grounds as these thereby becomes one who abides securely on the bodhisattva's Ground of Joyfulness.

Son of the Buddha, the bodhisattva who dwells on this Ground of Joyfulness is able to completely institute just such great vows entailing just such great heroic courage and just such great effective action. Specifically, they are:[46]

He brings forth a vast, pure, and resolute understanding through which he makes a vow to reverently present gifts of every form of offering to all buddhas without exception. His implementation of this vow is as vast as the Dharma realm and as extensive as empty space as it continues on incessantly until the end of future time and throughout all kalpas.

He also makes a great vow in which he vows to take on all buddhas' turning of the Dharma wheel, vows to take on [the realization of] all buddhas' bodhi, vows to protect all buddha's teaching, and vows to preserve all buddhas' Dharma. His implementation of this vow is as vast as the Dharma realm and as extensive as empty space as it continues on incessantly until the end of future time and throughout all kalpas.

He also makes a great vow in which he vows that, in all worlds, when the buddhas come forth into the world, descend from the Tuṣita Heaven Palace, enter the womb, abide in the womb, first take birth, leave behind the home life, achieve realization of the path, proclaim the Dharma, and finally enter nirvāṇa, in every instance, he will go forth to visit them, will draw close to them and make offerings to them, will serve them as a leader within their congregations, will take on the practice of right Dharma, and will proceed then to simultaneously turn the Dharma wheel in all places. His implementation of this vow is as vast as the Dharma realm and as extensive as empty space as it continues on incessantly until the end of future time and throughout all kalpas.

He also makes a great vow in which he vows to explain in accordance with their reality all of the bodhisattva practices, so vast, so immeasurable, indestructible, unalloyed in their purity, and inclusive of all the *pāramitās*, vows to explain the purifying cultivation of the grounds, their general characteristics, their specific characteristics, their common characteristics, their differentiating characteristics, the characteristics conducing to success in them, and the characteristics leading to ruination, vowing too to teach these matters to everyone, thus influencing them thereby to take on these practices and bring forth increasing resolve. His implementation of this vow is as vast as the Dharma realm and as extensive as empty space as it continues on incessantly until the end of future time and throughout all kalpas.

He also makes a great vow in which he vows: "I will teach all realms of beings in a manner influencing them to enter into the Dharma of the Buddha, influencing them to eternally cut off coursing in any of the destinies of worldly rebirth, and influencing them to become established in the path to the cognition of all-knowledge,[47] teaching all of them, whether they be possessed of form or formless, whether they be possessed of perception, free of perception, or abiding in a state of neither perception nor non-perception, whether they be egg-born, womb-born, moisture-born, or transformationally born, teaching all of them, no matter how they are connected to the triple world, no matter in which of the six destinies of rebirth they abide, and no matter in which place they have taken birth, teaching all beings possessed of name-and-form, teaching all such classes of beings as these." His implementation of this vow is as vast as the Dharma realm and as extensive as empty space as it continues on incessantly until the end of future time and throughout all kalpas.

He also makes a great vow in which he vows to directly know and perceive with utterly clear cognition all worlds in all their vastness and countless varieties, including the coarse, the subtle, the disordered, the inverted, and the upright, knowing them all, whether in entering them, coursing along within them, or emerging from them,[48] knowing them in their countlessly many different sorts of variations throughout the ten directions that are analogous [in their mutual relationship] to the net-like curtain of Indra. His implementation of this vow is as vast as the Dharma realm and as extensive as empty space as it continues on incessantly until the end of future time and throughout all kalpas.

He also makes a great vow in which he resolves to bring about the complete purification of all the measurelessly many buddha lands wherein all lands enter a single land, a single land enters all lands, and they are all adorned with many radiant phenomena, wherein they all become filled with measurelessly many wise beings[49] who have left behind all afflictions and perfected the path of purification, and wherein he everywhere enters the vast realms of all buddhas, accords with the mental dispositions of beings, and thus appears for them in a manner that causes them all to be pleased. His implementation of this vow is as vast as the Dharma realm and as extensive as empty space as it continues on incessantly until the end of future time and throughout all kalpas.

He also makes a great vow in which he vows to unite with all other bodhisattvas in practices with a single determined aim, doing so in a manner that remains free of enmity or jealousy, proceeding therein with the accumulation of all forms of roots of goodness, treating all bodhisattvas with universally equal regard and a singular objective basis for affinity, always gathering together with them and never allowing there to develop any mutual estrangement, doing so with a freely exercised ability to manifest all sorts of different buddha bodies, being able by resort to the capacities of his own mind to know all the domains, awesome powers, and wisdom[50] of all *tathāgatas*, being able thus to gain realization of the irreversible psychic powers through which one freely roams throughout all worlds, manifesting his physical presence in all of their assemblies, everywhere entering into all of stations of rebirth, perfecting the inconceivable Great Vehicle, cultivating the practices of the bodhisattvas. His implementation of this vow is as vast as the Dharma realm and as extensive as empty space as it continues on incessantly until the end of future time and throughout all kalpas.

He also makes a great vow in which he vows to take up the irreversible turning of the wheel, to course in the bodhisattva practices, to cultivate the refinement of physical, verbal, and mental karmic actions, to never neglect his endeavors in these matters, vowing too that, if anyone sees him, even if only momentarily, then he will thereby become bound for definite success in the Buddha's Dharma, vows that, if anyone hears his voice, even if only momentarily, then he will thereby become bound to gain genuine wisdom,[51] vows that, if one merely brings forth thoughts of pure faith, then he will thereby become bound to eternally cut off the afflictions, vows that he will succeed in becoming like a personification of the great king of medicine trees, that he will become like a personification of a wish-fulfilling jewel, and vowing that he will cultivate all of the bodhisattva practices. His implementation of this vow is as vast as the Dharma realm and as extensive as empty space as it continues on incessantly until the end of future time and throughout all kalpas.

He also makes a great vow in which he vows that he will gain realization of *anuttara-samyak-saṃbodhi* in all worlds, that he will not abandon even any of those places manifesting within the tip of a hair, that he will appear even in all those places manifesting within the tip of a hair the actions of taking on human birth, leaving behind the home life, arriving at the *bodhimaṇḍa,* realizing the right enlightenment, turning the wheel of Dharma, and entering nirvāṇa, that he will acquire the Buddha's realms of awareness and powers of great wisdom,[52] that even in every successive instant, adapting to the minds of every being, he will manifest for them the realization of buddhahood and cause them to succeed in achieving quiescent cessation themselves, that he will, through a single *saṃbodhi,* gain the realization of all dharma realms as characterized by identity with nirvāṇa, that, employing a single voice in the proclamation of Dharma, he will be able to cause the minds of all beings to become joyful, that, even though he manifests the appearance of entering the great nirvāṇa, he will still never cut off his coursing in the practices of the bodhisattva, that he will reveal the grounds of great wisdom[53] and the establishment of all dharmas, and that, in accomplishing this, he will employ the superknowledges associated with the cognition of dharmas, the superknowledges associated with the foundations of spiritual power, the conjuration-like superknowledges, and sovereignly masterful transformations that fill up the entire Dharma realm. His implementation of this vow is as vast as the Dharma realm and as extensive as empty space as it continues on incessantly until the end of future time and throughout all kalpas.

Son of the Buddha, the bodhisattva dwelling on this Ground of Joyfulness is able to bring forth such great vows, great heroic courage, and great effective action. Taking these ten vow gateways as foremost, he brings about the complete fulfillment of a hundred myriads of *asaṃkhyeyas* of great vows.

Son of the Buddha, these great vows are able to achieve their perfect completion on the basis of ten propositions on the ending [of various phenomena]. What then are those ten? They are:

The end of the realms of beings;
The end of worlds;
The end of the realms of empty space;
The end of the Dharma realm;
The end of the realm of nirvāṇa;
The end of the realms where the buddhas come forth and appear;
The end of the realm of the Tathāgata's knowledge;
The end of the realm of objects of mind;
The end of the realms of objective circumstances penetrated by the Buddha's cognition;
And the end of the realms of permutations of worlds, permutations of dharmas, and permutations of knowledge.

[Accordingly, he vows that]:

If the realms of beings come to an end, only then might my vows finally come to an end. If the worlds come to an end, and so forth on up to, if the realms of the permutations of worlds, permutations of dharmas, and permutations of knowledge come to an end, only then might my vows finally come to an end.

However, because the realms of beings cannot possibly ever come to an end, and so forth on up to because the realms of the permutations of worlds, permutations of dharmas, and permutations of knowledge cannot possibly ever come to an end, therefore the roots of goodness associated with these great vows of mine will never have an end.

Son of the Buddha, once the bodhisattva has made such vows as these, he then succeeds in acquiring:[54]

The beneficent mind;
The gentle mind;
The adaptive mind;
The serene mind;
The subdued mind;
The quiescent mind;
The humble mind;
The harmoniously smooth mind;
The unmoving mind;
And the unsullied mind.

He thereby succeeds in becoming one possessed of pure faith and possessed of the functional uses of faith, whereby he is able:[55]

To have faith in the original practices entered by the *tathāgatas;*
To have faith in the perfectibility of the *pāramitās;*
To have faith in the entry into the supreme grounds;
To have faith in the perfectibility of the powers;
To have faith in the complete fulfillment of the fearlessnesses;
To have faith in the production and development of the indomitable dharmas exclusive to the buddhas;
To have faith in the inconceivable Dharma of the buddhas;
To have faith in the generation of the Buddha's realm transcendent of either any middle or extremes;
To have faith in the entry into the Buddha's measureless domain;
And to have faith in the perfectibility of the resultant fruition.

To speak of the essentials, he has faith in all bodhisattva practices and the other related factors up to and including the Tathāgata's grounds of knowledge, proclamations, and powers.

Son of the Buddha, this bodhisattva has these additional thoughts:

The right Dharma of the buddhas is characterized by:
Such extreme profundity;
Such serenity;

Such quiescence;
Such emptiness;
Such signlessness;
Such wishlessness;
Such nondefilement;
Such measurelessness;
And such vastness.[56]

And yet common people:

Allow their minds to fall into wrong views;

Become covered over and blinded by ignorance;

Erect the lofty banner of arrogance;

Enter the net of craving;

Travel into the dense forest of flattery and deception and become unable to escape on their own;

Involve their minds in miserliness and jealousy, fail to relinquish them, and thus constantly create the causes and conditions conducing to rebirth in the various destinies;

Increase both day and night their accumulation of every sort of karmic activity based on greed, hatred, and delusion;

So set the wind of their anger and animosity blowing upon the flames of the mind's consciousness that they blaze incessantly.

Become such that whatever karmic actions they engage in are reflections of the inverted views;[57]

And become such that the flood of desire, the flood of becoming, the flood of ignorance, and the flood of views[58] continuously generate seeds associated with the mind and mental consciousness in the field of the three realms of existence that in turn grow forth the sprouts of suffering.

Specifically, this occurs as follows:

[The aggregates of] name-and-form[59] arise conjointly and inextricably.

This name-and-form develops and then produces the village of the six sense bases.[60]

In their corresponding pairings, these in turn produce contact.

As a result of the occurrence of contact, feelings then arise.

Because of feelings, there then follows the arising of craving.

Due to the growth of craving, there then occurs the generation of grasping.

Because of an increase in grasping, there then occurs the generation of becoming.

> Because of becoming, there then follow birth, aging, death, worry, sorrow, suffering, and the afflictions.

> It is in this manner that beings generate and proliferate a mass of suffering. In every case, everything therein is empty. Thus, absent the existence of any self or anything belonging to a self, there is no knowing, no awareness, nothing done, and nothing undergone. Thus these matters are all comparable to shrubs, trees, or a stone wall and are also comparable to mere reflected images. Still, beings remain unaware and unknowing of these circumstances.

On observing all beings in this circumstance wherein they are unable to escape from such a mass of suffering, the bodhisattva straightaway brings forth wisdom in association with the great compassion and then has this additional thought: "I should rescue and pull forth all these beings and see to their being placed in a circumstance of ultimate happiness." He therefore immediately brings forth radiant wisdom in association with the great kindness.

Son of the Buddha, when, in accordance with just such great compassion and great kindness as this, the bodhisattva-mahāsattva avails himself of deep and profound resolve and dwells on the first ground, he becomes free of any selfish cherishing for anything at all, pursues realization of the Buddha's great knowledge, and cultivates the great relinquishing through which he is able to bestow whatever he possesses as a gift. This includes his wealth, grain, the contents of his storehouses and granaries, gold, silver, *maṇi* jewels, true pearls, lapis lazuli, conch shells, jade, coral and other such things, precious jewels, necklaces, bodily adornments, elephants, horses, carriages, servants and workers, cities and villages, parks, forests, viewing terraces, wives, consorts, sons, daughters, members of his inner and outer retinue, and all other sorts of precious jewels and means of amusement. He is willing to also give even his head, eyes, hands, feet, blood, flesh, bones, marrow, and any other parts of his own body, bestowing all of these things without any selfish cherishing, and bestowing all these things in quest of the vast wisdom[61] of all buddhas. This is what constitutes the perfection of relinquishing carried out by the bodhisattva dwelling on the first ground.

Son of the Buddha, because of this mind of great giving imbued with kindness and compassion, the bodhisattva redoubles his quest to acquire every form of worldly and world-transcending beneficial means through which to facilitate the enactment of his aspiration to rescue and protect all beings. Through his tirelessness in this, he comes to perfect the tireless mind.

Having acquired the tireless mind, his mind then becomes entirely free of timidity with respect to pursuing the investigation of all scriptures and treatises. Because he is free of timidity in that regard, he then straightaway succeeds in acquiring the knowledge contained within all scriptures and treatises. Having acquired this knowledge, he is then well able to assess how he should and should not proceed in relating to all of the beings of superior, middling, and inferior capacities, adapting to what is appropriate for them, adapting to what suits their strengths, and adapting to whatever they are habitually accustomed to.

Due to proceeding in this manner, the bodhisattva succeeds in developing worldly wisdom. Having developed worldly wisdom, he then becomes aware of what constitutes correct timeliness and correct measure in those actions. Then, graced with a sense of shame and dread of blame, he diligently cultivates the path of simultaneously benefiting himself and benefiting others. Thus it is that he perfects the state of being graced by a sense of shame and dread of blame. As he engages in these practices, he diligently cultivates irreversible renunciation[62] and thus develops the power of enduring fortitude. Having developed the power of enduring fortitude, he then becomes diligent in making offerings to all buddhas and becomes able to practice in accord with the teaching dharmas proclaimed by the Buddha.

Son of the Buddha, thus it is that the bodhisattva perfects the ten dharmas employed in purifying the grounds, namely:[63]

Faith;
Compassion;
Kindness;
Renunciation;
Indefatigability;
Knowledge of the sutras and treatises;
Thorough comprehension of worldly dharmas;
A sense of shame and dread of blame;
The power of enduring fortitude;
The making of offerings to the buddhas while cultivating in accordance with the teachings.[64]

Son of the Buddha, having come to dwell on this Ground of Joyfulness, the bodhisattva, due to the power of his great vows, then becomes able to see many buddhas. That is to say that he becomes able to see many hundreds of buddhas, many thousands of buddhas, many hundreds of thousands of buddhas, many *koṭis* of buddhas, many hundreds of *koṭis* of buddhas, many thousands of *koṭis* of buddhas, many hundreds of thousands of *koṭis* of buddhas, many *koṭis* of *nayutas* of buddhas, many hundreds of *koṭis* of *nayutas* of buddhas, many thousands of *koṭis* of *nayutas* of buddhas, or many hundreds of thousands of *koṭis* of *nayutas* of buddhas, all of whom he reverently venerates with a magnanimous mind and resolute intentions as he serves them and makes offerings to them of robes, food and drink, bedding, medicines, and every sort of life-sustaining benefaction, all of which he offers up as gifts while also making offerings to all of the many members of the Sangha. He then dedicates all of the roots of goodness thereby created to the realization of the unsurpassable bodhi.

Son of the Buddha, on account of making offerings to the buddhas, this bodhisattva acquires the dharmas by which one brings about the maturation of beings. Employing the first two of the means of attraction, namely "giving" and "pleasing words," he draws forth beings. As for the remaining two means of attraction,[65] he only employs them in a manner commensurate with his powers of resolute faith, for his practice of them has not yet reached a state of consummate skillfulness.

Among the ten *pāramitās*, this bodhisattva becomes especially superior in his practice of *dāna pāramitā*. It is not, however, that he does not cultivate the remaining *pāramitās* at all. Rather, he simply accords them an amount of emphasis corresponding to his own strengths and to what is fitting.[66]

This bodhisattva, in accordance with whatever he is diligently cultivating, whether it be making offerings to buddhas or teaching beings, in every case does so through cultivating the grounds-purifying dharmas. He dedicates all of the associated roots of goodness to the acquisition of the ground of all-knowledge. As he does so, they become ever more radiant, pure, and pliant to the point that he becomes freely able to put them to use however he wishes.

Son of the Buddha, this circumstance is analogous to that of a goldsmith who, especially well-skilled in the refinement of gold, introduces it into the fire again and again, with the result that it shines ever more brightly, becomes ever more pure, and becomes ever more pliant to the point that, once this process is completed, he can then freely put it to use however he wishes.

The bodhisattva is just like this. His making of offerings to the buddhas and his teaching of beings is in every case done in the service of cultivating the dharmas employed in purification of the grounds. All of the roots of goodness thereby developed are dedicated to reaching the ground of all-knowledge. As he proceeds with this cultivation, they become ever more brightly shining, pure, and pliant to the point where he becomes freely able to put them to use.

Son of the Buddha, the bodhisattva-mahāsattva who dwells on the first ground should set forth searching questions in the presence of the buddhas, the bodhisattvas, and his good spiritual guides, insatiably requesting from them clarification of this ground's characteristic aspects and acquired fruits, doing so wishing to completely develop this ground's dharmas.

So too should he set forth searching questions in the presence of the buddhas, the bodhisattvas, and his good spiritual guides, insatiably requesting from them clarification regarding the second ground's characteristic aspects and acquired fruits, doing so wishing to completely develop that ground's dharmas.

So too should he set forth searching questions insatiably requesting clarification of the characteristic aspects and acquired fruits associated with the third, fourth, fifth, sixth, seventh, eighth, ninth, and tenth grounds, doing so wishing to completely develop those grounds' dharmas.

This bodhisattva then:

Thoroughly knows the obstacles encountered on the grounds as well as the means for countering them;

Thoroughly knows the means of achieving success or falling into ruination on the grounds;

Thoroughly knows the characteristic aspects and fruits associated with the grounds;

Thoroughly knows the attainment and cultivation of the grounds;

Thoroughly knows the grounds' purification of dharmas;

Thoroughly knows the progression in the successively adopted practices used in advancing from ground to ground;

Thoroughly knows with respect to each successive ground what is and is not the correct station;

Thoroughly knows with respect to each successive ground the type of especially superior knowledge associated with it;

Thoroughly knows with respect to each successive ground the means by which to prevent retreating from it;

And thoroughly knows how to bring about the purifying cultivation of all of the bodhisattva grounds on through to the point of progression into the ground of the Tathāgata.

Son of the Buddha, in this way, the bodhisattva thoroughly knows the characteristic features of the grounds beginning with the first ground, knows how one takes up the practices and carries them forward without interruption in this manner until one finally enters the tenth ground, continuing on in this without any instance of the practice being cut off. It is on account of the light associated with the knowledge of the grounds that he succeeds in developing the light of the Tathāgata's wisdom.[67]

Son of the Buddha, this circumstance is analogous to that of a leader of merchants who comes to know well the means employed when wishing to lead a group of merchants going off to some great city. Before embarking, he must first ask about the roads to be taken, inquiring about their fine qualities and their faulty aspects while also inquiring about the places where one might stop along the way, inquiring also as to whether the threats to security one might encounter along the way are surmountable or not. After doing this, he prepares the provisions to be used on the road and does all that one should do in preparing to embark.

Son of the Buddha, even though that great leader of merchants has not yet set foot on the road to be taken, he is nonetheless able to know all of the circumstances that might threaten their security along the path. He is skilled in applying his wisdom[68] in assessment and observation, in preparing whatever they will need, in ensuring that they will not run short of anything, and in safely leading the entire band of merchants all along the way until they reach that great city, doing so in a manner whereby he himself as well as that group of men will all be able to avoid encountering disastrous circumstances.

Son of the Buddha, so too it is with the bodhisattva in his acting like a leader of merchants. Even as he dwells on the first ground, he comes to know well the obstacles encountered on the grounds as well as the means for countering them. He comes to well know everything else as well, all the way on through to his knowing of the purifying cultivation of all of the bodhisattva grounds and the subsequent progression on forth into the ground of the Tathāgata. Having accomplished this, he next prepares the provisions of merit and knowledge with which he will be able to lead all beings through the hazardous and difficult regions within the vast wilderness of *saṃsāra*'s births and deaths so that they succeed in safely reaching the city of all-knowledge, all the while leading them along so neither he himself nor those beings are forced to go through calamitous and difficult circumstances.

Therefore, the bodhisattva should never slacken in his diligent cultivation of the most especially superior purifying karmic deeds on all the grounds on through to the point where he enters the ground of the Tathāgata's knowledge.

Son of the Buddha, this has been a summary discussion of the bodhisattva-mahāsattva's entry into the gateway of the first bodhisattva ground. Were one to present an extensive discussion of this, that would involve an incalculable and boundless number of hundreds of thousands of *asaṃkhyeyas* of differentiating factors.

Son of the Buddha, the bodhisattva-mahāsattva dwelling on the first ground often becomes a monarch reigning over the continent of Jambudvīpa who is a member of the aristocratic nobility that, acting with sovereign freedom, is able to draw forth beings through great giving. He is skilled in doing away with beings' filth of miserliness as he always practices endless great giving.

Even while pursuing the practices of giving, pleasing words, beneficial actions, and joint endeavors, in all these works that he carries out:

He never departs from mindfulness of the Buddha;
He never departs from mindfulness of the Dharma;
He never departs from mindfulness of the Sangha;
He never departs from mindfulness of the bodhisattvas engaged in the same practices;
He never departs from mindfulness of the bodhisattva conduct;
He never departs from mindfulness of the *pāramitās*;
He never departs from mindfulness of the grounds;
He never departs from mindfulness of the powers;
He never departs from mindfulness of the fearlessnesses;
He never departs from mindfulness of the dharmas exclusive to the Buddha;
And so forth until we come to his never departing from mindfulness of his quest to achieve complete fulfillment of the knowledge of all modes and the cognition of all-knowledge.

He also has this thought: "I should become one who serves these beings as a leader, as one who is supreme, as one who is most especially supreme, as one who is marvelous, as one who is most subtly marvelous, as one who is excellent, as one who is unexcelled, as one who is a guide, as one who is a general, one who is a supreme leader," and so forth until we come to "as one who relies on the cognition of all-knowledge."

If this bodhisattva wishes to relinquish the home life and take up the diligent practice of vigor in the Dharma of the Buddha, then he will be able to relinquish the household, his wife and children, and the five desires, and then rely on the teaching of the Tathāgata in his abandonment of the household and in his study of the path.

Having left behind the home life, if he diligently applies himself in the cultivation of vigor, in but a single moment:

He will be able to acquire a hundred samādhis, see a hundred buddhas, and know a hundred buddhas' spiritual powers;
He will be able to cause tremors in a hundred buddha worlds;
He will be able to travel across a hundred buddha worlds;
He will be able to illuminate a hundred buddha worlds;
He will be able to teach the beings in a hundred buddha worlds;
He will be able to remain for one hundred kalpas;
He will be able to know events occurring throughout a hundred kalpas of the past and future;
He will be able to enter a hundred Dharma gateways;
He will be able to manifest a hundred bodies;
And he will be able to manifest a hundred bodhisattvas to serve as the retinue for each and every one of those bodies.

Then, if he resorts to the power of the especially supreme vows of the bodhisattva, he will become freely able to bring forth manifestations beyond this number, such that one would never be able to count them even in a period of a hundred kalpas, a thousand kalpas, or a hundred thousand kalpas.

At that time, Vajragarbha Bodhisattva, wishing to once again proclaim his meaning, thereupon spoke these verses:

If someone accumulates the many sorts of good deeds,
perfects the hundred sorts of dharmas of purification,
makes offerings to those most honored among devas and men,
accords with the path of kindness and compassion,

possesses the most extremely vast sort of resolute faith,
and possesses resolve and delight that are pristinely pure,
then, for the sake of seeking the wisdom[69] of the Buddha,
he brings forth this unexcelled resolve.

In order to pursue the purification of all-knowledge, the powers, and the fearlessnesses,
to achieve the perfection of all dharmas of the Buddha, and
to draws in and rescue the many sorts of beings,

And in order to acquire the great kindness and compassion,
set turning the wheel of the supreme Dharma,
and adorn and purify buddha lands,
he brings forth this utterly supreme resolve.

In order, in a single moment, to know the three periods of time,
and still be free of discriminations about them,
in order, in all of the various eras, each different,
to manifest his presence within the world,

and, to state it briefly, in order to seek
all of the buddhas' supreme meritorious qualities,
he brings forth the vast resolve
equal in its scope to the realm of empty space.

Taking compassion as foremost and wisdom as primary,
adopting skillful means accordant with them,
being possessed of resolute faith and purified intentions,
availing himself of the Tathagata's measureless powers,

directly manifesting unimpeded knowledge,
bringing forth spontaneous understanding not reliant on others, and
gaining fulfillment herein that achieves parity with the Tathāgata,
he brings forth this most supreme resolve.

When a son of the Buddha first brings forth
such a marvelous jewel-like resolve as this,
he then steps beyond the position of the common person
and enters into the station in which the Buddha courses.

He is thus born into the family of the *tathāgatas,*
into that clan lineage utterly free of flaws, and
becomes one bound to become the equal of the buddhas
who will definitely realize the unexcelled enlightenment.

As soon as he brings forth such a resolve as this,
he straightaway succeeds in entering the first ground
and develops determination and delight as unshakable
as the great king of the mountains.

He experiences abundant joy, abundant cherishing delight,
and abundant pure-minded faith as well,
marshals a great and heroically brave resolve,
and avails himself of celebratory and exhilarated thought.

He abandons disputatiousness,
harmful behavior, and hatred,
and becomes humble, respectful, and straightforward in character
while also skillfully guarding the sense faculties.

Regarding those who are matchless in rescuing the world
and all of their many varieties of wisdom,[70]
he reflects: "This is the station that I am bound to realize,"
and, in bringing them to mind, he is filled with joy.

On first gaining entry into the first ground,
he straightaway oversteps five types of fearfulness:
failure to survive, death, ill repute,
the wretched destinies, and the awesome virtue of assemblies.

It is because they have no covetous attachment to a self
or to anything belonging to a self
that these sons of the Buddha
abandon all forms of fearfulness.

They always practice great kindness and sympathy
and constantly possess faith and reverence.
Replete in a sense of shame, a dread of blame, and the qualities,
they strive day and night to increase in good dharmas.
They delight in the genuine benefit conferred by the Dharma,
and are not fond of indulgence in the desires.

They contemplate the Dharma that they have learned
and leave far behind actions involving grasping and attachment.
They do not covet offerings or support,
only delight in the bodhi of the Buddha,

single-mindedly seek to acquire the Buddha's knowledge,
and focus intently on maintaining undistracted mindfulness.
They cultivate the *pāramitās*
and abandon flattery, falseness, and deception.

They cultivate in accordance with what has been proclaimed,
and establish themselves in truthful speech.
They refrain from defiling the house of the buddhas,
never relinquish the moral precepts of the bodhisattva,

do not delight in any sort of worldly matters,
and always benefit the world.
They are insatiable in the cultivation of what is good,
and strive ever more to reach increasingly superior paths.

In this manner, they are fond of and delight in dharmas
associated with meritorious qualities and whatever is meaningful.
They constantly raise up the resolve of their great vows,
vow to go and see the buddhas,

vow to guard and sustain all buddhas' Dharma, and
vow to gather and preserve the Great Rishi's teachings on the path.
They always bring forth vows such as these,
vowing to cultivate the most supreme practices.

They vow to bring all sorts of beings to maturation,
vow to carry forth the purification of the buddha lands,

vow to bring it about that, all buddha lands
shall become completely filled with sons of the Buddha,

vow that they shall maintain the same singular resolve as theirs,
vow that, whatever actions one does shall not have been in vain,
and vow that, even in those places within the tip of every hair,
they will, at once, manifest the realization of right enlightenment.

They make such great vows as these
that are measurelessly vast and boundless in their reach.
They declare: "If there were an end to empty space or beings,
an end to the Dharma realm or nirvāṇa,
an end to the worlds or the appearance of buddhas in the world,
an end to the buddhas' knowledge or to objects of mind,

an end to the realms entered by a *tathāgata's* knowledge
or to the three permutations [of worlds, dharmas, and knowledge]—
If all of these phenomena were to somehow come to an end,
my vows might then begin to come to an end.
But, just as all of those have no point at which they would end,
so too it is with these vows that I have made."

Thus it is that they bring forth great vows
with minds that are gentle, subdued, and adaptive.
Through their ability to maintain faith in the Buddha's qualities
and contemplate the realms of beings,

they realize their circumstances arise due to causes and conditions,
and then let flourish their kindly and mindful resolve,
wherein they reflect thus: "Suffering beings of this sort
are such as I should now rescue and liberate."

For the sake of these beings,
they then carry out the many different types of giving,
relinquishing the royal throne and jewels as well as
other possessions, including elephants, horses, and carriages,

their heads, eyes, hands, and feet,
even to the point of giving their entire body, its blood and its flesh.
They are able to relinquish absolutely everything
while still remaining free of any distress or regret in this.

They strive to study the many different scriptures
with minds tireless in this pursuit.
They skillfully comprehend their meaning and import,
and are able to adapt to the world in implementing their practices.

They grace themselves with a sense of shame and dread of blame
and become ever more solid in their cultivation.

They make offerings to countless buddhas,
doing so with respect and profound veneration.

Thus it is that they are always devoted to cultivation,
carrying it forward tirelessly, both day and night.
Their roots of goodness become ever more bright and pure
just as with true gold when it is refined in fire.

The bodhisattva dwelling herein
engages in the purifying cultivation of the ten grounds
and remains free of obstacles in all endeavors he pursues,
bringing them to completion without interruption.

In this, he is like a great leader of merchants
who, for the sake of benefiting an entire group of traders,
inquires about and learns the road's hazardous and easy conditions,
thus ensuring safe arrival at some great city.

The bodhisattva abiding on the first ground
should also be known as just like this.
Bringing heroic bravery to bear, he remains unimpeded
as he advances all the way to the tenth ground.

When he abides on this first ground,
he may become a monarch possessed of great meritorious qualities
who employs the Dharma in teaching beings
and uses the mind of kindness to refrain from inflicting injury

as he unites and leads the residents of Jambudvīpa
in a way that there are none not reached by his transformative acts.
Thus they are all caused to abide in that great relinquishing
through which they perfect the Buddha's wisdom.[71]

Then, wishing to pursue the most supreme of paths,
he relinquishes his position on the royal throne.
He becomes able in taking up the Buddha's teachings
to diligently pursue their cultivation with such heroic bravery

that he then succeeds in acquiring a hundred samādhis,
in seeing a hundred buddhas,
and in causing tremors throughout a hundred worlds.
His radiantly illuminating practices are also of this sort.

Thus he teaches the beings in a hundred lands,
enters a hundred gateways into the Dharma,
knows the events occurring for a hundred kalpas,
manifests a hundred bodies therein,

and manifests a hundred bodhisattvas
to serve in each of their retinues.

If he avails himself of his sovereign mastery over the power of vows,
he may extend his capacities beyond this to incalculable numbers.

I have provided here a summary description
of but a minor measure of this ground's meanings.
If one wished to comprehensively distinguish them all,
he could never finish it even in a *koṭi* of kalpas.

The supreme path of the bodhisattva
benefits all of the many types of beings.
I have hereby now concluded the explanation of
such dharmas of the first ground as these.

The Second Ground

The Stainlessness Ground

As the bodhisattvas listened to this description
of this especially superior and sublime ground,
their minds became entirely purified
and they were all filled with joy.

All of them then rose from their seats,
ascended upward, stood in empty space,
scattered the most marvelous blossoms everywhere,
and then simultaneously uttered praises together, saying:

"It is good indeed, Vajragarbha Bodhisattva,
that the greatly wise and fearless one
has so well described this ground
and the dharmas practiced by the bodhisattva."

Then, Liberation Moon Bodhisattva,
knowing that the minds of those in the assembly were pure
and knowing they would delight in hearing of the second ground
and all of its characteristic aspects of practice,

straightaway made a request of Vajragarbha Bodhisattva, saying:
"O You of Great Wisdom, we pray you will continue to expound,
for these sons of the Buddha would all delight in hearing
about the second of these grounds on which one may dwell."

At that time, Vajragarbha Bodhisattva informed Liberation Moon Bodhisattva, saying:

Son of the Buddha, the bodhisattva-mahāsattva who has already cultivated the first ground and then wishes to enter the second ground should bring forth ten types of resolute intentions.[72] What then are these ten? They are as follows:[73]

The resolute intention to be upright and straightforward;
The resolute intention to be gentle;
The resolute intention to be capable;
The resolute intention to be subdued;
The resolute intention to be serene;
The resolute intention to be thoroughly good;
The resolute intention to be unmixed [in moral purity];
The resolute intention to be unattached;
The resolute intention to be broadly inclusive;
And resolute intention to be magnanimous.

It is because of these ten types of resolute intentions that the bodhisattva succeeds in entering the second ground, the Ground of Stainlessness.

Son of the Buddha, the bodhisattva dwelling on the Ground of Stainlessness has naturally abandoned all killing of beings. He does not collect knives or staves, does not harbor feelings of animosity, is possessed of a sense of shame and dread of blame, is entirely complete in his humanity and consideration for others, and always brings forth thoughts of beneficial and kindly mindfulness for all beings including anything at all that is possessed of a life. This bodhisattva does not even produce evil thoughts envisioning his inflicting distress upon other beings, how much the less could it happen that he might, having formed the conception of the existence of a being, then proceed with deliberate intent to kill it.

He naturally refrains from stealing. As regards his own possessions and wealth, the bodhisattva is always easily satisfied. He feels kindness and consideration for others and so does not wish to appropriate what is theirs. If something belongs to someone else, he regards it as their property and hence never even thinks of stealing it. Hence, he will not take even a blade of grass or a leaf that has not been given. How much the less might he take anything else that serves to sustain another's life.

He naturally refrains from sexual misconduct. The bodhisattva is satisfied with his own wife and hence does not seek after the wives of others. As for the wives or consorts of others, women under the protection of others, female relatives, women whose marriage has already been arranged, and those who are under the protection of the Dharma, he does not even produce any thoughts defiled by desire, how much the less would he actually engage in any such action, and how much the less might he engage in behaviors involving a wrong physical orifice.

He naturally refrains from false speech. The bodhisattva always practices truthful speech, genuine speech, and timely speech, and, even in dreams, does not countenance speech aimed at concealment. He does not even generate any thought of wishing to commit such actions, how much the less might he commit a deliberate transgression.

He naturally refrains from divisive speech. The bodhisattva has no thought inclined toward instigating divisions between other beings, and has no thought to do harm to others. He does not report the words of this person to that one with the intention of breaking up that person's relationship with him, nor does he report to this person the words of that one with the intention of breaking up this person's relationship with him.

He does not cause the breaking apart of those who have not yet broken apart and, in the case of those who have already broken apart, he does not act in a way which might increase that schism. He does not rejoice in divisions that occur between others, does not delight in divisions between others, does not utter any speech that might create divisions between others, and does not pass on to anyone any talk that might create divisions between others, regardless of whether or not those reports might be truthful.

He naturally refrains from harsh speech such as poisonous and injurious speech, coarse and ferocious speech, speech inflicting suffering on others whether as direct statements or indirect statements, speech inciting hatred, vulgar speech, base speech, speech that no one would enjoy hearing, displeasing speech, angry speech, speech that makes others feel as if burned by fire, speech generating animosity, aggravating speech, speech one cannot appreciate, speech in which one can find no happiness, speech that may bring harm to either oneself or others, or any other such forms of speech, all of which one should abandon.

He always engages in soothingly smooth speech, pliant speech, pleasing speech, speech that may inspire happiness in the hearer, speech that one would be happy to hear, speech that delights the hearer, speech that skillfully enters others' minds, refined and principled speech, speech loved by the many, speech that many would find pleasing, and speech tending to cause an upwelling of delight in body and mind.

He naturally refrains from frivolous speech. The bodhisattva always delights in thoughtful and reasoned speech, timely speech, genuine speech, meaningful speech, Dharma speech, speech accordant with principle, skillfully subdued speech, and speech that accords with the right time, is always rooted in careful reflection, and is definite in its clarity. This bodhisattva, even in humorous speech, still always imbues it with thoughtfulness. How much the less would he deliberately indulge scattered and chaotically confused speech.

He naturally abstains from covetousness. The bodhisattva does not generate covetous thought, wishfulness, or craving to possess any of the wealth or possessions of others or anything others depend upon as a resource.

He naturally abandons ill will. The bodhisattva constantly brings forth kind thoughts, beneficial thoughts, pitying thoughts, joyful thoughts, harmoniously smooth thoughts, and inclusively accepting thoughts toward all beings. He has eternally relinquished ill will, animosity, injuriousness, and behavior intending to vex or torment others. Rather, he always engages in thoughtful and agreeably adaptive actions while also being motivated toward humanity, kindness, helpfulness, and the desire to serve the benefit of others.

He also abandons wrong views. The bodhisattva abides in the path of what is right. Thus he does not practice divination and does not seize on wrongly conceived rules for one's conduct. His mental perspective is correct, straightforward, and free of motivations toward deceptiveness or flattery. He brings forth and maintains resolute and definite faith in the Buddha, in the Dharma, and in the Sangha.

Son of the Buddha, it is in this manner that the bodhisattva-mahāsattva always and uninterruptedly guards and maintains his practice of the ten courses of good karmic action.

He also has this thought:

> Of all of the beings who descend into the wretched destinies, there are none who do not accomplish this by resort to the ten types of unwholesome karmic actions. Consequently, I should cultivate right conduct myself while also encouraging this in others in a manner that causes them to cultivate right conduct as well. Why does one proceed in this way? It is because, if one were to remain incapable of cultivating right conduct oneself while attempting to cause others to cultivate it, it would be impossible to succeed in this.

Son of the Buddha, this bodhisattva-mahāsattva also has this thought:

> The ten courses of unwholesome karmic action constitute the causes of rebirth in the hells, among animals, and among hungry ghosts, whereas the ten courses of good karmic action constitute the causes for rebirth among humans and devas and the other rebirth stations on up to the station at the peak of existence.
>
> Additionally, among these superior classes of those who adhere to the ten courses of good karmic action, there are those who rely on wisdom in cultivating them. Among them, there are those who, due to narrow and inferior resolve, due to fear of the three realms of existence, due to deficiency in the great compassion, and due to having achieved their understanding based on hearing the spoken teachings of others, they then achieve success in the *śrāvaka*-disciple vehicle.

Also, among these superior classes of those who adhere the ten courses of good karmic action, there are those whose cultivation is pure and who achieve self-awakening not derived from the teachings of others, but who, because of inadequacy in the great compassion and skillful means, and because they succeed in awakening through understanding the extremely profound dharma of causes and conditions, they then achieve success in the *pratyekabuddha* vehicle.

Then again, among these superior classes of those who adhere to the ten courses of good karmic action, there are those whose cultivation is pure, and who, because their minds are immeasurably vast, because they are complete in their development of compassion and pity, because their practice is subsumed within skillful means, because they have brought forth great vows, because they have not forsaken beings, because they strive to acquire the great knowledge of the buddhas, and because they carry out the purifying cultivation of the bodhisattva grounds, they then achieve success in the vast practices of the bodhisattva.

Furthermore, these who are most superior among those who are superior in the practice of the ten courses of good karmic action—because they purify the knowledge of all modes and so forth on up to the point of gaining realization of the ten powers and the four fearlessnesses, they therefore succeed in perfecting all dharmas of the Buddha.

Therefore I should now engage in the equal practice of all ten of these good deeds and should cause them all to become perfectly purified.

The bodhisattva should train in just such skillful means as these. Son of the Buddha, this bodhisattva-mahāsattva also has this thought:

The highest level of transgression in the ten courses of unwholesome karmic action constitutes the causal basis for rebirth in the hells. A middling level of such transgression constitutes the causal basis for rebirth as an animal. The lowest level constitutes the causal basis for rebirth as a hungry ghost.

Among these, the karmic offense of killing is able to cause beings to descend into the hell realms, animal realms, and hungry ghost realms. If they then achieve a human rebirth, they reap two types of retribution: First, a short life span. Second, extensive illness.

The karmic offense of stealing also causes beings to descend into the three wretched destinies. If they then achieve a human rebirth, they reap two types of retribution: First, poverty. Second, if they acquire any wealth, it is jointly held by others, thus preventing its independent use.

The karmic offense of sexual misconduct also causes beings to descend into the three wretched destinies. If they then achieve a human rebirth, they reap two types of retribution: First, their spouse is not virtuous. Second, they do not acquire a retinue responsive to their wishes.

The karmic offense of false speech also causes beings to descend into the three wretched destinies. If they then achieve a human rebirth, they reap two types of retribution: First, they are often slandered by others. Second, they are deceived by others.

The karmic offense of divisive speech also causes beings to descend into the three wretched destinies. If they then achieve a human rebirth, they reap two types of retribution: First, their retinue is fraught with mutually estranging divisions. Second, the members of their family and clan are corrupt and evil.

The karmic offense of harsh speech also causes beings to descend into the three wretched destinies. If they then achieve a human rebirth, they reap two types of retribution: First, they are always subjected to unpleasant sounds. Second, their conversation is characterized by abundant disputation.

The karmic offense of frivolous speech also causes beings to descend into the three wretched destinies. If they then achieve a human rebirth, they reap two types of retribution: First, nobody accepts their pronouncements. Second, their pronouncements fail to be clearly understood.

The karmic offense of covetousness also causes beings to descend into the three wretched destinies. If they then achieve a human rebirth, they reap two types of retribution: First, their minds are never satisfied. Second, they are extensively afflicted by insatiable desires.

The karmic offense of ill will also causes beings to descend into the three wretched destinies. If they then achieve a human rebirth, they reap two types of retribution: First, they are always subjected to others' criticism of their shortcomings. Second, they are constantly subjected to injurious torment by others.

The karmic offense of holding wrong views also causes beings to descend into the three wretched destinies. If they then achieve a human rebirth, they reap two types of retribution: First, they are always reborn into a household ruled by wrong views. Second, their own minds tend toward flattery and deviousness.

Son of the Buddha, the ten courses of unwholesome karmic action are able to generate such an aggregation of measurelessly and boundlessly many immense sufferings as these.

Consequently, the bodhisattva reflects thus: "I must entirely abandon the ten courses of unwholesome karmic action and instead take the ten courses of good karmic action as the gardens of the Dharma wherein I am delighted to abide, dwelling there myself while also encouraging others so that they too are caused to dwell therein."

Son of the Buddha, with regard to all beings, this bodhisattva-mahāsattva also brings forth:[74]

A mind resolved to serve their benefit;
A mind wishing to bring them peace and happiness;
A kind mind;
A compassionate mind;
An empathetically pitying mind;
A mind motivated to draw them forth;
A protective mind;
A mind that sees them as like oneself;
A mind that regards them as like teachers;
And a mind that regards them as like great teaching masters.

He reflects thus:

> These beings are so pitiable. They have fallen into wrong views, into perverse knowledge, into perverse inclinations, and into the entangling thicket of the unwholesome courses of karmic action. I should cause them to abide in right views and practice the genuine path.

He also thinks:

> All beings differentiate "other" as opposed to "self" and thus engage in mutually destructive actions, disputatiousness, and hatred that blazes incessantly. I should cause them to abide in the unsurpassable great kindness.

He also reflects thus:

> All beings are inclined toward insatiable covetousness and thus only seek to obtain wealth and self-benefit even to the point that they pursue wrong livelihoods to sustain their lives. I should cause them to abide in the dharma of right livelihood characterized by pure actions of body, speech, and mind.

He also thinks:

> All beings always follow along with the three poisons and the many different varieties of afflictions and, on account of that, they are as if ablaze. They fail to understand this and fail to bring forth the determination to seek the essential means to escape their circumstances. I should cause them to extinguish that great blaze

fed by all of their afflictions and to then become securely established in the station of nirvāṇa's clarity and coolness.

He also reflects:

Because the vision of all beings has been covered over by the deep darkness of delusion and the thick cataracts of false views, they have therefore strayed into a dark and dense thicket. Having lost the shining light of wisdom, they travel along on dangerous paths in a vast wilderness and bring forth all manner of wrong views. I should cause them to acquire the unimpeded purified wisdom eye with which they can know the true character of all dharmas in a manner not dependent upon the instruction of others.

He also thinks:

All beings abide on the hazardous road of cyclic births and deaths wherein they are bound to fall into the hell realms, the animal realms, and the realms of the hungry ghosts. They enter the net-trap of wrong views, become confused in the dense forest of delusions, and thus follow along with erroneous paths and pursue practices influenced by the inverted views. In this, they are like blind people with no guide. What is not a path of escape, they take to be a path of escape. They enter into Māra's realm, fall in with bands of evil thieves, follow the thoughts of Māra, and leave far behind the intentions of the Buddha. I should pull them out of these hazardous difficulties and cause them to abide in the fearless city of all-knowledge.

He also reflects:

All of these beings have become submerged in the waves of the great floods. They have been swept up by the flood of desire, the flood of existence, the flood of ignorance, and the flood of views and thus have become caught in the whirling currents of cyclic existence wherein they are tossed about and turned around in the river of craving as they are carried along in its racing rapids and bounding turbulence, finding no leisure in which to ponder their plight.

They are relentlessly driven along by desire-ridden thoughts, by thoughts motivated by hatred, and by thoughts intent on harming others. The *rākṣasa* of the view imputing the existence of a true self in association with one's body[75] seizes them and carries them off to dwell eternally within the dense forest of desire wherein they develop a deep defiling attachment for whatever they desire. They abide on the high plateau of arrogance and take up residence in the village of the six sense bases wherein they have no one well able to come to their rescue and no one who is able to liberate them.

> I should bring forth the mind of great compassion for them, should employ roots of goodness as means of rescuing them, should thus prevent their encountering calamitous disasters, and should thus assist their abandonment of defilement, their abiding in quiescent stillness, and their coming to dwell on the jeweled isle of all-knowledge.

He also thinks:

> All beings abide in the prison of worldly existence in which they are subjected to so much anguishing affliction. They always embrace love and hate and produce worries and fears for themselves. They are bound by the heavy shackles of desire, are covered over and obstructed by the dense forest of ignorance, and are stranded within the three realms of existence from which no one can escape on their own. I should cause them to abandon forever the three realms of existence so that they may come to dwell in the great nirvāṇa that is free of all obstacles.

He also reflects thus:

> All beings are attached to the existence of a self and do not seek to escape from their residence within the cave of the aggregates. In their reliance upon the empty village of the six sense bases, they engage in actions influenced by the four inverted views, are assailed and tormented by the toxic serpents of the four great elements, are subjected to death and injury at the hands of the hostile insurgents of the five aggregates, and thus consequently undergo immeasurably great suffering. I should cause them to take up residence in the most extremely superior station in which they are free of all attachments, namely, in the unexcelled nirvāṇa where all obstacles have been entirely destroyed.

He also has this thought:

> The minds of all beings are inferior and mean. They do not practice the most superior path, the path of all-knowledge. Although they might wish to make their escape, even then, they only delight in the vehicles of the *śrāvaka* disciples and the *pratyekabuddhas*. I must cause them to dwell in the Buddha's vast Dharma and vast wisdom.

Son of the Buddha, through his guarding and upholding of the moral precepts, the bodhisattva becomes well able to achieve growth in the mind of kindness and the mind of compassion.

Son of the Buddha, because of the power of his vows, the bodhisattva-mahāsattva who abides on the Ground of Stainlessness becomes able to see many buddhas. That is to say that he is able to see many hundreds of buddhas, many thousands of buddhas, many hundreds of thousands of buddhas, many *koṭis* of buddhas, many hundreds of *koṭis* of buddhas, many thousands of *koṭis* of buddhas, many hundreds of thousands of *koṭis* of buddhas, and so forth in this manner on up to his being able to see even many hundreds of thousands of *koṭis* of *nayutas* of buddhas.

Wherever the buddhas dwell, by resort to his vast resolve and resolute intentions, he acts with reverence and extreme veneration in serving and making offerings to them of robes, food and drink, bedding, medicines, and every form of life-supporting benefaction, all of which he offers up as gifts while also making offerings to their entire assembly of Sangha members. He then dedicates the roots of goodness associated with this to the realization of *anuttara-samyak-saṃbodhi*.

In addition, in the presence of all buddhas, bringing forth a mind of profound veneration, he undertakes the cultivation of the dharma of the ten courses of good karmic action, persisting in what he has undertaken all the way to the point of reaching the realization of bodhi, never in all that time neglecting or failing in such practice.

Because, for countless hundreds of thousands of *koṭis* of *nayutas* of kalpas, this bodhisattva has abandoned miserliness and any defilement arising from breaking the moral precepts, he achieves consummate purity in giving and the observance of the moral precepts. This is just as when one places real gold together with *kāsīsa*[76] and subjects it to standard refining processes, whereupon the gold leaves behind all impurities and becomes ever more radiant. So too it is in the case of this bodhisattva dwelling on the Ground of Stainlessness who, for countless hundreds of thousands of *koṭis* of *nayutas* of kalpas, in order to abandon miserliness and any defilement that would arise from breaking moral precepts, has practiced giving and upheld the moral precepts and has thus thereby achieved a state of consummate purity.

Son of the Buddha, among the four means of attraction, this bodhisattva focuses more strongly on "pleasing words" and, among the ten *pāramitās*, he focuses more strongly on upholding the moral precepts. It is not that he does not practice the others. Rather, he simply accords them an amount of emphasis corresponding to his own strengths and to what is fitting.

Son of the Buddha, this has been a summary discussion of the essentials of the bodhisattva-mahāsattva's second ground, the Ground of Stainlessness.

The bodhisattva abiding on this ground often becomes a wheel-turning sage king who serves as a great Dharma sovereign possessed of an abundance of the seven precious things and sovereign powers through which he is able to cause beings to do away with their miserliness and precept-breaking defilements. He employs skillful means to cause them to abide securely in the ten courses of good karmic action. He serves as a great benefactor to all, endlessly supplying provisions to everyone.

In his practice of giving, pleasing words, beneficial actions, and joint endeavors, and in all other such works as these, he never departs from mindfulness of the Buddha, never departs from mindfulness of the Dharma, never departs from mindfulness of the Sangha, and so forth until we come to his never departing from mindfulness of his quest to achieve complete fulfillment of the knowledge of all modes and the cognition of all-knowledge.

He also has this thought: "I should become one who serves these beings as a leader, as one who is supreme, as one who is most especially supreme, as one who is marvelous, as one who is most subtly marvelous, as one who is excellent, as one who is unexcelled," and so forth until we come to "as one who relies on the cognition of all-knowledge."

If this bodhisattva wishes to relinquish the home life and take up the diligent practice of vigor in the Dharma of the Buddha, then he will be able to relinquish the household, his wife and children, and the five desires, and having abandoned the home life, if he diligently applies himself in the practice of vigor, in but a single moment, he will acquire a thousand samādhis, will be able to see a thousand buddhas, will know the spiritual powers exercised by a thousand buddhas, will be able to cause tremors in a thousand world systems, and so forth until we come to his becoming able to manifest a thousand bodies and able to manifest a thousand bodhisattvas to serve in the retinue of each and every one of those bodies.

If he resorts to the power of the especially supreme vows of the bodhisattva, he will become freely able to bring forth a number of manifestations beyond even this such that one would never be able to count them even in a period of a hundred kalpas, a thousand kalpas, and so forth on up to a hundred thousand *koṭis* of *nayutas* of kalpas.

At that time, Vajragarbha Bodhisattva, wishing to again proclaim his meaning, thereupon spoke these verses:

The straightforward mind, the gentle mind, the capable mind,
the subdued mind, the serene mind, the mind of pure goodness,

the swift exits from *saṃsāra,* the broadly inclusive and great minds—
By employing these ten minds, one enters the second ground.[77]

Abiding herein, one perfects the qualities of the moral precepts,
departs far from killing, refrains from vexing or harming others,
and also abandons stealing as well as sexual misconduct and
speech that is either false, harsh, divisive, or meaningless.

He does not covet wealth, always feels kindness and pity,
walks the right path with a straight mind, has no flattery or falseness,
abandons treachery, casts off arrogance, is utterly subdued and pliant,
accords with the teachings in practice, and refrains from negligence.

One thinks, "The many sufferings endured in the hells, as animals,
and as hungry ghosts who, burning, spew forth fierce flames—
All of these are caused by karmic offenses.
I must abandon them and instead abide in the true Dharma.

Freely gaining rebirth among humans according to one's intentions,
and so on, up to *dhyāna* samādhi bliss in peak-of-existence heavens,
and the paths of *pratyekabuddha, śrāvaka,* and buddha vehicles—
All are gained with the ten good karmic actions as their cause."

One contemplates in this manner and thus refrains from negligence,
upholds pure precepts oneself, instructs others in guarding them,
and also, observing the many sufferings undergone by beings,
one thus ever increases the mind of great compassion.

"Foolish common people of faulty knowledge and wrong
understanding ever harbor hatred and engage in many disputes.
The objects of their covetousness never bring them satisfaction.
I should cause them to rid themselves of these three poisons.

"They are enveloped and blanketed by stupidity's great darkness,
fall into the net of wrong views on extremely hazardous paths,
and are trapped by adversaries in the cage of birth and death.
I should cause them to utterly defeat Māra's marauders.

"Swept away by the four floods, their minds become submerged.
They endure incalculable suffering as if burning in the three realms.
They conceive of the aggregates as a house in which a self abides.
Wishing to liberate them, I must diligently cultivate the path.

"Where they might seek escape, their minds being inferior and mean,
they have cast aside the Buddha's supremely excellent wisdom.
I wish to cause them to abide in the Great Vehicle
and bring forth diligent and tireless vigor in this."

The bodhisattva abiding herein accumulates meritorious qualities,
sees countless buddhas, presents offerings to them all,

and refines goodness to even greater brilliance for *koṭis* of kalpas
as if employing a fine elixir in refining real gold.

A son of the Buddha dwelling herein becomes a wheel-turning king
everywhere teaching beings to practice the ten good karmic deeds
while also cultivating all of the other good dharmas
in order to perfect the ten powers and rescue those in the world.

If he wishes to relinquish the royal throne, wealth, and jewels,
he thereupon abandons home life, accords with Buddha's teachings,
is valiant and energetic in diligence, and in a single moment,
acquires a thousand samādhis and sees a thousand buddhas.

The bodhisattva abiding on this ground is able to manifest
all the many different powers of the superknowledges,
and, through power of vows, his capabilities extend even beyond this
as, in countless ways, he freely liberates the many classes of beings.

As for these most supreme practices of the bodhisattva cultivated by
one who bestows benefit on everyone in the world,
all such meritorious qualities found on the second ground as these
have hereby been expounded on for the sake of the Buddha's sons.

The Third Ground

The Shining Light Ground

Of those sons of the Buddha hearing of this ground's practices
and of the inconceivable realms of the bodhisattva,
none failed to be moved to thoughts of reverence and delight.
Then, from the midst of space, they scattered blossoms as offerings.

Uttering praises, they said, "It is good indeed, Great Mountain King,
that, with compassionate mind, you think of beings with pity.
You have so well described the dharmas of moral virtue of the wise
as well as the practices and characteristics of the second ground.

The sublime practices of these bodhisattvas,
true, real, free of irregularities, and unvarying—
Wishing to benefit the many classes of beings,
you have thus expounded upon their supreme purity.

You to whom all humans and devas make offerings here,
we pray you will now expound on the third ground for their sakes
and hope you will entirely explain in accordance with their states
the Dharma-accordant works of the wise.

All of the Great Rishi's dharmas of giving, moral virtue,
patience, vigor, *dhyāna*, and wisdom,
as well as the path of skillful means, kindness, and compassion—
All these pure practices of the Buddha—please explain them all."

At that time, Liberation Moon repeated their request, saying:
"O fearless and greatly eminent master, Vajragarbha—
Please explain the manner of one's progression into the third ground
and all qualities of those there with pliant and harmonious minds."

At that time, Vajragarbha Bodhisattva informed Liberation Moon Bodhisattva, saying:

Son of the Buddha, the bodhisattva who has already accomplished the purification of the second ground and then wishes to enter the third ground should bring forth ten types of resolute intentions.[78] What then are these ten? They are:[79]

The resolute intention set on purity;
The resolute intention set on stable abiding;
The resolute intention set on renunciation;
The resolute intention set on abandoning desire;
The resolute intention set on irreversibility;

The resolute intention set on solidity;
The resolute intention set on flourishing brilliance;
The resolute intention set on heroic bravery;
The resolute intention set on being broadly inclusive;
And the resolute intention set on magnanimity.

The bodhisattva employs these ten types of resolute intentions to acquire entry into the third ground.

Son of the Buddha, after the bodhisattva-mahāsattva comes to abide on the third ground, he contemplates all conditioned dharmas in accordance with their true character, that is to say, they are characterized by:

Impermanence;
Suffering;
Impurity;
Instability;
Certainty of ruination;
Inability to long endure;
Production and destruction in each succeeding *kṣaṇa*;
Not coming forth from the past;
Not proceeding on to the future;
And not abiding in the present.

He also contemplates these dharmas:

As affording no protection;
As devoid of any refuge;
As accompanied by worry, sorrow, and anguish;
As bound up with love and hate;
As proliferating worry and sorrow;
As involving ceaseless accumulation;
As ablaze with the fire of desire, hatred, and stupidity that blaze on incessantly;
As enveloped by the many sorts of calamities;
As increasing day and night;
And as like magical conjurations in their unreality.

Having observed this, he doubly increases his renunciation of all conditioned things and progresses toward the wisdom of the Buddha. He perceives the wisdom of the Buddha:[80]

As inconceivable;
As unequaled;
As measureless;

As rarely encountered;
As unalloyed in its purity;
As beyond anguish;
As beyond worries;
As reaching all the way to the city of fearlessness;
As irreversible;
And as able to rescue countless beings beset with suffering and difficulty.

Once the bodhisattva has in this way observed the immeasurable benefit of the Tathāgata's wisdom and has likewise observed the countless faults and calamitous qualities of all that is conditioned, he then brings forth ten types of sympathetic mental intentions[81] toward all beings. What then are these ten? They are:[82]

He brings forth sympathetic mental intentions on observing that beings abide in solitude with no one upon whom they can depend;
He brings forth sympathetic mental intentions on observing that beings are poverty-stricken and destitute;
He brings forth sympathetic mental intentions on observing that beings are engulfed in the flames of the three poisons;
He brings forth sympathetic mental intentions on observing that beings are confined in the prison of the states of existence;
He brings forth sympathetic mental intentions on observing that beings are constantly covered over and obstructed by the dense forest of afflictions;
He brings forth sympathetic mental intentions on observing that beings are not skilled in contemplative thought;
He brings forth sympathetic mental intentions on observing that beings have no desire for good dharmas;
He brings forth sympathetic mental intentions on observing that beings have lost the buddhas' Dharma;
He brings forth sympathetic mental intentions on observing that beings flow along in the stream of cyclic births and deaths;
And he brings forth sympathetic mental intentions on observing that beings have lost the means of achieving liberation.

These are the ten.

Having thus observed the immeasurable suffering and anguish of the realms of beings' existence, the bodhisattva brings forth great vigor and thinks:[83]

I should rescue these beings;
I should liberate them;

I should establish them in purity;
I should take them on across;
I should see that they become situated in a place of goodness;
I should cause them to abide securely;
I should cause them to be filled with joy;
I should cause them to acquire knowledge and vision;
I should cause them to become well trained;
And I should cause them to reach nirvāṇa.

Having thus renounced all conditioned things, having thus become sympathetically mindful of all beings, having understood the supreme benefits of the cognition of all-knowledge, and wishing to rely on the Tathāgata's wisdom in rescuing beings, the bodhisattva reflects thus: "In this circumstance where all these beings have fallen into the great suffering of the afflictions, with what skillful means might I be able to extricate and rescue them so that they are caused to abide in the ultimate bliss of nirvāṇa?"

He then thinks:

> If one wishes to liberate beings and enable them to abide in nirvāṇa, this is inseparable from the unimpeded knowledge of liberation. The unimpeded knowledge of liberation is inseparable from awakening to all dharmas as they really are. The awakening to all dharmas as they really are is inseparable from the light of the practice wisdom that cognizes the nonexistence of action and nonproduction. The light of the practice wisdom that is cognizant of the nonexistence of action and nonproduction[84] is in turn inseparable from *dhyāna* meditation's skillful and definitive knowledge arising from contemplative investigation. *Dhyāna* meditation's skillful and definitive knowledge arising from contemplative investigation is in turn inseparable from skillful extensive learning.

Having contemplated and utterly realized this, the bodhisattva redoubles his diligent striving to cultivate right Dharma to the point that, day and night, he only wishes:[85]

To hear the Dharma;
To rejoice in the Dharma;
To delight in the Dharma;
To rely upon the Dharma;
To follow the Dharma;
To comprehend the Dharma;
To comply with the Dharma;
To arrive in the Dharma;

To abide in the Dharma;
And to practice the Dharma.

As in this way he diligently pursues his quest to acquire the Dharma of the Buddha, the bodhisattva retains no miserly cherishing for any precious possessions or wealth, for he does not perceive that there is any such thing that is worthy of being esteemed as rare. Rather, it is only the person who is able to explain the Buddha's Dharma that he conceives of as but rarely encountered.

Consequently, for the sake of his quest to acquire the Dharma of the Buddha, the bodhisattva is able to give away all his inward and outward wealth. There is no expression of reverence he would be unable to carry out, no form of pride he would be unable to relinquish, no form of service he would be unable to perform, and no form of intensely bitter suffering he would be unable to endure. If he were to be able to hear but a single sentence of Dharma he has never heard before, he would be filled with immense joy more abundant than what he would experience on receiving an entire great trichiliocosm full of precious jewels.

Were he to be able to hear but a single stanza of right Dharma he has not heard before, he would be filled with immense joy even more abundant than that experienced on acquiring the position of a wheel-turning sage king. Were he to succeed in acquiring but a single stanza of Dharma he had not heard before through which he might be able to purify his cultivation of the bodhisattva conduct, he would regard that as superior to ascending to the station of Indra or Brahmā where he might be able to abide in that manner for countless hundreds of thousands of kalpas.

Were someone to tell him: "I possess a single sentence of the Dharma spoken by the Buddha through which you will be able to purify your cultivation of the bodhisattva conduct, but I will only give it to you if you will now be able to plunge into a huge fire pit in which you will undergo the most extreme suffering," the bodhisattva would reflect in this way:

> If I were able to purify the cultivation of the bodhisattva conduct by acquiring this one stanza of Dharma spoken by the Buddha, then, even if an entire great trichiliocosm were filled with a great conflagration, I would still wish to throw my body down into it from the height of the Brahma Heaven in order to be able to personally acquire it. How much the less might it be that I would be unable to enter some small fire pit in order to acquire it? Hence, for the sake of seeking the Dharma of the Buddha, I should now even be willing to undergo all the many sufferings of the hells.

How much the less might I be unwilling to undergo any of the relatively minor sufferings encountered in the human realm?

In his practice of vigor in seeking the Buddha's Dharma, the bodhisattva brings forth just such diligence as this. He then implements the practice of contemplation and cultivation in accordance with whatsoever Dharma he has learned.

Having been able to hear the Dharma, this bodhisattva then focuses his mind and takes up peaceful dwelling in a secluded place, thinking, "It is only through cultivating in accordance with what has been taught that one then acquires the Buddha's Dharma. Achieving purification in these matters is not something one can accomplish solely through the spoken word."

Sons of the Buddha, when this bodhisattva comes to dwell on this Ground of Shining Light, he straightaway separates himself from desire and from evil and unwholesome dharmas. Still possessed of both ideation and mental discursion, he experiences the joy and the bliss arising from separation and abides in the first *dhyāna*.

Extinguishing both ideation and mental discursion, achieving inward purity, and anchoring the mind in a single place, he becomes free of ideation and free of mental discursion, experiences the joy and bliss generated through meditative concentration, and abides in the second *dhyāna*.

Separating himself from joy, abiding in equanimity, possessed of mindfulness and right knowing awareness, experiencing physical feeling of which the *āryas* are able to state that one is able to maintain equanimity toward it, and possessed of mindfulness while experiencing such bliss, he abides in the third *dhyāna*.

Cutting off bliss, having earlier already done away with suffering, having extinguished joy and sorrow, experiencing neither suffering nor bliss, and maintaining equanimity and mindfulness that are pure, he abides in the fourth *dhyāna*.

He transcends all perceptions of physical form, extinguishes all perceptions of [sensory] impingement, does not attend to any perceptions of diversity, enters a state characterized by boundless space, and thus then abides in the station of boundless space.

He entirely transcends the station of boundless space, enters a state characterized by boundless consciousness, and thus then abides in the station of boundless consciousness.

He entirely transcends the station of boundless consciousness, enters a state characterized by nothing whatsoever, and thus then abides in the station of nothing whatsoever.

He entirely transcends the station of nothing whatsoever and thus then abides in the station of neither perception nor nonperception.

Because he accords with the Dharma, he carries forth his practice without having anything to which he retains a pleasure-based attachment.

Son of the Buddha, this bodhisattva's mind pursues the cultivation of kindness to the point that it becomes vast, immeasurable, non-dual, free of enmity, free of any opposition, unimpeded, free of affliction, universally pervading everywhere throughout the Dharma realm and the realm of empty space, and extending universally to all worlds. His abiding in compassion, in sympathetic joy, and in equanimity are also just like this.

Son of the Buddha, this bodhisattva acquires the power of measureless spiritual superknowledges by which:

He is able to cause the entire great earth to tremor;

He is able to create many bodies from a single body and is able to make those many bodies become a single body, either making them hidden or making them visible;

He is able to pass unimpededly through the obstructions of rock, walls, and mountains just as if moving through empty space;

He is able to travel through empty space while remaining in full lotus position, just like a flying bird;

He is able to enter into the earth as if it were water;

He is able to walk on water as if it were the earth;

He is able to emit smoke and flames like a great bonfire;

He is also able to rain down water like a great cloud;

He also possesses that great and awesome power by which he is able to reach up with his hand and stroke the sun and the moon where they reside in space;

And he is able to freely transport his person wherever he pleases, even up to the Brahma World.

This bodhisattva possesses the heavenly ear that is purified and surpasses the human ear. Thus he is able to entirely hear all of the sounds of both humans and devas, whether they be near or far. He is also able even to entirely hear all of the sounds emitted by mosquitoes, gnats, and the various sorts of flies.

Employing the knowledge of others' thoughts, this bodhisattva knows in accordance with reality the thoughts of other beings. Specifically, when they have thoughts of desire, he knows in accordance with reality that they have thoughts of desire and when they have abandoned thoughts of desire, he knows in accordance with reality that they have abandoned thoughts of desire. In all cases, he knows in accordance with reality when they have:

> Thoughts of hatred or thoughts that have abandoned hatred;
> Deluded thoughts or thoughts that have abandoned delusion;
> Thoughts beset with afflictions or thoughts that are free of afflictions;
> Thoughts that are small in scope or thoughts that are vast in scope;
> Great thoughts or immeasurable thoughts;
> Thoughts that are general in nature or thoughts not general in nature;
> Scattered thoughts or thoughts that are not scattered;
> Concentrated thoughts or thoughts that are not concentrated;
> Liberated thoughts or unliberated thoughts;
> Surpassable thoughts or unsurpassable thoughts;
> Thoughts admixed with defilement or thoughts not admixed with defilement;
> And vast thoughts or thoughts that are not vast.

So it is that the bodhisattva uses the knowledge of others' thoughts to know beings' thoughts.

This bodhisattva remembers the details of countless past lives. Specifically, he remembers one life, two lives, three lives, four lives, and so forth on up to ten lives, twenty lives, thirty lives, and so forth on up to a hundred lives, countless hundreds of lives, countless thousands of lives, and countless hundreds of thousands of lives. He remembers the creation phase of the kalpa, the destruction phase of the kalpa, the creation and destruction phases of the kalpa, and remembers countless creation and destruction phases of kalpas. He remembers:

> I lived in such-and-such a place, was named this, was a member of this family, came from this caste, consumed these sorts of food and drink, lived a life of this length, dwelt for this amount of time, and experienced these sorts of suffering and happiness, after which I died in that place, was then reborn in such-and-such a place, after which I died in such-and-such a place, was then reborn in this place, possessed this sort of physical stature, was of this sort of appearance, and spoke with this sort of voice.

In this way, he entirely remembers countless details from his past.

This bodhisattva possesses the heavenly eye that is purified and surpasses the human eye. Thus he observes with respect to beings when they were born, when they died, whether they were of fine physical appearance or of hideous appearance, whether they dwelt in the destinies associated with goodness, whether they dwelt in the wretched destinies, and how they moved along in accordance with their karmic actions.

He is able as well to observe that, if some particular being had created bad physical karma, bad verbal karma, and bad mental karma, had slandered worthies and *āryas,* had become completely possessed of wrong views and the causes and conditions of karmic actions associated with wrong views, when his body perished and his life span came to an end, he then became bound for descent into the wretched destinies and was reborn into the hells.

He is also able to observe that, if yet some other being had created good physical karma, good verbal karma, and good mental karma, had refrained from slandering worthies and *āryas,* had become completely possessed of right views as well as the causes and conditions of karmic actions associated with right views, then, when his body perished and his life span came to an end, he then became bound for rebirth into the good destinies and for ascent into the heavens.

The bodhisattva's heavenly eye is able to observe all of these circumstances in accordance with the way they really are.

This bodhisattva, though well able to enter and emerge from the *dhyāna* samādhis and *samāpattis,* nonetheless does not acquiesce in their power when taking rebirth, but rather only acquiesces in rebirth to locations conducing to his ability to achieve complete fulfillment of the factors leading to the realization of bodhi. In this, availing himself of his mind's power of vows, he thereby achieves rebirth in those sorts of circumstances.

Son of the Buddha, due to the power of his vows, this bodhisattva who abides on this Ground of Shining Light becomes able to see many buddhas. That is to say that he may see many hundreds of buddhas, many thousands of buddhas, many hundreds of thousands of buddhas, and so forth until we come to his seeing many hundreds of thousands of *koṭis* of *nayutas* of buddhas, all of whom he reveres, venerates, and serves. He presents offerings to them of robes, food and drink, bedding, medicines, and all things supporting their lives, offering up all of these things with a vast mind and a deep mind. He also makes offerings of such requisites to everyone in their sangha assemblies and then dedicates these roots of goodness to the realization of *anuttara-samyak-saṃbodhi.* He listens respectfully to the Dharma in the presence of the buddhas. Having heard it, he retains it and cultivates it in a manner befitting his powers to do so.

This bodhisattva contemplates all dharmas as neither produced nor destroyed and as existing through the conjunction of causes and conditions.

Having first destroyed the bonds of views, the bonds of desire, the bonds of form, the bonds of becoming, and the bonds of ignorance all become ever more attenuated. Because, for countless hundreds of thousands of *koṭis* of *nayutas* of kalpas, they are no longer accumulated, wrong desire, wrong hatred, and wrong delusion are all entirely cut off. All of his roots of goodness then become ever more radiant.

Son of the Buddha, this is analogous to skillfully refining real gold to the point where its weight no longer diminishes with smelting and it shines ever more brightly in its purity. So too it is with the bodhisattva who dwells on the Ground of Shining Light. Because he no longer accumulates them, wrongly generated covetousness, wrongly generated hatred, and wrongly generated stupidity are all entirely cut off and his roots of goodness then shine ever more brightly.

This bodhisattva's inclination to be patient, his inclination to be gently harmonious, his inclination to be congenially adaptive, his inclination to be pleasingly sweet, his inclination to refrain from anger, his inclination to remain imperturbable, his inclination to remain unconfused, his inclination to refrain from judgments as to "superior" or "inferior," his inclination to not long for expressions of gratitude, his inclination to repay kindnesses, his inclination to refrain from flattery, his inclination to refrain from deviousness, and his inclination to refrain from treachery—all of these become ever more purified.[86]

Among the four means of attraction, this bodhisattva focuses more strongly on the practice of "beneficial actions" and, among the ten *pāramitās*, he focuses more strongly on the practice of the patience *pāramitā*.[87] It is not that he does not practice the others. Rather, he simply accords them an amount of emphasis corresponding to his own strengths and to whatever is fitting.

Son of the Buddha, this is what constitutes the bodhisattva's third ground, the Ground of Shining Light.

The bodhisattva dwelling on this ground often becomes a king of the Heaven of the Thirty-three who is able to employ skillful means to cause beings to abandon desire.

In his practice of "giving," "pleasing words," "beneficial actions," and "joint endeavors" and in all other such works as these, he never departs from mindfulness of the Buddha, never departs from mindfulness of the Dharma, never departs from mindfulness of the Sangha, and so forth until we come to his never departing from mindfulness of his quest to achieve complete fulfillment of the knowledge of all modes and the cognition of all-knowledge.

He also has this thought: "I should become one who serves these beings as a leader, as one who is supreme, as one who is most especially supreme, as one who is marvelous, as one who is most subtly marvelous, as one who is excellent, as one who is unexcelled," and so forth until we come to "as one who relies on the cognition of all-knowledge."

If he becomes diligent in the practice of vigor, then, in but a single moment, he will acquire a hundred thousand samādhis, will be able to see a hundred thousand buddhas, will know of the spiritual powers of a hundred thousand buddhas, will be able to cause tremors in a hundred thousand buddha worlds, and so forth until we come to his manifesting a hundred thousand bodies among which each and every one of those bodies manifests a hundred thousand bodhisattvas to serve as its retinue. If he uses the power of the bodhisattva's especially supreme vows, he will be freely able to bring forth manifestations beyond this number such that one could never count them all even in a hundred kalpas, a thousand kalpas, and so forth on up to a hundred thousand *koṭis* of *nayutas* of kalpas.

At that time, Vajragarbha Bodhisattva, wishing to again proclaim his meaning, thereupon spoke these verses:

The pure mind, stable abiding mind, mind of flourishing brilliance,
mind of renunciation, nondesiring mind, nonharming mind,[88]
the solid, valiant, broadly inclusive and magnanimous minds—
the wise resort to these in acquiring entry into the third ground.

The bodhisattva dwelling on this Ground of Shining Light
contemplates formative-factor dharmas as suffering, impermanent,
impure, bound to perish, rapidly bound to return to destruction,
as unenduring, as nonabiding, and as having no coming or going.

He contemplates conditioned dharmas as like a grave disease,
as bound up with worry, lamentation, suffering and anguish,
as constantly ablaze with the fierce fire of the three poisons
that, from beginningless time onward, has continued without cease.

He renounces the three realms, indulges no covetous attachment,
exclusively and without distraction pursues the Buddha's knowledge,

so difficult to fathom, difficult to conceive of, matchless,
immeasurable, boundless, and entirely free of torments.

Having observed the Buddha's knowledge, he feels pity for beings,
abiding alone, with no one to rely on or to rescue and protect them,
burned by the blazing fire of the three poisons, ever poverty-stricken,
dwelling in the prison of existence, always experiencing sufferings,

enveloped in and covered by the afflictions, blind, with no eyes,
aspiring to the inferior and mean, having lost the Dharma jewel,
swept along in cyclic births and deaths, frightened by nirvāṇa—
he thinks, "I should rescue them, bringing forth diligent vigor in this.

I shall seek the wisdom with which to benefit beings."
He reflects on which skillful means can cause their liberation and
realizes this is none other than the Tathāgata's unimpeded knowledge
that itself arises from the wisdom of nonproduction."

He reflects, "This wisdom is acquired through learning."
Having considered it thus, he then assiduously urges himself on
so that, day and night, he listens and practices incessantly,
taking only right Dharma as what is worthy of his esteem.

Whether it be countries, cities, wealth, the various precious jewels,
his wife, children, retinue, or even the royal throne—
for the sake of Dharma, the bodhisattva, with reverential mind,
is able to relinquish all such things.

Even his head, eyes, ears, nose, tongue, and teeth,
his hands, feet, bones, marrow, heart, blood and flesh—
relinquishing even such things as these, he does not deem difficult,
but rather only esteems the hearing of Dharma as most rare.

Should someone come and tell this bodhisattva,
"Whosoever is able to throw his body into a great bonfire—
I will bestow upon you a Dharma jewel of the Buddha,"
having heard this, he would feel no trepidation at leaping into it.

He instead thinks, "Even were there a fire filling up a trichiliocosm,
I would leap down into it from the height of the Brahma World,
for, to do this in search of the Dharma is not to be seen as difficult,
how much the less might I shrink from minor human sufferings."

Even all of the sufferings experienced in the Avīci Hells
from the time of his initial resolve until he achieves buddhahood—
he would be able to endure it all for the sake of hearing the Dharma.
How much the more would he endure all the sufferings of humans.

Having heard it, by right contemplation that accords with principle,
he gains in sequence the four *dhyānas*, four formless absorptions,

four equally regarding minds,[89] and five superknowledges,
yet does not acquiesce in their power to determine one's rebirths.

The bodhisattva dwelling herein sees many buddhas,
makes offerings to them, listens to them, and, with resolute mind,
severs erroneous views and delusions and becomes ever more pure,
as when refining true gold, its substance remains undiminished.

One who abides herein often becomes a Trāyastriṃśa Heaven King
teaching and guiding countless members of the assemblies of devas,
causing them to forsake the desire mind, abide in paths of goodness,
and proceed with singular devotion to seek the Buddha's qualities.

A son of the Buddha abiding herein who is diligently vigorous
perfectly acquires a hundred thousand samādhis,
sees a hundred thousand buddhas' bodies adorned with the marks,
and, if resorting to the power of vows, exceeds even this.

As for the universal benefiting of all beings
and all of those especially superior practices of the bodhisattvas
as well as all of the other such aspects of the third ground,
I have concluded their explanation according to their meaning.

The Fourth Ground

The Blazing Brilliance Ground

When those sons of the Buddha had heard of these vast practices
on this delightful, deeply sublime, and especially supreme ground,
their minds were exhilarated, they were filled with great joy, and
they scattered many flowers everywhere as offerings to the Buddha.

When such sublime Dharma had been proclaimed there,
the great earth trembled, the ocean's waters roiled,
and all of the celestial nymphs became joyful,
whereupon they all joined their marvelous voices in singing praises.

The Vaśavartin Heaven King, moved to immense celebratory delight,
rained down *maṇi* jewels as offerings to the Buddha,
and uttered praises: "The Buddha has come forth here for our sakes,
expounding the practices possessed of the foremost merit.

The meaning of the grounds taught by such a wise one as this
is extremely difficult to encounter in a hundred thousand kalpas.
We have now suddenly been able to hear this sublime Dharma voice
speak of a bodhisattva's supreme conduct.

We wish to additionally hear expounded the brilliantly wise one's
subsequent grounds on the definite path to the realm without residue
that bestows benefit on all devas and all humans.
All of these sons of the Buddha would delight in hearing this."

Then the heroically valiant one of great resolve, Liberation Moon,
posed a request to Vajragarbha, saying, "O Son of the Buddha,
please explain here all aspects of the practice involved in
turning from here to enter the fourth ground."

At that time, Vajragarbha Bodhisattva informed Liberation Moon Bodhisattva, saying:

O Son of the Buddha, as for the bodhisattva-mahāsattva who has already well purified his practice on the third ground and then wishes to enter the fourth ground, the Ground of Blazing Brilliance, he should cultivate ten gateways to the light of Dharma.[90] What are the ten? They are:

Contemplation of the realms of beings;
Contemplation of the Dharma realm;
Contemplation of the world realms;
Contemplation of the realms of empty space;

Contemplation of the realms of consciousness;
Contemplation of the desire realm;
Contemplation of the form realm;
Contemplation of the formless realm;
Contemplation of the realms of broadly inclusive resolute intentions and resolute convictions;[91]
And contemplation of the realms of magnanimous resolute intentions and resolute convictions.[92]

The bodhisattva employs these ten gateways to the light of Dharma to gain entry into the fourth ground, the Ground of Blazing Brilliance.

Son of the Buddha, if a bodhisattva comes to dwell on this Ground of Blazing Brilliance, then, by employing ten types of knowledge-maturing dharmas,[93] he becomes able to acquire its inner dharmas[94] and achieve birth into the clan of the *tathāgatas*. What then are those ten? They are:

Through possessing nonretreating resolute intentions;
Through bringing forth ultimately pure and indestructible faith in the Three Jewels;
Through contemplating the production and destruction of all karmic formative factors;
Through contemplating all dharmas as, by their very nature, unproduced;
Through contemplating the formation and destruction of worlds;
Through contemplating that it is on account of karmic actions that birth exists;
Through contemplating *saṃsāra* and nirvāṇa;
Through contemplating the karma associated with beings and lands;
Through contemplating the past and the future;
And through contemplating nonexistence and complete destruction.

These are the ten.

Son of the Buddha, the bodhisattva dwelling on this fourth ground employs the body-examining contemplation that takes his own body as the objective focus, employing diligent and robust mindfulness and knowing awareness[95] in ridding himself of desire and distress associated with the world. He employs the body-examining contemplation taking others' bodies as the objective focus, employing diligent and robust mindfulness and knowing awareness in ridding himself of desire and distress associated with the world. And he employs the body-examining contemplation that takes both his own body and others' bodies as the objective focus, employing diligent and robust mindfulness and knowing awareness in ridding himself of desire and distress associated with the world.

In this same manner, he also applies such contemplation to his own feelings, to the feelings of others, and to the feelings of both himself and others, applying the feeling-examining contemplation to those objective conditions.

He also applies such contemplation to his own mind, to the minds of others, and to the minds of both himself and others, employing the mind-examining contemplation to those objective conditions.

And, finally, he also applies such contemplation to subjectively related dharmas, to objectively related dharmas, and to dharmas that are both subjectively related and objectively related, employing the dharma-examining contemplation to those objective conditions.

Thus it is that he employs diligent and robust mindfulness and knowing awareness in ridding himself of desire and distress associated with the world.[96]

Additionally, for the sake of not generating evil and unwholesome dharmas that have not yet arisen, this bodhisattva strives to bring forth diligently applied vigor and resolves to cut off their arising.

For the sake of severing already-arisen evil and unwholesome dharmas, he strives to bring forth diligently applied vigor and resolves to cut them off.

For the sake of generating good dharmas not yet arisen, he strives to bring forth diligently applied vigor and resolves to proceed with their right practice.

And for the sake of ensuring that already-arisen good dharmas will continue and not be lost, and also in order to cultivate, increase, and broaden them, he strives to bring forth diligently applied vigor and resolves to engage in right practice.[97]

Additionally, this bodhisattva cultivates the severance practice associated with zeal-based concentration, this in order to completely establish the spiritual powers, doing so based upon detachment, based upon dispassion, based upon cessation, and directed toward relinquishment.[98] He also cultivates the severance practices associated with vigor-based concentration, associated with mind-based concentration, and associated with contemplation-based concentration, this in order to completely establish the spiritual powers, doing so based upon detachment, based upon dispassion, based upon cessation, and directed toward relinquishment.[99]

Additionally, this bodhisattva cultivates the root-faculty of faith, doing so based upon detachment, based upon dispassion, based upon cessation, and directed toward relinquishment, cultivates too the root-faculty of vigor, the root-faculty of mindfulness, the root-faculty of concentration, and the root-faculty of wisdom, in all cases doing so based upon detachment, based upon dispassion, based upon cessation, and directed toward relinquishment.[100]

Additionally, this bodhisattva cultivates the power of faith, doing so based upon detachment, based upon dispassion, based upon cessation, and directed toward relinquishment, cultivates the power of vigor, the power of mindfulness, the power of concentration, and the power of wisdom, doing so based upon detachment, based upon dispassion, based upon cessation, and directed toward relinquishment.[101]

Additionally, this bodhisattva cultivates the mindfulness limb of enlightenment, doing so based upon detachment, based upon dispassion, based upon cessation, and directed toward relinquishment, cultivates the dharma-differentiation limb of enlightenment, the vigor limb of enlightenment, the joyfulness limb of enlightenment, the pliancy limb of enlightenment, the concentration limb of enlightenment, and the equanimity limb of enlightenment, doing so based upon detachment, based upon dispassion, based upon cessation, and directed toward relinquishment.[102]

Additionally, this bodhisattva cultivates right views, doing so based upon detachment, based upon dispassion, based upon cessation, and directed toward relinquishment. So too, he cultivates right thought, right speech, right action, right livelihood, right effort, right mindfulness, and right concentration, doing so based upon detachment, based upon dispassion, based upon cessation, and directed toward relinquishment.[103]

The bodhisattva cultivates such meritorious qualities as these, engaging in such cultivation:

In order to refrain from forsaking all beings;
In order to be sustained by his original vows;
In order to make the great compassion foremost;
In order to perfect the great kindness;
In order to reflect upon and bear in mind the cognition of all-knowledge;
In order to completely accomplish the adornment of buddha lands;
In order to completely realize the Tathāgata's powers, fearlessnesses, dharmas exclusive to the buddhas, major marks, subsidiary signs, and voice;

In order to further his quest to acquire the most especially supreme path;[104]

In order to accord with what he has learned regarding the extremely profound liberation of the Buddha;

And in order to reflect upon greatly wise and good skillful means.

Son of the Buddha, the bodhisattva dwelling on the Ground of Blazing Brilliance, taking the view imputing the existence of a self associated with the body as chief among them, abandons all attachments that might be generated, including attachments to the existence of a self, to a person, to beings, to a life span, to the aggregates, to the sense realms, and to the sense bases, doing so because they arise and disappear in reliance on conceptual thought, because they are sustained through discursive thought, because they are but subsidiary to a self, because they are but its material possessions, and because they are but points of attachment. He entirely abandons them all.

Whenever this bodhisattva sees that particular karmic actions have been censured by the Tathāgata as defiled by the afflictions, he abandons all of them. Whenever he sees that particular karmic actions accord with the bodhisattva path and have been praised by the Tathāgata, he cultivates all of them.[105]

Son of the Buddha, this bodhisattva cultivates the path and the provisions assisting realization of the path[106] in a manner that befits the skillful means and wisdom he has developed. Proceeding in this manner, he thus acquires:[107]

The harmoniously smooth mind;

The gentle mind;

The congenially adaptive mind;

The mind that benefits and provides happiness to others;

The mind unmixed with defilement;

The mind that seeks ever more superior dharmas;

The mind that seeks especially supreme wisdom;

The mind that seeks to rescue everyone in the world;

The mind that respects those of venerable virtue and does not go against their teaching instructions;

And the mind that thoroughly cultivates in accordance with the Dharma one has learned.

This bodhisattva:[108]

Acknowledges kindnesses received;

Knows to repay kindnesses;

Has a mind that is extremely harmonious and good;

Dwells happily together with others;
Is endowed with a character that is straight-minded;
Is gentle and pliant;
Is free of behavior influenced by the dense forest [of afflictions];
Is free of arrogance;
Is one who skillfully accepts instruction;
And is one who well understands the intentions of those whose speech he hears.

It is in this way that this bodhisattva's patience becomes completely developed, in this way that his pliancy becomes completely developed, and in this way that his quiescence becomes completely developed. Having thus acquired completely developed patience, pliancy, and quiescence, he then purifies his karmic actions on the subsequent grounds.

At this time, as he proceeds with well-considered cultivation, he acquires:[109]

Unresting vigor;
Vigor unmixed with defiling factors;
Nonretreating vigor;
Vast vigor;
Boundless vigor;
Blazing vigor;
Matchless vigor;
Invincible vigor;
Vigor aimed at maturing all beings;
And vigor that is well able to distinguish what is and is not the path.

This bodhisattva's aspirations have become purified, his resolute intentions never wane, his awakened convictions are brilliant and sharp, and his roots of goodness increase.[110] He abandons the world's defiling turbidities, cuts off all doubts and uncertainties, achieves perfected clarity in severance, and is filled with delight. He is one of whom the buddhas are protectively mindful and his resolute intentions in relation to the immeasurable minds have become fully developed.[111]

Son of the Buddha, due to the power of his vows, the bodhisattva dwelling on this Ground of Blazing Brilliance is able to see many buddhas. That is to say that he can see many hundreds of buddhas, can see many hundreds of thousands of buddhas, and so forth until we come to his seeing of many hundreds of thousands of *koṭis* of *nayutas* of buddhas, all of whom he reveres, venerates, and serves, presenting offerings to them of robes, bedding, food and drink, medicines, and all amenities supporting their existence, offering up all of these things while also making offerings to those in all their sangha assemblies, proceeding then to dedicate the merit associated with these roots of goodness to *anuttara-samyak-saṃbodhi.*

So too does he then respectfully listen to the teachings on Dharma in the presence of those buddhas. Having heard these teachings, he takes them on, upholds them in practice, and entirely perfects their cultivation. Furthermore, during the Dharma reign of those buddhas, he leaves behind the home life to cultivate the path.

He also purifies his resolute intentions and resolute faith[112] as he passes through countless hundreds of thousands of *koṭis* of *nayutas* of kalpas wherein he causes his roots of goodness to shine ever more brightly in their purity.

Son of the Buddha, this is analogous to a goldsmith's refining of real gold to create objects of adornment unmatched in their perfection by anything made from other grades of gold. So too it is with this bodhisattva-mahāsattva. When he dwells on this ground, all of his roots of goodness are such that none of the roots of goodness of those on lower grounds could ever match them.

This circumstance is analogous to a *maṇi* jewel's orb of pure radiant light that is able to emit radiance of the sort that no other jewel's radiance can even approach, radiance that not even the conditions of wind, rain, and so forth are able to ruin. So, too, the bodhisattva-mahāsattva dwelling on this ground cannot be matched by any of the lower ground bodhisattvas, for he cannot be destroyed by any of the many sorts of *māras* or afflictions.

Among the four means of attraction, this bodhisattva most extensively devotes his practice to "joint endeavors," while, among the ten *pāramitās,* he most extensively practices the perfection of vigor. It is not that he does not practice the others. Rather, he simply accords them an amount of emphasis corresponding to his own strengths and to what is fitting.

Sons of the Buddha, this has been a concise explanation of the bodhisattva-mahāsattva's fourth ground, the Ground of Blazing Brilliance.

The bodhisattva dwelling on this ground often becomes the heavenly king Suyāma in which capacity he is equipped with skillful means by which he can influence beings to rid themselves of the view imputing the existence of a real self in association with the body[113] and other such delusions, thereby causing them to abide in right views.

In his practice of giving, pleasing words, beneficial actions, and joint endeavors and all other such works that he pursues, he never departs from mindfulness of the Buddha, never departs from mindfulness of the Dharma, never departs from mindfulness of the Sangha, and so forth until we come to his never departing from mindfulness of his quest to achieve complete fulfillment of the knowledge of all modes and the cognition of all-knowledge.

He also has this thought: "I should become one who serves these beings as a leader, as one who is supreme, as one who is most especially supreme, as one who is marvelous, as one who is most subtly marvelous, as one who is excellent, as one who is unexcelled," and so forth until we come to "as one who relies on the cognition of all-knowledge."

If this bodhisattva brings forth diligently vigorous practice, then, in but a moment, he will become able to enter a *koṭi* of samādhis, will be able to see a *koṭi* of buddhas, will become aware of the spiritual powers as exercised by a *koṭi* of buddhas, will be able to cause tremors in a *koṭi* of worlds, and so forth until we come to his being able to manifest a *koṭi* of bodies wherein each and every one of those bodies will itself become able to manifest a *koṭi* of bodhisattvas serving in his retinue. If he resorts to the power of the especially supreme vows of the bodhisattva, he will become freely able to bring forth manifestations beyond this number such that one would never be able to count them even in a period of a hundred kalpas, a thousand kalpas, and so forth until we come to a hundred thousand *koṭis* of *nayutas* of kalpas.

At that time, Vajragarbha Bodhisattva, wishing to once again proclaim the meaning of his discourse, thereupon spoke these verses:

The bodhisattva who has already purified the third ground
next contemplates beings, the worlds, the Dharma realm,
the realms of empty space and consciousness, the three realms,
intentions, and convictions. Fathoming these, he is able to enter.[114]

On first ascending to the flaming ground, as he increases in strength,
he is born into the *tathāgatas'* clan through never-retreating resolve,
indestructible faith in the Buddha, Dharma, and Sangha,
contemplating dharmas as impermanent and unproduced,

contemplating worlds' rise and fall, karma as the basis for birth,
saṃsāra and nirvāṇa, the karma associated with lands and such,
contemplating past and future, and also contemplating destruction.
Through just such cultivation as this, he is born into Buddha's clan.[115]

After acquiring these dharmas, his kindly sympathy increases,
he redoubles diligent cultivation of the four stations of mindfulness

and their inward and outward contemplation of body, feelings, mind,
and dharmas, thereby getting rid of and banishing all worldly desires.

The bodhisattva cultivates the four right efforts by which
bad dharmas are extinguished and good dharmas are increased.
Psychic power bases, faculties, and powers are all skillfully cultivated.
So too it is with the seven limbs of bodhi and the eightfold path.[116]

He cultivates those practices in order to liberate beings, to be guarded
by original vows, to perfect kindness, to make compassion foremost,
to aid his quest for all-knowledge and adornment of buddha lands,
and also to bear in mind acquisition of the Tathāgata's ten powers,

four fearlessnesses, the dharmas exclusive to the buddhas,
their special major marks, subsidiary signs, and fine voice.
He also cultivates those practices to pursue his quest for
the sublime path's stations of liberation and great skillful means.[117]

As for seeing a self related to the body, chief of the sixty-two views
that include conceiving of a self, its possessions, and countless other
attachments to aggregates, sense realms, sense bases, and such,
he abandons all of these on this fourth ground.

Because they are meaningless and unbeneficial, he cuts off all
affliction-ridden actions censured by the Tathāgata,
while, of the pure karmic actions cultivated by the wise,
there are none he fails to implement in order to liberate beings.

The bodhisattva, assiduous in cultivating, refrains from indolence,
straightaway achieves perfect fulfillment of ten types of mind,
focuses intently on tirelessly pursuing the path to buddhahood,
is resolute in aspiring to receive the consecration and liberate beings,

respectfully follows cultivation dharmas of the venerably virtuous,
acknowledges kindness, is easily taught, is free of enmity or temper,
forsakes pride, abandons flattery, has a subdued and pliant mind,
and increases in energetic diligence that then never retreats.

As for the bodhisattva dwelling on this Ground of Blazing Brilliance,
his intentions are purified and never are lost.
His awakened convictions are definite, his goodness increases, and
he entirely abandons the net of doubts and all defiling turbidity.

The bodhisattva on this ground, the most supreme of all men,
makes offerings to countless *nayutas* of buddhas,
listens to their right Dharma teaching, leaves the home life,
becomes impossible to impede, and becomes like real gold.

The bodhisattva abiding herein is replete with meritorious qualities.
He employs knowledge and skillful means in cultivating the path.

His resolve cannot be turned back by the many sorts of *māras*.
In this he becomes like a marvelous jewel that no one can ruin.

One abiding herein often becomes Suyāma, a king of the devas who,
masterfully adept in all dharmas and revered by the multitudes,
everywhere teaches all types of beings to be rid of wrong views and
focuses on seeking Buddha's knowledge and cultivating good karma.

This bodhisattva who is diligent in applying the power of vigor
acquires samādhis and other achievements, each a *koṭi* in number,
and, if he avails himself of the power of vows and knowledge, his acts
go beyond this number and exceed even the range of knowability.

Thus it is that the sublime path of the bodhisattva's fourth ground,
pure in its practices and mutually consistent with
the meritorious qualities, meaning, and knowledge,
has been explained by me for the Sons of the Buddha.

The Fifth Ground

The Difficult-to-Conquer Ground

On hearing of this ground's supreme practices,
the bodhisattvas awakened to this Dharma with joyous minds.
Blossoms rained down from the sky and praises resounded, saying:
"This is good indeed, O Great Eminence, Vajragarbha."

The Vaśavartin Deva King and his celestial host,
having heard this Dharma teaching, leapt up, stood in space,
and everywhere released all sorts of marvelous light clouds
as offerings to the Tathāgata, and everyone was filled with joy.

The celestial nymphs played heavenly music,
sang songs in praise of the Buddha,
and then, through the awesome spiritual power of the Bodhisattva,
from amidst the sounds of their voices, they uttered these words:

"The Buddha's vows, made so long ago, are now fulfilled.
The path of the Buddha, so long in its course, is now realized.
Śākyamuni Buddha has arrived at the celestial palace where
he who benefits both devas and humans, after so long, is now seen.

The Great Sea, so ancient and vast, for the first time, now moves.
The Buddha's light, so ancient and far-reaching, now shines forth.
Beings, after a long and distant past, for the first time, are happy.
The voice of the great compassion, after so long, is now heard.

[After such a long time, the Great Muni is now met.]
The far shore of all perfected qualities has been reached.
The darkness of all arrogance and pride has been dispelled
[The Great Śramaṇa, worthy of reverence, is revered.][118]

He who is possessed of utmost purity, like empty space,
undefiled by worldly dharmas, comparable to a lotus blossom,
the Great Muni, the Honored One, appears here in this world,
like Mount Sumeru rising up from the midst of the great ocean.

By making offerings to him, one becomes able to end all suffering.
By making offerings, one certainly acquires the buddhas' knowledge.
In this place of one worthy of offerings, we offer to one without peer.
Hence, with delighted minds, we present offerings to the Buddha."

After these countless daughters of the devas
had sung these phrases in praise,
everyone there was moved to reverence and was filled with joy.
They then gazed up at the Tathāgata who dwelt there in silence.

At this time, the great eminence, Liberation Moon,
again presented a request to the fearless one, Vajragarbha,
"We only pray, O Son of the Buddha, that you will explain for us
the practices and characteristic aspects of the fifth ground."

At that time, Vajragarbha Bodhisattva informed Liberation Moon Bodhisattva, saying:

O Son of the Buddha, the bodhisattva-mahāsattva who has already thoroughly and perfectly fulfilled the path of the fourth ground's practices and then wishes to enter the fifth ground, the "difficult-to-conquer" ground, should progress into it through the practice of ten kinds of equally regarding pure resolute intentions.[119] What then are these ten? They are:

- Equally regarding pure resolute intentions toward the Dharma of the buddhas of the past;
- Equally regarding pure resolute intentions toward the Dharma of the buddhas of the future;
- Equally regarding pure resolute intentions toward the Dharma of the buddhas of the present;
- Equally regarding pure resolute intentions toward the moral precepts;
- Equally regarding pure resolute intentions toward the mind;[120]
- Equally regarding pure resolute intentions toward ridding himself of views, doubts, and regretfulness;
- Equally regarding pure resolute intentions toward the knowledge of what is the path and what is not the path;
- Equally regarding pure resolute intentions toward the knowledge and vision associated with cultivating the practices;
- Equally regarding pure resolute intentions toward ever more superior contemplations of all the dharmas constituting the limbs of bodhi;
- And equally regarding pure resolute intentions toward teaching all beings.

The bodhisattva-mahāsattva uses these ten types of equally regarding pure resolute intentions to achieve entry into the fifth bodhisattva ground.

Son of the Buddha, once the bodhisattva-mahāsattva has come to dwell on this fifth ground, then:

- Due to thoroughly cultivating the dharmas of the limbs of bodhi;
- Due to thoroughly purifying the resolute intentions;[121]
- Due to further redoubled efforts in seeking the most supreme stations on the path;

Due to according with true suchness,
Due to being sustained by the power of vows;
Due to never relinquishing kindness and pity for all beings;
Due to accumulating the merit and knowledge constituting the provisions for realization of the path;
Due to energetic and ceaseless diligence in cultivation,
Due to bringing forth skillful means;
Due to contemplating and illuminating ever higher grounds;
Due to being guarded by the Tathāgata's protective mindfulness;
And due to being sustained by the power of mindfulness and wisdom,

He then acquires the irreversible resolve.

Son of the Buddha, this bodhisattva-mahāsattva knows in accordance with reality: "This is the *āryas'* truth of suffering, this is the Āryas' truth of the accumulation of suffering, this is the *āryas'* truth of the cessation of suffering, and this is the *āryas'* truth of the path to the cessation of suffering." He:

Knows well the conventional truth;[122]
Knows well the truth of the supreme meaning;[123]
Knows well the truth of characteristic signs;[124]
Knows well the truth of differentiating distinctions;[125]
Knows well the truth of establishment;[126]
Knows well the truth of phenomena;[127]
Knows well the truth of production;[128]
Knows well the truth of cessation with no further production;[129]
Knows well the truth of the knowledge associated with entering the path;[130]
Knows well the truth of the sequential and complete cultivation of all bodhisattva grounds, and so forth on up to his knowing well the truth associated with the complete cultivation of the Tathāgata's knowledge.[131]

This bodhisattva:

Knows the conventional truth through adapting to beings' mental dispositions and thereby causing them to be delighted;[132]
Knows the truth of the supreme meaning through achieving a penetrating comprehension of the one true character of all phenomena;[133]
Knows the truth of characteristic signs through comprehending the individual and shared characteristics of dharmas;[134]
Knows the truth of differentiating distinctions through completely comprehending the distinctions in dharmas' categorical differences;[135]

Knows the truth of establishment through skillfully distinguishing the aggregates, sense realms, and sense bases;[136]
Knows the truth of phenomena through being aware of the suffering and anguish inherent in body and mind;[137]
Knows the truth of production through being aware of the factors involved in the continuity of rebirths within the rebirth destinies;[138]
Knows the truth of complete cessation with no further production through the ultimate extinguishing of all inflaming afflictions;[139]
Knows the truth of the knowledge associated with entering the path through bringing forth the realization of non-duality;[140]
And knows well the truth of the sequential and continuous complete cultivation of all bodhisattva grounds on up to and including the complete cultivation of the Tathāgata's knowledge, accomplishing this through having become rightly aware of all aspects of the practices.[141]

It is through the power of knowledge associated with resolute faith[142] that he knows this, for this is not yet a case of knowing accomplished through the power of ultimately final knowledge.

Son of the Buddha, after this bodhisattva-mahāsattva has acquired the knowledge associated with these truths, he knows in accordance with reality that all conditioned dharmas are false and deceptive and that they thereby delude the foolish common person. At this time, the bodhisattva increases even more his great compassion for beings and brings forth the light of the great kindness.

Son of the Buddha, the bodhisattva-mahāsattva who has acquired such powers of knowledge never forsakes any being and always strives to acquire the Buddha's knowledge. He contemplates in accordance with reality all past and future conditioned actions and knows that it is from prior ignorance, existence, and craving that one therefore produces the flowing on and turning about in cyclic births and deaths wherein one is unable to move to escape the house of the aggregates and thus increases one's accumulation of suffering. He knows that there is no self, no entity possessed of a life span, no soul, and no one who yet again repeatedly takes up bodies in subsequent rebirth destinies. He knows that this all occurs entirely apart from any self or anything possessed by a self and knows that, just as this has been the case in the past, so too does it continue to be so in the future, for, in every case, none of these exist at all. And he knows whether or not there is any complete cessation and escape to be had from this covetous attachment to what is empty and false. He knows all of these matters in accordance with reality.

Son of the Buddha, this bodhisattva-mahāsattva has this additional thought:

> These common people, so deluded and devoid of wisdom, are so very pitiable. They have countless bodies that have already destroyed, are now being destroyed, and will be destroyed in the future. In this way, their bodies are all entirely destroyed and yet they are unable to bring forth any thought of renunciation toward the body, but rather instead ever increase the matters that are the mechanisms for producing suffering. Hence they flow along, following the current of births and deaths and remain unable to turn back against it.
>
> They do not seek to escape from the house of the aggregates and never know to become concerned about or fear the poisonous snakes of the four great elements. They are unable to extricate the arrows of pride and views, are unable to extinguish the fires of desire, hatred, and delusion, are unable to destroy the darkness of ignorance, and are unable to dry up the great sea of desire. They do not seek to encounter the great *ārya* and guide who possesses the ten powers but instead enter the entangling thicket of resolute intentions influenced by *māras*.[143] They then become swept up and drowned in the crashing surf of ideation and mental discursion.[144]

Son of the Buddha, this bodhisattva-mahāsattva has yet another thought:

> In their undergoing of such suffering, these beings are alone, poverty-stricken, and distressed by difficulties. They have no one to rescue them and no one to rely on. They are without an island, without a shelter, without a guide, and without eyes. They are covered over by ignorance and enveloped in darkness. For the sake of all those beings, I shall now cultivate merit and knowledge, the dharmas constituting provisions for the path. In doing so, I bring forth this resolve alone, not seeking any companions in this. Utilizing such meritorious qualities, I shall influence beings to achieve the ultimate purification and continue in this until they acquire the Tathāgata's ten powers and unimpeded wisdom.

Son of the Buddha, this bodhisattva-mahāsattva employing wisdom such as this, contemplates the roots of goodness that he cultivates as being dedicated entirely for the sake of:[145]

> Rescuing and protecting all beings;
> Benefiting all beings;
> Bringing happiness to all beings;

Bringing forth sympathetic pity for all beings;
Bringing about the complete success of all beings;
Liberating all beings;
Drawing in all beings;
Causing all beings to abandon suffering and anguish;
Causing all beings everywhere to acquire purity;
Causing all beings to adopt the training;
And causing all beings to achieve entry into *parinirvāṇa*.

Son of the Buddha, regarding the bodhisattva dwelling on this fifth ground, the Difficult-to-Conquer Ground:

He is one who is mindful, for he never forgets any dharma;
He is one who is wise, for he is able to skillfully and resolutely bring forth complete understanding;
He is one who comprehends implications, for he realizes the purport of the ideas contained in the scriptures and understands their order and their connections;
He is one possessed of a sense of shame and a dread of blame, for he guards himself while also protecting others;
He is one who is possessed of solidity, for he never abandons his practice of the moral precepts;
He is one who is possessed of awakened awareness,[146] for he is able to assess what is and is not possessed of correct bases;
He is one who accords with knowledge,[147] for he does not accord with anything aside from that;
He is one who accords with wisdom,[148] for he knows well the distinctions between principled and unprincipled statements;
He is one possessed of the spiritual superknowledges, for he skillfully cultivates the *dhyāna* absorptions;
He is one possessed of skillful means, for he is able to adapt to the ways of the world;
He is one possessed of insatiability, for he pursues the thorough accumulation of merit;[149]
He is one who is unresting, for he always seeks to acquire wisdom;[150]
He is one who is tireless, for he accumulates great kindness and compassion;[151]
He is one who pursues diligent cultivation on behalf of others, for he wishes to cause all beings to achieve entry into nirvāṇa;
He is one who is possessed of unrelenting diligence in the pursuit of his quest, for he seeks the Tathāgata's powers, fearlessness, and dharmas exclusive to the buddhas;

He is one who is able to carry out whatever he decides to do, for he perfects the adornment of the buddha lands;

He is one who diligently cultivates every sort of good karmic work, for he is able to completely fulfill [the bases for acquiring] the major marks and the subsidiary signs;

He is one who always cultivates with diligence, for he seeks to acquire the physical, verbal, and mental qualities adorning the Buddha;

He is one who greatly venerates and reveres the Dharma, for he practices in accordance with the teachings wherever all bodhisattva Dharma teachers reside;

He is one possessed of unimpeded resolve, for he adopts great skillful means as he always implements his practice in the world;

And he is one who, both day and night, abandons any other sorts of intentions, for he always delights in teaching all beings.

Son of the Buddha, as the bodhisattva-mahāsattva diligently cultivates in this manner:

He uses giving in teaching beings;

He uses pleasing words, beneficial actions, and joint endeavors in teaching beings;

He manifests form bodies in teaching beings;

He expounds on all dharmas in teaching beings;

He opens up and reveals the bodhisattva conduct in teaching beings;

He displays the immensely awe-inspiring powers of the Tathāgata in teaching beings;

He reveals the transgressions associated with *saṃsāra* in teaching beings;

He praises the benefits of the Tathāgata's wisdom in teaching beings;

He manifests the power of great spiritual superknowledges in teaching beings;

And he uses all different sorts of practices involving skillful means in teaching beings.

Son of the Buddha, even as the bodhisattva-mahāsattva is able in this fashion to diligently employ skillful means in teaching beings, his mind constantly progresses toward the Buddha's wisdom. He never turns back in his creation of roots of goodness, but rather always diligently cultivates and trains in the most especially supreme practice dharmas.

Son of the Buddha, in order to be of benefit to beings, there is no worldly skill or art that this bodhisattva-mahāsattva does not comprehensively practice. In particular, this refers to writing, mathematical calculation, drawing, writing, printing, and all of the different sorts of treatises devoted to the elements of earth, water, fire, and wind, all of which he completely comprehends. He is also thoroughly skilled in medicinal prescriptions and the treatment of all diseases, including insanity, the wasting diseases, possession by ghosts, and poisoning at the hands of sorcerers, all of which he is able to dispel. He is thoroughly skilled in all such matters as literary compositions, praises, chants, singing, dance, musical performance, humor, and explanatory discussion.

He is also skilled in the placement and arrangement of states, cities, villages, palaces, homes, parks, gardens, springs, flowing waters, reservoirs, ponds, grasses, trees, flowers, and medicinal plants so that they each find their most appropriate location. He also knows the hidden locations of gold, silver, *maṇi* jewels, pearls, lapis lazuli, conch shells, jade, coral, and other such things that he brings forth and reveals for others.

He is also skilled in the contemplative assessment of all such things as the sun, the moon and stars, the cries of birds, earthquakes, the auspicious or inauspicious significance of dreams, and the good and bad fortune associated with physical features, never erring even once in his judgment on these matters.

In order to benefit them and gradually influence them to become securely established in the unsurpassed Dharma of the Buddha, he thoroughly explains and reveals for beings such matters such as the observance of moral precepts, entry into the *dhyāna* absorptions, the spiritual superknowledges, the immeasurables, and the four formless absorptions as well as all other sorts of other matters having to do with the world. In this, his sole concern is that he never act in a manner harmful or distressing to beings.

Son of the Buddha, due to the power of his vows, the bodhisattva dwelling on this Difficult-to-Conquer Ground becomes able to see many buddhas. Specifically, he becomes able to see many hundreds of buddhas, many thousands of buddhas, many hundreds of thousands of buddhas, and so forth until we come to his becoming able to see many hundreds of thousands of *koṭis* of *nayutas* of buddhas, to all of whom he offers up his reverence, veneration, service, and offerings of robes, food and drink, bedding, medicines, and all amenities facilitating their lives and also makes offerings to all their Sangha assemblies. He dedicates all the merit associated with these roots of goodness to *anuttara-samyak-saṃbodhi* and, wherever those buddhas dwell, he goes and reverently listens to their teachings on Dharma, whereupon, having heard them, he accepts and upholds those teachings and cultivates them in a manner befitting his powers to do so.

Additionally, during the Dharma reign of those buddhas, he leaves the home life and, having left the home life, he listens to yet more teachings on Dharma, acquires *dhāraṇīs,* and becomes a master of the Dharma who, having heard the Dharma, upholds it and abides on this ground, passing through a hundred kalpas, passing through a thousand kalpas, and so forth up to the point that he even passes through countless hundreds of thousands of *koṭis* of *nayutas* of kalpas during which all of his roots of goodness shine forth with ever-increasing brightness.

Son of the Buddha, this is analogous to real gold that, as it is polished with *musāragalva*[152] to an ever more brilliant luster, shines forth with ever brighter purity. So too it is with all of the roots of goodness accumulated by this bodhisattva who dwells on this ground. As he employs his skillful means and wisdom in contemplative meditation, they shine forth with ever brighter purity.

Son of the Buddha, in the case of the bodhisattva who dwells on this Difficult-to-Conquer Ground, his use of skillful means and wisdom in perfecting meritorious qualities is such that the roots of goodness developed on lower grounds cannot even approach.

Son of the Buddha, this is just as with the sun, moon, stars, constellations, and the radiance of the celestial palaces wherein the wind-like forces supporting them are so irresistibly strong that none of the other winds could even slightly alter their course. So too it is with all the roots of goodness of the bodhisattva dwelling on this ground. Through his use of skillful means and wisdom in pursuing contemplative meditation, he becomes so invincible that he cannot be even slightly deflected from his path by anyone with only the roots of goodness of any *śrāvaka* disciple, *pratyekabuddha,* or worldly being.

Among the ten *pāramitās,* this bodhisattva most extensively practices the perfection of *dhyāna.* It is not that he does not practice the others. Rather, he simply accords them an amount of emphasis corresponding to his own strengths and to what is fitting.

Son of the Buddha, this has been a general explanation of the bodhisattva-mahāsattva's fifth ground, the Difficult-to-Conquer Ground.

The bodhisattva dwelling on this ground often becomes a Tuṣita Heaven king, one who in his interactions with other beings is possessed of sovereign mastery in all that he does. He utterly defeats in debate all proponents of the wrong views set forth by non-Buddhist traditions and he is able to influence other beings to abide in the real truth.

In his practice of giving, pleasing words, beneficial actions, joint endeavors, and all other such endeavors, he never departs from mindfulness of the Buddha, never departs from mindfulness of the Dharma, never departs from mindfulness of the Sangha, and so forth until we come to his never departing from mindfulness of his quest to achieve complete fulfillment of the knowledge of all modes and the cognition of all-knowledge.

He also has this thought: "I should become one who serves these beings as a leader, as one who is supreme, as one who is most especially supreme, as one who is marvelous, as one who is most subtly marvelous, as one who is excellent, as one who is unexcelled," and so forth until we come to "as one who relies on the cognition of all-knowledge."

If this bodhisattva brings forth diligently vigorous practice, then, in but a moment, he will become able to enter a thousand *koṭis* of samādhis, will be able to see a thousand *koṭis* of buddhas, will become aware of the spiritual powers as exercised by a thousand *koṭis* of buddhas, will be able to cause tremors in a thousand *koṭis* of worlds, and so forth until we come to his being able to manifest a thousand *koṭis* of bodies wherein each and every one of those bodies will itself be able to manifest a thousand *koṭis* of bodhisattvas serving in his retinue.

If he resorts to the power of the especially supreme vows of the bodhisattva, he will become freely able to bring forth manifestations beyond this number, such that one would never be able to count them even in a period of a hundred kalpas, a thousand kalpas, and so forth until we come to a hundred thousand *koṭis* of *nayutas* of kalpas.

At that time, Vajragarbha Bodhisattva, wishing to once again proclaim the meaning of his discourse, thereupon spoke these verses:

The bodhisattva who has achieved the fourth ground's purification
with equal dispositions contemplates the buddhas of the three times,
precepts, the mind, riddance of doubt, what is and is not the path,
and, through such contemplations, enters the fifth ground.

With stations of mindfulness as bow, sharpness of roots as arrows,
the right efforts as steed, the bases of psychic powers as his chariot,
and the five powers as sturdy shield, he crushes hostile adversaries,
and, with unretreating heroic valor, he then enters the fifth ground.

With senses of shame and blame as robes, limbs of bodhi as a garland,
pure moral precepts as incense, *dhyāna* meditation as perfume,
wisdom and skillful means as marvelous adornments,
he enters the *dhāraṇī* forest and the samādhi gardens.

With psychic powers as his feet, right mindfulness as his neck,
kindness and compassion as his eyes, and wisdom as his teeth,
with the roar of "non-self," the lion among men
crushes the affliction adversaries, and then enters the fifth ground.

The bodhisattva dwelling on this fifth ground
increases cultivation of the most supremely pure path,
is irreversible in his determined quest for the Buddha's Dharma, and
tireless in contemplative mindfulness of kindness and compassion.

He gathers the supreme qualities of merit and wisdom, possesses
energetic diligence and skillful means, contemplates higher grounds,
is aided by Buddha's powers, embodies mindfulness and wisdom,
and utterly knows all four truths in accordance with reality.

He knows well worldly truth, the truth of the supreme meaning,
the truths of characteristic signs, distinctions, and establishment,
the truths of phenomena, production, cessation, the path,
and so on up to the truth of what, for the Tathāgata, is unimpeded.[153]

Although such contemplation of truths is subtle and marvelous,
he has not yet realized the unimpeded supreme liberation.
In this way, he is able to generate great meritorious qualities
and therefore steps entirely beyond the sphere of worldly wisdom.

Having contemplated these truths, he realizes conditioned existence,
by its very nature, is false, deceptive, and devoid of solid reality.
He acquires the Buddha's radiant aspects of kindness and pity,
and seeks Buddha's knowledge in order to benefit beings.

He contemplates prior and later periods in conditioned existence
as beset by the darkness of ignorance and bound by bonds of craving
by which one flows onward cyclically, abiding in a mass of suffering,
wherein there is no self, no person, and no entity having a life span.

Craving and grasping are causes of their receiving future suffering
that, if one wished to seek its end, one could never find it.
"Confused by the false, they float on, never going against the flow.
Beings such as these are so pitiable. I should see to their liberation."

In the house of aggregates, snakes of sense realms, arrows of views,
the mind's flames blaze fiercely and delusion's darkness is heavy.
They drift and swirl in love's river with no leisure to contemplate it,
and, bereft of a brilliant guide, sink in the ocean of suffering's waters.

Having realized such things as these, he becomes diligent in vigor
and dedicates all of his actions to the liberation of beings.
He becomes one possessed of mindfulness, possessed of wisdom,
and so on up to his becoming one aware of the means of liberation.

He is insatiable in his cultivation of merit and wisdom,
tireless in his reverence for extensive learning,
and pursues adornment of all lands, the major marks, and the signs.
All such deeds are done for the sake of beings.

For the sake of teaching everyone in the world,
he knows well methods of writing, mathematics, printing and such,
also well understands medicinal prescriptions
and the treatment of the many diseases, all of which he can cure,

is marvelously skilled in all literary composition, songs, and dance,
assists secure placement of all palaces, homes, parks, and ponds,
shows others all locations of hidden jewels of not just a single sort,
and does all of this for the sake of benefiting countless beings.

He interprets the omens of the sun, moon, stars, earthquakes,
and other such things, including even people's physical features,
and, in order to be of benefit to the world, reveals for them the
four *dhyānas,* formless absorptions, and spiritual superknowledges.

Those wise ones who dwell on this Difficult-to-Conquer Ground
make offerings to *nayutas* of buddhas and listen to their Dharma.
Hence, just as when one uses a marvelous jewel to polish real gold,[154]
all of their roots of goodness shine ever more brightly in their purity.

Just as the stars and constellations residing in space,
supported by wind-like forces, are not shaken out of place,
and just as the blooming lotus is not attached to its waters,
so too does this great eminence travel along in the world.

Dwelling herein, he often becomes a Tuṣita Heaven King,
well able to utterly refute the wrong views of non-Buddhist paths.
The goodness he cultivates is done to acquire the Buddha's wisdom
and he vows to acquire the ten powers to thereby rescue beings.

He redoubles his cultivation of great vigor
and so straightaway makes offerings to a thousand *koṭis* of buddhas,
gains absorptions and shakes lands also as numerous as they are,
and, by the power of vows, surpasses even such numbers as these.

Thus it is that, using the power of all different sorts of skillful means,
this Difficult-to-Conquer Ground, the fifth ground
within the most supreme and genuine of all paths for humans,
has been explained by me for the Sons of the Buddha.

The Sixth Ground

The Direct Presence Ground

Having heard this teaching of supreme practices, the bodhisattvas'
minds were filled with joy, they rained down marvelous blossoms,
emanated pure light, sprinkled down precious jewels
as offerings to the Tathāgata, and praised his excellent discourse.

A hundred thousand assembled devas, full of celebratory delight,
at once scattered down from space the many jewels as offerings,
together with floral garlands, strands of pearls, banners,
jeweled canopies, and perfumes, all offered there to the Buddha.

The Vaśavartin Heaven King, together with his retinue,
all with minds filled with joyous delight, stood above in space,
scattered jewels forming a cloud that held their offerings, praised him,
and said, "O Buddha's Son, may you soon proclaim this teaching."

Countless celestial nymphs residing above in space
together made offerings of music and song in praise of the Buddha
wherein one heard amidst their voicings such words as these:
"The Buddha's discourse can expel the disease of the afflictions.

The nature of dharmas is originally quiescent, devoid of all signs,
and like empty space in that one makes no discriminations therein.
It transcends all attachments, reaches beyond the path of words,
and is genuine, uniformly equal, and eternally pure.

If one can completely comprehend the nature of dharmas,
his mind is unmoved by what exists or by what does not exist
as he cultivates diligently to rescue the inhabitants of the world.
This is a true son of the Buddha, born from the Buddha's mouth.

He does not seize on the various marks in his practicing of giving,
fundamentally cuts off all evil, and solidly upholds the precepts.
Knowing the Dharma, he is thus free of harming and always patient.
Knowing dharmas as by nature transcendent,[155] he is perfect in vigor.

Having ended the afflictions, he enters the *dhyānas*, and, in making
distinctions about dharmas, knows well they are empty of any nature.
Replete in wisdom power, he is able to extensively rescue beings and,
being rid of the many evils, he gains renown as a great eminence."

Having used such marvelous voices of a thousand myriad sorts
in offering praises, they then fell silent and gazed up at the Buddha.
Liberation Moon then set forth the request to Vajragarbha, "Through
which practice attributes does one enter the next ground?"

Vajragarbha Bodhisattva then informed Liberation Moon Bodhisattva, saying:

O Son of the Buddha, the bodhisattva-mahāsattva who has already completely fulfilled the fifth ground's practices and then aspires to enter the sixth ground, the Ground of Direct Presence, should then take up the contemplation of ten dharmas of identity.[156] What then are those ten? As follows, all dharmas:[157]

Are the same due to their signlessness;
Are the same due to their nonsubstantiality;
Are the same due to their being unproduced;
Are the same due to their being unborn;
Are the same due to their original purity;
Are the same due to their being beyond frivolous intellectual ideation;
Are the same due to their being beyond either grasping or relinquishing;
Are the same due to their quiescence.
Are the same due to their being like a conjured illusion, like a dream, like a shadow, like an echo, like the moon reflected on water, like an image in a mirror, like a mirage, and like a magical transformation;[158]
And are the same due to the non-duality in their existence and nonexistence.

The bodhisattva who contemplates all dharmas in this way realizes their nature is pure and practices in a manner that is consistent with this and that is free of anything that contradicts this. He thereby succeeds in entering the sixth ground, the Ground of Direct Presence, and acquires the acquiescent patience characterized by clarity and acuity.[159] Even so, he has not yet reached the realization of the unproduced-dharmas patience.

Son of the Buddha, once this bodhisattva-mahāsattva has come to contemplate in this manner, he then additionally takes the great compassion as what is foremost, the great compassion as what is to be increased, and the great compassion as what is to be brought to complete fulfillment.

He contemplates production and extinction as it takes place in the world, thinking, "Taking on rebirth in the world in every case arises through attachment to a self. Were one to abandon this attachment, then there would no longer be any basis for being reborn."

He additionally thinks:[160]

Common people, so unknowing, are attached to a self, always seek existence or nonexistence, engage in wrong thought, pursue falsely based actions, and follow erroneous paths wherein they accumulate and increase offense-generating actions, merit-generating actions, or imperturbable actions.[161] Through all courses of actions, they plant mental seeds associated with the contaminants and with the *grasping* that further precipitates subsequent *becoming, birth, aging,* and *death.* This is a circumstance said to be one wherein one's karmic *volitional actions* serve as a field, one's *consciousness* serves as seeds, *ignorance* keeps them covered in darkness, the water of *cravings* moistens them, and pride in oneself irrigates them.

As the net of views grows, the sprout of *name-and-form* is produced. As *name-and-form* develop, the five physical sense faculties are formed. With the oppositional impingement [of sense objects] on the sense faculties, *contact* is produced. This impingement-generated *contact* produces *feeling.* Subsequent wishing for further *feeling* produces *craving.* Increased *craving* brings about *grasping.* An increase in *grasping* produces *becoming.* Having produced *becoming,* it is one's generating of the five-aggregate bodies as one courses in the various destinies that constitutes *birth,* the deterioration following upon *birth* that constitutes *aging,* and the culmination of this process in mortality that brings about *death.* When *aging*-and-*death* arrive, one is seized by intense mental torment and, on account of this intense mental torment, one is then beset by distress, worry, sorrowful lamentation, and the accumulation of a multitude of sufferings.

Because this is all simply a product of causes and conditions, there is no entity for whom this accumulation takes place, and, even as this process proceeds on to destruction, there is still no existent entity that is destroyed, either.

The bodhisattva pursues just such an investigative contemplation of the characteristic features of causally based origination.

Son of the Buddha, this bodhisattva-mahāsattva also thinks thus:

It is the failure to utterly comprehend the ultimate truth that defines *ignorance.*

It is the fruition of karmic actions one has done that constitutes *volitional actions.*

The initial mental factor dependent on *volitional actions* is what constitutes *consciousness.*

The additional four appropriated aggregates arising together with *consciousness* are what constitute *name-and-form.*

The development of *name-and-form* creates *the six sense bases.*

The conjunction of the three phenomena of *sense faculties, sense objects,* and *consciousnesses,* constitutes *contact.*

Arising simultaneously with *contact,* there exists *feeling.*

The forming of a defiled attachment for *feeling* is what constitutes *craving.*

Based on an increase in *craving, grasping* then occurs.

Those karmic actions associated with the contaminants that arise as a consequence of *grasping* are what constitute *becoming.*

The arising of the aggregates resulting from such karmic actions is what constitutes *birth.*

The progressive maturation of the aggregates is what constitutes *aging.*

When the aggregates perish, this is what constitutes *death.*

The confusion and fond attachment attendant on the separation occurring at the time of dying that then manifest as agitation and depression of the heart—this is what is meant by *worry.*

Weeping and sniveling attended by regretful sighing—this is what is meant by *lamentation.*

That which occurs based on the five physical sense faculties constitutes *pain,* whereas what occurs based on the intellectual mind faculty constitutes *distress.*

As this distress and pain increase they result in *mental torment.*

In such circumstances as these, there is only a growing tree of suffering. There is no self in this, nothing belonging to a self, no agent of actions, and no entity undergoing experiences.

He has this additional thought: "If an agent of actions exists, then there exists an endeavor that is done. If no agent of actions exists, then there does not exist any endeavor that is done. From the perspective of ultimate truth, neither of them can even be found."

Son of the Buddha, this bodhisattva-mahāsattva has this additional thought:

Everything throughout the three realms of existence is only mind. Where the Tathāgata has, within this, distinguished and expounded upon these twelve factors comprising the bases of existence, they in every case rely on a single thought and are established on just such a basis. How is this the case?

In accordance with particular circumstances, desire arises together with the mind. In this, the mind constitutes the *consciousness,* whereas the particular circumstances themselves constitute the basis of *volitional actions.* The confusion that exists regarding *volitional actions* constitutes *ignorance.* That which is produced

> from the cooperation of *ignorance* and the mind is *name-and-form*. That which develops from *name-and-form* is *the six sense bases*. The threefold conjunction that occurs in association with *the six sense bases* constitutes *contact*. That which arises together with *contact* is *feeling*. Insatiability with respect to such *feeling* constitutes *craving*. *Craving* that becomes focused and is not relinquished culminates in *grasping*. That which all of these branches comprising existence produce is *becoming*. That which *becoming* brings forth is *birth*. The maturation of what has been born constitutes *aging*. The perishing brought on through *aging* is *death*.

Son of the Buddha, among these, *ignorance* has two types of karmic functions: First, it causes beings to be confused with respect to objective conditions. Second, it serves as a cause for the initiation of *volitional actions*.

Volitional actions also have two types of functions: First, they are capable of generating future retributions. Second, they serve as causes for the initiation of *consciousness*.

Consciousness also has two types of functions: First, it causes continuity of *becoming*. Second, it serves as a cause for the initiation of *name-and-form*.

Name-and-form also have two types of functions: First, they are mutually cooperative in their establishment. Second, they serve as the cause for the initiation of *the six sense bases*.

The six sense bases also have two types of functions: First, each of them clings to its own respective objective sense realm. Second, they serve as the cause for the initiation of *contact*.

Contact also has two types of functions: First, it is capable of touching its objective condition. Second, it serves as the cause for the initiation of *feeling*.

Feeling also has two types of functions: First it is capable of serving as the recipient of experiences that are craved, detested, and so forth. Second, it serves as the cause for the initiation of *craving*.

Craving also has two types of functions: First, it consists of a defiled attachment to whatsoever circumstances are deemed desirable. Second, it serves as the cause for the initiation of *grasping*.

Grasping also has two types of functions: First, it causes continuity of the afflictions. Second, it serves as the cause for the initiation of *becoming*.

Becoming also has two types of functions. First, it is capable of causing rebirth into the other destinies. Second, it serves as the cause for the initiation of *birth*.

Birth also has two types of functions. First, it is able to generate the aggregates. Second, it serves as the cause for the initiation of *aging*.

Aging also has two types of functions. First, it causes all of the sense faculties to undergo change. Second, it serves as the cause for the onset of *death*.

Death also has two types of functions. First, it is capable of destroying all actions. Second, because there is then no conscious awareness, it allows this process to continue on and not be cut off.

Son of the Buddha, in this circumstance wherein *ignorance* serves as a condition for *volitional actions,* and so on till we have *birth* serving as a condition for *aging-and-death,* it is because *ignorance* and so on up to *birth* serve as conditions that there then occurs the causation of *volitional actions* and so on up to *aging-and-death*. This occurs on account of [the prior conditions'] ceaseless facilitation of the establishment [of the subsequent conditions].

In the circumstances wherein, "if *ignorance* is extinguished, then *volitional actions* will be extinguished," and so forth until we come to "if *birth* is extinguished, then *aging-and-death* will be extinguished," this occurs because, in those circumstances, *ignorance* and so forth on up to *birth,* do not then any longer serve as conditions causing the initiation of *volitional actions* and so on up to *aging-and-death*. This extinguishing through severance occurs because there no longer occurs the [prior condition's] facilitating establishment [of the subsequent condition].

Son of the Buddha, among these, ceaseless *ignorance, craving,* and *grasping* constitute *the path of the afflictions*. Ceaseless *volitional actions* and *becoming* constitute *the path of karmic actions*. The ceaseless occurrence of the remaining factors constitutes *the path of suffering*. Analytic extinguishing of these prior and subsequent factors facilitates severance of all three paths.[162] [The factors comprising] these three paths exist apart from any self or possessions of a self and exist only as a process of production and extinction wherein they are analogous to standing sheaves of mutually supporting reeds.[163]

Additionally, where *ignorance* serves as the condition for the occurrence of *volitional actions,* this refers to past circumstances. The factors of *consciousness* on up to and including *feeling* refers to present circumstances. The factors of *craving* and so forth on up to and including *becoming* refer to future circumstances. Henceforth there occurs the unfolding of an ongoing continuity.

In those instances where the cessation of *ignorance* precipitates cessation of *volitional actions,* this is a case of severance occurring due to the dependency [of the latter conditions upon the prior conditions].

Additionally, the twelve factors comprising the bases of existence are synonymous with *the three sufferings*. Among these, *ignorance, volitional actions,* and so forth on up to and including *the six sense bases* collectively constitute *the suffering associated with the karmic formative factors.*[164] *Contact* and feeling constitute *the suffering of suffering.*[165] The remaining factors constitute *the suffering of deterioration.*[166]

Where the cessation of *ignorance* brings about the cessation of *volitional actions,* these three types of suffering are then cut off.

Additionally, in *ignorance*'s serving as a condition for the generation of *volitional actions,* ignorance is the cause and condition that can produce all manner of *volitional actions.* As for the circumstance wherein, once *ignorance* is extinguished, *volitional actions* are then extinguished, it is because, once there is an absence of *ignorance,* there are then no *volitional actions,* either. This same circumstance holds for all of the remaining factors as well.

Also, in *ignorance's* serving as a condition for the generation of *volitional actions,* this conduces to the generation of bondage. Where, with the extinguishing of *ignorance, volitional actions* are then extinguished, this then brings about the extinguishing of this bondage. This same principle holds for all of the remaining factors as well.

Then again, in *ignorance's* serving as a condition for the generation of *volitional actions,* this is a circumstance adaptable to the "nonexistence of anything whatsoever" contemplation. Where, with the extinguishing of *ignorance, volitional actions* are then extinguished, this is a circumstance adaptable to the "utter cessation of everything" contemplation. This same principle holds for all of the remaining factors as well.

Son of the Buddha, the bodhisattva-mahāsattva thus engages in ten types of sequential and counter-sequential contemplation of the factors involved in conditioned arising,[167] specifically:[168]

Contemplation of the sequential continuity in the existential factors.

Contemplation of their all being reducible to the one mind.

Contemplation of their each having their own distinct function.

Contemplation of their inseparability.

Contemplation of the non-severance of the three paths.[169]

Contemplation of their relationship to the past, the present, or the future.

Contemplation in terms of the accumulation of the three kinds of suffering.

Contemplation of their arising and ceasing through causes and conditions.

Contemplation in terms of the creation and destruction of bondage.

Contemplation in terms of "utter nonexistence" and "utter cessation."

Son of the Buddha, the bodhisattva-mahāsattva contemplates everything within the realm of conditioned arising in accordance with these ten characteristics. Thus he realizes that there is no self, no person, and no life span, that there is an absence of any inherently existent nature, and that there is also no agent of actions or anyone who undergoes experiences. He then immediately acquires the direct manifestation of *the emptiness gate to liberation*.[170]

He contemplates all of the factors associated with becoming as having the nature of cessation, as ultimately synonymous with liberation, and as not having even the smallest dharma characteristic that they produce. He then immediately acquires the direct manifestation of *the signlessness gate to liberation*.[171]

Having thus gained entry into both emptiness and signlessness, he then becomes entirely free of anything at all that he seeks with the sole exception of taking the great compassion as foremost in the transformative teaching of beings. He then immediately acquires the direct manifestation of *the wishlessness gate to liberation*.[172]

Thus it is that, in his cultivation of *the three gates to liberation*, the bodhisattva abandons conceptions of the existence of either others or a self, abandons conceptions of either any agent of actions or anyone who undergoes experiences, and abandons the conceptions of anything as either existent or nonexistent.

Son of the Buddha, this bodhisattva-mahāsattva's great compassion progressively increases. He is energetically diligent in his cultivation and, for the sake of bringing about the complete fulfillment of those factors facilitating bodhi he has not yet completely fulfilled, he reflects thus:

> All conditioned things possess an ongoing existence through a circumstance involving the conjunction of factors. Where there is no such circumstance involving the conjunction of factors, there is then no ongoing existence. When the conditions gather together, they may then possess an ongoing existence. When those conditions do not gather together, there is no ongoing existence.
>
> Thus I realize that, since conditioned dharmas are beset by many faults, I should cut off this conjunction of causes and conditions. However, for the sake of facilitating the successful

development of other beings, I shall nonetheless refrain from bringing about the ultimate extinguishing of all volitional actions.

Son of the Buddha, thus it is that the bodhisattva contemplatively investigates all conditioned things as possessed of many faults, as devoid of any inherently existent nature, as neither produced nor destroyed, and yet he nonetheless constantly generates the great compassion, refrains from abandoning beings, and then straightaway acquires the direct manifestation of the *prajñāpāramitā* known as the light of unimpeded wisdom.

Having successfully acquired such wisdom light, although he cultivates the causes and conditions related to the factors facilitating bodhi, he still refrains from abiding in the realm of conditioned things. And although he contemplates the nature of conditioned dharmas as that of quiescent cessation, he still does not abide in quiescent cessation either. This is because he has not yet achieved the complete fulfillment of the dharmas that lead to the realization of bodhi.

Son of the Buddha, the bodhisattva who dwells on this Ground of Direct Presence succeeds in entering:[173]

The penetration of emptiness samādhi;
The emptiness of any inherently existent nature samādhi;
The emptiness of the supreme meaning samādhi;
The foremost emptiness samādhi;
The great emptiness samādhi;
The emptiness of unities samādhi;
The emptiness of production samādhi;
The reality-accordant non-discriminating emptiness samādhi;
The non-abandonment emptiness samādhi;
And the transcendent yet not transcendent emptiness samādhi.

With these ten emptiness samādhis as foremost among them, this bodhisattva acquires the direct manifestation of every one of a hundred thousand emptiness samādhis. In this same way, with ten signlessness samādhis and ten wishlessness samādhis as foremost, he also acquires the direct manifestation of every one of a hundred thousand signlessness and wishlessness samādhis.

Son of the Buddha, the bodhisattva who dwells on this Ground of Direct Presence cultivates and completely perfects:[174]

The indestructible resolute intention;[175]
The definitely certain resolute intention;
The resolute intention of pure goodness;

The especially profound resolute intention;
The nonretreating resolute intention;
The unrelenting resolute intention;
The vast resolute intention;
The boundless resolute intention;
The knowledge-seeking resolute intention;
And the resolute intention joining skillful means and wisdom.

In every case, he brings all of these to a state of perfect fulfillment.

Son of the Buddha, in availing himself of these types of resolute intentions, the bodhisattva:

Accords with the bodhi of the buddhas;
Remains unfrightened by encounters with proponents of deviant doctrines;
Enters all the grounds of knowledge;
Abandons the paths of the Two Vehicles;
Progresses toward the knowledge of the Buddha;
Remains invulnerable to obstruction or ruination by any of the afflictions or *māras;*
Abides within the light of the bodhisattva's wisdom;
Skillfully cultivates and implements all the dharmas of emptiness, signlessness, and wishlessness;
In every case skillfully engages in the constantly conjoined practice of skillful means and wisdom;
And always implements and never relinquishes the dharmas assisting the realization of bodhi.

Son of the Buddha, the bodhisattva abiding on this Ground of Direct Presence acquires an especially supreme degree of realization in the practice of *prajñāpāramitā* and acquires the third of the patiences, the clear and sharp acquiescent patience,[176] this because of acting in accordance with and not contrary to the true character of dharmas.

Son of the Buddha, because of the power of his vows, the bodhisattva who has come to dwell on this Ground of Direct Presence succeeds in seeing many buddhas, that is to say, he can see many hundreds of buddhas and so forth until we come to his seeing of many hundreds of thousands of *koṭis* of *nayutas* of buddhas. In every instance, with a vast mind and a profound mind, he makes offerings to them, pays reverence to them, venerates them, praises them, and presents them with robes, food and drink, bedding, medicines, and all amenities supporting their existence, offering up all of these things while also making offerings to those within all their sangha assemblies. He then proceeds to dedicate the merit associated with these roots of goodness to *anuttara-samyak-saṃbodhi.*

So too does he then respectfully listen to the teachings on Dharma in the presence of those buddhas. Having heard these teachings, he takes them on and retains them, gains reality-concordant samādhis and the light of wisdom, and then accords with these in his cultivation, bearing them in mind and never relinquishing them.

He also gains access to the buddhas' treasuries of extremely profound Dharma and, passing through a hundred kalpas, passing through a thousand kalpas, and so forth on up to incalculably many hundreds of thousands of *koṭis* of *nayutas* of kalpas, his roots of goodness shine ever more brightly in their purity just as when a goldsmith uses a lapis lazuli gem to repeatedly polish real gold, causing it to shine with ever more brilliant purity. So too it is with all the roots of goodness of the bodhisattva who dwells on this ground. Through his use of skillful means and wisdom, in a manner corresponding to his pursuit of meditative contemplation, they become ever brighter and ever more imbued with quiescence to the point where they cannot be outshone by anyone and become like the light of the moon that shines on the bodies of beings and causes them to experience a sense of pristine coolness that the four kinds of wind are incapable of diminishing.

So too it is with all the roots of goodness of the bodhisattva on this ground who is able to use them to extinguish the blazing fires of affliction burning in incalculably many hundreds of thousands of *koṭis* of *nayutas* of beings. In this, they remain invulnerable to destruction by the paths of any of the four kinds of *māras.*

Among the ten *pāramitās,* this bodhisattva most extensively practices the *prajñā pāramitā.* It is not that he does not practice the others. Rather, he simply accords them an amount of emphasis corresponding to his own strengths and to what is fitting.

Sons of the Buddha, this has been a general explanation of the bodhisattva-mahāsattva's, sixth ground, the Ground of Direct Presence.

The bodhisattva dwelling on this ground often becomes a king of the Skillful Transformations Heaven[177] who, sovereignly masterful in all that he does, is one who cannot be driven into retreat or submission by any questioning challenge posed by any *śrāvaka* disciple. He is able to influence beings to do away with arrogance and to deeply enter into a comprehension of conditioned origination.

In his practice of giving, pleasing words, beneficial actions, and joint endeavors, and in all such works that he pursues, he never departs from mindfulness of the Buddha, and so forth until we come to his never departing from mindfulness of his quest to achieve complete fulfillment of the knowledge of all modes and the cognition of all-knowledge.

He also has this thought: "I should become one who serves these beings as a leader, as one who is supreme," and so forth until we come to "as one who relies on the cognition of all-knowledge."

If this bodhisattva brings forth diligently vigorous practice, then, in but a moment, he will be able to enter hundreds of thousands of *koṭis* of samādhis, and so forth until we come to his becoming able to transformationally manifest a hundred thousand *koṭis* of bodhisattvas to serve as his retinue. If he resorts to the power of vows, he will become freely able to manifest them in numbers beyond even this, such that one would never be able to count them even in a period of hundreds of thousands of *koṭis* of *nayutas* of kalpas.

At that time, Vajragarbha Bodhisattva, wishing to once again proclaim the meaning of his discourse, thereupon spoke these verses:

After entirely fulfilling the fifth ground's practices, the bodhisattva
sees dharmas as the same due to their being signless, natureless,
unproduced, unborn, originally pure,
beyond frivolous ideation, beyond grasping or relinquishing,

quiescent in substance and signs, and illusory, as well as
non-dual and beyond discrimination as existent or nonexistent.
Thus contemplating in accordance with the nature of dharmas,
those with this knowledge succeed in entering the sixth ground.

With clear and acute acquiescent patience and replete in knowledge,
he contemplates the world's aspects of production and destruction,
the world's production by the power of delusion's darkness, and sees,
if delusion's darkness were destroyed, the world would not exist.

He contemplates all causes and conditions as, in reality, empty,
yet does not contradict artificial names' use in designating constructs.
Even as there is no doer, no recipient, and no thinker of thoughts,
all actions arise and spread forth everywhere like clouds.

Failure to know the actual truth constitutes *ignorance.*
The *volitional actions* that are done are the fruit of delusion.
That which arises together with *consciousness* is *name-and-form.*
Thus it proceeds on forth until the manifold sufferings accumulate.

He utterly comprehends the three realms exist dependent on mind,
that the same is true of the twelve causes and conditions,
that birth and death in every case are created because of mind,
and that, if the mind itself is extinguished, then birth and death end.

That which *ignorance* brings about is in every case of two types:
Non-comprehension of conditions and the causes of *actions,*
This is so all the way through to *aging*'s end in *death.*
Suffering is generated endlessly from this.

So long as *ignorance* serves as a condition, these cannot be cut off, but,
if that condition is brought to an end, then these are all extinguished.
Ignorance, craving, and *grasping* are the factors belonging to afflictions.
Actions and *becoming* form karma, and the rest are suffering.

Ignorance up to *the six sense bases* relate to *formative-factor suffering.*
The proliferation of *contact* and *feeling* forms *the suffering of suffering.*
The rest of the existential factors relate to *the suffering of deterioration.*
If one sees nonexistence of "self," all three sufferings are destroyed.

Ignorance and *actions* both pertain to the past,
Consciousness on through to *feeling* continually unfold in the present.
Craving, grasping, and *becoming* generate future suffering.
If their interdependence is severed, such temporal phases all end.

When *ignorance* serves as a condition, it is this that creates the bonds.
Through abandoning such conditions, the bonds are thus ended.
Effects are produced from causes, but if abandoned, they are cut off.
By closely contemplating this, one realizes they are, by nature, empty.

Through following the course of *ignorance,* all existence arises.
If one but refrains from following its course, all existence is cut off.
If this exists, then that exists. So too it is for nonexistence as well.
Through the ten reflections, the mind abandons its attachments:

Continuity of existential factors; traceability to a single thought;
individual karma; inseparability; non-severance of three paths;
three times, three sufferings; generation by causes and conditions;
the rising and passing away of the fetters; nonexistence and cessation.

Thus he universally contemplates the course of conditioned arising,
realizing that it is devoid of any actor, recipient, or reality,
that it is like a conjuration, like a dream, like shadows,
or like a circumstance wherein a fool chases after a mere mirage.

Through just such analytic contemplation, he enters emptiness,
knows conditions as, by nature, separate, realizes signlessness,
utterly comprehends their falseness, and becomes free of any wish
with the sole exception of the desire to act with kindness for beings.

Thus this great eminence cultivating the three gates to liberation
ever increases great compassion and his quest for Buddha's Dharma.
He realizes all conditioned things are created as an assemblage and,
with resolute fondness for it, resolves to diligently practice the path.

He acquires a hundred thousand emptiness samādhi gateways.
and gains the same number for signlessness and wishlessness as well.
His *prajñā* and acquiescent patience both become ever more superior,
and his liberations and wisdom reach complete fulfillment.

With a deep mind, he also makes offerings to many buddhas
and cultivates the path through the instruction of those buddhas.
He gains buddhas' Dharma treasuries enhancing roots of goodness
just as when gold is subjected to polishing with a lapis lazuli gem.

Just as when the moon's pure and cool radiance shines on beings,
though the four winds may blow, none are able to interfere with it,
so too, this ground's bodhisattvas step over the paths of Māra
and extinguish the heat of all beings' afflictions.

On this ground, he is often King of the Fine Transformations Heaven,
one who teaches and guides beings in doing away with pridefulness.
All endeavors he pursues are done to seek all-knowledge, and they all
have already overstepped and become superior to the *śrāvaka* path.

The bodhisattva on this ground who is diligent in practice of vigor
acquires hundreds of thousands of *koṭis* of samādhis
and is also able to see countlessly many buddhas
that appear to him like suns shining in the midsummer sky.

This is extremely profound, sublime, and so difficult to know or see
that no *śrāvaka* disciple or *pratyekabuddha* could ever fully fathom it.
So it is that I have here explained the bodhisattva's sixth ground
for the sake of the Sons of the Buddha.

The Seventh Ground

The Far-Reaching Ground

Then the congregated devas, their minds filled with joy,
scattered jewels that formed a cloud hanging up in the sky,
whereupon they all sang with different sorts of sublime voices
addressed to The Most Supremely Pure One, saying:

"Having penetrated the supreme meaning, possessing masterful knowledge,
and having perfected a hundred thousand *koṭis* of fine qualities,
a lotus among men, entirely free of any attachments,
proclaims here the profound practices to benefit all beings."

The Vaśavartin Heaven King, abiding there in space,
emanated a great light that illuminated the Buddha's body
and spread forth the most superior sorts of sublime incense clouds,
all presented as offerings to he who dispels worries and afflictions.

Then, the entire congregation of devas, all of them joyful,
all sang beautiful sounds in a united chorus of praises:
"Having heard here of the qualities comprising this ground, we
have thence all reaped immense and fine benefit."

Then the celestial nymphs, their minds filled with celebratory delight,
vied in chorusing forth a thousand myriad musical sounds and then,
as all of them availed themselves of the Tathāgata's spiritual powers,
amidst all those sounds, they joined in uttering phrases like these:

"With peerless awe-inspiring presence and quiescent stillness, he
can train those difficult to train, is worthy of the world's gifts,
and, though he has already transcended all worlds,
he still travels forth in the world, extolling the marvelous path.

"Although he manifests incalculably many bodies of every kind,
he realizes each and every body is itself devoid of any existence.
He is skillful in the use of phrases in his explanation of all dharmas,
yet does not seize on any signs of words or sounds.

"He goes forth to a hundred thousand buddha lands
and presents all the most supreme gifts as offerings to those buddhas.
Through sovereign mastery of knowledge, he is free of all attachment
and so does not generate any conception of 'my own buddha land.'

"Although diligent in the teaching of all beings,
he does not have any thought conceiving of either 'other' or 'self.'
Although he has already cultivated vast goodness to perfection,
he still does not generate any attachment to good dharmas.

"Because he perceives that all worlds are always fiercely ablaze
with the fires of desire, hatred, and stupidity,
he has utterly transcended all forms of thought even as
he still brings forth the great compassion and the power of vigor."

After all of those devas and celestial nymphs
had finished presenting all different sorts of offerings and praises,
they all simultaneously fell silent and stood there,
gazing up at the most revered of men, wishing to hear the Dharma.

At that time, Liberation Moon Bodhisattva again set forth a request:
"The minds of everyone in this assembly are pure.
We wish only, O Son of the Buddha, that you will explain for us
the practices and characteristic aspects of the seventh ground."

At that time, Vajragarbha Bodhisattva addressed Liberation Moon Bodhisattva, saying:

O Son of the Buddha, the bodhisattva-mahāsattva who has already completed the sixth ground's practices and then aspires to gain entry into the seventh ground, the Far-Reaching Ground, should proceed in the cultivation of ten kinds of skillful means and wisdom,[178] thereby bringing forth the most especially supreme path. What then are those ten? Specifically, they are:

Although he has skillfully cultivated the emptiness, signlessness, and wishlessness samādhis, through the practice of kindness and compassion, he refrains from forsaking beings;

Although he has acquired the buddhas' dharma of uniform equality, he still delights in always making offerings to buddhas;

Although he has entered the gateway to wisdom of emptiness contemplation, he still diligently pursues the accumulation of merit;

Although he has become detached from the three realms of existence, he still engages in the adornment of the three realms of existence;

Although he has achieved the final extinguishing of the flames of all afflictions, he is still able for the sake of all beings to bring forth the means to extinguish the flames of their greed, hatred, and delusion;

Although he realizes that all dharmas are like conjurations, like dreams, like shadows, like echoes, like mirages, like transformations, like the moon reflected on water, and like images in a mirror, and realizes too that, in their essential nature, they are non-dual, he still accords with his resolve by performing works of countless different sorts;

Although he realizes that, by their very nature, all lands are like empty space, he is still able to use pure and sublime practices to adorn the buddha lands;

Although he realizes that the fundamental nature of all buddhas' Dharma body is free of any "body," he still adorns his own body with the major marks and subsidiary signs;

Although he realizes that, by its very nature, the voice of all buddhas is empty of inherent existence, quiescent, and ineffable, he is still able to accord with all beings by bringing forth for them many different sorts of pure voices;

And although he accords with all buddhas' complete fathoming of the three periods of time as reducible to but a single thought, he still accords with the differences in beings' minds and understandings by manifesting in many different sorts of appearances, many different temporal circumstances, and many different sorts of kalpas wherein he cultivates all the practices.

It is by resort to ten such types of skillful means and wisdom that the bodhisattva brings forth the especially supreme practices by which he leaves the sixth ground and enters the seventh ground. Once he has entered there, these practices always manifest directly before him and henceforth define his abiding on the seventh ground, the Far-Reaching Ground.

Son of the Buddha, after the bodhisattva-mahāsattva has achieved entry into the seventh ground:

He acquires a penetrating comprehension of the measurelessly many realms of beings;

He acquires a penetrating comprehension of the measurelessly many works carried out by the buddhas in their teaching of beings;

He acquires a penetrating comprehension of the measurelessly many networks of worlds;

He acquires a penetrating comprehension of the buddhas' measurelessly many pure lands;

He acquires a penetrating comprehension of the measurelessly many different sorts of dharmas;[179]

He acquires a penetrating comprehension of the measureless knowledge manifested by the buddhas' enlightenment;[180]

He acquires a penetrating comprehension of the enumeration of the measurelessly many kalpas;

He acquires a penetrating comprehension of the measureless knowledge of the three periods of time to which the buddhas have awakened;

He acquires a penetrating comprehension of beings' measurelessly many different sorts of resolute convictions;
He acquires a penetrating comprehension of the measurelessly many different sorts of name-and-form bodies manifested by the buddhas;[181]
He acquires a penetrating comprehension of the differences in beings' measurelessly many different mental dispositions and faculties;
He acquires a penetrating comprehension of the measurelessly many languages and voices through which the buddhas' inspire delight in beings;
He acquires a penetrating comprehension of beings' measurelessly many different courses of thought;
He acquires a penetrating comprehension of the buddhas' measurelessly many sorts of utterly complete understanding of vast knowledge;
He acquires a penetrating comprehension of the measurelessly many sorts of resolute convictions of adherents of the *śrāvaka*-disciple vehicle;
He acquires a penetrating comprehension of the measurelessly many proclamations of the path of wisdom set forth by the buddhas in inspiring resolute faith;
He acquires a penetrating comprehension of the measurelessly many accomplishments of *pratyekabuddhas;*
He acquires a penetrating comprehension of the buddhas' measurelessly many proclamations of gateways of extremely profound wisdom that cause others to enter therein;
He acquires a penetrating comprehension of the bodhisattvas' measurelessly many practices of skillful means;
And he acquires a penetrating comprehension of the measurelessly many works accumulated and accomplished in the Great Vehicle that, when described by the buddhas, then influence bodhisattvas to enter into them.

This bodhisattva reflects thus: "Such measureless domains of the *tathāgatas* as these could never be known even in a hundred thousand *koṭis* of *nayutas* of kalpas. I should therefore rather resort to the effortless and non-discriminating mind to succeed in achieving their perfect fulfillment."

Son of the Buddha, employing deep wisdom, this bodhisattva engages in such contemplative meditations as these whereby he always diligently cultivates these forms of skillful means and wisdom and thus brings forth this especially supreme path wherein he becomes so securely and unshakably established in it that there is not so much as a single moment in which he rests or desists. While walking, standing, sitting, lying down, and even in the midst of sleep and dreams, he never even briefly involves himself with any of the hindrances and he never abandons thought such as this.

In each successive moment, this bodhisattva is always able to completely fulfill the ten *pāramitās*. And how is this the case? This is because he takes the great compassion as foremost in every successive mind-moment as he cultivates the Buddha's Dharma and proceeds toward realization of the Buddha's knowledge. In particular:

He bestows on beings all roots of goodness he develops in the course of seeking to acquire the Buddha's knowledge. This is what constitutes *dāna pāramitā.*

He is able to extinguish the heat of the afflictions. This is what constitutes *śīla pāramitā.*

Taking kindness and compassion as foremost, he refrains from inflicting harm on beings. This is what constitutes *kṣānti pāramitā.*

He is insatiable in seeking supremely good dharmas. This is what constitutes *vīrya pāramitā.*

He always keeps the path of all-knowledge directly present before him, never becoming scattered or distracted. This is what constitutes *dhyāna pāramitā.*

He is able to patiently acquiesce in all dharmas as neither produced nor destroyed. This is what constitutes *prajñā pāramitā.*

He is able to bring forth measureless knowledge. This is what constitutes the *pāramitā* of skillful means.

He is able to seek out higher and higher levels of knowledge. This is what constitutes the *pāramitā* of vows.

None of the deviant doctrines or hordes of *māras* are ever able to obstruct him or bring about his ruination. This is what constitutes the *pāramitā* of powers.

He utterly knows all dharmas in accordance with reality. This is what constitutes the *pāramitā* of knowledge.

Son of the Buddha, this bodhisattva is able to completely fulfill all of these ten *pāramitās* in every successive mind-moment. It is in this way that, in each successive mind-moment, he is able to completely fulfill the four means of attraction, the four types of retention,[182] the thirty-seven factors conducing to enlightenment, the three gates to liberation, and, to state it briefly, all dharmas assisting the realization of bodhi.

At that time, Liberation Moon Bodhisattva asked Vajragarbha Bodhisattva, saying, "O Son of the Buddha, is it only on this seventh ground that the bodhisattva fulfills all dharmas assisting realization of bodhi?[183] Or is it rather that he is also able to completely fulfill them on all grounds?"

Vajragarbha Bodhisattva then replied:

O Son of the Buddha, the bodhisattva is able to completely fulfill the dharmas facilitating realization of bodhi on all ten grounds. Still, it is on the seventh ground where this ability becomes most especially supreme in its implementation. How is this the case? This is because it is on this seventh ground that his effortfully implemented practice becomes complete, thereby enabling his entry into practice characterized by sovereign mastery in wisdom.[184]

O Son of the Buddha, on the first ground, it is because of his aspiration taking all Buddha dharmas as its object that the bodhisattva perfects the dharmas assisting realization of bodhi.

On the second ground, this occurs due to his abandonment of the mind's defilements.

On the third ground, this occurs due to the ever-increasing strength of his vows and due to his acquiring the light of the Dharma.

On the fourth ground, this occurs through his entry into the path.

On the fifth ground, this occurs through his adaptation to the ways of the world.

On the sixth ground, this occurs through his entry into the extremely profound Dharma gateways.

On the seventh ground, it is due to bringing forth all Buddha dharmas and completely fulfilling all dharmas assisting realization of bodhi.

How is this the case? From the first ground through the seventh ground, the bodhisattva achieves the complete development of the effortfully implemented preliminary practice factors conducive to knowledge. It is due to the power produced by this that, from the eighth ground to the tenth ground, all of his effortless practices then become completely developed.

Son of the Buddha, it is as if there were two worlds of which one is characterized by admixture with defilements whereas the other is entirely pure and it is difficult to pass between them, the sole exception being in the case of the bodhisattva who possesses the powers of great skillful means, spiritual superknowledges, and vows.

Son of the Buddha, so too it is with the grounds of the bodhisattva wherein there are those in which the practices are admixed with defilement and there are those in which the practices are pure. It is difficult for anyone to pass between these two with the sole exception of the bodhisattva possessed of great vow power, skillful means, and wisdom who only then is able to pass between them.

Liberation Moon Bodhisattva then asked, "O Son of the Buddha, does this seventh ground bodhisattva engage in defiled practices or does he instead engage in pure practices?"

Vajragarbha Bodhisattva replied:

O Son of the Buddha, from the first ground to the seventh ground, all practices in which he engages involve abandoning affliction-related actions. This is because they are directed toward realizing unsurpassably supreme bodhi. However, because he has still only achieved a partial realization corresponding to the level of his position on the path, this still cannot be referred to as stepping completely beyond all affliction-related actions.

Son of the Buddha, this circumstance is comparable to that of a wheel-turning sage king who mounts his precious heavenly elephant and roams the four continents. In doing so, he becomes well aware that there are poverty-stricken people in difficult straits who are afflicted with suffering, even as he himself remains unsullied by those many disastrous situations. In such a circumstance, he would still not qualify as having truly stepped entirely beyond the position of being human.

Suppose, however, that he were to relinquish the body in which he serves as a king and then take rebirth in the Brahma Worlds where he would mount a heavenly palace from which he could view a thousand worlds as he roams throughout a thousand worlds manifesting the radiance and awesome qualities of a Brahma Heaven deva. In such a case, he would only then truly qualify as having stepped entirely beyond the station of being human.

Son of the Buddha, so too it is with the bodhisattva. Beginning with the first ground and going on through to the seventh ground, he mounts the vehicle of the *pāramitās*. As he roams about in the world, he becomes well aware of all the world's afflictions, faults, and disastrous aspects. Because he rides along on the path of right conduct, he remains unsullied by the faults associated with the afflictions. Still, he does not yet truly qualify as having stepped entirely beyond actions associated with afflictions.

However, if he were to then relinquish all of the effortfully implemented preliminary practices, he would then go forth from the seventh ground and enter the eighth ground and would then travel through the world mounted on the pure vehicle of the bodhisattva wherein he would be cognizant of the faults associated with the afflictions and yet would still remain unsullied by them. It is only then that he would qualify as having truly stepped entirely beyond the practices associated with the afflictions, this due to his having successfully stepped beyond them all.

Son of the Buddha, in coming to abide on this ground, this seventh ground bodhisattva has stepped entirely beyond the many sorts of afflictions such as abundant desire and the other sorts of afflictions. Abiding on this ground, he is not designated as someone who possesses the afflictions and yet he is not designated as entirely devoid of the afflictions, either. How is this the case? This is because, since none of the afflictions directly manifest in his practice, he is not designated as possessing them. However, because he seeks to acquire the Tathāgata's knowledge and his intentions have not yet become completely fulfilled, he is not yet designated as entirely free of them, either.

Son of the Buddha, through profound purified intentions, the bodhisattva abiding on the seventh ground perfects his physical karma actions, perfects his verbal karmic actions, and perfects mental karmic actions. He has already entirely abandoned all bad courses of karmic action criticized by the Tathāgata and he always thoroughly cultivates all good courses of karmic actions praised by the Tathāgata. As for everything related to the world's classical texts, skills, and arts, his actions here are as described earlier in relation to the fifth ground. He naturally practices all of these without having to expend any particular effort in doing so.

This bodhisattva serves as a greatly illustrious teacher for those throughout the worlds of a great trichiliocosm, one who, with the sole exceptions of the *tathāgatas* and those on the eighth ground and above, is unmatched by any of the other bodhisattvas in his resolute intentions and the marvelousness of his practice. All of the *dhyāna* samādhis, *samāpattis,* spiritual superknowledges, and liberations become directly manifest for him. Still, their cultivation and development here is not like that occurring on the eighth ground wherein they become completely realized as a function of karmic reward. In every successive mind-moment, the bodhisattva on this ground completely cultivates the power of skillful means and wisdom as well as all dharmas assisting realization of bodhi, all of which become ever more supremely fulfilled herein.

Son of the Buddha, the bodhisattva abiding on this ground enters:[185]

The bodhisattva's skillful investigative contemplation samādhi;
The skillful consideration of meanings samādhi;
The most supreme intelligence samādhi;
The distinguishing of the treasury of meanings samādhi;
The distinguishing of meaning in accordance with reality samādhi;
The skillful abiding in solidly established roots samādhi;
The gateway to knowledge and spiritual superknowledges samādhi;
The works throughout the Dharma realm samādhi;
The supreme benefit of the Tathāgata samādhi;
And the samādhi of the treasury of many different meanings and the gateway to *saṃsāra* and nirvāṇa.

He enters hundreds of myriads of samādhis such as these that are gateways to complete fulfillment of great knowledge and spiritual superknowledges whereby he is able to carry out the purifying cultivation of this ground.

Having acquired these samādhis, due to thoroughly purifying skillful means and wisdom and due to the power of the great compassion, this bodhisattva steps beyond the Two Vehicles' grounds and reaches the wisdom contemplation ground.[186]

Son of the Buddha, because the bodhisattva dwelling on this ground well purifies countless signlessness practices related to physical karma, well purifies countless signlessness practices related to verbal karma, and well purifies countless signlessness practices related to mental karma, he consequently acquires the light of the unproduced-dharmas patience.

Liberation Moon Bodhisattva then asked, "O Son of the Buddha, how could it be that all of the measurelessly many physical, verbal and mental deeds performed by each of the bodhisattvas from the first ground onward have not already stepped entirely beyond the Two Vehicles' practices?"

Vajragarbha Bodhisattva then replied:

Son of the Buddha, all of those bodhisattvas do step entirely beyond them, however, they do so only due to their aspiration to acquire the Dharma of all buddhas. It is not due to their own cognition's power of meditative contemplation.[187] Now, however, on this seventh ground, it is because of their own power of cognition that Two Vehicles practitioners are unable to even approach them.

This circumstance is analogous to that of a prince born of a queen into the house of a king entirely possessed of all of the marks of a king. Right at birth, he is immediately deemed superior even to all of the government ministers. This, however, is solely due to the power associated with kingship and not due to any power he as yet possesses himself. If as he grows to adulthood he becomes accomplished in the various sorts of skills, it will only then be due to his own powers that he steps entirely beyond everyone else.

So too it is with the bodhisattva-mahāsattva. When he first brings forth the resolve, because he has established the great Dharma as the goal of his determination, he right then steps entirely beyond all *śrāvaka* disciples and *pratyekabuddhas*. Now, in dwelling on this ground, it is due to the power of wisdom that he surpasses all adherents of the Two Vehicles.

Son of the Buddha, the bodhisattva dwelling on this seventh ground acquires the ability to engage in extremely profound and secluded non-practice even as he still always practices deeds of body, speech, and mind through which he diligently pursues the supreme path, thus never abandoning that quest. Therefore, although the bodhisattva practices in accordance with ultimate reality,[188] he still refrains from bringing about its complete realization.

Liberation Moon Bodhisattva then asked, "O Son of the Buddha, beginning with which ground can the bodhisattva enter the cessation concentration?"

Vajragarbha Bodhisattva replied:

Son of the Buddha, it is from the sixth ground onward that the bodhisattva has the ability to enter the cessation concentration. Now, as he abides on this ground, he can enter it in each successive mind-moment and can also arise from it in each successive mind-moment and yet still refrain from bringing about its complete realization. So it is that this bodhisattva is known as one who has completely developed inconceivable deeds of body, speech, and mind.

His practicing in accordance with ultimate reality even while still refraining from bringing about its complete realization is analogous to someone who sets sail in a boat out onto the open ocean and who then, by resorting to the power of his skillfulness, remains able to avoid disastrous difficulties out on those waters. So too it is with the bodhisattva dwelling on this ground. He sets sail in the ship of the *pāramitās* out onto the ocean of ultimate reality and, in doing so, through his reliance on the power of vows, he still refrains from bringing about the complete realization of cessation.

Son of the Buddha, having acquired powers of samādhi and knowledge such as these, he employs great skillful means by which:

Although he manifests within *saṃsāra*, he still constantly abides in nirvāṇa;
Although surrounded by a retinue, he still always delights in detachment;
Although, by resort to the power of vows, he takes birth in the three realms, he still remains undefiled by worldly dharmas;
Although he always abides in a state of quiescence, through the power of skillful means, he is as if ablaze, but, although ablaze, he remains unburned;
Although he proceeds in accordance with the knowledge of the Buddha, he may still manifest entry into the grounds of the *śrāvaka* disciples and the *pratyekabuddhas;*
Although he has acquired the treasury of the Buddha's realms of cognition,[189] he may still manifest as dwelling in the realms of *māras;*[190]
Although he has stepped beyond the paths of the *māras*, he may still manifest as practicing the dharmas of *māras;*
Although he may manifest practices identical to those of non-Buddhist traditions, he still never relinquishes the Dharma of the Buddha;
Although he manifests in ways that adapt to those in all worlds, he still always practices all world-transcending dharmas;
And although all of his adorning phenomena[191] surpass anything possessed by any of the devas, dragons, *yakṣas, gandharvas, asuras, garuḍas, kiṃnaras, mahoragas,* humans, non-humans, Śakra Devānām-Indra, the Brahma Heaven King, the Four Heavenly Kings, or anyone else, he still never relinquishes the mind that delights in the Dharma.

Son of the Buddha, the bodhisattva who has completely developed wisdom such as this abides on the Far-Reaching Ground.

Due to the power of his vows he succeeds in seeing many buddhas, that is to say, he can see many hundreds of buddhas and so forth until we come to his seeing of many hundreds of thousands of *koṭis* of *nayutas* of buddhas. He goes forth wherever those buddhas dwell and then, with a vast mind and with an especially supreme mind, he makes offerings to them, pays reverence to them, venerates them, praises them, presents them with robes, food and drink, bedding, medicines, and all amenities supporting their existence, offering up all of these things while also making offerings to those within all of their sangha assemblies. He then dedicates the merit associated with these roots of goodness to *anuttara-samyak-saṃbodhi.* So too does he then respectfully listen to the teachings on Dharma in those places where those buddhas dwell. Having heard these teachings, he takes them on and retains them, gains reality-concordant samādhis and the light of wisdom, and then accords with these in his cultivation.

Wherever the buddhas dwell, he guards and preserves right Dharma. He is always one whom the *tathāgatas* praise and express delight in. No proponent of the Two Vehicles can cause him to retreat or prevail over him through questioning or challenging him. His benefiting of beings purifies his realization of the patience with respect to dharmas. He passes through incalculably many hundreds of thousands of *koṭis* of *nayutas* of kalpas in this way during which all of his roots of goodness achieve ever greater supremacy.

This circumstance is comparable to when one inlays in real gold many sorts of marvelous gems as adornments, thereby making it ever more superior in quality and thereby redoubling its radiance to the point that no other article of adornment can rival it in these respects. All of the roots of goodness of the bodhisattva who dwells on the seventh ground are of just this very sort. Employing the power of skillful means and wisdom, he brings them to a state of ever-increasing brightness and purity unrivaled by any followers of the Two Vehicles.

Son of the Buddha, this circumstance is comparable to the light of the sun which the light cast by the stars, the moon, and other heavenly bodies cannot even approach it in its brilliance that is even able to dry up all of the marshes on the entire continent of Jambudvīpa. So too it is with the bodhisattva on this Far-Reaching Ground who cannot be rivaled by any follower of the Two Vehicles, for he is able to entirely dry up all of the marshes of delusion possessed by all beings.

Among the ten *pāramitās*, this bodhisattva most extensively practices the *pāramitā* of skillful means. It is not that he does not practice the others. Rather, he simply accords them an amount of emphasis corresponding to his own strengths and to what is fitting.

Son of the Buddha, this has been a general explanation of the bodhisattva-mahāsattva's seventh ground, the Far-Reaching Ground.

The bodhisattva dwelling on this ground often becomes a Vaśavartin Heaven king who, through skillfully explaining for beings the means to achieve the realization of knowledge, thereby induces them to realize and enter it.

In his practice of giving, pleasing words, beneficial actions, and joint endeavors and in all such works that he pursues, he never departs from mindfulness of the Buddha, and so forth until we come to his never departing from mindfulness of his quest to achieve complete fulfillment of the knowledge of all modes and the cognition of all-knowledge.

He also has this thought: "I should become one who serves these beings as a leader, as one who is supreme," and so forth until we come to "as one who relies on the cognition of all-knowledge."

If this bodhisattva brings forth diligently vigorous practice, then, in but a moment, he will become able to enter hundreds of thousands of *koṭis* of samādhis, and so forth until we come to his becoming able to transformationally manifest hundreds of thousands of *koṭis* of bodhisattvas to serve as his retinue. If he resorts to the especially supreme power of the bodhisattva's vows, he will become freely able to manifest them in numbers beyond even this, even to the point that one could never calculate their number even in a period of hundreds of thousands of *koṭis* of *nayutas* of kalpas.

At that time, Vajragarbha Bodhisattva, wishing to once again proclaim the meaning of his discourse, thereupon spoke these verses:

As, on the path of the supreme meaning's knowledge and samādhi,
his sixth ground mind cultivation reaches complete fullness,
he straightaway perfects skillful means and wisdom.
It is due to this that the bodhisattva enters the seventh ground.

Though awakened to three liberations, he is kind and compassionate.
Though the same as *tathāgatas,* he is diligent in offerings to buddhas.
Though contemplating emptiness, he still accumulates merit.
Through these things, a bodhisattva ascends to the seventh ground.

He has become detached from the three realms yet still adorns them.
He's put out his own delusions' fires, yet douses others' fires as well.
He knows dharmas' non-duality and yet is diligent in doing works.
He fathoms all lands as empty, yet delights in adorning lands.

Even knowing the body as unmoving, he embodies all of its signs.
Though aware the voice is by nature transcendent, he is skilled in discourse.
Though he fathoms all as one thought, he distinguishes all matters.
It is due to this that the wise ascend to the seventh ground.

Closely contemplating these dharmas, he gains utter illumination,
broadly brings forth benefit for the multitudes who are so confused,
and enters the boundlessly many realms of beings as well as
the buddhas' acts of transformative teaching that are also countless.

All lands, all dharmas, and all categories of kalpas,
beings' convictions and mental dispositions—he enters them all,

proclaiming Three Vehicles Dharma in a manner equally boundless,
carrying forth in this way the teaching of all the multitudes of beings.

The bodhisattva diligently pursues the supreme path
and, moving or still, never forsakes skillful means and wisdom.
He dedicates each and every act to gaining Buddha's bodhi,
and, in each successive mind-moment, he perfects the *pāramitās*.

Generating the resolve and making dedications constitute giving.
Extinguishing delusions is moral virtue and nonharming is patience.
Insatiable pursuit of goodness—this is vigor's goad.
Being unshakable on the path is the cultivation of *dhyāna*.

Patient acquiescence in the unproduced is what constitutes prajñā.
Dedicating merit constitutes skillful means. Aspirations form vows.
Invincibility is the mark of powers. Skillful fathoming is knowledge.
It is in this way that he develops all of these to complete fullness.

On the first ground, grasping fine qualities' conditions is fulfilled.
On the second, one abandons defilement. The third: Disputes cease.
On the fourth, one enters the path. The fifth: Practice is compliant.
On the sixth, light shines from wisdom that fathoms the unproduced.

On the seventh, merit from the bodhi practices becomes full
and all the different types of great vows become perfectly complete.
It is because of this that one is able to cause
everything one does on the eighth ground to become entirely pure.

This ground is difficult to traverse. With wisdom, one steps beyond.
This is analogous to going between two worlds and
also like a sage king's degree of freedom from defiling attachment,
for it does not yet qualify as totally stepping beyond it.

When he comes to abide on the eighth ground of knowledge
he then passes on beyond those domains of mind.
As Brahmā deva, viewing the world, steps beyond the human realm,
and like a lotus atop the water, he is then free of defiling attachments.

Although on this ground one oversteps the many sorts of afflictions,
one is not said either to have afflictions or to be free of afflictions.[192]
This is because there are no afflictions that are active therein even as
the mind seeking Buddha's knowledge has not yet become fulfilled.

He entirely fathoms all of the many types of worldly skills,
the classical texts, books, literary skills, and polemics while, as for the
dhyāna concentrations, samādhis, and spiritual superknowledges,
he cultivates all such endeavors to the point of complete mastery.

In cultivating and perfecting the path of the seventh ground,
the bodhisattva steps entirely beyond all Two Vehicles' practices.

First ground success arises from vows. Here it is from knowledge.
This is analogous to a prince whose powers are utterly perfected.

Though perfect in the very profound, he still advances on the path.
His every moment is quiescent cessation, yet he forgoes realization.
It is just as when one goes forth in a boat out into the open ocean,
and yet still keeps from being capsized by its waters.

His practice of skillful means and wisdom and perfection of qualities
are such that no one in the entire world can completely fathom.
Through offerings to many buddhas and his mind's growing radiance
he becomes like gold that has been adorned with marvelous gems.

The wisdom of this ground's bodhisattva is the most brilliant of all.
Like flourishing sunlight, it dries up the waters of craving.
He also serves as a lord of the Paranirmita Vaśavartin Heaven
who teaches and guides beings in the cultivation of right knowledge.

If he resorts to the power of valiant and vigorous diligence,
he acquires numerous samādhis and sees multitudes of buddhas,
hundreds of thousands of *koṭis* of *nayutas* in number.
With freely exercised vow power, the number goes even beyond this.

This is the bodhisattva's Far-Reaching Ground,
the path of the purification of skillful means and wisdom.
It is such that no deva, human, *śrāvaka* disciple, or *pratyekabuddha*
anywhere in any world would be able to comprehend it.

The Eighth Ground

The Immovability Ground

At that time, the Deva King and those in the deva assembly,
hearing of these supreme practices, were filled with joyous delight.
Wishing to make offerings to the Tathāgata
and to that boundless congregation of great bodhisattvas,

they rained down marvelous blossoms, banners, canopies,
incenses, floral garlands, necklaces, and jeweled robes,
measurelessly and boundlessly many, of a hundred thousand sorts,
all of which were adorned with *maṇi* jewels.

Celestial nymphs simultaneously chorused forth heavenly music,
sending everywhere about many different sorts of sublime voices
as offerings to the Buddha as well to those sons of the Buddha there,
all together singing forth these words that they offered in praise:

"The All Seeing One most revered among all two-legged beings,
out of kindly pity for these beings, manifests his spiritual powers,
causing these many sorts of celestial music and sublime sounds
to come forth from everywhere so that everyone is able to hear.

On each hair tip, there are a hundred thousand *koṭis*
of *nayutas* of lands as numerous as atoms
wherein just such a measureless number of *tathāgatas*
abide there, proclaiming the sublime Dharma.

Within each hair pore there are countless lands,
each of which has its four continents and great oceans
as well as Mount Sumeru and the Iron Ring Mountains,
all of which are seen therein without being cramped for space.

Within the tip of each hair, there exist the six destinies of rebirth,
the three wretched destinies, as well as men and devas,
all of the multitudes of dragons and spirits, and the *asuras*, wherein
each undergoes retribution in accordance with his karma.

In all of those lands, there are *tathāgatas*
expounding teachings with their marvelous voices,
adapting to the minds of all of the different sorts of beings
in order to turn the wheel of the supremely pure Dharma.

In those lands, the beings have all different sorts of bodies.
Within their bodies, there are in turn many different types of lands.
Humans, devas, the other destinies—each is different from the others.
The Buddha, having fully known them, speaks Dharma for them all.

Large lands, in response to thought, transform, becoming small.
Small lands, in response to thought, transform, becoming large.
He has such spiritual superknowledges that are so measureless that,
even if worldlings all described them at once, they could never finish."

Having sent forth everywhere these sublime sounds
praising the meritorious qualities of the Tathāgata,
those assembled there, filled with joyous delight, became silent
and then single-mindedly gazed up, wishing to hear an explanation.

At that time, Liberation Moon Bodhisattva again set forth a request:
"Everyone in this assembled congregation has become still and quiet.
We pray that you will describe the practice aspects
that one sequentially enters in reaching the eighth ground."

At that time, Vajragarbha Bodhisattva informed Liberation Moon Bodhisattva, saying:

O Son of the Buddha, here we have the bodhisattva-mahāsattva who, on seven grounds:

Has well cultivated skillful means together with wisdom;
Has well purified the paths;
Has well accumulated the dharmas assisting realization of the path;
Has been sustained by the power of great vows;[193]
Has received the assistance of the Tathāgata's powers;[194]
Has been supported by the power of his own goodness;[195]
Has remained always mindful of the Tathāgata's powers, fearlessnesses, and dharmas exclusive to the buddhas;[196]
Has well purified his higher aspirations and intentions;[197]
Has become able to completely develop merit and wisdom;[198]
And has practiced the great kindness and the great compassion by which he never forsakes any being. So it is that he enters the path of measureless knowledge.[199]

He penetratingly comprehends all dharmas:[200]

As originally unproduced;
As non-arising;
As signless;
As neither created nor destroyed;
As inexhaustible and undergoing no transformation;
As having the nature of being devoid of any inherent nature;
As of uniformly equal character in the past, present, and future;
As being amenable to penetration by nondiscriminating suchness-cognizing knowledge;

As being beyond the range of discriminating concepts associated with the mind or mind consciousness;
And as, in the manner of empty space, devoid of any basis for grasping or attachment.

This penetrating comprehension of all dharmas as comparable in their nature to empty space is synonymous with the realization of the unproduced-dharmas patience.

Son of the Buddha, when the bodhisattva acquires this patience, he immediately achieves entry into the eighth ground, the Ground of Immovability, and becomes a "profound practice" bodhisattva who is unfathomable and free of any discriminations, one who has transcended all signs, all conceptual thought, and all attachments, one who has reached a state that is immeasurable and boundless, one who cannot be matched by any *śrāvaka* disciple or *pratyekabuddha,* one who has abandoned all contentiousness, and one in whom quiescence is directly manifest.

This circumstance is comparable to that of a bhikshu who has perfected the spiritual superknowledges and whose mind has achieved sovereign mastery, one who has proceeded through the sequential development of the absorptions to the point of entering the absorption of complete cessation and has become one wherein all movement of the mind, all recollective thought, and all discriminations have entirely ceased.

In just such a way, when this bodhisattva-mahāsattva comes to dwell on the Ground of Immovability, he immediately relinquishes all deliberately effortful practice and acquires the dharma of effortlessness. As for any undertakings of body, speech, and mind as well as any mental exertion, these all completely cease. He then abides in practice accomplished as the fruit of karmic rewards.[201]

His situation is like that of a person who, in the midst of a dream, sees that he has tumbled into the waters of a great river, and then, wishing to get across, brings forth great bravery and pursues some means to accomplish this. Then, due to bringing forth great bravery and enacting some means to accomplish this, he suddenly wakes up. Having awoken, he then desists from everything he was doing.

So too it is with the bodhisattva. Having seen that beings are being swept along in the four floods,[202] he exerts himself with great bravery and brings forth great vigor to rescue them and bring them across. Due to his bravery and vigor, he then succeeds in reaching the Ground of Immovability. Then, having reached this station, there is none of his deliberate effortfulness that does not cease entirely. He then no longer manifests any duality-based practice or practice grounded in phenomenal characteristics.

Son of the Buddha, this situation is comparable to what occurs when one is reborn into the Brahma World wherein, of all the afflictions associated with the desire realm, none of them fail to cease. So too it is when one comes to dwell on the Ground of Immovability. All activity associated with the mind or mind consciousness no longer manifests. This bodhisattva-mahāsattva no longer even manifests the arising of any thought associated with being a bodhisattva, any thought associated with buddhahood, any thought associated with bodhi, or any thought associated with nirvāṇa, how much the less would he bring forth any sort of thought associated with the world.

Son of the Buddha, on account of the power of his original vows, the buddhas, the *bhagavats*, personally manifest directly before the bodhisattva who dwells on this ground, bestowing on him the knowledge of the *tathāgatas*, causing him to pass through the gateway leading into the flow of the Dharma.

They then speak as follows:

> This is good indeed, good indeed. Son of Good Family, this patience is the foremost among them all, one that accords with all dharmas of the buddhas. Still, Son of Good Family, you have not yet acquired all of our ten powers, our fearlessnesses, and our eighteen dharmas exclusive to the buddhas. Hence, out of a desire to perfectly realize these dharmas, you should bring forth the diligent application of vigor even while, at the same time, you must never relinquish this gateway of patience.
>
> Furthermore, Son of Good Family, although you have indeed acquired this quiescent liberation, still, the foolish common people have not yet been able to acquire that realization. All of the different sorts of afflictions continue to manifest in them and all the different sorts of ideation and discursive thought always assail and injure them. Out of kindly pity, you should bear in mind the plight of these beings.
>
> Additionally, Son of Good Family, you should bear in mind your original vow to bestow great and universal benefit on all beings, in every instance causing them to enter the gateway of inconceivable wisdom.
>
> Also, Son of Good Family, this essential nature of all dharmas[203] always abides and never changes whether buddhas come forth into the world or do not come forth into the world. It is not through acquiring this dharma that they are designated as

"*tathāgatas*." Even all those who pursue the Two Vehicles practice are equally able to acquire this dharma that is free of discriminating thought.

Furthermore, Son of Good Family, you should behold the measurelessness of our physical signs, the measurelessness of our wisdom, the measurelessness of our lands, the measurelessness of our skillful means, the measurelessness of our light auras,[204] and also the measurelessness of our pure voices. It is only fitting that you should now perfect these phenomena yourself.

Additionally, Son of Good Family, you have just now acquired this one Dharma light,[205] namely that all dharmas are unproduced and devoid of any differentiating distinctions.[206] Son of Good Family, the Dharma light that the *tathāgatas* have acquired is possessed of so countlessly many circumstances it enters, so countlessly many implementations, and so countlessly many permutations that, even in hundreds of thousands of *koṭis* of *nayutas* of kalpas, one could still never succeed in knowing them all. You should cultivate and perfect this dharma.

Also, Son of Good Family, as you contemplate throughout the ten directions the many different distinctions in the immeasurably many lands, the immeasurably many beings, and the immeasurably many dharmas, you should penetrate and comprehend them all in accordance with reality.

Son of the Buddha, the buddhas, the *bhagavats*, bestow upon these bodhisattvas just so countlessly many gateways to the generation of knowledge, thus enabling them to generate countlessly and boundlessly many different works arising from their knowledge.

Son of the Buddha, if the buddhas did not bestow on these bodhisattvas these gateways to the generation of knowledge, they would otherwise straightaway enter final nirvāṇa and abandon all of their works carried out for the benefit of beings. It is because the buddhas bestow on them just so countlessly and boundlessly many gateways for the generation of wisdom that the wisdom-implementing works these bodhisattvas then generate in but a single mind-moment become so numerous that all of the practices they have cultivated from the time of bringing forth their initial resolve all the way on through to the seventh ground could not even equal a hundredth part, and so forth until we come to their being in aggregate unable to equal even a single part in a hundred thousand *koṭis* of *nayutas* of parts and, in this same way, unable to equal even a single part in an *asaṃkhyeya* of parts, in a *kalā* of parts, in the highest number of parts reachable by calculation, in the highest number of parts describable by analogy, or even in an *upaniṣad*'s number of parts.

And why is this? Son of the Buddha, this bodhisattva formerly employed but one single body in developing his practice. Now, in coming to dwell on this ground, he acquires countless bodies, countless voices, and measureless wisdom while also taking on countless rebirths whereby he engages in the purification of countless pure lands, teaches countless beings, makes offerings to countless buddhas, enters countless gateways into the Dharma, equips himself with countless sorts of spiritual superknowledges, becomes possessed of countless different *bodhimaṇḍa* congregations, abides in countless different sorts of physical, verbal, and mental deeds, and accumulates all of the bodhisattva practices, accomplishing all of this by relying on the dharma of immovability.

Son of the Buddha, in this, he is comparable to someone who boards a ship wishing to set sail out onto the great ocean. Before he has actually reached the ocean, he must tax his strength by devoting much deliberate effort to this end. If he manages to make his way out to sea, he then need only accord with the prevailing winds in continuing to travel along, doing so with no further requirement of human exertion.

Then, due to having finally reached the great ocean, the distance he can then travel in but a single day becomes so great that, were one to compare it with his progress before reaching the ocean, it could not be matched by even a hundred years of those previous methods.

Son of the Buddha, so too it is with bodhisattva-mahāsattva. Once he has accumulated such a vast store of roots of goodness and sets sail in the ship of the Great Vehicle out onto the ocean of bodhisattva practices, then, in but a single mind-moment, he is able to employ effortlessly implemented knowledge to proceed so far into the realm of the cognition of all-knowledge that his progress then could not be rivaled by even countless hundreds of thousands of *koṭis* of *nayutas* of kalpas of his former deliberately effortful practices.

Son of the Buddha, by using effortlessly manifest awakened intelligence produced by great skillful means and cleverly invoked knowledge, the bodhisattva dwelling on the eighth ground contemplates the realm in which the cognition of all-knowledge is implemented.

In particular, he contemplates the creation of worlds and the destruction of worlds and thus knows that they are created from the accumulation of these particular sorts of karmic deeds, that they are destroyed through the exhaustion of the effects of these particular sorts of karmic deeds, knows when their creation phase occurs, knows when their destruction phase occurs, knows how long their creation phase endures, and knows how long their destruction phase endures. He knows all of these things in accordance with reality.

He also knows with respect to the sphere of the earth-element its character on a small scale, its character on a large scale, its character when manifest on an immeasurable scale, and its character in its different manifestations. So too does he know of the spheres of the water, fire, and wind elements their character on a small scale, their character on a large scale, their character on an immeasurable scale, and their character in their different manifestations.

So too does he know of the atoms their character as minutely manifest, their character in their different manifestations, and their character in their different manifestations when manifest on an immeasurable scale. He knows of whichever worlds what constitutes their entire accumulation of atoms as well as the character of those atoms' different manifestations, knowing all of these phenomena in accordance with reality.

So too does he know of whichever world, how many such atoms constitute each of its elemental spheres of earth, water, fire, and wind, how many such atoms form all of their precious things, how many such atoms constitute the bodies of all the beings there, and how many such atoms form the physical mass of those lands, knowing all of these phenomena in accordance with reality.

So too does he know of those beings, both of those who are physically large and of those who are physically small, how many such atoms collectively compose their bodies, knowing this as well of the bodies of the hell-dwellers, the bodies of the animals, the bodies of the hungry ghosts, the bodies of the *asuras,* the bodies of the devas, and the bodies of the humans, knowing of each of them of how many such atoms they are composed.

He acquires just such knowledge as this whereby he knows even of atoms their different sorts of manifestations.

So too, he knows of the desire realm, the form realm, and the formless realm the circumstances of their creation, knows of the desire realm, the form realm, and the formless realm the circumstances of their destruction, knows of the desire realm, the form realm, and the formless realm their character on a small scale, their character on a large scale, their character when manifest on an immeasurable scale, and their character in their different manifestations.

He acquires just such knowledge as this whereby he contemplates the different manifestations within the three realms of existence.

Son of the Buddha, this bodhisattva also brings forth the light of knowledge by resort to which he teaches beings. In particular, he thereby becomes thoroughly aware of the different physical bodies of beings, thoroughly distinguishes the character of these beings' physical bodies, and thoroughly contemplates the stations of rebirth into which these beings are born. He then manifests bodies for them in ways adapted to what is appropriate for them, whereupon he then teaches them and brings them to maturation.

This bodhisattva employs his light of knowledge to manifest the taking on of rebirths everywhere throughout an entire great trichiliocosm, doing so in a manner adapted to the differences in beings' bodies and resolute convictions.

So too, everywhere throughout the worlds within two or three great trichiliocosms, within a hundred thousand great trichiliocosms, and even within ineffably many great trichiliocosms, he manifests this taking on of births in a manner adapted to the differences in beings' bodies and resolute convictions.

Because this bodhisattva has perfected wisdom such as this, even as his body remains motionless within a single buddha land, he manifests his bodies everywhere, doing so in the midst of assembled congregations in up to an ineffably great number of buddha lands.

Son of the Buddha, this bodhisattva, adapting to all of the different variations in beings' bodies, minds, and resolute convictions, manifests his own bodies in the midst of the assembled congregations within those buddha lands. In particular, within assemblies of *śramaṇas,* he appears in the form of a *śramaṇa,* within assemblies of brahmins, he appears in the form of a brahmin, and within assemblies of *kṣatriyas,* he appears in the form of a *kṣatriya.* He appears in this same manner within assemblies of *vaiśyas,* within assemblies of *śūdras,* within assemblies of householders, within assemblies in the Heaven of the Four Heavenly Kings, within assemblies in the Heaven of the Thirty-three, within assemblies in the Yāma Heaven, within assemblies in the Tuṣita Heaven, within assemblies in the Transformation of Bliss Heaven, within assemblies in the Paranirmita Vaśavartin Heaven, within assemblies of *māras,* within assemblies in the Brahma Heaven, and so forth on up to his manifestations that appear within assemblies in the Akaniṣṭha Heaven. In each of these cases, he manifests in a form adapted to the particular sorts of beings there.

Also, for the sake of those who should most readily achieve liberation through someone manifesting in the form of a *śrāvaka* disciple, he then manifests in the form of a *śrāvaka* disciple. For the sake of those who should most readily achieve liberation through someone manifesting in the form of a *pratyekabuddha,* he then manifests in the form of a *pratyekabuddha.* For the sake of those who should most readily achieve liberation through someone manifesting in the form of a bodhisattva, he then manifests in the form of a bodhisattva. And for the sake of those who should most readily achieve liberation through someone manifesting in the form of a *tathāgata,* he then manifests in the form of a *tathāgata.*

Son of the Buddha, it is in this way that the bodhisattva manifests bodies in all of these ineffably many buddha lands, doing so in accordance with the distinct differences in beings' resolute convictions.

Son of the Buddha, this bodhisattva has completely abandoned all discriminations associated with the perceptions of bodies and abides in the awareness of uniform equality in such things.

This bodhisattva knows:

The bodies of beings;
The bodies of lands;
The bodies received as karmic retribution;
The bodies of *śrāvaka* disciples;
The bodies of *pratyekabuddhas;*
The bodies of bodhisattvas;
The bodies of *tathāgatas;*
The knowledge body;
The Dharma body;
And empty space bodies.

This bodhisattva, knowing beings' resolute convictions, is able to use a being's body to form his own body. So too is he able to turn it into the body of a land, a body received as karmic retribution, or any of the other sorts of bodies, up to and including an empty space body.

He is also able, knowing beings' resolute convictions, to turn the body of a land into his own body. So too is he able to turn it into the body of a being, a body received as karmic retribution, or any of the other sorts of bodies, up to and including an empty space body.

He is also able, knowing what pleases the minds of beings, to turn a karmic retribution body into his own body. So too is he able to turn it into the body of a being, the body of a land, or any of the other sorts of bodies up to and including an empty space body.

He is also able, knowing beings' resolute convictions, to turn his own body into the body of another being, the physical body of a land, and so forth on up to and including an empty space body.

So it is that, adapting to beings' different resolute convictions, he then employs these sorts of bodies to manifest for them just these very sorts of physical forms.

This bodhisattva knows beings' bodies associated with the accumulation of karmic actions, their karmic retribution bodies, their bodies associated with the afflictions, their form-realm bodies, and their formless-realm bodies.

He also knows with regard to the bodies of lands:

Their characteristics when small;
Their characteristics when large;
Their characteristics when immeasurable;
Their characteristics when defiled;
Their characteristics when pure;
Their characteristics when vast;
Their characteristics when inverted;
Their characteristics when upright;
Their characteristics when they are universally pervasive;
And their different sorts of characteristics when existing as parts of a spatially distributed network.

He knows with respect to bodies received as karmic retribution, the distinctions in the conventional names applied to them and knows with respect to the bodies of *śrāvaka* disciples, the bodies of *pratyekabuddhas*, and the bodies of bodhisattvas, the distinctions in the conventional names applied to them.

He knows with respect to the bodies of *tathāgatas*, their possession of:

Bodhi bodies;
Bodies associated with vows;
Transformationally produced bodies;
Bodies sustained through their powers;
Bodies graced with the major marks and subsidiary signs;
Bodies possessed of awe-inspiring strength;
Mind-generated bodies;
Merit bodies;
The Dharma body;
And the knowledge body.

He knows with respect to the knowledge body:

Its characteristic of skillful deliberation;
Its characteristic of selective judgment in accordance with reality;
Its characteristics associated with the practices leading to the fruits of the path;
Its characteristics associated with the distinctions between what is worldly and what is world-transcending;
Its characteristics associated with distinctions in the Three Vehicles;
Its characteristics when shared;
Its characteristics when exclusive;
Its characteristics when associated with emancipation;
Its characteristics when associated with an unemancipated state;
Its characteristics when associated with the stages of the learner;
And its characteristics when associated with the stage of those beyond learning.

He knows with respect to the Dharma body its characteristic of uniform equality and its characteristic of indestructibility, knows the characteristics associated with the differentiation in conventional names when adapted to times and when adapted to mundane circumstances, knows the characteristic distinctions in the dharmas associated with beings as opposed to those associated with non-beings, and knows the characteristic distinctions in the dharmas associated with the buddhas, the Dharma, and the Ārya Sangha.

He knows with respect to the empty space body its characteristic of immeasurability, its characteristic of universal pervasion, its characteristic of formlessness, its characteristic of nondifferentiation, its characteristic of boundlessness, and its characteristic of revealing the existence of form bodies.

Son of the Buddha, having completely developed such knowledge with respect to bodies as this, this bodhisattva acquires:

Sovereign mastery in life span;
Sovereign mastery of mind;
Sovereign mastery in wealth;
Sovereign mastery in karmic deeds;
Sovereign mastery in births;
Sovereign mastery in vows;
Sovereign mastery in resolute faith;[207]
Sovereign mastery in psychic power;
Sovereign mastery in knowledge;
And sovereign mastery of the Dharma.

Due to having acquired these ten types of sovereign mastery, he then becomes one whose knowledge is inconceivable, one whose knowledge is measureless, one whose knowledge is vast, and one whose knowledge is invincible.

Having achieved just such penetrating comprehension as this and having achieved just such consummate realization as this, he thus becomes:

One who is absolutely free of fault in physical karmic actions, free of fault in verbal deeds, and free of fault in mental deeds;
One in whom all physical, verbal, and mental karmic acts are carried forth in accordance with knowledge;
One in whom the *prajñāpāramitā* is dominant;
One in whom the great compassion has become the foremost priority;
One whose expedient means are skillful;
One who is well able to make distinctions;
One who is excellent in bringing forth great vows;
One who is protected by the power of the Buddha;
One who always diligently cultivates knowledge directed toward benefiting beings;
And one who dwells everywhere throughout the boundlessly many different worlds.

Son of the Buddha, to state this in terms of the most essential point, the bodhisattva dwelling on this Ground of Immovability is able to gather all dharmas of the Buddha in all that he does through his physical, verbal, and mental deeds.

Son of the Buddha, the bodhisattva dwelling on this ground:

Becomes well established in the power of the resolute intentions[208] because none of the afflictions function in him;
Becomes well established in the power of the supreme mind through never departing from the path;
Becomes well established in the power of the great compassion through never relinquishing his benefiting of beings;
Becomes well established in the power of the great kindness through striving to rescue and protect everyone abiding in all worlds;
Becomes well established in power of the *dhāraṇīs* through never forgetting any dharma;
Becomes well established in power of eloquence through skillfully contemplating and distinguishing all dharmas;

Becomes well established in the power of the spiritual superknowledges through going forth everywhere throughout the boundlessly many worlds;

Becomes well established in the power of the great vows through never relinquishing any of the bodhisattva endeavors;

Becomes well established in the power of the *pāramitās* through perfecting all dharmas of the Buddha;

And acquires the power of being protected and borne in mind by the *tathāgatas* through his being directed toward the knowledge of all modes and the cognition of all-knowledge.

This bodhisattva who has acquired such powers of knowledge as these is able to manifest all endeavors that are to be accomplished while remaining free of fault in all those endeavors.

Son of the Buddha, this bodhisattva ground of knowledge:

Is known as the Ground of Immovability because no one is able to obstruct or overcome him;

Is known as the ground of irreversibility because his wisdom never retreats;

Is known as the ground that is difficult to acquire because no one in the world is able to fathom it;

Is known as the ground of the pure youth[209] because he has abandoned all faults;

Is known as the ground of birth because he possesses sovereign mastery in doing whatever he pleases;

Is known as the ground of completion because there is nothing more to be done;

Is known as the ultimate ground because his wisdom has become resolutely decisive;

Is known as the ground of transformations because he achieves complete success in whatever he wishes to do;

Is known as the ground of sustenance through power because others are unable to move him;

And is known as the ground of effortlessness because, earlier on, he has already achieved complete development.

Son of the Buddha, the bodhisattva who has developed wisdom such as this gains entry into the domain of the buddhas, becomes illuminated by the Buddha's merit, and accords with the Buddha's awe-inspiring deportment. With the direct manifestation of the realms of the buddhas, he is always protected and borne in mind by the *tathāgatas*. Brahmā, Śakra, the Four Heavenly Kings, and the Vajra-wielding protectors constantly follow and protect him. He never leaves the great samādhis and is able to manifest countless different sorts of bodies each and every one of which is possessed of immense strength. As karmically generated effects, he acquires spiritual superknowledges and samādhis in which he has sovereign mastery.[210] Wherever there are beings amenable to being taught, he manifests the realization of right enlightenment.

Son of the Buddha, it is in this way that the bodhisattva enters the assembly of those who abide in the Great Vehicle, acquires great spiritual superknowledges, emits immensely radiant light, and is unimpeded in entering the Dharma realm. He knows the different variations among the worlds. He manifests all of the magnificent meritorious qualities, has sovereign mastery in whatever he directs his mind to, is well able to bring forth an utterly penetrating comprehension of both the past and the future, and is able to everywhere overcome all of the paths of Māra's deviance. He deeply enters the realms in which the *tathāgatas* course and cultivates the bodhisattva practices in countless lands. It is because he has been able to acquire the dharma of irreversibility that he is described as dwelling on the Ground of Immovability.

Son of the Buddha, having come to dwell on this Ground of Immovability, this bodhisattva, through the power of samādhi, is then always able to directly see measurelessly many buddhas. He never relinquishes his practice of serving and making offerings to them. In each and every kalpa and in each and every world, this bodhisattva sees measurelessly many hundreds of buddhas, measurelessly many thousands of buddhas, and so forth on up to measurelessly many hundreds of thousands of *koṭis* of *nayutas* of buddhas, all of whom he reveres, venerates, serves, and presents with offerings. He offers up and bestows upon them all amenities facilitating the sustenance of their lives.

Wherever the buddhas dwell, he acquires the *tathāgatas'* treasuries of extremely profound Dharma and receives from them measureless Dharma light pertaining to the differences among worlds and other such phenomena. Should anyone approach him and challenge him by posing difficult questions regarding any of the distinctions among worlds or other such matters, no one can prevail over him.

He continues on in this way passing through a period of measurelessly many hundreds of kalpas, measurelessly many thousands of kalpas, and so on up to measurelessly many hundreds of thousands of *koṭis* of *nayutas* of kalpas during which his roots of goodness become ever more radiant in their purity like the real gold that is fashioned into a jeweled crown to be placed on the head of the sage king ruling over the continent of Jambudvīpa. It is of a sort that none of the adornments possessed by any of his government ministers or any of his people could ever rival it.

So too it is with all the roots of goodness possessed by the bodhisattva dwelling on this ground, for they are such that they could never be rivaled by any roots of goodness possessed by followers of the Two Vehicles or by bodhisattvas dwelling on any of the first seven grounds.

Due to dwelling on this ground, the light of his great wisdom is able to everywhere extinguish the darkness of beings' afflictions. This is because he is well able to open up and expound upon the gateways to wisdom.

Son of the Buddha, just as that lord of a thousand worlds, the king of the Great Brahma Heaven, is able to everywhere extend his mind of kindness and everywhere send forth light that fills up a thousand worlds, so too it is with the bodhisattva dwelling on this ground. He is able to send forth light that illuminates worlds as numerous as the atoms in hundreds of myriads of buddha lands that extinguishes the flames of afflictions of the beings therein and causes them to experience clarity and coolness.

Among the ten *pāramitās*, this bodhisattva is especially superior in his practice of the *pāramitā* of vows. It is not that he does not practice the other *pāramitās*. Rather, he simply accords them an amount of emphasis corresponding to his own strengths and to what is fitting.

This has been a summary discussion of all bodhisattva-mahāsattvas' eighth ground, the Ground of Immovability. Were one to speak of it extensively, one could pursue the discussion for measurelessly many kalpas and yet still be unable to find the end of it.

Son of the Buddha, the bodhisattva-mahāsattva dwelling on this ground often serves as a king of the Great Brahma Heaven, the lord over a thousand worlds, who, supreme in his sovereign mastery, is well able to discourse on any principle and is able to bestow the path of the *pāramitās* on *śrāvaka* disciples, *pratyekabuddhas,* and bodhisattvas. Should anyone challenge his explanations of the differences in world realms, no one is able to prevail over him.

In his practice of giving, pleasing words, beneficial actions, and joint endeavors as well as any of the other such endeavors he pursues, he never departs from mindfulness of the Buddha, and so forth on up to his never departing from mindfulness of the knowledge of all modes and the cognition of all-knowledge.

He also has this thought: "I should become one who serves these beings as a leader, as one who is supreme," and so forth until we come to "as one who relies on the cognition of all-knowledge."

If this bodhisattva brings forth the power of great vigor, then, in but a moment, he acquires a number of samādhis as numerous as the atoms in the worlds contained within a hundred myriads of great trichiliocosms. And so it goes on up to his then being able to manifest a following of bodhisattvas serving in his retinue as numerous as the atoms in all the worlds in a hundred myriads of great trichiliocosms.

If this bodhisattva chooses to avail himself of the power of his especially supreme vows, he becomes able then to freely manifest these phenomena in numbers well beyond these, such that one would never be able to count them even in hundreds of thousands of *koṭis* of *nayutas* of kalpas.

At that time, Vajragarbha Bodhisattva, wishing to proclaim his meaning once more, thereupon spoke these verses:

Having on seven grounds cultivated expedients and wisdom, having
thoroughly assembled path-assisting practices and great vow power,
having become supported by those most honored among men, and
seeking to acquire supreme knowledge, he ascends to the eighth ground.

He perfects meritorious qualities,[211] is constant in kindliness and pity,
possesses wisdom as vast as empty space, and is then able
by hearing Dharma, to initiate the power of resolute decisiveness and
enter the quiescent unproduced-dharmas patience.

He knows dharmas as unproduced, unarisen, signless,
as uncreated, undestroyed, endless, not undergoing transformation,
as beyond existence, uniformly equal, cutting short discriminations,
as stepping beyond the range of thought, and as abiding like space.

Having perfected this patience, he transcends frivolous theorizing,
abides in very deep, motionless, and constant quiescence
such as no one in the entire world could ever comprehend,
and such as abandons all thoughts, signs, grasping, and attachment.

Dwelling on this ground, he makes no discriminations,
like the bhikshu who has entered the cessation absorption, like
one in a river-fording dream who, awakening, sees it is nonexistent,
and like one who, born in the Brahma Heaven, severs base desires.

By power of original vows, he receives encouragement and guidance,
is praised for gaining supreme patience, is given a crown anointing,
and is told, "The many Buddha dharmas that we possess,
you have now still not acquired. You must bring forth diligent vigor.

Although you have already extinguished the afflictions' fires,
the flaming afflictions of the world's beings still blaze on.
You must recall your original vow to help beings cross beyond,
and influence them all to cultivate the causes leading to liberation.

True constancy of Dharmas' nature and separation from thoughts
are of the sort that even adherents of the Two Vehicles can realize.
Hence it is not due to this that we are the World Honored Ones,
rather it is solely due to extremely deep and unimpeded knowledge."

In this way, those worthy of the offerings of men and devas
bestow this wisdom on him, causing him to deeply contemplate it.
Thus they completely develop boundlessly many buddha dharmas
and, in a single moment, step beyond their many previous practices.

When the bodhisattva dwells on this ground of sublime knowledge,
he then acquires vast spiritual superknowledges' powers whereby,
in a moment, his transformation bodies pervade the ten directions
as he becomes like a ship gone out to sea, carried across by the wind.

The mind effortlessly avails itself of the power of knowledge,
entirely knows the creation, destruction, and abiding of lands,
all of the differences in each of the different sorts of realms,
and is able to utterly know them when small, large, or boundless.

The four great elements throughout the trichiliocosms' worlds,
the different sorts of bodies of the beings in the six rebirth destinies,
as well as even the atoms forming the many jewels—
with his knowledge, he contemplates all of these without exception.

This bodhisattva is also able to know all of the types of bodies
and take on the same forms as theirs for the sake of teaching beings.
In the countless lands with their many different types, he manifests
his forms for them, with none wherein he is not everywhere present.

Like the sun and moon that, abiding in space,
display their reflections in all of the bodies of water,
he abides in the Dharma realm, remaining motionless, even as,
adapting to beings' minds, he manifests reflections in this same way.

Adapting to their minds' predilections[212] that differ in each case,
he manifests bodies in the presence of all beings,
doing so with bodies of *śrāvakas, pratyekabuddhas,* bodhisattvas,
or buddhas, having no type of body that he does not manifest.

Bodies of beings, bodies of lands, karmic retribution bodies,
bodies of the various *āryas*, the knowledge body, the Dharma body,
and the space-like body, all uniformly equal in character—
he manifests them everywhere for the sake of beings.

With ten *ārya* knowledges,[213] his contemplation extends everywhere.
He also adapts kindness and compassion to doing many works,
entirely develops all dharmas of a buddha,
and, in upholding moral precepts, is as immovable as Mount Sumeru.

Completely developed in ten powers, he cannot be moved or shaken,
cannot be turned back by any of Māra's hordes,
is held in mindfully protected by buddhas, is revered by deva kings,
and is constantly served and guarded by traceless vajra-bearers.

The meritorious qualities of those on this ground are boundless,
indescribable even in thousands of myriads of *koṭis* of kalpas.
He continues by offerings to buddhas to skillfully increase in radiance
that thus becomes like that of the adornments on the head of a king.

The bodhisattva dwelling on this eighth ground
often serves as a Brahma Heaven king, lord of a thousand realms,
who expounds endlessly on the Three Vehicles, everywhere shines
forth his light of kindness, and dispels the afflictions of the many.

The samādhis he acquires in but a single moment
equal in number the atoms in a hundred myriads of worlds.
So too is the number of endeavors that he accomplishes,
and yet, through vow power, he may even manifest yet more.

The bodhisattva's eighth ground, the Ground of Immovability
has thus been summarily explained by me for the sake of all of you.
Were one to pursue a vast, sequentially presented analysis of this,
even expounding on it for a *koṭi* of kalpas, one still could never finish.

The Ninth Ground

The Excellent Intelligence Ground

Once the eighth bodhisattva ground's explanation had concluded,
the Tathāgata manifested great spiritual superknowledges' powers,
causing tremors in an inconceivable and incalculable number of *koṭis*
of lands throughout the ten directions.

The body of that all-knowing and seeing Supremely Honored One
then sent forth everywhere immensely radiant light
that illuminated with dazzling brilliance all those countless lands,
causing all beings therein to be filled with happiness.

The incalculably many hundreds of thousands of *koṭis* of bodhisattvas
simultaneously ascended into space where they remained
and presented offerings superior even to the devas' marvelous gifts
to he whose proclamations are the most superior of all.

The Great Vaśavartin Heaven King and the Vaśavartin devas
then all together and with unified minds felt measureless joy.
They each then presented all different sorts of the many types of gifts
as offerings to the extremely deep ocean of meritorious qualities.

A thousand myriads *koṭis* of celestial nymphs were also present
who, filled with joyous exultation in body and mind,
each played measurelessly many kinds of music
as offerings to the great guiding teacher among humans.

Then the many sorts of music played simultaneously
a hundred thousand myriads of *koṭis* of countless musical variations
that, by the awe-inspiring spiritual power of the Well Gone One,
uttered praises with sublime voices, saying:

"The quiescent and pliant one free of defilements or injuriousness
skillfully cultivates whichever ground he enters.
Possessed of a mind like space, he goes forth to the ten directions,
broadly proclaiming the Buddha's path to awaken the many beings.

In all places throughout the heavens and among men,
he manifests incomparably marvelous adornments
arising from the meritorious qualities of the Tathāgata
that cause those who observe them to delight in Buddha's wisdom.

Without leaving that single land, he goes to visit the many lands.
In this, he is like the moon everywhere illuminating the entire world.
Even as his voice's conceptual thoughts have all become quiescent,[214]
like echoes in a valley, there is no place where they do not resound.

Where there are beings of lesser resolve,
he expounds for them the practices of *śrāvaka* disciples.
If their minds are bright, sharp and pleased by the *pratyeka* vehicle,[215]
then he discourses for them on the path of that intermediate vehicle.

For the kind and compassionate who delight in beneficence,
he explains for them the deeds practiced by bodhisattvas.
For those with the resolve to acquire the most superior wisdom,
he shows them the unsurpassable Dharma of the Tathāgata.

In this, he is like a conjurer in his creation of many phenomena
wherein none of those forms or features are real.
So too it is with these conjurations born of this bodhisattva's wisdom.
though it shows all things, it transcends existence and nonexistence."

Having thus sung with a thousand myriad beautiful sounds
these songs praising the Buddha, they all then stood there in silence.
Liberation Moon then spoke, saying: "This congregation is now pure.
Please expound now on the path as practiced on the ninth ground."

At that time, Vajragarbha Bodhisattva informed Liberation Moon Bodhisattva, saying:

O Son of the Buddha, here we have the bodhisattva-mahāsattva who, resorting to such measurelessly vast knowledge as this, has pursued reflective meditative contemplations and has additionally sought:

To seek out ever more supreme realizations of quiescent liberation;

To further cultivate the wisdom of the Tathāgata;

To access the secret dharmas of the Tathāgata;

To contemplate the nature of inconceivably great knowledge;

To purify all gateways to *dhāraṇīs* and samādhis;

To become equipped with the great spiritual superknowledges;

To enter the different sorts of worlds;

To cultivate the powers, fearlessnesses, and dharmas exclusive to the buddhas;

To accord with all buddhas in turning the wheel of the Dharma;

And to never relinquish his greatly compassionate original vows.

It is he who then succeeds in entering the bodhisattva's ninth ground, the Ground of Excellent Intelligence.

Son of the Buddha, the bodhisattva-mahāsattva dwelling on this Ground of Excellent Intelligence knows in accordance with reality:

The effects of practicing[216] dharmas that are good, bad, and karmically neutral;

The effects of practicing dharmas either associated with or free of the contaminants;
The effects of practicing worldly dharmas and world-transcending dharmas;
The effects of practicing dharmas that are conceivable and dharmas that are inconceivable;
The effects of practicing the dharmas that are definite and the dharmas that are indefinite;
The effects of practicing *śrāvaka* dharmas and dharmas of *pratyekabuddhas*;
The effects of practicing the bodhisattva practice dharmas;
The effects of practicing dharmas of the Tathāgata's ground;
The effects of practicing conditioned dharmas;
And the effects of practicing unconditioned dharmas.

This bodhisattva uses such wisdom to know in accordance with reality the entangling thickets[217] in beings' minds, specifically knowing:[218]

The entangling thicket of the afflictions;
The entangling thicket of karmic actions;
The entangling thicket of the faculties;
The entangling thicket of resolute beliefs;[219]
The entangling thicket of the sense realms;[220]
The entangling thicket of resolute intentions;[221]
The entangling thicket of latent tendencies;[222]
The entangling thicket of births;[223]
The entangling thicket of the continuity of karmic propensities;[224]
And the entangling thicket associated with the differences among the three groups of beings.[225]

This bodhisattva knows in accordance with reality all of the different sorts of characteristics of beings' minds, specifically knowing:

The characteristic of arising with diverse character;
The characteristic of swift transformation;
The characteristic of either being destroyed or undestroyed;
The characteristic of having no physical form;[226]
The characteristic of becoming boundless;[227]
The characteristic of purity;
The characteristic of being either defiled or undefiled;
The characteristic of being either held in bondage or freed of bondage;
The characteristic of being deceptive about its endeavors;

And the characteristic of manifesting in accordance with the destinies of rebirth.

So it is that he knows in accordance with reality such characteristics numbering in the hundreds of thousands of myriads of *koṭis*, knowing characteristics that in number extend to the point of incalculability.

So too does he know all of the different characteristics of the afflictions, specifically knowing:

Their characteristic of following one long and far;

Their characteristic of possessing boundlessly many bases for their arising;

Their characteristic of accompanying [the mind] in their arising and thus not being abandoned;

Their characteristic of possessing the same quality in both their latent and arisen states;

Their characteristic of being either associated with mind or disassociated from mind;

Their characteristic of abiding in a manner corresponding to the destiny of rebirth one enters;

Their characteristic of differing in each of the three realms of existence;

The characteristic of craving, views, ignorance, and pride to be as calamitous as deeply penetrating arrows;

And their characteristic of uninterrupted continuity in serving as causes and conditions of the three categories of karmic actions.

Briefly stated, he knows in accordance with reality all such characteristics, thus knowing even up to eighty-four thousand such characteristics.

So too does he know the characteristics of all of the different sorts of karmic actions, specifically knowing:

Their characteristic of being either good, bad, or neutral;

Their characteristic of being either manifest or not manifest;

Their characteristic of arising in association with and not separate from mind;

Their characteristic of being, due to their very nature, extinguished in every *kṣaṇa* even as there occurs the sequential accumulation of karmic fruits that are never lost;

Their characteristic of involving or not involving karmic retribution;

Their characteristic of involving the undergoing of multiple sorts of karmic retributions as when black actions are rewarded with black retributions, and so forth;[228]

Their characteristic of being comparable to immeasurably vast farm fields [in which their karmic causes are planted];[229]
Their characteristic of possessing differences as performed by the foolish common people and by the *āryas;*
Their characteristic of involving the undergoing of their retribution in the present life, in the immediately ensuing rebirth, or in some subsequent life;
And their characteristic of being either definite or indefinite as determined by their association with any of the vehicles or non-association with any of the vehicles.

Briefly stated, he knows in accordance with reality all such characteristics, thus knowing even up to eighty-four thousand such characteristics.

So too does he know the characteristics of the various faculties, specifically knowing:

Their characteristic of being either weak, middling, or superb;
Their characteristic of possessing or not possessing distinct differences between the past and the future;
Their characteristic of existing in association with what is either superior, middling, or inferior;
Their characteristic of arising in association with and being inseparable from the afflictions;
Their characteristic of being either definite or indefinite as determined by their association with any of the vehicles or nonassociation with any of the vehicles;
Their characteristic of being entirely ripened and trained to the point of pliancy;
Their characteristic of vulnerability, as befits the state of the individual web of faculties, to transformation and destruction;
Their characteristic of becoming so especially superb that they are insuperable by anyone;
Their characteristic of differing as regards their reversibility or irreversibility;
And their characteristic of possessing differences in the degree to which they continue even distantly to accompany one in their arising.

Briefly stated, he knows in accordance with reality all such characteristics, thus knowing even up to eighty-four thousand such characteristics.

So too does he know:

With respect to resolute beliefs,[230] the degree to which they may be either weak, middling, or superior;

With respect to sense realms,[231] the degree to which they may be either weak, middling, or superior;

With respect to resolute intentions,[232] the degree to which they may be either weak, middling, or superior.

With respect to all of these matters, briefly stated, he knows all of their associated characteristics, thus knowing of each of them even up to eighty-four thousand such characteristics.

He also knows with respect to the latent tendencies,[233] all of their different sorts of characteristics, specifically knowing:

Their characteristic of arising in association with resolute intentions;[234]

Their characteristic of arising in association with thought;

Their characteristic of differing when concomitant with mind or not concomitant with mind;

Their characteristic of following one long and far;

Their characteristic of having existed beginninglessly and thus never having been extricated;

Their characteristic of running counter to the realization of any and all of the *dhyāna* absorptions, liberations, samādhis, *samāpattis,* and spiritual superknowledges;

Their characteristic of being what holds one in bondage to continuous rebirth within the three realms;

Their characteristic of causing the boundlessly continuous manifestation of mind;

Their characteristic of opening the gateway to all of the sense bases;

Their characteristic of possessing such solidity as to be difficult to counteract;

Their characteristic of determining success or failure in acquisition of any of the grounds as stations of the path;

And their characteristic of being only such as may be extricated through the path of the *āryas.*

He also knows with respect to the taking on of rebirths, all of their different sorts of characteristics, specifically knowing:

The characteristic of taking on rebirths in accordance with one's karmic deeds;

The characteristics associated with differences in the six rebirth destinies;

The characteristics associated with differences between form realm and formless realm rebirth;

The characteristics associated with differences between rebirths with perception and rebirths without perception;

The characteristics associated with karmic action acting as a field, craving as moistening water, ignorance as sheltering darkness, and consciousness as a seed giving birth to the sprout of subsequent becoming;

The characteristics of simultaneous arising and inseparability of name-and-form;

The characteristic of delusion and craving to seek continued existence;

The characteristic of beginningless desirous attachment to desire feelings and to desire rebirth;

And the characteristic of erroneously thinking one has already escaped the desires involved in existence within the three realms.

He also knows with respect to the habitual karmic propensities,[235] all their different sorts of characteristics, specifically knowing:

The characteristic of differing when active or inactive;

The characteristic of their imbued impressions to follow into the rebirth destinies;

The characteristic of their imbued impressions to accord with beings' actions;

The characteristic of their imbued impressions to accord with karma and afflictions;

The characteristic of their imbued impressions to accord with what is karmically good, bad, or neutral;

The characteristic of their imbued impressions to follow one into subsequent existences;

The characteristic of their creation of imbued impressions to occur in a sequential manner;

The characteristic of their imbued impressions to be associated with ceaseless afflictions that follow one afar and are not relinquished;

The characteristic of their imbued impressions to be associated with what is substantially true or associated with what is not substantially true;

And the characteristic of their imbued impressions to be associated with observing, listening to, and drawing near to either *śrāvaka* disciples, *pratyekabuddhas*, bodhisattvas, or *tathāgatas*.

He also knows with respect to beings the characteristics of being fixed in what is right, fixed in what is wrong, or unfixed, specifically knowing:[236]

The characteristic of being fixed in what is right through the possession of right views;
The characteristic of being fixed in what is wrong through the possession of wrong views;
The characteristic of being unfixed in both of these respects;
The characteristic of being fixed in what is wrong through the five heinous karmic offenses;[237]
The characteristic of being fixed in what is right through the five root faculties;
The characteristic of being unfixed in both of these respects;
The characteristic of being fixed in what is wrong through following the eightfold wrong path;
The characteristic of being fixed in what is right through following what is right by its very nature;
The characteristic of being unfixed in either respect by no longer engaging in either [what is right or what is wrong], thus separating from both;
The characteristic of being fixed in what is wrong through being deeply attached to wrong dharmas;
The characteristic of being fixed in what is right through habitual practice of the path of the *āryas;*
And the characteristic of being unfixed in either respect through abandoning both [what is right and what is wrong].

Son of the Buddha, the bodhisattva who accords with knowledge such as this is said to dwell on the Ground of Excellent Intelligence. Having come to dwell on this ground, he completely knows all the different aspects of beings' actions, teaches and trains them, and thereby causes them to gain liberation.

Son of the Buddha, this bodhisattva is well able to expound on the dharmas of the *śrāvaka*-disciple vehicle, the dharmas of the *pratyekabuddha* vehicle, the dharmas of the bodhisattva vehicle, and the dharmas of the ground of the Tathāgata.

Because, in all aspects of practice, he acts in accordance with such knowledge, he is able to adapt to variations in beings' faculties, natures, desires, understandings, and practices as well as to differences in their groups.[238] He also accords with whichever destiny they have been born into as well as with their particular afflictions, latent tendencies, karmic bonds, karmic actions, and habitual karmic propensities. Having done so, he then explains the Dharma for them accordingly, thereby causing them to develop resolute belief,[239] to increase their wisdom, and to then achieve liberation through whichever vehicle is appropriate for them.

Son of the Buddha, the bodhisattva who dwells on this Ground of Excellent Intelligence becomes a great expounder of the Dharma[240] thoroughly equipped with the practice appropriate to an expounder of the Dharma. He is thus well able to preserve and protect the Dharma treasury of the Tathāgata.

Availing himself of immeasurably vast knowledge, he brings forth the four types of unimpeded knowledge and uses the bodhisattva's command of phrasing to expound the Dharma. This bodhisattva always accords with permutations of the four kinds of unimpeded knowledge[241] and never abandons them even briefly. What then are those four? They are:

Unimpeded knowledge of Dharma;
Unimpeded knowledge of meaning;
Unimpeded knowledge of language;
And unimpeded knowledge of eloquence.

It is through unimpeded knowledge of Dharma that this bodhisattva knows the specific characteristics of individual dharmas, through unimpeded knowledge of meaning that he knows the differentiating characteristics of dharmas, through unimpeded knowledge of language that he remains free of errors in his discourse, and through unimpeded knowledge of eloquence that his discourse is neither interrupted nor exhausted.

Additionally, it is through unimpeded knowledge of Dharma that he knows the nature of dharmas, through unimpeded knowledge of meaning that he knows the production and destruction of dharmas, through unimpeded knowledge of language that he establishes [the conventional designations of] all dharmas and discourses on them continuously,[242] and through unimpeded knowledge of eloquence that he presents boundless discourses that accord with and do no violence to [those conventional designations] he has established.

Also, it is through unimpeded knowledge of Dharma that he knows the distinctions among present dharmas, through unimpeded knowledge of meaning that he knows the distinctions among past and future dharmas, through unimpeded knowledge of language that he discourses without error on past, future, and present dharmas, and it is through unimpeded knowledge of eloquence that he discourses completely and with boundless Dharma light on each of the periods of time.

Then again, it is through unimpeded knowledge of Dharma that he knows the differences among dharmas, through unimpeded knowledge of meaning that he knows the differences among meanings, through unimpeded knowledge of language that he accords with others' language in his discourse, and through unimpeded knowledge of eloquence that he adapts to others' mental dispositions.

Additionally, it is through unimpeded knowledge of Dharma that he uses Dharma knowledge to know differentiating and non-differentiating aspects. It is through unimpeded knowledge of meaning that he employs comparative knowledge to know differences in accordance with reality. It is through unimpeded knowledge of language that he uses worldly knowledge to discourse on differentiating aspects. And it is through unimpeded knowledge of eloquence that he uses the knowledge of ultimate truth to discourse skillfully.

Also, it is through unimpeded knowledge of Dharma that he knows dharmas' singular and indestructible character. It is through unimpeded knowledge of meaning that his knowing of the aggregates, the sense realms, the sense bases, the truths, and conditioned origination is skillful. It is through unimpeded knowledge of language that he is able to employ in his discourse a beautifully sublime voice and choice of phrasing that are easily and completely understood by all inhabitants of the world. And it is through unimpeded knowledge of eloquence that he becomes ever more supremely able to discourse with boundless Dharma light.

Then again, it is through unimpeded knowledge of Dharma that he knows the uniformly equal nature of the One Vehicle, through unimpeded knowledge of meaning that he knows the different natures of all the vehicles, through unimpeded knowledge of language that he expounds on the absence of differences among all of the vehicles, and through unimpeded knowledge of eloquence that he expounds on each and every one of the vehicles with boundless Dharma [light].[243]

Also, it is through unimpeded knowledge of Dharma that he knows the practices of all bodhisattvas, the practice of knowledge, the practice of the Dharma, and the realizations following from knowledge. It is through unimpeded knowledge of meaning that he knows the differences in meaning associated with the stations on ten grounds. It is through unimpeded knowledge of language that he discourses on the aspects of the path of the grounds that do not differ. And it is through unimpeded knowledge of eloquence that he expounds on the boundless practice aspects of each and every one of the grounds.

Then again, it is through unimpeded knowledge of Dharma that he knows the realization of the right enlightenment in but a single mind-moment as achieved by all *tathāgatas*. It is through unimpeded knowledge of meaning that he knows the individual distinctions in the many different times, the many different places, and so forth. It is through unimpeded knowledge of language that he expounds on the different aspects associated with the realization of right enlightenment. And it is through unimpeded knowledge of eloquence that he may discourse on each and every sentence of Dharma for measurelessly many kalpas and yet still not come to the end of it.

Also, it is through unimpeded knowledge of Dharma that he knows the corresponding realizations associated with all *tathāgatas'* proclamations, powers, fearlessnesses, dharmas exclusive to buddhas, great kindness, great compassion, eloquence, skillful means, turning of the Dharma wheel, and cognition of all-knowledge. It is through unimpeded knowledge of meaning that he knows the means by which the Tathāgata's voice adapts to beings' eighty-four thousand different implementations of resolute intentions,[244] different faculties, and different resolute beliefs.[245] It is through unimpeded knowledge of language that, adapting to all of the courses of action engaged in by beings, he uses the voice of the Tathāgata to present different explanations to them. And it is through unimpeded knowledge of eloquence that, adapting to beings' resolute convictions,[246] he uses the Tathāgata's knowledge and perfectly pure practice to discourse for them.

Son of the Buddha, the bodhisattva dwelling on the ninth ground acquires just such skill in the unimpeded knowledges, acquires the Tathāgata's treasury of sublime Dharma, becomes a great master of the Dharma, and also acquires the meanings *dhāraṇī*, the Dharma *dhāraṇī*, the wisdom *dhāraṇī*, the radiant illumination *dhāraṇī*, the good intelligence *dhāraṇī*, the manifold wealth *dhāraṇī*, the awe-inspiring virtue *dhāraṇī*, the unimpeded gateway *dhāraṇī*, the boundless *dhāraṇī*, and the variety of meanings *dhāraṇī*. He acquires in their fullness a hundred myriads of *asaṃkhyeyas* of *dhāraṇī* gateways and he employs a hundred myriads of *asaṃkhyeyas* of gateways of skillfulness in voice and eloquence with which he expounds the Dharma.

Having acquired hundreds of myriads of *asaṃkhyeyas* of *dhāraṇīs* such as these, this bodhisattva, appearing before each and every one of measurelessly many buddhas wherever those buddhas dwell, then uses hundreds of myriads of *asaṃkhyeyas* of *dhāraṇī* gateways such as these in listening to their teachings of right Dharma. Then, having heard them, he never forgets them. He then takes up those measurelessly many different gateways and expounds on them for others.

When this bodhisattva first enters the presence of a buddha, he bows, head to the ground, in reverential obeisance, and then, straightaway, in their very presence, acquires measurelessly many gateways into the Dharma. These dharmas that he acquires are so extensive that, even in a hundred thousand kalpas, none of the great *śrāvaka* disciples who are skillful in learning and retention could ever be able to absorb them.

Having acquired such *dhāraṇīs* and such unimpeded knowledges as these, even as this bodhisattva sits on the Dharma throne and expounds on Dharma, he is just then explaining it for the beings abiding throughout the worlds of a great trichiliocosm, doing so in a manner adapted to their different mental dispositions.[247] With the sole exception of the buddhas and those bodhisattvas who have already received the consecration, there is no one in any other assembly whose awe-inspiring virtue and brilliant radiance could ever rival that which he manifests.

When this bodhisattva sits on the Dharma throne:

He may wish to use but a single voice to cause everyone within a great assembly to gain complete comprehension, whereupon they will immediately acquire complete comprehension.

He may wish to employ many different sorts of voices to cause everyone in an entire great assembly to equally develop an understanding.

He may at times wish, by emanating great radiant light, to thereby proclaim gateways to the Dharma.

He may at times wish for the sound of Dharma to be proclaimed from each and every single hair pore on his body.

He may at times wish to cause all things with and without form throughout the worlds of a great trichiliocosm to simultaneously send forth the sublime sounds of Dharma.

He may at times wish to utter the sound of a single word that will then pervade the entire Dharma realm, causing all within it to achieve complete comprehension.

He may at times wish for the sounds of all words to emanate the sound of the Dharma, doing so in a way that constantly endures and never fades away.

He may at times wish for all musical sounds throughout all worlds, including those of flutes, pipes, bells, drums, songs, and chants, to proclaim in unison the sounds of the Dharma.

He may at times wish for but a single word to become entirely replete in itself with all of the words contained in all utterances of Dharma.

He may at times wish to cause each and every one of the finest atoms comprising the four great elements of earth, water, fire, and wind throughout an ineffable and measureless number of worlds to each proclaim an ineffable number of Dharma gateways.

In just this way, whatever he brings to mind comes to pass in accordance with his intentions so that none of them do not do so.

Son of the Buddha, even if all the beings within the worlds of a great trichiliocosm all came before this bodhisattva, and each and every one of them, using measurelessly many words, let flourish questions wherein each and every one of those questions was different from the others, this bodhisattva would still be able in but a single mind-moment to absorb them all and then, employing but a single voice, he would be able to explain and resolve every one of those questions, thereby causing each individual to become delighted in a manner accordant with whatever suits his mental disposition.

In this same way, even if each and every one of all the beings in an inexpressibly great number of worlds were, in but a single *kṣaṇa,* to use measurelessly many words as they let flourish questions wherein each and every one of those questions was different from the others, in but a single mind-moment, this bodhisattva would be able to absorb them all and, employing but a single voice, he would be able to explain and resolve every one of them, thereby causing each individual to become delighted in a manner accordant with his mental disposition.

So, too, even were this to be the case with all the beings filling up an ineffably great number of ineffably many worlds, this bodhisattva would still be able to explain the Dharma for each of them, in every case according with whatever suits each being's mental disposition, suits his faculties, and suits his resolute beliefs.

So it is that, receiving the assistance of the buddhas' spiritual powers, he engages on a vast scale in accomplishing the Buddha's works, everywhere serving as someone upon whom everyone can rely.

Son of the Buddha, this bodhisattva redoubles his application of vigor in order to perfect the light of knowledge, doing so even to this degree: Suppose that on the tip of every single hair there were buddha assemblies as numerous as the atoms in an ineffably great number of worlds. Suppose as well that, in every one of those assemblies, there were beings as numerous as the atoms in an ineffably great number of worlds, each and every one of which beings possessed individual dispositions as numerous as the atoms in an ineffably great number of worlds. Suppose also that all of those buddhas bestowed on those beings a gateway into the Dharma suited to those beings' individual dispositions. And suppose too that this circumstance existing in this one single place on the tip of a single hair was also true of all other places throughout the entire Dharma realm. Even so, this bodhisattva would still be able in but a single mind-moment to take in and never forget even all of those measurelessly many gateways to the Dharma as have been described herein.

Son of the Buddha, the bodhisattva dwelling on this ninth ground is intensely focused in the diligence of his practice both day and night, never indulging any other thought other than his aspiration that is solely devoted to entering the realm in which the Buddha courses,[248] to drawing close to the Tathāgata, and to entering the extremely profound liberations of all bodhisattvas. He always abides in samādhi, constantly sees the buddhas, and never relinquishes this circumstance.

In each and every kalpa, he sees measurelessly many buddhas, measurelessly many hundreds of buddhas, measurelessly many thousands of buddhas, and so forth on up to his seeing of measurelessly many hundreds of thousands of *koṭis* of *nayutas* of buddhas. He pays reverence to, venerates, renders service to, and presents offerings to those buddhas. He also presents inquiries to them on many different sorts of difficult topics and acquires the *dhāraṇīs* facilitating the proclamation of Dharma.

All of his roots of goodness become ever more bright in the radiance of their purity in a manner comparable to the real gold that would be crafted by a skillful goldsmith into a jeweled crown made to adorn the head of a wheel-turning sage king, one that could never be rivaled by any adornment in the possession of any of the lesser kings, ministers, or citizens anywhere else on the four continents. Just so are the roots of goodness of this bodhisattva dwelling on the ninth ground, for they are such that none of the roots of goodness of any *śrāvaka* disciple, *pratyekabuddha*, or bodhisattva dwelling on a lesser ground could ever rival.

Son of the Buddha, this circumstance is comparable to that of a king of the Great Brahma Heaven, a lord of two thousand worlds, whose body emanates such radiant light that it illuminates with dazzling brilliance even the most dark and distant places throughout those two thousand worlds, thus dispelling all darkness therein. So too it is with all the roots of goodness of the bodhisattva dwelling on this ground, for he is thereby enabled to emanate such brilliant light that it illuminates the minds of beings and thus causes all the darkness of their afflictions to become entirely extinguished.

Among the ten *pāramitās,* this bodhisattva has become most supreme in his perfection of the powers *pāramitā.* It is not that he does not practice the others. Rather, he simply accords them an amount of emphasis corresponding to his own strengths and to what is fitting.

Son of the Buddha, this has been a general explanation of the bodhisattva-mahāsattva's, ninth ground, the Ground of Excellent Intelligence. Were one to discourse on this extensively, then one would remain unable to finish the discussion of it even if one carried it forth for measurelessly many kalpas.

Son of the Buddha, the bodhisattva dwelling on this ground often becomes a king of the Great Brahma Heaven, a lord ruling over two thousand worlds who is well able to govern and liberally serve the benefit of others with sovereign mastery. He is able to differentially expound on the practice of the *pāramitās* for the sake of all *śrāvaka* disciples, *pratyekabuddhas,* and bodhisattvas. In this, he adapts to beings' mental dispositions[249] and, in addressing all of their challenging questions, there is no one who can prevail over him.

In his practice of giving, pleasing words, beneficial actions, and joint endeavors, and, in all such works that he pursues, he never departs from mindfulness of the Buddha, and so forth until we come to his never departing from mindfulness of the knowledge of all modes and the cognition of all-knowledge.

He also has this thought: "I should become one who serves these beings as a leader, as one who is supreme," and so forth until we come to "as one who relies on the cognition of all-knowledge."

If this bodhisattva brings forth diligently vigorous practice, then, in but a moment, he will become able to enter samādhis as numerous as the atoms in hundreds of myriads of *asaṃkhyeyas* of lands, and so forth until we come to his becoming able to transformationally manifest bodhisattvas to serve as his retinue that are as numerous as the atoms in hundreds of myriads of *asaṃkhyeyas* of lands. If he resorts to the power inherent in the bodhisattva's especially supreme vows, he becomes able then to freely manifest numbers beyond even this, such that one would never be able to count them even in a period of hundreds of thousands of *koṭis* of *nayutas* of kalpas.

At that time, Vajragarbha Bodhisattva, wishing to restate his meaning, thereupon spoke these verses:

Through skillful meditation with measureless wisdom power
that is the most supremely subtle and difficult for the world to know,
he everywhere enters the Tathāgata's secret places,
and, serving the benefit of beings, enters the ninth ground.

Exercising sovereign mastery in both *dhāraṇis* and samādhis and
gaining great spiritual superknowledges, he enters the many lands.
Equipped with the powers, wisdom, fearlessness, exclusive dharmas,
vow power, and compassionate mind, he enters the ninth ground.

Dwelling on this ground he preserves the treasury of Dharma
and utterly knows: what is good, bad, or neutral; what possesses
or is free of the contaminants; what is worldly or world-transcending;
and what is conceivable or inconceivable. He well knows them all.

As for whether any dharma is definite or indefinite as well as what
Three Vehicle's adherents do, he meditatively contemplates it all.
Regarding the differences in conditioned and unconditioned actions,
he knows them just as they are and thus enters the worlds.

If he wishes to know beings' minds, he can use knowledge to know
as they truly are their many characteristics including whether
they are diversely arising, swiftly transformed, deteriorating,
not deteriorating, insubstantial, boundless, and so forth.

He knows afflictions as boundless, as in constant accompaniment, as
of the same quality, latent or arising, as continuing in the destinies,
knows karmic actions' varying natures, each different, destruction of
of causes, and accrual of effects. He is able to know all of these.

All the different faculties, inferior, middling, or superior,
their past and future differences, countless other distinctions,
resolute beliefs, sense realms, and resolute intentions—
of eighty-four thousand aspects, there are none he does not know.

[He knows] beings' afflictions and views that ever follow and bind,
their beginningless entangling thickets, never yet cut down, the
[latent tendencies] arising with intentions and together with mind,
and their always restraining and binding them, never being severed.

He knows they are merely erroneous thought, are unreal phenomena,
are inseparable from the mind, are devoid of any place they dwell, are
still able to cause retreat after being dispelled by *dhyāna* samādhis,
and are extinguished on the vajra path and then are finally ended.

He knows that taking birth in the six destinies, each case differs,
that karma is the field, cravings are moisture, ignorance is covering,

consciousness is the seed, name-and-form are the sprout, and these
cause beginningless ever continuous becoming in the three realms.

He knows afflicted acts and mental habits cause birth in the destinies,
knows that, if one abandons these, there will be no further births,
and knows beings as all existing within one of three groupings,[250]
and as either drowning among views or else as practicing the path.

Dwelling on this ground, he is skillful in meditative contemplation,
adapts to their dispositions, faculties, and resolute beliefs, and,
always employs the unimpeded knowledges and sublime eloquence
by which he teaches each differently as befits what is appropriate.

As he sits on the Dharma throne, he is like a lion,
also is like the king of bulls, the king of jewel mountains,
or a king of dragons who spreads forth dense clouds,
showers down the sweet-dew rain, and thus fills the great oceans.

He knows well the nature of dharmas and their abstruse meanings,
is able with concordant verbal expressions to expound eloquently,
and, possessed of a hundred myriad *asaṃkhyeyas* of *dhāraṇīs*, retains
everything, just as the great ocean takes in the many showers of rain.

With *dhāraṇīs* and samādhis that are all pure,
he is able in but a single mind-moment to see the many buddhas,
listens to the Dharma in the presence of each and every buddha,
and then in turn expounds on it with a sublimely wondrous voice.

Whenever he wishes, throughout the worlds of a great trichiliocosm,
he teaches all of the many classes of beings, becoming in this
like a vastly spreading cloud that has no place it fails to reach as he
adapts to their faculties and predilections, causing all to feel joyful.

Even with countless buddha assemblies on the tips of every hair
and even with beings' mental predilections also being endless,
they respond to all their minds in the bestowing of Dharma gates,
doing so in this same manner throughout the entire Dharma realm.

The bodhisattva diligently applies the power of vigor and thereby
gains yet more meritorious qualities, ever more supremely refined.
His hearing and retaining of so very many Dharma gateways as this
is comparable to the earth's ability to retain all seeds.

If the countless beings throughout the ten directions
all came and drew close to where he sits in the midst of an assembly,
in but a moment, he would adapt to their minds as each poses queries
and then, with a single voice, he would respond and satisfy them all.

Dwelling on this ground, he serves as a king of Dharma, adapting
to beings' potentials, tirelessly providing teaching and inducement.

Day and night, he sees the buddhas, never relinquishes that vision,
and enters deeply quiescent knowledge and liberation.

He makes offerings to buddhas, skillfully refines his brilliance
so that it shines like the Sage King's marvelously bejeweled crown
and also causes the darkness of beings' afflictions to be extinguished
just as when the Brahma Heaven King's light illuminates every place.

Dwelling herein, he often becomes king of a Great Brahma Heaven
who employs the Dharma of the Three Vehicles to teach beings.
The good works he does are everywhere and liberally beneficial
all the way on to his future realization of all-knowledge.

The samādhis he enters in but a single mind-moment
number as the atoms comprising an *asaṃkhyeya* of lands.
So too is the number of buddhas he sees proclaiming the Dharma.
Through the power of vows these extend in number even beyond this.

This has been the ninth, the Ground of Excellent Intelligence,
the station in which bodhisattvas of great knowledge practice,
one that is extremely profound, sublime, and recondite.
I have now finished its explanation for the Sons of the Buddha.

The Tenth Ground

The Dharma Cloud Ground

Having heard of the supreme practices carried out on this ground,
the *nayutas* of Pure Dwelling Heaven devas
who were up in the sky sprang up in delight and then,
united in deep sincerity, presented offerings to the Buddha.

That inconceivably vast assembly of bodhisattvas
that was also there in the sky was immensely delighted.
They all lit the most supremely mind-pleasing incenses
that everywhere permeated that assembly, causing it to be purified.

The Paranirmita Vaśavartin Heaven King with his heavenly host
of countless *koṭis* of devas that were there in the sky scattered
everywhere heavenly raiment as offerings to the Buddha which
floated down in a profusion of a hundred thousand myriad sorts.

Of the heavenly nymphs there in measureless numbers,
none failed to then joyfully present offerings to the Buddha
as they each played all sorts of sublime music and
all together used these phrases in offering their praises:

"Even as this body of the Buddha sits securely in a single land,
he manifests bodies in all worlds, wherein, in stately adornment,
countless *koṭis* of his physical appearances are seen,
entirely filling the Dharma realm in all its vastness.

Within a single hair pore, he emanates light
that everywhere extinguishes the darkness of the world's afflictions.
Though one might be able to know a land's number of atoms,
one could still never measure these light rays' number.

One may see the Tathāgata there replete with all his many signs,
turning the unsurpassable wheel of right Dharma.
One may see him roaming forth to all of the buddha lands,
or one may see him still, at peace, unmoving.

Or he may manifest as dwelling in the Tuṣita Heaven Palace,
or may manifest as descending into his mother's womb,
or may appear as dwelling in the womb or emerging from the womb,
in all such cases causing this to be observable in countless lands.

He may manifest as leaving home, cultivating the path in the world,
as appearing in the *bodhimaṇḍa,* and as realizing right enlightenment.
He may manifest as proclaiming the Dharma and as entering nirvāṇa,
everywhere causing there to be none in ten directions not seeing this.

Just as a master conjurer skilled in the techniques of conjuration
performs his many feats in the midst of a great crowd,
so too it is in the case of the Tathāgata's wisdom by which
he manifests his bodies everywhere throughout the worlds.

The Buddha dwells within dharmas' extremely profound true nature
that is quiescent, signless, and like space
even as, from within ultimate truth,
he manifests the many different deeds that he performs.

All those endeavors performed for the benefit of beings,
come into existence in dependence upon the very nature of dharmas.
That possessed of signs and the signless have no differentiation,
for, with entry into the ultimate, they are all signless.

If one wishes to acquire the knowledge of the Tathāgata,
one should abandon all false discriminations, utterly comprehend
existents and nonexistents all abide in a state of uniform equality,
and thus swiftly become a great guide for humans and devas."

Having offered up these praises with many different phrases,
this countless and boundlessly vast assemblage of celestial nymphs
fell silent in both body and mind, and, united in their happiness,
gazed up at the Tathāgata as they stood there quietly.

Then Liberation Moon Bodhisattva,
aware that everyone in the great assembly was now still and silent,
straightaway addressed Vajragarbha Bodhisattva, saying:
"O, Great Fearless One, True Son of the Buddha,"

"we pray that you who possess such intelligence and wisdom
will expound here on all the meritorious qualities, aspects of practice,
spiritual superknowledges, and transformational deeds that are
involved in advancing from the ninth ground into the tenth ground."

At that time, Vajragarbha Bodhisattva-mahāsattva informed Liberation Moon Bodhisattva, saying:

O Son of the Buddha, from the first ground through the ninth ground, having employed such measureless wisdom as this in meditative contemplation and awakening, the bodhisattva-mahāsattva:

- Engages in thorough meditative contemplation on cultivation;[251]
- Thoroughly fulfills the pristinely white dharmas;
- Assembles boundlessly many dharmas constituting the provisions for the path;
- Increases his immense stock of merit and wisdom;
- Cultivates the great compassion on a vast scale;
- Comes to know the aspects distinguishing the worlds;

Penetrates the entangling thickets of the realms of beings;[252]
Enters the domain in which the Tathāgata courses;
Accords with the Tathāgata's quiescence practices;
And always carries on meditative contemplations focused on the *tathāgatas'* powers, fearlessnesses, and dharmas exclusive to the buddhas.

Having done so, he is then said to have reached the station wherein one receives the consecration of imminent acquisition of the knowledge of all modes and the cognition of all-knowledge.

Son of the Buddha, once this bodhisattva-mahāsattva has employed wisdom such as this to enter the ground of consecration, he straightaway acquires:[253]

The bodhisattva's stainless samādhi;
The entering the distinctions within the dharma realm samādhi;
The adornment of the *bodhimaṇḍa* samādhi;
The radiance of every kind of flower samādhi;
The oceanic treasury samādhi;
The oceanic reflection samādhi;
The vastness of empty space samādhi;
The contemplation of the nature of all dharmas samādhi;
The knowledge of the minds and actions of all beings samādhi;
And the direct manifestation of all buddhas samādhi.

A hundred myriads of *asaṃkhyeyas* of other samādhis such as these also all manifest directly before him. In all of these samādhis, the bodhisattva, whether entering them or arising from them, in all cases achieves a state of consummate skillfulness while also comprehending well the differences in the functional uses to which all of these samādhis are devoted. The very last samādhi to manifest for him is the one known as "the station of the acquisition of the supreme consecration of all-knowledge."[254]

When this samādhi manifests directly before him, an immense bejeweled lotus flower suddenly emerges, one whose blossom is so immense that it equals in volume the breadth of a hundred myriad great trichiliocosms. It is inlaid and adorned with the many sorts of marvelous precious gems and presents an appearance that surpasses any realm of objective phenomena observed in any world. This is a phenomenon that comes forth from his world-transcending roots of goodness and that is perfected by his many practices utilizing the knowledge that all dharmas are by nature like mere illusions.

It constantly radiates brilliant light that everywhere illuminates the Dharma realm. This is a phenomenon that is not found even in any of the celestial abodes. Its stem is made of beryl and *maṇi* jewels. Its dais consists of sandalwood incense. Emeralds compose its floral stamens and its petals are made of *jambunada* gold. Its blossom always emanates countless light rays. The many sorts of precious jewels compose its inner chamber, and it is covered over by a bejeweled net canopy. Lotus blossoms as numerous as the atoms in ten great trichiliocosms make up its retinue.

At this time, as the bodhisattva then sits atop the flower throne, the scale of his physical appearance precisely matches that of the throne itself. Measurelessly many bodhisattvas serve as his retinue, with each of them sitting upon one of the other lotus blossoms completely encircling him. Each and every one of them, having thereupon acquired a hundred myriad samādhis, then single-mindedly gazes up at this great bodhisattva.

Son of the Buddha, when this great bodhisattva together with his retinue are all sitting there on their lotus thrones, all of those light rays as well as the sound of his words then everywhere fill all ten directions of the Dharma realm, those worlds all quake, the wretched destinies become stilled, and all lands then became adorned and purified. Of all the bodhisattvas engaged in the same practices, none of them do not then come and assemble there.

The musical sounds of men and devas then simultaneously resound as all of those beings experience feelings of happiness and then present offerings of inconceivable gifts to all the buddhas. All of the assemblies of the buddhas then became visibly manifest.

Son of the Buddha, as this bodhisattva sits there atop that immense lotus blossom throne, from the bottom of his two feet, he releases a hundred myriads of *asaṃkhyeyas* of light rays that everywhere illuminate all the great hell realms throughout the ten directions and extinguish the sufferings undergone by the beings dwelling in them.

From his two kneecaps, he releases a hundred myriads of *asaṃkhyeyas* of light rays that everywhere illuminate all the ten directions' animal rebirth destinies and extinguish the sufferings of the beings dwelling in them.

From the center of his navel, he releases a hundred myriads of *asaṃkhyeyas* of light rays that everywhere illuminate the ten directions' realms of King Yama and extinguish the sufferings of the beings residing in them.[255]

From his left and right sides, he releases a hundred myriads of *asaṃkhyeyas* of light rays that everywhere illuminate all the realms of the human destinies throughout the ten directions and extinguish the sufferings of the beings residing in them.

From his two hands, he releases a hundred myriads of *asaṃkhyeyas* of light rays that everywhere illuminate all the palaces of the devas and *asuras* throughout the ten directions.

From atop his two shoulders, he releases a hundred myriads of *asaṃkhyeyas* of light rays that everywhere illuminate all the *śrāvaka* disciples throughout the ten directions.

From the back of his neck, he releases a hundred myriads of *asaṃkhyeyas* of light rays that everywhere illuminate the bodies of all the *pratyekabuddhas* throughout the ten directions.

From his face, he releases a hundred myriads of *asaṃkhyeyas* of light rays that everywhere illuminate the bodies of all the bodhisattvas throughout the ten directions, inclusive of those who have newly brought forth the initial resolve on up to all those dwelling on the ninth ground.

From between his eyebrows, he releases a hundred myriads of *asaṃkhyeyas* of light rays that everywhere illuminate all the bodhisattvas throughout the ten directions who had received the consecration while also causing the palaces of the *māras* to no longer appear.

From the crown of his head, he then releases light rays as numerous as the atoms in a hundred myriads of *asaṃkhyeyas* of great trichiliocosms that everywhere illuminate the assemblies attending upon the *bodhimaṇḍas* of all the buddhas, the *tathāgatas,* throughout all worlds of the ten directions.

Those rays then circle around them ten times in a rightward direction and, having ascended into the midst of space, they dwell there and form a net-like canopy of bright light known as "Flaming Radiance" that then sends forth all sorts of different offerings to the buddhas.

Those offerings are so numerous that the offerings of all the other bodhisattvas from those who have but newly brought forth the resolve on through to those who dwell on the ninth ground could not compare to even a hundredth part and so forth until we come to their being unable to compare at all even by resort to calculation or analogy.

That canopy of brilliant light rains down offerings before each and every one of the *tathāgatas* and their assemblies everywhere throughout the ten directions, raining down the many sorts of marvelous incenses, floral garlands, raiment, banners, bejeweled canopies, various *maṇi* jewels, and other sorts of adornments, all of which are presented there as offerings. In every case, these offerings issue from world-transcending roots of goodness and surpass anything found in any worldly realm. Were there to be any being at all who might observe this occurrence, they would all be those who had already reached the stage of irreversibility with respect to the realization of *anuttara-samyak-saṃbodhi.*

Son of the Buddha, once this immense aggregation of light rays has finished these acts of offering, it then once again circles around each and every one of the *bodhimaṇḍa* assemblies of all buddhas throughout all worlds of the ten directions. After it has finished circling around them ten times, it then enters the bottoms of the feet of all *tathāgatas.*

It is at this time that all buddhas and bodhisattvas realize that, in this particular world system, a particular bodhisattva-mahāsattva has been able to perform such immensely expansive practices and has thus reached the stage of receiving the consecration.

Son of the Buddha, at this time, the congregation of all the measurelessly and boundlessly many bodhisattvas throughout the ten directions inclusive of those who have reached the ninth ground then arrives there. They circumambulate him, reverently present offerings, and then enter a state of single-minded meditative contemplation. At the very time when they enter into this state of meditative contemplation, each of these bodhisattvas acquires a myriad samādhis.

Just at that very time, all the bodhisattvas throughout the ten directions who have already received the consecration emanate from their chests' vajra adornment meritorious-qualities symbol an immense beam of bright light known as "able to destroy Māra's enmity," one attended by a hundred myriads of *asaṃkhyeyas* of light rays that form its retinue. It everywhere illuminates all of the ten directions and manifests incalculably many permutations of the spiritual superknowledges. After it has finished carrying out these actions, it then comes and enters the vajra adornment virtuous-qualities mark on this bodhisattva's chest. After that light has entered, it then causes all of the wisdom and powers of this bodhisattva to increase more than a hundred thousandfold.

At that time, all buddhas throughout the ten directions put forth a pure beam of light from between their eyebrows known as "enhancer of all-knowledge's superknowledges," one attended by countless light rays that form its retinue. It everywhere illuminates all worlds throughout the ten directions, circling them ten times in a rightward direction, manifesting the *tathāgatas'* vast powers of sovereign mastery and instigating the awakening of a congregation of incalculably many hundreds of thousands of *koṭis* of *nayutas* of bodhisattvas, everywhere causing the quaking of all buddha lands, extinguishing the sufferings in all the wretched destinies, covering over and hiding the palaces of the *māras*, and revealing the adornments and awe-inspiring qualities in all the assemblies at those *bodhimaṇḍas* wherein the buddhas have achieved realization of bodhi.

After having everywhere illuminated all worlds even to the ends of empty space and throughout the entire Dharma realm, it then comes and, arriving in the assembly of this bodhisattva, circles ten times around in a rightward direction, revealing all of the different sorts of adornments there. After having revealed these phenomena, it then enters into the crown of this great bodhisattva. Its retinue light rays also each enter the crowns of those other bodhisattvas in attendance there.

At that very time, this bodhisattva acquires a hundred myriad samādhis he has never before acquired and becomes known[256] as one who has reached the station of consecration and has entered the realm of the buddhas wherein, having completely developed the ten powers, he joins the ranks of the buddhas.

Son of the Buddha, in this circumstance he is comparable to a crown prince born to a wheel-turning sage king whose mother is the chief queen and who is himself completely endowed with the physical marks. That wheel-turning king orders this prince to sit on the throne of marvelous gold atop his white elephant treasure, raises the great canopy, plants the great banner, burns incense, scatters flowers, plays all sorts of music, takes up water from each of the four great seas, and places it into the vase of gold.

The King then takes up this vase and pours the liquid out over the crown of the prince's head. From this very moment on he is known as one who has reached the stage of receiving royal consecration at which point he then joins the ranks of the consecrated *kṣatriyan* kings. He then straightaway becomes able to completely fulfill the ten courses of good karmic action and is then also able to become known as a wheel-turning sage king.

So too it is in the case of this bodhisattva who has received the consecration. Because the waters of all buddhas' knowledge have been poured onto the crown of his head, he is then known as one who has received the consecration. It is on account of his complete development of the Tathāgata's ten powers that he then joins the ranks of the buddhas.

Son of the Buddha, this is what is what is known as the bodhisattva's great knowledge consecration. It is because of this great knowledge consecration that this bodhisattva is then able to engage in incalculably many hundreds of thousands of myriads of *koṭis* of *nayutas* of difficult-to-practice practices and increase his growth in incalculably many sorts of wisdom and meritorious qualities. So it is that he is then known as one who abides securely on the Dharma Cloud Ground.

Son of the Buddha, the bodhisattva-mahāsattva dwelling on this Dharma Cloud Ground knows in accordance with reality:

Attainment as it takes place in the desire realm;[257]
Attainment as it takes place in the form realm;
Attainment as it takes place in the formless realm;
Attainment as it takes place within the worldly realms;
Attainment as it takes place within the Dharma realm;
Attainment as it takes place within the conditioned realm;
Attainment as it takes place within the unconditioned realm;
Attainment as it takes place within the realms of beings;
Attainment as it takes place within the realms of consciousness;
Attainment as it takes place within the realm of empty space;
And attainment as it takes place within the realm of nirvāṇa.

This bodhisattva also knows in accordance with reality:

The attainment of karmic actions associated with the views and the afflictions;
Knows attainment as it takes place in the production and destruction of worlds;
Knows the attainment of *śrāvaka*-disciple practices;
Knows the attainment of *pratyekabuddha* practices;
Knows the attainment of bodhisattva practices;
Knows attainment as it takes place in a *tathāgata*'s powers, fearlessnesses, form bodies, and Dharma body;
Knows attainment of the knowledge associated with the knowledge of all modes and all-knowledge;
Knows attainment as it occurs in the manifestation of the appearance of realizing bodhi and turning the Dharma wheel;
And knows attainment as it takes place in entering the knowledge that is decisive in its distinguishing of all dharmas.

To speak of what is essential in this, he employs all-knowledge to know all processes of attainment.

Son of the Buddha, this bodhisattva-mahāsattva resorts to just such supremely awakened wisdom to know in accordance with reality:

Transformation as it takes place in beings' karmic actions;
Transformation as it takes place in the afflictions;
Transformation as it takes place in the views;
Transformation as it takes place in the worlds;
Transformation as it takes place in the Dharma realm;
Transformation as it takes place among *śrāvaka* disciples;
Transformation as it takes place among *pratyekabuddhas*;
Transformation as it takes place among bodhisattvas;
Transformation as it takes place among *tathāgatas*;
And transformation as it takes place in the presence and absence of differences.

He also knows in accordance with reality all of the other such sorts of transformations.

So too does he know in accordance with reality:

The sustaining bases[258] of the Buddha.
The sustaining bases of the Dharma;
The sustaining bases of the Sangha;
The sustaining bases of karma;
The sustaining bases of the afflictions;
The sustaining bases of time;
The sustaining bases of vows;
The sustaining bases of offerings;
The sustaining bases of practices;
The sustaining bases of kalpas;
And the sustaining bases of knowledge.

He also knows in accordance with reality all of the other such sorts of phenomena.

So too does he know in accordance with reality all buddhas', all *tathāgatas'*, knowledge that enters into all sorts of subtlety, specifically knowing:

Their knowledge regarding the subtleties involved in cultivation;
Their knowledge regarding the subtleties involved in the ending of a lifetime;[259]
Their knowledge regarding the subtleties involved in the taking on of birth;
Their knowledge regarding the subtleties involved in abandoning the home life;

Their knowledge regarding the subtleties involved in the manifesting of the spiritual superknowledges;
Their knowledge regarding the subtleties involved in achieving realization of the right enlightenment;
Their knowledge regarding the subtleties involved in turning the wheel of Dharma;
Their knowledge regarding the subtleties involved in abiding throughout a life span;
Their knowledge regarding the subtleties involved in [passing into] nirvāṇa;
And their knowledge regarding the subtleties involved in the endurance of their teaching Dharma.

He also knows all of the other such sorts of phenomena in accordance with reality.

So too does he enter into the *tathāgatas'* secrets, specifically entering:

Their secrets associated with the body;
Their secrets associated with speech;
Their secrets associated with the mind;
Their secrets associated with the assessment of timeliness and untimeliness;
Their secrets associated with the bestowing of predictions upon bodhisattvas;
Their secrets associated with the attraction of beings;
Their secrets associated with the many different sorts of vehicles;
Their secrets associated with the root faculties and practices of all beings;
Their secrets associated with the functioning of karmic actions;
And their secrets associated with acquisition of the practices associated with bodhi.

He also knows all other such sorts of phenomena in accordance with reality.

So too does he know all of the knowledge of the buddhas with regard to the interpenetration of kalpas [and other such measures of time], specifically knowing:

How a single kalpa may enter into an *asaṃkhyeya* kalpa;
How an *asaṃkhyeya* kalpa may enter into a single kalpa;
How an enumerated number of kalpas may enter into innumerable kalpas;
How innumerable kalpas may enter into an enumerated number of kalpas;

How a single mind-moment may enter into a kalpa;
How a kalpa may enter into a single mind-moment;
How a kalpa may enter into what does not constitute a kalpa;
How what does not constitute a kalpa may enter into a kalpa;
How a kalpa in which there is a buddha may enter into a kalpa in which there is no buddha;
How a kalpa with no buddha may enter into a kalpa in which there is a buddha;
How past and future kalpas may enter into the present kalpa;
How the present kalpa may enter into past and future kalpas;
How past kalpas may enter into future kalpas;
How future kalpas may enter into past kalpas;
How long kalpas may enter into short kalpas;
And how short kalpas may enter into long kalpas.

He also knows all the other such sorts of phenomena in accordance with reality.

So too does he know all of the types of penetrating knowledge that the Tathāgata possesses, specifically knowing:

The penetrating knowledge[260] that knows the realms of ordinary common people;[261]
The penetrating knowledge that knows atoms;
The rightly enlightened penetrating knowledge that knows [buddha] land bodies;[262]
The rightly enlightened penetrating knowledge that knows the beings' bodies;
The rightly enlightened penetrating knowledge that knows beings' minds;
The rightly enlightened penetrating knowledge that knows beings' actions;
The rightly enlightened penetrating knowledge that knows adaptation to all places;
The penetrating knowledge that knows the manifestation of universally pervasive practices;
The penetrating knowledge that knows the manifestation of adaptive practices;
The penetrating knowledge that knows the manifestation of contrary practices;
The penetrating knowledge that knows the manifestation of conceivable and inconceivable practices and knows the manifestation of practices either completely comprehensible to the world or not completely comprehensible to the world;

And the penetrating knowledge that knows the manifestation of the practices of *śrāvaka* disciples, *pratyekabuddhas*, bodhisattvas, and *tathāgatas*.

Son of the Buddha, in every case, the bodhisattva dwelling on this ground is able to have penetrating knowledge of all the vast and measureless wisdom possessed by all buddhas.

Son of the Buddha, the bodhisattva-mahāsattva dwelling on this ground immediately acquires:

The bodhisattva's inconceivable liberation;
The unimpeded liberation;
The pure contemplation liberation;
The universal illumination liberation;
The *tathāgata* treasury liberation;
The compliance with the unimpeded wheel liberation;
The penetrating comprehension of the three periods of time liberation;
The Dharma realm treasury liberation;
The circle of liberation's light liberation;
And the realm of remainderless totality liberation.

These ten are those that are chief among them. There are incalculably many hundreds of thousands of *asaṃkhyeyas* of other such gateways to liberation that are all acquired on this tenth ground.

In this same way, there are also even as many as measurelessly many hundreds of thousands of *asaṃkhyeyas* of samādhi gateways, measurelessly many hundreds of thousands of *asaṃkhyeyas* of *dhāraṇī* gateways, and measurelessly many hundreds of thousands of *asaṃkhyeyas* of spiritual superknowledge gateways that, in every case, he also succeeds in completely developing.

Son of the Buddha, this bodhisattva-mahāsattva develops a penetrating comprehension of wisdom such as this that accords with measureless bodhi. He also develops such powers of skillful memory that, in a single mind-moment, he is in every case able to accommodate, able to take in, able to absorb, and is able to retain all of the measureless great Dharma light, great Dharma illumination, and great Dharma rain of all of the measurelessly many buddhas throughout the ten directions.

Just as it is the case that, with the sole exception of the great ocean, all other places are in every case unable to accommodate, unable to take in, unable to absorb, and unable to retain the great rains poured down by Sāgara, the dragon king, so too it is with the great Dharma light, the great Dharma illumination, and the great

Dharma rain coming forth from the secret treasury of the Tathāgata. With the sole exception of the tenth ground bodhisattvas, all other beings including *śrāvaka* disciples, *pratyekabuddhas,* and bodhisattvas up through the ninth ground are all unable to accommodate it, unable to take it in, unable to absorb it, and unable to retain it.

Son of the Buddha, in this, he is comparable to the great ocean that is able to accommodate, able to take in, able to absorb, and able to retain those great rains poured down by one of the great dragon kings, two of them, three of them, and so forth on up to the rains poured down by countless dragon kings. In but a single mind-moment, it is able to accommodate, able to take in, able to absorb, and able to retain all the rain that they all simultaneously pour down. And why is it able to do this? It is because it is a vessel possessed of an immeasurably vast capacity.

So too it is with this bodhisattva who dwells on the Dharma Cloud Ground who is himself able to accommodate, able to take in, able to absorb, and able to retain the Dharma light, the Dharma illumination, and the Dharma rain brought forth by one buddha, two, three, and so forth on up to measurelessly many buddhas, being able to take it all in in this very same manner, even if it were all to be simultaneously expounded to him in but a single mind-moment. It is for this very reason that this ground is known as the Dharma Cloud Ground.

Liberation Moon Bodhisattva then asked, "O Son of the Buddha, from how many *tathāgatas* is the bodhisattva dwelling on this ground able in but a single mind-moment to accommodate, take in, absorb, and retain their great Dharma light, their great Dharma illumination, and their great Dharma rain?"

Vajragarbha Bodhisattva replied:

O Son of the Buddha, this is something that cannot be known merely by resort to numerical calculations. I shall provide an analogy for you.

Son of the Buddha, suppose for instance that there existed in each of the ten directions worlds as numerous as the atoms in ten ineffably numerous hundreds of thousands of *koṭis* of *nayutas* of buddha lands, and in each of those worlds each and every one of the beings residing therein had all acquired the "hearing-and-retaining" *dhāraṇī,* had served as a buddha's attendant, was foremost in learning among everyone within the assembly of *śrāvaka* disciples, was one comparable to Great Supremacy Bhikshu[263] residing in the dwelling place of Vajra Lotus Blossom Supremacy Buddha,[264] while

> the Dharma received by each of these beings was not the same as that received by any of the others.
>
> Son of the Buddha, what do you think? Is all of the Dharma received by all of these beings measurable or immeasurable?

Liberation Moon Bodhisattva replied, "That is an exceedingly great amount, one that is measureless and boundless."

Vajragarbha Bodhisattva then said:

> Son of the Buddha, I will explain this matter for you in a manner that will cause you to comprehend it.
>
> Son of the Buddha, that great Dharma light, great Dharma illumination, and great Dharma rain constituting the Dharma treasury of the three periods of time that this Dharma Cloud Ground bodhisattva is able to accommodate, take in, absorb, and retain from but one single buddha in just a single mind-moment is such that all the Dharma heard and retained by all of those beings in those previously described world systems could not even compare to a hundredth part of it and is such that one could not adequately compare the two even by resort to analogy.
>
> And just as this is the case with the Dharma taken in from but a single Buddha, so too it is for all those other buddhas as numerous as the atoms in all those previously described worlds throughout the ten directions wherein this number is exceeded immeasurably and boundlessly, for this bodhisattva is able in every case to accommodate, able to take in, able to absorb, and able to retain all of their Dharma light, Dharma illumination, and Dharma rain that constitute the Dharma treasury of the three periods of time as it is brought forth by each and every one of those *tathāgatas*. It is for this reason that this is known as the Dharma Cloud Ground.
>
> Son of the Buddha, through the power of his own vows, the bodhisattva dwelling on this ground spreads forth the clouds of the great compassion, brings on the quaking of the great Dharma thunder, uses his superknowledges, clarities, and fearlessnesses as the flashing of his lightning, and brings forth his merit and wisdom as dense rain clouds. He manifests all different kinds of bodies that circulate everywhere, going forth and returning, and, in but a single mind-moment, they everywhere pervade the ten directions, going forth to a number of lands as numerous as the atoms in hundreds of thousands of *koṭis* of *nayutas* of worlds wherein they expound the great Dharma and utterly defeat Māra's hordes.
>
> In yet greater numbers than these, in lands as numerous as the atoms in measurelessly many hundreds of thousands of *koṭis* of

nayutas of worlds, he adapts to the dispositions of the beings therein and pours down the rain of sweet-dew *amṛta,* thus extinguishing the smoke and flames of beings' afflictions. It is for this reason that this is known as the Dharma Cloud Ground.

Son of the Buddha, from the time he descends from a particular world's Tuṣita Heaven on through to the time he enters nirvāṇa, the bodhisattva dwelling on this ground adapts to the minds of the beings he should bring to liberation and then manifests the works of a buddha. So too does he carry this out in the same way in two worlds, three worlds, and so forth on up to his doing so in lands as numerous as the above-described atoms, even doing so in a number of lands beyond even these, in even up to lands as numerous as the atoms in measurelessly many hundreds of thousands of *koṭis* of *nayutas* of worlds. It is for this reason that this ground is known as the Dharma Cloud Ground.

Son of the Buddha, the bodhisattva dwelling on this ground is possessed of such brightly penetrating wisdom and sovereign mastery of the spiritual superknowledges that he is able in accordance with whatever he wishes to transform a narrow world into a broad world, transform a broad world into a narrow world, transform a defiled world into a pure world, transform a pure world into a defiled world, and is able, too, to mutually transform every type of world into the other, including those that are chaotically arranged, those that are arranged in an orderly fashion, those that are upside down, those that are right-side up, and those that are of countless other different varieties.

Or it may also be that, in accordance with whatever he wishes, he may also place within a single atom an entire world with its Mount Sumerus as well as all of its other mountains and rivers, doing so even while keeping the appearance of an atom just as it was before and while also ensuring that world is not reduced in scale.

Or then again, it may also be that, within but a single atom, he may place two, place three, or place even up to an ineffably great number of worlds with their Mount Sumerus and other such mountains and rivers, doing so even while the physical appearance of that atom remains just as it originally was and doing so even while the world system within it is able to remain entirely and clearly manifest.

Or it may also be that, in accordance with whatever he wishes, he may manifest in a but a single world the adornments of two worlds, and so forth until we come to his placing the adornments of an ineffably great number[265] of worlds into the adornments of but a single world.

Or it may also be that, in the adornment of a single world, he may manifest two worlds and so forth on up to an ineffably great number of worlds.

Or it may also be that, in accordance with whatever he wishes, he may place the beings from an ineffably great number of worlds into but a single world.

Or it may also be that, in accordance with whatever he wishes, he places the beings from a single world into an ineffably great number of worlds and yet does so without disturbing or harming any of those beings in any way.

Or it may also be that, in accordance with whatever he wishes, he manifests in a single hair pore all the adornments associated with the realms of all buddhas.

Or it may also be that, in accordance with whatever he wishes, in but a single mind-moment, he manifests bodies as numerous as the atoms in an ineffably great number of worlds, each and every one of those bodies then manifests hands as numerous as that same number of atoms, and each and every one of those hands holds a Ganges' sands number of trays of flowers, cases of incense, floral garlands, canopies, flags, and banners that are then presented as offerings to the buddhas everywhere throughout the ten directions.

Additionally, each and every one of those bodies may manifest with a number of heads matching this same number of atoms as each and every one of those heads manifests a number of tongues matching this same number of atoms and, in each and every mind-moment, their utterances reach everywhere throughout the ten directions with praises of the buddhas' meritorious qualities.

Or it may also be that, in accordance with whatever he wishes, in but a single mind-moment, he thus manifests everywhere throughout the ten directions the appearances of realizing the right enlightenment and the other associated events on through to the nirvāṇa along with the associated lands and their adornments.

Or it may be that he manifests bodies everywhere throughout the three periods of time while revealing within each of his bodies an incalculably great number of buddhas as well as their buddha lands, their adornments, and the creation and destruction of worlds, revealing all of these things in a manner whereby none of these phenomena fail to completely manifest therein.

Or it may also be that, from a single hair pore in his own body, he sends forth every variety of wind that, even so, does no harm to any being.

Or it may also be that, in accordance with whatever he wishes, he transformationally manifests therein boundlessly many worlds forming a single great ocean and then manifests in the middle of this sea's waters a great lotus blossom that, with its radiance and graceful adornment, everywhere covers measurelessly and boundlessly many worlds as he manifests therein a great bodhi tree with all its adornments, and so forth on through to his manifestation of the realization of the knowledge of all modes.

Or it may also be that, even within his own body, he manifests every sort of light, including that of precious *maṇi* pearls, the sun, the moon, the stars, lightning in the clouds, and so forth, so that there are none that do not manifest therein.

Or it may also be that, employing the breath from his mouth, he is able to move the incalculably many worlds throughout the ten directions and yet still not cause any of the beings therein to give rise to thoughts of terror.

Or it may also be that he manifests the appearance of the wind disasters, fire disasters, and water disasters throughout the ten directions.

Or it may also be that, adapting to beings' predilections, he manifests form bodies that are entirely replete in their adornment.

Or it may also be that, even within his own body, he manifests the body of a buddha or else manifests his own body within the body of a buddha. Or it may also be that, within the body of a buddha, he manifests his own land, or else, within his own land, manifests the body of a buddha.

Son of the Buddha, this bodhisattva dwelling on the Dharma Cloud Ground is able to manifest such phenomena as these as well as measurelessly many other hundreds of thousands of *koṭis* of *nayutas* of such appearances produced through his sovereign mastery of the spiritual powers.

At that time, the bodhisattvas within the assembly as well as the devas, dragons, *yakṣas, gandarvas, asuras,* the Four World-Protecting kings, Śakra Devānām Indra, the Brahma Heaven devas, and the devas' sons of the Pure Dwelling Heavens and Maheśvara Heavens all had this same thought: "If a bodhisattva is able to employ the power of spiritual superknowledges and the power of his knowledge in ways such as this, what more in addition to that could be done even by a buddha?"

At that time, Liberation Moon Bodhisattva, aware of the thoughts in the minds of everyone within that assembly, then addressed

Vajragarbha Bodhisattva, saying: "O Son of the Buddha, having heard of this bodhisattva's power of spiritual superknowledges and wisdom, the members of this great assembly have now fallen into a net of doubts. It would be good indeed, O Humane One, if, for the sake of cutting off their doubts, one were to briefly reveal those phenomena associated with the spiritual powers and adornments of the bodhisattva."

At this time, Vajragarbha Bodhisattva immediately entered "the nature of the physical form of all buddha lands samādhi."[266] When he entered this samādhi, the bodhisattvas as well as the entire great assembly all viewed their own bodies residing within the body of Vajragarbha Bodhisattva and, within it, they observed all the many different sorts of adornments within the great trichiliocosm that were such that, even were one to attempt to describe them for an entire *koṭi* of kalpas, one would never be able to come to the end of them.

They also observed therein a bodhi tree, the trunk of which had the circumference of ten myriads of great trichiliocosms and a height that reached to a hundred myriads of great trichiliocosms. The span of the shade cast by its branches and leaves was of the same scale, matching the shape and size of the tree.

There was a lion throne there upon which sat a buddha named King of Omniscience and Superknowledges.[267] The entire great assembly observed that buddha sitting there beneath the bodhi tree on a lion throne adorned with many different characteristics that were such that, even in a *koṭi* of kalpas, one could never completely describe them.

Having manifested such great powers of spiritual superknowledges as these, Vajragarbha Bodhisattva caused each individual in the assembly to return to his original place. At that time, that great assembly, having experienced what it never experienced before, brought forth thoughts of amazement at the rarity of what they had experienced and then remained there quietly, single-mindedly gazing up at Vajragarbha Bodhisattva.

At that time, Liberation Moon Bodhisattva said, "O Son of the Buddha, this samādhi is extremely rare and possessed of immense power. What is its name?"

Vajragarbha Bodhisattva replied, "This samādhi is known as 'the nature of the physical form of all buddha lands samādhi.'"

He also asked, "What is the range of this samādhi's objective domain?"

Vajragarbha Bodhisattva then replied:

> Son of the Buddha, if a bodhisattva were to cultivate this samādhi, then in accordance with whatever he wishes, he would be able to manifest within his own body a number of buddha lands as numerous as the atoms in a Ganges' sands number of worlds or even a number yet greater than this extending up to a measurelessly and boundlessly great number.
>
> Son of the Buddha, the bodhisattva dwelling on the Dharma Cloud Ground acquires measurelessly many hundreds of thousands of other great samādhis such as these. Consequently this bodhisattva's body and his physical deeds are impossible to completely fathom. So too, his speech, his verbal deeds, his mind, his mental deeds, his sovereign mastery of the spiritual superknowledges, his contemplation of the three periods of time, the objective domains of his samādhis, the objective domains of his wisdom, his wandering and sporting in all the gates to liberation, the transformations he performs, what he accomplishes through the use of spiritual powers, the works his rays of light perform and, to state it briefly, everything he does up to and including every raising up and setting down of his feet—absolutely everything he does all the way along cannot be known by any bodhisattva up to and including those who have reached the Ground of Excellent Intelligence who dwell therein at the station of the Dharma Prince.
>
> Son of the Buddha, to state it briefly, all of the objective domains of this bodhisattva dwelling on the Dharma Cloud Ground are of this very sort. If one were to attempt an extensive explanation of it, one would still be unable to finish it even in measurelessly many hundreds of thousands of *asaṃkhyeyas* of kalpas.

Liberation Moon Bodhisattva said, "O Son of the Buddha, if the objective domains of this bodhisattva's spiritual superknowledges are of this sort, then what additional factors must characterize the powers of a buddha's spiritual superknowledges?"

Vajragarbha Bodhisattva replied:

> O Son of the Buddha, by way of comparison, suppose there was someone who picked up a clump of soil from somewhere on the four continents and asked, 'Which is of greater volume? Is it all of that soil that comprises all the great earths in the boundlessly many worlds, or is it instead this clump of earth that I am holding here?' I see this question you have asked as of this very sort. The Tathāgata's wisdom is boundless and unequaled by anyone. How then could it possibly be compared to that of a bodhisattva?

Additionally, Son of the Buddha, it is just as when one picks up a small clump of earth from somewhere on the four continents and what remains is incalculable in volume. Were one to attempt to describe the spiritual superknowledges and wisdom of this bodhisattva on the Dharma Cloud Ground, even if one were to attempt to describe them for measurelessly many kalpas, one could only succeed in describing a minor portion of them. How much the more so then would this be the case if one were to attempt to describe them as they relate to one who abides on the ground of the Tathāgata?

Son of the Buddha, I will now bring forth a circumstance for you that will attest to the truth of this matter and thereby cause you to be able to understand the realm of the Tathāgata. Son of the Buddha, suppose that in each and every one of the ten directions there were buddha lands as numerous as the atoms in boundlessly many worlds, and suppose too that each and every one of those lands was so completely filled with bodhisattvas abiding on this ground that they could be compared to dense thickets of sugar cane stalks, bamboo, reeds, paddy rice, or hemp. Even all the wisdom arising from the bodhisattva practices cultivated by all of those bodhisattvas across the course of hundreds of thousands of *koṭis* of *nayutas* of kalpas could not compare to even a hundredth part of that possessed by a single *tathāgata,* and so forth until we come to its inability to equal even the smallest fraction of an *upaniṣad* when compared with the wisdom possessed by a single *tathāgata.*

Son of the Buddha, abiding in wisdom of this sort, this bodhisattva is no different from the Tathāgata in his actions of body, speech, and mind. He never relinquishes the power of any of the bodhisattva samādhis. Across the course of countless kalpas, he renders service to and makes offering to all buddhas and, in each and every kalpa, he presents every sort of gift to them as offerings. He is aided by the spiritual powers of all buddhas. The light of his wisdom becomes ever more supremely bright. Hence he is able to skillfully resolve all the difficult challenging questions throughout the Dharma realm, becoming one over whom no one can prevail even if they were to challenge him for a hundred thousand *koṭis* of kalpas.

Son of the Buddha, it is as if there were a goldsmith who, using the most supremely fine real gold, created articles of physical adornment to be personally worn by the Vaśavartin Heaven King,[268] adornments in which he inlaid large *maṇi* jewels, thereby creating adornments that could not be rivaled by those worn by any of the other devas.

So too it is in the case of the bodhisattva dwelling on this ground. His wisdom is such that it cannot be rivaled by all of the wisdom-based conduct of all bodhisattvas dwelling on the first ground through the ninth ground. The wisdom light of the bodhisattva dwelling on this ground is even able to cause beings to reach all the way through to the point of entering the cognition of all-knowledge. None of the wisdom light of those others is able to compare to this.

Son of the Buddha, this is analogous to the light of the Maheśvara Heaven King[269] that is able to cause the bodies and minds of beings to become clear and cool and, as such, is of a sort that cannot be rivaled by the light of any other beings.

So too it is with the wisdom light of the bodhisattva dwelling on this ground. It is able to cause all beings to acquire clarity and coolness and progress on through to the point where they themselves dwell in the cognition of all-knowledge. As such, it is of a sort that it cannot be rivaled by the wisdom light of any *śrāvaka* disciple, *pratyekabuddha,* or bodhisattva on any ground up to and including the ninth ground.

Son of the Buddha, though this bodhisattva-mahāsattva already possesses the ability to be established in wisdom such as this, the buddhas, the *bhagavats,* additionally expound for his sake on the "the knowledge of the three periods of time," "the knowledge of the Dharma realm's distinctions," "the knowledge that extends to all worlds," "the knowledge that illuminates all worlds," "the knowledge that bears all beings in mind with kindness," and, to speak of what is essential, they expound for his sake on all the types of knowledge up to and including that which culminates in gaining the cognition of all-knowledge.

Among the ten *pāramitās,* this bodhisattva has become most especially superior in his perfection of the *pāramitā* of knowledges, though it is not the case that he does not cultivate the others.

Son of the Buddha, this has been a summary explanation of the bodhisattva-mahāsattva's, tenth ground, the Ground of the Dharma Cloud. Were one to discourse on it extensively, even if one were to do so for measurelessly many *asaṃkhyeyas* of kalpas, one would still be unable to come to the end of it.

Son of the Buddha, the bodhisattva-mahāsattva dwelling on this ground often becomes a Maheśvara Heaven King who possesses sovereign mastery of the Dharma and who is able to transmit on to beings the practices of *śrāvaka* disciples and *pratyekabuddhas* as well as the practice of the bodhisattvas' *pāramitās.* Even if challenged with all the difficult questions from throughout the entire Dharma realm, there would still be no one able to prevail over him.

In his practice of giving, pleasing words, beneficial actions, joint endeavors, and all other such karmic works he pursues, he never departs from mindfulness of the Buddha, and so forth until we come to his never departing from mindfulness of his quest to achieve complete fulfillment of the knowledge of all modes and the cognition of all-knowledge.

He also has this thought: "I should become one who serves these beings as a leader, as one who is supreme," and so forth until we come to "as one who relies on the cognition of all-knowledge."

If he applies himself diligently to the practice of vigor, then, in but the instant of a single mind-moment, he succeeds in acquiring samādhis as numerous as the atoms in ineffably many hundreds of thousands of *koṭis* of *nayutas* of buddha lands. And so it goes on up to his then being able to manifest the acquisition of a following of bodhisattvas serving in his retinues as numerous as just that many atoms.

If this bodhisattva chooses to avail himself of the power of his especially supreme vows, he becomes able then to freely manifest such phenomena in numbers well beyond these, even to the point that, whether we speak of his cultivation, the adornments he creates, his resolute faith, what he accomplishes through physical or verbal actions, his light, his faculties, his spiritual transformations, his voice, or the domain of his practices, one would still be unable to enumerate them even if one were to attempt to do so for a hundred thousand *koṭis* of *nayutas* of kalpas.

Son of the Buddha, this bodhisattva-mahāsattva's aspects of practice on the ten grounds are such that, so long as he causes them to become directly and sequentially manifest, he will thereby become able to progress into the cognition of all-knowledge.

This circumstance is analogous to Lake Anavatapta that sends forth the four great rivers, the flowing waters of which circulate throughout the continent of Jambudvīpa. Because these waters are never exhausted, they ever increase in volume until they enter the ocean and cause it to become full.

Son of the Buddha, so too it is with this bodhisattva. From the point of his initial resolve to realize bodhi, he continually streams forth the waters of his roots of goodness and great vows, employing the four means of attraction to completely fulfill the needs of beings. Not only are these waters inexhaustible, they are moreover ever increasing until they ultimately pour forth into the ocean of all-knowledge and cause it to become full.

Son of the Buddha, due to the Buddha's knowledge, the ten grounds of the bodhisattva have distinct differences. This is just as when, due to the great earth, there exist the ten kings of mountains. What then are those ten? They are: the Snow Mountain King, the Fragrance Mountain King, the Vaidharī Mountain King, the Rishi Mountain King, the Yugaṃdhara Mountain King, the Horse Ear Mountain King, the Nimindhara Mountain King, the Cakravāḍa Mountain King, the Ketumat Mountain King, and the Sumeru Mountain King.

Son of the Buddha, just as on the Snow Mountain King, every sort of herb grows there so abundantly that one could never harvest them all, so too it is on the bodhisattva's Ground of Joyfulness, for all the world's classical texts, skills and arts, literature, verses, mantras and other occult techniques—these are all so completely present therein that one could never exhaustively describe them all.

Son of the Buddha, just as on the Fragrance Mountain King, every sort of incense is all accumulated there and is so abundantly present there that one could never harvest it all, so too it is on the bodhisattva's Ground of Stainlessness, for the bodhisattva's moral precept practices and standards of awesome deportment are all so completely present therein that one could never exhaustively describe them all.

Son of the Buddha, just as the Vaidharī Mountain King is so entirely composed of jewels that the many different kinds of precious jewels are so abundantly present therein that one could never extract them all, so too it is on the bodhisattva's Ground of Shining Light, for the world's *dhyāna* absorptions, spiritual superknowledges, liberations, samādhis, and *samāpattis* are all so completely present therein that one could never exhaustively describe them all.

Son of the Buddha, just as the Rishi Mountain King composed entirely of jewels has rishis possessed of the five spiritual superknowledges in such abundance that they are endlessly numerous, so too it is with the bodhisattva's Ground of Blazing Brilliance, for the forms of especially supreme wisdom from all paths are so completely present therein that one could never exhaustively describe them all.

Son of the Buddha, just as on the Yugaṃdhara Mountain King composed entirely of jewels, the *yakṣas,* those great spirits, live there in such abundance that one could never come to the end of them, so too it is on the bodhisattva's Difficult-to-Conquer Ground, for all types of sovereign masteries, psychic powers, and spiritual superknowledges are so completely present therein that one could never exhaustively describe them all.

Son of the Buddha, just as on the Horse Ear Mountain King composed entirely of jewels, all the various fruits are so abundantly present there that one could never harvest them all, so too it is on the bodhisattva's Ground of Direct Presence, for those who have penetrated the principle of conditioned arising corresponding to the realizations of *śrāvaka* disciples' fruits of the path are all so completely present therein that one could never exhaustively describe them all.

Just as on the Nimindhara Mountain King composed entirely of jewels, all the greatly powerful dragon spirits are so abundantly present there that one could never come to the end of them, so too it is on the bodhisattva's Far-Reaching Ground, for the skillful means, wisdom, and realizations corresponding to the fruits of a *pratyekabuddha*'s path are all so completely present therein that one could never exhaustively describe them all.

Just as on the Cakravāda Mountain King composed entirely of jewels, the congregation of those possessed of sovereign mastery is so abundantly present that one could never come to the end of them, so too it is on the bodhisattva's Ground of Immovability, for all bodhisattvas' sovereign masteries in traveling to different worlds are all so completely present therein that one could never exhaustively describe them all.

Just as on the Ketumat Mountain King composed entirely of jewels, all the *asura* kings possessed of great awe-inspiring virtue who dwell there are so abundantly present that one could never come to the end of them, so too it is on the bodhisattva's Ground of Excellent Intelligence, for all forms of knowledge and practice pertaining to the creation and destruction of worlds are all so completely present therein that one could never exhaustively describe them all.

Just as on the Sumeru Mountain King that is entirely composed of precious jewels, the devas possessed of greatly awe-inspiring virtue are so abundantly present there that one could never come to the end of them, so too it is on the bodhisattva's Dharma Cloud Ground, for the Tathāgata's powers, fearlessnesses, exclusive dharmas, and matters pertaining to buddhahood are all so completely present therein along with their abundantly present facility in questions, answers, and proclamations that one could never come to the end of them all.

Son of the Buddha, these ten jeweled mountain kings all identically reside within the great ocean and achieve their names based on their differences. So too it is with the bodhisattva's ten grounds. They all identically reside within all-knowledge and acquire their names based on their differences.

Son of the Buddha, [these ten bodhisattva grounds] are comparable to the great ocean that, on the basis of ten characteristic features, acquires the inalterably exclusive designation "great ocean."[270] What then are those ten? They are:

First, it progresses gradually from its shallows to its depths;
Second, it refuses to accept dead bodies;
Third, upon flowing into it, all other waters thereby lose their original names;
Fourth, it is everywhere of the same singular flavor;
Fifth, it holds incalculably many truly precious jewels;
Sixth, nobody is able to go all the way down to its bottom;
Seventh, it is incalculably vast;
Eighth, it is a place in which beings with huge bodies reside;
Ninth, its tides do not reach beyond its shoreline;
Tenth, it everywhere takes in the great rains without overflowing.

So too it is with the practices of the bodhisattva that on the basis of ten characteristic features acquire the inalterably exclusive designation "bodhisattva practices." What then are those ten? They are:

On the Ground of Joyfulness this is because it is therein that the production of great vows gradually and sequentially deepens;
On the Ground of Stainlessness this is because it refuses to accept the dead bodies of those who break the precepts;
On the Ground of Shining Light this is because that is where one relinquishes the world's false designations;
On the Ground of Blazing Brilliance this is because it is of the same singular flavor as the Buddha's meritorious qualities;
On the Difficult-to-Conquer Ground this is because this is where one produces incalculably many skillful means and spiritual superknowledges whereby what one does in the world constitutes a multitude of precious jewels;
On the Ground of Direct Presence this is because that is where one contemplates the extremely profound principles of conditioned arising;
On the Far-Reaching Ground this is because that is where one employs vast enlightened intelligence in skillful investigative contemplation;
On the Ground of Immovability this is because that is where one manifests vast works of adornment;
On the Ground of Excellent Intelligence this is because that is where one acquires profound liberation and, in one's practice within the world, one's awareness accords with reality and never extends beyond boundaries;

And on the Dharma Cloud Ground this is because that is where one becomes able to insatiably take on all the rain of the Buddha's, the Tathāgata's, great Dharma light.

Son of the Buddha, this circumstance is analogous to that of a large *maṇi* jewel that by virtue of possessing ten characteristic qualities surpasses all the many other sorts of jewels. What then are those ten? They are:

First, it comes forth from the great ocean;
Second, it is enhanced by the refinements of a skilled artisan;
Third, it is perfect and entirely free of flaws;
Fourth, it is possessed of stainless purity;
Fifth, its brightly penetrating brilliance shines both inwardly and outwardly;
Sixth, it has been skillfully drilled through;
Seventh, it is strung with precious thread;
Eighth, it is mounted at the very tip of a tall flagpole made of lapis lazuli;
Ninth, it shines forth everywhere with all the many different kinds of light;
Tenth, it is able to rain down the many sorts of precious things in response to the wishes of the King and is able to fulfill the wishes arising in beings' minds.

Son of the Buddha, so too it is with the bodhisattva who, in this same manner, by virtue of possessing ten characteristic features, surpasses the qualities of the many other *āryas*. What then are these ten?

First, he has brought forth the resolve to gain all-knowledge;
Second, in his observance of the moral precepts and his cultivation of the *dhūta* practices, he is possessed of radiantly pure right practice;
Third, he is possessed of perfectly full and flawless practice of all the *dhyāna* samādhis;
Fourth, his path practices are pure white and free from all stains and defilements;
Fifth, his skillful means and spiritual superknowledges are possessed of a penetrating brilliance that shines both inwardly and outwardly;
Sixth, his wisdom with respect to the process of conditioned arising has the capacity to be skillfully penetrating;
Seventh, [his practice] is strung through with the thread of the many different applications of skillful means and wisdom;

Eighth, he is placed high atop the pillar of the sovereign masteries;
Ninth, he contemplates beings' actions and emanates the light of learning and retention;
Tenth, having received the buddhas' consecration of his knowledge, he then falls in among those counted as buddhas and thus becomes able, for the sake of beings, to carry out on a vast scale the works of the buddhas.

Son of the Buddha, as for this chapter on the bodhisattva practice gateways by which one accumulates the meritorious qualities associated with the knowledge of all modes and all-knowledge, if any being had not himself already planted roots of goodness, he would be unable to even obtain a hearing of it.

Liberation Moon Bodhisattva then asked, "How much merit might one acquire due to having heard [this chapter that describes] these Dharma gateways?"

Vajragarbha Bodhisattva replied:

The merit associated with simply hearing these Dharma gateways is of the same sort as the merit of all-knowledge. How could that be? It could not be that one might have resolute faith in, accept, uphold, study, and recite these Dharma gateways to the meritorious qualities if one had not heard them. How much the less might one then proceed to vigorously pursue their cultivation in accordance with the way they were explained. Therefore, one should realize that it is essential that one gain a hearing of these Dharma gateways to the accumulation of the meritorious qualities associated with all-knowledge in order to then be able to have resolute faith in them, accept them, uphold them in practice, and thus later succeed in reaching the ground of all-knowledge.

At that time, because of the spiritual powers of the Buddha and because of the very nature of the Dharma, in each of the ten directions, worlds as numerous as the atoms in ten *koṭis* of buddha lands underwent the six types and eighteen varieties of characteristic movements, namely: movement, universal movement, equal-and-universal movement, rising, universal rising, equal-and-universal rising, upward thrusting, universal upward thrusting, equal-and-universal upward thrusting, shaking, universal shaking, equal-and-universal shaking, roaring, universal roaring, equal-and-universal roaring, striking, universal striking, and equal-and-universal striking. This was accompanied by the raining down of the many sorts of heavenly flower blossoms, heavenly floral garlands, heavenly raiment, and also heavenly jewels, articles of adornment, flags, banners, silken canopies, the playing of heavenly instruments and singing in which the sounds were harmonious and refined and accompanied by the simultaneous sounding of voices in praise of all the meritorious qualities of the ground of all-knowledge.

Just as this proclamation of this Dharma was taking place in the palace of this world's Paranirmita Vaśavartin Heaven, so too was it also taking place in this very fashion in all worlds of the ten directions.

Additionally, at that time, again on account of the spiritual powers of the Buddha, there came to this assembly from beyond worlds as numerous as the atoms in ten *koṭis* of buddha lands bodhisattvas as numerous as the atoms in ten *koṭis* of buddha lands who then spoke these words:

> It is good indeed, good indeed, O Vajragarbha, that you have discoursed so directly on this dharma. We too carry the name "Vajragarbha" and the worlds in which we dwell with all their differences, are all named, "Vajra Qualities." Our buddha is called "Vajra Banner." All of us, receiving the benefit of the spiritual powers of the Tathāgata, proclaim this very Dharma in those worlds in which we dwell and from which we come. Our assemblies are all also entirely identical. The language, the phrases, and the meanings are also neither enhanced nor reduced in comparison to what is set forth here.
>
> That all of us have come to this assembly is entirely because of the Buddha's spiritual powers through which we have come to offer this certifying corroboration. Just as we have now come and entered this world, so too is it the case that, in this same manner, we go forth to all the worlds of the ten directions to offer just such certifying corroboration there as well.

At that time, Vajragarbha Bodhisattva regarded that entire congregation that had assembled from the ten directions throughout the entire Dharma realm and, wishing to praise the generation of the resolve to gain realization of the cognition of all-knowledge, wishing to reveal the realms of the bodhisattvas, wishing to reveal the purification of the practices and powers of the bodhisattva, wishing to discourse on the acquisition of the path to the knowledge of all modes, wishing to discourse on the extinguishing of all forms of worldly defilement, wishing to bestow all-knowledge, wishing to reveal the adornments associated with inconceivable knowledge, wishing to reveal all the meritorious qualities of all bodhisattvas, and wishing to cause such meanings associated with the grounds to become yet more clearly revealed, he availed himself of the spiritual power of the Buddha and then proceeded to utter verses, saying:

With a mind abiding in quiescence, forever tamed,
and as uniformly the same and unobstructed as space itself,
he abandons the turbidity of all defilements and abides in the path.
You should listen to such especially supreme practices as these.

For a hundred thousand *koṭis* of kalpas, he cultivates every good,
presents offerings to incalculably and boundlessly many buddhas,
and to *śrāvaka* disciples and *pratyekabuddhas* as well
and, in order to benefit beings, brings forth the great resolve.

He diligently upholds moral precepts, is always pliantly patient,
is replete in senses of shame and blame and merit and knowledge,
resolutely seeks Buddha's knowledge, cultivates vast intelligence,
and, vowing to acquire the ten powers, brings forth the great resolve.

He makes offerings to all buddhas of the three periods of time,
adorns and purifies all lands,
utterly realizes all dharmas' uniform equality,
and, for the sake of benefiting beings, brings forth the great resolve.[271]

Dwelling on the first ground, he brings forth this resolve,
forever abandons the many evils, and always abides in joyfulness.
Through the power of vows, he vastly cultivates all good dharmas,
and, through compassionate empathy, enters the next station.

Entirely replete in precepts and learning and mindful of beings,
he washes away defilements, his mind becomes radiantly pristine,
he contemplates the world's fires of the three poisons,
and, with vast comprehension, proceeds on to the third ground.

Seeing the three realms of existence as entirely impermanent,
as ablaze with sufferings akin to when an arrow is shot into the body,
he renounces all that is conditioned, pursues the Buddha's Dharma,
and, as one with great wisdom, enters the Blazing Ground.

Fully replete in mindfulness and wisdom, he gains path knowledge,
makes hundreds of thousands of offerings to countless buddhas,
and always contemplates all of the most supreme qualities,
whereupon this person then enters the Difficult-to-Conquer Ground.

Employing wisdom and skillful means, he skillfully contemplates,
brings forth all different sorts of manifestations to rescue beings,
again makes offerings to the unexcelled Honored One of ten powers,
and enters the unproduced and the Direct Presence Ground.

He becomes able to know what is difficult for a worldling to know,
does not accept any self, transcends existence and nonexistence,
knows dharmas' basic stillness, adapts to conditions' transformations,
and, having gained these sublime states, enters the seventh ground.

With wisdom, skillful means, and a vast mind, [he masters] what is
hard to practice, hard to overcome, and hard to entirely know.
Though he has realized quiescent cessation, he cultivates diligently
and is able to enter the space-like Ground of Immovability.

Encouraged by Buddha, he is caused to rise from quiescent cessation,
takes up vast cultivation of many different deeds rooted in wisdom.
Equipped with ten sovereign masteries, he contemplates the world,
and, due to this, ascends to the Ground of Excellent Intelligence.

With subtle and marvelous wisdom, he contemplates beings'
thickets of mental actions, karmic actions, afflictions, and such,
and, wishing to teach them and cause them to enter the path,
he then expounds on all buddhas' treasury of the supreme meaning.

He sequentially cultivates to completion the many forms of goodness,
accumulates merit and wisdom up through the ninth ground,
always pursues all buddhas' most supreme dharmas, and gains
the consecration with Buddha's wisdom waters poured on his crown.

He acquires measurelessly many samādhis and
also thoroughly and completely understands their functions.
The very last samādhi is known as "Receiving the Consecration"
wherein he dwells in a vast realm, forever unmoving.

When this bodhisattva acquires this samādhi,
an immense bejeweled lotus blossom suddenly appears,
whereupon, with a body of matching size, he sits down in its middle,
surrounded by those buddha's sons, all in the same contemplation.

He emanates a hundred thousand *koṭis* of great light beams
that extinguish the sufferings of all beings
and also emanates beams of light from his crown that
everywhere enter the assemblies of the buddhas of the ten directions.

They all remain there in space, forming a net-like canopy of light
that, after making offerings to the buddhas, then enters their feet.
The buddhas all then immediately know,
"This Buddha's son has now ascended to the consecration stage."

The bodhisattvas from the ten directions come to observe
this great consecration-receiving eminence pour forth illumination.
The buddhas then also release light from between their eyebrows
that, after producing illumination everywhere, then enters his crown.

All worlds of the ten directions are then beset with tremors
and all the sufferings experienced in the hells are extinguished.
It is at this very time that the buddhas confer their consecration
just as a wheel-turning king confers a consecration on his eldest son.

When one receives this anointing of the crown by the buddhas, then
this is what is known as ascending to the Dharma Cloud Ground.
His wisdom continues to grow boundlessly to include
[the means of] awakening everyone in all worlds.

The desire realm, the form realm, the formless realm,
the Dharma realm, the worldly realms, and the realms of beings.
Whether calculable, incalculable, or in the realms of empty space,
he acquires a penetrating comprehension of all such things as these.

In all his transformations, he employs greatly awe-inspiring powers
and receives the buddhas' augmenting support in subtle knowledge.
As for the esoteric, kalpa enumerations, ordinary beings, and such,
he can contemplate them all in accordance with reality.

He takes on birth, leaves the home life, realizes right enlightenment,
turns the wheel of the wondrous Dharma, and enters nirvāṇa.
Everything up to the dharma of quiescent liberation as well as
what has not yet been taught—he is able to completely fathom it all.

The bodhisattva dwelling on this Dharma Cloud Ground,
entirely perfect in mindfulness power, retains the Buddha's Dharma.
Just as the great ocean takes in the dragon's rains,
so too is his ability to take in and retain the Dharma on this ground.

Compared to all buddha dharmas countless beings in ten directions
who had the hearing-and-retaining [samādhi] would be able to retain,
the Dharma that he hears [and retains] in the place of a single buddha
exceeds that number by a measurelessly great amount.

Using the power of wisdom, past vows, and awesome spiritual might,
in but a single mind-moment, he pervades the ten directions' lands,
pours down the rain of sweet-dew elixir, and extinguishes afflictions.
Hence the Buddha referred to this as "the Dharma Cloud Ground."

What his superknowledges manifest throughout the ten directions
so surpasses such things in the worldly sphere of humans and devas,
exceeding their number so incalculably many *koṭis* of times, assessing
them by worldly knowledge, one is sure to become confused and discouraged.

Even everyone up through the ninth ground cannot know how
much knowledge and merit is involved in his merely raising his foot.
How much less might this be known by any ordinary being
or even by any *śrāvaka* disciple or *pratyekabuddha*.

The bodhisattva dwelling on this ground makes offerings to buddhas
in the lands throughout the ten directions
while also making offerings to all present-era assemblies of *āryas*
and completely fulfilling his adornment with a buddha's qualities.

As he dwells on this ground, they additionally discourse for him
on unimpeded knowledge of the three times, the Dharma realm,
and in the same manner, on beings, on lands,
and so forth on up to all of the Buddha's meritorious qualities.

The wisdom light of the bodhisattva dwelling on this ground
is able to reveal to beings the road of right Dharma.
As the Maheśvara Heaven King's light dispels worldly darkness,
so too this light of his dispels darkness in just that same manner.

Dwelling herein, one often becomes a king within the three realms
well able to expound on Dharma according to the Three Vehicles.
Incalculably many samādhis are acquired in but a mind-moment
and the number of buddhas he sees is of that same order.

I have now concluded a summary explanation of this ground.
If one wished to discourse on it extensively, it would be endless.
Just so, the grounds exist in reliance on the Buddha's wisdom just as
the ten mountain kings, towering, abide [in reliance on the earth].

Culturally supportive works done on the first ground are endless,
comparable to the density of the many herbs on Snow Mountain.
Second ground precepts and learning are like Incense Mountain.
The third is like the fine flowers that come forth on Vaidharī.

The jewels of the path on the "Blazing Brilliance" ground are endless,
comparable to the worthies skillfully dwelling on Rishi Mountain.
The spiritual powers on the fifth ground are like on Yugaṃdhara.
The many fruits on the sixth are like on Horse Ear Mountain.

The seventh ground's great wisdom is analogous to Nimindhara.
The sovereign masteries on the eighth ground are like Cakravāda.
The ninth is like Ketumat in its assembling of unimpeded knowledge.
The tenth is like Sumeru in its repletion with the manifold virtues.

The first ground is chief in vows, the second in upholding precepts,
the third ground in virtues, the fourth in singular focus,
the fifth ground in sublimity, the sixth in extreme profundity,
the seventh in vast wisdom, and the eighth in adornment.

The ninth is foremost in the contemplation of sublime meanings
in a manner that surpasses that of all the world's paths.
On the tenth ground, one takes on and preserves Buddha dharmas.
It is in this way that the ocean of practices is inexhaustible.

Ten practices overstep the worldly, the first is generating the resolve,
upholding precepts is second, *dhyāna* is third,
purification of practices is fourth, fulfillment is fifth, conditioned
arising is sixth, his threading of [means and wisdom] is seventh,

the eighth is placement atop the vajra pillar,
the ninth is contemplation of the beings' thickets,
the tenth is the anointing of the crown according to the King's intent.
It is in this way that the jewel of virtue gradually becomes purified.

Even if, having crushed the ten directions' lands to dust,
one could know in but a single mind-moment their number of dusts,
and, even if one could measure the size of space with a hair tip, still,
one could not finish describing [the grounds] even in a *koṭi* of kalpas.

The End of Chapter Twenty-Six

Chapter 27
The Ten Samādhis

At that time, the Bhagavat was in the state of Magadha abiding at the site of his enlightenment in accordance with the *araṇya* dharma where, having first realized right enlightenment, in the Hall of Universal Radiance, he entered all buddhas' *kṣaṇa*-boundary samādhi and, with the spiritual power inherent in all-knowledge, he manifested the Tathāgata's body, pure and unimpeded, not depending on anything, free of any clinging to conditions, dwelling in *śamathā*'s most ultimate quiescence, possessed of great awesome virtue, free of all defiling attachments, able to cause all who saw him to become awakened, manifesting in accordance with what is fitting, never missing the right time, always abiding in the one sign, namely signlessness.

He was together with bodhisattva-mahāsattvas as numerous as the atoms in ten buddha *kṣetras*, none of whom had not already entered the crown-anointing stage of consecration, already become fully possessed of bodhisattva practices as measureless and boundless as the Dharma realm, and already acquired all bodhisattvas' universal vision samādhi. With the great compassion, they bestowed peace and security on all beings. They possessed sovereign mastery of the spiritual superknowledges identical to that of the Tathāgata. With deeply penetrating wisdom, they expounded the true meaning and, possessed of all-knowledge, subdued the many *māras*. Although they had entered the world, their minds were constantly quiescent and dwelt in the bodhisattva's non-abiding liberation. Their names were:

Vajra Wisdom Bodhisattva,
Peerless Wisdom Bodhisattva,
Wisdom of Meaningful Words Bodhisattva,
Supreme Wisdom Bodhisattva,
Always Equanimous Wisdom Bodhisattva,
Nāga Wisdom Bodhisattva,
Consummate Wisdom Bodhisattva,
Harmonious Wisdom Bodhisattva,
Great Powers Wisdom Bodhisattva,
Inconceivable Wisdom Bodhisattva,

Unimpeded Wisdom Bodhisattva,
Especially Superior Wisdom Bodhisattva,
Everywhere Offering Wisdom Bodhisattva,
Noumenal Wisdom Bodhisattva,
Skillful Wisdom Bodhisattva,
Sovereign Dharma Wisdom Bodhisattva,
Dharma Wisdom Bodhisattva,
Quiescent Wisdom Bodhisattva,
Spacious Wisdom Bodhisattva,
Single Sign Wisdom Bodhisattva,
Good Wisdom Bodhisattva,
Illusoriness-Cognizing Wisdom Bodhisattva,
Vast Wisdom Bodhisattva,
Powerful Wisdom Bodhisattva,
World Wisdom Bodhisattva,
Buddha Ground Wisdom Bodhisattva,
Genuine Wisdom Bodhisattva,
Honored and Victorious Wisdom Bodhisattva,
Sagacious Light Wisdom Bodhisattva,
Boundless Wisdom Bodhisattva,
Mindfulness Adornment Bodhisattva,
Space Boundary Penetrating Bodhisattva,
Nature Adornment Bodhisattva,
Extremely Profound Realm Bodhisattva,
Skillful Knower of the Possible and Impossible Bodhisattva,
Great Radiance Bodhisattva,
Ever Radiant Bodhisattva,
Knower of the Buddha Lineage Bodhisattva,
Mind King Bodhisattva,[272]
Single Practice Bodhisattva,
Always Manifest Spiritual Superknowledges Bodhisattva,
Wisdom Sprout Bodhisattva,
Meritorious Qualities Abode Bodhisattva,
Dharma Lamp Bodhisattva,
World Illuminating Bodhisattva,
World Supporting Bodhisattva,
Most Secure Bodhisattva,
Most Superior Bodhisattva,
Unsurpassed Bodhisattva,
Incomparable Bodhisattva,
Peerless Bodhisattva,

Unimpeded Practice Bodhisattva,
Flaming Radiance Bodhisattva,
Moonlight Bodhisattva,
Single Object Bodhisattva,
Solid Practice Bodhisattva,
Drenching Dharma Rain Bodhisattva,
Supreme Banner Bodhisattva,
Universal Adornment Bodhisattva,
Wisdom Eye Bodhisattva,
Dharma Eye Bodhisattva,
Wisdom Cloud Bodhisattva,
Dhāraṇī King Bodhisattva,
Non-Abiding Vows Bodhisattva,
Wisdom Treasury Bodhisattva,
Mind King Bodhisattva,
Inward Awakening Wisdom Bodhisattva,
Abiding in Buddha Wisdom Bodhisattva,
Stalwart Dhāraṇī Powers Bodhisattva,
Earth-Supporting Powers Bodhisattva,
Marvelous Moon Bodhisattva,
Sumeru Summit Bodhisattva,
Bejeweled Summit Bodhisattva,
Universal Illumination Bodhisattva,
Awesome Virtue King Bodhisattva,
Wisdom Wheel Bodhisattva,
Magnificent Awesome Virtue Bodhisattva,
Great Dragon Sign Bodhisattva,
Straightforward Practice Bodhisattva,
Non-Retreating Bodhisattva,
Upholding the Dharma Banner Bodhisattva,
Never Forgetful Bodhisattva,
Attracting Those from All Destinies Bodhisattva,
Inconceivable and Decisive Wisdom Bodhisattva,
Easeful Mastery of Boundless Wisdom Bodhisattva,
Endless Treasury of Sublime Dharma Bodhisattva,
Wisdom Sun Bodhisattva,
Dharma Sun Bodhisattva,
Wisdom Treasury Bodhisattva,
Wisdom Meadow Bodhisattva,
Universal Vision Bodhisattva,

Never Seen in Vain Bodhisattva,
Vajra Penetration Bodhisattva,
Vajra Wisdom Bodhisattva,
Vajra Flame Bodhisattva,
Vajra Intelligence Bodhisattva,
Universal Eye Bodhisattva,
Buddha Sun Bodhisattva,
Retainer of the Buddha's Vajra Secret Meaning Bodhisattva, and
Adorned With the Wisdom of the Universal Eye Realm Bodhisattva.

There were bodhisattva-mahāsattvas such as these as numerous as the atoms in ten buddha *kṣetras,* all of whom had in the past cultivated together with Vairocana Tathāgata the practices producing the bodhisattva's roots of goodness.

At that time, Universal Eye Bodhisattva-mahāsattva, aided by the Buddha's spiritual powers, rose from his seat, bared his right shoulder, knelt with his right knee on the ground, placed his palms together, and addressed the Buddha, saying, "O Bhagavat, I have a question I wish to ask of the Tathāgata, the Arhat, the one of Right and Perfect Enlightenment. Please permit me to ask it."

The Buddha replied, "Universal Eye, feel free to ask whatever you wish. I will then speak about it for you and cause your mind to feel joyful."

Universal Eye Bodhisattva then asked, "How many samādhis and liberations have been perfected by Samantabhadra Bodhisattva and the multitudes of bodhisattvas who abide in all the practices and vows of Samantabhadra that they may enter, may emerge from, and may at times peacefully dwell in the bodhisattva's great samādhis and, because they skillfully enter and emerge from these inconceivably vast bodhisattva samādhis, they are able in all those samādhis to ceaselessly exercise sovereign mastery in the spiritual superknowledges and transformations?"

The Buddha replied, "It is good indeed, Universal Eye, that in order to benefit the multitudes of past, future, and present bodhisattvas, you have inquired into the meaning of this. Universal Eye, Samantabhadra is now here. He has already been able to perfect inconceivably many sovereign spiritual superknowledges to a degree that surpasses all other bodhisattvas and is only rarely ever encountered.

He is one who has been born from the countless bodhisattva practices and who has already purified all the bodhisattva's great vows.

He has attained irreversibility in all the practices that he practices. He has already gained unimpeded purity in all the countless *pāramitā* gateways, in all the unimpeded *dhāraṇī* gateways, and in all the gateways of inexhaustible eloquence. His great compassion benefits all beings and the power of his original vows is such that he shall tirelessly continue in them to the very end of future time. You should ask him and he will explain for you his samādhis, his sovereign masteries, and his liberations."

At that time, when the multitude of bodhisattvas in that congregation heard Samantabhadra's name, they immediately acquired an inconceivable and measureless samādhi in which their minds became unimpeded, quiescent, unmoving, in which they possessed vast and unfathomably deep wisdom, and in which they possessed an extremely profound sphere of cognition to which none could compare, one in which they saw all the countless buddhas manifest directly before them. They acquired the powers of the Tathāgata, became of the same nature as the Tathāgata, and had nothing in the past, future, or present that they did not clearly illuminate. All of their inexhaustible merit and all of their spiritual superknowledges all became completely fulfilled.

The minds of all those bodhisattvas were filled with reverential esteem for Samantabhadra and they urgently wished to see him. Although they looked everywhere throughout that congregation, they were finally unable to see him and were also unable even to see the seat on which he sits. That this occurred was because of the effect of Tathāgata's awesome powers and was also because of Samantabhadra's sovereign mastery of the spiritual superknowledges.

At that time, Universal Eye Bodhisattva asked the Buddha, "O Bhagavat, where is Samantabhadra Bodhisattva now?"

The Buddha replied, "Universal Eye, Samantabhadra Bodhisattva is now close to me in this congregation at the site of enlightenment. From the very beginning, he has not moved at all."

Universal Eye and the other bodhisattvas looked again throughout the congregation at the site of enlightenment, searching everywhere, and then said to the Buddha, "O Bhagavat, we are now still unable to see Samantabhadra Bodhisattva or the seat on which he sits."

The Buddha replied, "So it is. Son of Good Family, why is it that you are all still unable to see him? Son of Good Family, this is because Samantabhadra Bodhisattva's dwelling place is so extremely profound as to be indescribable. Samantabhadra Bodhisattva has acquired the gateway to boundless wisdom, has entered the lion-sprint meditative absorption, has acquired the functions of unexcelled sovereign mastery by which he has entered the realm of unimpeded purity, has developed the Tathāgata's ten powers, has taken the treasury of the Dharma realm as his body, has become one who is regarded with protective mindfulness by all *tathāgatas*, and has become able in but a single mind-moment to realize and enter the undifferentiated wisdom of all buddhas of the three periods of time. It is for these reasons that you have all remained unable to see him."

Then, on hearing the Tathāgata describe Samantabhadra Bodhisattva's pure meritorious qualities, Universal Eye Bodhisattva acquired a myriad *asaṃkhyeyas* of samādhis and then used the power of those samādhis to again look everywhere, strongly wishing to see Samantabhadra Bodhisattva. However, he was still unable to see him. Everyone else in that multitude of bodhisattvas was also still unable to see him.

Universal Eye Bodhisattva then emerged from those samādhis and addressed the Buddha, saying: "O Bhagavat, although I have entered ten thousand *asaṃkhyeyas* of samādhis in which I have searched for Samantabhadra, I have still remained unable to find him. I have not seen his body or physical actions, his speech or verbal actions, his mind or mental actions, his seat, or his dwelling place. I have not seen any of these."

The Buddha replied, "So it is. So it is. Son of Good Family, you should realize that this is all because of Samantabhadra Bodhisattva's power from dwelling in inconceivable liberations. Universal Eye, what do you think? Would it be possible for anyone to describe the location of various illusory images spoken of in magically conjured writings?"

He replied, "No. It would not."

The Buddha told Universal Eye, "If one cannot even describe the illusory images in a magical conjuration, how much the less could one enter into or see Samantabhadra Bodhisattva's secret spheres of physical action, secret spheres of verbal actions, or secret spheres of mental actions. Why is this the case? It is because Samantabhadra Bodhisattva's spheres of action are extremely deep, inconceivable, and so measureless as to have passed beyond all means of measurement.

To speak of what is essential, Samantabhadra Bodhisattva uses the vajra wisdom to everywhere enter all worlds of the Dharma realm even as he has no place to which he travels and no place in which he dwells. He knows the bodies of all beings to all be just non-bodies which have neither any going nor any coming. He has acquired never-ending nondiscriminating sovereign mastery of the spiritual superknowledges by which he has nothing on which he depends, nothing that he does, and also has no movement even as he reaches the most ultimately distant boundaries of the Dharma realm.

Son of Good Family, if one is able to see Samantabhadra Bodhisattva, serve him, hear his name, meditate on him, bear him in mind, develop resolute faith in him, diligently contemplate him, begin to follow him, rightly search for him, or make vows connected to him, doing so continuously and uninterruptedly, then in all such cases, one will gain benefit from this and will not have done these things in vain."

Then Universal Eye and all of the others in that multitude of bodhisattvas, longing to see Samantabhadra Bodhisattva, spoke in this way: "*Namo* to all buddhas. *Namo* to Samantabhadra Bodhisattva,"[273] doing so three times as they bowed their heads [to the ground] in reverential respect.

The Buddha then told Universal Eye Bodhisattva and those in the congregation, "Sons of the Buddha, it would be fitting for you to again bow down in reverence to Samantabhadra to express the earnestness of your wish to see him. You should then also contemplate the ten directions with single-minded intent, visualizing Samantabhadra's body manifesting directly before you as you contemplate his being present everywhere throughout the Dharma realm. With deep resolve and resolute faith, renounce everything and vow to take up the same conduct and vows as Samantabhadra, penetrating the dharma of nondual reality. His bodies appear everywhere in all worlds where they all know all the different faculties of beings. Pervading all places, they accumulate the path of Samantabhadra. If one is able to make great vows such as these, then he should be able to see Samantabhadra Bodhisattva."

At this time, having heard these words from the Buddha, Universal Eye and the other bodhisattvas simultaneously bowed down in reverence, requesting to be able to see Samantabhadra, the great eminence.

Then, using the powers of the liberation's superknowledges, Samantabhadra Bodhisattva, according with what was fitting, manifested his form body for them, thereby enabling everyone in that multitude of bodhisattvas to see Samantabhadra near the Tathāgata, sitting on a lotus flower throne in the midst of this congregation of all bodhisattvas. They also witnessed his sequential and continuous arrival into all those other worlds, reaching the abodes of all buddhas. They also saw him in the abodes of all buddhas, expounding on all the bodhisattva practices, explaining the path to the wisdom of all-knowledge, elucidating all the spiritual superknowledges of all bodhisattvas, distinguishing the awesome virtues of all bodhisattvas, and revealing all buddhas of the three periods of time.

Then when Universal Eye Bodhisattva and the congregation of all those bodhisattvas witnessed these spiritual transformations, they were filled with exultation and great happiness. There were none among them who did not then bow down in reverence to Samantabhadra Bodhisattva. They felt reverential esteem for him the same as if they were seeing all buddhas of the ten directions.

Then, because of the great awesome spiritual powers of the Buddha, the power of the resolute faith of those bodhisattvas, and the power of Samantabhadra Bodhisattva's original vows, there spontaneously rained down a myriad kinds of clouds, including:

Clouds of all different kinds of flowers;
Clouds of all different kinds of garlands;
Clouds of all different kinds of fragrances;
Clouds of all different kinds of powdered incense;
Clouds of all different kinds of canopies;
Clouds of all different kinds of robes;
Clouds of all different kinds of adornments;
Clouds of all different kinds of precious jewels;
Clouds of all different kinds of burning incense; and
Clouds of all different kinds of silk streamers.

In an ineffable number of worlds, there occurred the six kinds of moving and shaking together with the playing of celestial music the sounds of which could be heard from afar. In an ineffable number of worlds, great light was emanated which produced universal illumination. In an ineffable number of worlds, the three wretched destinies were all caused to completely disappear. An ineffable number of worlds became purified. An ineffable number of bodhisattvas were caused to enter the practices of Samantabhadra. An ineffable number of bodhisattvas perfected the practices of Samantabhadra. And an ineffable number of bodhisattvas were able to completely fulfill the conduct and vows of Samantabhadra and attain *anuttarasamyaksaṃbodhi*.

Then Universal Eye Bodhisattva addressed the Buddha saying, "O Bhagavat, Samantabhadra Bodhisattva is one who abides in great awesome virtue, who abides in incomparability, who abides in unsurpassability, who abides in irreversibility, who abides in equanimity, who abides in indestructibility, who abides in all different dharmas, who abides in all undifferentiated dharmas, who abides where the mind of expedients for all beings abides, and who abides in the samādhi of the liberation of sovereign mastery in all dharmas."

The Buddha replied, "So it is. So it is, Universal Eye. It is just as you have stated. Samantabhadra Bodhisattva has *asaṃkhyeyas* of pure meritorious qualities, for instance: the meritorious quality of incomparable adornments, the meritorious quality of countless jewels, the meritorious quality of oceans of inconceivability, the meritorious quality of measureless signs, the meritorious quality of boundless clouds, the meritorious quality of boundlessness beyond the reach of praises, the meritorious quality of endless Dharma, the meritorious quality of ineffability, the meritorious qualities of all buddhas, and the meritorious qualities which can never be completely praised."

The Tathāgata then told Samantabhadra Bodhisattva:

> Samantabhadra, you should explain the ten samādhis for the benefit of Universal Eye and the multitudes of bodhisattvas in this assembly, thereby enabling them to skillfully enter and completely fulfill all the conduct and vows of Samantabhadra. It is because all bodhisattva-mahāsattvas explain these ten samādhis that the bodhisattvas of the past have succeeded in gaining emancipation, the bodhisattvas of the present now succeed in gaining emancipation, and the bodhisattvas of the future shall succeed in gaining emancipation. What are these ten? They are:
>
> First, the great samādhi of universal light;
> Second, the great samādhi of sublime light;
> Third, the great samādhi of
> sequential visitation of all buddha lands everywhere;
> Fourth, the great samādhi of pure and deep-minded practice;
> Fifth, the great samādhi of the knowledge of the treasury of past adornments;
> Sixth, the great samādhi of a treasury of wisdom light;
> Seventh, the great samādhi of the complete knowledge of all worlds' buddha adornments;
> Eight, the great samādhi of all beings' different bodies;

Ninth, the great samādhi of sovereign mastery throughout the Dharma realm; and

Tenth, the great samādhi of the unimpeded wheel.

All great bodhisattvas then become able to skillfully enter these ten great samādhis. They have been explained, will be explained, and are now explained by all buddhas of the past, the future, and the present. If bodhisattvas delight in, esteem, and tirelessly cultivate them, then they will succeed in perfecting them. A person such as this is then known as a buddha, is then known as a *tathāgata,* is also then known as a person who has acquired the ten powers, is also known as a master guide, is also known as a great master guide, is also known as omniscient, is also known as all-seeing, is also known as abiding in the unimpeded, is also known as comprehending all spheres of experience, and is also known as having sovereign mastery in all dharmas. This bodhisattva:

Everywhere enters all worlds and yet has no attachments in any world;

Everywhere enters all realms of beings and yet is free of any seizing on the existence of any being;

Everywhere enters all bodies and yet remains unimpeded by any body;

Everywhere enters the entire Dharma realm and yet knows the Dharma realm as boundless, draws close to all buddhas of the three periods of time, clearly perceives the Dharma of all buddhas, skillfully speaks in all languages, fully comprehends all conventional designations, perfects the pure path of all bodhisattvas, and securely abides in all the different practices of all bodhisattvas, and in but a single mind-moment, he:

Everywhere acquires all-knowledge of the three periods of time;

Everywhere knows all dharmas of the three periods of time;

Everywhere expounds on the teachings of all buddhas;

Everywhere turns the irreversible wheel of Dharma;

Everywhere realizes all paths leading to bodhi in every world throughout the past, the future, and the present; and

Everywhere comprehends the utterances of all buddhas regarding every one of these types of bodhi.

These constitute:

The gateways to all characteristics of the dharmas of all bodhisattvas;

The gateways to the knowledge and awakening of bodhisattvas;

The gateways to the banner of invincibility of the knowledge of all modes;

The gateways to all of Samantabhadra's conduct and vows;
The gateways to especially sharp spiritual superknowledges and vows;
The gateways to all the complete-retention [*dhāraṇīs*] and eloquence;
The gateways to the distinctions among all dharmas of the three periods of time;
The gateways to all the manifestations of all buddhas;
The gateways to establishing all beings with all-knowledge; and
The gateways to purifying all worlds with the Buddha's spiritual powers.

If the bodhisattva enters these samādhis:

He acquires inexhaustible powers within the Dharma realm;
He acquires unimpeded travel through empty space;
He acquires the measureless sovereign powers of the position of the Dharma King just like someone in the world who receives the summit-anointing consecration;
He acquires boundless wisdom by which he has a penetrating comprehension of all things;
He acquires ten types of complete fulfillment of vast powers;
He perfects the mind of noncontentiousness;
He penetrates to the very bounds of quiescence;
He acquires great compassion and fearlessness like that of a lion;
He becomes a greatly wise man who lights the bright lamp of right Dharma;
He becomes possessed of meritorious qualities which praises could never reach the end of and which no *śrāvaka* disciple or *pratyekabuddha* could even conceive of;
He acquires the wisdom of the Dharma realm;
He abides at the very bounds of motionlessness and yet is still able to use all kinds of different discourse to accord with mundane conventions;
He abides in signlessness even as he skillfully penetrates the characteristic signs of dharmas;
He acquires the treasury of the pure individual nature and is born into the pure family of the Tathāgata;
He skillfully opens the many different kinds of Dharma gateways even as, by resort to wisdom, he completely realizes that none of them exist;
He is skillful in knowing the right time as he constantly practices the giving of Dharma, awakens everyone, and becomes renowned as a sage;

He everywhere gathers in beings and enables them all to attain purity;

He uses his knowledge of skillful means to demonstrate the attainment of buddhahood, and yet he still always and endlessly cultivates the bodhisattva practices;

He enters the sphere of expedient means for the attainment of all-knowledge; and

He manifests many different kinds of vast spiritual superknowledges.

Therefore, Samantabhadra, you should now clearly distinguish and extensively explain the ten great samādhis of all bodhisattvas. Everyone in this congregation now wishes to hear this.

Then, having received the Tathāgata's instructions, Samantabhadra Bodhisattva regarded Universal Eye and the other bodhisattvas in that multitude and said to them:

Sons of the Buddha, what then is meant by the bodhisattva-mahāsattva's "samādhi of universal light"? Sons of the Buddha, this bodhisattva-mahāsattva has ten kinds of inexhaustible dharmas. What are those ten? They are:

Inexhaustible knowledge of all buddhas' appearances in the world;

Inexhaustible knowledge of beings' transformations;

Inexhaustible knowledge of the world as like mere reflections;

Inexhaustible knowledge of deep entry into the Dharma realm;

Inexhaustible knowledge of how to skillfully gather in bodhisattvas;

Inexhaustible knowledge of the bodhisattva's irreversibility;

Inexhaustible knowledge of skillfully contemplating the meanings of all dharmas;

Inexhaustible knowledge of skillfully preserving the powers of the mind;

Inexhaustible knowledge of abiding in the vast bodhi resolve; and

Inexhaustible knowledge of abiding in the dharmas of all buddhas and in the power of the vow to attain all-knowledge.

Sons of the Buddha, these are the bodhisattva-mahāsattva's ten inexhaustible dharmas.

Sons of the Buddha, this bodhisattva-mahāsattva makes ten kinds of boundless resolve. What are those ten? They are:

He makes the boundless resolve to liberate all beings;

He makes the boundless resolve to serve all buddhas;

He makes the boundless resolve to give offerings to all buddhas;

He makes the boundless resolve to everywhere see all buddhas;
He makes the boundless resolve to preserve all dharmas of the buddhas and never forget them;
He makes the boundless resolve to manifest the countless spiritual transformations of all buddhas;
He makes the boundless resolve to never relinquish any of the bodhi practices in order to acquire the powers of the Buddha;
He makes the boundless resolve to everywhere enter the subtle sphere of all-knowledge and expound on all dharmas of the Buddha;
He makes the boundless resolve to everywhere enter the inconceivably vast sphere of the Buddha;
He makes the boundless resolve to arouse the deep aspiration to acquire the Buddha's eloquence and receive all dharmas of the Buddha; and
He makes the boundless resolve to manifest the many different kinds of bodies possessed of sovereign powers and enter the sites of enlightenment and congregations of all *tathāgatas*.

These are the ten.[274]

Sons of the Buddha, this bodhisattva-mahāsattva has ten kinds of knowledge of different ways of entering samādhi. What are these ten? They are [knowledge with regard to]:

Entering samādhi in the east and emerging in the west;
Entering samādhi in the west and emerging in the east;
Entering samādhi in the south and emerging in the north;
Entering samādhi in the north and emerging in the south;
Entering samādhi in the northeast and emerging in the southwest;
Entering samādhi in the southwest and emerging in the northeast;
Entering samādhi in the northwest and emerging in the southeast;
Entering samādhi in the southeast and emerging in the northwest;
Entering samādhi in the nadir and emerging in the zenith; and
Entering samādhi in the zenith and emerging in the nadir.

These are the ten.

Sons of the Buddha, this bodhisattva-mahāsattva has ten kinds of knowledge of skillful means in entering the great samādhis. What are these ten? Sons of the Buddha:

The bodhisattva-mahāsattva forms a great trichiliocosm into a single lotus flower;
He manifests a body that sits in the full lotus posture atop this lotus flower, covering its entire upper surface;
Within his body, he further manifests a trichiliocosm;

Within it are a hundred *koṭīs* of fourfold continents;
On every one of those continents, he manifests a hundred *koṭīs* of bodies;
Every one of those bodies enters into a hundred *koṭīs* times a hundred *koṭīs* of great trichiliocosms;
On every one of those worlds' fourfold continents, he manifests a hundred *koṭīs* times a hundred *koṭīs* of bodhisattvas engaged in cultivation;
Every one of those cultivating bodhisattvas produces a hundred *koṭīs* times a hundred *koṭīs* of kinds of definite understanding;
Every one of those instances of definite understanding enables the complete fulfillment of a hundred *koṭīs* times a hundred *koṭīs* of fundamental natures; and
Every one of those fundamental natures accomplishes a hundred *koṭīs* times a hundred *koṭīs* of irreversible implementations of the bodhisattva's Dharma.

In this circumstance, the bodies that he manifests are neither one nor many and there is no error in any instance of their entering samādhi or emerging from samādhi.

Sons of the Buddha, this is like the case of Rāhu, the king of the *asuras*. His original body is seven hundred *yojanas* tall. He manifests a form one hundred and sixty-eight thousand *yojanas* tall that, when it stands in the ocean, half of his body extends above the surface of the water to a height precisely equal to that of Mount Sumeru.

Sons of the Buddha, although that king of the *asuras* transformationally manifests a body one hundred and sixty-eight thousand *yojanas* in height, this still does not damage any of the features of his original body, for all of its aggregates, sense realms, and sense bases all remain just as they originally were. Nor does his mind then make mistakes, for it does not conceive of that transformationally created body as "other," nor does it somehow regard his original body as no longer his own.

The body he originally received at birth is constantly enjoying every sort of pleasure even as his transformation body is forever manifesting all different kinds of sovereign mastery in the use of the awesome powers of the spiritual superknowledges.

Sons of the Buddha, although the *asura* king is possessed of greed, hatred, and delusion and is full of arrogance and pride, he is still able to transform his body in ways such as these. How much the more so then would a bodhisattva-mahāsattva be able to reach a deep and complete comprehension of the mind and dharmas as being like mere conjurations, the entire world as being like a dream, all buddhas coming forth into the world as being like reflected images, all worlds as being like transformationally created phenomena, and speech and sounds as being like mere echoes.

He perceives dharmas in accordance with reality and takes dharmas accordant with reality as constituting his own body. He realizes all dharmas are possessed of a fundamentally pure nature and completely realizes that both body and mind are devoid of any genuine substantiality. His bodies everywhere abide in countless realms as, using the vast radiance of the Buddha's wisdom, he purifies and cultivates all the practices leading to bodhi.

Sons of the Buddha, when the bodhisattva-mahāsattva abides in this samādhi, he so transcends the world and becomes so detached from the world that no one can disturb him and no one can overpower him.

Sons of the Buddha, just as when a bhikshu contemplates the inside of the body and abides in the meditative contemplation of impurity[275] in which he explores his own body and sees that his body is entirely impure, so too it is with the bodhisattva-mahāsattva when he abides in this samādhi. As he contemplates the Dharma body, he sees all worlds as entering into his own body and thus clearly sees all worlds and all worldly dharmas inside of it, this even as he remains free of any attachment to any worlds or any worldly dharmas.

Sons of the Buddha, this is what constitutes the knowledge of skillful means as it relates to the bodhisattva-mahāsattva's first great samādhi, "the great samādhi of universal light."

What then is meant by the bodhisattva-mahāsattva's "samādhi of sublime light"? Sons of the Buddha, this bodhisattva-mahāsattva is able to enter great trichiliocosms as numerous as the atoms in a great trichiliocosm in which he is able to manifest in every one of those worlds bodies as numerous as the atoms in a great trichiliocosm, causing every one of those bodies to emanate light rays as numerous as the atoms in a great trichiliocosm, causing every one of those light rays to manifest colors as numerous as the atoms in a great trichiliocosm, every one of which colors illuminates worlds as numerous as the atoms in a trichiliocosm. He is able in every one of those worlds to train beings as numerous as the atoms in a great trichiliocosm.

The bodhisattva knows the many kinds of differences in all these worlds, in particular knowing these worlds' defilement, these worlds' purity, these worlds' causes, these worlds' establishment, these worlds' coexistence, these worlds' radiance and colors, and these worlds' comings and goings. The bodhisattva knows all matters such as these. The bodhisattva enters all these worlds and they all also come and enter the bodhisattva's body, doing so without any intermixing or disorderliness occurring in any of these worlds, and doing so without any destruction occurring in any of these many different phenomena.

Sons of the Buddha, this circumstance is analogous to when the sun comes forth and circles around Mount Sumeru, illuminating the seven jeweled mountains. As this occurs, those seven jeweled mountains and the areas in between those jeweled mountains all manifest reflections that all appear clearly. Of all those reflections of the sun from the mountains, none fail to appear in the reflections appearing in the areas between the mountains. All the reflections of the sun in the areas between those seven mountains also appear in the reflections on the mountains. In this way, they continuously beam reflections back and forth on each other.

One could say that the sun's reflections come forth from the seven jeweled mountains, could say that the sun's reflections come forth from the area between the mountains, could say that the sun's reflections enter the seven jeweled mountains, or could say that the sun's reflections enter the areas between the seven mountains, yet, in these circumstances, these reflections from the sun cause each of them to illuminate each other, doing so boundlessly in this way, even as any substantial nature in them is neither existent nor nonexistent. They do not abide either on the mountains or apart from the mountains and do not abide in the waters or apart from the waters.

Sons of the Buddha, so too it is with the bodhisattva-mahāsattva. As he abides in this vast "samādhi of sublime light," he does not interfere with any of the features established in the world, does not alter the nature of any of the world's dharmas, does not abide within the world, does not abide outside of the world, is free of all discriminations regarding the world, and also does not interfere with any of the features of the world. He contemplates all dharmas as possessed of a single sign, that of being signless, this as he also does not interfere with the nature of any dharmas. He abides in the nature of true suchness and never departs from it.

Sons of the Buddha, this circumstance is analogous to that of a conjurer skilled in the techniques of conjuration who, at a crossroads, manifests all kinds of conjured phenomena in which he is able to manifest in but a single moment on a single given day the appearance of the events of a whole day, a whole night, seven days and seven nights, a half-month, a full month, a year, or a hundred years, being freely able as befits his wishes to conjure a city, a village, a spring, creek, river, or ocean, the sun, the moon, the clouds, the rain, palaces, buildings, homes, all such things as these, none of which are not completely manifested there. In doing this, no interference occurs between the originally existing day or hour and the conjuration's apparent passage of years. Nor is it the case that the extreme brevity and rapidity of that originally existent time frame interferes in the least with the conjuration's manifestation of the passing of a day, a month, a year, or years. The conjuration's images appear there clearly even as that original day's time duration is not somehow thereby ruined.

So too it is with this bodhisattva-mahāsattva who enters this vast "samādhi of sublime light" who brings forth the appearance of an *asaṃkhyeya* of worlds entering one of those worlds. Every one of those *asaṃkhyeyas* of worlds is possessed of earth, water, fire, and wind, the great seas and mountains, cities and villages, parks, forests, buildings and houses, celestial palaces and dragon palaces, *yakṣa* palaces, *gandharva* palaces, *asura* palaces, *garuḍa* palaces, *kiṃnara* palaces, and *mahoraga* palaces, all of which are entirely complete in all of their many different kinds of adornments.

They appear complete with desire realms, form realms, formless realms, small chiliocosms, large chiliocosms, karmic actions and their rewards and retributions, death in this place, rebirth in that place, all of the world's time periods consisting of instants, days and nights, half months, full months, single years, and centuries, the kalpas of creation, the kalpas of destruction, defiled lands, pure lands, vast lands, small lands, and lands with buddhas within them manifesting their appearances in the world in buddha *kṣetras* that are pure, attended there by congregations of bodhisattvas gathered around them as, with sovereign mastery in the spiritual superknowledges, they engage in the teaching of beings.

The places in which those lands are located are all full of populations of countless people. All the different kinds of beings of different forms and various destinies are countlessly, boundlessly, and inconceivably numerous. The power of pure karma of the past, future, and present produces countless supremely marvelous precious jewels. All kinds of phenomena such as these appear as entering a single world.

The bodhisattva clearly observes all these phenomena, enters them all, contemplates them all, reflects on them all, completely understands them all, and, with his inexhaustible wisdom, understands them all in accordance with reality.

In this circumstance, it is not the case that the multiplicity of those many worlds somehow interferes with [perceiving] the integrity of this one world, nor is it the case that the integrity of this one world somehow interferes with [perceiving] the multiplicity of those many worlds. And how is this so? It is because this bodhisattva realizes all dharmas are devoid of any inherent self-existence. Hence he is known as one who has penetrated the dharma of the nonexistence of a life span and the dharma of the nonexistence of anything at all that is created.

Because this bodhisattva diligently cultivates the dharma of noncontentiousness in all worlds, he is known as one who abides in the dharma of the nonexistence of anything constituting a self. Because this bodhisattva perceives in accordance with reality that all bodies are created from conditions, he is known as one who abides in the dharma of the nonexistence of anything constituting a being. Because this bodhisattva realizes that all dharmas that are produced and destroyed arise from causes, he is known as one who abides in the dharma of the nonexistence of anything constituting a *pudgala*.[276] Because this bodhisattva realizes that the fundamental nature of all dharmas is the same, he is known as one who abides in the dharma of the nonexistence of anything constituting a human being[277] or a *māṇava*.[278] Because this bodhisattva realizes that the fundamental nature of all dharmas is quiescent, he is known as one who abides in the dharma of quiescence. Because this bodhisattva realizes that all dharmas have but a single sign, he is known as one who abides in the dharma of nondiscrimination. Because this bodhisattva realizes that the Dharma realm is devoid of any of the many different kinds of dharmas, he is known as one who abides in the dharma of the inconceivable. Because this bodhisattva diligently cultivates all skillful means and skillfully trains beings, he is known as one who abides in the dharma of great compassion.

Sons of the Buddha, it is in this way that the bodhisattva is able to place *asaṃkhyeyas* of worlds into a single world. He knows all the different kinds of distinctions among the countlessly many beings, sees every one of the innumerable bodhisattvas setting forth [on the bodhisattva path], and contemplates innumerable buddhas appearing in the world in place after place. All those bodhisattvas are able to receive all the Dharma expounded by all those *tathāgatas* and they also see themselves cultivating among them. Even so, they never leave this place to see themselves in that place and never leave that place to see themselves in this place. Those bodies and this body are no different, for he has entered the Dharma realm. He is always and incessantly diligent in meditative contemplation and never relinquishes his wisdom for he has become one who is irreversible [on the path].

Just as when a conjurer performs a conjuration in any particular place, in conjuring some illusory spot of earth, he does not destroy his original spot of earth on which he stood, and in conjuring some other illusory day, he does not destroy the original day in which he existed, so too it is with the bodhisattva-mahāsattva when he manifests a land's existence where no land exists, manifests the nonexistence of a land where a land does exist, manifests the nonexistence of a being where a being does exist, manifests the existence of a being where no being exists, manifests the appearance of forms where no forms exist, or manifests the nonexistence of forms where forms do exist. In doing so, does not allow the former circumstance to interfere with the latter circumstance and does not allow the latter circumstance to interfere with the former circumstance.

The bodhisattva's complete understanding of all worldly dharmas is just like this, for he knows them all to be the same as illusory conjurations. Because he knows the illusory nature of dharmas, he knows the illusory nature of knowledge. Because he knows the illusory nature of knowledge, he knows the illusory nature of karmic deeds. Having come to know the illusory nature of knowledge and the illusory nature of karmic deeds, he then brings forth that illusion-perceiving wisdom with which he contemplates all karmic deeds.

Just as when a conjurer produces illusions in the world, it is not the case that he manifests such illusions somewhere outside of his current location nor is it the case that the current location is somewhere outside of the conjured illusion, so too it is with the bodhisattva-mahāsattva for whom it is not the case that he enters worlds somewhere outside of empty space. Nor is it the case that he enters empty space somewhere beyond the world.

Why is this the case? This is because empty space[279] and the world are no different. As he abides in the world, he also abides in empty space. In the midst of empty space, the bodhisattva-mahāsattva is still able to see and is still able to cultivate all of his many different marvelously adorning karmic deeds in all worlds.

In but a single mind-moment, he is able to completely know with regard to innumerable worlds their creations and their destructions while also knowing with regard to all kalpas their continuity and sequences. He is able to manifest innumerable kalpas in a single mind-moment even as he still does not cause that single mind-moment to become vastly long.

The bodhisattva-mahāsattva reaches the far shore of perfection in the attainment of inconceivable liberations and illusion-perceiving knowledge. He abides at the very boundary of the illusory and enters the analytical knowledge[280] of the world's illusory nature. He reflects upon all dharmas as illusory, does not oppose the illusory world, and attains the ultimate in illusion-perceiving knowledge within it.

He completely realizes that the three periods of time are no different from an illusory conjuration and has a definite penetrating comprehension of the mind as boundless. Just as all *tathāgatas* abide with equanimous minds in the wisdom that perceives the illusion-like nature of phenomena, so too it is with the bodhisattva-mahāsattva. He knows that all worlds are like illusory conjurations and, wherever he is, he remains free of attachment and free of anything he considers to be "mine."

In this, he is just like that conjurer in his creation of illusory phenomena for whom, although he does not abide with those illusory phenomena, he still remains free of any confusion regarding those illusory phenomena. So too it is with this bodhisattva-mahāsattva, for his realization of the nature of all dharmas has reached the farthest shore of perfection in which his mind does not impute the existence of any "self." He is able to enter into dharmas, and yet he remains free of any error or confusion with regard to any dharmas. This is what constitutes the knowledge of skillful means as it relates to the bodhisattva-mahāsattva's second great samādhi, "the great samādhi of sublime light."

Sons of the Buddha, what then is meant by the bodhisattva-mahāsattva's "spiritual superknowledge samādhi of sequential visitation of all buddha lands everywhere"? Sons of the Buddha, this bodhisattva-mahāsattva goes past countless worlds to the east and then, additionally goes on beyond a number of worlds as numerous as the atoms in all those worlds, entering this samādhi in all those worlds:

Perhaps entering for a *kṣaṇa;*
Perhaps entering for a moment;
Perhaps entering continuously;
Perhaps entering for the first part of the day;
Perhaps entering for the middle part of the day;
Perhaps entering for the final part of the day;
Perhaps entering for the first part of the night;
Perhaps entering for the middle part of the night;

Perhaps entering for the final part of the night;
Perhaps entering for an entire day;
Perhaps entering for five days;
Perhaps entering for a half-month;
Perhaps entering for an entire month;
Perhaps entering for an entire year;
Perhaps entering for a hundred years;
Perhaps entering for a thousand years;
Perhaps entering for a hundred thousand years;
Perhaps entering for a *koṭī* of years;
Perhaps entering for a hundred thousand *koṭīs* of years;
Perhaps entering for a hundred thousand *nayutas* of *koṭīs* of years;
Perhaps entering for an entire kalpa;
Perhaps entering for a hundred kalpas;
Perhaps entering for a hundred thousand kalpas;
Perhaps entering for a hundred thousand *nayutas* of *koṭīs* of kalpas;
Perhaps entering for numberless kalpas
Perhaps entering for measurelessly many kalpas;
Perhaps entering for boundlessly many kalpas;
Perhaps entering for incomparably many kalpas
Perhaps entering for innumerably many kalpas;
Perhaps entering for indescribably many kalpas;
Perhaps entering for inconceivably many kalpas;
Perhaps entering for immeasurably many kalpas;
Perhaps entering for an ineffable number of kalpas; or
Perhaps entering for an ineffable-ineffable number of kalpas.

Whether it is with respect to its long duration or short duration or to the dharmas or the timing, there are many different distinctions in this. In all those circumstances, the bodhisattva makes no discriminations and his mind remains free of any defiling attachments. He does not impute duality or non-duality, does not impute universality and does not impute uniqueness. Although he abandons these kinds of discriminations, he still uses skillful means involving the spiritual superknowledges so that, when he emerges from this samādhi, he does not ever forget or lose any of its dharmas. In this, he is like the solar *devaputra*, the sun, which goes around on a cycle of illumination, never stopping, day or night. When the sun rises, this is designated as "daytime," and when the sun sets, this is designated as "nighttime." It is neither born in [the beginning of] the day nor dies at night. When this bodhisattva-mahāsattva has been abiding within this spiritual superknowledge samādhi in countless worlds and then finishes with that period of abiding in samādhi, his still continuing to clearly behold all of those countlessly many worlds is a matter of this very same sort.

Sons of the Buddha, this is what constitutes the knowledge of skillful means as it relates to the bodhisattva-mahāsattva's third great samādhi, "the great spiritual superknowledge samādhi of visitation to all buddha lands everywhere."

Sons of the Buddha, what then is meant by the bodhisattva-mahāsattva's "samādhi of pure and deep-minded practice"? Sons of the Buddha, this bodhisattva-mahāsattva knows that the number of buddhas is equal to the number of other beings. He sees countless buddhas more numerous than the atoms in an *asaṃkhyeya* of worlds and, wherever those *tathāgatas* are:

He makes offerings to them of all different kinds of marvelous incense;
He makes offerings to them of all different kinds of marvelous flowers;
He makes offerings to them of all different kinds of canopies as large as an *asaṃkhyeya* of buddha *kṣetras;*
He makes offerings to them of all different kinds of supremely marvelous adornments surpassing those in all worlds;
He makes offerings to them by scattering all different kinds of jewels;
He makes offerings to them of all different kinds of adornments to beautify those places where they practice walking meditation;
He makes offerings to them of all kinds of treasuries containing countless supremely marvelous *maṇi* jewels; and
He makes offerings to them of superior flavors of beverages and foods flowing from the Buddha's spiritual powers which surpass even those in the heavens.

He is able to use spiritual powers to everywhere gather together all different kinds of supremely marvelous offering gifts from all buddha *kṣetras* to then use in making offerings. To every one of those *tathāgatas,* he pays respects and honors them, bowing his head down to the ground in reverence as he prostrates his entire body before them, poses questions about the dharmas of the Buddha, praises the impartiality of the Buddha, extols all buddhas' vast meritorious qualities, enters the great compassion entered by all buddhas, acquires the Buddha's equal and unimpeded powers, and, in but a single mind-moment, earnestly seeks the sublime Dharma from all buddhas.

In so doing, he finds nothing at all that is apprehensible [as inherently existent] in such signs[281] [in the lives] of the buddhas as their appearing in the world or entering *parinirvāṇa*. Just as when someone with a scattered mind distinguishes objective conditions, he might remain unable to know due to which conditions thoughts arise when they arise and due to which conditions thoughts are extinguished when they are extinguished, so too it is with this bodhisattva, for he never makes discriminations regarding the signs associated with the Tathāgata's appearance in the world or his entering nirvāṇa.

Sons of the Buddha, this circumstance is analogous to that of a mirage which does not come forth from the clouds, does not come forth from a pond, does not abide on the land, does not abide in the waters, is neither existent nor nonexistent, is neither good nor bad, is neither clear nor turbid, cannot be drunk, cannot be made dirty, is neither substantial nor insubstantial, and is neither possessed of flavor nor flavorless. Still, due to its particular causes and conditions, when it is perceived by the consciousness, it presents the appearance of water. Hence, when one looks at it from a great distance, perceptions arise imagining there to be water in the distance. Yet, when one draws closer, that appearance no longer manifests and the perceptions imagining the existence of water naturally cease. So too it is in the case of the bodhisattva-mahāsattva, for he remains unable to apprehend [any inherent existence] in the signs such as the Tathāgata's appearing in the world or entering nirvāṇa. The [perceptions of] the existence or nonexistence of the signs of all buddhas' [appearance in the world] all arise from discriminations made by the perceiving mind.

Sons of the Buddha, this samādhi is known as "the samādhi of pure and deep-minded practice." When, after having entered this samādhi, this bodhisattva-mahāsattva subsequently emerges from it, he does not lose what he has experienced within it. This is analogous to when a person awakens from sleeping and remembers the events in his dreams. Although, once he has awakened, those spheres of experience associated with the dream no longer exist, he is still able to recall them because his mind does not forget them.

So too it is with this bodhisattva-mahāsattva. When he enters this samādhi, he sees the Buddha and hears the Dharma. When he emerges from meditative absorption, he remembers these experiences, does not forget them, and then uses them in instructing the congregations in all those sites of enlightenment and in adorning all those buddha lands. He acquires a clear comprehension of countless meanings and their import, purifies all the gateways to the Dharma, lights the wisdom torch, extends the lineage of the buddhas, and becomes completely endowed with fearlessness and inexhaustible eloquence with which he explains and expounds upon the extremely deep treasury of Dharma.

This is what constitutes the knowledge of skillful means as it relates to the bodhisattva-mahāsattva's fourth great samādhi, "the great samādhi of pure and deep-minded practice."

What then is meant by the bodhisattva-mahāsattva's "samādhi of the knowledge of the treasury of past adornments"? Sons of the Buddha, the bodhisattva-mahāsattva is able to know the appearance in the world of the buddhas of the past, in particular knowing:

The sequence of all *kṣetras* within the sequence of kalpas;
The sequence of kalpas within the sequence of *kṣetras;*
The sequence of the buddhas' appearances in the world within the sequence of kalpas;
The sequence of discourses on the Dharma as they occur in the midst of the sequence of buddhas' appearances in the world;
The sequence in the arising of earnest aspirations as they arise during the sequence of discourses on the Dharma;
The sequence in the [development of] faculties within the sequence of earnest aspirations;
The sequence of training within the sequence in the [development of] faculties;
The sequence in the life spans of all buddhas within the sequence of training; and
The sequence of knowing *koṭīs* of *nayutas* of durations in years within the sequence of those life spans.

Sons of the Buddha, because this bodhisattva-mahāsattva acquires knowledge with respect to boundlessly many sequences such as these:

He then knows the buddhas of the past;
He then knows the *kṣetras* of the past;
He then knows the Dharma gateways of the past;
He then knows the kalpas of the past;
He then knows the dharmas of the past;
He then knows the minds of the past;
He then knows the understandings of the past;
He then knows the beings of the past;
He then knows the afflictions of the past;
He then knows the ceremonial protocols of the past; and

He then knows the purity of the past.

Sons of the Buddha, this samādhi is known as "the treasury of past pure [adornments]" in which, in but a single mind-moment:

He is able to enter a hundred kalpas;
He is able to enter a thousand kalpas;
He is able to enter a hundred thousand kalpas;
He is able to enter a hundred thousand *koṭīs* of *nayutas* of kalpas;
He is able to enter a numberless number kalpas;
He is able to enter a measureless number of kalpas;
He is able to enter a boundless number of kalpas;
He is able to enter an incomparable number of kalpas;
He is able to enter an innumerable number of kalpas;
He is able to enter an indescribable number of kalpas;
He is able to enter an inconceivable number of kalpas;
He is able to enter an incalculable number of kalpas;
He is able to enter an ineffable number of kalpas; and
He is able to enter an ineffable-ineffable number of kalpas.

Sons of the Buddha, when that bodhisattva-mahāsattva enters this samādhi, it is not that he extinguishes the present and it is not that he then takes the past as an objective condition. Sons of the Buddha, when that bodhisattva emerges from this samādhi, he receives ten kinds of inconceivable crown-anointing consecration dharmas from the Tathāgata which he acquires, purifies, perfects, enters, realizes, fulfills, upholds, and equally and completely knows while maintaining purity of the three factors.[282] What are these ten? They are:

First, He speaks with eloquence that does not contradict its meaning;
Second, he is inexhaustible in teaching the Dharma;
Third, his teachings are impeccable;
Fourth, he is incessantly eloquent;
Fifth, his mind is free of fear;
Sixth, his speech is definitely truthful;
Seventh, he is relied on by beings;
Eighth, he rescues and liberates the beings in the three realms of existence;
Ninth, he possesses the most supreme roots of goodness; and
Tenth, he provides training and guidance in the sublime Dharma.

Sons of the Buddha, these are ten types of dharmas associated with receiving this crown-anointing consecration. When a bodhisattva enters this samādhi, upon emerging from this samādhi, he instantly attains them just as, when a *kalala*[283] enters the womb, its consciousness takes birth in it in but a single mind-moment. So too it is with the bodhisattva-mahāsattva, for, when he emerges from this samādhi, in but a single mind-moment, he acquires these ten kinds of dharmas from the Tathāgata.

Sons of the Buddha, this is what constitutes the knowledge of skillful means as it relates to the bodhisattva-mahāsattva's fifth great samādhi, "the great samādhi of the knowledge of the treasury of past adornments."

Sons of the Buddha, what then is meant by the bodhisattva-mahāsattva's "samādhi of a treasury of wisdom light"? Sons of the Buddha, when that bodhisattva-mahāsattva abides in this samādhi, he is able to know with respect to all buddhas in all worlds in all kalpas of the future their various names, each of which are different, whether they have already commenced their proclamations or have not yet commenced their proclamations, and whether they have already received their predictions or have not yet received their predictions, in particular knowing:

Their countlessly many names;
Their measurelessly many names;
Their boundlessly many names;
Their incomparably many names;
Their innumerably many names;
Their indescribably many names;
Their inconceivably many names;
Their incalculably many names;
Their ineffably many names;
That they will appear in the world;
That they will benefit beings;
That they will serve as Dharma kings;
That they will accomplish the buddha works;
That they will proclaim the benefit of merit;
That they will praise the meaningfulness of goodness;
That they will explain the meaningfulness of purity;[284]
That they will purify all kinds of evil;
That they will establish themselves in meritorious qualities;
That they will explain the ultimate truth;
That they will enter the position of the crown-anointing consecration;
That they will accomplish the realization of all-knowledge;
That those *tathāgatas* will cultivate the perfectly complete practices;

That they will make the perfectly complete vows;
That they will enter the perfectly complete wisdom;
That they will possess the perfectly complete community;
That they will become replete in the perfectly complete adornments;
That they will accumulate the perfectly complete meritorious qualities;
That they will awaken to the perfectly complete Dharma;
That they will attain the perfectly complete fruits [of the path];
That they will possess the perfectly complete signs; and
That they will achieve the perfectly complete enlightenment.

Those *tathāgatas'* names, clan lineages, skillful means, spiritual superknowledges, spiritual transformations, ripening of beings, entry into *parinirvāṇa*, and all other such matters—they will fully know them.

In but a single mind-moment, this bodhisattva is able:

To enter a single kalpa, a hundred kalpas, a thousand kalpas, a hundred thousand kalpas, or a hundred thousand *koṭīs* of *nayutas* of kalpas;
To enter kalpas as numerous as the atoms in the continent of Jambudvīpa;
To enter kalpas as numerous as the atoms in all four of the continents;
To enter kalpas as numerous as the atoms in a small chiliocosm;
To enter kalpas as numerous as the atoms in a chiliocosm;
To enter kalpas as numerous as the atoms in a great trichiliocosm;
To enter kalpas as numerous as the atoms in a buddha *kṣetra;*
To enter kalpas as numerous as the atoms in a hundred thousand buddha *kṣetras;*
To enter kalpas as numerous as the atoms in a hundred thousand *koṭīs* of *nayutas* of buddha *kṣetras;*
To enter kalpas as numerous as the atoms in numberless buddha *kṣetras;*
To enter kalpas as numerous as the atoms in a measureless number of buddha *kṣetras;*
To enter kalpas as numerous as the atoms in a boundless number of buddha *kṣetras;*
To enter kalpas as numerous as the atoms in an incomparable number of buddha *kṣetras;*
To enter kalpas as numerous as the atoms in an innumerable number of buddha *kṣetras;*

To enter kalpas as numerous as the atoms in an indescribable number of buddha *kṣetras;*

To enter kalpas as numerous as the atoms in an inconceivable number of buddha *kṣetras';*

To enter kalpas as numerous as the atoms in an immeasurable number of buddha *kṣetras;*

To enter kalpas as numerous as the atoms in an ineffable number of buddha *kṣetras';* and

To enter kalpas as numerous as the atoms in an ineffable-ineffable number of buddha *kṣetras.*

In this way, he is able to use his wisdom to fully know the number of kalpas in all future worlds. Because he completely knows them, his mind is also able to enter ten kinds of gateways to retention. What are those ten? They are:

Due to entering that of upholding the Buddha, he acquires the protective mindfulness of buddhas as numerous as the atoms in an ineffable number of buddha *kṣetras;*

Due to entering that of upholding the Dharma, he acquires the endless eloquence provided by the light of ten kinds of *dhāraṇīs;*

Due to entering that of upholding the practices, he achieves the complete fulfillment of especially supreme vows;

Due to entering that of upholding the powers, he becomes one whom no one can overcome or vanquish;

Due to entering that of upholding wisdom, he becomes free of obstacles in whichever buddha dharmas he practices;

Due to entering that of upholding the great compassion, he turns the irreversible wheel of the pure Dharma;

Due to entering that of upholding the different skillful expedient statements, he turns the wheel of all language and words and purifies the ground of all Dharma gateways;

Due to entering that of upholding the dharma of the lion's birth, he is able to open the Dharma's gate lock and escape from the mire of desires;

Due to entering that of upholding the wisdom powers, he never rests in his cultivation of the bodhisattva practices;

Due to entering that of upholding the power of the good spiritual guide, he is able to enable boundlessly many beings to become purified;

Due to entering that of upholding the power of non-abiding, he enters an ineffable-ineffable number of vast kalpas; and

Due to entering that of upholding the power of Dharma, he uses unimpeded skillful means and wisdom to realize the purity of all dharmas' inherent nature.[285]

Sons of the Buddha, after this bodhisattva-mahāsattva has come to abide in this samādhi:

He skillfully abides in an ineffable-ineffable number of kalpas;
He skillfully abides in an ineffable-ineffable number of *kṣetras;*
He skillfully knows an ineffable-ineffable number of different kinds of beings;
He skillfully knows an ineffable-ineffable number of beings' different characteristics;
He skillfully knows an ineffable-ineffable number of identical and different karmic retributions;
He skillfully knows an ineffable-ineffable number of different practices as they relate to vigor, individual faculties, habitual karmic propensities, and continuity;
He skillfully knows an ineffable-ineffable number of beings' countless different kinds of defiled and pure ways of thinking;
He skillfully knows an ineffable-ineffable number of ways of expressing the Dharma's many different meanings with countless ways of using the language of the texts to expound upon them;
He skillfully knows an ineffable-ineffable number of buddhas' many different appearances [in the world], their clan lineages, their times, their manifestations of signs, their teaching of the Dharma, their accomplishing of buddha works, and their entry into *parinirvāṇa;*
He skillfully knows an ineffable-ineffable number of gateways of boundless wisdom; and
He skillfully knows an ineffable-ineffable number of the countless transformations manifested with all the spiritual superknowledges.

Sons of the Buddha, it is just as when the sun rises, all the world's many different sorts of things such as the villages and encampments, cities and towns, palaces and houses, mountains and swamps, birds and beasts, trees and groves, and flowers and fruit are then clearly seen by anyone who has eyes. Sons of the Buddha, the sunlight shines equally on everything without discriminating and thus it is able to allow the eyes to see the many different appearances of these phenomena.

So too it is with this great samādhi. Its essential nature is one of impartiality and nondiscrimination by which it is able to allow the bodhisattva to know an ineffable-ineffable number of hundreds of thousands of *koṭīs* of *nayutas* of different signs. Sons of the Buddha, when this bodhisattva-mahāsattva possesses such complete knowing of this sort he enables all beings to acquire ten kinds of fruitfulness.[286] What are those ten? They are:

First, the fruitfulness of seeing him by which he enables beings to produce roots of goodness;

Second, the fruitfulness of being heard by which he enables beings to become ripened;

Third, the fruitfulness of abiding together with him by which he enables beings' minds to become trained;

Fourth, the fruitfulness of starting out by which he enables beings to act in accordance with their statements and gain a penetrating comprehension of the meaning of all dharmas;

Fifth, the fruitfulness of practice by which he enables the purification of boundlessly many worlds;

Sixth, the fruitfulness of drawing near by which, in the presence of an ineffable-ineffable number of buddhas, he severs the doubts of an ineffable-ineffable number of beings;

Seventh, the fruitfulness of vows by which he enables all beings of whom he is mindful to make supreme offerings and thus accomplish all their vows;

Eighth, the fruitfulness of skillful expedient dharmas by which he enables everyone to succeed in abiding in unimpeded liberations and pure wisdom;

Ninth, the fruitfulness of raining the Dharma rain by which, among beings possessed of an ineffable-ineffable number of various faculties, he uses skillful means to explain the practices leading to all-knowledge, thus enabling them to abide in the path to buddhahood; and

Tenth, the fruitfulness of his manifestations by which he manifests boundlessly many signs by which he enables all beings to receive his illumination.

Sons of the Buddha, when this bodhisattva-mahāsattva abides in this samādhi and [those beings] gain these ten kinds of fruitfulness:

The heavenly kings and their congregations all come and bow down in reverence to him;

The dragon kings and their congregations spread great clouds of incense all about;

The *yakṣa* kings prostrate themselves in reverence at his feet;

The *asura* kings present respectful offerings to him;

The *garuḍa* kings circumambulate him;

The Brahma Heaven kings all come and present their invitations to speak the Dharma;

The *kiṃnara* kings and the *mahoraga* kings all utter praises in unison.
The *gandharva* kings always come and draw near to him; and
The human kings and their congregations serve him and make offerings to him.

Sons of the Buddha, this is what constitutes the knowledge of skillful means as it relates to the bodhisattva-mahāsattva's sixth great samādhi, "the great samādhi of a treasury of wisdom light."

Sons of the Buddha, what then is meant by the bodhisattva-mahāsattva's "samādhi of the complete knowledge of all worlds' buddha adornments"? Sons of the Buddha, why is this samādhi called "the complete knowledge of all worlds' buddha adornments"?

Sons of the Buddha, the bodhisattva-mahāsattva who abides in this samādhi is able to successively enter the worlds to the east and is able to successively enter the worlds of the south, the west, the north, the four midpoints, the zenith, and the nadir. In this way, he is able to successively enter all worlds. In all of them:

He sees all buddhas appearing in the world;
He also sees all the spiritual powers of those buddhas;
He also sees all the feats of easeful mastery of all buddhas;
He also sees the vast awesome virtue of all buddhas;
He also sees the supreme sovereign masteries of all buddhas;
He also sees all buddhas' great lion's roar;
He also sees all the practices cultivated by all buddhas;
He also sees all the many different kinds of adornments of all buddhas;
He also sees all buddhas' supernatural psycho-spiritual powers and transformations; and
He also sees all buddhas' congregations gathering together like clouds, the purity of the congregations, the vastness of the congregations, the congregations' signs of unity, the congregations' signs of multiplicity, the dwelling places of the congregations, the abiding of the congregations, the ripening of the congregations, the training of the congregations, and the awesome virtue of the congregations.

He sees all things such as these with complete clarity. Moreover:

He also sees congregations equal in size to the continent of Jambudvīpa;
He also sees congregations equal in size to all four continents;
He also sees congregations equal in size to a small chiliocosm;
He also sees congregations equal in size to an intermediate chiliocosm;

He also sees congregations equal in size to a great trichiliocosm;
He also sees congregations that would fill a hundred thousand *koṭīs* of *nayutas* of buddha *kṣetras;*
He also sees congregations that would fill an *asaṃkhyeya* of buddha *kṣetras;*
He also sees congregations that would fill buddha *kṣetras* as numerous as the atoms in a hundred buddha *kṣetras;*
He also sees congregations that would fill buddha *kṣetras* as numerous as the atoms in a thousand buddha *kṣetras;*
He also sees congregations that would fill buddha *kṣetras* as numerous as the atoms in a hundred thousand *koṭīs* of *nayutas* of buddha *kṣetras;*
He also sees congregations that would fill buddha *kṣetras* as numerous as the atoms in a numberless number of buddha *kṣetras;*
He also sees congregations that would fill buddha *kṣetras* as numerous as the atoms in a measureless number of buddha *kṣetras;*
He also sees congregations that would fill buddha *kṣetras* as numerous as the atoms in a boundless number of buddha *kṣetras;*
He also sees congregations that would fill buddha *kṣetras* as numerous as the atoms in an incomparable number of buddha *kṣetras;*
He also sees congregations that would fill buddha *kṣetras* as numerous as the atoms in an innumerable number of buddha *kṣetras;*
He also sees congregations that would fill buddha *kṣetras* as numerous as the atoms in an unspeakable number of buddha *kṣetras;*
He also sees congregations that would fill buddha *kṣetras* as numerous as the atoms in an inconceivable number of buddha *kṣetras;*
He also sees congregations that would fill buddha *kṣetras* as numerous as the atoms in an immeasurable number of buddha *kṣetras;*
He also sees congregations that would fill buddha *kṣetras* as numerous as the atoms in an ineffable number of buddha *kṣetras;*
He also sees congregations that would fill buddha *kṣetras* as numerous as the atoms in an ineffable-ineffable number of buddha *kṣetras;* and

He also sees buddhas in those congregations' sites of enlightenment manifesting many different signs, many different times, many different lands, many different transformations, many different spiritual superknowledges, many different adornments, many different sovereign masteries, many different physical sizes, and many different works.

The bodhisattva-mahāsattva also sees himself going to those congregations, also sees himself speaking the Dharma in those places, also sees himself receiving and preserving the words of those buddhas, also sees himself there coming to thoroughly know conditioned arising, also sees himself there abiding in empty space, also sees himself abiding within the Dharma body, also sees himself refraining from developing defiling attachments, also sees himself refraining from abiding in discriminations, also sees himself remaining free of weariness, also sees himself everywhere penetrating all varieties of wisdom, also sees himself everywhere knowing all meanings, also sees himself everywhere entering all grounds, also sees himself everywhere entering all of the rebirth destinies, also sees himself everywhere knowing skillful means, also sees himself everywhere abiding in the presence of the buddhas, also sees himself everywhere entering all the powers, also sees himself everywhere entering true suchness, also sees himself everywhere entering noncontentiousness, and also sees himself everywhere entering all dharmas.

When he sees these things he does not make discriminations regarding lands, he does not make discriminations regarding beings, he does not make discriminations regarding buddhas, he does not make discriminations regarding dharmas, he does not become attached to the body, he does not become attached to the body's actions, he does not become attached to the mind, and he does not become attached to the intellectual mind.

Just as dharmas themselves do not make discriminations with regard to their own essential nature and do not make discriminations regarding sounds, and yet, even so, do not relinquish their own essential nature and do not thus experience the disappearance of their names, so too it is with the bodhisattva-mahāsattva. He does not relinquish the practices and adapts to what the world does, and yet he has no attachment to either of these two.

Sons of the Buddha, the bodhisattva-mahāsattva sees the Buddha's countless manifestations of light and color and his countless forms and signs that are completely perfected, equal, and pure, seeing every one of them directly before him, clearly evident and fully realized, perhaps seeing the many different kinds of light emanated by the Buddha's body, or seeing the fathom-wide aura of light surrounding the Buddha's body, or seeing the Buddha's body the color of the blazing sun, or seeing the sublime radiance and colors of the Buddha's body, or seeing the pure colors emanating from the Buddha's body, or seeing the Buddha's body when he makes it the color of yellow gold, or seeing the Buddha's body when he makes it the color of vajra, or seeing the Buddha's body when he makes it violet in color, or seeing the Buddha's body when he makes it manifest boundlessly many colors, or seeing the Buddha's body when he makes it the color of a sapphire, or seeing the Buddha's body as seven cubits tall, or seeing the Buddha's body as eight cubits tall, or seeing the Buddha's body as nine cubits tall, or seeing the Buddha's body as ten cubits tall, or seeing the Buddha's body as twenty cubits tall, or seeing the Buddha's body as thirty cubits tall or up to a hundred cubits tall or a thousand cubits tall, or seeing the Buddha's body as one *krośa*[287] tall, or seeing the Buddha's body as half a *yojana* tall, or seeing the Buddha's body as one *yojana* tall, or seeing the Buddha's body as ten *yojanas* tall, or seeing the Buddha's body as a hundred *yojanas* tall, or seeing the Buddha's body as a thousand *yojanas* tall, or seeing the Buddha's body as a hundred thousand *yojanas* tall, or seeing the Buddha's body as having the height of Jambudvīpa's breadth, or seeing the Buddha's body as having the height of all four continents' breadth, or seeing the Buddha's body as having the height of a small chiliocosm, or seeing the Buddha's body as having the height of an intermediate-sized chiliocosm, or seeing the Buddha's body as having the height of a great chiliocosm, or seeing the Buddha's body as having the height of a hundred great chiliocosms, or seeing the Buddha's body as having the height of a thousand great chiliocosms, or seeing the Buddha's body as having the height of a hundred thousand great chiliocosms, or seeing the Buddha's body as having the height of a hundred thousand *koṭīs* of *nayutas* of great chiliocosms, or seeing the Buddha's body as having the height of a numberless number of great chiliocosms, or seeing the Buddha's body as having the height of a measureless number of great chiliocosms, or seeing the Buddha's body as having the height of a boundless number of great chiliocosms, or seeing the Buddha's body as having the height of an incomparable number of great chiliocosms, or seeing the Buddha's body as having the height of an innumerable number of great chiliocosms, or seeing the Buddha's body as having the height of an unspeakable number of great chiliocosms, or seeing the Buddha's body as having the height of an inconceivable number of great chiliocosms, or seeing the Buddha's body as having the height of an immeasurable number of great chiliocosms, or seeing the Buddha's body as having the height of an ineffable number of great chiliocosms, or seeing the Buddha's body as having the height of an ineffable-ineffable number of great chiliocosms.

Sons of the Buddha, in this way, the bodhisattva-mahāsattva sees countless colors and signs, countless forms and appearances, countless manifestations, countless rays of light, and countless nets of light. The range of that light is commensurate with the Dharma realm. It has nothing in the Dharma realm it does not illuminate and it everywhere enables the development of unsurpassably great wisdom. He also sees the Buddha's body as entirely free of any defiling attachment, as free of all obstacles, and as supremely marvelous and pure.

Sons of the Buddha, the bodhisattva sees the body of the Buddha in these ways and yet the Tathāgata's body neither increases nor decreases in size. Just as it is with empty space which, even when residing in the hole made in a mustard seed by an insect, does not shrink in size, and even when abiding in the midst of countless worlds, still does not increase in its vastness, so too it is with the Buddha's body. When one sees it as large, it still does not increase and when one sees it as small, it still does not shrink.

Sons of the Buddha, just as the orb of the moon appears to be only a small form when seen by those living in Jambudvīpa even though it still has not shrunk in size, and appears to be a very large form when seen by someone standing on the moon even though it still has not increased in size, so too it is with the bodhisattva-mahāsattva. When he abides in this samādhi, in accordance with whatever he wishes for, he sees the Buddha's body taking on all kinds of different transformations in its appearance. When in those circumstances he listens there to the words and phrases of the Dharma being expounded, taking them in, retaining them, and not forgetting them, the Tathāgata's body neither increases in size nor decreases in size.

Sons of the Buddha, just as when, right after a being's life has ended and he is about to take rebirth, this is not apart from his mind and what he then looks upon as pure,[288] so too it is with the bodhisattva-mahāsattva for whom this is not apart from this extremely deep samādhi and what he sees in it as pure.

Sons of the Buddha, when the bodhisattva-mahāsattva abides in this samādhi, he perfects ten kinds of swiftness dharmas. What are those ten? They are:

Swiftness in increasing all the practices and achieving complete fulfillment of great vows;

Swiftness in using the light of Dharma to brightly illuminate the world;

Swiftness in using skillful means to turn the wheel of the Dharma and liberate beings;

Swiftness in adapting to beings' karma by revealing the pure lands of all buddhas;

Swiftness in using equanimous wisdom in progressing into the ten powers;

Swiftness in coming to abide together with all *tathāgatas*;

Swiftness in using the power of the great kindness to vanquish the armies of Māra;

Swiftness in severing beings' doubts and enabling them to be happy;

Swiftness in manifesting spiritual transformations adapted to beings' convictions; and

Swiftness in using all different kinds of words and phrases of sublime Dharma to purify all worlds.

Sons of the Buddha, this bodhisattva-mahāsattva also acquires ten kinds of Dharma seals with which he imprints all dharmas. What are these ten? They are:

First, that of possessing the same roots of goodness as those of all buddhas of the past, the future, and the present;

Second, that of acquiring a Dharma body possessed of boundless wisdom the same as that of all *tathāgatas*;

Third, that of abiding in the non-duality of dharmas the same as all *tathāgatas*;

Fourth, that of contemplating just as the *tathāgatas* do the identity of all the countless spheres of experience of the three periods of time;

Fifth, that of acquiring just as the *tathāgatas* do the complete comprehension of the unimpeded sphere of the Dharma realm;

Sixth, that of perfecting the ten powers and becoming unimpeded in action just as the *tathāgatas* do;

Seventh, that of forever severing the two types of actions[289] and then dwelling in the dharma of noncontentiousness just as the *tathāgatas* do;

Eighth, that of engaging in the ceaseless teaching of beings just as the *tathāgatas* do;

Ninth, that of being able to skillfully contemplate skillful means in wisdom and skillful means in meaning just as the *tathāgatas* do; and

Tenth, that of becoming the same as and no different from all buddhas just as the *tathāgatas* do.

Sons of the Buddha, when a bodhisattva-mahāsattva perfects the gateways of skillful expedient means associated with this "great samādhi of the complete knowledge of all worlds' buddha adornments":

He becomes one who has no teacher who, unaided by others' instruction, penetrates all dharmas of the Buddha on his own;

He becomes one who is an eminent man because he is able to awaken all beings;

He becomes one who is pure because he realizes the fundamental purity of the nature of the mind;

He becomes one who is foremost because he is able to liberate the beings in all worlds;

He becomes one who is a provider of comfort because he is able to instruct and awaken understanding in all beings;

He becomes one who establishes [others] because he enables those not yet abiding in the lineage of the Buddha to abide in it;

He becomes one who is possessed of genuine knowing because he enters the gateway of all-knowledge;

He becomes one who is free of all variant conceptions because he does not speak in two different ways;

He becomes one who abides in the treasury of Dharma because he has vowed to completely know all dharmas of the Buddha; and

He becomes one who is able to rain the Dharma rain because he adapts to beings' inclinations and thus enables them all to become completely satisfied.

Sons of the Buddha, this circumstance is analogous to that of Śakra who places a *maṇi* jewel into his topknot. Because of the power of that jewel, his awe-inspiring radiance increases. When Śakra the deva king first acquires this jewel, he acquires ten dharmas in which he surpasses all the devas in the Trāyastriṃśa Heaven. What are those ten? They are:

First, in terms of his physical signs;

Second, in terms of his physical form;

Third, in terms of his manifestations;

Fourth, in terms of his retinue;

Fifth, in terms of his possessions;

Sixth, in terms of his voice;

Seventh, in terms of his spiritual superknowledges;

Eighth, in terms of his kinds of sovereign mastery;

Ninth, in terms of his wise understanding; and

Tenth, in terms of the uses of his wisdom.

It is in ten qualities such as these that he surpasses all the devas in the Trāyastriṃśa Heaven. So too it is with the bodhisattva-mahāsattva, for, from the point when he first gains this samādhi, he then acquires ten kinds of treasuries of vast knowledge. What are those ten? They are:

First, the knowledge that brightly illuminates all buddha *kṣetras*;

Second, the knowledge by which he knows the rebirths of all beings;

Third, the knowledge by which he everywhere manifests transformations throughout the three periods of time;

Fourth, the knowledge by which he everywhere enters the body of all buddhas;[290]

Fifth, the knowledge by which he possesses a penetrating comprehension of all dharmas of the Buddha;

Sixth, the knowledge by which he everywhere gathers all pure dharmas;

Seventh, the knowledge by which he everywhere enables all beings to enter the Dharma body;

Eighth, the knowledge by which he directly perceives all dharmas with the purified universal eye;

Ninth, the knowledge by which he gains sovereign mastery in all things that has reached the far shore of perfection; and

Tenth, the knowledge by which he everywhere becomes securely established in all vast dharmas without exception.

Sons of the Buddha, when this bodhisattva-mahāsattva abides in this samādhi, he also acquires a body possessed of ten kinds of supreme purity and awesome virtue. What are those ten? They are:

First, to brightly illuminate an ineffable-ineffable number of worlds, he emanates an ineffable-ineffable number of spheres of light;

Second, to purify all worlds, he emanates an ineffable-ineffable number of spheres of light of countless colors and appearances;

Third, to train beings, he emanates an ineffable-ineffable number of spheres of light;

Fourth, to draw near to all buddhas, he transformationally creates an ineffable-ineffable number of bodies;

Fifth, to serve and make offerings to all buddhas, he rains down an ineffable-ineffable number of clouds of many different kinds of especially marvelous incense and flowers;

Sixth, to serve and make offerings to all buddhas and to train all beings, he transformationally creates an ineffable-ineffable number of many different kinds of musical sounds which emanate from every one of his pores;

Seventh, to ripen beings, he manifests an ineffable-ineffable number of various kinds of masterful spiritual transformations;

Eighth, to inquire about the Dharma from all the buddhas of many different names throughout the ten directions, in a single step, he passes beyond an ineffable-ineffable number of worlds;

Ninth, to enable all beings who see him or hear his voice to have not done so in vain, he manifests an ineffable-ineffable number of many different kinds of pure form bodies of countless colors and appearances, all of which possess the summit which no one can see; and

Tenth, to provide beings with instruction in countless esoteric dharmas, he utters an ineffable-ineffable number of sounds and words.

Sons of the Buddha, after the bodhisattva-mahāsattva has acquired these ten kinds of supremely pure and awesomely virtuous bodies, he can enable beings to acquire ten kinds of complete fulfillment. What are these ten? They are:

First, he can enable beings to succeed in seeing the Buddha;

Second, he can enable beings to develop deep faith in the Buddha;

Third, he can enable beings to succeed in hearing the Dharma;

Fourth, he can enable beings to know that there are worlds in which there are buddhas;

Fifth, he can enable beings to see the Buddha's spiritual superknowledges;

Sixth, he can enable beings to recall the karma that they have accumulated;

Seventh, he can enable beings to achieve complete fulfillment of the mind of meditative absorption;

Eighth, he can enable beings to enter into the purity of the Buddha;

Ninth, he can enable beings to make the resolve to attain bodhi; and

Tenth, he can enable beings to achieve complete fulfillment of the Buddha's wisdom.

Sons of the Buddha, after the bodhisattva-mahāsattva has enabled beings to acquire these ten kinds of complete fulfillment, he also accomplishes ten kinds of buddha works for the sake of beings. What are those ten? They are:

He uses sounds in accomplishing buddha works to ripen beings;
He uses physical forms in accomplishing buddha works to train beings;
He uses remembrance in accomplishing buddha works to purify beings;
He uses the shaking of worlds in accomplishing buddha works to enable beings to abandon the wretched destinies;
He uses skillful means to instigate awakening in accomplishing buddha works to enable beings to not lose their mindfulness;
He uses the manifestation of signs in dreams in accomplishing buddha works to enable beings to constantly abide in right mindfulness;
He uses the emanation of great light in accomplishing buddha works to everywhere gather in all beings;
He uses the cultivation of the bodhisattva practices in accomplishing buddha works to enable beings to abide in the supreme vows;
He uses the realization of the right and perfect enlightenment in accomplishing buddha works to enable beings to realize the illusory nature of dharmas;
He uses the turning of the wheel of the sublime Dharma in accomplishing buddha works to speak the Dharma for beings without missing the right time;
He uses the manifestation of the appearance of abiding for a particular life span in accomplishing buddha works to train all beings; and
He manifests the appearance of entering *parinirvāṇa* in accomplishing buddha works, knowing that beings will then develop feelings of weariness [of *saṃsāra*].

Sons of the Buddha, this is what constitutes the knowledge of skillful means as it relates to the bodhisattva-mahāsattva's seventh great samādhi, "the great samādhi of the complete knowledge of all worlds' buddha adornments."

Sons of the Buddha, what then is meant by the bodhisattva-mahāsattva's "samādhi of all beings' different bodies"? Sons of the Buddha, the bodhisattva-mahāsattva who abides in this samādhi acquires ten kinds of nonattachment. What are those ten? They are:

Nonattachment to any of the *kṣetras;*
Nonattachment to any of the directions;
Nonattachment to any of the kalpas;
Nonattachment to any of the congregations;
Nonattachment to any of the dharmas;

Nonattachment to any of the bodhisattvas;
Nonattachment to any of the bodhisattva vows;
Nonattachment to any of the samādhis;
Nonattachment to any of the buddhas; and
Nonattachment to any of the grounds.

These are the ten.

Sons of the Buddha, how is it that the bodhisattva-mahāsattva enters this samādhi and how is it that he emerges from it? Sons of the Buddha, in this samādhi, this bodhisattva-mahāsattva does so:

By entering within the body and emerging outside the body;
By entering outside the body and emerging inside the body;
By entering in the same body and emerging in a different body;
By entering in a different body and emerging in the same body;
By entering in a human body and emerging in a *yakṣa*'s body;
By entering in a *yakṣa*'s body and emerging in a dragon's body;
By entering in a dragon's body and emerging in an *asura*'s body;
By entering in an *asura*'s body and emerging in a deva's body;
By entering in a deva's body and emerging in a brahma heaven king's body;
By entering in a brahma heaven king's body and emerging in a desire-realm body;
By entering in the heavens and emerging in the hells;
By entering in the hells and emerging in the human realm;
By entering in the human realm and emerging in any of the other rebirth destinies;
By entering in a thousand bodies and emerging in a single body;
By entering in a single body and emerging in a thousand bodies;
By entering in a *nayuta* of bodies and emerging in a single body;
By entering in a single body and emerging in a *nayuta* of bodies;
By entering among the population of beings in Jambudvīpa and emerging among the population of beings in Avaragodānīya;
By entering among the population of beings in Avaragodānīya and emerging among the population of beings in Uttarakuru;
By entering among the population of beings Uttarakuru and emerging among the population of beings in Pūrvavideha;
By entering among the population of beings in Pūrvavideha and emerging among the population of beings in any of the other three continents;
By entering among the population of beings in any of the other three continents and emerging among the population of beings in the fourth of the continents;

By entering among the population beings in any of the four continents and emerging among the population of beings in any of the oceans;

By entering among the population of beings in any of the oceans and emerging among the population of spirits in any of the oceans;

By entering among the population of spirits in any of the oceans and emerging in the water element of all the oceans;

By entering in the water element of all the oceans and emerging in the earth element of all the oceans;

By entering in the earth element of all the oceans and emerging in the fire element of all the oceans;

By entering in the fire element of all the oceans and emerging in the wind element of all the oceans;

By entering in the wind element of all the oceans and emerging in all four elements;

By entering in all four elements and emerging in unproduced dharmas;

By entering in unproduced dharmas and emerging in the Wonderfully Tall Mountain, [Mount Sumeru];

By entering in the Wonderfully Tall Mountain and emerging in the seven jeweled mountains;

By entering in the seven jeweled mountains and emerging in any of the earth's many different kinds of grains, trees, forests, or black mountains;

By entering in any of the earth's many different kinds of grains, trees, forests, or black mountains and emerging in any of the adornments consisting of marvelous kinds of incense, flowers, or jewels;

By entering in any of the adornments consisting of marvelous kinds of incense, flowers, or jewels and emerging among any of the beings born on any of the four continents or in any of the regions below them or above them;

By entering among any of the beings born on any of the four continents or in any of the regions below them or above them and then emerging among the population of beings in a small chiliocosm;

By entering among the population of beings in a small chiliocosm and emerging among the population of beings in an intermediate chiliocosm;

By entering among the population of beings in an intermediate chiliocosm and emerging among the population of beings in a large chiliocosm;

By entering among the population of beings in a large chiliocosm and emerging among the population of beings in a hundred thousand *koṭīs* of *nayutas* of great trichiliocosms;

By entering among the population of beings in a hundred thousand *koṭīs* of *nayutas* of great trichiliocosms and emerging among the population of beings in numberless worlds;

By entering among the population of beings in numberless worlds and emerging among the population of beings in measureless worlds;

By entering among the population of beings in measureless worlds and emerging among the population of beings in boundlessly many buddha *kṣetras;*

By entering among the population of beings in boundlessly many buddha *kṣetras* and emerging among the population of beings in incomparably many buddha *kṣetras;*

By entering among the population of beings in incomparably many buddha *kṣetras* and emerging in among the population of beings in numberless worlds;

By entering among the population of beings in numberless worlds and emerging among the population of beings in an unspeakable number of worlds;

By entering among the population of beings in an unspeakable number of worlds and emerging among the population of beings in an inconceivable number of worlds;

By entering among the population of beings in an inconceivable number of worlds and emerging among the population of beings in an immeasurable number of worlds;

By entering among the population of beings in an immeasurable number of worlds and emerging among the population of beings in an ineffable number of worlds;

By entering among the population of beings in an ineffable number of worlds and emerging among the population of beings in an ineffable-ineffable number of worlds;

By entering among the population of beings in an ineffable-ineffable number of worlds and emerging among the population of defiled beings;

By entering among the population of defiled beings and emerging among the population of pure beings;

By entering among the population of pure beings and emerging among the population of defiled beings;

By entering in the eye sense base and emerging in the ear sense base;

By entering in the ear sense base and emerging in the eye sense base;
By entering in the nose sense base and emerging in the tongue sense base;
By entering in the tongue sense base and emerging in the nose sense base;
By entering in the body sense base and emerging in the mind sense base;
By entering in the mind sense base and emerging in the body sense base;
By entering in his own sense bases and emerging in the sense bases of someone else;
By entering in the sense bases of someone else and emerging in his own sense bases;
By entering in a single atom and emerging in the atoms of numberless worlds;
By entering in the atoms of numberless worlds and emerging in a single atom;
By entering among *śrāvaka* disciples and emerging among *pratyekabuddhas;*
By entering among *pratyekabuddhas* and emerging among *śrāvaka* disciples;
By entering in his own body and emerging in the body of a buddha;
By entering in the body of a buddha and emerging in his own body;
By entering in but a single mind-moment and emerging in a *koṭī* of kalpas;
By entering in a *koṭī* of kalpas and emerging in but a single mind-moment;
By entering in the same mind-moment and emerging in another time;
By entering in another time and emerging in the same mind-moment;
By entering in the past and emerging in the future;
By entering in the future and emerging in the past;
By entering in the past and emerging in the present;
By entering in the present and emerging in the past;
By entering in the three periods of time and emerging in a single *kṣaṇa;*
By entering in a single *kṣaṇa* and emerging in the three periods of time;

By entering in true suchness and emerging in speech; or
By entering in speech and emerging in true suchness.

Sons of the Buddha, this is just as when there is someone possessed by a ghost whose body then trembles so that he is unable to calm himself. Even though the ghost does not reveal his own body, he causes another's body to become this way. So too it is with the bodhisattva-mahāsattva who abides in this samādhi. He may enter meditative absorption in his own body and emerge in the body of another or may enter meditative absorption in the body of another and emerge in his own body.

Sons of the Buddha, this is just as when, due to the power of a spell, a corpse is then able to get up and walk around and succeed in accomplishing whatever task it is doing. Although the corpse and the spell are different, together they are able to accomplish that task. So too it is with the bodhisattva-mahāsattva who abides in this samādhi. He may enter meditative absorption in the same objective sphere and emerge in a different objective sphere and may enter in a different objective sphere and emerge in the same objective sphere.

Sons of the Buddha, this is just as when a bhikshu attains sovereign mastery over the mind and may then use a single body to create many bodies or may use many bodies to create a single body. It is not that the one body passes away and many bodies are then born. Nor is it the case that many bodies pass away and then a single body is born. So too it is with the bodhisattva-mahāsattva who abides in this samādhi. He may enter meditative absorption in a single body and emerge in many bodies or may enter meditative absorption in many bodies and emerge in a single body.

Sons of the Buddha, just as the great earth has but a single flavor, yet the seedlings and grains growing from it have many different flavors so that, even though there is no difference in the earth, the resulting flavors have extraordinary differences, so too it is with the bodhisattva-mahāsattva who abides in this samādhi. He does not engage in any discriminations, yet he may enter meditative absorption in a single circumstance and emerge from it in many different circumstances or may enter meditative absorption in many different circumstances and emerge from it in but a single kind of circumstance.

Sons of the Buddha, when the bodhisattva-mahāsattva abides in this samādhi, he acquires ten kinds of praiseworthy dharmas due to which he is praised. What are those ten? They are:

Due to entering true suchness, he is known as a *tathāgata*;

Due to awakening to all dharmas, he is known as a buddha;

Due to being praised by everyone in the world, he is acknowledged as a master of the Dharma;

Due to knowing all dharmas, he is known as one possessed of all-knowledge;

Due to being one in whom everyone in the world takes refuge, he is known as a refuge;

Due to completely comprehending the skillful means to be used with all dharmas, he is known as a master guide;

Due to leading all beings into the path to omniscience, he is known as a great master guide;

Due to serving as a lamp for the entire world he is known as a light;

Due to being one possessed of completely fulfilled resolve who has successfully realized both meaning and benefit, who has done what is to be done, and who abides in unimpeded wisdom by which he clearly distinguishes and utterly knows all dharmas, he is acknowledged as one possessed of sovereign mastery in the ten powers; and

Due to his having attained a penetrating comprehension of the wheel of all dharmas, he is known as one who sees everything.

These are the ten.

Sons of the Buddha, when the bodhisattva-mahāsattva abides in this samādhi, he additionally acquires ten kinds of radiant illumination. What are those ten? They are:

He acquires the light of all buddhas because of his equality with them;

He acquires the light of all worlds because he is everywhere able to adorn them;

He acquires the light of all beings because he goes forth to train them all;

He acquires the measureless light of fearlessness because he takes the Dharma realm as the site in which he expounds [on the Dharma];

He acquires the light of nondifferentiation because he knows all dharmas do not have many different kinds of individual natures;

He acquires the light of skillful means because, having reached the apex of dispassion for all dharmas, he has thereby realized entry into them;

He acquires the light of the genuine truth because, having reached the apex of dispassion for all dharmas, his mind has become equanimous;

He acquires the light of spiritual transformations which pervades all worlds because he receives incessant empowerment by the Buddha;
He acquires the light of skillful contemplative thought because he has reached the far shore of perfection in the sovereign mastery of all buddhas; and
He acquires the light of the true suchness of all dharmas because, even within a single pore, he is well able to explain everything.

These are the ten.

Sons of the Buddha, when the bodhisattva-mahāsattva abides in this samādhi, he also acquires ten kinds of effortlessness. What are these ten? They are:

Effortlessness in physical deeds;
Effortlessness in verbal deeds;
Effortlessness in mental deeds;
Effortlessness in spiritual superknowledges;
Effortlessness in completely understanding that all dharmas have no inherently existent nature;
Effortlessness in knowing that karma is never destroyed;
Effortlessness in the possession of nondiscriminating wisdom;
Effortlessness in the wisdom of the unproduced;
Effortlessness in knowing dharmas as undestroyed; and
Effortlessness in according with texts without contradicting their meaning.

These are the ten.

Sons of the Buddha, when the bodhisattva-mahāsattva abides in this samādhi, the countless spheres of experience have many kinds of differences, in particular:

Entering as single and emerging as multiple;
Entering as multiple and emerging as single;
Entering as the same and emerging as different;
Entering as different and emerging as the same;
Entering as fine and emerging as coarse;
Entering as coarse and emerging as fine;
Entering as large and emerging as small;
Entering as small and emerging as large;
Entering in accordance and emerging in opposition;
Entering in opposition and emerging in accordance;
Entering without a body and emerging with a body;
Entering with a body and emerging without a body;
Entering in signlessness and emerging in signs;

Entering in signs and emerging in signlessness; and
Entering in emerging and emerging in entering.

All such circumstances as these are masterful spheres of experience characteristic of this samādhi.

Sons of the Buddha, this is just as when the spell chanted by a conjurer becomes efficacious, it is then able to manifest many different kinds of forms and appearances. The spell and the conjuration are different and yet they are able to create a conjured illusion. The spell is just sound and yet it is able to conjure various forms perceived through the eye consciousness, various sounds perceived through the ear consciousness, various smells perceived through the smell consciousness, various flavors perceived through the taste consciousness, various physical sensations perceived through the body consciousness, and various spheres of experience perceived by the mind consciousness. So too, when the bodhisattva-mahāsattva abides in this samādhi, he enters in the midst of what is the same and emerges in the midst of what is different, enters in the midst of what is different and merges in the midst of what is the same.

Sons of the Buddha, this is just as it is when the Trāyastriṃśa Heaven devas battled with the *asuras*, the devas emerged victorious and the *asuras* retreated in defeated. Although the body of the *asura* king was seven hundred *yojanas* tall and he was surrounded and guarded by fourfold armies consisting of numberless thousands of myriads of soldiers, he was able to use the power of conjuring techniques to all at once lead his entire army away into a hole in a lotus root.

So too it is with the bodhisattva-mahāsattva. He has already thoroughly perfected the wisdom ground in which everything is understood as like an illusion. In this circumstance, the illusion-cognizing wisdom is identical to the bodhisattva and the bodhisattva is identical to the illusion-cognizing wisdom. He is therefore able to enter meditative absorption in undifferentiated dharmas and emerge from it in dharmas that are different from each other. He is also able to enter meditative absorption in dharmas that are different from each other and then emerge from it in undifferentiated dharmas.

Sons of the Buddha, just as when a farmer plants a seed in his field, the seed is planted down below and the fruit grows forth above, so too it is with the bodhisattva-mahāsattva abiding in this samādhi. He may enter meditative absorption in oneness and emerge from it in multiplicity and may also enter meditative absorption in multiplicity and emerge from it in oneness.

Sons of the Buddha, this is just as when a man and a woman engage in "joining the red and the white,"[291] there may be a being who takes rebirth in the midst of this. At that time, it is referred to as being at the embryonic *kalala* stage from which it sequentially grows as it resides in the mother's womb for the full ten months and, through the power of its good karmic deeds, undergoes complete development of all of its physical parts in which none of its faculties are deficient and its mind is completely clear.

That embryonic *kalala* and the six sense faculties differ in substance and appearance, yet, through the power of its [previous] karma, it is then able to cause them to undergo their sequential and complete development and undergo all different kinds of similar and different karmic rewards and retributions. So too it is with the bodhisattva-mahāsattva who, beginning from the embryonic *kalala* stage of omniscience, gradually grows and develops through the power of resolute faith and vows. His mind becomes vast and takes on the ability to act with sovereign mastery in entering meditative absorption in the nonexistent and emerging in the existent and in entering in the existent and emerging in the nonexistent.[292]

Sons of the Buddha, this is analogous to the circumstance in which the dragon palace is built on ground and not in the sky and the dragons themselves live in their palaces and also do not live in the sky. Even so, they are still able to spread forth clouds that completely fill the sky. As for the palaces that a person might see when gazing upward, one should realize that they are the cities of *gandharvas* and are not the palaces of the dragons.

Sons of the Buddha, although the dragons dwell down below, still, their clouds are spread forth up above. So too it is with the bodhisattva-mahāsattva who abides in this samādhi. He may enter meditative absorption in the signless and emerge in what is possessed of signs and may enter in what is possessed of signs and emerge in the signless.

Sons of the Buddha, this is analogous to the case of the palace where the Great Brahma Heaven king known as Sublime Light dwells. It is called "Treasury of the Most Supreme Purity in All Worlds." From within this great palace, one everywhere sees everything contained within the great trichiliocosm including all four continents, the celestial palaces, the dragon palaces, the *yakṣa* palaces, the *gandharva* palaces, the *asura* palaces, the *garuḍa* palaces, the *kiṃnara* palaces, the *mahoraga* palaces, the abodes of the humans, the three wretched rebirth destinies, all the different mountains such as Mount Sumeru, the great oceans and rivers, the ponds, marshes, and springs, the cities, their surrounding districts, the villages, the forests, the many kinds of jewels, all the many other adornments such as these, all the great surrounding mountain rings, all their boundaries, and even the subtlest floating dust motes in empty space. None of these phenomena are not entirely and clearly visible within that Brahma Heaven palace just as one would see the image of one's own face reflected in a brightly lit mirror.

When the bodhisattva-mahāsattva abides in this "great samādhi of all beings' different bodies," he knows the many different *kṣetras,* sees the many different buddhas, liberates the many different kinds of beings, realizes the many different dharmas, perfects the many different practices, fulfills the many different liberations, enters the many different kinds of samādhis, produces the many different spiritual superknowledges, acquires the many different types of wisdom, and abides in many different kinds of *kṣaṇa* moments.

Sons of the Buddha, this bodhisattva-mahāsattva reaches the far shore of perfection in ten kinds of spiritual superknowledges. What are those ten? They are:

He reaches the far shore of perfection in the spiritual superknowledges of all buddhas throughout empty space and the Dharma realm;

He reaches the far shore of perfection in the bodhisattva's ultimately undifferentiated and masterful spiritual superknowledges;

He reaches the far shore of perfection in the spiritual superknowledges by which he is able to bring forth the bodhisattva's great conduct and vows, enter the gateway of the Tathāgata, and accomplish buddha works;

He reaches the far shore of perfection in the spiritual superknowledges by which he is able to cause all worlds and all realms to become purified;

He reaches the far shore of perfection in the spiritual superknowledges by which he is able to freely know the inconceivable karmic rewards of all beings as like illusory conjurations or transformations;

He reaches the far shore of perfection in the spiritual superknowledges by which he is able to freely know the different coarse and subtle signs of entry into and emergence from all samādhis;

He reaches the far shore of perfection in the spiritual superknowledges by which he is able to courageously enter the realms of the Tathāgata and bring forth the great vows within them;

He reaches the far shore of perfection in the spiritual superknowledges by which he is able to transformationally create buddhas and transformationally turn the Dharma wheel to train beings, thereby enabling them to be born into the lineage of the Buddha, and thereby enabling them to enter and achieve rapid success in the buddha vehicle;

He reaches the far shore of perfection in the spiritual superknowledges by which he is able to completely understand all the ineffably many statements in the esoteric texts and turn the Dharma wheel, thereby enabling the purification of hundreds of thousands of *koṭīs* of *nayutas* of ineffable-ineffables of Dharma gateways; and

He reaches the far shore of perfection in the spiritual superknowledges by which he is able in but a single mind-moment to manifest all three periods of time without being limited in doing so to any particular number of days, nights, years, months, or kalpas.

These are the ten. Sons of the Buddha, this is what constitutes the knowledge of skillful means as it relates to the bodhisattva-mahāsattva's eighth great samādhi, "the great samādhi of all beings' different bodies."

Sons of the Buddha, what then is meant by the bodhisattva-mahāsattva's "samādhi of sovereign mastery throughout the Dharma realm"?

Sons of the Buddha, on his own eye sense base and so forth, up to and including on his own mind sense base, this bodhisattva-mahāsattva enters a samādhi called "the samādhi of sovereign mastery throughout the Dharma realm." The bodhisattva enters this samādhi in every pore of his own body and is then spontaneously able to know the entire world, to know all worldly dharmas, to know all worlds, to know *koṭīs* of *nayutas* of worlds, to know *asaṃkhyeyas* of worlds, and to know worlds as numerous as the atoms in an ineffable number of buddha *kṣetras*.

In all those worlds, he sees buddhas appearing together with congregations of bodhisattvas completely filling them who are radiant, pure, unalloyed in their complete goodness, arrayed with vast adornments, and beautified with many different kinds of jewels. Within them, the bodhisattva never rests in cultivating the bodhisattva practices, cultivating them for perhaps a kalpa, or a hundred kalpas, or a thousand kalpas, or a *koṭī* of kalpas, or a hundred thousand *koṭīs* of *nayutas* of kalpas, or numberless kalpas, or measureless kalpas, or boundlessly many kalpas, or incomparably many kalpas, or innumerably many kalpas, or unspeakably many kalpas, or inconceivably many kalpas, or immeasurably many kalpas, or ineffably many kalpas, or for an ineffable-ineffable number of kalpas, or for kalpas as numerous as the atoms in an ineffable-ineffable number of buddha *kṣetras*.

Moreover, he abides in this samādhi during measurelessly many kalpas such as these during which he also enters it, also emerges from it, also perfects worlds, also trains beings, also becomes present everywhere throughout the Dharma realm, also everywhere knows all three periods of time, also expounds on all dharmas, and also manifests great spiritual superknowledges and many different kinds of skillful means, accomplishing all of these things without attachment and without obstruction.

Due to attaining sovereign mastery throughout the Dharma realm, he skillfully distinguishes factors related to the eye, skillfully distinguishes factors related to the ear, skillfully distinguishes factors related to the nose, skillfully distinguishes factors related to the tongue, skillfully distinguishes factors related to the body, and skillfully distinguishes factors related to the mind, skillfully distinguishing to their limits all of the many different kinds of distinctions such as these.

Having acquired such skill in knowledge and vision as this, the bodhisattva accomplishes the following things:

He is able to produce the light of a myriad *koṭīs* of *dhāraṇī* dharmas;
He perfects a myriad *koṭīs* of pure practices;
He acquires a myriad *koṭīs* of faculties;
He fulfills a myriad *koṭīs* of spiritual superknowledges;
He becomes able to enter a myriad *koṭīs* of samādhis;
He perfects a myriad *koṭīs* of spiritual powers;
He develops and nurtures a myriad *koṭīs* of powers;
He fulfills a myriad *koṭīs* of kinds of profound thought;
He implements a myriad *koṭīs* of means of attaining power;
He manifests a myriad *koṭīs* of spiritual transformations;
He perfects a myriad *koṭīs* of unimpeded abilities;
He fulfills a myriad *koṭīs* of provisions for the bodhisattva path;
He accumulates a myriad *koṭīs* of treasuries;
He clearly illuminates a myriad *koṭīs* of bodhisattva skillful means;
He expounds on a myriad *koṭīs* of meanings;
He fulfills a myriad *koṭīs* of vows;
He produces a myriad *koṭīs* of dedications;
He facilitates the purification of the right and fixed position[293] for a myriad *koṭīs* of bodhisattvas;
He completely understands a myriad *koṭīs* of Dharma gateways;

He provides instruction in a myriad *koṭīs* of discourses; and
He cultivates a myriad *koṭīs* of types of bodhisattva purity.

Sons of the Buddha, the bodhisattva-mahāsattva also possesses numberless meritorious qualities, measureless meritorious qualities, boundless meritorious qualities, incomparably many meritorious qualities, innumerably many meritorious qualities, indescribably many meritorious qualities, inconceivably many meritorious qualities, immeasurably many meritorious qualities, ineffably many meritorious qualities, and endlessly many meritorious qualities.

Sons of the Buddha, as for these meritorious qualities, this bodhisattva has already fully prepared them, has already accumulated them all, has already adorned them all, has already purified them all, has already made them radiantly clear, has already integrated them, has already become able to produce them, has already made them praiseworthy, has already made them enduring, and he has already completely perfected them.

Sons of the Buddha, when this bodhisattva-mahāsattva abides in this samādhi, he is taken into the care of buddhas to the east with names as numerous as the atoms in a myriad *asaṃkhyeyas* of buddha *kṣetras* among whom there are in turn an additional number of buddhas bearing each of these names as numerous as the atoms in a myriad *asaṃkhyeyas* of buddha *kṣetras*, every one of whom is different from each other. And just as this is so in the east, so too is this also so in the same way in the south, west, north, the four midpoints, the zenith, and the nadir as well. All of these buddhas appear directly before him, whereupon:

They show him all buddhas' pure *kṣetras*;
They tell him about the measureless body of all buddhas;
They tell him about the inconceivable eyes of all buddhas;
They tell him about the measureless ears of all buddhas;
They tell him about the pure nose of all buddhas;
They tell him about the pure tongue of all buddhas;
They tell him about the non-abiding mind of all buddhas;
They tell him about the unexcelled spiritual superknowledges of all *tathāgatas*;
They enable him to cultivate the Tathāgata's unexcelled bodhi;
They enable him to acquire the Tathāgata's pure voice;
They explain the Tathāgata's irreversible wheel of Dharma;
They reveal the Tathāgata's boundless congregation;
They enable him to enter the Tathāgata's boundless secrets;
They praise all the Tathāgata's roots of goodness;

They enable him to enter the Tathāgata's equal dharmas;
They expound upon the Tathāgata's lineage extending throughout the three periods of time;
They reveal the Tathāgata's measureless physical marks;
They extol the dharmas of which the Tathāgata is protectively mindful;
They expound on the Tathāgata's sublime Dharma voice;
They clearly distinguish the worlds of all buddhas;
They promulgate all buddhas' samādhis;
They reveal the sequence of all buddhas' congregations;
They protect the inconceivable Dharma of all buddhas;
They explain how all dharmas are like illusory conjurations;
They make it clear that the nature of dharmas is motionless;
They reveal all instances of [the turning of] the wheel of the unexcelled Dharma;
They praise the exquisiteness of the Tathāgata's countless meritorious qualities;
They enable him to enter the clouds of all samādhis; and
They enable him to realize that one's mind is like a boundless and endless conjured illusion or magical transformation.

Sons of the Buddha, when this bodhisattva-mahāsattva abides in this "samādhi of sovereign mastery throughout the Dharma realm," he is simultaneously regarded with protective mindfulness by all those *tathāgatas* in each of the ten directions possessed of names as numerous as the atoms in a myriad *asaṃkhyeyas* of buddha *kṣetras* among whom there are in turn an additional number of such buddhas bearing each of these names as numerous as the atoms in a myriad *asaṃkhyeyas* buddha *kṣetras*.

They enable this bodhisattva to acquire a boundless body;
They enable this bodhisattva to acquire an unimpeded mind;
They enable this bodhisattva to acquire unforgetting mindfulness of all dharmas;
They enable this bodhisattva to acquire definite wisdom regarding all dharmas;
They enable this bodhisattva to acquire ever-increasing brilliant intelligence regarding all dharmas by which they are able to absorb them all;
They enable this bodhisattva to completely understand all dharmas;
They enable this bodhisattva to acquire fiercely sharp faculties by which he is able to attain skill in the dharmas of the spiritual superknowledges;

They enable this bodhisattva to acquire an unimpeded sphere of action in which he is able to constantly and incessantly travel everywhere throughout the Dharma realm;

They enable this bodhisattva to acquire ultimately purified unimpeded wisdom; and

They enable this bodhisattva to use the power of the spiritual superknowledges to manifest the realization of buddhahood in all worlds.

Sons of the Buddha, when the bodhisattva-mahāsattva abides in this samādhi, he acquires ten kinds of oceans. What are those ten? They are as follows:

He acquires the ocean of all buddhas because he sees them all;

He acquires the ocean of beings because he trains them all;

He acquires the ocean of all dharmas because he is able to use wisdom to completely know them all;

He acquires the ocean of all *kṣetras* because he uses the spiritual superknowledges of the absence of inherent existence and wishlessness to go and visit them all;

He acquires the ocean of meritorious qualities because he fulfills the cultivation of them all;

He acquires the ocean of spiritual superknowledges because he is able to extensively manifest them to enable awakening;

He acquires the ocean of all faculties because he thoroughly knows all their various differences;

He acquires the ocean of all minds because he knows the countless minds of all beings with their many and various differences;

He acquires the ocean of all practices because he is able to use the power of vows to completely fulfill them all; and

He acquires the ocean of all vows because he maintains perpetual purity in accomplishing them all.

Sons of the Buddha, after the bodhisattva-mahāsattva acquires these ten kinds of oceans, he also acquires ten kinds of extraordinary supremacy. What are those ten? They are as follows:

First, he becomes foremost among all beings;

Second, even among all the devas, he is the most extraordinary;

Third, even among all the Brahma Heaven kings, he possesses the most ultimate powers of sovereign mastery;

Fourth, he remains free of any defiling attachment to anything in any world;

Fifth, there is no one in any world who is able to overcome him;

Sixth, none of the *māras* are able to delude or confuse him;
Seventh, he remains unhindered in entering all the rebirth destinies;
Eighth, in whichever of the many different places he takes rebirth, he remains aware that they are not durable;
Ninth, he attains sovereign mastery in all dharmas of the Buddha; and
Tenth, he is able to manifest all the spiritual superknowledges.

Sons of the Buddha, after the bodhisattva-mahāsattva acquires these ten kinds of extraordinary excellence, he also acquires ten kinds of powers with which he cultivates all the practices in the realms of beings. What are those ten? They are as follows:

The first is the power of courage and strength, because of which he trains those in the world;
The second is the power of vigor, because of which he never retreats;
The third is the power of nonattachment, because of which he abandons all defilements;
The fourth is the power of quiescence, because of which he remains free of contentiousness regarding any dharma;
The fifth is the power to deal with both opposition and agreeableness, because of which his mind is at ease with all dharmas;
The sixth is the power of [realizing] the nature of dharmas, because of which he gains sovereign mastery of all meanings;
The seventh is the power of being unimpeded, because of which his wisdom is vast;
The eighth is the power of fearlessness, because of which he is able to discuss all dharmas;
The ninth is the power of eloquence because of which he is able to retain all dharmas; and
The tenth is the power of explanation, because of which his wisdom is boundless.

Sons of the Buddha, as for these ten kinds of powers, they are vast powers, supreme powers, invincible powers, measureless powers, skillfully accumulated powers, unshakable powers, solidly enduring powers, wisdom powers, powers of accomplishment, powers of supreme meditative absorption, pure powers, ultimately purified powers, Dharma body powers, Dharma light powers, Dharma lamp powers, Dharma gateway powers, indestructible powers, ultimately courageous powers, powers of a great man, powers of a good man's cultivation, powers of the realization of right enlightenment, powers of roots of goodness accumulated in the past, powers of establishment in measureless roots of goodness, powers associated with abiding in the powers of a *tathāgata*, powers of the mind's contemplative reflections, powers that increase a bodhisattva's happiness, powers that produce pure faith in the bodhisattva, powers that increase the bodhisattva's courage, powers produced by the resolve to attain bodhi, powers of the bodhisattva's pure profound mind, powers of the bodhisattva's especially supreme profound mind, powers produced by the influential effect of a bodhisattva's roots of goodness, powers produced by achieving the ultimate in all dharmas, powers associated with the unimpeded body, powers produced by entering the Dharma gateways of skillful expedient means, powers of the pure and sublime Dharma, powers arising from becoming established in the great strength by which he cannot be shaken by anyone in the world, and powers which no being can overcome.

Sons of the Buddha, as for the dharmas of measureless meritorious qualities such as these, this bodhisattva-mahāsattva: is able to produce them, is able to perfect them, is able to completely fulfill them, is able to illuminate them, is able to embody them, is able to everywhere embody them, is able to make them vast, is able to make them steadfast, is able to increase them, is able to purify them, and is able to everywhere purify them.

This bodhisattva becomes such that no one could fully describe the bounds of his meritorious qualities, the bounds of his wisdom, the bounds of his cultivation, the bounds of his Dharma gateways, the bounds of his sovereign masteries, the bounds of his practice of the austerities, the bounds of his development, the bounds of his purity, the bounds of his emancipation, or the bounds of his sovereign mastery in the Dharma.

This bodhisattva also becomes such that, even in an ineffable number of kalpas, no one could completely describe all the Dharma gateways that he has acquired, that he has developed, that he has entered into, that he has directly manifested, that he has fathomed their spheres of experience, that he has contemplated, that he has realized and entered, that he has purified, that he has come to completely know, or that he has established.

Sons of the Buddha, when this bodhisattva-mahāsattva abides in this samādhi, he becomes able to completely know all the numberlessly many, measurelessly many, boundlessly many, incomparably many, innumerably many, unspeakably many, inconceivably many, immeasurably many, ineffably many, and ineffably-ineffably many samādhis. All the spheres of experience of every one of those samādhis are measurelessly vast. Whether in entering into, emerging from, or abiding in those spheres of experience, there are none of them for which he does not clearly see all their appearances, all their manifestations, all their stations of practice, all their similar consequences, all their individual natures, all the factors that they extinguish, and all the emancipation that they bring about.

Sons of the Buddha, he is like the palace of the great dragon king, Anavatapta, "Free of Heat," from which there flow four rivers that are free of turbidity, free of the various pollutants, free of any defiling filth, and that have waters that are as clear as space. The four sides of that lake each have a single mouth and from every one of those mouths, there flows a river. The Ganges River flows from an elephant's mouth, the Śītā River flows from a lion's mouth, the Sindhu River flows from an ox's mouth, and the Vākṣu River flows from a horse's mouth.

As the four great rivers flow out, the mouth that sends forth the Ganges River spills forth silver sands, the mouth that sends forth the Śītā River spills forth vajra sands, the mouth that sends forth the Sindhu River spills forth gold sands, and the mouth that sends forth the Vākṣu River spills forth lapis lazuli sands. The Ganges River becomes the color of white silver at its mouth, the Śītā River becomes the color of vajra at its mouth, the Sindhu River becomes the color of yellow gold at its mouth, and the Vākṣu River becomes the color of lapis lazuli at its mouth.

Each of these rivers is a *yojana* wide at its mouth. Having poured forth in this manner, the four rivers each wind around that great lake seven times and then are diverted away toward their respective directions to which they send their vast and bounding currents rushing away to flow into the great ocean. As those rivers wind around in their circular flow, in the areas between each of their courses there are *utpala* flowers, *padma* flowers, *kumuda* flowers, and *puṇḍārīka* flowers made of jewels from the heavens. They emanate their exotic fragrances and are exquisite in their colors and purity. All their many different flower petals and many different pods and stamens are all made of many kinds of precious jewels that, naturally possessed of translucent brilliance, emanate light producing mutually reflected illumination.

Anavatapta, the Heat-Free Lake, round and vast, is fifty *yojanas* across. Its bottom is everywhere spread with marvelous sands made of the many kinds of precious gems. Ornamented with all the many different kinds of *maṇi* jewels, its banks are all adorned with countless jewels. The marvelous fragrance of sandalwood incense spreads about everywhere there. *Utpala* flowers, *padma* flowers, *kumuda* flowers, and *puṇḍārīka* flowers as well as all the other kinds of bejeweled flowers everywhere fill those areas. A subtle breeze wafts through, causing the fragrant scent to spread afar. The area is completely surrounded by groves of flowering bejeweled trees. When the sun rises, it everywhere illuminates both within and beyond the waters of the lake and its rivers. All those many phenomena receive its reflections and display interlaced rays of brilliant light that form a net of bright illumination.

All the many kinds of phenomena such as these, whether they be near or far, high or low, vast or constricted, coarse or fine, even down to those that are the most extremely tiny things such as a grain of sand or a mote of dust—they all consist of exquisite jewels whose radiance emanates penetrating reflections. None of them fail to display reflected images of the sun's orb that in turn progressively reflect back ever more such radiance each upon the other. The many reflections such as these neither increase nor decrease and neither mix together nor dissipate. They all retain their original character by which they are all able to be clearly discerned.

Sons of the Buddha, just as four rivers flow forth into the great ocean from the four river mouths of Anavatapta, the Heat-Free Lake, so too it is with the bodhisattva-mahāsattva, for it is from his four types of eloquence[294] that all the practices flow forth and ultimately lead into the ocean of all-knowledge.

Just as the great Ganges River flows out over silver sands from the silver-colored elephant's mouth, so too it is with the bodhisattva-mahāsattva who, with eloquence with respect to meanings,[295] expounds upon all the gateways to meaning taught by all *tathāgatas*, thereby giving birth to all the pure dharmas that ultimately lead into the ocean of unimpeded knowledge.

Just as the great Śītā River flows out over vajra sands from the vajra-colored lion's mouth, so too it is with the bodhisattva-mahāsattva who, with eloquence with respect to dharmas,[296] expounds for all beings on the Buddha's vajra statements, drawing forth vajra knowledge that ultimately leads into the ocean of unimpeded knowledge.

Just as the great Sindhu River flows out over gold sands from the gold-colored ox's mouth, so too it is with the bodhisattva-mahāsattva who, with eloquence with respect to the language of the teachings,[297] expounds on the skillful means by which one accords with conditioned arising as it operates in the world, thereby awakening beings, delighting them, training them, and ripening them so that they ultimately enter the ocean of skillful means based on conditioned arising.

And just as the great Vākṣu River flows out over lapis lazuli sands from the lapis lazuli-colored horse's mouth, so too it is with the bodhisattva-mahāsattva who, with endless eloquence,[298] rains down a rain of hundreds of thousands of *koṭīs* of *nayutas* of ineffable numbers of dharmas, enabling all those who hear him to receive its drenching moisture and thus ultimately enter the Dharma ocean of all buddhas.

Just as, after, following their courses in flowing around Anavatapta, the Heat-Free Lake, the four rivers then flow off in four directions and enter the ocean, so too it is with the bodhisattva-mahāsattva who, in developing compliant physical actions, compliant verbal actions, and compliant mental actions, perfects wisdom as the guide in physical actions, wisdom as the guide in verbal actions, and wisdom as the guide in mental actions and then flows off in the four directions and ultimately enters the ocean of all-knowledge.

Sons of the Buddha, what then is meant by "the four directions" as they apply to the bodhisattva? Sons of the Buddha, these refer to:

Seeing all buddhas and then becoming awakened;
Hearing, absorbing, retaining, and never forgetting all dharmas;
Achieving the fulfillment of all of the *pāramitā* practices; and
Using great compassion to teach the Dharma and satisfy beings.

Just as when those four great rivers flow around that great lake, the areas between each of their courses are all filled with *utpala* flowers, *padma* flowers, *kumuda* flowers, and *puṇḍārīka* flowers, so too it is with the bodhisattva-mahāsattva who, in his bodhi resolve, never relinquishes beings. He speaks the Dharma for them, trains them, and enables them all to completely fulfill the practice of countless samādhis with which they see the adorned and purified buddha lands.

Just as Anavatapta, the Heat-Free Lake, is surrounded by bejeweled trees, so too it is with the bodhisattva-mahāsattva when he reveals the buddha lands surrounded by adornments and thus enables all beings to progress toward bodhi.

Just as Anavatapta, the Heat-Free Lake, is fifty *yojanas* long and wide, pure, and free of turbidity, so too it is with the bodhisattva-mahāsattva, for his bodhi resolve is possessed of boundless capacity, is completely full of roots of goodness, and is pure and free of turbidity.

Just as Anavatapta, the Heat-Free Lake, has banks adorned with countless jewels and has sandalwood incense scattered all around in it, so too it is with the bodhisattva-mahāsattva, for the banks of his great vow of bodhi resolve are adorned with hundreds of thousands of *koṭīs* of wisdom jewels of ten different types and are everywhere sprinkled with the exquisite fragrance of all his many varieties of goodness.

Just as the bottom of Anavatapta, the Heat-Free Lake, is spread with gold sands and is adorned with inlaid *maṇi* jewels of many different sorts, so too it is with the bodhisattva-mahāsattva as he everywhere contemplates with his sublime wisdom inlaid and adorned with the Dharma jewels of his inconceivable bodhisattva liberations, acquires the unimpeded radiance of all dharmas, dwells where all buddhas dwell, and enters all the extremely profound skillful means.

Just as the dragon king Anavatapta has forever abandoned all the heat afflictions of dragons, so too it is with the bodhisattva-mahāsattva, for he has forever abandoned all of the world's misery and afflictions and, although he manifests the appearance of taking on rebirths, he still remains free of defiling attachments even as he does so.

Just as the four great rivers provide moisture to all the lands on the continent of Jambudvīpa and, after providing that moisture, they then enter the great ocean, so too it is with the bodhisattva-mahāsattva, for he provides the moisture of his four rivers of wisdom to the devas, humans, *śramaṇas*, and brahmans and enables them all to enter the great ocean of the wisdom of *anuttarasamyaksaṃbodhi* adorned with the ten powers.

What then are those four rivers? They are:

First, the river of the knowledge of vows by which he ceaselessly rescues, protects, and trains all beings;

Second, the river of the knowledge of the *pāramitās* by which he continuously and endlessly cultivates the bodhi practices and benefits beings in the past, future, and present ages, thus bringing about their ultimate entry into the ocean of all buddhas' wisdom;

Third, the river of the knowledge of the bodhisattva's samādhis which is adorned with numberless samādhis by which one sees all buddhas and enters the ocean of all buddhas; and

Fourth, the river of the knowledge of great compassion in which, with sovereign mastery in great kindness, he everywhere rescues beings, incessantly uses skillful means to gather them in, cultivates the gateways to secret meritorious qualities, and ultimately enters the great ocean of the ten powers.

Just as, after the four great rivers flow forth from Anavatapta, the Heat-Free Lake, they flow on endlessly and ultimately enter the great ocean, so too it is with the bodhisattva-mahāsattva who, using the power of great vows, cultivates the bodhisattva practices and, with sovereign mastery of inexhaustible knowledge and vision, ultimate enters the ocean of all-knowledge.

Just as, when the four great rivers proceed toward their entry into the great ocean, there is nothing that is able to obstruct them and prevent them from entering it, so too it is with the bodhisattva-mahāsattva, for there is nothing that impedes his constant and diligent cultivation of Samantabhadra's conduct and vows, his complete development of the light of all wisdom, his dwelling in the bodhi dharmas of all buddhas, and his entry into the wisdom of the Tathāgata.

Just as the four great rivers never weary of sending their bounding flow on into the ocean even throughout the course of kalpa after kalpa, so too it is with the bodhisattva-mahāsattva, for, even to the very end of all kalpas of the future, he never wearies of using the conduct and vows of Samantabhadra to cultivate the bodhisattva practices and enter the ocean of the *tathāgatas*.

Sons of the Buddha, just as when the sun rises, reflections of the sun appear in the gold sands, silver sands, vajra sands, lapis lazuli sands, and all the many other different kinds of bejeweled things in the waters of Anavatapta, the Heat-Free Lake, and just as the gold sands and other bejeweled objects in turn each mutually and unimpededly manifest penetrating reflections of each other's images, so too it is with the bodhisattva-mahāsattva when, abiding in this samādhi, he sees in every pore of his own body buddhas, *tathāgatas,* as numerous as the atoms in an ineffable-ineffable number of buddha *kṣetras.* He also sees all the lands of those buddhas, their sites of enlightenment, and their congregations. He listens to Dharma teachings from each of those buddhas, absorbs and retains them, develops resolute faith, and makes offerings. In each instance, he passes through an ineffable-ineffable number of *koṭīs* of *nayutas* of kalpas and yet does not conceive of those spans of time as either long or short or those congregations as crowded. Why is this? This is:

Because, with a sublime mind, he enters the boundless Dharma realm;

Because he enters incomparably many different fruitions of karma;

Because he enters the spheres of experience of inconceivably many samādhis;
Because he enters the spheres of experience of inconceivably many types of meditative contemplation;
Because he enters the spheres of experience of all buddhas' sovereign mastery;
Because he is regarded with protective mindfulness by all buddhas;
Because he acquires all buddhas' great spiritual transformations;
Because he acquires all *tathāgatas'* rare and recondite ten powers;
Because he enters the completely fulfilled sphere of experience of Samantabhadra Bodhisattva's practices; and
Because he acquires all buddhas' tireless powers of the spiritual superknowledges.

Sons of the Buddha, as for this bodhisattva-mahāsattva:

Although he is able to enter and emerge from meditative absorption in but a single mind-moment, he still does not dispense with remaining in meditative absorption for a long time, nor does he have any attachment to it;
Although he enters these spheres of experience, he does not depend on them or dwell in them, and yet he still does not abandon all those with whom he has developed karmic conditions;
Although he is well able to enter even the boundaries of a *kṣaṇa,* he is still tireless in manifesting a buddha's spiritual superknowledges to benefit all beings;
Although he equally enters the entire Dharma realm, he still never reaches its boundaries;
Although he has no abiding or any place in which he abides, he still constantly progresses into the path to all-knowledge and uses his powers to create transformations to everywhere enter the countless congregations of beings and completely adorn all worlds;
Although he has abandoned the discriminations associated with the world's inverted views and has stepped beyond all the grounds in which discriminations take place, he still does not abandon the many different kinds of signs;
Although he is able to completely perfect skillful expedient means, he still achieves the ultimate in purity; and
Although he does not make discriminations regarding the bodhisattva's grounds, he still has already skillfully entered them.

Sons of the Buddha, just as, although empty space is able to embrace all things, it is still apart from existence or nonexistence, so too it is with the bodhisattva-mahāsattva in these respects:

Although he everywhere enters all worlds, he still abandons any conception of "the world";

Although he diligently liberates all beings, he still abandons any conception of "beings";

Although he deeply knows all dharmas, he still abandons any conception of "dharmas";

Although he delights in seeing all buddhas, he still abandons any conception of "buddhas";

Although he skillfully enters many different samādhis, he still realizes that the inherent nature of all dharmas is suchness and thus remains free of any defiling attachments;

Although he uses boundless eloquence to expound on endless Dharma statements, his mind still forever abides apart from the dharmas of language;

Although he delights in contemplating the wordless Dharma, he still constantly manifests his pure voice;

Although he abides at the very limits of all language-transcending dharmas, he still constantly reveals many different kinds of forms and characteristics;

Although he teaches beings, he still realizes all dharmas are ultimately empty by nature;

Although he diligently cultivates the great compassion and liberates beings, he still realizes the realms of beings are endless and will never be subject to dissolution;

Although he fully comprehends that the Dharma realm is everlasting and unchanging, he still constantly and ceaselessly uses the three spheres[299] to train beings; and

Although he always securely abides where the Tathāgata abides, he still uses his pure wisdom and fearless mind to distinguish and expound on many different kinds of dharmas as he constantly and ceaselessly turns the wheel of the Dharma.

Sons of the Buddha, this is what constitutes the knowledge of skillful means as it relates to the bodhisattva-mahāsattva's ninth great samādhi, "the great samādhi of sovereign mastery throughout the Dharma realm."

Sons of the Buddha, what then is meant by the bodhisattva-mahāsattva's "samādhi of the unimpeded wheel"?

Sons of the Buddha, when the bodhisattva-mahāsattva enters this samādhi, he abides in unimpeded physical actions, unimpeded verbal actions, and unimpeded mental actions, he abides in unimpeded buddha lands, he acquires the wisdom by which he is unimpeded in ripening beings, he gains the wisdom by which he is unimpeded in training beings, he emanates unimpeded radiance, he manifests a net of unimpeded light, he manifests unimpeded vast transformations, he turns the unimpeded wheel of the pure Dharma, he acquires the bodhisattva's unimpeded sovereign masteries, he everywhere enters all the powers of the Buddha, he everywhere abides in the wisdom of all buddhas, he accomplishes what the Buddha accomplishes, he purifies whatever the Buddha purifies, he manifests the Buddha's spiritual superknowledges, he pleases the Buddha, he practices the Tathāgata's practices, he abides in the Tathāgata's path, he is always able to draw near to countless buddhas, he accomplishes the Buddha's works, and he carries on the lineage of all buddhas.

Sons of the Buddha, after the bodhisattva-mahāsattva has come to abide in this samādhi, he contemplates all-knowledge, he contemplates all-knowledge in general, he contemplates all-knowledge in terms of its specific aspects, he accords with all-knowledge, he reveals all-knowledge, he takes all-knowledge as the object of his attention, he perceives all-knowledge, he comprehensively perceives all-knowledge, and he perceives all-knowledge in terms of its specific aspects.

In his cultivation of Samantabhadra Bodhisattva's vast vows, vast resolve, vast practices, vast destinies, vast places entered, vast radiance, vast manifestations, vast protective mindfulness, vast transformations, and vast path, he never interrupts it, never retreats from it, never rests from it, never discontinues it, never grows weary of it, never relinquishes it, never becomes distracted in it, never becomes confused in it, always increases his progress in it, and constantly continues in it.

And why is this? This bodhisattva-mahāsattva has perfected great vows in relation to all dharmas, has set out in the practice of the Great Vehicle, and has entered the ocean of skillful means of the Buddha's Dharma. By the power of supreme vows, he has developed brightly illuminating wisdom and skillful means in cultivating the practices that all bodhisattvas practice. He has perfected the bodhisattva's spiritual superknowledges and transformations and is well able to regard all beings with protective mindfulness just as all buddhas of past, future, and present eras regard them with protective mindfulness. He constantly arouses the great compassion for all beings and achieves success in the unchanging Dharma of the Tathāgata.

Sons of the Buddha, just as when someone attaches a *maṇi* jewel to a colored robe, that *maṇi* jewel takes on the same color as the robe yet does not relinquish its own nature, so too it is with the bodhisattva-mahāsattva, for when he perfects wisdom as the jewel of the mind, contemplates all-knowledge, and makes it everywhere clearly apparent, he still never relinquishes his cultivation of the bodhisattva practices.

And why is this? The bodhisattva-mahāsattva has made great vows to benefit all beings, to liberate all beings, to serve all buddhas, to purify all worlds, to comfort beings, to deeply enter the ocean of Dharma, to manifest great sovereign mastery in order to purify the realms of beings, to provide for and give to beings, to everywhere illuminate the world, and to enter the Dharma gateway of boundless illusory conjurations without retreating or turning back and without tiring or becoming weary of this.

Sons of the Buddha, just as empty space holds the many worlds whether they are coming into being or abiding, doing so without wearying, without tiring, without deteriorating, without decaying, without dissolution, without damage, without change, without varying, without difference, and without relinquishing its own nature, doing so because it is the nature of empty space for it to be this way, so too it is with the bodhisattva-mahāsattva who establishes countless great vows to liberate all beings with a mind that remains free of any weariness in doing so.

Sons of the Buddha, this circumstance is analogous to that of nirvāṇa which never grows weary even as the countless beings of the past, the future, and the present pass into extinction within it. And why is this so? It is because the original nature of all dharmas is pure. This is what is referred to as "nirvāṇa." How then could it somehow grow weary of this? So too it is with the bodhisattva-mahāsattva. It is for the very purpose of fulfilling his wish to liberate all beings and enable their emancipation that he appears in the world. How then could his mind somehow become weary of this?

Sons of the Buddha, this is just as it is with all-knowledge which can enable all bodhisattvas of the past, future, and present to already be born, now be born, or be born in the future into the family of all buddhas and then eventually enable them to attain unexcelled bodhi. And why is this so? It is because all-knowledge and the Dharma realm are no different and because it has no attachment to any dharmas. So too it is with the bodhisattva-mahāsattva, for his mind abides with equanimity in all-knowledge. How then could he have a mind that grows weary of this?

Sons of the Buddha, this bodhisattva-mahāsattva has a lotus flower that is so vast that it extends to the very boundaries of the ten directions. It is adorned with an ineffable number of petals, an ineffable number of jewels, and an ineffable number of fragrances. Its ineffable number of jewels in turn reveal many different kinds of pristine and exquisite jewels arranged in the finest ways. That flower always emanates lights of many different colors which are unimpeded in their pervasive illumination of all worlds throughout the ten directions. Suspended over it is a net made of real gold which is hung with jeweled bells that slowly sway and emanate sublime sounds. Those sounds expound on the dharma of all-knowledge. This immense lotus flower possessed of the pure adornments of the Tathāgata is produced from all his roots of goodness, is a manifestation of auspiciousness made visible through spiritual powers, is a reflection of a myriad *asaṃkhyeyas* of pure meritorious qualities perfected during the course of the bodhisattva's marvelous path, and is a phenomenon that has flowed forth from the resolve to attain all-knowledge. Reflected images of the buddhas of the ten directions are displayed within it. Those in the world gaze up at it with admiration as if it were a buddha stupa and, of those beings who do see it, there are none who do not bow down in reverence before it. It arises from the right Dharma by which one is able to fully understand the illusory and it is such that there is nothing in the world which could compare to it.

When the bodhisattva-mahāsattva sits down on this lotus flower in the lotus posture, the size of his body matches that of the flower. Aided by the spiritual powers of all buddhas, every pore of the bodhisattva's body emanates rays of light as numerous as the atoms in a hundred myriad *koṭīs* of *nayutas* of ineffables of buddha *kṣetras*. Every light ray in turn manifests *maṇi* jewels as numerous as the atoms in a hundred myriads of *koṭīs* of *nayutas* of ineffables of buddha *kṣetras*. Those jewels are all known as "treasuries of universal light" which are adorned with many different colors and characteristics and which are the product of countless meritorious qualities. Suspended over it is a net made of many jewels and flowers which spreads about hundreds of thousands of *koṭīs* of *nayutas* of especially supreme and sublime fragrances and many different adornments of different colors and appearances. There also appears a canopy suspended over it which is adorned with inconceivable jewels.

Every one of those *maṇi* jewels manifests towers as numerous as the atoms in a hundred myriads of *koṭīs* of *nayutas* of ineffables of buddha *kṣetras*.

Every one of those towers manifests lotus flower dais lion thrones as numerous as the atoms in a hundred myriads of *koṭīs* of *nayutas* of ineffables of buddha *kṣetras*.

Every one of those lion thrones manifests rays of light as numerous as the atoms in a hundred myriads of *koṭīs* of *nayutas* of ineffables of buddha *kṣetras*.

Every one of those rays of light manifests forms and appearances as numerous as the atoms in a hundred myriads of *koṭīs* of *nayutas* of ineffables of buddha *kṣetras*.

Every one of those forms and appearances manifests orbs of light as numerous as the atoms in a hundred myriads of *koṭīs* of *nayutas* of ineffables of buddha *kṣetras*.

Every one of those orbs of light manifests *vairocana maṇi* jewel flowers as numerous as the atoms in a hundred myriads of *koṭīs* of *nayutas* of ineffables of buddha *kṣetras*.

Every one of those flowers manifests pedestals as numerous as the atoms in a hundred myriads of *koṭīs* of *nayutas* of ineffables of buddha *kṣetras*.

Every one of those pedestals manifests buddhas as numerous as the atoms in a hundred myriads of *koṭīs* of *nayutas* of ineffables of buddha *kṣetras*.

Every one of those buddhas manifests spiritual transformations as numerous as the atoms in a hundred myriads of *koṭīs* of *nayutas* of ineffables of buddha *kṣetras*.

Every one of those spiritual transformations purifies congregations of beings as numerous as the atoms in a hundred myriads of *koṭīs* of *nayutas* of ineffables of buddha *kṣetras*.

Every one of those congregations of beings manifests sovereign masteries of the buddhas as numerous as the atoms in a hundred myriads of *koṭīs* of *nayutas* of ineffables of buddha *kṣetras*.

Every one of those sovereign masteries rains down dharmas of the Buddha as numerous as the atoms in a hundred myriads of *koṭīs* of *nayutas* of ineffables of buddha *kṣetras*.

Every one of those dharmas of the Buddha has sutras as numerous as the atoms in a hundred myriads of *koṭīs* of *nayutas* of ineffables of buddha *kṣetras*.

Every one of those sutras expounds on gateways to the Dharma as numerous as the atoms in a hundred myriads of *koṭīs* of *nayutas* of ineffables of buddha *kṣetras*.

Every one of those gateways to the Dharma is possessed of types of Dharma wheels penetrated by vajra wisdom, each discoursing in different words as numerous as the atoms in a hundred myriads of *koṭīs* of *nayutas* of ineffables of buddha *kṣetras*.

Every one of those Dharma wheels ripens realms of beings as numerous as the atoms in a hundred myriads of *koṭīs* of *nayutas* of ineffables of buddha *kṣetras*.

And every one of those realms of beings is possessed of beings receiving training in dharmas of the Buddha as numerous as the atoms in a hundred myriads of *koṭīs* of *nayutas* of ineffables of buddha *kṣetras*.

Sons of the Buddha, the bodhisattva-mahāsattva who abides in this samādhi manifests countless transformations such as these from the realms of his spiritual superknowledges. He realizes that they are all like illusory conjurations and thus does not have any defiled attachment to them. He securely abides in the inherently pure nature of the boundlessly and ineffably many dharmas, in the true character of the Dharma realm, in the lineage of the *tathāgatas*, at the very boundaries of the unimpeded, where there is neither any going nor coming, where there is nothing that is either prior or subsequent, where it is so extremely profound as to be bottomless, and in what is realized through direct perception. By resort to wisdom, he enters on his own and does not depend on others for his awakening. His mind remains unconfused and also free of discriminations.

He becomes one who is praised by all buddhas of the past, future, and present who flows forth from the power of the buddhas and enters the sphere of all buddhas. His purified eyes directly realize the reality-accordant essential nature. His wisdom eye possesses universal vision. He perfects the buddha eye, becomes a bright lamp for the world, courses in spheres of cognition known by the wisdom eye, and is able to extensively explain the gateways to the sublime Dharma.

He attains success in his resolve to realize bodhi, progresses toward the state of the most supreme of men, becomes unimpeded in all spheres of experience, enters the lineage of the wise, brings forth all forms of wisdom, abandons the dharmas associated with taking birth in the world, and yet manifests as taking rebirth and uses transformations produced by spiritual superknowledges as skillful means to train beings. In all these matters, there is nothing that does not involve skillful means.

His meritorious qualities, understandings, and aspirations are all pure, are all possessed of the most ultimate degree of sublimity, and are completely and perfectly full in their development. His wisdom is as vast as empty space. He is well able to contemplate the spheres of cognition of the many *āryas*. His faith, practice, and power of vows are unshakably solid. His meritorious qualities are endless and are praised by those in the world. He gathers the many marvelous jewels from the treasury beheld by all buddhas, from the station of the great bodhi, and from the ocean of all-knowledge and thus becomes one possessed of great wisdom. His nature is as pure as a lotus flower. When beings see him, they are all delighted and they all benefit from it. The light of his wisdom is pervasively illuminating. He sees countless buddhas and purifies all dharmas.

In all that he practices, he is quiescent, and in the dharmas of all buddhas, he is ultimately unimpeded. He constantly uses skillful means in dwelling in the bodhi of the Buddha and it is from within the practice of the meritorious qualities that he is born. He embodies the wisdom of the bodhisattva, becomes chief among the bodhisattvas, and is regarded with protective mindfulness by all buddhas. He acquires the awesome spiritual powers of a buddha and succeeds in developing the Dharma body of a buddha. With his inconceivable power of mindfulness, he focuses on a single object and yet he still has nothing at all that he takes as an objective condition. His practice is vast, signless, unimpeded, and commensurate in scope with the immeasurability and boundlessness of the Dharma realm itself. The bodhi that he has realized is as boundless as empty space and he is entirely free of bonds or attachments.

His pervasive benefiting of the entire world flows forth from his roots of goodness in the ocean of all-knowledge. He is able to completely comprehend countless spheres of experience and he has already skillfully perfected the dharma of pure giving. He abides in the bodhisattva resolve, purifies the bodhisattva seed by which he is able in the course of things to give birth to the bodhi of all buddhas. He acquires skill in all dharmas of all buddhas. He embodies the subtle and marvelous practices and perfects the solidly enduring powers.

The bodhisattva comes to fully know all the masterful awesome spiritual powers of all buddhas which beings rarely even hear of. He enters the gateway of the non-dual and abides in the dharma of signlessness. Even though he has forever relinquished all signs, he is still able to extensively expound upon the many different dharmas. Adapting to beings' mental dispositions and aspirations, he enables them all to undergo the training and causes them all to be filled with joyous delight.

He takes the Dharma realm as his own body and remains free of discriminations. The sphere of his wisdom is inexhaustible, his determination is always intrepid, and his mind is constantly equanimous. He sees the entire extent of all buddhas' meritorious qualities, completely understands the differences and sequences in all kalpas, explains all dharmas, abides securely in all kṣetras, purifies all buddha lands, manifests the light of all right Dharma, expounds on all dharmas of the buddhas of the past, the future, and the present, reveals the stations in which all bodhisattvas dwell, serves as a bright lamp for the world, develops all roots of goodness, forever transcends the world, and always takes birth in the presence of the Buddha.

He attains the Buddha's wisdom and become foremost in understanding it with complete clarity. He is drawn forth and taken in by all buddhas, and has already entered the ranks of the *tathāgatas* of the future. He is one born from all good spiritual guides. Of all things that he aspires to, there are none of them that do not come to fruition.

He possesses great awe-inspiring virtue, abides in especially supreme intentions, is well able to explain all that he ever hears, also explaining it for others so that, on hearing the Dharma, they develop roots of goodness and come to dwell in the sphere of the apex of reality. His mind is unimpeded in all dharmas, he never relinquishes any of the practices, and he abandons all discriminations.

No thought moves in his mind regarding any dharma. He acquires the light of wisdom with which he extinguishes the darkness of delusion and brightly illuminates all dharmas of the Buddha. He does not create any interference in any of the realms of existence and yet takes on rebirths within them. He completely realizes that, even from their very origin on forward to the present, all the realms of existence have never had any movement at all. All of his physical, verbal, and mental karmic deeds are boundless.

Although he adapts to the world by using countless kinds of language to expound on many different topics, he still never contradicts the Dharma beyond words. He enters deeply into the ocean of the buddhas, realizes that all dharmas are merely artificial designations, and remains free of any bonds or attachments to anything in any spheres of experience. He completely understands that all dharmas are empty and devoid of anything at all that exists. The practices that he cultivates all come forth from the Dharma realm. Like empty space, they are all signless and formless. He deeply enters the Dharma realm and adapts to beings in expounding on it. Through the gateway of a single sphere of experience, he gives birth to all-knowledge.

He contemplates the ground of the ten powers and uses wisdom in cultivation and training. He takes wisdom as the bridge to all-knowledge, uses the wisdom eye to remain unimpeded in seeing the Dharma, and skillfully enters all the grounds. He knows the many different kinds of meanings, is able to completely understand every one of all the Dharma gateways, and, of all the great vows, there are none that he does not completely fulfill.

Sons of the Buddha, it is in this way that the bodhisattva-mahāsattva reveals the undifferentiated nature of all *tathāgatas*. This is the gateway of unimpeded skillful means. This is able to produce congregations of bodhisattvas. This dharma consists solely of spheres of experience of samādhi. This enables courageous entry into all-knowledge. This is able to reveal all the gateways into samādhi. This enables unimpeded entry into all *kṣetras* everywhere. This enables the training of all beings. This enables one to abide at the very bounds of the nonexistence of beings. This enables the explanation of all dharmas of the Buddha. And this finds nothing at all that is apprehensible in any sphere of experience.

Although he is always expounding and explaining, he still constantly abandons erroneous conceptions and discriminations.

Although he knows all dharmas have nothing that they do, he is still able to show all kinds of actions that he accomplishes.

Although he knows all buddhas have no signs of duality, he is still able to reveal all buddhas.

Although he knows forms do not exist, he still expounds on all forms.

Although he knows feelings do not exist, he still expounds on all feelings.

Although he knows perceptions do not exist, he still expounds on all perceptions.

Although he knows karmic formative factors do not exist, he still expounds on all karmic formative factors.

Although he knows consciousnesses do not exist, he still expounds on all consciousnesses and constantly uses the wheel of the Dharma to instruct everyone.

Although he knows dharmas are unproduced, he still constantly turns the wheel of Dharma.

Although he knows dharmas are free of any differences, he still speaks of all the gateways to differentiation.

Although he knows all dharmas are neither produced nor destroyed, he still speaks of all the signs of production and destruction.

Although he knows all dharmas are free of any signs of either coarseness or subtlety, he still speaks of all dharmas' signs of coarseness and subtlety.

Although he knows all dharmas have no supremacy, mediocrity, or inferiority, he is still able to expound on the most supreme of all dharmas.

Although he knows all dharmas cannot be described in words, he is still able to expound on them with pure words and phrases.

Although he knows all dharmas have no inward or outward, he still speaks of all inward and outward dharmas.

Although he knows all dharmas cannot be completely known, he still speaks of many different kinds of wise contemplation.

Although he knows all dharmas have no reality, he still speaks of the genuine path to emancipation.

Although he knows all dharmas are ultimately endless, he still expounds on the ending of all the contaminants.

Although he knows all dharmas are devoid of any bases for opposition or contentiousness, it is still not the case that there are no differences between self and other.

Although he knows all dharmas ultimately do not require a teacher, he still always reveres all teachers and seniors.

Although he knows all dharmas do not require [teaching by] others for one to awaken to them, he still always reveres all good spiritual guides.

Although he knows dharmas have no turning,[300] he still turns the wheel of the Dharma.

Although he knows dharmas have no arising, he still reveals all their causes and conditions.

Although he knows all dharmas have no past, he still speaks extensively about the past.

Although he knows all dharmas have no future, he still speaks extensively about the future.

Although he knows all dharmas have no present, he still speaks extensively about the present.

Although he knows all dharmas have no creator, he still speaks about all the actions by which they are created.

Although he knows all dharmas have no causes or conditions, he still speaks about all of their accumulated causes.

Although he knows all dharmas have no equal, he still speaks about the path of equality and inequality.

Although he knows all dharmas are beyond words and speech, he still makes definite statements about the dharmas of the three periods of time.

Although he knows all dharmas have nothing upon which they depend, he still speaks of relying on wholesome dharmas to then succeed in gaining emancipation.

Although he knows all dharmas have no body at all, he still speaks extensively about the Dharma body.

Although he knows all buddhas of the three periods of time are boundlessly many, he is still able to speak extensively about there only being one buddha.

Although he knows dharmas are formless, he still manifests many different forms.

Although he knows dharmas have no views, he still speaks extensively about all views.

Although he knows dharmas are signless, he still speaks of many different signs.

Although he knows all dharmas have no spheres of cognition, he still speaks extensively of wise spheres of cognition.

Although he knows all dharmas have no differences, he still speaks of the many kinds of differences in the fruits of the practices.

Although he knows all dharmas have no emancipation,[301] he still speaks about the pure practices for gaining emancipation.

Although he knows all dharmas are originally eternally abiding, he still speaks of all the dharmas involved in flowing along in cyclic existence.

And although he knows all dharmas have no illumination, he still speaks about the dharmas used to produce illumination.

Sons of the Buddha, if the bodhisattva-mahāsattva enters the spheres of cognition of great awesome samādhis such as this, then he is able realize all dharmas of the Buddha, he is able to progress into all dharmas of the Buddha, he is able to completely accomplish them, he is able to perfectly fulfill them, he is able to accumulate them, he is able to purify them, he is able to securely abide in them, and he is able to completely comprehend them and abide in conformity with the essential nature of all dharmas. This being so, this bodhisattva-mahāsattva does not have thoughts such as these: "There are a certain number of bodhisattvas," "a certain number of bodhisattva dharmas," "a certain number of bodhisattva ultimates," "a certain number of illusory ultimates," "a certain number of transformational ultimates," "a certain number of complete accomplishments of the spiritual superknowledges," "a certain number of complete accomplishments of cognition," "a certain number of meditative reflections," "a certain number of realizations and entries," "a certain number of modes of progression," or "a certain number of spheres of experience."

And why is this? This is because the bodhisattva's samādhi has an essential nature such as this, boundlessness such as this, and extraordinary supremacy such as this. This samādhi involves many different kinds of spheres of cognition, many different kinds of awesome powers, and many different kinds of deep entry, namely:

Entry into an ineffable number of wisdom gateways;
Entry into adornments apart from discriminations;
Entry into boundlessly many extraordinarily supreme *pāramitās;*
Entry into numberless *dhyāna* absorptions;
Entry into hundreds of thousands of *koṭīs* of *nayutas* of ineffables of forms of vast knowledge;
Entry into the vision of supremely marvelous treasuries of boundlessly many buddhas;
Entry into spheres of cognition which do not cease;
Entry into the enlightenment factors with pure resolute faith;
Entry into the great spiritual superknowledges with fiercely sharp faculties;
Entry into spheres of cognition with an unimpeded mind;
Entry into the eye which sees the equality of all buddhas;
Entry into the accumulation of Samantabhadra's supreme resolve and practices;
Entry into dwelling in the marvelous wisdom body of a *nārāyaṇa;*[302]
Entry into the proclamation of the Tathāgata's ocean of wisdom;
Entry into the generation of countless kinds of masterful spiritual transformations;
Entry into the gateway by which one produces the inexhaustible wisdom of all buddhas;
Entry into dwelling in the directly experienced sphere of action of all buddhas;
Entry into the purification of the sovereign wisdom of Samantabhadra Bodhisattva;
Entry into the revelation of the incomparable wisdom of the universal gateway;
Entry into the universal knowledge of all the Dharma realm's extremely subtle spheres of cognition;
Entry into the universal manifestation of all the Dharma realm's extremely subtle spheres of cognition;
Entry into the extraordinarily supreme light of wisdom;
Entry into the farthest reaches of all the sovereign masteries;
Entry into the farthest reaches of all the Dharma gateways of eloquence;

Entry into the wisdom body that everywhere pervades the Dharma realm;
Entry into perfecting the path by which one travels to all places everywhere;
Entry into skillfully abiding in all the different samādhis; and
Entry into knowing the minds of all buddhas.

Sons of the Buddha, this bodhisattva-mahāsattva abides in the practices of Samantabhadra and, in each successive mind-moment, enters a hundred *koṭīs* of ineffables of samādhis and yet does not see any beginning to Samantabhadra Bodhisattva's samādhis or the adornments of the Buddha's spheres of cognition. And why is this? This is:

Because he knows all dharmas are ultimately endless;
Because he knows all buddha *kṣetras* are boundless;
Because he knows all realms of beings are inconceivable;
Because he knows the past has no beginning;
Because he knows the future is endless;
Because he knows the present is as boundless as the entirety of empty space throughout the Dharma realm;
Because he knows the spheres of cognition of all buddhas are inconceivably many;
Because he knows all the bodhisattva practices are numberless;
Because he knows the spheres of cognition described by all buddhas' eloquence are ineffably and boundlessly many; and
Because he knows all dharmas taken as objective conditions by the mind which knows all as illusory are measurelessly many.

Sons of the Buddha, just as a wish-fulfilling jewel provides whatever is wished for, satisfying all wishes even when what is sought for is endless, and yet the power of jewel is still never exhausted, so too it is with the bodhisattva-mahāsattva when he enters this samādhi. He realizes that the mind is like an illusory conjuration that everywhere endlessly, inexhaustibly and ceaselessly, produces all the spheres of experience associated with all dharmas. How is this so? This is because, in perfecting Samantabhadra's unimpeded practices and wisdom, the bodhisattva-mahāsattva contemplates the measurelessly vast illusory objective realms as like reflected images and as neither increased nor decreased.

Sons of the Buddha, just as all the thoughts produced by each common person in the past, the present, and the future are boundless, uninterrupted, and endless so that the flowing on of their thoughts is continuous, ceaseless, and inconceivable, so too it is with the bodhisattva-mahāsattva, for when he enters this samādhi of the gateway to the universal illusion, it is boundless and unfathomable. And how is this so? It is because he completely comprehends the countless dharmas of Samantabhadra Bodhisattva's gateway of universal illusion.

Sons of the Buddha, this is just as when Nanda, Upananda, Manasvin, and the other great dragon kings send down the rain. Raindrops the size of cart hubs may fall throughout a boundless area and, even though the rain is of this sort, the clouds are still never exhausted. This is the effortless sphere of the dragons.

So too it is with the bodhisattva-mahāsattva, for when he abides in this samādhi, he enters all the gateways of Samantabhadra Bodhisattva's samādhis, including:

The gateway to wisdom;
The gateway to Dharma;
The gateway to seeing all buddhas;
The gateway to travel in all directions;
The gateway to sovereign mastery of the mind;
The gateway to empowerment;
The gateway to spiritual transformations;
The gateway to spiritual superknowledges;
The gateway to illusory conjurations;
The gateway to all dharmas as illusory;
The gateway filled with an ineffable-ineffable number of bodhisattvas;
The gateway to drawing near to *tathāgatas,* rightly enlightened ones, as numerous as the atoms in an ineffable-ineffable number of buddha *kṣetras;*
The gateway to entering an ineffable-ineffable number of vast webs of illusion;
The gateway to knowing an ineffable-ineffable number of different vast buddha *kṣetras;*
The gateway to knowing an ineffable-ineffable number of substantial and insubstantial worlds;
The gateway to knowing the thoughts of an ineffable-ineffable number of beings;
The gateway to knowing an ineffable-ineffable number of differences in time;
The gateway to knowing the creation and destruction of an ineffable-ineffable number of worlds; and
The gateway to knowing an ineffable-ineffable number of inverted and upright buddha *kṣetras.*

In but a single mind-moment, he knows them all in accordance with reality. When he enters them in these ways, they are boundless and endless. He does not become tired and does not grow weary of this. He never stops, never rests, never retreats, and never loses [his resolve].

In all these dharmas, he does not abide in wrong objects, constantly abides in right meditative reflection, and does not allow either sinking or restless mind states. He never retreats from his quest to gain all-knowledge and, for all buddha *kṣetras,* becomes a bright lamp that illuminates the world and turns the wheel of Dharma in an ineffable-ineffable number of circumstances, using marvelous eloquence in freely and endlessly inquiring of the *tathāgatas.* He manifests as gaining enlightenment in boundlessly many circumstances and, in training beings, he never abandons them. He always diligently cultivates Samantabhadra's conduct and vows and never rests in doing so. He incessantly manifests an ineffable-ineffable number of form bodies.

And how is this so? Just as whenever a burning flame comes into contact with a suitable object, a fire starts and does not cease to burn, so too it is with the bodhisattva-mahāsattva. Contemplating the realms of beings, the Dharma realm, and all worlds as just as boundless as empty space, he is then able in but a single mind-moment to go to visit buddhas as numerous as the atoms in an ineffable-ineffable number of buddha *kṣetras.* In the presence of every one of those buddhas, he enters an ineffable-ineffable number of many different dharmas of all-knowledge with which he enables the beings in an ineffable-ineffable number of realms of beings to leave behind the home life for the sake of the path and then diligently cultivate roots of goodness by which they attain ultimate purity. So too he enables an ineffable-ineffable number of bodhisattvas as yet not definitely committed to the conduct and vows of Samantabhadra to then become definitely committed to them and then establish themselves in the gateways of Samantabhadra's wisdom.

Using countless skillful means, throughout the three periods of time, he enters an ineffable-ineffable number of different vast kalpas of creation, abiding, and destruction and enters different realms within an ineffable-ineffable number of worlds in their creation, abiding, and destruction phases where he arouses just so very many greatly compassionate great vows to train all those countless beings without exception. And how is this so? It is because, due to his desire to liberate all beings, this bodhisattva-mahāsattva cultivates

Samantabhadra's practices, develops Samantabhadra's wisdom, and completely fulfills all the conduct and vows of Samantabhadra.

Therefore all bodhisattvas should diligently cultivate kinds of actions such as these, spheres of experience such as these, awesome virtue such as this, vastness such as this, measurelessness such as this, inconceivability such as this, universal illumination such as this, dwelling in the direct presence of all buddhas in this way, being regarded with protective mindfulness by all *tathāgatas* in this way, developing past roots of goodness in this way, and entering samādhi such as this in which their minds are unimpeded and unshakable, abandoning all the feverish afflictions, remaining tireless in this, maintaining irreversible resolve in this, establishing profound aspirations, remaining courageous and free of trepidation, according with the spheres of experience in samādhi, entering the grounds of inconceivable wisdom, not relying on language, not being attached to the world, not seizing on any dharma, not making discriminations, not having any defiling attachments to worldly matters, and not making discriminations regarding the spheres of experience.

As for the knowledge of all dharmas, they should simply establish themselves in it and should not attempt to measure it, which is to say:

[They should] draw near to those possessed of all-knowledge, awaken to the bodhi of the Buddha, perfect the light of the Dharma, bestow roots of goodness on all beings, extricate beings from the realms of the *māras*, enable them to enter the realm of the Buddha's Dharma, enable them to never relinquish the great vows, diligently contemplate the path of emancipation, broaden the sphere of purity, completely develop all the perfections, and arouse deep resolute faith in all buddhas;

They should always contemplate the nature of all dharmas and never relinquish this for even a moment;

They should realize that their own bodies and the nature of all dharmas are all the same;

They should clearly understand the actions of those in the world and then instruct them with wisdom and skillful means in accordance with the Dharma;

They should forever remain incessantly vigorous;

They should contemplate the scarcity of their own roots of goodness;

They should be diligent in increasing others' roots of goodness;

They should persist in their own cultivation of the path to all-knowledge;

They should diligently increase their own sphere of bodhisattva actions;
They should delight in drawing near to all good spiritual guides;
They should engage in joint practice with them and dwell together with them;
They should not discriminate among buddhas;
They should never relinquish mindfulness;
They should always abide in Dharma realm of equality;
They should realize that all manifestations of the mind and consciousness are like conjured illusions;
They should realize that all worldly actions are like a dream;
They should realize that the manifestations of all buddhas' power of vows are like reflected images;
They should realize that all vast karmic works are like supernatural transformations;
They should realize that all words and speech are like echoes;
They should contemplate all dharmas as like illusions;
They should realize that all dharmas that are produced and destroyed are like mere passing sounds;
They should realize that all buddha *kṣetras* to which they go are devoid of any essential nature;
They should never weary of inquiring of the *tathāgatas* about the Dharma of the Buddha;
They should be diligent in providing instruction to awaken everyone in the world and they should never abandon them; and
They should never rest in their efforts to know the right time to teach the Dharma to train all beings.

Sons of the Buddha, it is in these ways that the bodhisattva-mahāsattva cultivates Samantabhadra's practices, in these ways that he achieves perfect fulfillment of the bodhisattva's sphere of action, in these ways that he acquires a penetrating comprehension of the path to emancipation, in these ways that he absorbs and retains the Dharma of all buddhas of the three periods of time, in these ways that he contemplates the gateways to all-knowledge, in these ways that he reflects on the unchanging Dharma, in these ways that he brightens and purifies his especially supreme aspiration, in these ways that he develops resolute faith in all *tathāgatas*, in these ways that he acquires a complete awareness of the Buddha's vast powers, in these ways that he develops decisive and unimpeded resolve, and in these ways that he attracts and takes in all beings.

Sons of the Buddha, when the bodhisattva-mahāsattva enters this samādhi of such great wisdom in which Samantabhadra abides, buddhas from an ineffable-ineffable number of lands in each of the ten directions manifest directly before him. In every one of those lands there are *tathāgata* names as numerous as the atoms in an ineffable-ineffable number of buddha *kṣetras*, and, for every one of those names, there are buddhas as numerous as the atoms in an ineffable-ineffable number of buddha *kṣetras*, all of whom, having appeared directly before him, then:

Bestow on him the memory power of the Tathāgata, thereby enabling him to never forget the Tathāgata's sphere of cognition;

Bestow on him ultimate wisdom with respect to all dharmas, thereby enabling him to enter all-knowledge;

Bestow on him decisive wisdom in knowing the many different meanings of all dharmas, thereby enabling him to absorb and retain all dharmas of the Buddha and become unimpeded in penetrating [their meaning];

Bestow on him the unexcelled bodhi of the Buddha, thereby enabling him to enter all-knowledge and awaken to the Dharma realm;

Bestow on him the bodhisattva's ultimate wisdom, thereby enabling him to acquire the light of all dharmas and become free of all darkness;

Bestow on him the bodhisattva's irreversible wisdom, thereby enabling him to know what is and is not the appropriate time and which skillful means should be used in training beings;

Bestow on him the bodhisattva's unimpeded eloquence, thereby enabling him to awaken to and understand boundlessly many dharmas and then expound on them endlessly;

Bestow on him the power of spiritual superknowledges and transformations, thereby enabling him to manifest an ineffable-ineffable number of different bodies with boundlessly many different forms and appearances with which to awaken beings;

Bestow on him the perfectly complete voice, thereby enabling him to awaken beings by manifesting an ineffable-ineffable number of voices in many different languages; and

Bestow on him the power to not do anything in vain, thereby enabling all beings who succeed in seeing his physical form or hearing his Dharma teachings to then meet with success so that they will not have encountered him in vain.

Sons of the Buddha, because the bodhisattva-mahāsattva fulfills Samantabhadra's practices in this way, he acquires the Tathāgata's powers, purifies the path of emancipation, achieves the fulfillment of all-knowledge, and uses unimpeded eloquence together with spiritual superknowledges and transformations to accomplish the ultimate training of all beings. Possessed of the awesome virtue of the Buddha, he purifies the practices of Samantabhadra and abides in the path of Samantabhadra. Wishing to train all beings, he turns the wheel of all buddhas' sublime Dharma to the very end of future time. Why? Sons of the Buddha, if this bodhisattva-mahāsattva becomes accomplished in such extraordinary and supreme great vows and bodhisattva practices, then:

He becomes a master of Dharma for the entire world;
He becomes a Dharma sun for the entire world;
He becomes a wisdom moon for the entire world;
He becomes for the entire world a Sumeru king of mountains of towering height and unshakable solidity;
He becomes an ocean of boundless wisdom for the entire world;
He becomes a bright lamp of right Dharma for the entire world who everywhere provides boundless, continuous, and unending illumination;
He instructs all beings in boundlessly many pure meritorious qualities, thereby enabling them all to abide in meritorious qualities and roots of goodness, to accord with [the path to] all-knowledge and great impartial vows, and to cultivate the vast practices of Samantabhadra; and
He is always able to encourage countless beings to abide in and manifest great sovereign mastery in this samādhi of an ineffable-ineffable number of vast practices.

Sons of the Buddha, this bodhisattva-mahāsattva acquires wisdom such as this, realizes dharmas such as these, investigates, abides in, and clearly perceives dharmas such as these, acquires spiritual powers such as these, abides in spheres of cognition such as these, manifests spiritual transformations such as these, brings forth spiritual superknowledges such as these, always abides in the great compassion, and always benefits beings. He instructs beings in becoming securely established in the right path, in erecting the great radiant banner of merit and wisdom, in realizing inconceivable liberations, in dwelling in the liberations of all-knowledge, in reaching the far shore of perfection in the liberations of all buddhas, and in training in the gateways to inconceivable liberations and skillful means.

He has already succeeded in becoming accomplished in the different gateways for entering the Dharma realm without error or confusion. He attains easeful mastery in the ineffable-ineffable number of samādhis of Samantabhadra and abides with unimpeded mind in the lion-sprint wisdom.

His mind constantly abides in the ten great Dharma treasuries. What are those ten? They are as follows:

He abides in the recollection of all buddhas;
He abides in the recollection of all dharmas of the Buddha;
He abides in the use of great compassion in training all beings;
He abides in the wisdom that reveals inconceivable pure lands;
He abides in the decisive understanding with which he deeply enters the spheres of cognition of all buddhas;
He abides in the bodhi of the same character as that of all buddhas of the past, the future, and the present;
He abides in the most ultimate degree of unimpeded action and nonattachment;
He abides in the signless nature of all dharmas;
He abides in the same roots of goodness as all buddhas of the past, the future, and the present; and
He abides in the wisdom that guides the undifferentiated physical, verbal, and mental actions throughout the Dharma realm of all *tathāgatas* of the past, the future, and the present.

[Moreover], he abides in the contemplation in which the taking birth, leaving the home life, arriving at the site of enlightenment, realizing right enlightenment, turning the Dharma wheel, and entering *parinirvāṇa* of all buddhas of the three periods of time are all subsumed within the boundaries of a single *kṣaṇa*. Sons of the Buddha, the contents of these ten great Dharma treasuries are vast, measureless, innumerable, indescribable, inconceivable, ineffable, inexhaustible, hard to bear, and such that, not even anyone equipped with all worldly knowledge could ever fully describe them.

Sons of the Buddha, this bodhisattva-mahāsattva has already reached the far shore of perfection in Samantabhadra's practices, has realized the dharma of purity, has become possessed of vast power of resolve, and instructs beings in the accumulation of measureless roots of goodness and in the growth of all powers of the bodhisattva. In each successive mind-moment, he fulfills all meritorious qualities of the bodhisattva, perfects all practices of the bodhisattva, acquires the *dhāraṇī* dharmas of all buddhas, and absorbs and retains everything ever spoken by all buddhas.

Although he always abides securely in the apex of reality of true suchness, he still adapts to all the varieties of worldly discourse and thereby manifests as one who trains all beings. And how is this the case? This is because this is the very nature of the dharma of this samādhi in which the bodhisattva-mahāsattva abides.

Sons of the Buddha, because of this samādhi, this bodhisattva-mahāsattva acquires the vast wisdom of all buddhas; acquires the masterful eloquence by which he skillfully expounds on all vast dharmas; acquires the dharmas of purity and fearlessness that are the most especially supreme in all worlds; acquires the wisdom by which he enters all samādhis; acquires all bodhisattvas' skillful means; acquires the gateways to the light of all dharmas; reaches the far shore of perfection in the dharmas with which he provides comfort to the entire world; knows with respect to all beings what is and is not the right time; illuminates all places throughout the worlds of the ten directions and enables all beings to acquire supreme wisdom; and serves the entire world as an unsurpassable teacher, securely abides in all of the meritorious qualities, and instructs all beings in the pure samādhis by which they are enabled to enter into the most superior wisdom.

And how is so? If the bodhisattva-mahāsattva cultivates in this way, then he benefits beings, he increases in the great compassion, he draws near to good spiritual guides, he sees all buddhas, he completely understands all dharmas, he goes to all *kṣetras*, he enters all regions, he enters all worlds, he awakens to the identical nature of all dharmas, he knows the identical nature of all buddhas, and he abides in the identical nature of all-knowledge.

In this dharma, he engages in actions such as these and does not engage in any other kinds of actions. He abides in the mind that is not yet satisfied, he abides in the mind that is not distracted or confused, he abides in the singularly focused mind, he abides in the diligently cultivating mind, he abides in the resolutely decisive mind, and he abides in the unchanging mind. He reflects in this way, he acts in this way, and he reaches the ultimate in this way.

Sons of the Buddha, the bodhisattva-mahāsattva has no contradictory speech and has no contradictory actions, but rather is one who is consistent in his speech and consistent in his actions. Why? Just as vajra takes its name from its indestructibility and never has a time when it departs from indestructibility, so too it is with the bodhisattva-mahāsattva who takes his name from the practice dharmas and never has a time when he departs from the practice dharmas.

Just as real gold takes its name from its possession of its marvelous color and never has a time when it departs from its marvelous color, so too it is with the bodhisattva-mahāsattva who takes his name from all good karmic deeds and never has a time when he departs from all good karmic deeds.

Just as the solar *devaputra* takes his name from his orb of light and never has a time when he departs from his orb of light, so too it is with the bodhisattva-mahāsattva who takes his name from the light of wisdom and never has a time when he departs from his light of wisdom.

Just as Sumeru, the king of mountains, takes its name from the four jeweled peaks due to which it towers high above its place in the midst of the great ocean and never has a time when it departs from its four peaks, so too it is with the bodhisattva-mahāsattva who takes his name from his roots of goodness due to which he towers high above his place in the world and never has a time when he departs from his roots of goodness.

Just as the great earth takes its name from its ability to support all things and never has a time when it departs from its ability to support all things, so too it is with the bodhisattva-mahāsattva who takes his name from his ability to liberate everyone and never has a time when he departs from the great compassion.

Just as the great ocean takes its name from its ability to take in the many waters and never has a time when it departs from those waters, so too it is with the bodhisattva-mahāsattva who takes his name from his great vows and never has a time when he departs from his vows to liberate beings.

Just as a general takes his name from his ability to skillfully implement the methods of war and never has a time when he abandons this ability, so too it is with the bodhisattva-mahāsattva who takes his name from his ability to skillfully use samādhis such as these and, even up to the time when he perfects the wisdom of all-knowledge, never has a time when he departs from this practice.

Just as in his governance of the four continents a wheel-turning monarch is always diligent in guarding all beings, protecting them from untimely death, and ensuring that they will always enjoy happiness, so too it is with the bodhisattva-mahāsattva who enters great samādhis such as these and always diligently teaches and liberates all beings until he enables them to attain ultimate purity.

Just as when a seed is planted in the ground, it is then eventually able to cause the growth of a stem and leaves, so too it is with the bodhisattva-mahāsattva who cultivates the practices of Samantabhadra until he is able to cause all beings to grow in their good dharmas.

Just as the great clouds in the hot summer months send down great drenching rains that eventually bring about growth in all seeds, so too it is with the bodhisattva-mahāsattva who enters great samādhis such as these, cultivates the bodhisattva practices, and rains down the great Dharma rain that eventually causes all beings to attain ultimate purity, ultimate nirvāṇa, ultimate peace and security, ultimate arrival at the far shore of perfection, ultimate joyous delight, and the ultimate severance of doubts as he serves all beings as an ultimate field of merit by which he enables them all to purify their giving karma, enables them all to dwell irreversibly in the path, enables them all to equally acquire the wisdom of all-knowledge, enables them all to gain emancipation from the three realms of existence, enables them all to acquire ultimate wisdom, enables them all to acquire the most ultimate dharmas of all buddhas, the *tathāgatas*, and thereby establishes all beings in the station of all-knowledge.

Why is this so? When the bodhisattva-mahāsattva perfects these dharmas, his wisdom becomes completely clear, he enters the gates of the Dharma realm, and he becomes able to purify the bodhisattva's countless inconceivable practices. That is to say, he is able to purify all knowledge because he seeks to attain all-knowledge, he is able to purify beings because he enables their training, he is able to purify the *kṣetras* because he always engages in dedications [of merit], he is able to purify all dharmas because he completely understands them all, he is able to purify the fearlessnesses because he is free of timidity, he is able to purify unimpeded eloquence because of his skillfulness in expounding [the Dharma], he is able to purify the *dhāraṇīs* because he attains sovereign mastery in all dharmas, and he is able to purify the practice of drawing near because he always witnesses all buddhas appearing in the world.

Sons of the Buddha, when the bodhisattva-mahāsattva abides in this samādhi, he acquires hundreds of thousands of *koṭīs* of *nayutas* of ineffable-ineffables of pure meritorious qualities such as these:

Due to gaining sovereign mastery in the spheres of experience of samādhis such as these;
Due to being empowered by all buddhas;
Due to what flows from the power of their own roots of goodness;
Due to the great awesome power of entering the wisdom grounds;
Due to the power of the guidance provided by all his good spiritual guides;
Due to the power by which he vanquishes all demons;

Due to the power of the complete purity of his roots of goodness of the same class;
Due to the power of his zeal in the vast vows;
Due to the power of the ripening of the roots of goodness he has planted; and
Due to the unopposable power of his inexhaustible merit which is superior to that of anyone in the world.

Sons of the Buddha, by abiding in this samādhi, the bodhisattva-mahāsattva acquires ten kinds of dharmas that are the same as those of all buddhas of the past, the future, and the present. What are those ten? They are as follows:

His attainment of the major marks, the secondary characteristics, and the many different kinds of adornments is the same as that of all buddhas;
His ability to emanate immense nets of pure light is the same as that of all buddhas;
His use of the spiritual superknowledges and transformations to train beings is the same as that of all buddhas;
His boundlessly many form bodies and his pure and perfect voice are the same as those of all buddhas;
His manifestation of pure buddha lands in accordance with the karma of beings is the same as that of all buddhas;
His ability to acquire all the languages of all beings and then never forget or lose them is the same as that of all buddhas;
His use of inexhaustible eloquence adapted to the minds of beings in turning the Dharma wheel and enabling them to develop wisdom is the same as that of all buddhas;
His fearlessness in roaring the lion's roar and using countless dharmas to awaken the many kinds of beings is the same as that of all buddhas;
His use of great spiritual superknowledges to everywhere enter the three periods of time in but a single mind-moment is the same as that of all buddhas; and
His ability to everywhere reveal to all beings the buddhas' adornments, the buddhas' awesome powers, and the buddhas' sphere of endeavors is the same as that of all buddhas.

At that time, Universal Eye Bodhisattva addressed Samantabhadra Bodhisattva, saying:

O Son of the Buddha, given that this bodhisattva-mahāsattva has acquired dharmas such as these that are the same as those of all *tathāgatas*:

Why is he not referred to as a buddha?

Why is he not referred to as possessed of the ten powers?

Why is he not referred to as possessed of all-knowledge?

Why is he not referred to as one who has realized bodhi with regard to all dharmas?

Why can he not be referred to as [one possessed of] the universal eye?

Why is he not referred to as one who possesses the unimpeded vision of all realms?

Why is he not referred to as one who has awakened to all dharmas?

Why is he not referred to as one who abides together with all buddhas of the three periods of time in a state of non-duality?

Why is he not referred to as one who abides in the apex of reality?

Why has he not already ceased the cultivation of Samantabhadra's conduct and vows?

Why is he not able to achieve that ultimately final realization of the Dharma realm by which he would relinquish the bodhisattva path?

At that time, Samantabhadra Bodhisattva told Universal Eye Bodhisattva:

It is good indeed, O Son of the Buddha, that you have posed questions such as these beginning with "If this bodhisattva-mahāsattva has become identical in these respects to all buddhas, why is he not referred to as a buddha?" and continuing on through to "Why is he still unable to relinquish the bodhisattva path?"

Son of the Buddha, if this bodhisattva-mahāsattva has already become able to cultivate all the many different kinds of practices and vows of all bodhisattvas of the past, the future, and the present and has penetrated the realms of wisdom, then he may be referred to as a buddha. [However], if he incessantly cultivates the bodhisattva practices in the presence of a *tathāgata*, then he is referred to as a bodhisattva.

If he has already penetrated all the powers of the Tathāgata, then he may be referred to as one possessed of the ten powers. [However], if even though he has successively developed the ten powers, he still incessantly cultivates Samantabhadra's practices, then he is referred to as a bodhisattva.

If he knows all dharmas and is able to expound upon them, he may be referred to as one possessed of all-knowledge. [However], if although he is able to expound on all dharmas, he still never ceases to engage in skillful meditative reflection on every dharma, then he is referred to as bodhisattva.

If he knows all dharmas are non-dual, he is then referred to as awakened to all dharmas. If he is engaged in incessant and ever-increasing skillful contemplation of the path of all dual and non-dual dharmas' differences, then he is referred to as a bodhisattva.

If he has already become able to clearly see the objective spheres observed by the universal eye, he is then known as [one possessed of] the universal eye. If, although he is able to realize and acquire the objective sphere of the universal eye, he ceaselessly continues to increase in this in each successive mind-moment, then he is referred to as a bodhisattva.

If he is able to brightly illuminate all dharmas and leave behind all obstructions imposed by darkness, he is referred to as one of unimpeded vision. If he always diligently recollects those of unimpeded vision, then he is referred to as a bodhisattva.

If he has already acquired the wisdom eye of all buddhas, then in this case he is referred to as awakened to all dharmas. If he contemplates all *tathāgatas'* wisdom eye of right enlightenment and remains free of neglectfulness in this, then he is referred to as a bodhisattva.

If he abides where the Buddha abides and is no different from the Buddha, then he is known as one who in abides in non-duality with the Buddha. If he is drawn forth by the Buddha and cultivates all types of wisdom, then he is referred to as bodhisattva.

If he always contemplates the apex of reality of all worlds, then he is referred to as one who abides at the apex of reality. If, al-though he always contemplates the apex of reality of all dharmas, he still neither realizes and enters it nor abandons it, then he is referred to as a bodhisattva.

If he neither goes nor comes and is neither the same nor different and he forever puts to rest all discriminations such as these, then he is known as one who has ceased the pursuit of those vows. If he never retreats from the vast cultivation of their perfectly complete fulfillment, then he is referred to as one who has not yet ceased his pursuit of Samantabhadra's vows.

If he completely realizes that the Dharma realm is boundless and that all dharmas have a single sign, namely that of signlessness, then he is known as one who has achieved the ultimate realization of the Dharma realm and relinquished the bodhisattva path. If, although he realizes the Dharma realm is boundless, he still knows all of the many kinds of different signs, arouses the mind of great compassion, liberates beings, and does so to the end of future time without becoming weary of this, then he is referred to as a universally worthy bodhisattva.[303]

Son of the Buddha, this circumstance is analogous to that of the elephant king Airāvaṇa, who dwells in the seven-jeweled cave on Golden Flanks Mountain. All around his cave, there are seven-jeweled railings and jeweled *tāla* palm trees arranged in orderly rows with gold nets suspended over them. That elephant's body is as immaculately white as jade or snow. There is a gold banner raised above it and it is adorned with gold necklaces, a jeweled net which covers its trunk, and hanging bells adorned with jewels. It is fully developed in its seven parts and possessed of six tusks. It is so handsome and fully formed that all who lay eyes on it are delighted. It is well-trained, obedient, and has a mind free of rebelliousness.

Whenever Śakra, the celestial lord, wishes to travel about, that elephant king immediately realizes his intentions and then causes his form to disappear from his jeweled cave and appear in the Trāyastriṃśa Heaven in the presence of Lord Śakra. Through the use of all kinds of transformations accomplished with the spiritual superknowledges, he is able to cause his body to appear with thirty-three heads, on each of which he conjures seven tusks. On each of those tusks, he creates seven ponds, and in each of those ponds, there are seven lotus flowers on each one of which there are seven maidens all of whom simultaneously sing a hundred thousand celestial songs.

Then Lord Śakra, having mounted that jewel-adorned elephant goes forth from his Invincible Palace out to his flower garden park which is filled with *puṇḍarīka* lotus flowers. Then, after Lord Śakra reaches his flower garden park, he dismounts from his elephant and enters a palace adorned with all kinds of jewels followed by countless maidens who serve him, singing and playing music, and allowing him to enjoy every sort of bliss. Then that elephant king once again uses his spiritual superknowledges to cause his elephant form to disappear and be replaced with his conjured creation of the body of a deva who, with the Trāyastriṃśa Heaven devas and maidens, sports about and enjoys the pleasures in the *puṇḍarīka* flower gardens during which, the appearance of the body he has manifested, its radiance and clothes, its going and coming, its moving and stopping, its speech and laughter, are all observed to be so identical and no different from any of those other devas that no one could distinguish any difference. This elephant and these devas, when compared with each other, appear to be the same.

Son of the Buddha, when that elephant king, Airāvaṇa, dwells in the seven-jeweled cave on Golden Flanks Mountain, he does not undergo any transformations. However, when he goes to the Trāyastriṃśa Heaven, wishing to make offerings to Śakra Devānām Indra, he then conjures all different kinds of delightful things and enjoys the celestial blisses in a manner no different from the devas themselves.

Son of the Buddha, so too it is with the bodhisattva-mahāsattva. He cultivates Samantabhadra Bodhisattva's conduct, vows, and samādhis. It is these that serve as his jeweled adornments.

The seven limbs of bodhi serve as the bodhisattva's body. The light that he emanates forms a net. He raises the great Dharma banner, rings the great Dharma bell, takes the great compassion as his cave, and takes his solid vows as his tusks. The fearlessness of his wisdom is like that of a lion. He ties up his topknot with the headband of the Dharma, reveals the esoteric, and reaches the far shore of perfection in the conduct and vows of all bodhisattvas.

Wishing to become securely established on the seat of enlightenment, realize all-knowledge, and attain the utmost right enlightenment, he increases his cultivation of the great conduct and vows of Samantabhadra, never retreating, never resting, never interrupting it, and never relinquishing it. Continuing with great compassion and vigor to the very end of future time, he liberates all suffering and afflicted beings and never abandons the path of Samantabhadra.

He manifests the realization of the utmost right enlightenment, manifests an ineffable-ineffable number of gateways to realization of right enlightenment, manifests an ineffable-ineffable number of gateways to the turning of the Dharma wheel, manifests an ineffable-ineffable number of gateways to dwelling in the profound mind, manifests the gateways to the transformation of nirvāṇa in an ineffable-ineffable number of vast lands, manifests taking rebirth and cultivating Samantabhadra's practices in an ineffable-ineffable number of different worlds, and manifests an ineffable-ineffable number of *tathāgatas* realizing the utmost right enlightenment beneath the bodhi tree in an ineffable-ineffable number of vast lands, closely surrounded by a congregation consisting of an ineffable-ineffable number of bodhisattvas.

It may be that he cultivates Samantabhadra's practices for a mind-moment and then attains right enlightenment, or does so for an instant, for an hour, for a day, for a half-month, for a month, for a year, for countless years, for a kalpa, or even for an ineffable-ineffable number of kalpas during which he cultivates Samantabhadra's practices and then attains right enlightenment.

He also serves as the leader among those in all buddha *kṣetras* who draws near to the buddhas, bows down to them in reverence, makes offerings to them, poses questions to them, contemplates the spheres of experience as like illusions, purifies and cultivates the bodhisattva's countless practices, countless types of knowledge, various spiritual transformations, various forms of awesome virtue, various types of wisdom, various spheres of cognition, various spiritual superknowledges, various types of sovereign mastery, various liberations, various types of Dharma light, and various types dharmas used in teaching and training.

Son of the Buddha, the original body of the bodhisattva-mahāsattva does not disappear even as he uses the power of conduct and vows to everywhere produce transformations such as these. Why?

Because he wishes to use the sovereign spiritual powers of Samantabhadra to train all beings;

Because he wishes to enable an ineffable-ineffable number of beings to attain purity;

Because he wishes to enable them to forever cut off [cyclic existence in] the wheel of *saṃsāra*;

Because he wishes to purify vast worlds;

Because he wishes to always see all *tathāgatas*;

Because he wishes to deeply enter the stream of the Dharma of all buddhas;

Because he wishes to bear in mind the lineage of all buddhas of the three periods of time;

Because he wishes to bear in mind the Dharma and Dharma body of all buddhas of the ten directions;

Because he wishes to everywhere cultivate and completely fulfill the practices of all bodhisattvas; and

Because he wishes to enter the stream of Samantabhadra and be freely able to realize all-knowledge.

Son of the Buddha, you should observe that this bodhisattva-mahāsattva does not abandon Samantabhadra's practices, that he does not cut off [his cultivation of] the bodhisattva path, that he sees all buddhas, that he realizes all-knowledge, that he is masterful in his use of the dharmas of all-knowledge, that he is like the elephant king, Airāvaṇa, who does not relinquish his elephant body even when going to the Trāyastriṃśa Heaven where he is ridden by the deva, enjoys the celestial pleasures, engages in celestial play, serves that lord of the devas, and engages in delightful pleasures with the celestial nymphs in the same way as the devas and no differently.

Son of the Buddha, so too it is with the bodhisattva-mahāsattva who does not abandon Samantabhadra's Great Vehicle practices, who does not retreat from the vows, who acquires the sovereign masteries of the Buddha, who possesses all-knowledge, who realizes the Buddha's unobstructed and unimpeded liberations, who, in his perfection of purification, is free of defiling attachments in all lands, and who is free of discriminations with regard to the dharmas of the Buddha.

Although he realizes that all dharmas are the same and nondual, he still constantly and clearly sees all buddha lands. Although he has already become the equal of all buddhas of the three periods of time, he still continuously and ceaselessly cultivates the bodhisattva practices.

Son of the Buddha, wherever a bodhisattva-mahāsattva has become securely established in practices and vows of Samantabhadra such as these, one should realize that this person's mind has become purified.

Sons of the Buddha, this is what constitutes the vast knowledge of the extraordinarily superior mind in the bodhisattva-mahāsattva's tenth great samādhi, "the great samādhi of the unimpeded wheel."

Sons of the Buddha, this is what constitutes the sphere of the ten great samādhis of the practices of Samantabhadra in which this bodhisattva-mahāsattva dwells.

The End of Chapter Twenty-Seven

Chapter 28
The Ten Superknowledges

At that time, Samantabhadra Bodhisattva-mahāsattva told all the bodhisattvas:

Sons of the Buddha, the bodhisattva-mahāsattva has ten superknowledges. What are those ten? Sons of the Buddha, using the superknowledge that knows the minds of others, the bodhisattva-mahāsattva knows the different thoughts of the beings within a great trichiliocosm, in particular knowing their good thoughts, bad thoughts, vast thoughts, narrow thoughts, great thoughts, small thoughts, thoughts acquiescing in *saṃsāra,* thoughts opposing *saṃsāra, śrāvaka* disciples' thoughts, *pratyekabuddhas'* thoughts, bodhisattvas' thoughts, *śrāvaka* disciples' practice-related thoughts, *pratyekabuddhas'* practice-related thoughts, bodhisattvas' practice-related thoughts, devas' thoughts, dragons' thoughts, *yakṣas'* thoughts, *gandharvas'* thoughts, *asuras'* thoughts, *garuḍas'* thoughts, *kiṃnaras'* thoughts, *mahoragas'* thoughts, humans' thoughts, non-humans' thoughts, hell-dwellers' thoughts, animals' thoughts, thoughts associated with the realm of King Yama,[304] hungry ghosts' thoughts, and the thoughts of beings residing in the difficulties.[305]

He distinguishes and knows all the different thoughts of countless beings such as these. And just as this is so for a single world, so too is this so in this same way for the beings in a hundred worlds, a thousand worlds, a hundred thousand worlds, a hundred thousand *koṭīs* of *nayutas* of worlds, and so forth until we come to worlds as numerous as the atoms in an ineffable-ineffable number of buddha *kṣetras* in which he distinguishes and knows the minds of all those beings. This is what is known as the first of the bodhisattva-mahāsattva's superknowledges, the spiritual superknowledge by which he thoroughly knows the minds of others.

Sons of the Buddha, using the superknowledge of the unimpeded and pure heavenly eye, the bodhisattva-mahāsattva sees with regard to the beings in worlds as numerous as the atoms in countlessly many ineffable-ineffables of buddha *kṣetras* their dying here and being reborn there, their being born in either a fortunate rebirth destiny or in one of the wretched destinies, their being possessed of the signs of merit or the signs of karmic offenses, their being either fine-looking or ugly, and their being either defiled or pure. He knows this of groups of countless types of beings such as these, namely: devas, dragons, *yakṣas, gandharvas, asuras, garuḍas, kiṃnaras, mahoragas,* humans, nonhumans, beings possessed of tiny bodies, and beings possessed of immense bodies, whether they be of small groups, large groups, or any of the other groups of the many different kinds of beings.

Using the unimpeded eye, he is able to completely and clearly see whatever karma they have accumulated, whatever suffering and happiness they have experienced, whatever thoughts they have, whatever discriminations they make, whatever views they hold, whatever words they speak, whatever causes they establish, whatever karma they commit, and whatever conditions are involved, so that whatever arises, he completely sees it all without error. This is what is known as the second of the bodhisattva-mahāsattva's superknowledges, the spiritual superknowledge of the unimpeded heavenly eye.

Sons of the Buddha, using the superknowledge that knows past lives at will, the bodhisattva-mahāsattva is able to know the matters associated with his own past lives and those of all the beings in worlds as numerous as the atoms in an ineffable-ineffable number of buddha *kṣetras,* knowing these with regard to all the lifetimes throughout kalpas as numerous as the atoms in an ineffable-ineffable number of buddha *kṣetras.*

In particular, he knows that they were born in such-and-such a place, that they were called this name, that they had this surname, that they were from this clan, that they ate and drank these things, and that they underwent these various kinds of sufferings and pleasures. He knows due to which particular causes and conditions, since the inception of their beginningless lifetimes up until the present, they have therefore circulated within and grown up in the midst of all the various realms of existence, following a particular sequence that has continued on in unending cyclic existences among the many different kinds of species, within the many different lands, and within the many different destinies of rebirth, taking on the many different kinds of forms and appearances, engaging in the many different kinds of karmic actions, becoming entangled in the many different kinds of fetters, thinking the many different kinds of thoughts, involving themselves in the many different kinds of causes and conditions, and taking on the various kinds of rebirths. He knows all matters such as these.

He also recalls that in the past, during a period of kalpas as numerous as the atoms in this particular number of buddha *kṣetras*, in worlds as numerous as the atoms in this particular number of buddha *kṣetras*, there were buddhas as numerous as the atoms in this particular number of buddha *kṣetras*, remembering for each and every one of those buddhas that they bore this name, appeared in the world in this way, had this congregation, had these parents, had this attendant, had these *śrāvaka* disciples among which these two were the most superior disciples, that he dwelt near this city, that he left the home life in this way, that he then realized the utmost right enlightenment beneath this bodhi tree, that he sat on this type of throne in this particular place, that he proclaimed this number of these particular kinds of sutras, that he benefited in these ways this particular number of beings, that he dwelt for a life span of this duration, that he carried out this number of these kinds of buddha works, that, in reliance on the realm of the *parinirvāṇa* without residue, he entered *parinirvāṇa*, and that, having entered *parinirvāṇa*, his Dharma then remained for this length of time. He is able to remember all matters such as these.

He also remembers the names of buddhas as numerous as the atoms in an ineffable-ineffable number of buddha *kṣetras*, and, among them, remembers for every one of those names the buddhas of that same name as numerous as the atoms in an ineffable-ineffable number of buddha *kṣetras*, recalling for each of them how, from the point when they first made the resolve, that they made these vows, cultivated these practices, made offerings to these buddhas, trained these beings, proclaimed the Dharma in the midst of these congregations, had a life span of this particular length, possessed spiritual superknowledges with which they performed these transformations, and so forth until they entered the nirvāṇa without residue and, after having entered *parinirvāṇa*, their Dharma then remained for this length of time during which they had commemorative stupas and temples built for them with these various kinds of adornments that then influenced beings to plant roots of goodness.

He is able to completely know all these things. This is what is known as the third of the bodhisattva-mahāsattva's superknowledges, the spiritual superknowledge that knows the past lives of beings throughout the kalpas of the past.

Sons of the Buddha, using the superknowledge that knows the kalpas of the future even to the end of future time, the bodhisattva-mahāsattva knows for each and every one of all future kalpas how they will transpire in worlds as numerous as the atoms in an ineffable-ineffable number of buddha *kṣetras,* knowing with respect to all beings how it will be that, having reached the end of their lives, they will then take on a particular rebirth, doing so continuously in all the realms of existence in accordance with the rewards and retributions of their karmic actions, knowing whether they will be good or not good, whether they will attain emancipation or will fail to attain emancipation, whether their liberation is certain or whether their liberation is uncertain,[306] whether they are fixed in what is wrong or fixed in what is right, whether their roots of goodness will involve latent defilements or their roots of goodness will not involve latent defilements, whether their roots of goodness will reach full development or their roots of goodness will fail to reach full development, whether they will consolidate their roots of goodness or will fail to consolidate their roots of goodness, whether they will accumulate roots of goodness or they will fail to accumulate roots of goodness, and whether they will accumulate the dharmas of karmic offenses or whether they will refrain from accumulating the dharmas of karmic offenses. He is able to know all such circumstances as these.

He also knows with respect to worlds as numerous as the atoms in an ineffable-ineffable number of buddha *kṣetras* that there will be kalpas on to the end of future time as numerous as the atoms in an ineffable-ineffable number of buddha *kṣetras,* knows that every kalpa has buddhas' names as numerous as the atoms in an ineffable-ineffable number of buddha *kṣetras,* knows that for every one of those names there are buddhas, *tathāgatas,* as numerous as the atoms in an ineffable-ineffable number of buddha *kṣetras,* and knows with respect to every one of those *tathāgatas,* from the point when they will first make the resolve, that they will make these vows, will establish these practices, will make offerings to these buddhas, will teach these beings, will proclaim the Dharma in the midst of these congregations, will abide for a life span of this duration, will possess these superknowledges with which they perform these transformations, and so forth until we come to his knowing their entry into the nirvāṇa without residue and, after they will have entered *parinirvāṇa,* that their Dharma will remain for this long during which they will have commemorative stupas and temples built for them with various kinds of adornments that will then influence beings to plant roots of goodness.

He is able to completely know all matters such as these. This is what is known as the fourth of the bodhisattva-mahāsattva's superknowledges, the spiritual superknowledge that knows all kalpas to the end of future time.

Sons of the Buddha, the bodhisattva-mahāsattva perfects the unimpeded and purified heavenly ear, bringing it to the complete fulfillment of vastly penetrating acuity that transcends all obstacles and achieves complete and unimpeded comprehension. He completely perfects the sovereign mastery of the ability with regard to all sounds to either hear or not hear any sound at will.

Sons of the Buddha, there are buddhas in the east as numerous as the atoms in an ineffable-ineffable number of buddha *kṣetras*. Whatever those buddhas proclaim, reveal, explain, or expound, whatever they establish or teach, whomever they train or bear in mind, and whatever they distinguish in all of its extreme depth, vastness, and various different aspects—he is able to hear and retain all of these things along with their countless skillful means and countless skillful and pure dharmas.

Furthermore, within all of this, whether it was a matter of meaning or words, whether it occurred with a single person or with a group, in accordance with their language, in accordance with their wisdom, in accordance with their comprehension, in accordance with what manifested, in accordance with those who were trained, in accordance with their spheres of cognition, in accordance with what was relied upon, and in accordance with their paths of emancipation, he is able to completely remember and retain it all. He does not forget it, does not lose it, does not experience interruptions in it, and it does not dissipate. He remains free of any confusion and delusion about it. He is able to expound on these matters for others, thereby enabling them to acquire an awakened understanding. In doing so, he never forgets so much as a single phrase or statement.

And just as this is so with respect to those in the east, so too is this so in this very same way with respect to those in the south, west, north, the four midpoints, the zenith, and the nadir.

This is what is known as the fifth of the bodhisattva-mahāsattva's superknowledges, the spiritual superknowledge of the unimpeded and purified heavenly ear.

Sons of the Buddha, the bodhisattva-mahāsattva abides in the insubstantiality superknowledge, in the effortless superknowledge, in the uniform equality superknowledge, in the vastness superknowledge, in the measureless superknowledge, in the independent superknowledge, in the superknowledge responsive to thought, in the origination superknowledge, in the nonorigination superknowledge, in the nonretreating superknowledge, in the uninterrupted superknowledge, in the indestructible superknowledge, in the growth-producing superknowledge, and in the superknowledge of going wherever one wishes.

This bodhisattva hears the names of all buddhas even in the most extremely distant worlds, that is to say he hears the names of those in innumerable many worlds, the names of those in measurelessly many worlds, and so forth on up to his hearing the names of all buddhas in a number of worlds as numerous as the atoms in an ineffable-ineffable number of worlds. Having heard their names, he immediately sees himself in the presence of those buddhas.

In all those worlds, whether upward-facing or inverted, in each of their different conformations, in each of their different places, in each of their boundlessly many and unimpededly many different types, in all the many different kinds of lands, in all the different times and kalpas, each possessed of countless qualities, each different in its adornments, each of those *tathāgatas* appears within them, manifesting spiritual transformations, announcing their names, incalculably and innumerably many, each of them different from those of the others.

On once being able to hear those *tathāgatas'* names, even without moving from his original place, this bodhisattva sees his own body in the places where those buddhas dwell, bowing down in reverence before them, serving them, making offerings to them, posing questions to them about the dharmas of the bodhisattva, penetrating the wisdom of the buddhas, becoming completely able to fully comprehend all those buddhas' lands, their sites of enlightenment, and their congregations as well as the Dharma that they proclaim, achieving the ultimate in all these matters while still remaining free of any attachment to them.

In this way, he passes through kalpas as numerous as the atoms in an ineffable-ineffable number of buddha *kṣetras* during which he goes everywhere throughout the ten directions and yet has no place to which he goes. Thus he visits the buddha *kṣetras*, contemplates those buddhas, listens to their Dharma, and requests their teachings on the path, doing so unremittingly and endlessly, never abandoning this, never resting in this, and never wearying of this. He cultivates the bodhisattva practices and perfects the great vows, bringing them all to complete fulfillment and never retreats from this, proceeding in this way in order to ensure that the vastly long lineage of the Tathāgata is never cut off.

This is what is known as the sixth of the bodhisattva-mahāsattva's superknowledges, the spiritual superknowledge in which he abides in the absence of any substantial nature, remains motionless, and does nothing whatsoever even as he travels to all the buddha *kṣetras.*

Sons of the Buddha, using the superknowledge that skillfully distinguishes the languages of all beings, the bodhisattva-mahāsattva knows the different kinds of languages of beings as numerous as the atoms in an ineffable-ineffable number of buddha *kṣetras*, in particular knowing the languages of *āryas*, the languages of non-*āryas*, the languages of devas, the languages of dragons, the languages of *yakṣas*, the languages of *gandharvas, asuras, garuḍas, kiṃnaras, mahoragas*, humans, and nonhumans and so forth until we come to his knowing all the languages of an ineffable-ineffable number of beings in all the different ways each of them manifests. So it is that he completely knows them all.

Whichever worlds this bodhisattva enters, he is able to know with regard to all the beings within them all their individual natures and propensities. Then, in accordance with their natures and propensities, he utters the words by which they are all enabled to achieve complete understanding and become free of doubts or delusions. Just as when the light of sun shines forth and everywhere illuminates the many forms, it enables everyone with eyes to clearly see all things, so too it is with the bodhisattva-mahāsattva. Using the wisdom that skillfully distinguishes all languages, he deeply penetrates all the languages within the cloud of all languages and thus enables all intelligent beings in the world to achieve complete understanding.

This is what is known as the seventh of the bodhisattva-mahāsattva's superknowledges, the spiritual superknowledge that skillfully distinguishes all languages.

Sons of the Buddha, using the superknowledge of the emanation of countless *asaṃkhyeyas* of form body adornments, the bodhisattva-mahāsattva knows all dharmas are apart from forms and signs, have no differentiating signs, have no signs of variety, have no signs of measurelessness, have no signs subject to discrimination, and have no signs of blue, yellow, red, or white.

It is in this way that the bodhisattva who enters the Dharma realm is able to manifest his body and create many different kinds of forms, namely:[307]

> Boundless forms, measureless forms, pure forms, adorning forms, pervasive forms, incomparable forms, universally illuminating forms, especially supreme forms, non-opposing forms, and forms replete with all the signs;[308]

Forms free of the many kinds of evil, forms possessed of great awesome powers, forms worthy of veneration, inexhaustible forms, forms possessed of the many and various marvelous aspects, extremely beautiful forms, immeasurable forms, forms providing excellent protection, forms able to facilitate ripening, and forms that adapt to those who are being taught;

Unimpeded forms, forms with extremely penetrating brightness, forms free of defiling turbidity, forms with the most ultimate clarity and purity, greatly courageous stalwart forms, forms possessed of inconceivable skillful means, indestructible forms, forms free of defects, forms free of obstructive dimness, and skillfully established forms;

Marvelously adorned forms, forms with majestic signs, forms with the various subsidiary signs, greatly venerated forms, forms with marvelous realms, well-polished forms, forms with pure and profound minds, forms full of blazing brilliance, supremely vast forms, and uninterrupted forms;

Independent forms, peerless forms, forms filling ineffably many buddha *kṣetras*, growing forms, forms with enduring attraction, forms with supreme meritorious qualities, forms adaptive to mental dispositions, forms with pure and complete understanding, forms collecting the many marvelous qualities, and forms with skillful decisiveness;

Unobstructed forms, bright and pure space-like forms, pure and delightful forms, forms free of all defilements, incalculable forms, visually exquisite forms, universally seen forms, forms manifested in accordance with the time, quiescent forms, and forms free of desire;

Forms which are genuine fields of merit, forms able to create peace and security, forms free of all fear, forms free of deluded actions, forms with wisdom and courage, forms with unimpeded physical signs, forms that roam everywhere, forms with independent minds, forms produced by great kindness, and forms manifested by great compassion;

Equally emancipating forms, forms replete with merit, forms that accord with recollections, forms adorned with infinite marvelous jewels, forms of the light emanated by jewel treasuries, forms associated with beings' faithful aspiration, forms in which all-knowledge is manifested, forms with joyously delighted eyes, forms with the foremost multi-jeweled adornments, and forms having no place in which they reside;

Forms manifested with sovereign mastery, forms with many different spiritual superknowledges, forms associated with birth into the family of the *tathāgatas,* forms surpassing description even by analogies, forms that pervade the Dharma realm, forms to which the multitudes all travel to visit, forms of many different types, perfected forms, forms leading to emancipation, and forms adapting to the deportment of those to be taught;

Forms that the viewer never tires of observing, forms possessing various types of radiant purity, forms able to emanate nets consisting of countless rays of light, forms with an ineffable number of many different kinds of lights, forms emanating inconceivable fragrance and radiance superior to any existing within the three realms, forms emanating the measureless dazzling illumination of the solar orb, forms manifesting the incomparable body of the moon, forms consisting of clouds of countless lovely flowers, forms emanating clouds of all kinds of different lotus flower garland adornments, and forms everywhere emanating fragrance and flaming brilliance superior to any existing in the world;

Forms associated with the treasury of all *tathāgatas,* forms emanating an ineffable number of voices explaining and expounding on all dharmas, and forms replete with all the practices of Samantabhadra.

Sons of the Buddha, the bodhisattva-mahāsattva who deeply enters a formless Dharma realm such as this is able to manifest these many different kinds of form bodies with which:

He enables those being taught to see them;

He enables those being taught to be mindful of them;

He turns the Dharma wheel for the sake of those being taught;

He adapts to the time appropriate for those being taught;

He adapts to the characteristics of those being taught;

He enables those being taught to draw near;

He enables those being taught to awaken;

He brings forth many different kinds of spiritual superknowledges for those being taught;

He manifests all kinds of different sovereign masteries for those being taught; and

He bestows many different kinds of abilities on those being taught.

This is what is known as the eighth of the bodhisattva-mahāsattva's superknowledges, the spiritual superknowledge of the countless form bodies which he diligently cultivates and perfects for the sake of liberating all beings.

Sons of the Buddha, using the spiritual superknowledge that knows all dharmas, the bodhisattva-mahāsattva knows all dharmas as nameless, as devoid of any lineage, as neither coming nor going, as neither differentiated nor nondifferentiated, as neither various nor non-various, as neither dual nor non-dual, as devoid of a self, as incomparable, as neither produced nor destroyed, as unmoving, as not deteriorating, as devoid of reality and devoid of falseness, as of but a single sign and yet signless, as neither nonexistent nor existent, as neither Dharma nor non-Dharma, as neither adapting to the conventional nor not adapting to the conventional, as neither karma nor non-karma, as neither karmic consequences nor not karmic consequences, as neither conditioned nor unconditioned, as neither ultimate truth nor not ultimate truth, as neither path nor not path, as neither emancipated nor unemancipated, as neither measurable nor immeasurable, as neither worldly nor world-transcending, as neither arising from causes nor not arising from causes, as neither definite nor indefinite, as neither complete nor incomplete, as neither emergent nor non-emergent, as neither discriminated nor not discriminated, and as neither according with principle nor not according with principle.

This bodhisattva does not seize upon mundane conventional truth, nor does he abide in ultimate truth. He does not make discriminations regarding dharmas and does not establish words [alone as sacred]. He accords with the quiescent nature but never forsakes any of his vows. He perceives meaning, knows dharmas, spreads forth the Dharma cloud, and sends down the Dharma rains.

Although he realizes the true character of dharmas cannot be described in words, he still uses skillful means and inexhaustible eloquence with which, adapting to dharmas and adapting to meanings, he presents orderly explanations of it.

By having developed excellent skill in explaining dharmas with eloquent phrasing and by having already purified great kindness and great compassion, he is able to explain dharmas that are beyond words with words that accord with and do not contradict those dharmas and their meanings. In explaining dharmas for others, he describes them as all arising from conditions.

Although he does present verbal descriptions, he is free of any attachment to them. He expounds on all dharmas with inexhaustible eloquence, making distinctions among them, establishing them, explaining them, and providing guidance through them. He causes the nature of all dharmas to become entirely and clearly revealed, rends the net of the many doubts, and thus facilitates everyone's realization of purity.

Although he does draw forth beings, in doing so, he never abandons what is genuine and never retreats from the dharma of non-duality. He is ever able to expound upon the gateways to the unimpeded Dharma. He uses many marvelous verbal presentations adapted to beings' minds with which he everywhere rains down the Dharma rain and never misses the right time in doing so.

This is what is known as the ninth of the bodhisattva-mahāsattva's superknowledges, the spiritual superknowledge that knows all dharmas.

Sons of the Buddha, using the superknowledge of the complete cessation of all dharmas samādhi, the bodhisattva-mahāsattva is able in every successive mind-moment to enter the samādhi of the complete cessation of all dharmas but still does not retreat from the bodhisattva path, does not abandon the bodhisattva works, and does not relinquish the mind of great kindness and great compassion. He never rests in his continuous cultivation of the *pāramitās* and never wearies of contemplating the lands of all buddhas. He does not give up his vows to liberate beings, does not interrupt his endeavors in turning the wheel of Dharma, does not diminish his works in teaching beings, does not relinquish his practice of making offerings to all buddhas, does not relinquish the gateways to sovereign mastery in all dharmas, does not relinquish always going to see all buddhas, and does not relinquish always listening to all dharmas.

He realizes all dharmas exist in a state of unimpeded equality, possesses sovereign mastery in perfecting all dharmas of the Buddha, and achieves the complete fulfillment of all his supreme vows. He completely knows all the distinctions in all lands, and, in entering the lineage of the Buddha, he reaches the far shore of perfection. He is able to train in all dharmas in all those other worlds while completely understanding the signlessness of dharmas.

He realizes that all dharmas arise from conditions and are devoid of any essential nature of their own and yet he still accords with the realm of the mundane and conventional by using skillful means in expounding on them. Although, even in the midst of all dharmas, his mind has no place it dwells, he still adapts to beings' faculties and aspirations by using skillful means to explain the many different kinds of dharmas for them.

As this bodhisattva abides in samādhi, according to his mental disposition, he may abide in it for a kalpa, may abide in it for a hundred kalpas, may abide in it for a thousand kalpas, may abide in it for a *koṭī* of kalpas, may abide in it for a hundred *koṭīs* of kalpas, may abide in it for a thousand *koṭīs* of kalpas, may abide in it for a hundred thousand *koṭīs* of kalpas, may abide in it for a *nayuta* of *koṭīs* of kalpas, may abide in it for a hundred *nayutas* of *koṭīs* of kalpas, may abide in it for a thousand *nayutas* of *koṭīs* of kalpas, may abide in it for a hundred thousand *nayutas* of *koṭīs* of kalpas, may abide in it for innumerable kalpas, may abide in it for measurelessly many kalpas, and so forth on up to his perhaps abiding in it for an ineffable-ineffable number of kalpas.

Although the bodhisattva may enter this samādhi of the complete cessation of all dharmas and remain in it throughout just so very many kalpas, his body still never disintegrates, never atrophies, and never changes. Remaining neither visible nor invisible, it is never destroyed, never ruined, never worn out, never quits, and remains inexhaustible.

Even though he does not engage in any endeavors at all in any sphere of existence or nonexistence, he is still able to continue accomplishing all kinds of bodhisattva works. That is to say, he never abandons all beings, but rather constantly teaches and trains them, never missing the appropriate time in doing so. Thus he enables them to grow in all dharmas of the Buddha and enables them to achieve complete fulfillment of all the bodhisattva practices. Because he wishes to benefit all beings, he never desists from using his spiritual superknowledges and transformations for their sake. These manifest like reflected images that appear everywhere for everyone even as he all the while remains quiescent and unmoving in this samādhi.

This is what is known as the tenth of the bodhisattva-mahāsattva's superknowledges, the spiritual superknowledge of entering the samādhi of the complete cessation of all dharmas.

Sons of the Buddha, this bodhisattva-mahāsattva's abiding in these ten kinds of superknowledges is inconceivable to all devas and humans, is inconceivable to all beings, and is inconceivable to all *śrāvaka* disciples, to all *pratyekabuddhas,* and to all the other members of the bodhisattva sangha. It is such that none of these beings can even conceive of it. This bodhisattva's physical karmic deeds are inconceivable, his verbal karmic deeds are inconceivable, his mental karmic deeds are inconceivable, his samādhis and sovereign masteries are inconceivable, and his wisdom's spheres of cognition are inconceivable. Aside from the buddhas and the bodhisattvas who have acquired these spiritual superknowledges, there is no one else even able to adequately describe and proclaim the praises of the meritorious qualities of a person such as this.

Sons of the Buddha, these are the bodhisattva-mahāsattva's ten kinds of spiritual superknowledges. If bodhisattva-mahāsattvas abide in these spiritual superknowledges, they all acquire all the spiritual superknowledges of unimpeded knowledge throughout all three periods of time.

The End of Chapter Twenty-Eight

Chapter 29
The Ten Patiences

At that time, Samantabhadra Bodhisattva told the bodhisattvas:

Sons of the Buddha, the bodhisattva-mahāsattva has ten kinds of patience. If one acquires these kinds of patience, then he will succeed in reaching the ground of all bodhisattvas' unimpeded patience and will become endlessly unimpeded in all dharmas of the Buddha. What are these ten? They are as follows:

Patience with the sounds [of the teachings];
Acquiescent patience;
Unproduced-dharmas patience;
Patience [due to seeing all as] like a conjured illusion;
Patience [due to seeing all as] like a mirage;
Patience [due to seeing all as] like a dream;
Patience [due to seeing all as] like echoes;
Patience [due to seeing all as] like reflections;
Patience [due to seeing all as] like transformations; and
Patience [due to seeing all as] like space.

These ten kinds of patience have been proclaimed, are now proclaimed, and will be proclaimed by all buddhas of the three periods of time.

Sons of the Buddha, what is meant by the bodhisattva-mahāsattva's patience with the sounds [of the teachings]? This means that, when one hears the Dharma proclaimed by all buddhas, one is not alarmed, is not frightened, and is not intimidated, but rather responds with deep faith, awakened understanding, fond delight, attraction toward it, focused attention on it, recollection of it, cultivation of it, and secure establishment in it. This is what is meant by the first of the bodhisattva-mahāsattva's kinds of patience, patience with the sound [of the teaching].

Sons of the Buddha, what is meant by the bodhisattva-mahāsattva's acquiescent patience? This refers to reflecting upon and contemplating all dharmas equally and without opposition, acquiescing in and completely understanding them, enabling one's mind to remain in a state of purity, rightly abiding in cultivating them, entering them, and perfecting them. This is what is meant by the second of the bodhisattva-mahāsattva's kinds of patience, acquiescent patience.

Sons of the Buddha, what is meant by the bodhisattva-mahāsattva's unproduced-dharmas patience? Sons of the Buddha, this bodhisattva-mahāsattva does not perceive that there is even the most minor dharma that is ever produced and also does not perceive that there is even the most minor dharma that is destroyed. Why is this? If they are not produced, then they are not destroyed. If they are not destroyed, then they are endless. If they are endless, then they are free of defilement. If they are free of defilement, then they are devoid of differences. If they are devoid of differences, then they have no place in which they abide. If they have no place in which they abide, then they are quiescent. If they are quiescent, then they are apart from desire. If they are apart from desire, then there is nothing they do. If there is nothing that they do, then they are wishless. If they are wishless, then they have no abiding. And if they have no abiding, then they have neither any going nor any coming. This is what is meant by the third of the bodhisattva-mahāsattva's patiences, the unproduced-dharmas patience.

Sons of the Buddha, what is meant by the bodhisattva-mahāsattva's patience due to seeing all as like a conjured illusion?[309] Sons of the Buddha, this bodhisattva-mahāsattva realizes that all dharmas are like conjured illusions and that they arise through causes and conditions. In but a single dharma, he understands many dharmas and in many dharmas, he understands any single dharma.

Having realized that all dharmas are like conjured illusions, this bodhisattva comprehends lands, comprehends beings, comprehends the Dharma realm, comprehends the equality of the world, comprehends the equality of the buddhas' appearances in the world, comprehends the equality of the three periods of time, and perfects many different kinds of spiritual superknowledges and spiritual transformations.

Just as the contents of conjured illusions are not elephants, are not horses, are not chariots, are not soldiers,[310] not men, not women, not boys, not girls, not trees, not leaves, not flowers, not fruits, not earth, not water, not fire, not wind, not daytime, not nighttime, not days, not months, not a half-month, not one month, not one year, not centuries, not one kalpa, not many kalpas, not concentration, not confusion, not purity, not admixture, not unity, not difference, not vastness, not constriction, not abundance, not scarcity, not measurability, not immeasurability, not coarseness, and not refinement, and are not actually any of these many different kinds of things—and just as the many different kinds of phenomena are not illusions and illusions are not the many different kinds of phenomena, but rather it is merely because of conjured illusions that there are any of those manifestations of the many different kinds of phenomena—so too it is with the bodhisattva-mahāsattva in his contemplation of all worlds as like mere illusions, as for instance with his contemplations of the world of karmic actions, the world of the afflictions, the world of lands, the world of dharmas, the world of time, the world of the destinies of rebirth, worlds being formed, worlds being destroyed, worlds in motion, and the world of endeavors.

When the bodhisattva-mahāsattva is contemplating all worlds as like mere illusions, he does not perceive the creation of any being, does not perceive the destruction of any being, does not perceive the creation of any land, does not perceive the destruction of any land, does not perceive the creation of any dharma, does not perceive the destruction of any dharma, does not perceive any past about which one may make discriminations, does not perceive any future in which one may initiate endeavors, does not perceive any present that abides for even a single mind-moment, does not contemplate bodhi, does not make discriminations regarding bodhi, does not perceive any buddha that appears in the world, does not perceive any buddha who enters nirvāṇa, does not perceive any abiding in great vows, does not perceive any entry into the right and fixed position,[311] and does not [perceive anything that] goes beyond the uniformly equal nature.

Although this bodhisattva develops buddha lands, he realizes there are no differences between lands;

Although he develops realms of beings, he realizes there are no differences between beings;

Although he everywhere contemplates the Dharma realm, he abides securely, quiescent and unmoving, in the nature of dharmas;

Although he comprehends the uniform equality of the three periods of time, he still does not oppose making distinctions among the dharmas of the three periods of time;

Although he develops the aggregates and the sense bases, he still forever severs all points of dependence;

Although he liberates beings, he still completely realizes the uniform equality of the Dharma realm in which there are none of the many kinds of differences;

Although he realizes that all dharmas go beyond the reach of language and cannot be described in words, he still always expounds on the Dharma with endless eloquence;

Although he does not seize on or become attached to the work of teaching beings, he still never relinquishes the great compassion and so continues to turn the Dharma wheel to liberate everyone; and

Although he explains past causes and conditions for beings, he still realizes that the very nature of causes and conditions has no movement or transformation at all.

This is what is meant by the fourth of the bodhisattva-mahāsattva's patiences, patience due to seeing all as like conjured illusions.

Sons of the Buddha, what is meant by the bodhisattva-mahāsattva's patience due to seeing all as like a mirage? Sons of the Buddha, this bodhisattva-mahāsattva realizes that the entire world is the same as a mirage. Just as a mirage has no actual place, is neither inwardly existing nor outwardly existing, is neither existent nor nonexistent, is neither instantaneous nor eternal, is not of only a single form, is not of multiple forms, and is not formless, but rather is something manifested solely based on conventional worldly discourse, so too, when the bodhisattva contemplates in accordance with reality in this way, he comes to completely understand all dharmas, directly realizing that this [mirage-like nature] is true of them all. Thus he is enabled to attain complete fulfillment [of this realization]. This is what is meant by the fifth of the bodhisattva-mahāsattva's patiences, patience due to seeing all as like a mirage.

Sons of the Buddha, what is meant by the bodhisattva-mahāsattva's patience due to seeing all as like a dream? Sons of the Buddha, this bodhisattva-mahāsattva realizes that the entire world is like a dream. Just as a dream is neither within the world nor apart from the world, is not connected to the desire realm, is not connected to the form realm, is not connected to the formless realm, is neither produced nor destroyed, and is neither defiled nor immaculate, yet nonetheless does have an appearance, so too, the bodhisattva-mahāsattva realizes that the entire world is the same as a dream: because of the absence of change; because its inherent nature is dreamlike; because attachment to it is like attaching to something in a dream; because, like a dream, it is by nature disconnected; because its original nature is like that of a dream; because all that appears in it is dreamlike; because, as in a dream, it is has no differentiating aspects; because all discriminations in one's perceptions are like those in a dream; and because, when one awakens, it is as if one were awakening from a dream. This is what is meant by the sixth of the bodhisattva-mahāsattva's patiences, patience due to seeing all as like a dream.

Sons of the Buddha, what is meant by the bodhisattva-mahāsattva's patience due to seeing all as like echoes? Sons of the Buddha, when this bodhisattva-mahāsattva hears the Buddha teaching the Dharma, he contemplates the nature of all dharmas, cultivates the training to the far shore of perfection, and realizes that all sounds are like echoes in that, although they have neither any coming nor any going, they still manifest in this way.

Sons of the Buddha, in contemplating the voice of the Tathāgata, this bodhisattva-mahāsattva observes that it does not emanate from within, does not emanate from without, and does not emanate from both within and without. Although he completely understands that this voice does not emanate from within, from without, or from both within and without, it is still able to manifest excellent skillful means in the use of designations and statements in producing perfectly complete expositions. [He observes that] it is like echoes in a valley which arise from conditions and yet it does not contradict the nature of dharmas as it enables beings to acquire understanding suited to their individual type so that they may cultivate and pursue the training.

Just as Indra's wife, Śācī, the daughter of an *asura* king, emanates a thousand voices from within her single voice even without consciously intending to cause them to emerge in this way, so too it is with the bodhisattva-mahāsattva who enters the realm of non-discrimination and perfects the voice possessed of skillful means adapted to the beings' individual types as he constantly turns the wheel of Dharma in boundlessly many worlds. This bodhisattva is well able to contemplate all beings and use the sign of the vast and long tongue to expound the Dharma for them. His voice is unimpeded in its reach which extends everywhere throughout the lands of the ten directions and enables the beings within them to hear individually different Dharma teachings suited to what is most fitting for each of them.

Although he realizes that sounds have no arising, he nonetheless manifests his voice everywhere. Although he realizes that nothing whatsoever is said, he still extensively expounds on all dharmas with a sublime voice that equally adapts to everyone so that, in accordance with their type, beings are all able to use their own wisdom to fully comprehend these teachings.

This is what is meant by the seventh of the bodhisattva-mahāsattva's patiences, patience due to seeing all as like echoes.

Sons of the Buddha, what is meant by the bodhisattva-mahāsattva's patience due to seeing all as like reflections? Sons of the buddha, this bodhisattva-mahāsattva is not born into the world, does not die in the world, does not exist in the world, does not exist outside of the world, does not act within the world nor not act within the world, is not the same as the world, is not different from the world, does not go forth into the world nor not go forth into the world, does not abide within the world nor not abide within the world, is not of the world, has not gone beyond the world, does not cultivate the bodhisattva practices, does not abandon the great vows, is not real, and is not unreal. Although he constantly practices all dharmas of the Buddha, he is still able to carry out all kinds of endeavors in the world. He does not follow along with the flow of the world nor does he dwell in the flow of the Dharma.

Just as the sun, moon, men, women, houses, mountains, forests, rivers, springs, and all other such things have their images reflected by the surfaces of oil, water, beings' bodies, jewelry, bright mirrors, and other such immaculate things—

And just as those reflections are neither one with nor different from and neither apart from nor united with those surfaces of the oil and other such things—

And just as they do not float along in the current of the river and do not sink down into and disappear within those ponds and wells—

And just as, although those reflections appear within them, they do not become attached to them or sullied by them—

And just as beings know that as these images appear in this place even as they realize that none of those things, whether far away or near, actually exist within these reflections—

And just as, although all of these things appear in these reflections, the appearances portrayed by the reflections do not correspond to the actual proximity or distance of the reflected phenomena—

So too it is with the bodhisattva-mahāsattva, for he is able to realize that his own physical being and the physical beings of others in all cases are simply spheres of cognition. Thus he does not engage in duality-based modes of understanding by which he would be of the opinion that he is different from others even as they each differently and simultaneously everywhere appear in their own lands and the lands of others.

Just as a seed contains no roots, sprouts, stems, branching limbs, or leaves, and yet it is still able to produce them, so too it is with the bodhisattva-mahāsattva who, even in the midst of non-dual dharmas, distinguishes dual characteristics and thus brings forth skillful means by which he enables the development of unimpeded penetrating comprehension.

This is what is meant by the eighth of the bodhisattva-mahāsattva's patiences, patience due to seeing all as like reflections. When the bodhisattva-mahāsattva perfects this patience, even though he may not travel to pay his respects in the lands of the ten directions, he is still able to appear everywhere in all buddha *kṣetras* even as he does not leave this particular place and does not go to those places.

Just as those reflections appear everywhere, so too is he unimpeded in his ability to go everywhere, enabling all beings to see different bodies identical in the solidity of their appearances to those otherwise found in the world. Even so, these differences are just nondifferences, for these differing and nondiffering factors have no inherent mutual interference. This bodhisattva is born from within the lineage of the Tathāgata and, as such, his physical, verbal, and mental actions are pure and unimpeded. Therefore he is able to acquire the pure body possessed of the boundless physical signs.

Sons of the Buddha, what is meant by the bodhisattva-mahāsattva's patience due to seeing all as like transformations?[312] Sons of the Buddha, this bodhisattva-mahāsattva realizes that the entire world is comparable to [supernaturally produced] transformations. That is to say: all beings are transformations of mental deeds produced because of ideation and perceptions; all worlds are transformations of actions produced because of discriminations; all pain and pleasure are transformations of inverted views produced because of erroneous grasping; all worlds are transformations of unreal dharmas appearing as conventions based on language; and all afflictions are transformations of discriminations produced because of perceptions and thoughts.

There are also: the transformational effects of purifying training which appear because of nondiscrimination; the transformation of not changing during the three periods of time which occurs through [realizing] the equality of the unproduced; the transformational effects of bodhisattvas' vow power occurring because of their vast cultivation; the transformational effects of the *tathāgatas'* great compassion appearing because of their skillful means; and the transformational effects of the skillful means used in turning the wheel of the Dharma occurring because of what is proclaimed with wisdom, fearlessness, and eloquence.

It is in these ways that the bodhisattva completely knows both the worldly and world-transcending types of transformations through directly realized knowing, through vast knowing, through boundless knowing, through knowing that accords with phenomena, through knowing with sovereign mastery, and through genuine knowing. He is not one who can be shaken even in the slightest by false views. He adapts to the practices occurring in the world and yet does not commit errors or become corrupted in so doing.

Just as transformations: do not arise from the mind, do not arise from mind dharmas, do not arise from karma, and do not experience karmic rewards and retributions; are not produced by the world and are not destroyed by the world; cannot be pursued and cannot be grasped or touched; do not abide for a long time and do not abide for but an instant; do not act within the world and are not apart from the world; are not connected with only one region and do not belong to all regions; are neither measurable nor measureless; do not become weary and do not rest nor do they not become weary and rest; are not associated with the common person and are not associated with *āryas*; are not defiled and are not pure; are not born and do not die; are not wise and are not foolish; are not seen and are not unseen; are not dependent on the world and are not penetrating the dharma realm; are not clever and are not dull; are not grasping and are not free of grasping; are not of *saṃsāra* and are not of nirvāṇa; and are not existent and are not nonexistent—so too it is with the bodhisattva in his use of skillful means as he moves through the world cultivating the bodhisattva path. Completely understanding the dharmas of the world, he transformationally creates division bodies and transformationally goes forth into it, remaining unattached to the world, not seizing on these as his own bodies, and having no discriminations with regard to either the world or those bodies. He does not dwell in the world and yet does not leave the world behind. He does not dwell in dharmas and yet does not leave dharmas behind.

Because of his original vows, he never abandons even a single realm of beings and does not merely train realms occupied by only a few beings. He does not make discriminations with regard to dharmas and yet it is not that he does make any discriminations at all. He realizes that the nature of dharmas neither comes nor goes. Although nothing at all exists, he still achieves the complete fulfillment of the dharmas of buddhahood and completely realizes dharmas are like transformations which are neither existent nor nonexistent.

Sons of the Buddha, even as the bodhisattva-mahāsattva abides in this way in the patience due to seeing all as like transformations, he is still able to completely fulfill the path to the bodhi of all buddhas and benefit beings.

This is what is meant by the ninth of the bodhisattva-mahāsattva's patiences, patience due to seeing all as like [magical] transformations. When the bodhisattva-mahāsattva perfects this patience, everything he does is like a mere transformation. Like a magician, in all buddha *kṣetras,* he has nothing at all on which he depends. He has nothing in the world that he seizes upon or becomes attached to. He does not produce discriminations regarding any of the Buddha's dharmas and yet progresses on toward the bodhi of the Buddha without negligence or weariness. In cultivating the bodhisattva practices, he abandons all inverted views. Although he has no body, he manifests all kinds of bodies. Although he does not dwell anywhere, he still dwells in the many lands. Although he is formless, he still everywhere manifests the many kinds of forms. Although he is not attached to the apex of reality, he still brightly illuminates the equally immanent and perfect nature of dharmas.

Sons of the Buddha, it is by having no dharma whatsoever on which he depends that this bodhisattva is known as one who is liberated. It is by having abandoned all faults that he is known as one who is well trained. It is by remaining motionless and never retreating that he everywhere enters the congregations of all *tathāgatas* and is known as one possessed of the spiritual superknowledges. It is by having already realized consummate skillfulness in the dharma of the unproduced that he is known as one who is irreversible. It is by possessing all the powers and becoming one whom not even Mount Sumeru or the Iron Ring Mountains could obstruct that he is known as one who is unimpeded.

Sons of the Buddha, what is meant by the bodhisattva-mahāsattva's patience due to seeing all as like space? Sons of the Buddha, this bodhisattva-mahāsattva understands the entire Dharma realm as like space because of its signlessness, understands all worlds as like space because of their non-arising, understands all dharmas as like space because of their non-duality, understands the actions of all beings as like space because they have nothing they enact, understands all buddhas as like space because they are free of discriminations, understands the powers of all buddhas as like space because they are no different, understands all *dhyāna* absorptions as like space because they are the same throughout all three periods of time, understands all dharmas that have been spoken as like space because they cannot be described in words, and understands the bodies of all buddhas as like space because they are free of attachments and are unimpeded. It is in these ways that the bodhisattva uses the skillful means of seeing all as like space to understand all dharmas as entirely nonexistent.

Sons of the Buddha, when the bodhisattva-mahāsattva uses the wisdom of the patience due to seeing all as like space to understand all dharmas, he acquires a spacelike body and physical actions, he acquires spacelike speech and verbal actions, and he acquires a spacelike mind and mental actions.

Just as space is depended upon by all dharmas and is not born and does not die, so too it is with the bodhisattva-mahāsattva, for his Dharma body is not born and does not die.

Just as space is indestructible, so too it is with the bodhisattva-mahāsattva, for his wisdom and powers are indestructible.

Just as space is that in which all worlds reside and yet it has nothing on which it depends, so too it is with the bodhisattva-mahāsattva, for he is one in whom all dharmas reside and yet he has nothing on which he depends.

Just as space is neither created nor destroyed and yet it is able to support the creation and destruction of all worlds, so too it is with the bodhisattva-mahāsattva, for, although he has no progression and no attainment, he is still able to manifest progression and attainment and everywhere enable those in the world to cultivate purity.

Just as space itself has no directions or locales, yet it is able to reveal boundless directions and locales, so too it is with the bodhisattva-mahāsattva, for he has neither karmic actions nor karmic consequences, yet he is able to reveal the many different kinds of karmic actions and karmic consequences.

Just as space is not walking or standing and yet it is able to reveal the many different kinds of deportment, so too it is with the bodhisattva-mahāsattva, for he neither moves along nor remains still, yet he is able to distinguish all actions.

Just as space is neither form nor non-form, yet it is able to reveal the many different kinds of forms, so too it is with the bodhisattva-mahāsattva, for he is neither worldly form nor world-transcending form, yet he is able to manifest all kinds of forms.

Just as space is neither far nor near, yet it is able to abide forever, revealing all things, so too it is with the bodhisattva-mahāsattva, for he is neither far nor near, yet he is able to abide forever, revealing all the practices carried out by bodhisattvas.

Just as space itself is neither clean nor dirty, yet it is never apart from whatever is clean or dirty, so too it is with the bodhisattva-mahāsattva, for he is neither obstructed or not obstructed, yet he is never apart from obstruction and non-obstruction.

Just as everything in the world appears to space, yet it does not appear to everything in the world, so too it is with the bodhisattva-mahāsattva, for all dharmas appear before him, yet he does not appear before all dharmas.

And just as space everywhere enters into everything and is boundless, so too it is with the bodhisattva-mahāsattva, for he everywhere penetrates all dharmas and his bodhisattva resolve is boundless.

Why is this? This is because whatever the bodhisattva does is like space. That is to say, all of his cultivation, all of his purification, and all that he brings to completion are in every case equal, of a single substance, and of a single type of capacity whereby, like space itself, they are pure and pervade all places. It is in this way that he achieves realized knowing of all dharmas even as he remains free of discriminations regarding any dharma.

He purifies all buddha lands and achieves perfect fulfillment of the body that depends on nothing. He discerns all directions without confusion, possesses all the powers, becomes invincible, and completely fulfills all the boundlessly many meritorious qualities.

He has already reached all the most extremely profound stations of the Dharma, has attained the penetrating comprehension of the path of all the *pāramitās*, and everywhere sits on all the vajra thrones. He everywhere emanates the voice that adapts to all types of beings, turns the wheel of the Dharma for those throughout the entire world, and never misses the appropriate time in doing so.

This is what is meant by the tenth of the bodhisattva-mahāsattva's patiences, patience due to seeing all as like space. When the bodhisattva-mahāsattva perfects this patience, he acquires a body that has no coming because it has no going. He acquires a body that has no creation because it has no destruction. He acquires a body that does not move because it is not subject to deterioration. He acquires a body that is not substantial through having transcended whatever is false. He acquires a body with but a single sign through the realization of signlessness. He acquires an immeasurable body because of the immeasurable powers of the Buddha. He acquires a body of uniform equality because of its identity with suchness. He acquires a body free of all differentiations through equal contemplation of all three periods of time. He acquires a body that reaches all places through the unimpeded and pervasive illumination provided by his purified eyes. He acquires a body that has abandoned the realm of desire through realization that all dharmas have no unification or dissolution. He acquires a body of boundless space through possession of a treasury of merit that is as endless as empty space. He acquires a body possessed of uninterrupted and inexhaustible eloquence due to realizing that the signs of all dharmas consist of but a single sign and that, like space, their nature is an absence of any inherent nature. He acquires a body possessed of the measureless and unimpeded voice through becoming as unimpeded as space. He acquires a body completely possessed of all skillful means and pure bodhisattva practices through becoming everywhere as unimpeded as space. He acquires a body of the sequential continuity of the oceans of all buddha dharmas through becoming as interminable as space. He acquires a body that manifests countless buddha *kṣetras* in all buddha *kṣetras* through having abandoned all desire-based attachments and through having become as boundless as space. He acquires a body that ceaselessly manifests all of the dharmas of sovereign mastery through becoming as boundless as the great ocean of space. He acquires an indestructibly solid and powerful body through becoming like space in his ability to support all worlds. He acquires a body possessed of brilliantly sharp faculties which is as solid and indestructible as vajra through becoming as invulnerable as empty space to being burned up by the kalpa-consuming fires. And he acquires a body possessed of the power to sustain all worlds through wisdom power as boundless as space.

Sons of the Buddha, these are what constitute the bodhisattva-mahāsattva's ten kinds of patience.

At that time, wishing to restate his meaning, Samantabhadra Bodhisattva-mahāsattva then spoke these verses:

It is as if there were some person in the world
who heard of a place with a treasury of jewels
and, because he realized he could obtain them,
his mind was then filled with great joy.

So too it is with the greatly wise bodhisattva
who is a true son of the Buddha
when he hears of the Dharma of all buddhas
that is extremely profound and characterized by quiescence.

When he hears of this profound Dharma,
his mind then feels peaceful and secure
and is not alarmed, frightened,
or filled with dread.

When this great eminence pursues his quest for bodhi
and hears this sound with such vast reach,
his mind becomes purified, able to abide in patience,
and free of all doubts about this.

He brings to mind the fact that, because of hearing this
extremely profound and sublime Dharma,
he is then bound to attain the realization of all-knowledge
and thus become a great guide for both humans and devas.

When the bodhisattva hears this sound,
his mind is filled with great and joyous delight
and he then makes the solidly enduring resolve
by which he vows to seek the Dharma of all buddhas.

Because of his delight in bodhi,
his mind becomes gradually trained,
his faith is thus caused to increase,
and he never opposes or disparages the Dharma.

Therefore, on hearing this sound,
his mind then acquires the patiences
by which he securely and unshakably abides
in the cultivation of the bodhisattva practices.

In order to pursue his quest to realize bodhi,
he focuses his practice on progressing along that path,
maintaining vigor, becoming irreversible,
and never casting off the yoke of goodness.

Because of his quest to realize bodhi,
his mind then becomes free of fear.
When he hears the Dharma, his courage then increases
and he makes offerings to buddhas that please them.

Just as when a person with great merit
acquires a treasury of real gold,
he uses it to make whatever adornments
that he then deems it fitting for him to wear.

So too it is with the bodhisattva,
for when he hears these extremely profound meanings,
he reflects upon them, thus increasing his ocean of wisdom,
and thus cultivating the dharma of compliance.

The existence of dharmas, he also compliantly knows.
The nonexistence of dharmas, he also compliantly knows.
By according with the suchness of those dharmas,
he thus comes to know all the dharmas.[313]

He accomplishes the purification of the mind,
acquires penetrating brilliance and immensely joyous delight,
and, realizing that dharmas all arise from conditions,
he becomes courageous and diligent in his cultivation.

He contemplates all dharmas equally,
completely knows their inherent nature,
does not contradict anything in Buddha's Dharma treasury,
and attains a universal awakening to all dharmas.

His aspiration is forever solid
as he purifies the bodhi of the Buddha,
becomes as unshakable as Mount Sumeru,
and single-mindedly pursues right enlightenment.

By bringing forth vigorous resolve
while also cultivating the path of samādhi,
for countless kalpas, he diligently practices
and still never retreats or loses the path.

The dharmas into which the bodhisattva enters
are the stations of practice of the buddhas themselves.
As he becomes able to completely know these,
his mind remains forever free of weariness or indolence.

In accordance with what the Peerless One has proclaimed,
he equally contemplates all dharmas,
and, with the patience that is never impartial,
he is able to perfect the wisdom that knows equality.

Complying with what has been proclaimed by the Buddha,
he perfects this gateway of patience,
and thus completely knows it in accordance with the Dharma
and yet still does not make discriminations regarding dharmas.

In the Trāyastriṃśa Heaven,
all of those sons of the devas
eat there from but a single vessel,
yet what each of them consumes is different.

The many different kinds of food that they eat
do not arrive there from the ten directions,
rather it is according to the deeds they have cultivated
that they all spontaneously appear in that vessel.

So too it is with the bodhisattva
in his contemplative investigation of all dharmas
in which he sees that they all arise from causes and conditions,
sees that, because they have no arising, they have no destruction,

sees that, because they have no destruction, they are endless,
and sees that, because they are endless, they are free of all defilements.
Regarding the world's changing dharmas,
he fully realizes that they have no changes that they undergo.

If they have no change, then they have no abiding.
If they have no abiding, then they are quiescent.
Thus his mind remains free of all defiling attachments
and he vows to liberate all the many kinds of beings.

He focuses his mindfulness on the Buddha's Dharma,
never becomes scattered or perturbed,
and thus proceeds with the resolve of his compassionate vows
to use skillful means in acting within the world.

He diligently pursues acquisition of the ten powers,
resides within the world and yet does not abide in it.
He has neither any coming nor any going
and uses expedients to skillfully expound on the Dharma.

This patience is of the most supreme sort
whereby one completely understands the infinity of dharmas
and enters into the true Dharma realm
even as, in truth, there is no place one enters.

The bodhisattva abiding in this patience
everywhere sees all *tathāgatas*
simultaneously bestowing a prediction on him.
This is what is known as receiving the buddhas' consecration.

He fully comprehends that the dharmas of the three periods of time
are characterized by quiescence and purity
and thus he becomes able to teach beings
and set them on the path of goodness.

The many different dharmas of the world
are all comparable to conjured illusions.
If one is able to know them in this way,
then his mind will become unshakable.

Because all actions arise from the mind,
it is therefore said that the mind is like a conjured illusion.
If one abandons this engaging in discriminations,
one thereby extinguishes all the destinies of rebirth.

Just as a master conjurer
might everywhere manifest forms and images
that cause the multitude to crave them in vain
since they ultimately have nothing at all they acquire,

So too it is with the world
in which everything is like illusory conjurations
which, though both devoid of any inherent nature and unproduced,
still manifest the appearance of the existence of various phenomena.

Striving to liberate all beings,
he enables them to realize dharmas are like illusory conjurations.
Beings themselves are no different from illusory conjurations.
On completely understanding illusions, one sees no beings exist at all.

Beings as well as lands
and all dharmas of the three periods of time—
all things such as these, entirely and without exception,
are all in every case like conjured illusions.

The conjured shapes of men and women
as well as of elephants, horses, oxen, sheep,
and types of things such as buildings, homes, ponds, and springs
as well as parks, groves, blossoms, fruit, and so forth—

Those conjured phenomena have no knowing awareness
and also have no place where they abide.
They are ultimately characterized by quiescence
and only appear in accordance with one's discriminations.

The bodhisattva is able in this same way
to every perceive all of the entire world's
existent and nonexistent dharmas
and fully comprehend them all as like illusory conjurations.

Beings as well as lands
are created by the many different kinds of karmic deeds.
By entering the sphere in which one sees all as illusory conjurations,
one becomes free of dependence on them or attachment to them.

It is in this way that one acquires skillful means,
develops quiescence, and becomes free of conceptual proliferation.
Then, dwelling on the ground of the unimpeded,
one everywhere manifests great awe-inspiring powers.

The courageous son of all buddhas
compliantly accords with and enters the sublime Dharma
and skillfully contemplates all perceptions
as like a net that entangles one within the world.

The many perceptions are like mirages
that cause beings to develop inverted understandings.
The bodhisattva skillfully understands perceptions
and thus abandons all inverted views.

Beings are each distinctly different
and their forms and types are not of but a single sort.
He fully comprehends that they are all only perceptions
and that everything is devoid of any reality.

All beings throughout the ten directions
are covered over by their perceptions.
If one is able to relinquish one's inverted views,
then one extinguishes worldly perceptions.

The world is comparable to a mere mirage
that possesses its differences due to one's perceptions.
He realizes that those in the world abide in their perceptions
and leaves the three types of inverted mental factors far behind.[314]

Just as a mirage appearing in the hot season
when seen by those in the world is thought to be water
when in truth there is no water there
and the wise find it unworthy of pursuing,

so too it is with beings,
for whatever they pursue in the world is nonexistent.
Just as with a mirage, those things abide [only] in their perceptions.
This is the sphere of cognition of those with unimpeded minds.

If one abandons all such perceptions,
then one also abandons all conceptual proliferation.
Thus the foolish who are attached to thoughts
may all be enabled to attain liberation.

Leaving the arrogant mind far behind,
extinguishing worldly perceptions,
and dwelling in the station of both the finite and the infinite—
This is a bodhisattva's skillful means.

The bodhisattva understands all worldly dharmas
as being in every case like dreams.
Neither having nor not having any place they dwell,
their essential nature is constantly quiescent.

All dharmas are devoid of differences
and, like dreams, they are not different from the mind.
All worlds throughout the three periods of time
are all of this very sort.

The substance of dreams has no creation or destruction
and also has no location at all.
So too it is with the three realms of existence.
Whoever perceives this has a liberated mind.

Dreams do not reside within the world
nor do they reside beyond the world.
When one makes no discriminations between these two,
one succeeds then in entering the ground of patience.

Just as one sees within a dream
various kinds of differing appearances,
so too it is with the world itself,
for there are no differences between it and a dream.

Those who abide in the dream-like meditative absorption
understand that everything in the world is like a dream.
They are neither identical nor different
and neither singular nor multifarious.

The karmic deeds of the beings in all lands,
whether defiled or pure—
He completely understands all such things
as in every case equivalent to the contents of dreams.

The practices the bodhisattva pursues
as well as all of his great vows,
he fully understands to all be like a dream
and also in no way different from the world.

He understands the world as entirely empty and quiescent
yet does not interfere with any worldly dharmas.
They are like what one sees within a dream,
with all kinds of forms that are long, short, and so forth.

This is what is meant by patience due to seeing all as like a dream.
Because of this, he completely understands the world's dharmas,
swiftly realizes unimpeded wisdom,
and extensively liberates the many kinds of beings.

Through cultivating practices such as these,
one then develops vast understanding,
skillfully knows the nature of all dharmas,
and acquires a mind free of attachment to any dharmas.

The many different kinds of sounds
heard within all worlds
are neither inward nor outward.
He understands them all as like mere echoes.

Just as when one hears the many different kinds of echoes,
one's mind does not pursue discriminations about them,
so too, when the bodhisattva hears sounds,
his mind is just this way.

He gazes up in admiration at all the *tathāgatas*
and also listens to the sound of their teaching the Dharma
as they thus expound on countless sutras.
Though listening to all this, he has nothing to which he is attached.

Just as echoes have no place from which they come,
so too it is with these voices that he hears,
and yet he is able to distinguish their dharmas
and avoid any contradictions or errors regarding any dharma.

Though he thoroughly understands all sounds,
he still does not make discriminations about such sounds.
He knows sounds as all empty and quiescent,
and as everywhere emanating the sounds of purity.

He understands the Dharma does not reside in words
and skillfully enters the realm beyond words
even as he is able to manifest speech
that, like echoes, resounds throughout the world.

He fully understands the path of words and speech
and develops the completely perfected voice.
He realizes the nature of sounds is empty and quiescent
and yet uses the language of the world to speak.

In accordance with the sounds of all the world's languages,
he reveals both the same and different dharmas.
His voice pervades all places
and awakens all the many kinds of beings.

The bodhisattva acquiring this patience
uses his pure voice to teach those in the world,
skillfully speaking the Dharma throughout the three periods of time
while still remaining free of any attachment to the world.

Because of his wish to benefit those in the world,
he single-mindedly seeks to realize bodhi
and thus always penetrates the nature of dharmas
and stays free of any discriminations about them.

He everywhere contemplates all worlds
as quiescent and devoid of any essential nature
and yet he constantly benefits others
and cultivates with unwavering resolve.

He does not abide within the world,
nor does he abandon the world.
He has nothing in the world on which he depends,
for no point of dependence can be apprehended at all.

He fully understands the nature of the world
while staying free of any defiling attachment to its nature.
Although he does not depend on the world,
he teaches those in the world and enables their liberation.

He fully knows the inherent nature
of all dharmas of the world,
realizes the non-duality of those dharmas,
and also remains free of attachment even to non-duality.

His mind does not abandon the world
and also does not abide within the world,
for it is not beyond the world
that one cultivates the realization of all-knowledge.

Just as reflections appearing on water
are neither in it nor outside of it,
so too, the bodhisattva in quest of bodhi
realizes that the world is not a world.

He neither resides within nor leaves the world,
for the world is beyond description.
Nor does he reside within it or outside of it,
for his appearance in the world is like that of reflection.

He penetrates this extremely profound meaning,
abandons defilement, and completely understands everything.
He never relinquishes his resolve to fulfill his original vow
to serve as a lamp of wisdom illuminating all.

Although the worlds are boundlessly vast,
his wisdom penetrates them all equally.
He everywhere teaches the many kinds of beings
and enables them to relinquish their many attachments.

He contemplates the extremely profound Dharma,
and thus benefits the many kinds of beings.
After this, they attain entry into wisdom
and cultivate all of its paths.

When the bodhisattva contemplates dharmas, he examines them,
realizes they all are like magically transformed phenomena,
and then practices the transformation-like practice,
never relinquishing it even to the very end.

It is in accordance with the essential nature of these transformations
that he cultivates the path leading to bodhi.
Just as all dharmas are like transformationally created phenomena,
so too is this so of the bodhisattva's practice.

Everything in all worlds
as well as the measurelessly many karmic deeds
are all equally comparable to transformationally created phenomena
that all ultimately abide in quiescence.

All buddhas of the three periods of time
are all also like magically created transformations
whose original vows and cultivation of all the practices
transformed them into *tathāgatas*.

Using their great kindness and compassion,
the buddhas liberate beings who are themselves like transformations.
That process of liberating them is like a transformation as well, and
it is by the power of transformation that they speak Dharma for them.

He knows the world is all like transformationally created phenomena
and does not make discriminations about the world.
Transformational phenomena are of many distinctly different kinds,
all of which arise from differences in karmic actions.

He cultivates the practices leading to bodhi,
thus adorning a treasury of transformations.
Adorning it with countless kinds of goodness
he makes the world in accordance with such deeds.

Transformationally created phenomena go beyond discriminations.
So too, he does not make discriminations with regard to dharmas.
These two are both [by nature] quiescent.
The practices of the bodhisattva are just like this.

The ocean of transformations is fathomed by wisdom.
The world is imprinted with the transformation-like nature.
Transformations are not dharmas which are produced or destroyed.
Wisdom, too, is just like this.

The tenth kind of patience is the clear contemplation
of beings as well as dharmas, seeing them all as having
an essential nature of complete quiescence
by which, like space, they have no location.

One who acquires this knowledge of all as like space
forever abandons all grasping and attachment
and becomes, like space, free of the many different kinds of things
and unimpeded wherever he goes in the world.

He perfects the power of this "patience due to seeing all as like space"
which, like space, is inexhaustible.
Though his sphere of cognition is as vast as space,
he makes no discriminations regarding what is empty.

Space is devoid of any essential nature at all,
is also not such that it can be cut off or extinguished,
and is also devoid of the various kinds of differentiating aspects.
So too is this true of his power of wisdom.

Empty space has no beginning
just as it also has neither any middle nor end.
Its capacity could never be deduced.
So too is this true of the bodhisattva's wisdom.

In this way he contemplates the nature of dharmas
as in every case like empty space,
and as neither produced nor destroyed.
This is what the bodhisattva has realized.

He himself abides in this dharma of seeing all as like space
while he also explains it for the sake of beings,
and succeeds in vanquishing all the *māras*,
all due to using the skillful means of this kind of patience.

All differences in the characteristic signs of the world
are in every case empty and signless.
He enters into the station of signlessness
in which all signs are the same [in this way].

It is through but a single skillful means
that he everywhere enters the many worlds,
namely, by realizing the dharmas of the three periods of time
all equally have the nature of being like space.

As for the wisdom, the voice,
and the body of the bodhisattva,
their nature is like empty space
and all of them are quiescent.

The ten kinds of patience such as these
are what this son of the Buddha cultivates.
His mind is skillfully and securely established in them
and he extensively explains them for beings.

He skillfully cultivates and trains in these
and thus develops vast powers,
the power of the Dharma as well as the power of wisdom,
which serve as skillful means enabling the realization of bodhi.

Through penetrating comprehension of these gateways to patience
he thereby develops unimpeded wisdom
with which he steps beyond all the multitudes
and turns the unsurpassed wheel [of the Dharma].

These vast practices that he cultivates
are such that one could never discover their full measure.
Only with the ocean of wisdom of the Master Trainer
could one then be able to distinguish and know them.

By relinquishing the self and then cultivating the practices,
he penetrates the nature of the profound Dharma.
His mind forever dwells in the pure Dharma
and then bestows this on the many beings.

Though one might conceivably be able to know the number
of all the beings and the atoms in all *kṣetras.*
Even so, no one could ever measure the bounds
of all of this bodhisattva's meritorious qualities.

The bodhisattva is able to perfect
the ten kinds of patience such as these.
His wisdom and all that he practices
are such that no being could ever fathom them.

The End of Chapter Twenty-Nine

Chapter 30

Asaṃkhyeyas[315]

At that time, Mind King Bodhisattva addressed the Buddha, saying, "O Bhagavat, when expounding on the Dharma, the buddhas, the *tathāgatas*, use such numbers as '*asaṃkhyeya*,' 'measureless,' 'boundless,' 'incomparable,' 'innumerable,' 'indescribable,' 'inconceivable,' 'incalculable,' 'ineffable,' and 'ineffable-ineffable.' O Bhagavat, what is meant by '*asaṃkhyeya*' and so forth until we come to 'ineffable-ineffable'?"

The Buddha then informed Mind King Bodhisattva, saying, "It is good indeed, good indeed, O Son of Good Family, that, wishing to enable all those in the world to penetrate the meaning of these denominations of measurement known by the Buddha, you now ask the Tathāgata, the Arhat, the One of Right and Universal Enlightenment, about this matter. Son of Good Family, listen carefully, listen carefully, and skillfully ponder this as I now explain this for you."

Then Mind King Bodhisattva replied, "I wish only to receive this very instruction."

The Buddha then said, "Oh Son of Good Family":

A hundred *lakṣas* equals a *koṭī*.[316]
A *koṭī* times a *koṭī* equals an *ayuta*.
An *ayuta* times an *ayuta* equals a *nayuta*.
A *nayuta* times a *nayuta* equals a *viṃvara*.
A *viṃvara* times a *viṃvara* equals a *kaṅkara*.
A *kaṅkara* times a *kaṅkara* equals an *agāra*.
An *agāra* times an *agāra* equals a *pravara*.
A *pravara* times a *pravara* equals a *mavara*.
A *mavara* times a *mavara* equals an *avara*.
An *avara* times an *avara* equals a *tavara*.
A *tavara* times a *tavara* equals a *sīmā*.
A *sīmā* times a *sīmā* equals a *hūma*.
A *hūma* times a *hūma* equals a *nema*.
A *nema* times a *nema* equals an *avaga*.
An *avaga* times an *avaga* equals a *mīgava*.
A *mīgava* times a *mīgava* equals a *viraga*.
A *viraga* times a *viraga* equals a *vigava*.

A *vigava* times a *vigava* equals a *saṃkrama*.
A *saṃkrama* times a *saṃkrama* equals a *visara*.
A *visara* times a *visara* equals a *vijambha*.
A *vijambha* times a *vijambha* equals a *vijāga*.
A *vijāga* times a *vijāga* equals a *visota*.
A *visota* times a *visota* equals a *vivāha*.
A *vivāha* times a *vivāha* equals a *vibhakti*.
A *vibhakti* times a *vibhakti* equals a *vikhyāta*.
A *vikhyāta* times a *vikhyāta* equals a *tulana*.
A *tulana* times a *tulana* equals a *dharaṇa*.
A *dharaṇa* times a *dharaṇa* equals a *vipatha*.
A *vipatha* times a *vipatha* equals a *viparya*.
A *viparya* times a *viparya* equals a *samarya*.
A *samarya* times a *samarya* equals a *viturṇa*.
A *viturṇa* times a *viturṇa* equals a *hevara*.
A *hevara* times a *hevara* equals a *vicāra*.
A *vicāra* times a *vicāra* equals a *vicasta*.
A *vicasta* times a *vicasta* equals an *atyudgata*.
An *atyudgata* times an *atyudgata* equals a *viśiṣṭa*.
A *viśiṣṭa* times a *viśiṣṭa* equals a *nevala*.
A *nevala* times a *nevala* equals a *hariva*.
A *hariva* times a *hariva* equals a *vikṣobha*.
A *vikṣobha* times a *vikṣobha* equals a *halibhu*.
A *halibhu* times a *halibhu* equals a *harisa*.
A *harisa* times a *harisa* equals a *heluga*.
A *heluga* times a *heluga* equals a *drabuddha*.
A *drabuddha* times a *drabuddha* equals a *haruṇa*.
A *haruṇa* times a *haruṇa* equals a *maluda*.
A *maluda* times a *maluda* equals a *kṣamuda*.
A *kṣamuda* times a *kṣamuda* equals an *elada*.
An *elada* times an *elada* equals a *maluma*.
A *maluma* times a *maluma* equals a *sadama*.
A *sadama* times a *sadama* equals a *vimuda*.
A *vimuda* times a *vimuda* equals a *vaimātra*.
A *vaimātra* times a *vaimātra* equals a *pramātra*.
A *pramātra* times a *pramātra* equals an *amātra*.
An *amātra* times an *amātra* equals a *bhramātra*.
A *bhramātra* times a *bhramātra* equals a *gamātra*.
A *gamātra* times a *gamātra* equals a *namātra*.
A *namātra* times a *namātra* equals a *hemātra*.

A *hemātra* times a *hemātra* equals a *vemātra*.
A *vemātra* times a *vemātra* equals a *paramātra*.
A *paramātra* times a *paramātra* equals a *śivamātra*.
A *śivamātra* times a *śivamātra* equals an *ela*.
An *ela* times an *ela* equals a *vela*.
A *vela* times a *vela* equals a *tela*.
A *tela* times a *tela* equals a *gela*.
A *gela* times a *gela* equals a *svela*.
A *svela* times a *svela* equals a *nela*.
A *nela* times a *nela* equals a *kela*.
A *kela* times a *kela* equals a *sela*.
A *sela* times a *sela* equals a *phela*.
A *phela* times a *phela* equals a *mela*.
A *mela* times a *mela* equals a *saraṭa*.
A *saraṭa* times a *saraṭa* equals a *meruda*.
A *meruda* times a *meruda* equals a *kheluda*.
A *kheluda* times a *kheluda* equals a *mātula*.
A *mātula* times a *mātula* equals a *samula*.
A *samula* times a *samula* equals an *ayava*.
An *ayava* times an *ayava* equals a *kamala*.
A *kamala* times a *kamala* equals a *magava*.
A *magava* times a *magava* equals an *atara*.
An *atara* times an *atara* equals a *heluya*.
A *heluya* times a *heluya* equals a *veluva*.
A *veluva* times a *veluva* equals a *kalāpa*.
A *kalāpa* times a *kalāpa* equals a *havava*.
A *havava* times a *havava* equals a *vivara*.
A *vivara* times a *vivara* equals a *navara*.
A *navara* times a *navara* equals a *malara*.
A *malara* times a *malara* equals a *savara*.
A *savara* times a *savara* equals a *meruṭu*.
A *meruṭu* times a *meruṭu* equals a *camara*.
A *camara* times a *camara* equals a *dhamara*.
A *dhamara* times a *dhamara* equals a *pramāda*.
A *pramāda* times a *pramāda* equals a *vigama*.
A *vigama* times a *vigama* equals an *upavarta*.
An *upavarta* times an *upavarta* equals a *nirdeśa*.
A *nirdeśa* times a *nirdeśa* equals an *akṣaya*.
An *akṣaya* times an *akṣaya* equals a *sambhūta*.
A *sambhūta* times a *sambhūta* equals an *amama*.

An *amama* times an *amama* equals an *avānta.*
An *avānta* times an *avānta* equals an *utpala.*
An *utpala* times an *utpala* equals a *padma.*
A *padma* times a *padma* equals a *saṃkhyā.*
A *saṃkhyā* times a *saṃkhyā* equals a *gati.*
A *gati* times a *gati* equals an *upagama.*
An *upagama* times an *upagama* equals an *asaṃkhyeya.*
An *asaṃkhyeya* times an *asaṃkhyeya* equals an *asaṃkhyeya-parivarta.*[317]
An *asaṃkhyeya-parivarta* times an *asaṃkhyeya-parivarta* equals an *aparimāṇa.*
An *aparimāṇa* times an *aparimāṇa* equals an *aparimāṇa-parivarta.*
An *aparimāṇa-parivarta* times an *aparimāṇa-parivarta* equals an *aparyanta.*
An *aparyanta* times an *aparyanta* equals an *aparyanta-parivarta.*
An *aparyanta-parivarta* times an *aparyanta-parivarta* equals an *asamanta.*
An *asamanta* times an *asamanta* equals an *asamanta-parivarta.*
An *asamanta-parivarta* times an *asamanta-parivarta* equals an *agaṇeya.*
An *agaṇeya* times an *agaṇeya* equals an *agaṇeya-parivarta.*
An *agaṇeya-parivarta* times an *agaṇeya-parivarta* equals an *atulya.*
An *atulya* times an *atulya* equals an *atulya-parivarta.*
An *atulya-parivarta* times an *atulya-parivarta* equals an *acintya.*
An *acintya* times an *acintya* equals an *acintya-parivarta.*
An *acintya-parivarta* times an *acintya-parivarta* equals an *ameya.*
An *ameya* times an *ameya* equals an *ameya-parivarta.*
An *ameya-parivarta* times an *ameya-parivarta* equals an *anabhilāpya.*
An *anabhilāpya* times an *anabhilāpya* equals an *anabhilāpya-parivarta.*
An *anabhilāpya-parivarta* times an *anabhilāpya-parivarta* equals an *anabhilāpyānabhilāpya.*[318]
This *anabhilāpyānabhilāpya,* times an *anabhilāpyānabhilāpya* equals an *anabhilāpyānabhilāpya-parivarta.*

At that time, the Bhagavat spoke these verses for Mind King Bodhisattva:

An ineffable number of ineffably many phenomena
fill up all of the ineffably many phenomena.
Even in an ineffable number of kalpas, one could never finish
describing the ineffable number of those phenomena within them.[319]

If one were to take an ineffable number of buddha *kṣetras*
and grind them all into atoms,
the *kṣetras* contained in a single atom would still be ineffably many.
And just as this is true of one, so too is this true of all others as well.

If, in every mind-moment, one ground to atoms an ineffable number
of these ineffably many buddha *kṣetras*
and the *kṣetras* ground up in all ensuing mind-moments were the same
as one constantly did so in this same way for ineffably many kalpas,

the *kṣetras* contained in these atoms would be ineffably numerous.
If these *kṣetras* were also reduced to atoms, it would be harder yet to describe them.
Even if one used an ineffable number of methods of calculation
and continued to count them in this way for ineffably many kalpas—

Even if one uttered praises for kalpas as numerous as these atoms,
allotting ten myriads of ineffables of kalpas for each of those atoms,
praising one Samantabhadra for just so very many kalpas,
no one could ever exhaust his full measure of meritorious qualities.

On the tip of a single fine hair,
there are an ineffable number of Samantabhadras
and this is also true of the tip of every hair.
So too is this true throughout the entire Dharma realm.

All the *kṣetras* on the tip of a single hair
are such that their number amounts to countless ineffables.
Every one of the hair tips throughout the realm of empty space
also contain just such an extensive number of *kṣetras*.

All the lands residing on the tips of all those hairs
consist of those with immeasurably many different ways they abide.
And just as there are ineffably many different types of *kṣetras*,
so too are there ineffably many *kṣetras* of the very same sort.

On each of the ineffably many places on the tips of hairs,
there are pure *kṣetras* which themselves are ineffably numerous,
each possessed of various adornments of ineffably many types.
Their various kinds of unique marvels are also ineffably many.

In the places on the tip of every one of those hairs,
the names of an ineffable number of buddhas are recited.
Every single one of those names corresponds to a number of *tathāgatas*
of whom there are an ineffable-ineffable number.

On the bodies of every one of those buddhas
there appear an ineffable number of pores,
and in every one of those pores,
there appear an ineffable number of many forms and images.

That ineffable number of pores
all emanate an ineffable number of light rays.
In every one of those light rays,
there are manifested an ineffable number of lotus flowers.

In every one of those lotus flowers,
there are an ineffable number of flower petals
and in the ineffable number of flowers and their many petals,
there appear an ineffable number of forms and images.

Within each of those ineffably many forms,
there in turn appear an ineffable number of petals.
Within the petals, there are an ineffable number of light rays
and the forms and images appearing in the light are ineffably many.

Every one of these ineffably many forms and images
displays within it an ineffable number of light rays.
Within this light, there appear an ineffable number of moons
and those moons in turn manifest ineffably many more moons.

From within every one of these ineffably many moons
there are manifested ineffably many rays of light
and from within every one of those rays of light
there are in turn also manifested an ineffable number of suns.

From within every one of these ineffably many suns,
ineffably many colors are displayed
and within every one of those colors
there are also manifested an ineffable number of light rays.

Within each of those rays of light,
there appear an ineffable number of lion thrones,
the adornments of every one of which are ineffably many,
and the rays of light shining from each of which are ineffably many.

The marvelous colors within these light rays are ineffably many
and the pure lights within those colors are also ineffably many.
From within every one of those pure light rays
there are in turn manifested many different types of marvelous lights.

This light in turn manifests many different lights
which are themselves of an ineffable-ineffable number.
Within each of the many different light rays such as these,
there appear marvelous Sumeru-like jewels.

The jewels manifested within every ray of light
are of an ineffable-ineffable number
and each one of those marvelous Sumeru-like jewels
manifests an ineffable number of *kṣetras*.

All of those Sumeru-like jewels without exception
in every case manifest just such an array of *kṣetras*
and, were one to grind to atoms any single one of those *kṣetras*,
one would find ineffably many forms and images in every atom.

Were one to reduce the many *kṣetras* to atoms, the images in the atoms
would be of an ineffable-ineffable number.
All the many different images in atoms such as these
in every case would emanate an ineffable number of light rays.

The buddhas appearing within these lights are ineffably many
and the dharmas taught by those buddhas are ineffably many.
The marvelous verses within that Dharma are ineffably many.
Understandings gained from hearing those verses are ineffably many.

In every mind-moment, ineffably many understandings
bring about ineffably many revelations of the truths.
Manifested therein are all buddhas of the future
forever and endlessly expounding on the Dharma.

Dharmas proclaimed by each of the buddhas are ineffably many.
Their varieties of purity are ineffably many.
The marvelous voices they utter are ineffably many.
And their turnings of the wheel of right Dharma are ineffably many.

In every one of their turnings of the wheel of Dharma,
they expound on an ineffable number of sutras.
Within every one of those sutras,
they distinguish an ineffable number of gateways into the Dharma.

Within every one of those gateways into the Dharma,
they also explain an ineffable number of dharmas.
Through the use of every one of those dharmas,
they train an ineffable number of beings.

They may also always dwell for an ineffable number of kalpas
within those places on the tip of but a single hair.
Just as this is so of a single hair tip, so too is this also true of all others
in which the number of kalpas they dwell there are all just the same.

Their minds are unimpeded in ineffably many ways.
Their transformationally created buddhas are of an ineffable number.
Every one of those transformationally created *tathāgatas*
in turn manifests ineffably many other such transformations.

The Dharma body of those buddhas is itself ineffable
and those buddha's division bodies are of an ineffable number.
Their countless adornments are of an ineffable number
and the places in the ten directions they visit are also ineffably many.

The lands in which they everywhere travel are ineffably many
and the beings they contemplate are ineffably many.
The beings they purify are ineffably many
and the beings they train are ineffably many.

All their adornments are ineffably many.
All their spiritual powers are ineffably many.
All their types of sovereign mastery are ineffably many.
And all their spiritual transformations are ineffably many.

All their spiritual superknowledges are ineffably many.
All their spheres of cognition are ineffably many.
All their empowerments are ineffably many.
And all the worlds in which they dwell are ineffably many.

Their teachings of the pure true character [of dharmas][320]
are ineffably many, their teachings of sutras are ineffably many,
and the Dharma gateways on which they expound
in every one of those sutras are ineffably many.

The dharmas which they additionally teach
within each of those Dharma gates are ineffably many.
In every one of those dharmas,
all their definitive teachings are ineffably many.

In each of those definitive teachings,
they train an ineffable number of beings.
Using ineffably many similar kinds of dharmas,
ineffably many similar kinds of thought,

ineffably many different kinds of dharmas,
ineffably many different kinds of thought,
ineffably many different kinds of faculties,
and ineffably many different kinds of discourse,

in all stations of practice and in each successive mind-moment,
they engage in the training of ineffably many beings
using ineffably many spiritual transformations,
all the manifestations of which are themselves ineffably many.

The time in which they do so consists of ineffably many kalpas
and the differences in how they do so are ineffably many.
The bodhisattva is able to distinguish and explain all these matters,
but no mathematician could even differentiate them.

All the large and small *kṣetras* residing on the tip of but a single hair,
whether they be defiled, pure, coarse, or refined *kṣetras*—
All of those of types such as these are ineffably many.
He is able to distinguish and clearly understand every one of them.

If one were to grind to atoms a single one of these lands,
those atoms would be so countless as to be ineffably many.
The boundless *kṣetras* such as these as numerous as those atoms
all come and gather together on the tip of but a single hair.

All of these ineffably many lands
are all gathered together in the tip of a hair without being crowded
and without causing the tip of that hair to increase in size,
and yet those lands all come and gather together there.

All the lands therein maintain their shapes and appearances
just as they originally existed, doing so without becoming mixed up.
And just as any single land does not cause disorder in the others,
so too is this true of all the other lands in this same way.

Even all the boundless realms of empty space
are entirely spread forth within a hair tip, filling it up entirely.
All lands such as these that are found abiding in a single hair tip,
the bodhisattva is able to expound on in but a single mind-moment.

An ineffable number of *kṣetras* may all enter in an orderly manner
even into but a single tiny pore.
That pore is able to hold all those *kṣetras*
and those *kṣetras* are still unable to completely fill up that pore.

The number of kalpas of their interpenetration are ineffably many.
The number of kalpas of their being held therein are ineffably many.
The time during which they reside therein in such an orderly way
consists of such a number of kalpas, no one could describe them all.

After they have been absorbed and securely dwell there in this way,
all those realms contained within it are then ineffably many.
The means employed in their entering there are ineffably many
and all the actions done after entering there are ineffably many.

The things clearly known by his mind faculty are ineffably many.
The regions that he roams through there are ineffably many.
The instances of his courageous vigor are ineffably many.
The masterfully enacted spiritual transformations are ineffably many.

His meditations are ineffably many,
his great vows are ineffably many,
his spheres of cognition are ineffably many,
and his penetrating realizations are ineffably many.

His pure physical karmic actions are ineffably many,
his pure verbal karmic actions are ineffably many,
his pure mental karmic actions are ineffably many,
and his pure resolute beliefs are ineffably many.

His instances of marvelous cognition are ineffably many,
his instances of marvelous wisdom are ineffably many,
his instances of fathoming dharmas' true character are ineffably many,
and his instances of severing doubts and delusions are ineffably many.

His instances of emancipation from *saṃsāra* are ineffably many,
his ascents to the right and fixed position are ineffably many,[321]
his extremely deep samādhis are ineffably many,
and his comprehensions of everything are ineffably many.

All beings are ineffably many,
all buddha *kṣetras* are ineffably many,
his insights regarding beings' bodies are ineffably many,
and his insights into beings' mental dispositions are ineffably many.

His insights about the fruits of their karma are ineffably many,
his insights about their mental inclinations are ineffably many,
his insights about their different types are ineffably many,
and his insights about their individual natures are ineffably many.

His insights about their taking on of bodies are ineffably many,
his insights about their birth places are ineffably many,
his insights about the time when they are born are ineffably many,
and his insights about the time after their birth are ineffably many.

His insights about their understandings are ineffably many,
his insights about their inclinations are ineffably many,
his insights about their languages are ineffably many,
and his insights about their actions are ineffably many.

With such great kindness and compassion as this, the bodhisattva
benefits everyone throughout all worlds,
everywhere manifests ineffably many bodies,
and enters into all the ineffably many buddha *kṣetras*.

He goes to see ineffably many bodhisattvas.
develops ineffably many types of wisdom,
poses ineffably many requests to receive teaching on right Dharma,
and his efforts to propagate the Buddha's teaching are ineffably many.

His manifestations of many different bodies are ineffably many,
his instances of paying respects in all lands are ineffably many,
his manifestations of spiritual superknowledges are ineffably many,
and his visits throughout the ten directions are ineffably many.

His emanations of division bodies everywhere are ineffably many,
his instances of drawing near to all buddhas are ineffably many,
his creations of all kinds of offering gifts are ineffably many,
and his countless offerings of all kinds of gifts are ineffably many.

Using ineffably many pure jewels,
using ineffably many marvelous lotus flowers,
and using ineffably many supremely fragrant garlands,
his offerings to *tathāgatas* are ineffably many.

His thoughts of pure faith are ineffably many,
his supremely awakened realizations are ineffably many,
his supreme aspirations are ineffably many,
and his acts of reverential respect for all buddhas are ineffably many.

His acts of cultivating giving are ineffably many,
his past instances of resolving [to give] have been ineffably many,
his gifts of all that is requested to supplicants are ineffably many.
and his instances of giving away everything are ineffably many.

His acts of purely observing moral precepts are ineffably many,
his instances of pure thought are ineffably many,
his praises of all buddhas are ineffably many,
and his acts of devotion to right Dharma are ineffably many.

His instances of perfecting patiences are ineffably many,
his instances of unproduced-dharmas patience are ineffably many,
his instances of complete fulfillment of quiescence are ineffably many,
and the times he dwelt on the quiescence ground are ineffably many.

His instances of rousing great vigor are ineffably many,
his past resolutions [to rouse vigor] were ineffably many.
his instances of irreversible resolve are ineffably many.
and his instances of unshakeable [vigor] are ineffably many.

His treasuries of all meditative absorptions are ineffably many,
his contemplations of dharmas are ineffably many,
his instances of quiescent abiding in absorptions are ineffably many,
and his complete penetrations of all the *dhyānas* are ineffably many.

His instances of wise penetrating cognition are ineffably many,
his sovereign masteries of samādhi are ineffably many,
his instances of complete cognition of dharmas are ineffably many,
and his clear visions of all buddhas are ineffably many.

His acts of cultivating countless practices are ineffably many,
his instances of making vast vows are ineffably many,
his extremely profound spheres of cognition are ineffably many,
and his pure Dharma gateways are ineffably many.

His bodhisattva Dharma powers are ineffably many,
his bodhisattva Dharma dwellings are ineffably many,
his instances of right mindfulness are ineffably many,
and his realms of Dharma are ineffably many.

His acts of cultivating wisdom in skillful means are ineffably many,
his trainings in extremely profound wisdom are ineffably many,
his instances of measureless wisdom are ineffably many,
and his expressions of ultimate wisdom are ineffably many.

His types of Dharma wisdom are ineffably many,
his [turnings of] the pure Dharma wheel are ineffably many,
his acts of [spreading forth] the Dharma cloud are ineffably many,
and his acts of raining the great Dharma rain are ineffably many.

His spiritual powers are ineffably many,
his skillful means are ineffably many,
his entries into empty and quiescent wisdom are ineffably many,
and his continuations of it in every mind-moment are ineffably many.

His measureless practice gateways are ineffably many,
his constant acts of abiding in them in every *kṣaṇa* are ineffably many,
[the lands in] the ocean of all buddha *kṣetras* are ineffably many,
and his abilities to go and visit them all are ineffably many.

The differences among all the *kṣetras* are ineffably many,
their many different types of purification are ineffably many,
their different kinds of adornments are ineffably many,
and their boundless forms and appearances are ineffably many.

The many different varieties of inlays are ineffably many,
the many different types of exquisite aspects are ineffably many,
the pure buddha lands are ineffably many,
and the defiled worlds are ineffably many.

His complete cognitions of beings are ineffably many,
his cognitions of their individual natures are ineffably many,
his cognitions of their karmic retributions are ineffably many,
and his cognitions of their mental behavior are ineffably many.

His cognitions of the nature of their faculties are ineffably many,
his cognitions of their understandings and desires are ineffably many,
[his cognitions of] their defilement and purity are ineffably many,
and his contemplations and trainings of them are ineffably many.

His sovereign masteries of transformations are ineffably many,
his manifestations of various different bodies are ineffably many,
his ways of cultivating vigor are ineffably many,
and his liberations of beings are ineffably many.

His manifestations of spiritual transformations are ineffably many,
his emanations of great radiance are ineffably many,
his different kinds of forms and appearances are ineffably many,
and his acts enabling beings to attain purity are ineffably many.

The number of each of his pores is ineffably many,
their emanations of nets of light are ineffably many,
the colors displayed by those nets of light are ineffably many,
and the buddha *kṣetras* that are all illuminated are ineffably many.

His acts of courage and fearlessness are ineffably many,
his uses of skillful expedient means are ineffably many,
his instances of training beings are ineffably many,
and the times he enables their escape from *saṃsāra* are ineffably many.

His pure physical actions are ineffably many,
his pure verbal actions are ineffably many,
his boundless mental actions are ineffably many,
and his especially supreme and marvelous actions are ineffably many.

His perfections of the jewel of wisdom are ineffably many,
his deep penetrations into the Dharma realm are ineffably many,
his bodhisattva's complete-retention *dhāraṇīs* are ineffably many,
and his instances of being well able to cultivate the training are ineffably many.

His voices of the wise are ineffably many,
his pure voices are ineffably many,
the genuine aspects of his right mindfulness are ineffably many,
and his awakenings of beings are ineffably many.

The ways he fulfills the awesome deportment are ineffably many,
his acts of pure cultivation are ineffably many,
his perfections of fearlessness are ineffably many,
and his ways of training those in the world are ineffably many.

His congregations of sons of the Buddha are ineffably many,
his pure and supreme practices are ineffably many,
his eulogizing exaltations of the buddhas are ineffably many,
and his endless proclamations of their praises are ineffably many.

The guides of the world[322] are ineffably many,
his discourses devoted to their praises are ineffably many,
all those bodhisattvas are ineffably many,
and their pure meritorious qualities are ineffably many.

The bounds [of their meritorious qualities] are ineffably [far-reaching],
those able to abide in them are ineffably many,
the types of wisdom by which they dwell in them are ineffably many,
and the kalpas exhausted dwelling in them are ineffably many.

The ways in which he is devoted to the buddhas are ineffably many,
the ways in which his wisdom is impartial are ineffably many,
the ways he skillfully penetrates dharmas are ineffably many,
and the ways he is unimpeded in the Dharma are ineffably many.

The ways he is like space in all three times are ineffably many,
his types of wisdom in all three times are ineffably many,
his ways of comprehending the three times are ineffably many,
and his ways of abiding in wisdom are ineffably many.

His especially supreme and marvelous practices are ineffably many,
his measureless great vows are ineffably many,
his pure great vows are ineffably many,
and the ways he realizes bodhi are ineffably many.

The bodhi of all buddhas is ineffable,
the wisdom they produce is ineffable,
the principles they distinguish are ineffable,
and their knowledge of all dharmas is ineffable.

The purification of buddha *kṣetras* is ineffable,
the cultivation of the powers is ineffable,
the length of time devoted to cultivation is ineffable,
and what is awoken to in but a single mind-moment is ineffable.

The sovereign masteries of all buddhas are ineffable,
their vast proclamations of right Dharma are ineffable,
their many different kinds of spiritual powers are ineffable,
and their manifestations within the world are ineffable.

The wheel of the pure Dharma is ineffable,
the courage in being able to turn it is ineffable,
the various means of explanatory discourse are ineffable,
and the acts of deep pity for those in the world are ineffable.

Though one might praise his ineffably many meritorious qualities
for an ineffable number of all kalpas,
although one might reach the end of those ineffably many kalpas,
one could never reach the end of those ineffably many qualities.

Even if ineffably many *tathāgatas*
praised with ineffably many tongues
the Buddha's ineffably many qualities for ineffably many kalpas,
still, none of them would ever be able to come to the end of them.

Even if all beings throughout the ten directions
simultaneously attained the realization of right enlightenment,
and every one of those resulting buddhas everywhere manifested
ineffably many bodies of all types,

whereupon each one of those ineffably many bodies
then manifested ineffably many heads,
and each one of those ineffably many heads
then manifested ineffably many tongues,

whereupon each one of those ineffably many tongues
then manifested ineffably many voices,
and each one of those ineffably many voices
then continued on for the duration of ineffably many kalpas,

and just as this was so with one, so too it was so with all buddhas,
and just as this was so with one, so too it was with all those bodies,
and just as this was so with one, so too it was with all those heads,
and just as this was so with one, so too it was with all those tongues,

and just as this was so with one, so too it was with all those voices
that they constantly praised the Buddha for ineffably many kalpas,
even were it possible to exhaust all those ineffably many kalpas,
still, no one could ever finish praising all the Buddha's qualities.

But a single fine atom is able to completely hold within it
ineffably many lotus flower worlds,
and in every one of those lotus flower worlds,
there are ineffably many Foremost Worthy Tathāgatas

who pervade even all places throughout the Dharma realm,
residing in all the atoms within it.
All the worlds therein, whether being created, abiding, or declining,
exist in such numbers as to be immeasurably and ineffably many.

The capacity of the area within a single atom is so boundless
that immeasurably many *kṣetras* are all able to enter there within it.
In the ten directions, these exist with ineffably many differences.
Those spread throughout the ocean of *kṣetras* are ineffably many.

Within every *kṣetra* there are *tathāgatas*
possessed of lifespans stretching on for ineffably many kalpas.
The actions carried out then by buddhas are ineffably many.
Their extremely deep and marvelous dharmas are ineffably many.

Their great powers of spiritual superknowledges are ineffably many,
their unimpeded knowledges are ineffably many,
their penetrations even into pores are ineffably many,
and those pores' causes and conditions are ineffably many.

Their perfections of the ten powers are ineffably many,
their awakenings to bodhi are ineffably many,
their penetrations of the pure Dharma realm are ineffably many,
and their acquisitions in deep wisdom's treasury are ineffably many.

The various ways of numerical measurement are ineffably many.
He is entirely able to know them just as they all are.
The many different forms are ineffably many.
Of these, there are none that he does not entirely comprehend.

His many different samādhis are ineffably many.
He is able in all of them to pass through ineffably many kalpas.
His pure practices in the presence of ineffably many buddhas
are themselves also ineffably many.

He acquires ineffably many varieties of unimpeded mind,
goes to pay his respects in ineffably many places in the ten directions,
brings forth ineffably many manifestations of spiritual power,
and carries out ineffably many boundless practices.

He goes forth to visit the multitudes of ineffably many *kṣetras,*
attains full comprehension of ineffably many buddhas,
practices ineffably many kinds of courageous vigor,
and gains ineffably many penetrating comprehensions with wisdom.

Neither practicing nor not practicing Dharma,
he enters ineffably many spheres of cognition
and, throughout ineffably many great kalpas,
constantly roams the ten directions to ineffably many places.

His expedient expressions of wisdom are ineffably many,
his expressions of genuine wisdom are ineffably many,
his wise uses of spiritual superknowledges are ineffably many,
and such manifestations in every mind-moment are ineffably many.

He achieves ineffably many complete cognitions of each one
of the ineffably many dharmas of the buddhas.
He is able to attain the realization of bodhi at one time
or instead attains such realization and entry at many different times.

The buddha *kṣetras* on the tip of a single hair are ineffably many,
and the buddha *kṣetras* in an atom are ineffably many.
He is able to go and pay respects to all buddha *kṣetras* such as these
and thereby see all the ineffably many *tathāgatas.*

His penetrating comprehensions of one reality are ineffably many
and his skillful entries into the Buddha's lineage are ineffably many.
The lands of all buddhas are ineffably many.
He is able to go, pay respects in them all, and then realize bodhi.

The differences present in the essential natures
of lands, beings, and buddhas are all ineffably many.
Their manifestations such as these in the three times are boundless.
The bodhisattva clearly sees them all.

The End of Chapter Thirty

Chapter 31
Life Spans[323]

At that time, Mind King Bodhisattva-mahāsattva told the bodhisattvas in that congregation:

Sons of the Buddha, a single kalpa in Śākyamuni Buddha's buddha *kṣetra* equals a single day and a single night in Amitābha Buddha's buddha *kṣetra* known as the World of Ultimate Bliss.

A single kalpa in the World of Ultimate Bliss equals a single day and a single night in Vajra Solidity Buddha's[324] buddha *kṣetra* known as Kaṣāya Banner World.

A single kalpa in the Kaṣāya Banner World equals a single day and a single night in Lotus Blooming in Excellent Light Buddha's[325] buddha *kṣetra* known as Voice of the Irreversible Wheel.[326]

A single kalpa in the Voice of the Irreversible Wheel World equals a single day and a single night in Dharma Banner Buddha's[327] buddha *kṣetra* known as the Stainlessness World.

A single kalpa in the Stainlessness World equals a single day and a single night in Lion Buddha's[328] buddha *kṣetra* known as the Lamp of Goodness World.

A single kalpa in the Lamp of Goodness World equals a single day and a single night in Light Treasury Buddha's buddha *kṣetra* known as the Sublime Light World.

A single kalpa in the Sublime Light World equals a single day and a single night in Lotus Blooming in Dharma Light Buddha's buddha *kṣetra* known as the Unsurpassable World.

A single kalpa in the Unsurpassable World equals a single day and a single night in Light of All Superknowledges Buddha's buddha *kṣetra* known as the Wisdom Adornment World.

A single kalpa in the Wisdom Adornment World equals a single day and a single night in Lunar Intelligence Buddha's[329] buddha *kṣetra* known as the Mirror Light World.

Sons of the Buddha, following an orderly sequence such as this on through beyond a hundred myriads of *asaṃkhyeyas* of worlds, a kalpa in the very last of those worlds is equal to a day and a night in Worthy Supremacy Buddha's buddha *kṣetra* known as the Supreme Lotus World. It is completely filled with bodhisattvas such as Samantabhadra Bodhisattva and other such bodhisattvas who cultivate the same practices.

The End of Chapter Thirty-One

Chapter 32
The Bodhisattva Abodes

At that time, Mind King Bodhisattva-mahāsattva told the bodhisattvas in that congregation:

Sons of the Buddha, there is a place off to the east known as Rishi Mountain in which, from the distant past until now, a congregation of bodhisattvas has dwelt and where there is now a bodhisattva named Vajra Supremacy who dwells there with a retinue consisting of a multitude of bodhisattvas, three hundred in all, among whom he always resides, expounding on the Dharma.

There is a place off to the south known as Supreme Peak Mountain in which, from the distant past until now, a congregation of bodhisattvas has dwelt. There is now a bodhisattva there named Dharma Wisdom who dwells there with a retinue consisting of a multitude of bodhisattvas, five hundred in all, among whom he always resides, expounding on the Dharma.

There is a place off to the west known as Vajra Flaming Light Mountain in which, from the distant past until now, a congregation of bodhisattvas has dwelt. There is now a bodhisattva there named Vigorous and Fearless Practice who dwells there with a retinue consisting of a multitude of bodhisattvas, three hundred in all, among whom he always resides, expounding on the Dharma.

There is a place off to the north known as Incense Accumulation Mountain in which, from the distant past until now, a congregation of bodhisattvas has dwelt. There is now a bodhisattva there named Gandhahastin, or "Fragrant Elephant," who dwells there with a retinue consisting of a multitude of bodhisattvas, three thousand in all, among whom he always resides, expounding on the Dharma.

There is a place off to the northeast known as Clear and Cool Mountain in which, from the distant past until now, a congregation of bodhisattvas has dwelt. There is now a bodhisattva there named Mañjuśrī who dwells there with a retinue consisting of a multitude of bodhisattvas, ten thousand in all, among whom he always resides, expounding on the Dharma.

There is a place out in the ocean known as Vajra Mountain in which, from the distant past until now, a congregation of bodhisattvas has dwelt. There is now a bodhisattva there named Risen from

Dharma who dwells there with a retinue consisting of a multitude of bodhisattvas, twelve hundred in all, among whom he always resides, expounding on the Dharma.

There is a place off to the southeast known as Caitya Mountain in which, from the distant past until now, a congregation of bodhisattvas has dwelt. There is now a bodhisattva there named Celestial Crown who dwells there with a retinue consisting of a multitude of bodhisattvas, a thousand in all, among whom he always resides, expounding on the Dharma.

There is a place off to the southwest known as Radiance Mountain in which, from the distant past until now, a congregation of bodhisattvas has dwelt. There is now a bodhisattva there named Worthy Supremacy who dwells there with a retinue consisting of a multitude of bodhisattvas, three thousand in all, among whom he always resides, expounding on the Dharma.

There is a place off to the northwest known as Fragrant Breeze Mountain in which, from the distant past until now, a congregation of bodhisattvas has dwelt. There is now a bodhisattva there named Fragrant Light who dwells there with a retinue consisting of a multitude of bodhisattvas, five thousand in all, among whom he always resides, expounding on the Dharma.

There is an additional place out in the great ocean named Adorned Cave in which, from the distant past until now, a congregation of bodhisattvas has been dwelling.

South of Vaiśālī, there is a dwelling place known as Root of Fine Abiding in which, from the distant past until now, a congregation of bodhisattvas has been dwelling.

In the city of Mathurā, there is a dwelling place known as Fulfillment Cave in which, from the distant past until now, a congregation of bodhisattvas has been dwelling.

In the city of Kuṇḍina, there is a dwelling place known as Dharma Throne in which, from the distant past until now, a congregation of bodhisattvas has been dwelling.

In the city of Pure Perfection there is a dwelling place known as Mucilinda Cave in which, from the distant past until now, a congregation of bodhisattvas has been dwelling.

In the state of Marūndha, there is a dwelling place known as Established by the Unimpeded Dragon King in which, from the distant past until now, a congregation of bodhisattvas has been dwelling.

In the state of Kamboja, there is a dwelling place known as Generating Kindness in which, from the distant past until now, a congregation of bodhisattvas has been dwelling.

In China, there is a dwelling place known as Nārāyaṇa Cave in which, from the distant past until now, a congregation of bodhisattvas has been dwelling.

In Kashgar, there is a dwelling place known as Ox Head Mountain in which, from the distant past until now, a congregation of bodhisattvas has been dwelling.

In Kashmir, there is a dwelling place known as Sequential Order in which, from the distant past until now, a congregation of bodhisattvas has been dwelling.

In the city of Increasing Delight, there is a dwelling place known as Cave of the Venerables in which, from the distant past until now, a congregation of bodhisattvas has been dwelling.

In the state of Ambulima, there is a dwelling place known as Vision of the Light from a Koṭī of Treasuries in which, from the distant past until now, a congregation of bodhisattvas has been dwelling.

And in Gandhāra, there is a dwelling place known as Śaṃbala Cave in which, from the distant past until now, a congregation of bodhisattvas has been dwelling.

The End of Chapter Thirty-Two

Chapter 33
The Inconceivable Dharmas of the Buddhas

At that time, within that great congregation, there were bodhisattvas who had these thoughts:

How are the lands of the buddhas inconceivable?
How are the original vows of the buddhas inconceivable?
How is the lineage of the buddhas inconceivable?
How are the buddhas' appearances in the world inconceivable?
How are the bodies of the buddhas inconceivable?
How are the voices of the buddhas inconceivable?
How is the wisdom of the buddhas inconceivable?
How are the sovereign powers[330] of the buddhas inconceivable?
How are the unimpeded qualities of the buddhas inconceivable?
And how are the liberations of the buddhas inconceivable?

At that time, the Bhagavat, aware of the thoughts in the bodhisattvas' minds, then used his spiritual powers to aid them, used his wisdom to embrace them, used his radiance to illuminate them, and then filled them with his awesome strength. He then enabled Blue Lotus Treasury Bodhisattva to abide in the Buddha's fearlessness, to enter the Buddha's Dharma realm, to acquire the Buddha's awesome virtues and sovereign mastery of the spiritual superknowledges, to attain the Buddha's unimpeded vast contemplations, to know the order of succession in the lineages of all buddhas, and to dwell in the ineffably many skillful means in the Buddha's Dharma.

At that time, Blue Lotus Treasury Bodhisattva was then able to gain a penetrating comprehension of the unimpeded Dharma realm, was then able to securely abide in the profound practice free of obstacles, was then able to completely fulfill the great vows of Samantabhadra, and was then able to know and see the dharmas of all buddhas.

Contemplating beings with the mind of great compassion, he wished to enable them to attain purity and engage in intensely diligent cultivation free of weariness or indolence as they take on the practice of all bodhisattva dharmas. In but a single mind-moment, he then produced the wisdom of the Buddha, fully understood all the gateways to inexhaustible wisdom, and became fully possessed of all the complete-retention *dhāraṇīs* and eloquence. Then, aided by the Buddha's spiritual powers, he told Lotus Treasury Bodhisattva:

Sons of the Buddha, all buddhas, the *bhagavats,* have countless abodes, for example: the abode in which they forever dwell in great compassion; the abode in which, with many different types of bodies, they do the works of all buddhas; the abode in which, with an impartial mind, they turn the wheel of the pure Dharma; the abode in which, using the eloquence of the four unimpeded knowledges, they explain countless dharmas; the abode of the inconceivable dharmas of all buddhas; the abode in which their pure voices pervade countless lands; the abode of ineffably many extremely profound realms of Dharma; and the abode in which they manifest all of the most supreme spiritual superknowledges and are able to reveal and explain the unimpeded and ultimate Dharma.

Sons of the Buddha, all buddhas, the *bhagavats,* have ten kinds of dharmas with which they go everywhere throughout the measureless and boundless Dharma realm. What are those ten? They are as follows:

All buddhas have the boundless body possessed of pure physical signs that everywhere enters all rebirth destinies and yet remains free of any defiling attachments;

All buddhas have the boundlessly unimpeded eye faculty with which they are able to clearly see all dharmas;

All buddhas have the boundlessly unimpeded ear faculty with which they are able to completely comprehend all sounds;

All buddhas have the boundlessly sensitive olfactory faculty with which they are able to reach the far shore of perfection in all buddhas' sovereign powers;

All buddhas have the vast and long tongue that produces their marvelous voice which reaches throughout the Dharma realm;

All buddhas have the boundless body that, in response to the minds of beings, enables them all to see them;

All buddhas have the boundless mind faculty that abides within the unimpeded and universally pervasive Dharma body;

All buddhas have the boundlessly unimpeded liberations with which they manifest endless powers of the great spiritual superknowledges;

All buddhas have boundless pure worlds with which, in accordance with beings' dispositions, they manifest a multitude of buddha lands replete with countless different kinds of adornments and yet do not cause them to engender any defiling attachment to them; and

All buddhas have the boundless conduct and vows of the bodhisattvas, acquire perfectly fulfilled wisdom, attain easeful mastery of the miraculous powers, and are entirely able to fully comprehend all dharmas of the Buddha.

Sons of the Buddha, these are the ten kinds of dharmas of the Tathāgata, the Arhat, the Right and Perfectly Enlightened One, everywhere throughout the boundless Dharma realm.

Sons of the Buddha, all buddhas, the *bhagavats*, have ten kinds of knowledge which they produce in each successive mind-moment. What are those ten? They are as follows:

In but a single mind-moment, all buddhas are able to manifest descent from the heavens in countless worlds;

In but a single mind-moment, all buddhas are able to manifest the bodhisattva's taking birth in countless worlds;

In but a single mind-moment, all buddhas are able to manifest leaving the home life and training in the path in countless worlds;

In but a single mind-moment, all buddhas are able to manifest realization of the universal and right enlightenment beneath the bodhi tree in countless worlds;

In but a single mind-moment, all buddhas are able to manifest the turning of the wheel of the sublime Dharma in countless worlds.

In but a single mind-moment, all buddhas are able to manifest the teaching of beings and the making of offerings to all buddhas in countless worlds;

In but a single mind-moment, all buddhas are able to manifest an ineffable number of many different kinds of buddha bodies in countless worlds;

In but a single mind-moment, all buddhas are able to manifest all the many different kinds of adornment and numberlessly many adornments in countless worlds along with the Tathāgata's sovereign masteries and treasury of all-knowledge;

In but a single mind-moment, all buddhas are able to manifest incalculably and innumerably many pure beings in countless worlds; and

In but a single mind-moment, all buddhas are able in countless worlds to manifest the many different kinds of faculties, many different kinds of vigor, and many different kinds of practice and understanding of all buddhas of the three periods of time and realize the universal and right enlightenment throughout the three periods of time.

These are the ten.

Sons of the Buddha, all buddhas, the *bhagavats,* have ten ways in which they do not miss the right time. What are those ten? They are as follows: All buddhas never miss the right time in realizing the universal and right enlightenment. All buddhas never miss the right time in ripening beings with whom they have affinities based on karmic conditions. All buddhas never miss the right time in bestowing predictions on bodhisattvas. All buddhas never miss the right time in manifesting spiritual powers adapted to the minds of beings. All buddhas never miss the right time in manifesting buddha bodies in accordance with beings' understandings. All buddhas never miss the right time in abiding in the great relinquishment. All buddhas never miss the right time in entering villages. All buddhas never miss the right time in attracting those with pure faith. All buddhas never miss the right time in training evil beings. And all buddhas never miss the right time in manifesting the inconceivable spiritual superknowledges of all buddhas. These are the ten.

Sons of the Buddha, all buddhas, the *bhagavats,* have ten kinds of incomparable and inconceivable spheres of action. What are those ten? They are as follows: When all buddhas sit in the lotus position, they fill up all worlds throughout the ten directions. When all buddhas utter a sentence with a single meaning, they are thereby able to explain all dharmas of the Buddha. When all buddhas emanate a single ray of light, they are able to illuminate all worlds. All buddhas are able with but a single body to manifest all bodies. All buddhas are able to reveal all worlds in but a single place. All buddhas are able with but a single type of knowledge to attain an unimpeded and decisive understanding of all dharmas. All buddhas are able in but a single mind-moment to go forth everywhere throughout the worlds of the ten directions. All buddhas are able in but a single mind-moment to manifest the Tathāgata's countless awesome virtues. All buddhas are able in but a single mind-moment to focus on all buddhas and beings of the three periods of time without experiencing any disorderliness in their own minds. And, in but a single mind-moment, all buddhas abide in substantially identical and non-dual identity with all buddhas of the past, future, and present. These are the ten.

Sons of the Buddha, all buddhas, the *bhagavats,* are able to produce ten kinds of wisdom. What are those ten? They are as follows: All buddhas know all dharmas have no tendencies, and yet they are able to produce the wisdom that makes dedications and vows. All buddhas know all dharmas have no body, and yet they are able to produce the wisdom that manifests pure bodies. All buddhas know all dharmas are fundamentally non-dual, and yet they are able to produce the wisdom that enables awakening. All buddhas know all dharmas are devoid of any self and devoid of any being, and yet they are able to produce the wisdom with which they train beings. All buddhas know all dharmas are fundamentally signless, and yet they are able to produce the wisdom that understands all signs. All buddhas know all worlds have no creation or destruction and yet they are able to produce the wisdom that understands all creation and destruction. All buddhas know all dharmas have no endeavors in which they engage, and yet they are able to produce the wisdom that knows the retributions of karmic actions. All buddhas know all dharmas have no words or speech, and yet they are able to produce the wisdom that understands words and speech. All buddhas know all dharmas have no defilement or purity, and yet they are able to produce the wisdom that knows defilement and purity. And all buddhas know all dharmas have no arising or cessation, and yet they are able to produce the wisdom that understands arising and cessation. These are the ten.

Sons of the Buddha, all buddhas, the *bhagavats*, have ten kinds of dharmas of pervasive entry. What are those ten? They are as follows: All buddhas have a pure and marvelous body that everywhere enters the three periods of time. All buddhas have completely perfected all three kinds of sovereign mastery with which they everywhere teach beings.[331] All buddhas have completely perfected all of the *dhāraṇīs* by which they are everywhere able to take on and uphold all dharmas of the buddhas. All buddhas have completely perfected the eloquence of the four types of unimpeded knowledge by which they everywhere turn the wheel of the pure Dharma. All buddhas have completely perfected the impartial great compassion by which they never abandon any being. All buddhas have completely perfected the extremely deep *dhyāna* absorptions through which they constantly contemplate all beings everywhere. All buddhas have completely perfected the roots of goodness arising from benefiting others by which they ceaselessly engage in the training of beings. All buddhas have completely perfected the unimpeded mind by which they are everywhere able to securely abide throughout the entire Dharma realm. All buddhas have completely perfected the unimpeded spiritual powers by which, in but a single mind-moment, they everywhere manifest all buddhas of the three periods of time.[332] All buddhas have completely perfected the unimpeded wisdom by which, in but a single mind-moment, they everywhere establish all the numerical categories of kalpas throughout the three periods of time. These are the ten.

Sons of the Buddha, all buddhas, the *bhagavats,* have ten kinds of vast dharmas that are difficult to believe in or accept. What are those ten? They are as follows: All buddhas are able to vanquish all *māras.* All buddhas are able to overcome the proponents of all non-Buddhist paths. All buddhas are able to train all beings and enable them all to be pleased. All buddhas are able to travel to visit all worlds, teaching and guiding the many kinds of beings. All buddhas are able with wisdom to attain realized knowledge of the extremely deep Dharma realm. All buddhas are able to use the non-dual body to manifest many different kinds of bodies that completely fill the world. All buddhas are able to use their pure voices to bring forth the eloquence of the four kinds of unimpeded knowledge to expound without interruption on the Dharma so that whoever accepts it with faith will not have done so in vain. All buddhas are able in but a single pore to ceaselessly manifest all buddhas as numerous as the atoms in all worlds. All buddhas are able to reveal multitudes of *kṣetras* within a single atom that are as numerous as the atoms in all worlds, all of which are replete with all different kinds of supremely marvelous adornments, this as they constantly turn the wheel of the sublime Dharma within them, thereby teaching beings, doing so even as those dust motes are not increased in size and those worlds are not made smaller, and as they always use realized wisdom to securely abide throughout the Dharma realm. All buddhas are able to completely penetrate the pure Dharma realm and use the light of wisdom to dispel the darkness of delusion among those abiding in the world, thereby enabling them to awaken to the Buddha's Dharma and follow the Tathāgata in coming to abide in the ten powers. These are the ten.

Sons of the Buddha, all buddhas, the *bhagavats,* possess ten kinds of great meritorious qualities embodying faultless purity. What are those ten? They are as follows:

All buddhas possess the faultless purity by which they possess great awesome virtue;

All buddhas possess the faultless purity of birth into the family of all *tathāgatas* of the three periods of time, the clan of those trained in goodness;

All buddhas possess the faultless purity by which, to the very end of future time, their mind has no place in which it dwells;

All buddhas possess the faultless purity by which they have no attachment to any dharmas throughout the three periods of time;

All buddhas possess the faultless purity by which they realize that the many different kinds of nature are but a single nature which has no place from which it has come;

All buddhas possess the faultless purity of endless past and future karmic merit commensurate in its vastness with the entire Dharma realm;

All buddhas possess the faultless purity of the mark of the boundless body by which they pervade the *kṣetras* of the ten directions and adapt to the time in training all beings;

All buddhas possess the faultless purity of having acquired the four fearlessnesses by which they have abandoned all fearfulness in roaring the great lion's roar in the midst of the assembled congregation and by which they clearly distinguish all dharmas;

All buddhas possess the faultless purity by which, when they enter *parinirvāṇa* in an ineffable-ineffable number of kalpas, beings who hear their names acquire measureless merit indistinguishable from and just the same as if the buddhas were even now still residing in the world; and

All buddhas possess the faultless purity by which, even if beings dwell at a great distance an ineffable-ineffable number of worlds away, so long as they engage in single-minded right mindfulness of those buddhas, they will then be able to see them.

These are the ten.

Sons of the Buddha, all buddhas, the *bhagavats*, possess ten kinds of ultimate purity. What are those ten? They are as follows: All buddhas' past vows are ultimately pure. All buddhas' *brahmacarya* is ultimately pure. All buddhas' separation from the many delusions of the world is ultimately pure. All buddhas' adornments of lands are ultimately pure. All buddhas' retinues are ultimately pure. All buddhas' lineages are ultimately pure. All buddhas' physical marks and secondary signs are ultimately pure. All buddhas' undefiled Dharma body is ultimately pure. All buddhas' unimpeded wisdom of all-knowledge is ultimately pure. All buddhas' liberations and sovereign masteries by which they have done what is to be done and reached the far shore—these are ultimately pure. These are the ten.

Sons of the Buddha, all buddhas, the *bhagavats*, in all worlds and at all times, have ten kinds of buddha works. What are those ten? They are as follows: First, if beings are single-mindedly mindful of them, they will manifest directly before them. Second, if beings have untrained minds, then they will speak Dharma for their sakes.

Third, if beings are able to develop pure faith, they will definitely enable them to acquire measureless great roots of goodness. Fourth, if beings are able to achieve entry into the Dharma position,[333] then they will all manifest direct realizations by which they have nothing they do not completely understand. Fifth, they never weary of teaching beings. Sixth, in traveling to all buddha *kṣetras,* they are unimpeded in coming and going. Seventh, their great compassion is such that they never abandon any being. Eighth, they manifest transformation bodies constantly and incessantly. Ninth, their sovereign mastery of the spiritual superknowledges is incessant. And tenth, they dwell in the Dharma realm and are able to carry out contemplations everywhere. These are the ten.

Sons of the Buddha, all buddhas, the *bhagavats,* have ten kinds of dharmas associated with their inexhaustible ocean of wisdom. What are those ten? They are as follows: The inexhaustible ocean-of-wisdom dharma of all buddhas' boundless Dharma body. The inexhaustible ocean-of-wisdom dharma of all buddhas' measureless buddha works. The inexhaustible ocean-of-wisdom dharma of all buddhas' sphere of cognition with the buddha eye. The inexhaustible ocean-of-wisdom dharma of all buddhas' measureless, innumerable, and inconceivable roots of goodness. The inexhaustible ocean-of-wisdom dharma of all buddhas' all-pervasive raining down of every kind of sublime elixir of immortality dharma. The inexhaustible ocean-of-wisdom dharma of all buddhas' praising of the Buddha's meritorious qualities. The inexhaustible ocean-of-wisdom dharma of all buddhas' many different kinds of vows and conduct cultivated in the past. The inexhaustible ocean-of-wisdom dharma of all buddhas' constant doing of buddha works to the end of future time. The inexhaustible ocean-of-wisdom dharma of all buddhas' complete knowing of all beings' mental actions. The inexhaustible ocean-of-wisdom dharma of all buddhas' adornment with merit and wisdom which no one can surpass. These are the ten.

Sons of the Buddha, all buddhas, the *bhagavats,* have ten kinds of dharmas which they always manifest. What are those ten? They are as follows: All buddhas always practice all of the *pāramitās.* All buddhas always abandon delusion regarding all dharmas. All buddhas always possess the great compassion. All buddhas always possess the ten powers. All buddhas always turn the wheel of Dharma. [All buddhas always liberate all beings.][334] All buddhas always demonstrate for beings the realization of the right enlightenment. All buddhas always delight in training all beings. All buddhas always maintain right mindfulness of the dharma of non-duality. All buddhas always demonstrate entry into the nirvāṇa without residue after they have finished teaching beings, doing so because the realm of all buddhas is boundless. These are the ten.

Sons of the Buddha, all buddhas, the *bhagavats*, have ten kinds of discourse on the countless Dharma gateways of all buddhas. What are those ten? They are as follows: All buddhas expound on the countless gateways related to the realms of beings. All buddhas expound on the countless gateways related to beings' actions. All buddhas expound on the countless gateways related to beings' karmic retributions. All buddhas expound on the countless gateways used in teaching beings. All buddhas expound on the countless gateways used in the purification of beings. All buddhas expound on the countless gateways related to the bodhisattva practices. All buddhas expound on the countless gateways related to the bodhisattva vows. All buddhas expound on the countless gateways related to the formation and destruction of the kalpas in all worlds. All buddhas expound on the countless gateways related to the bodhisattva's deep resolve to purify buddha *kṣetras*. All buddhas expound on the countless gateways related to the orderly appearance in all worlds and in each kalpa of all buddhas of the three periods of time. All buddhas expound on the wisdom gateways of all buddhas. These are the ten.

Sons of the Buddha, all buddhas, the *bhagavats*, have ten ways in which they do buddha works for beings. What are those ten? They are as follows: All buddhas manifest form bodies to accomplish buddha works for beings. All buddhas emanate sublime voices to accomplish buddha works for beings. All buddhas have that which they accept to accomplish buddha works for beings. All buddhas have that which they do not accept to accomplish buddha works for beings. All buddhas use earth, water, fire, and wind to accomplish buddha works for beings. All buddhas use sovereign mastery of spiritual powers to manifest all kinds of objective phenomena to accomplish buddha works for beings. All buddhas use all kinds of different names to accomplish buddha works for beings. All buddhas use buddha *kṣetra* realms to accomplish buddha works for beings. All buddhas purify buddha *kṣetras* to accomplish buddha works for beings. All buddhas may remain silent and refrain from speaking to accomplish buddha works for beings. These are the ten.

Sons of the Buddha, all buddhas, the *bhagavats*, have ten kinds of supreme dharmas. What are those ten? They are as follows:

All buddhas' great and solid vows cannot be impeded. They definitely do whatever they say they will do. Hence their actions and their words do not differ.

All buddhas tirelessly cultivate the bodhisattva practices to the end of future kalpas because they wish to achieve complete fulfillment of all meritorious qualities.

All buddhas go forth to an ineffable-ineffable number of worlds because they wish to train all beings, ceaselessly engaging in their efforts on behalf of all beings.

All buddhas have great compassion by which they are impartial and no different in their universal regard for two kinds of beings, those who are faithful and those who disparage them.

All buddhas, from the time they make their initial resolve until they realize buddhahood, never retreat from their bodhi resolve.

All buddhas accumulate measureless excellent meritorious qualities and dedicate them all to the realization of all-knowledge while still never forming any defiling attachment to anything in the world.

All buddhas cultivate and train in the three kinds of karmic actions in the presence of all buddhas, only practice the practices associated with buddhahood, not the practices associated with the Two Vehicles, and then dedicate all of this to the realization of all-knowledge and the attainment of the utmost, right, and perfect bodhi.

All buddhas emanate great radiance, the light from which equally illuminates all places while also illuminating the Dharma of all buddhas, thereby enabling all bodhisattvas to attain purity of mind and fulfill all-knowledge.

All buddhas relinquish the pleasures of the world, do not crave them, are not defiled by them, and yet make the universal vow wishing to enable everyone in the world to leave suffering, attain bliss, and become free of all conceptual proliferation.

All buddhas, pitying all beings, undergo all different kinds of suffering as they guard and preserve the lineage of the buddhas, practice the Buddha's spheres of action, attain emancipation from *saṃsāra,* and arrive at the ground of the ten powers.

These are ten.

Sons of the Buddha, all buddhas, the *bhagavats,* have ten kinds of unimpeded abiding. What are those ten? They are as follows: All buddhas have the unimpeded abiding by which they are all able to go forth to all worlds. All buddhas have the unimpeded abiding by which they are all able to abide in all worlds. All buddhas have the unimpeded abiding by which they are all able to walk, stand, sit, and lie down in all worlds. All buddhas have the unimpeded abiding by which they are all able to expound on right Dharma in all worlds. All buddhas have the unimpeded abiding by which they are all able to dwell in the Tuṣita Heaven Palace in all worlds. All buddhas have the unimpeded abiding by which they are all able to enter the Dharma realm in all three periods of time. All buddhas have the unimpeded abiding by which they are all able to sit in all sites of enlightenment in the Dharma realm. All buddhas have the unimpeded abiding by which they are all able in each successive mind-moment to contemplate the mental actions of all beings and use their three kinds of sovereign mastery to teach and train them. All buddhas have the unimpeded abiding by which they are all able with but a single body to abide in all of the countless inconceivable abodes of all buddhas as well as all other places, bestowing benefit on beings. All buddhas have the unimpeded abiding by which they are all able to reveal and explain the right Dharma proclaimed by the incalculably many buddhas. These are the ten.

Sons of the Buddha, all buddhas, the *bhagavats*, have ten kinds of supreme and unsurpassable adornments. What are those ten? They are as follows:

All buddhas have completely perfected all of the major marks and secondary signs. This is the first of the buddhas' unsurpassably supreme adornments, those associated with the body.

All buddhas have completely perfected the sixty kinds of voices in every one of which there are five hundred subtypes in every one of which there are countless hundreds of thousands of pure voices which serve as fine adornments. They are able to fearlessly roar the great lion's roar in the midst of all assemblies throughout the Dharma realm, expounding on the Tathāgata's extremely profound meanings of the Dharma. When beings hear this, none of them are not delighted. In accordance with their faculties and inclinations, they are all able to receive the training. This is the second of the buddhas' unsurpassably supreme adornments, those associated with their speech.

All buddhas possess the ten powers, the great samādhis, and the eighteen dharmas exclusive to the buddhas which serve as adornments of their mental actions. In the sphere of cognition in which they act, they have an unimpededly penetrating comprehension of all dharmas of the Buddha. They all acquire as their adornments all of the Dharma realm's adornments without exception. In but a single mind-moment, they are able to clearly see every one of the different past, future, and present mental actions of all beings throughout the Dharma realm. This is the third of the buddhas' unsurpassably supreme adornments, those associated with their minds.

All buddhas are able to emanate countless light rays, every ray of which has a retinue of an ineffable number of light nets. They everywhere illuminate all buddha lands, extinguish the darkness in all worlds, and reveal the countless buddhas' coming forth and appearing in the world. Their bodies are all equal and they are all pure. Of all the buddha works that they accomplish, none of them are done in vain. They are thereby able to cause beings to reach irreversibility. This is the fourth of the buddhas' unsurpassably supreme adornments, those associated with their radiance.

When all buddhas manifest a subtle smile, they all emanate hundreds of thousands of *koṭīs* of *nayutas* of *asaṃkhyeyas* of light rays from their mouths, every ray of which possesses incalculably and inconceivably many different colors which everywhere illuminate all worlds of the ten directions and send forth in the midst of the great assembly the truthful speech that bestows the *anuttarā-samyak-saṃbodhi* prediction on incalculably, innumerably, and inconceivably many beings. This is the fifth of the buddhas' unsurpassably supreme adornments, those which transcend the world's delusions and are associated with their subtle smile.

All buddhas possess the pure and unimpeded Dharma body and have an ultimately penetrating comprehension of all dharmas. It abides in the Dharma realm and is boundless. Although they reside in the world, they do not mix with the world. They completely understand the true nature of the world and practice the world-transcending dharmas that cut short the path of words and speech and go beyond the aggregates, the sense realms and the sense bases. This is the sixth of the buddhas' unsurpassably supreme adornments, those associated with their Dharma body.

All buddhas have countless ever-marvelous lights which have an ineffable-ineffable number of various kinds of colors and appearances as their fine adornments. These form a treasury of light that sends forth countless spheres of light which everywhere and unimpededly illuminate the ten directions. This is the seventh of the buddhas' unsurpassably supreme adornments, those associated with their ever-marvelous lights.

All buddhas have boundlessly many marvelous forms, lovely marvelous forms, pure marvelous forms, marvelous forms appearing in response to whatever they wish, marvelous forms outshining everything throughout the three realms of existence, and unsurpassably marvelous forms which reach the far shore of perfection. This is the eighth of the buddhas' unsurpassably supreme adornments, those associated with their marvelous forms.

All buddhas are born into the lineage of all buddhas of the three periods of time in which they accumulate the many jewels of goodness, attain ultimate purity, become free of all faults, leave behind all of the world's censure and slander, adorn themselves with the most especially supreme purity in the practice of all dharmas, completely fulfill the wisdom of all-knowledge, and become possessed of the pure clan lineage which no one can criticize or disparage. This is the ninth of the buddhas' unsurpassably supreme adornments, those associated with their lineage.

All buddhas adorn themselves with the power of the great kindness, achieve the most ultimate purity, become free of all cravings, forever put to rest all physical actions, achieve thorough liberation of mind, become those whom no one ever wearies of seeing, use the great compassion to rescue and protect everyone in the world, serve as the foremost of all fields of merit unsurpassably supreme in their worthiness to accept offerings, deeply sympathize with and benefit all beings, and enable them all to increase their accumulations of measureless merit and wisdom. This is the tenth of the buddhas' unsurpassably supreme adornments, those associated with their meritorious qualities of great kindness and great compassion.

These are the ten.

Sons of the Buddha, all buddhas, the *bhagavats,* have ten kinds of dharmas of sovereign mastery. What are those ten? They are as follows:

All buddhas have achieved sovereign mastery in all dharmas by which they have a clear comprehension of the many different kinds of statements and syllables[335] and expound on all dharmas with unimpeded eloquence. This is the first of the buddhas' dharmas of sovereign mastery.

All buddhas never miss the right time in teaching beings. Adapting to their aspirations, they ceaselessly explain right Dharma for them, thereby enabling their training. This is the second of the buddhas' dharmas of sovereign mastery.

All buddhas are able to cause the six kinds of quaking in all of the incalculably and innumerably variously adorned worlds throughout all realms of space, thereby causing those worlds to rise or fall, to expand or contract, or to come together or scatter apart, doing so in a manner whereby not even a single being in them is ever subjected to distress or injury, and doing so in a manner whereby the beings in them are entirely unaware, unknowing, free of doubts, and unsurprised. This is the third of the buddhas' dharmas of sovereign mastery.

Using the power of spiritual superknowledges, all buddhas are able to engage in the purification of all worlds whereby, in but a single mind-moment, they may everywhere manifest adornments of all worlds. These adornments are such that one could never finish describing them even in countless kalpas. They are all free of defilements and are incomparably pure. They are able to cause all of the purifying phenomena throughout all buddha *kṣetras* to equally enter into but a single *kṣetra*. This is the fourth of the buddhas' dharmas of sovereign mastery.

When all buddhas observe any single being who should be taught, they may extend their own life spans for even up to an ineffable-ineffable number of kalpas which may extend to the end of future time during which time they may continue to sit in the lotus posture free of any weariness in either body or mind with their minds focused on and mindful of this being, never forgetting him as they use skillful means to train him, ensuring that they never miss the right time in doing so. Just as they may do this for a single being, so too may they also do this for all beings in the very same way. This is the fifth of the buddhas' dharmas of sovereign mastery.

All buddhas are able to go everywhere in all worlds to the places where all *tathāgatas* travel and yet never even briefly leave any other place throughout the entire Dharma realm. In every one of the different regions throughout the ten directions, there are oceans of countless worlds, and in every one of those oceans of worlds, there are countless world systems. Using their spiritual powers, in but a single mind-moment, the buddhas are able to go to all of them and turn the wheel of the unimpeded pure Dharma. This is the sixth of the buddhas' dharmas of sovereign mastery.

Wishing to train all beings, in each successive mind-moment, all buddhas manifest the realization of *anuttarā-samyak-saṃbodhi* even as, with respect to all dharmas of a buddha, they are not such as have already awakened or are now awakening, are not such as will be awakened in the future, and are not such as abide on the ground of those still in training. Still, they are possessed of the complete knowledge and vision by which they command unimpeded penetrating comprehension, measureless wisdom, and measureless sovereign mastery with which they teach and train all beings. This is the seventh of the buddhas' dharmas of sovereign mastery.

All buddhas are able with the eye sense base to do the buddha works of the ear sense base, are able with the ear sense base to do the buddha works of the nose sense base, are able with the nose sense base to do the buddha works of the tongue sense base, are able with the tongue sense base to do the buddha works of the body sense base, are able with the body sense base to do the buddha works of the mind sense base, are able with the mind sense base to abide in all worlds in the many different kinds of worldly and world-transcending realms, and are able in every one of those realms to do the incalculably many vast works of the Buddha. This is the eighth of the buddhas' dharmas of sovereign mastery.

Every one of the pores on the body of all buddhas is able to contain all beings even as every one of those beings' bodies, commensurate in size with an ineffable number of buddha *kṣetras,* remains entirely unconstricted within it. Every one of those beings is able with every step to pass by countless worlds. And so this may continue to the point that, continuing to the very end of countless kalpas, they see all buddhas coming forth into the worlds, teaching beings, turning the wheel of pure Dharma, and offering instruction in an ineffable number of dharmas of the past, future, and present, this even as all beings throughout the realm of space continue to take on bodies in all the rebirth destinies, continuing to go and come in their various ways of comporting themselves, and fully possessed of the various kinds of objects from which they derive their enjoyments. In all of this, no mutually obstructive interferences occur at all. This is the ninth of the buddhas' dharmas of sovereign mastery.

All buddhas are able in but a single mind-moment to reveal all buddhas as numerous as the atoms in all worlds with each of those buddhas throughout the entire Dharma realm in vastly adorned lotus flower worlds of many wonders seated on lotus dais lion thrones, realizing the perfect and right enlightenment, manifesting all buddhas' sovereign mastery of the spiritual powers.

And just as this occurs in this way in the vastly adorned lotus flower worlds of many wonders, so too does this also occur everywhere throughout the entire Dharma realm in an ineffable-ineffable number of pure worlds possessed of many different kinds of adornments, many different kinds of realms, many different kinds of forms and appearances, many different kinds of manifestations, and many different kinds of numbers of kalpas.

And just as this is the case in a single mind-moment, so too is this also so in all the mind-moments in incalculably and boundlessly many *asaṃkhyeyas* of kalpas in which, in every single mind-moment, everything appears in this way, and in every single mind-moment, these incalculably many phenomena all abide therein, even as, in all of this, they are never required to use even the slightest sort of power of expedient means to cause this to occur in this way. This is the tenth of the buddhas' dharmas of sovereign mastery.

Sons of the Buddha, all buddhas, the *bhagavats*, have ten kinds of measureless and inconceivable perfectly fulfilled buddha dharmas. What are those ten? They are as follows: Every one of the pure marks of all buddhas embodies a hundredfold measure of merit. All buddhas perfect all the dharmas of a buddha. All buddhas perfect all roots of goodness. All buddhas perfect all meritorious qualities. All buddhas are able to teach all beings. All buddhas are able to serve as leaders for beings. All buddhas perfect pure buddha *kṣetras*. All buddhas perfect the wisdom of all-knowledge. All buddhas perfect the form body with its major marks and secondary signs that enables all who see it to acquire such benefit that their efforts will not have been in vain. All buddhas possess the equal and right Dharma of all buddhas. After all buddhas have completed their buddha works, none of them do not manifest the appearance of entering nirvāṇa. These are the ten.

Sons of the Buddha, all buddhas, the *bhagavats*, have ten kinds of skillful means. What are those ten? They are as follows:

All buddhas completely know all dharmas transcend all conceptual proliferation and thus they are able to reveal and provide instruction in all buddhas' roots of goodness. This is the first of their skillful means.

All buddhas realize that all dharmas have nothing they perceive, that each of them has no mutual awareness of any other, that they have no bondage and have no liberation, that they have no experiencing of anything and have no accumulation, and that they have no accomplishment, yet they independently ultimately reach the far shore of perfection. Thus they realize that the reality of all dharmas does not involve any differentiation or particularity and thus they attain sovereign mastery. They realize there is no self or anything that experiences and thus they do not contradict the apex of reality. They have already succeeded in reaching the ground of great sovereign mastery and are thereby always able to contemplate the entire Dharma realm. This is the second of their skillful means.

All buddhas have forever transcended all phenomenal characteristics. Their minds have no place in which they dwell and yet they are able to know them all in a way that is not disordered and that is not erroneous. Although they know all such characteristics have no inherent existence of their own, they are still able to skillfully penetrate them in a manner accordant with their essential nature and are still able to manifest countless form bodies and use the inexhaustible phenomenal characteristics associated with every sort of adornment in all pure buddha lands and accumulate lamps of wisdom to extinguish the delusions of beings. This is the third of their skillful means.

As all buddhas abide in the Dharma realm, they do not abide in the past, the future, or the present because, in the nature of suchness, there is no past, future, or present, the signs of the three periods of time. Even so, they are still able to expound on the coming forth into the world of the countless buddhas of the past, the future, and the present, thus enabling those who hear this to everywhere see the realms of all buddhas. This is the fourth of their skillful means.

In the physical, verbal, and mental actions of all buddhas, there is nothing that they do. They have no coming, no going, and no abiding. They transcend all dharmas of enumeration, reach the far shore of perfection in all dharmas, and yet become a treasury of the many dharmas possessed of measureless wisdom. They have a completely penetrating comprehension of the many different kinds of worldly and world-transcending dharmas and possess unimpeded wisdom. They manifest countless kinds of masterfully implemented spiritual powers and train all the beings of the Dharma realm. This is the fifth of their skillful means.

All buddhas know that all dharmas are imperceptible, neither singular nor different, neither measurable nor measureless, neither coming nor going, and in every case devoid of any inherently existent nature even as they still do not contradict [the conventional existence of] worldly dharmas. For those possessed of all-knowledge perceive all dharmas even in the midst of what is devoid of any inherent nature. With sovereign mastery in all dharmas, they extensively expound on all dharmas even as they still always securely abide in the true nature of true suchness. This is the sixth of their skillful means.

All buddhas know all times in any single time. They possess pure roots of goodness and achieve entry into the right and fixed position,[336] and yet remain free of anything to which they are attached. They neither dwell within nor relinquish any of the creations and destructions occurring in days, months, years, kalpas, and other such periods of time, and yet they are able to manifest within them. Whether it be the beginning, middle, or ending periods of the day or the night, a single day, seven days, a half month, a month, a year, a century, one kalpa, many kalpas, inconceivably many kalpas, an ineffable number of kalpas, and so forth on through to the exhaustion of all kalpas of the future, they constantly and uninterruptedly turn the wheel of the sublime Dharma for the benefit of beings, never retreating from this and never resting in this. This is the seventh of their skillful means.

All buddhas constantly abide in the Dharma realm, perfect in the countlessly many fearlessnesses of all buddhas as well as their innumerable types of eloquence, their incalculable forms of eloquence, their interminable eloquence, their uninterrupted eloquence, their boundless eloquence, their exclusive forms of eloquence, their inexhaustible eloquence, their genuine eloquence, their eloquence that employs skillful means in the explanation of all statements, and their eloquence with respect to all dharmas. They adapt to beings' faculties and natures as well as to their aspirations and understandings, using then all kinds of different Dharma gateways to proclaim the ineffable-ineffable number of hundreds of thousands of *koṭīs* of *nayutas* of sutras that are good in the beginning, good in the middle, and good in the end, all of which are possessed of complete ultimacy. This is the eighth of their skillful means.

All buddhas abide in the pure Dharma realm knowing that all dharmas are fundamentally nameless, having no past names, no present names, no future names, no names of beings, no names of non-beings, no country names, no non-country names, no dharma names, no non-dharma names, no meritorious quality names, no non-meritorious quality names, no bodhisattva names, no buddha names, no numerical names, no non-numerical names, no names associated with production, no names associated with destruction, no names associated with existence, no names associated with nonexistence, no singular kinds of names, and no different kinds of names. And why is this? This is because the essential nature of all dharmas is indescribable. All dharmas are devoid of direction, devoid of place, indescribable in the aggregate, indescribable when scattered, indescribable with a single way of speaking, indescribable through multiple ways of speaking, entirely inaccessible to description by voice, and such as cut short any attempt to describe them with words and speech. Although [the buddhas] do conform to the many different kinds of worldly verbal discourse, in doing so, they have no objective conditions that they seize upon and have nothing that they create. They abandon all attachments to false conceptions. In all such matters they reach the most ultimately far shore of perfection. This is the ninth of their skillful means.

All buddhas know that the fundamental nature of all dharmas is quiescence. Because they are unproduced, they are not associated with the form aggregate. Because they are not accessible through conceptual proliferation, they are not associated with the feeling aggregate. Because they are devoid of any names or numerical categories, they are not associated with the perception aggregate. Because they are devoid of anything that is done, they are not associated with the karmic formative factor aggregate. Because they are devoid of any grasping at anything at all, they are not associated with the consciousness aggregate. Because they have no point of access, they are not associated with any of the sense bases. Because they are devoid of anything that is apprehensible, they are not associated with any of the sense realms. Even though this is the case, there is still no damage done to [the conventional existence of] any dharma. Their fundamental nature has no arising, for it is like empty space.

All dharmas are empty and quiescent, without any karmic retributions, without any cultivation, without any accomplishment, and without any production. They are neither enumerated nor non-enumerated, neither existent nor nonexistent, neither produced nor destroyed, neither defiled nor immaculate, neither entered nor exited, neither abiding nor non-abiding, neither associated with training nor unassociated with training, neither associated with beings nor unassociated with beings, neither consistent with a life span nor inconsistent with the existence of a life span, and they are neither within the sphere of causes and conditions nor devoid of causes and conditions. Even so, [the buddhas] are able to completely know [with regard to beings] whether they are in the group of those fixed in the path of what is right, in the group of those fixed in the path of what is wrong, or in the group of those whose destiny is still unfixed. They expound on the sublime Dharma for all beings and thereby enable them to reach the far shore of liberation, to fully develop the ten powers and the four fearlessnesses, become able to roar the lion's roar, become possessed of all-knowledge, and dwell in the Buddha's sphere of cognition. This is the tenth of their skillful means.

Sons of the Buddha, these are what constitute all buddhas' perfection of the ten kinds of skillful means.

Sons of the Buddha, all buddhas, the *bhagavats*, have ten kinds of vast buddha works that are measureless, boundless, inconceivable, such as none of the world's devas or humans could ever know, such as no *śrāvaka* disciple or *pratyekabuddha* could ever know, and such as only can be known through the awesome spiritual powers of the Tathāgata. What are those ten? They are as follows:

Sons of the Buddha, when all buddhas are dwelling in the Tuṣita Heavens in all worlds to the very ends of empty space throughout the Dharma realm, they all manifest the taking on of births in which they cultivate bodhisattva practices and accomplish the great buddha works, appearing then with countless forms and appearances, countless kinds of awesome deportment, countless kinds of light, countless kinds of voices, countless kinds of language, countless samādhis, and countless spheres of cognition imbued with wisdom by all of which they draw forth all humans, devas, *māras*, Brahma Heaven devas, *śramaṇas*, brahmans, *asuras*, and others of these sorts, using their unimpeded great kindness and their ultimate great compassion to equally benefit all beings, perhaps enabling them to be born as devas, perhaps enabling them to be born as humans, perhaps purifying their faculties, perhaps training their minds, sometimes speaking for their benefit of three different vehicles, and sometimes speaking for their benefit of the perfectly complete One Vehicle, thereby rescuing and liberating them all through enabling them to escape from *saṃsāra*. This is the first of their vast buddha works.

Sons of the Buddha, when all buddhas spiritually descend from the Tuṣita Heaven into their mother's womb, they use the most ultimate samādhi to contemplate the dharmas involved in taking birth as like a magical conjuration, like a transformation, like a reflection, like space, or like a mirage in the hot season. It is in accordance with what pleases them that they take this on in a manner that is measurelessly unimpeded, enter into the dharma of noncontentiousness, bring forth unattached wisdom that is apart from desire and pure, perfect a treasury of vast and marvelous adornments, and then take on that very last body. They abide there in a great tower adorned with jewels, doing the Buddha's works, sometimes using their spiritual powers to do the Buddha's works, sometimes using right mindfulness to do the Buddha's works, sometimes manifesting the spiritual superknowledges to do the Buddha's works, sometime manifesting the wisdom sun to do the Buddha's works, sometimes manifesting the vast realms of the buddhas to do the Buddha's works, sometimes manifesting the measureless radiance of all buddhas to do the Buddha's works, sometimes entering into countless vast samādhis to do the Buddha's works, and sometimes manifesting their emergence from those samādhis to do the Buddha's works.

Sons of the Buddha, at that time, even as the Tathāgata resides in his mother's womb, because he wishes to benefit all beings, he may bring forth many different kinds of manifestations in doing the Buddha's works. For example, he may manifest his first taking birth, may manifest his existence as a youth, may manifest his residing within the palace, may manifest his leaving the home life, may once again manifest his realization of the perfect and right enlightenment, may once again manifest his turning of the wheel of the sublime Dharma, or may manifest his entry into *parinirvāṇa*. In this way, he always uses these many different kinds of skillful means in every region, in all the networks, in all the clans, in all the lineages, and in all the worlds as he accomplishes the Buddha's works. This is the second of their vast buddha works.

Sons of the Buddha, all buddhas have already achieved complete purity in all good karmic actions. All of their knowledge regarding the taking on of births having already become radiantly immaculate, they use the dharma of taking birth to gather in and guide the many confused beings, thus enabling them to awaken and completely practice the many kinds of goodness.

For the sake of beings, they manifest the appearance of being born into the palace of a king. All buddhas have already relinquished all sensual desires and pleasures of the palace life for they have nothing at all that they desire. They always contemplate all aspects of existence as empty and devoid of any essential nature and always contemplate all objects of pleasure as unreal. They have achieved the most ultimate and perfect fulfillment in observing a buddha's pure moral precepts.

In contemplating their wives, consorts, and retainers within the inner palace, they bring forth the pity of the great compassion for them. Contemplating all beings as false and unreal, they bring forth the mind of great kindness for them. Contemplating all worlds as devoid of anything in which one could delight, they bring forth the great sympathetic joy. And with their minds' acquisition of sovereign mastery in all dharmas, they bring forth the great equanimity.

Completely possessed of the meritorious qualities of a buddha, they manifest birth into the Dharma realm in bodies perfectly complete in their physical marks and are attended by retinues which are pure and thus they are free of any sort of attachment to any of them. With their voices adapted to the various types of beings, they expound on the Dharma for the sake of the many, thereby enabling those beings to bring forth a deep renunciation of worldly dharmas.

In accordance with the actions in which they engage, they instruct beings in the fruits that will thereby accrue to them. They also use skillful means adapted to those who should receive the benefit of their teachings. Those who have not yet become ripened, they enable to become ripened. Those who have already become ripened, they enable to attain liberation. So that they may do the works of the buddhas, they enable them to attain irreversibility.

Furthermore, they use their vast minds of kindness and compassion to constantly expound on the many different dharmas for the benefit of beings. They also manifest for them their three kinds of sovereign mastery, thus enabling them to awaken and achieve the purification of their own minds. Although they dwell within the inner palace where they are all seen by the multitudes, they still engage in the Buddha's works in all worlds. With great wisdom and with great vigor, they manifest many different kinds of unimpeded and endless acts of the Buddha's spiritual superknowledges. They constantly abide in the three kinds of expedient actions, namely the ultimate purity of their physical actions, the constant accordance of their verbal actions with wisdom, and their extremely profound and unimpeded mental actions. They use these skillful means to benefit beings. This is the third of their vast buddha works.

Sons of the Buddha, all buddhas manifest residence within palaces with all kinds of adornments and then contemplate them, renounce them, and abandon them to leave behind the home life. They wish to influence beings to fully realize that the dharmas of the world are all false conceptions which are impermanent and bound for destruction so that they will bring forth deep renunciation of them, so that they will not generate a defiling attachment to them, and so that they will forever cut off the world's desire-based afflictions and then cultivate the pure conduct and benefit beings.

When they are about to leave the home life, they relinquish the behavior of the common person, abide within the dharma of non-contentiousness, fulfill the incalculable meritorious qualities of their original vows, use the great light of their wisdom to extinguish the darkness of the world's delusions, and serve as unexcelled fields of merit for the entire world. For the sake of beings, they always praise the meritorious qualities of the Buddha, thereby causing them to plant roots of goodness in relation to the buddhas. They use the wisdom eye to perceive the genuine meaning. For beings' sakes, they also praise the purity, absence of faults, and eternal emancipation associated with leaving the home life and then forever serving for the world as a highly placed banner of wisdom. This is the fourth of their vast buddha works.

Sons of the Buddha, all buddhas, being possessed of all-knowledge, have already come to completely know and see all of the countlessly many dharmas. They realize the utmost right enlightenment beneath the bodhi tree, vanquish the many *māras*, and become possessed of the most especially revered kinds of awesome virtue. Their bodies completely fill all worlds. What they accomplish through their spiritual powers is boundless and endless. They all attain sovereign mastery in the meaning of the practices related to all-knowledge. They have all already perfectly fulfilled the cultivation of every form of meritorious quality. Their bodhi thrones are perfectly complete in their adornments and everywhere pervade all the worlds of the ten directions. The buddhas abide on them, turning the wheel of the sublime Dharma, expounding on the practices and vows of all bodhisattvas, revealing and explaining the spheres of action of all the countlessly many buddhas, enabling all bodhisattvas to succeed in awakening to and entering them, enabling them also to cultivate the many different kinds of pure and marvelous practices, and, additionally, enabling them to instruct and guide all beings, enabling them to plant roots of goodness, to become born onto the level ground of the Tathāgata, to dwell in the boundless and marvelous practices of all bodhisattvas, and to perfect all the supreme dharmas of the meritorious qualities.

They skillfully and completely know all worlds, all beings, all buddha *kṣetras*, all dharmas, all bodhisattvas, all teachings, all three periods of time, all means of training, all the spiritual transformations, and all those matters that the minds of beings delight in and desire. So it is that they engage in doing the Buddha's works. This is the fifth of their vast buddha works.

Sons of the Buddha, all buddhas turn the irreversible Dharma wheel to enable all bodhisattvas to attain irreversibility. They turn the measureless Dharma wheel to enable the entire world to reach complete understanding. They turn the Dharma wheel that awakens everyone to enable the attainment of the great fearlessnesses and the roaring of the lion's roar. They turn the Dharma wheel of the treasury of the knowledge of all dharmas to open the gates of the Dharma treasury and eliminate the obstacles associated with benightedness. They turn the unimpeded Dharma wheel to enable becoming the same as empty space. They turn the Dharma wheel of nonattachment to enable contemplation of all dharmas as neither existent nor nonexistent. They turn the world-illuminating Dharma wheel to enable all beings to purify the Dharma eye. They turn the Dharma wheel that explains the all-knowledge which completely extends to all dharmas of the three periods of time. They turn the Dharma wheel that is the same for all buddhas because the dharmas of all buddhas are not mutually contradictory. All buddhas use incalculable and innumerable hundreds of thousands of *koṭīs* of *nayutas* of kinds of Dharma wheels such as these to adapt to the differences in the mental actions of beings and thus accomplish their inconceivable buddha works. This is the sixth of their vast buddha works.

Sons of the Buddha, when all buddhas enter the capital cities of all kings, they accomplish buddha works for the sake of all beings. That is to say, when the buddhas enter the city gates of the cities of human kings, deva kings, dragon kings, *yakṣa* kings, *gandharva* kings, *asura* kings, *garuḍa* kings, *kiṃnara* kings, *mahoraga* kings, *rākṣasa* kings, *piśāca* kings, and other such kings, the great earth quakes, light illuminates everything, the blind gain sight, the deaf gain hearing, the insane come to their right minds, those who have no clothes obtain robes, all who are distressed and afflicted with suffering become happy, the musical instruments sound of their own accord without being played, all adornments, whether worn or not worn, emanate marvelous sounds, and, of all beings who hear this, there are none who are not pleased.

All buddhas have pure form bodies complete with all the major marks and secondary signs which, whoever beholds them, never wearies of seeing them. They are able to use them to perform the buddha works for the sake of beings. For example, whether they turn and look at a being, contemplate them, turn around, bend down or straighten up, walk along or stand, sit down or lie down, remain silent or speak, manifest spiritual superknowledges, speak

Dharma for them, or provide them with instructions, in all such cases as these, they are doing buddha works for the sake of beings.

Everywhere in all the countless worlds, in the midst of the ocean of mental dispositions of the many different kinds of beings, all buddhas encourage and enable them to practice mindfulness of the Buddha, to always diligently practice meditative contemplation, to plant roots of goodness, and to cultivate the bodhisattva practices. They praise the buddha's physical signs as the most sublime of all, as rarely encountered by any being, as being such that, if beings are able to see them and then bring forth minds of faith, then they will produce all of the countless good dharmas, will accumulate the buddhas' meritorious qualities, and will all become purified.

Having praised the Buddha's meritorious qualities in these ways, they send forth division bodies that go forth everywhere throughout the worlds of the ten directions, thus enabling all beings to look up with reverence, reflect upon, contemplate, serve, and make offerings to buddhas, thereby planting all kinds of roots of goodness, thereby eliciting the pleased approval of the buddhas, and thereby extending the lineage of the buddhas as they all become buddhas in the future.

It is through practices such as these that they accomplish buddha works. For beings' sakes, they sometimes manifest form bodies, sometimes speak with sublime voices, or sometimes simply smile a subtle smile that causes beings to bring forth resolute faith, to bow down in reverence, to bend low their bodies with pressed palms, to utter praises, to half-bow, or to stand up in respect. It is in ways such as these that they accomplish buddha works.

All buddhas use incalculably, innumerably, ineffably, and inconceivably many different kinds of buddha works such as these with which, in all worlds, they adapt to all beings' mental dispositions. Using the power of their original vows, the power of great kindness and great compassion, and the power of all-knowledge, they use skillful means to teach beings and enable them all to take on the training. This is the seventh of their vast buddha works.

Sons of the Buddha, all buddhas may abide in an *araṇya,* a forest dwelling, and thus accomplish buddha works, may abide in a quiet place and thus accomplish buddha works, may abide in a deserted place and thus accomplish buddha works, may abide where the Buddha dwells and thus accomplish buddha works, may abide in samādhi and thus accomplish buddha works, may dwell alone in a garden or grove and thus accomplish buddha works, may hide their bodies and not appear at all and thus accomplish buddha works, may abide in extremely deep wisdom and thus accomplish buddha works, may abide in all buddhas' incomparable spheres of action and thus accomplish buddha works, or they may abide in all different kinds of invisible physical actions adapted to beings' mental dispositions, desires, and understandings, ceaselessly using skillful means in teaching and thus accomplish buddha works.

They may use the body of a deva seeking all-knowledge and thus accomplish buddha works, may use the body of a dragon, the body of *yakṣa,* the body of a *gandharva,* the body of an *asura,* the body of a *garuḍa,* the body of a *kiṃnara,* the body of a *mahoraga,* or the body of a human or nonhuman that, in each case, is seeking all-knowledge and thus accomplish buddha works, may use the body of a *śrāvaka* disciple, the body of a *pratyekabuddha,* or the body of a bodhisattva seeking all-knowledge and thus accomplish buddha works, may engage in speaking the Dharma or remain silent and thus accomplish buddha works, may speak of but a single buddha or speak of many buddhas and thus accomplish buddha works, may speak of all practices or all vows of bodhisattvas as but a single practice or vow and thus accomplish buddha works, or they may speak of a single practice or a single vow of bodhisattvas as constituting countless practices or vows and thus accomplish buddha works.

They may speak of the Buddha's realms as just the world's realms and thus accomplish buddha works, may speak of the world's realms as just the Buddha's realm and thus accomplish buddha works, or may speak of the Buddha's realms as not being realms at all and thus accomplish buddha works or, for the sake of all beings, they may remain for one day, one night, a half month, a whole month, a whole year, and so forth on up to their sometimes abiding even for an inexpressibly great number of kalpas and thus accomplish buddha works. This is the eighth of their vast buddha works.

Sons of the Buddha, all buddhas are a treasury which produces pure roots of goodness. They enable beings to develop pure resolute faith in the Buddha's Dharma, to acquire training of their faculties, and to forever transcend the world. They enable bodhisattvas to develop perfectly realized wisdom light on the path to bodhi and also cause them to acquire the awakening that does not depend on anyone else. For example, they may manifest entry into nirvāṇa and thus accomplish buddha works, may reveal all worlds as impermanent and thus accomplish buddha works, may speak of the body of the Buddha and thus accomplish buddha works, may speak of having already done what is to be done and thus accomplish buddha works, may speak of achieving perfectly fulfilled and flawless meritorious qualities and thus accomplish buddha works, may speak of forever severing the root of all realms of existence and thus accomplish buddha works, may enable beings to renounce the world and follow in accordance with the Buddha's resolve and thus accomplish buddha works, may speak of the life span as inevitably bound to end and thus accomplish buddha works, or they may speak of the world as devoid of even a single delightful thing and thus accomplish buddha works.

They may expound on the practice of making offerings to all buddhas to the end of the future and thus accomplish buddha works, may speak of all buddhas turning the wheel of the pure Dharma, thereby causing those who hear to be filled with great joy, and thus accomplish buddha works, may expound on all buddhas' spheres of action, thereby causing others to bring forth the resolve and cultivate all the practices and thus accomplish buddha works, may expound on the mindfulness of the Buddha samādhi, thereby causing others to bring forth the resolve by which they always delight in seeing the Buddha and thus accomplish buddha works, may expound on the purification of all one's faculties and the diligent pursuit of the path to buddhahood with a resolve that never rests or retreats and thus accomplish buddha works, may visit all buddha lands, contemplating the many different causes and conditions associated with all realms and thus accomplish buddha works, or they may unite the bodies of all beings into the body of a buddha, thereby causing all indolent and neglectful beings to abide in the pure moral precepts of the Tathāgata. This is the ninth of their vast Buddha works.

Sons of the Buddha, when all buddhas enter nirvāṇa, countless beings wail piteously, weep and cry, are beset with immense distress and affliction, and then look to each other and say, "The Tathāgata, the Bhagavat, possessed of the great kindness and compassion, deeply pities and benefits the entire world and serves beings as a rescuer and a refuge. The Tathāgata's appearance in the world is only rarely ever encountered. The most supreme of all fields of merit has now forever entered nirvāṇa." By causing beings to wail piteously and long for the Buddha in this way, they also accomplish buddha works.

Moreover, to teach and liberate all the devas, dragon spirits, *yakṣas, gandharvas, asuras, garuḍas, kiṃnaras, mahoragas,* humans, and nonhumans, they adapt to their aspirations, even grinding up their own bodies to serve as incalculably and innumerably many inconceivable *śarīra* relics which serve to cause beings to bring forth thoughts of pure faith, respect, reverence, and joyous delight in making offerings and cultivating all the meritorious qualities to complete fulfillment. They also erect stupas with all different kinds of adornments and make offerings in celestial palaces, dragon palaces, *yakṣa* palaces, and palaces of *gandharvas, asuras, garuḍas, kiṃnaras, mahoragas,* humans, nonhumans, and others.

They may also erect commemorative stupas to the buddhas' teeth, nails, or hair relics which inspire all those who see them to become mindful of the Buddha, mindful of the Dharma, and mindful of the Sangha while also causing them to develop unremitting resolute faith, to bring forth sincere respect and reverential esteem, to make gifts of offerings in place after place, and to cultivate all the meritorious qualities. Because of this merit, those beings may be reborn in the heavens or may come to dwell among humans in an honorable and illustrious clan where they are well endowed with wealth and possessions, are attended by a retinue of pure beings, and never enter the wretched destinies, but rather are always reborn in the good destinies where they are always able to see the Buddha, perfect the many dharmas of pristine purity, and swiftly succeed in gaining emancipation from the three realms of existence as they each reap the fruits of their own vehicles in accordance with whatever they have vowed to accomplish and then recognize and repay kindnesses bestowed on them by the *tathāgatas* and thus forever serve as those in whom those in the world can take refuge.

Sons of the Buddha, although all buddhas, the *bhagavats,* enter *parinirvāṇa,* they still continue to serve beings as inconceivable fields of pure merit and as the most supreme of all fields of merit for the generation of endless meritorious qualities, doing so in ways which enable all beings to fully develop roots of goodness and acquire the complete fulfillment of merit. This is the tenth of their vast buddha works.

Sons of the Buddha, these works of the buddhas are so immeasurably vast and so inconceivable that no deva or human in the entire world and no past, future, or present *śrāvaka* disciple or *pratyekabuddha* could ever know them unless they were aided by the awesome spiritual powers of the Tathāgata.

Sons of the Buddha, all buddhas, the *bhagavats,* have ten kinds of dharmas of masterful action in which it could not be otherwise. What are those ten? They are as follows: All buddhas are able to bestow predictions in which it definitely could not be otherwise.[337] All buddhas are able to adapt to the thoughts in beings' minds and enable their wishes to be fulfilled and it definitely could not be otherwise. All buddhas are able to manifest awakening to all dharmas and expound on their meaning and it definitely could not be otherwise. All buddhas are able to completely fulfill the wisdom of all buddhas of the past, future and present periods of time and it definitely could not be otherwise. All buddhas realize that all *kṣaṇa*-instants throughout the three periods of time are but a single *kṣaṇa*-instant and it definitely could not be otherwise. All buddhas realize that all buddha *kṣetras* of the three periods of time enter into a single buddha *kṣetra* and it definitely could not be otherwise. All buddhas realize that all speech of all buddhas of the three periods of time is identical to the speech of any single buddha and it definitely could not be otherwise. All buddhas realize that the essential nature of all buddhas of the three periods of time and the essential nature of all the beings they teach are identical and it definitely could not be otherwise. All buddhas realize that the nature of worldly dharmas and the nature of all buddhas' dharmas do not differ and it definitely could not be otherwise. All buddhas realize that all roots of goodness of all buddhas of the three periods of time are the same as any one of their roots of goodness and it definitely could not be otherwise. These are the ten.

Sons of the Buddha, all buddhas, the *bhagavats*, have ten kinds of abiding in which they abide in all dharmas. What are those ten? They are as follows: All buddhas abide in awakening to the entire Dharma realm. All buddhas abide in greatly compassionate speech. All buddhas abide in original great vows. All buddhas abide in the practice of not abandoning their training of beings. All buddhas abide in the dharma of the nonexistence of any inherent nature. All buddhas abide in impartially benefiting beings. All buddhas abide in never forgetting any dharma. All buddhas abide in the unimpeded mind. All buddhas abide in the mind of constant right meditative concentration. All buddhas abide in the equal penetration of all dharmas and never contradicting their having the characteristic [nature of] the apex of reality. These are the ten.

Sons of the Buddha, all buddhas, the *bhagavats*, have ten kinds of knowing of all dharmas without exception. What are those ten? They are as follows: They know all dharmas of the past without exception. They know all dharmas of the future without exception. They know all dharmas of the present without exception. They know all speech dharmas without exception. They know all worldly paths without exception. They know the thoughts of all beings without exception. They know without exception all of the superior, middling, and inferior roots of goodness of all bodhisattvas as well as all their many different stations on the path. They know all without exception, neither more nor less, of all buddhas' perfectly fulfilled types of knowledge and roots of goodness. They know that all dharmas without exception arise from conditions. They know all the different world systems without exception. They know all the different phenomena without exception throughout the entire Dharma realm are like the net of Indra. These are the ten.

Sons of the Buddha, all buddhas, the *bhagavats,* have ten kinds of powers. What are those ten? They are as follows: vast powers, supreme powers, measureless powers, powers of great awesome virtue, powers that are difficult to acquire, irreversible powers, solidly enduring powers, indestructible powers, powers inconceivable to anyone in the world, and powers that cannot be shaken by any being. These are the ten.

Sons of the Buddha, all buddhas, the *bhagavats,* have ten kinds of great *nārāyaṇa* banner dharmas of bravery and strength. What are those ten? They are as follows:

All buddhas have indestructible bodies and lives which cannot be cut short. They cannot be poisoned by the world's poisons. Not even all the world's water, fire, and wind disasters can injure the Buddha's body. Even if all the demons, devas, dragons, *yakṣas, gandharvas, asuras, garuḍas, kiṃnaras, mahoragas,* humans, nonhumans, *piśācas, rākṣasas,* and other such beings all exhausted all of their strength in raining down great vajras as immense as Mount Sumeru or the Iron Ring Mountains all over all worlds of the entire great trichiliocosm, raining them down all at once, they would still remain unable to cause any fear in the mind of the Buddha, would still be unable to shake even a single hair on his body, and, even from the very beginning, would still be unable to cause any change at all in his walking, standing, sitting, or lying down. Wherever the Buddha dwells, whether near or far, if he does not allow them to descend, then they would be unable to rain down. And even if he did not restrain them and they then did in fact rain down, they would still remain unable to do him any harm. Not even any being supported by the Buddha or sent as an emissary of the Buddha could be the least bit harmed, how much the less could harm befall the body of the Tathāgata himself. This is the first of all buddhas' great *nārāyaṇa* banner dharmas of bravery and strength.

Sons of the Buddha, all buddhas may place into a single pore all of the contents of all the worlds throughout the entire Dharma realm, including Sumeru, the king of mountains, the Iron Ring Mountains, the Great Iron Ring Mountains, the great oceans, the mountains, the forests, the palaces, the buildings, and the dwellings, doing so even to the very end of future kalpas even as all beings remain entirely unaware and incognizant of this unless they are assisted by the Tathāgata's spiritual powers.

Sons of the Buddha, at that time when the buddhas hold within a single pore all of those so very many worlds even to the very end of all kalpas of the future, whether they be walking, standing, sitting, or lying down, they never have even a single thought of weariness in this regard. Sons of the Buddha, just as empty space everywhere holds within it all the worlds throughout the entire Dharma realm without ever becoming wearied by this, so too it is with all buddhas as they hold all worlds within but a single pore. This is the second of all buddhas' great *nārāyaṇa* banner dharmas of bravery and strength.

Sons of the Buddha, all buddhas are able in but a single mind-moment to take a number of steps equal to the number of atoms in an ineffable-ineffable number of worlds and, in so doing, pass with every step beyond a number of worlds equal to the atoms contained within an ineffable-ineffable number of buddha *kṣetras* so that, as they walk along in this way, they may pass through a number of kalpas equal to the number of atoms contained in all worlds.

Sons of the Buddha, suppose that there was a great vajra mountain the size of which was precisely commensurate with all those buddha *kṣetras* that were passed by in the above description, and suppose too that there was a number of such great vajra mountains equal to the number of atoms in an ineffable-ineffable number of buddha *kṣetras*. The buddhas are able to take all such mountains and place them all inside of a single one of their pores. Even supposing that the number of pores on a buddha's body were equivalent to all the pores existing on the bodies of all beings throughout the entire Dharma realm, in every one of their pores, they can place just so very many great vajra mountains as this and, taking along just so very many mountains as this, they can then roam about throughout the ten directions, entering all the worlds throughout the entirety of empty space, doing so from the beginning of time on through to the end of all kalpas of the future, doing so without ever resting. and doing so without any injury to the Buddha's body, also doing so without any weariness occurring as a result of this, and doing so with the mind constantly residing in meditative concentration, entirely free of any scattering or disorder at all. This is the third of all buddhas' great *nārāyaṇa* banner dharmas of bravery and strength.

Sons of the Buddha, after all buddhas have taken their meal in a single sitting, sitting in the lotus posture, they may pass through an ineffable number of kalpas of the past and future, immersed in the inconceivable bliss experienced by buddhas as, securely abiding there, their bodies remain quiescent and unmoving, this even as they still never desist from their work of teaching beings.

Sons of the Buddha, suppose there was a person who used the tip of a single hair to sequentially measure every one of the worlds throughout empty space. All buddhas are able to sit in the lotus position on the tip of but a single hair, doing so to the very end of all kalpas of the future. And just as this is so in the case of a single hair tip, so too may they do this on the tips of all hairs in the very same way.

Sons of the Buddha, suppose that every being among all the beings in all worlds throughout the ten directions was of a size equal to that of the aggregate of a number of worlds equivalent to the number of atoms in an ineffable number of buddha *kṣetras*. Suppose too that this was true of their weight as well. Even so, all buddhas would be able to place all those beings onto the tip of but a single one of their fingers, doing so on through to the end of all kalpas of the future while also doing so on each of their other fingertips in just this same way. They would be able to carry all of these very many beings into all places within every one of the worlds throughout all of empty space, doing so throughout all parts of the entire Dharma realm without exception, doing so without there ever being any weariness in either body or mind on the part of the buddhas. This is the fourth of all buddhas' great *nārāyaṇa* banner dharmas of bravery and strength.

Sons of the Buddha, all buddhas are able to transformationally manifest on but a single body a number of heads as numerous as the atoms within an ineffable-ineffable number of buddha *kṣetras* and are able to transformationally manifest on every one of those heads a number of tongues as numerous as the atoms in an ineffable-ineffable number of buddha *kṣetras*. In association with every one of those tongues, they are able to transformationally manifest a number of different voices as numerous as the atoms in an ineffable-ineffable number of buddha *kṣetras*, voices which no being anywhere in the Dharma realm could fail to hear.

With every one of those voices, they are able to expound upon a number of repositories of sutras as numerous as the atoms contained in an ineffable-ineffable number of buddha *kṣetras*. In association with every one of those repositories of sutras, they are able to expound on a number of dharmas equal in number to all the atoms contained in an ineffable-ineffable number of buddha *kṣetras*. In association with every one of those dharmas, there are a number of passages, words, statements, and meanings as numerous as the atoms contained in an ineffable-ineffable number of buddha *kṣetras*.

They may expound in this way for a number of kalpas equal to all the atoms contained in an ineffable-ineffable number of *kṣetras*. Then, having exhausted so very many kalpas as these in doing so, they may yet again expound in this way throughout a number of kalpas as numerous as the atoms contained in an ineffable-ineffable number of buddha *kṣetras*. They may continue on sequentially in this way until they exhaust a number of kalpas equivalent to the atoms contained in all worlds and then exhaust a number of kalpas equivalent to the number of thoughts had by all beings.

Although one might conceivably exhaust all the kalpas of the future, the number of Dharma wheels turned by all transformation bodies of the Tathāgata are endless. This refers in particular to: the Dharma wheel of wise discourse, the Dharma wheel that severs all doubts, the Dharma wheel that illuminates all dharmas, the Dharma wheel that opens the treasury of the unimpeded, the Dharma wheel that enables the happiness and training of countless beings, the Dharma wheel that reveals and explains all bodhisattva practices, the Dharma wheel of the perfectly full sun of great wisdom that has risen high in the sky, the Dharma wheel of the brightly shining lamp of wisdom that everywhere illuminates the world, and the Dharma wheel adorned in many ways with fearless eloquence.

And just as a single buddha body, using the powers of spiritual superknowledges, turns so many different Dharma wheels as these that no analogy using worldly dharmas could describe them all, so too and in this very same way, throughout all realms of empty space, in every one of those places the size of the tip of a single hair, there are worlds as numerous as the atoms in an ineffable-ineffable number of buddha *kṣetras* and, within every one of those worlds, there are manifested in each successive mind-moment a number of transformation bodies as numerous as the atoms in an ineffable-ineffable number of buddha *kṣetras* in which the sounds of the teaching of passages, words, statements, and meanings uttered by every one of those transformation bodies also and in the very same way completely fill up the entire Dharma realm. All the beings within it are able to completely understand all of them. And as this occurs, the sound of those buddhas' words continues on, unchanged, uninterrupted, and without end. This is the fifth of all buddhas' great *nārāyaṇa* banner dharmas of bravery and strength.

Sons of the Buddha, all buddhas have the sign of virtue adorning their chests and are all just as invulnerable to injury as vajra. Seated in the lotus posture beneath the bodhi tree, they are confronted by the boundless hordes of the king of the *māras* who appear in all kinds of different extremely fearsome forms such that, were beings to see them, none would not shrink in terror, be driven wildly insane, or perhaps even drop dead in fear.

In this circumstance, even though hordes of *māras* such as these completely fill all of empty space, when the Tathāgata sees them, his mind remains free of fear and his countenance remains unchanged. Not even a single hair is caused to rise on his body. Neither shaken nor flustered, he does not even indulge in any discriminations in this regard. He remains free of either joy or anger, remains in a state of serene purity, abides as a buddha abides, and embodies the power of kindness and compassion, with all of his faculties trained and restrained, and with his mind in a state of complete fearlessness. He is not one whom any of the armies of Māra could cause to quaver even slightly. Rather, he is able to vanquish all the armies of Māra and cause them all to change their minds, bow down their heads in reverence, and take refuge in him. He later uses the three spheres of action[338] to teach them and inspire them to bring forth the forever irreversible resolve to realize *anuttarā-samyak-saṃbodhi.* This is the sixth of all buddhas' great *nārāyaṇa* banner dharmas of bravery and strength.

Sons of the Buddha, all buddhas possess an unimpeded voice the sound of which reaches everywhere throughout the worlds of the ten directions. When beings hear it, they become spontaneously inclined to take on the training. The sound sent forth by all *tathāgatas* is such that it cannot be blocked by Mount Sumeru or any of the other mountains, cannot be blocked by any of the palaces of the devas, palaces of the dragons, palaces of the *yakṣas,* or palaces of any of the *gandharvas, asuras, garuḍas, kiṃnaras, mahoragas,* humans, nonhumans, or any other class of being, and is such that it cannot be blocked by any of the loudest sounds from anywhere in any world. In accordance with whichever beings should be taught, there are none of them who do not then fully hear and succeed in completely understanding its passages, words, statements, and meanings. This is the seventh of all buddhas' great *nārāyaṇa* banner dharmas of bravery and strength.

Sons of the Buddha, all buddhas' minds are unimpeded. For hundreds of thousands of *koṭīs* of *nayutas* of ineffable-ineffable numbers of kalpas, they have constantly dwelt in goodness and purity. They are of the same single essential nature as that of all buddhas of the past, the future, and the present. They are free of all turbidity, are free of all obscurations, are devoid of any self or possessions of a self, and are neither inward nor outward. They realize the emptiness and quiescence of the objective realms, do not produce any erroneous perceptions, have nothing on which they depend and nothing they do, do not dwell on signs, and forever sever all discriminations. Their original nature is pure, they abandon all thought inclined to seize on objective conditions, they are ever free of any opposition or disputation regarding any dharmas, and they abide in the apex of reality. They have attained the purity apart from desires, and have entered the true Dharma realm where they expound on the Dharma endlessly. They have left behind all erroneous mental discursions associated with either perception or mistaken perception and have cut off all discussions of both the conditioned and the unconditioned.

They have already achieved a penetrating comprehension of an ineffable number of boundless realms. They possess unimpeded and endless wisdom and skillful means and have perfected the pure adornments of all of the meritorious qualities associated with the ten powers. They expound on the many different immeasurable dharmas in ways that never contradict the true character of dharmas. They have attained equal and indistinguishable ultimate sovereign mastery in all dharmas throughout the Dharma realm and the three periods of time. They have entered the supreme treasury of all dharmas and remain in a state of undeluded right mindfulness of all dharmas. They securely abide in all buddha *kṣetras* throughout the ten directions and yet remain motionless. They have acquired the uninterrupted wisdom that knows in the most ultimate way all dharmas without exception. They have put an end to all contaminants, have acquired the mind that is well liberated, have acquired the wisdom that is well liberated, and abide in an unimpeded penetrating comprehension of the apex of reality. Their minds are always in right meditative concentration and they are able in but a single mind-moment to attain an utterly penetrating and unimpeded comprehension of the mental activity of all beings throughout the three periods of time. This is the eighth of all buddhas' great *nārāyaṇa* banner dharmas of bravery and strength.

Sons of the Buddha, all buddhas have: the same single Dharma body; the body possessed of countless objective realms; the body possessed of boundless meritorious qualities; the body that is endlessly present in the world; the body that remains undefiled by the three realms of existence; the body that manifests in accordance with thoughts; the body that, neither real nor false, is possessed of uniformly equal purity; the body that neither comes nor goes, that is unconditioned, and that is never destroyed; the body with the inherent nature of dharmas that has the single sign of signlessness; the body that, having no location and no region, pervades all places; the body possessed of masterful spiritual transformations with boundless forms and appearances; the body that possesses many different kinds of manifestations and everywhere enters all places; the body possessed of the sublime Dharma's skillful means; the body with the pervasive illumination of the treasury of wisdom; the body that reveals the uniform equality of dharmas; the body that everywhere pervades the Dharma realm; the body that is unmoving, free of all discriminations, neither existent nor nonexistent, and always pure; the body that is neither expedient nor nonexpedient, neither destroyed nor undestroyed, and that manifests in ways adapted to the many different kinds of resolute faith possessed by all beings who should be provided with teaching; the body that is born from the jewels of every sort of meritorious quality; the body possessed of the true suchness of the Dharma of all buddhas; the body with the original nature of unimpeded quiescence; the body that perfects all unimpeded dharmas; the body that abides everywhere throughout the pure Dharma realm; the body that divides its form and pervades all worlds; and the body free of grasping at objective conditions which is irreversibly and forever liberated, which is possessed of all-knowledge, and which has a complete comprehension of everything. This is the ninth of all buddhas' great *nārāyaṇa* banner dharmas of bravery and strength.

Sons of the Buddha, all buddhas have equally awakened to all dharmas of the *tathāgatas* and have equally cultivated all the bodhisattva practices. Whether it be their vows or their knowledge, they are pure, impartial, and as vast as the great ocean. Their practices and powers are venerable and supreme. They have never retreated in timidity from their cultivation. They abide in the measureless spheres of cognition of all samādhis. They provide instruction in all aspects of the paths, encouraging goodness and warning against evil. Their power of wisdom is foremost. They are fearless in expounding on the Dharma. They are able to offer skillful replies to whatever is asked. Their wisdom in teaching the Dharma is uniformly pure and their physical, verbal, and mental actions are all free of any impurities. They dwell where the buddhas dwell, in the lineage of all buddhas. They use the Buddha's wisdom to do the buddha works and, dwelling in all-knowledge, they expound on the countless dharmas as devoid of any foundation or boundaries. Their spiritual superknowledges and wisdom are inconceivable and such that no one in the world is able to completely fathom them. Their wisdom with which they deeply penetrate and perceive all dharmas is sublime, vast, measureless, and boundless. With it, they have attained a thorough and penetrating comprehension of all Dharma gateways of the three periods of time. They are able to awaken those in all worlds. They use world-transcending wisdom to accomplish an ineffable number of buddha works of all different kinds everywhere in the world. Having realized irreversible wisdom, they have entered the ranks of all buddhas.

Although they have already realized the indescribable Dharma that transcends the written word, they are still able to explain all the many different kinds of expressions in language. Using the wisdom of Samantabhadra, they have accumulated all good practices and have perfected the sublime wisdom that responds in but a single mind-moment. They are able to command complete enlightenment with respect to all dharmas and, as befits all the beings they have just brought to mind, they rely on their individual vehicle and then proceed to give them their appropriate dharma. All dharmas, all worlds, all beings, and everything in the three periods of time—with their unimpeded wisdom, they are able to know and see all the boundless realms such as these throughout the Dharma realm.

Sons of the Buddha, in accordance with the needs of those who should be taught and in but a single mind-moment, all buddhas appear in the world. They dwell in pure lands, realize the perfect and right enlightenment, manifest the powers of their spiritual superknowledges, and awaken the minds, intentions, and consciousnesses of all beings of the three periods of time, never missing the appropriate time in doing so.

Sons of the Buddha, beings are boundless, worlds are boundless, the Dharma realm is boundless, the three periods of time are boundless, and all buddhas, the most supreme ones, are also boundless. [The buddhas] all manifest the realization of the perfect and right enlightenment in the midst of them all and are tireless in using a buddha's wisdom and skillful means to awaken them.

Sons of the Buddha, all buddhas use the power of their spiritual superknowledges to manifest their supremely marvelous bodies and dwell in boundlessly many places in which, with their great compassion, skillful means, and unimpeded minds, at all points in time, they forever expound on the sublime Dharma for the benefit of beings. This is the tenth of all buddhas' great *nārāyaṇa* banner dharmas of bravery and strength.

Sons of the Buddha, these great *nārāyaṇa* banner dharmas of bravery and strength of all buddhas are measureless, boundless, inconceivable, and such that they could never be completely understood by any of the beings or adherents of the Two Vehicles of the past, future or present with the sole exception of those who are aided by the spiritual powers of the Tathāgata.

Sons of the Buddha, all buddhas, the *bhagavats,* have ten kinds of definite dharmas. What are those ten? They are as follows: At the end of their lives in the Tuṣita Heaven, all buddhas then definitely descend to take birth. All buddhas definitely manifest the taking on of birth, dwelling in the womb for ten months. All buddhas definitely renounce the mundane ways of the world and delight in the quest to leave the home life. All buddhas definitely sit beneath the bodhi tree, realize the perfect and right enlightenment, and awaken to all the dharmas of buddhahood. All buddhas definitely awaken to all dharmas in but a single mind-moment and then manifest their spiritual powers in all worlds. All buddhas are definitely able to respond in accordance with the right time and turn the wheel of the sublime Dharma. All buddhas are definitely able to accord with the roots of goodness planted by others by speaking the Dharma for them at the appropriate time and then bestowing predictions for their benefit. All buddhas are definitely able to accord with the appropriate time in order to accomplish the buddha works. All buddhas are definitely able to bestow predictions for the sake of all fully accomplished bodhisattvas. And all buddhas are definitely able to reply in but a single mind-moment to all questions posed by any being. These are the ten.

Sons of the Buddha, all buddhas, the *bhagavats,* have ten kinds of swiftness dharmas. What are those ten? They are as follows: Whoever sees any buddha will swiftly leave all of the wretched rebirth destinies far behind. Whoever sees any buddha will swiftly succeed in the complete fulfillment of the especially supreme meritorious qualities. Whoever sees any buddha will swiftly become able to fully develop vast roots of goodness. Whoever sees any buddha will swiftly succeed in gaining rebirth into pure and marvelous heavens. Whoever sees any buddha will swiftly become able to cut off all their doubts. Whoever, having already resolved to attain bodhi, sees any buddha—they will swiftly succeed in developing vast resolute faith, perpetual irreversibility, and the ability to teach beings in accordance with whatever is appropriate for them, whereas, in the case of those who have not yet resolved to attain bodhi, they will then swiftly be able to resolve to realize *anuttarā-samyak-saṃbodhi*. Whoever sees any buddha while not yet having entered the right and fixed position[339] will swiftly enter the right and fixed position. Whoever sees any buddha will swiftly be able to purify all worldly and world-transcending faculties. Whoever sees any buddha will swiftly succeed in eliminating all their obstacles. And whoever sees any buddha will swiftly be able to acquire fearless eloquence. These are the ten.

Sons of the Buddha, all buddhas, the *bhagavats*, have ten kinds of pure dharmas that one should always bear in mind. What are those ten? They are as follows: All bodhisattvas should always bear in mind all buddhas' past causes and conditions. All bodhisattvas should always bear in mind all buddhas' pure and supreme practices. All bodhisattvas should always bear in mind all buddhas' fulfillment of all the perfections. All bodhisattvas should always bear in mind all buddhas' perfection of great vows. All bodhisattvas should always bear in mind all buddhas' accumulation of roots of goodness. All bodhisattvas should always bear in mind all buddhas' past perfection of *brahmacarya*. All bodhisattvas should always bear in mind all buddhas' manifesting the realization of right enlightenment. All bodhisattvas should always bear in mind all buddhas' countless form bodies. All bodhisattvas should always bear in mind all buddhas' measureless spiritual superknowledges. And all bodhisattvas should always bear in mind all buddhas' ten powers and fearlessnesses. These are the ten.

Sons of the Buddha, all buddhas, the *bhagavats*, have ten kinds of omniscient abiding. What are those ten? They are as follows: In but a single mind-moment, all buddhas completely know all the actions of each successive thought of all beings throughout the three periods of time. In but a single mind-moment, all buddhas completely know all the karma and karmic retributions accumulated by all beings throughout the three periods of time. In but a single mind-moment, all buddhas completely know what is fitting for all beings in their use of the three spheres of action[340] to teach and train them. In but a single mind-moment, all buddhas exhaustively know with regard to all beings in the Dharma realm all their mental characteristics in response to which they then everywhere manifest the appearance of buddhas and enable those beings to see them and be gathered in through the use of skillful means. In but a single mind-moment, all buddhas everywhere adapt to the inclinations, desires, and understandings of all beings throughout the Dharma realm and then manifest the speaking of Dharma for them to enable them to be trained. In but a single mind-moment, all buddhas completely know what delights the minds of all beings throughout the Dharma realm and then manifest spiritual powers for their sakes. In but a single mind-moment, all buddhas go forth to all places everywhere and, adapting to all those beings who should receive the teaching, they then manifest their appearance in the world and explain for beings that the body of the buddha is not graspable. In but a single mind-moment, all buddhas go everywhere throughout the Dharma realm into all the paths of all beings. In but a single mind-moment, all buddhas, in accordance with all beings who bring them to mind, go forth to every one of their locations, having none to whom they do not go in response. And, in but a single mind-moment, all buddhas completely know the understandings and desires of all beings and manifest countlessly many forms and appearances for their sakes. These are the ten.

Sons of the Buddha, all buddhas, the *bhagavats,* have ten kinds of measureless and inconceivable buddha samādhis. What are those ten? They are as follows: All buddhas constantly abide in right meditative concentration and, in but a single mind-moment, pervade all places, everywhere extensively expounding on the sublime Dharma for the benefit of beings. All buddhas constantly abide in right meditative concentration and, in but a single mind-moment, pervade all places, everywhere expounding for beings on the ultimate meaning of non-self. All buddhas constantly abide in right meditative concentration and, in but a single mind-moment, pervade all places, everywhere entering the three periods of time. All buddhas constantly abide in right meditative concentration and, in but a single mind-moment, pervade all places, everywhere entering the vast buddha *kṣetras* throughout the ten directions. All buddhas constantly abide in right meditative concentration and, in but a single mind-moment, pervade all places, everywhere manifesting incalculably many kinds of buddha bodies. All buddhas constantly abide in right meditative concentration and, in but a single mind-moment, pervade all places, manifesting physical, verbal, and mental deeds adapted to beings' many different types of inclinations. All buddhas constantly abide in right meditative concentration and, in but a single mind-moment, pervade all places, expounding on all dharmas, transcendence of desire, and the apex of reality. All buddhas constantly abide in right meditative concentration and, in but a single mind-moment, pervade all places, expounding on the essential nature of everything arising through conditions. All buddhas constantly abide in right meditative concentration and, in but a single mind-moment, pervade all places, manifesting countless vast worldly and world-transcending adornments by which they enable all beings to always succeed in seeing the Buddha. And all buddhas constantly abide in right meditative concentration and, in but a single mind-moment, pervade all places, enabling beings to acquire a penetrating comprehension of all buddha dharmas, to achieve measureless liberation, and to ultimately reach the far shore of unsurpassed perfection. These are the ten.

Sons of the Buddha, all buddhas, the *bhagavats*, have ten kinds of unimpeded liberation. What are those ten? They are as follows: All buddhas are able to manifest within a single atom an ineffable-ineffable number of buddhas coming forth and appearing in the world. All buddhas are able to manifest within a single atom an ineffable-ineffable number of buddhas turning the wheel of the pure Dharma. All buddhas are able to manifest within a single atom an ineffable-ineffable number of beings receiving teaching and training. All buddhas are able to manifest within a single atom an ineffable-ineffable number of buddha lands. All buddhas are able to manifest within a single atom an ineffable-ineffable number of bodhisattvas receiving their predictions of buddhahood. All buddhas are able to manifest within a single atom all buddhas of the past, the future, and the present. All buddhas are able to manifest within a single atom all world systems of the past, the future, and the present. All buddhas are able to manifest within a single atom all spiritual superknowledges of the past, the future, and the present. All buddhas are able to manifest within a single atom all beings of the past, the future, and the present. And all buddhas are able to manifest within a single atom all buddha works throughout the past, the future, and the present. These are the ten.

The End of Chapter Thirty-Three

Chapter 34
The Ocean of Major Marks of the Tathāgata's Ten Bodies

At that time, Samantabhadra Bodhisattva-mahāsattva informed the bodhisattvas, saying:

Sons of the Buddha, I shall now explain for you the ocean of the Tathāgata's marks.[341] Sons of the Buddha, on the top of the Tathāgata's head, there is a mark of the great man adorned with thirty-two jewels. Among them is one of the marks of a great man that is known as "the light that illuminates all regions, everywhere emanating an immeasurably vast net of light rays." It is adorned with all kinds of marvelous jewels. All of his jewel-adorned hair is soft and dense. Every one of its strands emanates the light of *maṇi* jewels which completely fills all the boundlessly many worlds and completely reveals the perfect fulfillment of the buddha body's physical marks. This is the first.

Next, there is a mark of the great man known as "the cloud of light of the buddha eye." Adorned with all kinds of sovereign *maṇi* jewels, it emanates golden light like the light emanated by the hair mark between the Buddha's brows. Its light everywhere illuminates all worlds. This is the second.

Next, there is a mark of the great man known as "the cloud that fills the Dharma realm." Adorned with supremely marvelous jeweled spheres, it emanates the lamp light of the Tathāgata's merit and wisdom which pervasively illuminates the ocean of worlds throughout the ten directions of the entire Dharma realm and everywhere reveals all the buddhas and bodhisattvas within them. This is the third.

Next, there is a mark of the great man known as "the cloud that manifests pervasive illumination." Arrayed with many different kinds of adornments made of real gold and *maṇi* jewel adornments, its marvelous jewels all emanate light which illuminates inconceivably many buddha lands in which all buddhas appear. This is the fourth.

Next, there is a mark of the great man known as "the cloud that emanates the light of jewels." It is arrayed with pure adornments consisting of sovereign *maṇi* jewels. The stamens of the flowers are made of *vaiḍūrya* jewels. Its light illuminates the ten directions of the entire Dharma realm, everywhere revealing many different kinds of spiritual transformations praising the Tathāgata's past practice of wisdom and meritorious qualities. This is the fifth.

Next, there is a mark of the great man known as "the cloud that reveals the great sovereign mastery of the Tathāgata throughout the Dharma realm." His crown is made of flaming jewel light *maṇi* jewels created by bodhisattvas' spiritual transformations and his floral chaplet is made of spheres of the flaming light of all jewels with the Tathāgata's power to awaken all beings. Their radiance illuminates all worlds throughout the ten directions and reveals all the *tathāgatas* in them sitting at their sites of enlightenment as clouds of all-knowledge everywhere fill empty space throughout the measureless Dharma realm. This is the sixth.

Next, there is a mark of the great man known as "the Tathāgata's cloud of universally pervasive lamplight" which is adorned with an ocean of great sovereign power jewels able to cause the quaking of all worlds throughout the Dharma realm. It emanates a pure radiance that completely fills the Dharma realm, revealing within it the ocean of meritorious qualities of all bodhisattvas throughout the ten directions as well as an ocean of wisdom banners of all buddhas of the past, the present, and the future. This is the seventh.

Next, there is a mark of the great man known as "the vast cloud that everywhere illuminates all buddhas." It is adorned with Indra jewels, sovereign wish-granting jewels, and sovereign *maṇi* jewels and always emanates the light of bodhisattvas' flaming lamps which everywhere illuminate all worlds of the ten directions and reveals the oceans of the many forms and appearances of all buddhas within them, their oceans of sounds, and their oceans of pure powers. This is the eighth.

Next, there is a mark of the great man known as "the cloud of light spheres." It is adorned with many different kinds of supremely marvelous bejeweled flowers made of *vaiḍūrya* and sovereign *maṇi* jewels. All those many jewels spread forth immense nets of flaming light which fill all the worlds of the ten directions. All the beings within them see the Tathāgata appearing, sitting directly before them, praising the meritorious qualities of the Dharma body of all buddhas and bodhisattvas, enabling them to enter the pure realms of the Tathāgata. This is the ninth.

Next, there is a mark of the great man known as "the light cloud that everywhere illuminates the treasury of all bodhisattvas' practices." Adorned with marvelous flowers made of the many kinds of jewels, its jewel light everywhere illuminates countless worlds. Its flaming jewel light spreading everywhere over all lands throughout the ten directions of the Dharma realm is unimpeded in its pervasive penetration. It emanates the quake-inducing sound of the Buddha widely and freely expounding on the ocean of dharmas. This is the tenth.

Next, there is a mark of the great man known as "the universally illuminating cloud of dazzling light." It is adorned with *vaiḍūrya,* Indra jewels, vajra, and *maṇi* jewels. The colors of the light from the *vaiḍūrya* jewels brightly interpenetrate and everywhere illuminate the ocean of all worlds. It also sends forth marvelous sounds that fill the Dharma realm. All phenomena such as these are transformationally created manifestations produced from all buddhas' ocean of wisdom and great meritorious qualities. This is the eleventh.

Next, there is a mark of the great man known as "the cloud of the right enlightenment." It is adorned with flowers made of the various kinds of precious jewels. All those bejeweled flowers emanate rays of light in each of which there is a *tathāgata* seated in a site of enlightenment. They fill up all the boundless worlds, causing all those worlds to become purified and forever severing all erroneous thinking and discriminations. This is the twelfth.

Next, there is a mark of the great man known as "the cloud of dazzling light." It is adorned with an ocean of flaming jewel light treasuries and mind-king *maṇi* jewels which emanate a great light in which are revealed countless bodhisattvas and bodhisattva practices along with an ocean of forms and appearances of all *tathāgatas'* wisdom bodies and Dharma body which fills the Dharma realm. This is the thirteenth.

Next, there is a mark of the great man known as "the cloud of universally illuminating adornments." Adorned with vajra flowers and *vaiḍūrya* jewels, it emanates rays of light in which there are great fully adorned jeweled lotus thrones that spread all over the Dharma realm, spontaneously expounding on the four bodhisattva practices,[342] the sound from which everywhere pervades the ocean of the Dharma realm. This is the fourteenth.

Next, there is a mark of the great man known as "the cloud revealing the practice of the Buddha's ocean of samādhis." In but a single mind-moment, it reveals all the Tathāgata's measureless adornments that everywhere adorn the entire Dharma realm's inconceivable ocean of worlds. This is the fifteenth.

Next, there is a mark of the great man known as "the universally illuminating cloud of the ocean of transformations." It is adorned with a marvelous bejeweled lotus flower comparable to Mount

Sumeru. The light of its many jewels arises from the Buddha's vows and reveals all of his endless transformations. This is the sixteenth.

Next, there is a mark of the great man known as "the cloud of all *tathāgatas'* liberations." Adorned with the pure and marvelous jewels, it emanates a great light that serves to adorn the lion thrones of all buddhas and reveal the physical appearances of all buddhas as well as the countless dharmas of the Buddha and the ocean of all buddha *kṣetras*. This is the seventeenth.

Next, there is a mark of the great man known as "the universally illuminating cloud of freely implemented expedient means." It is adorned with flowers made of *vaiḍūrya*, flowers made of real gold, sovereign *maṇi* jewel lamps, and clouds of the sublime Dharma's flaming radiance. It emanates a dense cloud of all buddhas' flaming jewel radiance, the pure light from which fills the Dharma realm and everywhere reveals within it all of its marvelously fine adornments. This is the eighteenth.

Next, there is a mark of the great man known as "the cloud instigating awakening to the lineage of the buddhas." Adorned with countless rays of jeweled light, it contains a thousand spheres and is possessed of inward and outward purity arising from past roots of goodness. Its radiance everywhere illuminates the worlds of the ten directions and ignites the light of the wisdom sun which proclaims the ocean of dharmas. This is the nineteenth.

Next, there is a mark of the great man known as "the cloud of sovereign powers revealing the marks of all *tathāgatas*." Adorned with necklaces of the many kinds of jewels and flowers made of *vaiḍūrya* jewels, it spreads forth the flaming radiance of immense jewels that fills up the Dharma realm and everywhere reveals within it countless past, future, and present buddhas as numerous as the atoms in all buddha *kṣetras* who are as courageous and fearless as the king of lions and who are replete in their physical marks and wisdom. This is the twentieth.

Next, there is a mark of the great man known as "the cloud that everywhere illuminates the entire Dharma realm." It possesses the pure adornments of the Tathāgata's precious signs and emanates a great radiance that everywhere illuminates the Dharma realm and reveals the marvelous treasury of wisdom possessed by all the countlessly and boundlessly many buddhas and bodhisattvas. This is the twenty-first.

Next, there is a mark of the great man known as "the cloud of Vairocana Tathāgata's marks." Adorned with supremely marvelous jewel flowers as well as with pure and marvelous moons made of *vaiḍūrya,* it emanates countless hundreds of thousands of myriads of *koṭīs* of *maṇi* jewel light rays that fill up all of empty space and the Dharma realm and reveal the countless buddha *kṣetras* therein, in each of which there sits a *tathāgata* seated in the lotus posture. This is the twenty-second.

Next, there is a mark of the great man known as "the light cloud that everywhere illuminates all buddhas." Adorned with marvelous lamps made of many kinds of jewels, it emanates pure light that pervasively illuminates all worlds of the ten directions, revealing in all of them the buddhas turning the wheel of the Dharma. This is the twenty-third.

Next, there is a mark of the great man known as "the cloud that everywhere reveals all adornments." Adorned with the many different kinds of flaming jewel light, it emanates pure radiance that fills the Dharma realm and, in each successive mind-moment, forever reveals an ineffable-ineffable number of all buddhas and bodhisattvas sitting in the sites of enlightenment. This is the twenty-fourth.

Next, there is a mark of the great man known as "the cloud that emanates all sounds of the Dharma realm." Adorned with oceans of *maṇi* jewels and supremely marvelous sandalwood, it spreads forth a great net of flaming radiance that fills the Dharma realm and everywhere emanates sublime voices instructing beings on the ocean of all karma. This is the twenty-fifth.

Next, there is a mark of the great man known as "the cloud that everywhere illuminates the sphere of all buddhas' spiritual transformations." Adorned by the pure eyes of the Tathāgata, its light illuminates all worlds of the ten directions and everywhere reveals within them all the adornments of all buddhas of the past, the future, and the present while also emanating sublime voices expounding on the inconceivably vast ocean of Dharma. This is the twenty-sixth.

Next, there is a mark of the great man known as "the cloud whose light illuminates the ocean of buddhas." Its light everywhere unimpededly illuminates all worlds throughout the entire Dharma realm, revealing them all as having *tathāgatas* in them who are seated in the lotus posture. This is the twenty-seventh.

Next, there is a mark of the great man known as "the cloud of bejeweled lamps." It emanates the vast radiance of the *tathāgatas* which everywhere illuminates the ten directions of the entire Dharma realm and reveals within it all buddhas as well as all bodhisattvas and the inconceivable ocean of all beings. This is the twenty-eighth.

Next, there is a mark of the great man known as "the cloud of the undifferentiated Dharma realm." It emanates the light of the Tathāgata's great wisdom which everywhere illuminates the lands of all buddhas of the ten directions, all their congregations of bodhisattvas at their sites of enlightenment, and their measureless ocean of Dharma, everywhere revealing within them their many different kinds of spiritual superknowledges while also emanating marvelous voices which, adapting to beings' mental dispositions, expound on the conduct and vows of Samantabhadra Bodhisattva and inspire those beings to dedicate [their cultivation to emulating it]. This is the twenty-ninth.

Next, there is a mark of the great man known as "the pervasively illuminating cloud that abides in the ocean of all worlds." It emanates a jewel radiance that fills all of empty space and the Dharma realm and everywhere reveals the pure and marvelous sites of enlightenment within them as well as the signs adorning the bodies of the buddhas and bodhisattvas, thereby enabling all who behold this to gain the realization in which nothing whatsoever is perceived. This is the thirtieth.

Next, there is a mark of the great man known as "the cloud of all jewels' pure flaming radiance." It emanates the pure light of the countless buddhas, bodhisattvas, and marvelous *maṇi* jewels, everywhere illuminates the ten directions of the entire Dharma realm, and everywhere reveals the ocean of bodhisattvas within it, none of whom have not completely developed the Tathāgata's spiritual powers by which they forever roam about in the network of all *kṣetras* throughout the ten directions of space. This is the thirty-first.

Next, there is a mark of the great man known as "the cloud that everywhere illuminates the entire Dharma realm's adornments." It is located right in the very center where it gradually bulges upward [on the top of the Buddha's head]. It is adorned with an Indra's net of *jambūnada* gold and emanates a cloud of pure light that fills the Dharma realm. In each successive mind-moment, it forever reveals the congregations of all buddhas and bodhisattvas at the sites of enlightenment in all worlds. This is the thirty-second.

Sons of the Buddha, on the summit of the Tathāgata's head, there are thirty-two marks of the great man such as these which serve there as fine marks of adornment.

Sons of the Buddha, between the Tathāgata's eyebrows, there is a mark of the great man known as "the light cloud that pervades the Dharma realm." Adorned with flowers made of *maṇi* jewels, it emanates a great light that includes the colors of the many kinds of jewels. Like the pure penetrating light of the sun and moon, its light everywhere illuminates the lands of the ten directions and reveals the bodies of all buddhas within them while also emanating a marvelous voice that sends forth proclamations of the ocean of dharmas. This is the thirty-third.

The Tathāgata's eyes have a mark of the great man known as "the cloud of independent pervasive vision." Adorned with many kinds of marvelous jewels, its *maṇi* jewel light's pure and penetrating brightness everywhere unimpededly sees all things. This is the thirty-fourth.

The Tathāgata's nose has a mark of the great man known as "the cloud of all spiritual superknowledges and wisdom." Adorned with pure and marvelous jewels, the colored light of the many kinds of precious gems spreads forth over all of it and reveals countless transformation buddhas in it who sit on bejeweled lotus flowers and go forth to all worlds, expounding on the inconceivable ocean of the Dharma of all buddhas for the benefit of all bodhisattvas and all beings. This is the thirty-fifth.

The Tathāgata's tongue has a mark of the great man known as "the cloud that manifests sounds and reflected images." It is adorned with marvelous multi-colored jewels and it is produced through roots of goodness created in former lifetimes. His tongue is vast and long and everywhere covers the oceans of all worlds. If perhaps the Tathāgata at times happily and subtly smiles, it certainly then emanates the radiance of all kinds of *maṇi* jewels, the light from which everywhere illuminates the ten directions of the Dharma realm in which it is able to bring about clarity and coolness in everyone's minds. All buddhas of the past, the future, and the present appear brilliantly shining within that radiance, all of them expounding with a vastly resonant and sublime voice that pervades all *kṣetras* and remains within them for countless kalpas. This is the thirty-sixth.

The Tathāgata's tongue also has a mark of the great man known as "the Dharma realm cloud." Its surface is perfectly flat and adorned with the many kinds of jewels. It emanates marvelous jewel light with perfect forms and appearances which is like the light emanated from between his brows. Those lights everywhere illuminate all buddha *kṣetras*, revealing them to be composed solely of atoms and hence entirely devoid of any inherently existent nature of their own. Those lights also reveal the countless buddhas all sending forth sublime voices expounding on all dharmas. This is the thirty-seventh.

The tip of the Tathāgata's tongue has a mark of the great man known as "the light cloud that illuminates the Dharma realm." Adorned with sovereign wish-fulfilling gems, it spontaneously and constantly sends forth golden flaming jewel radiance in which the ocean of all buddhas is reflected. In addition, it emanates marvelous quake-inducing voices which fill all the boundlessly many worlds. In every one of those voices are contained all voices, all of which expound on the sublime Dharma, delighting the minds of all who hear them. This continues on for countless kalpas during which it continues to be appreciated and never forgotten. This is the thirty-eighth.

The tip of the Tathāgata's tongue has another mark of the great man known as "the cloud that illuminates the Dharma realm with dazzling radiance." Adorned with sovereign *maṇi* jewels, it emanates streams of sublime light of many colors which fill the countless lands of the ten directions throughout the Dharma realm, thereby purifying them all. Present within it are countless buddhas and bodhisattvas speaking in sublime voices with which they offer many different explanatory instructions to which all bodhisattvas directly listen. This is the thirty-ninth.

The upper palate of the Tathāgata's mouth has a mark of the great man known as "the cloud that reveals the inconceivable Dharma realm." Adorned with Indra jewels and *vaiḍūrya* gems, it emanates fragrant flaming lamplight in clouds of pure radiance which everywhere fill the ten directions of the Dharma realm and reveal the many different kinds of spiritual superknowledges and skillful means while also expounding on the extremely profound and inconceivable Dharma everywhere throughout the oceans of worlds. This is the fortieth.

The Tathāgata's lower right front teeth have a mark of the great man known as "the buddha tooth cloud." Adorned with the many kinds of precious gems and *maṇi* jewels forming *svastika*-emblem wheels, it emanates a great radiance that everywhere illuminates the Dharma realm and reveals everywhere within it the bodies of all buddhas flowing forth everywhere in the ten directions, awakening the many kinds of beings. This is the forty-first.

The Tathāgata's upper right front teeth have a mark of the great man known as "the cloud of flaming jewel light Sumeru treasuries." Adorned with treasuries of *maṇi* jewels, it emanates fragrant flaming vajra radiance, the pure light from each and every ray of which fills up the Dharma realm, revealing the spiritual powers of all buddhas while also revealing the pure and marvelous sites of enlightenment throughout all worlds of the ten directions. This is the forty-second.

The Tathāgata's lower left front teeth have a mark of the great man known as "the universally illuminating cloud of jewel lamplight." Adorned with all kinds of marvelous jewels and emitting the fragrance of blooming flowers, it emanates a cloud of flaming lamplight, the pure radiance from which fills up all the oceans of worlds, revealing within it all their buddhas sitting on lotus dais lion thrones, surrounded by congregations of bodhisattvas. This is the forty-third.

The Tathāgata's upper left front teeth have a mark of the great man known as "the cloud that illuminates the Tathāgatas." Adorned with pure light, *jambūnada* gold, jeweled nets, and bejeweled flowers, it emanates a great orb of flaming radiance which fills the Dharma realm and everywhere reveals within it all buddhas using the powers of their spiritual superknowledges to distribute throughout space a flow of Dharma milk, Dharma lamplight, and Dharma jewels that teaches the congregations of all bodhisattvas. This is the forty-fourth.

The Tathāgata's teeth have a mark of the great man known as "the cloud that manifests light everywhere." Between each of his teeth, there are oceans of adorning signs. Whenever he smiles even slightly, they emanate jewel-colored light and the flaming light of *maṇi* jewels which circumambulate in a rightward direction, flowing throughout the Dharma realm, completely filling it, expounding with the voice of the Buddha on the practices of Samantabhadra. This is the forty-fifth.

The Tathāgata's lips have a mark of the great man known as "the cloud that reflects the light of all jewels." It emanates vast radiance the color of real *jambūnada* gold, the color of lotus flowers, and the color of every kind of jewel that illuminates the Dharma realm and causes everything to become purified. This is the forty-sixth.

The Tathāgata's neck has a mark of the great man known as "the cloud that everywhere illuminates all worlds." Adorned with sovereign *maṇi* jewels, possessed of the fully developed *kamboja*[343] feature, soft, and smooth, it emanates pure *vairocana* light that fills all worlds of the ten directions and everywhere reveals all the buddhas within them. This is the forty-seventh.

The Tathāgata's right shoulder has a mark of the great man known as "the Buddha's vast cloud of every kind of jewel." It emanates lights the colors of all kinds of jewels, the color of real gold, and the color of lotus flowers that form a web of flaming jewel light everywhere illuminating the Dharma realm, revealing all the bodhisattvas within it. This is the forty-eighth.

The Tathāgata's right shoulder also has a mark of the great man known as "the cloud of supreme jewels' universal illumination." With colors as pure as *jambūnada* gold, it emanates *maṇi* jewel light that fills the Dharma realm and everywhere illuminates all the bodhisattvas within it. This is the forty-ninth.

The Tathāgata's left shoulder has a mark of the great man known as "the cloud of supreme light that illuminates the Dharma realm." Like that of the many different kinds of adornments on his summit and between his brows, it emanates light of the many kinds of jewels that is the color of *jambūnada* gold and lotus flowers and which forms a great net of flaming radiance that fills the Dharma realm and reveals all the spiritual powers being used within it. This is the fiftieth.

The Tathāgata's left shoulder also has a mark of the great man known as "the cloud of universally illuminating light." That mark swirls around in a rightward direction and is characterized by adornments the color of *jambūnada* gold and sovereign *maṇi* jewels. It emanates the light of flowers made of the many kinds of jewels and fragrant flaming light that pervasively fills the Dharma realm and everywhere reveals all the buddhas within it as well as all of their adorned pure lands. This is the fifty-first.

The Tathāgata's left shoulder also has a mark of the great man known as "the cloud of universally illuminating dazzling light." That mark swirls around in a rightward direction, is possessed of subtle and fine adornments, and emanates clouds of the Buddha's flaming lamplight. Its pure light everywhere fills the Dharma realm and reveals the many different kinds of adornments of all of the bodhisattvas within it, all of which are marvelously fine. This is the fifty-second.

The Tathāgata's chest has a mark of the great man shaped like a *svastika* emblem that is known as "the cloud of the ocean of auspiciousness." Adorned with flowers made of *maṇi* jewels, it emanates all kinds of flaming light spheres the color of every kind of jewel which fill the Dharma realm and cause everything to be purified while also sending forth marvelous sounds that freely propagate [the teachings in] the ocean of Dharma. This is the fifty-third.

To the right of this mark of auspiciousness, there is a mark of the great man known as "the cloud that manifests radiant illumination." Adorned by Indra's net, it emanates immense spheres of light which fill the Dharma realm and everywhere reveal the countless buddhas within it. This is the fifty-fourth.

To the right of the mark of auspiciousness, there is also a mark of the great man known as "the cloud that everywhere reveals the *tathāgatas*." Adorned with bodhisattva *maṇi* jewel crowns, it emanates great radiance that everywhere illuminates all worlds of the ten directions, purifying them all and revealing the buddhas of the past, the future, and the present, seated in their sites of enlightenment, everywhere manifesting spiritual powers and extensively propagating [the teachings in] the ocean of Dharma. This is the fifty-fifth.

To the right of the mark of auspiciousness, there is also a mark of the great man known as "the cloud of blooming flowers." Adorned with flowers made of *maṇi* jewels, it emanates pure light from bejeweled fragrant flaming radiance lamps shaped like lotus flowers that fill the worlds. This is the fifty-sixth.

To the right of the mark of auspiciousness, there is also a mark of the great man known as "the delightful golden cloud." Adorned with sovereign *maṇi* jewels from the mind king treasury of all jewels, it emanates pure light that illuminates the Dharma realm, everywhere revealing within it vast radiant *maṇi* jewel treasuries resembling the eyes of the Buddha. This is the fifty-seventh.

To the right of the mark of auspiciousness, there is also a mark of the great man known as "the cloud of the ocean of buddhas." Adorned with *vaiḍūrya* gems, fragrant lamps, and floral garlands, it emanates the pure light filling empty space from sovereign *maṇi* jewels and fragrant lamps' great flaming radiance which pervades all lands of the ten directions and everywhere reveals within them the congregations at their sites of enlightenment. This is the fifty-eighth.

To the left of the mark of auspiciousness, there is a mark of the great man known as "the cloud that manifests light." Adorned with countless bodhisattvas sitting on bejeweled lotus flowers, it emanates the flaming light of many different kinds of jewels inlaid among sovereign *maṇi* jewels which everywhere purifies the entire ocean of the Dharma realm and reveals the countless buddhas within it while also making apparent the voices of those buddhas expounding on all dharmas. This is the fifty-ninth.

To the left of the mark of auspiciousness, there is also a mark of the great man known as "the cloud that manifests light throughout the Dharma realm." Adorned with an ocean of *maṇi* jewels, it emanates great light that pervades all *kṣetras* and everywhere reveals all the bodhisattvas within them. This is the sixtieth.

To the left of the mark of auspiciousness, there is also a mark of the great man known as "the cloud of universal supremacy." Adorned with sunlight sovereign *maṇi* jewels, jeweled spheres, and garlands, it emanates a great flaming radiance that fills the oceans of worlds throughout the Dharma realm and reveals all the worlds, all the *tathāgatas,* and all the beings within them. This is the sixty-first.

To the left of the mark of auspiciousness, there is also a mark of the great man known as "the cloud of the marvelous sounds of turning the Dharma wheel." Adorned with all kinds of Dharma lamps and stamens exuding pure fragrance, it emanates a great radiance that fills the Dharma realm and everywhere reveals the ocean of all marks and the ocean of the mind of all buddhas. This is the sixty-second.

To the left of the mark of auspiciousness, there is also a mark of the great man known as "the cloud of adornments." Adorned with the ocean of all buddhas of the past, the future, and the present, it emanates a pure light that purifies all buddha lands and everywhere reveals within them all buddhas and bodhisattvas of the ten directions as well as all the practices they follow. This is the sixty-third.

The Tathāgata's right hand has a mark of the great man known as "the cloud of oceanic illumination." Adorned with the many kinds of jewels, it constantly emanates the pure radiance of shimmering moonlight that fills all the worlds throughout empty space and sends forth a great voice praising all the bodhisattva practices. This is the sixty-fourth.

The Tathāgata's right hand also has a mark of the great man known as "the cloud that reflects dazzling illumination." Adorned with flowers made of *vaiḍūrya,* sapphires, and *maṇi* jewels, it emanates a great radiance that everywhere illuminates all the lotus treasury worlds, *maṇi* jewel treasury worlds, and other worlds in which the bodhisattvas of the ten directions dwell while revealing the countless buddhas within them who, in reliance on the pure Dharma body, sit beneath the bodhi trees and cause all lands throughout the ten directions to quake. This is the sixty-fifth.

The Tathāgata's right hand also has a mark of the great man known as "the universally purifying cloud of flaming lamplight and garlands." Adorned with *vairocana* jewels, it emanates a great radiance that forms a net of transformations and everywhere reveals the congregations of bodhisattvas within it, all of whom wear jeweled crowns and expound upon the ocean of all practices. This is the sixty-sixth.

The Tathāgata's right hand also has a mark of the great man known as "the cloud that everywhere reveals all *maṇi* jewels." Adorned with flaming lotus lamplight radiance, it emanates oceanic treasuries of light which fill the Dharma realm and everywhere reveal within them the countless buddhas sitting on lotus flower thrones. This is the sixty-seventh.

The Tathāgata's right hand also has a mark of the great man known as "the cloud of radiance." Adorned with an ocean of *maṇi* jewel flaming radiance, it emanates the pure light of the flaming radiance of the many kinds of jewels, the flaming radiance of incenses, and the flaming radiance of flowers which fills the net of all worlds and everywhere reveals within them the sites of enlightenment of all buddhas. This is the sixty-eighth.

The Tathāgata's left hand has a mark of the great man known as "the cloud of pure *vaiḍūrya* lamplight." Adorned with the marvelous colors of grounds made of jewels, it emanates the golden light of the Tathāgata and, in each successive mind-moment, forever reveals all the supremely marvelous adornments. This is the sixty-ninth.

The Tathāgata's left hand also has a mark of the great man known as "the cloud of voices of the lamps of wisdom throughout all *kṣetras*." Adorned with the net of Indra and vajra flowers, it emanates the pure light of *jambūnada* gold that everywhere illuminates all worlds of the ten directions. This is the seventieth.

The Tathāgata's left hand also has a mark of the great man known as "the cloud of light dwelling in a jeweled lotus." Adorned with marvelous flowers made of the many kinds of jewels, it emanates a great radiance as if from a lamp the size of Mount Sumeru which everywhere illuminates all worlds of the ten directions. This is the seventy-first.

The Tathāgata's left hand also has a mark of the great man known as "the cloud that everywhere illuminates the Dharma realm." Adorned with marvelous jeweled garlands, jeweled spheres, jeweled vases, Indra's nets, and the many marvelous of emblematic signs, it emanates a great radiance that everywhere illuminates all lands of the ten directions and reveals all the *tathāgatas* sitting on lotus flower thrones within the ocean of all worlds throughout the entire Dharma realm. This is the seventy-second.

The fingers of the Tathāgata's right hand have a mark of the great man known as "the swirling cloud revealing the ocean of all kalpas and *kṣetras*." Adorned with the sovereign *maṇi* jewels of the water moon's treasury of flaming radiance and flowers made of all kinds of jewels, it emanates a great light that fills the Dharma realm and constantly sends forth from within it sublime voices that fill the *kṣetras* of the ten directions. This is the seventy-third.

The fingers of the Tathāgata's left hand have a mark of the great man known as "the cloud that rests on all kinds of jewels." Adorned with sapphires and vajra gems, it emanates the light of sovereign *maṇi* jewels and the many kinds of precious gems which fill the Dharma realm, everywhere revealing all the buddhas and bodhisattvas within it. This is the seventy-fourth.

The Tathāgata's right palm has a mark of the great man known as "the cloud of dazzling illumination." Adorned with sovereign *maṇi* jewels and thousand-spoked jeweled wheels, it emanates the light of jewels that swirls around to the right and then fills the Dharma realm, everywhere revealing all the buddhas within it, the flaming light and blazing radiance of every one of their buddha bodies, as well as their speaking of Dharma to liberate people and their purification of all worlds. This is the seventy-fifth.

The Tathāgata's left palm has a mark of the great man known as "the cloud of flaming light spheres that everywhere increase the transformationally manifested sites of enlightenment throughout the Dharma realm." Adorned with thousand-spoked wheels of sovereign sunlight *maṇi* jewels, it emanates a great radiance that fills all the oceans of worlds and reveals all the bodhisattvas within them as they expound on Samantabhadra's ocean of practices and everywhere enter the lands of all buddhas where they each awaken countless beings. This is the seventy-sixth.

The Tathāgata's characteristic sign of genital ensheathment has a mark of the great man known as "the cloud that everywhere streams forth the voice of the Buddha." Adorned with every sort of marvelous jewel, it emanates the flaming floral light of *maṇi* jewel lamps, the light from which blazes fully with the colors of the many kinds of jewels, everywhere illuminates all of empty space and the Dharma realm, and everywhere reveals within them all the buddhas going forth and coming back as they everywhere roam about to place after place. This is the seventy-seventh.

The Tathāgata's right hip has a mark of the great man known as "the universally illuminating cloud of bejeweled lamps and garlands." Adorned with all kinds of *maṇi* jewels, it emanates an ineffable number of rays of flaming jewel radiance which spread forth across the entire Dharma realm. It is of the same single characteristic as the realm of empty space and the Dharma realm, and yet it is able to produce all the signs, each sign of which reveals the masterfully implemented spiritual transformations of all buddhas. This is the seventy-eighth.

The Tathāgata's left hip has a mark of the great man known as "the cloud that reveals the light of the ocean of the entire Dharma realm and blankets empty space." Adorned with pure and marvelous jewels resembling lotus flowers, it emanates a net of light that everywhere illuminates the ten directions of the entire Dharma realm and everywhere reveals within it the many different kinds of clouds of signs. This is the seventy-ninth.

The Tathāgata's right thigh has a mark of the great man known as "the universally revealing cloud." Adorned with *maṇi* jewels of many different colors, above and below, his thighs and calves are proportionate in size and emanate flaming *maṇi* jewel radiance and the light of the sublime Dharma which, in but a single mind-moment, are able to everywhere reveal all the Jewel Kings'[344] freely roaming in the ocean of signs. This is the eightieth.

The Tathāgata's left thigh has a mark of the great man known as "the cloud that reveals the ocean of the countless signs of all buddhas." Adorned with an ocean of all kinds of jewels that follow along and remain with them in their vast roaming travels, they emanate a pure light that everywhere illuminates beings and causes them all to aspire to seek the unsurpassable Dharma of the Buddha. This is the eighty-first.

The Tathāgata's right calf, resembling that of the *aiṇeya* antelope, has a mark of the great man known as "the cloud of all of empty space and the Dharma realm." Adorned with marvelous radiant jewels and characterized by being round, straight, and well able to stride along in his wandering, it emanates the pure light of *jambūnada* gold that everywhere illuminates the worlds of all buddhas while also sending forth a great sound that everywhere causes a shaking movement. It also reveals the lands of all buddhas abiding in space, adorned with flaming jewel radiance, and it reveals as well the countless bodhisattvas transformationally manifested from within them. This is the eighty-second.

The Tathāgata's left calf, resembling that of the *aiṇeya* antelope, has a mark of the great man known as "the cloud of an ocean of adornments." Having a color like that of real gold, it is able to roam about, traveling everywhere to all the buddha *kṣetras*. It emanates the pure light of all the many kinds of jewels that fills the Dharma realm and performs buddha works. This is the eighty-third.

The hair on the Tathāgata's jewel-adorned calves has a mark of the great man known as "the cloud that everywhere reveals reflected images of the Dharma realm." Those hairs grow in a right-ward spiraling direction and the tips of every one of those hairs emanates the light of jewels which fills the ten directions of the entire Dharma realm, revealing the spiritual powers of all buddhas. Those hair pores all emanate a radiance in which all buddha *kṣetras* are shown. This is the eighty-fourth.

The bottom of the Tathāgata's feet have a mark of the great man known as "the cloud in which the ocean of all bodhisattvas resides." It has a color like that of vajra, *jambūnada* gold, and pure lotus flowers and emanates a jewel radiance that everywhere illuminates the ocean of all worlds throughout the ten directions. A cloud of fragrant flaming jewel light spreads about everywhere into place after place. Whenever he raises a foot to begin a step, fragrant mists the colors of the many kinds of jewels flow about everywhere, filling the Dharma realm. This is the eighty-fifth.

The top of the Tathāgata's right foot has a mark of the great man known as "the light cloud that everywhere illuminates everything." Adorned with all of the many kinds of jewels, it emanates a great light that fills the Dharma realm and reveals all the buddhas and bodhisattvas. This is the eighty-sixth.

The top of the Tathāgata's left foot has a mark of the great man known as "the cloud that everywhere reveals all buddhas." Adorned with jewel treasury *maṇi* jewels, it emanates the light of jewels which in each successive mind-moment reveal all buddhas' spiritual superknowledges and transformations as well as their ocean of Dharma and the sites of enlightenment in which they sit uninterruptedly to the very end of all kalpas of the future. This is the eighty-seventh.

The spaces between the toes of the Tathāgata's right foot have a mark of the great man known as "the cloud that brightly illuminates the ocean of the entire Dharma realm." Adorned in all kinds of different ways with *sumeru* lamps, sovereign *maṇi* jewels, and thousand-spoked wheels of flaming radiance, they emanate a great light that fills all the oceans of worlds throughout the ten directions of the entire Dharma realm and everywhere reveal within them all the buddhas as well as all their many different kinds of signs adorned with jewels. This is the eighty-eighth.

The spaces between the toes of the Tathāgata's left foot have a mark of the great man known as "the cloud that reveals the ocean of all buddhas." Adorned with *maṇi* jewel flowers, fragrantly flaming lamps, garlands, and wheels made of every kind of jewel, they constantly emanate the pure light of an ocean of jewels that fills empty space and everywhere reaches all worlds throughout the ten directions, revealing all the buddhas and bodhisattvas within them as well as their perfectly full voices, their *svastika* emblems, and other such signs with which they benefit all the countlessly many beings. This is the eighty-ninth.

The Tathāgata's right heel has a mark of the great man known as "the cloud of freely shining dazzling illumination." Adorned with powdered sapphires, it always emanates the radiance of the Tathāgata's marvelous jewels, the marvelously fine light of which, all of it of the same appearance, free of any differences, fills the Dharma realm and reveals all the buddhas within it seated in their sites of enlightenment, expounding on the sublime Dharma. This is the ninetieth.

The Tathāgata's left heel has a mark of the great man known as "the cloud that reveals the marvelous voice expounding on the ocean of all dharmas." Adorned with ocean-of-transformations *maṇi* jewels, ocean-of-fragrant-flaming-light *sumeru* flower *maṇi* jewels, and *vaiḍūrya,* it emanates a great light that fills the Dharma realm and everywhere reveals within it the spiritual powers of all buddhas. This is the ninety-first.

The Tathāgata's right ankle has a mark of the great man known as "the light cloud that reveals all adornments." Possessed of the most ultimately marvelous adornments made of the many kinds of jewels, it emanates pure light the color of *jambūnada* gold that everywhere illuminates the ten directions of the Dharma realm. The appearance of its radiance is like that of a great cloud that everywhere covers the sites of enlightenment of all buddhas. This is the ninety-second.

The Tathāgata's left ankle has a mark of the great man known as "the cloud that reveals the many forms and appearances." Adorned with *vairocana* jewels and sapphires from the treasury of the shimmering light of all moons, in every mind-moment, it travels through all oceans of the Dharma realm emanating the fragrant flaming light of *maṇi* lamps. Its radiance everywhere fills the entire Dharma realm. This is the ninety-third.

The four-part circumference of the Tathāgata's right foot has a mark of the great man known as "the cloud of the universal treasury." Adorned with sapphire gems, and vajra jewels, it emanates the light of jewels that fills empty space and reveals within it all buddhas sitting in their sites of enlightenment on lion thrones made of sovereign *maṇi* jewels. This is the ninety-fourth.

The four sides of the Tathāgata's left foot have a mark of the great man known as "the cloud whose light everywhere illuminates the Dharma realm." Adorned with *maṇi* jewel flowers, it emanates a great radiance of the same single character that fills the Dharma realm and reveals within it the sovereign spiritual powers of all buddhas and bodhisattvas as well as their use of a loud and sublime voice with which they expound on the endless Dharma gateways of the Dharma realm. This is the ninety-fifth.

The tips of the Tathāgata's right toes have a mark of the great man known as "the cloud that reveals adornments." Adorned with extremely lovely pure *jambūnada* gold, it emanates a great radiance that fills the ten directions of the Dharma realm, revealing within it all buddhas and bodhisattvas, their endless ocean of dharmas, their many different kinds of meritorious qualities, and the transformations produced by their spiritual superknowledges. This is the ninety-sixth.

The tips of the Tathāgata's left toes have a mark of the great man known as "the cloud that reveals the spiritual transformations of all buddhas." Adorned with the inconceivable light of the Buddha, the universally pervasive fragrance of shimmering moonlight, and wheels of flaming *maṇi* jewel radiance, it emanates a pure light the color of the many kinds of jewels that fills all the oceans of worlds, revealing within them all buddhas and bodhisattvas expounding on the ocean of the Dharma of all buddhas. This is the ninety-seventh.

Sons of the Buddha, Vairocana Tathāgata has marks of the great man such as these as numerous as the atoms in ten oceans of worlds such as the Flower Treasury World. Every one of the parts of his body is adorned with marvelous signs made of the many kinds of jewels.

The End of Chapter Thirty-Four

Chapter 35
The Qualities of the Light of the Tathāgata's Secondary Signs

At that time, the Bhagavat told Jewel Hand Bodhisattva:

O Son of the Buddha, the Tathāgata, the Arhat, the One of Right and Perfect Enlightenment, has a subsidiary sign known as "the king of perfect fulfillment." From within this subsidiary sign there comes forth a great light known as "flourishing abundance" with a retinue consisting of seven hundred myriads of *asaṃkhyeyas* of light rays.

Son of the Buddha, when I was the bodhisattva abiding in the Tuṣita Heaven Palace, I emanated a great light known as "the king of light banners" that illuminated worlds as numerous as the atoms in ten buddha *kṣetras*. When the beings in the hells associated with those worlds encountered this light, their many sorts of sufferings ceased and they acquired ten kinds of pure eyes. So too did this occur with their ears, noses, tongues, bodies, and minds. They were all filled with joy and danced with celebratory delight. After their lives there came to an end, they were born in the Tuṣita Heaven. In that heaven, there was a drum called "delightful." After they were born in that heaven, this drum emanated a voice which announced to them: "Sons of the Devas, because your minds were not neglectful, because you planted roots of goodness with the Tathāgata, because you drew near to good spiritual guides in the past, and because of the great awesome spiritual powers of Vairocana, when your lives there came to an end, you came to be born in this heaven."

Sons of the Buddha, the thousand-spoked wheel emblem on the bottom of the bodhisattva's feet is known as "the king of universally illuminating light." This has a subsidiary sign known as "the king of perfect fulfillment" which always emanates forty kinds of light among which one of those lights is known as "pure meritorious qualities." It is able to illuminate worlds as numerous as the atoms in a *koṭī* of *nayutas* of buddha *kṣetras* and, adapting to all beings' many different kinds of karmic actions and many different sorts of aspirations, it enables them to become fully ripened. When beings undergoing the most extreme sufferings in the Avīci Hells encounter this light, once they all reach the end of their lives there, they are born in the Tuṣita Heaven. Having been reborn in this heaven, they then hear the sound of the celestial drum telling them: "Good indeed. Good indeed. Sons of the Devas, Vairocana Bodhisattva has entered the stainless samādhi. You should go and bow in reverence to him."

At that time, having heard this sound from the celestial drum encouraging and instructing them in this way, those devas' sons all have this thought: "How strange and rare! Why does it emanate this sublime sound?"

At this time, that celestial drum tells these devas' sons:

This sound that I have sent forth is produced by the power of all sorts of roots of goodness. Sons of the Devas, just as when I refer to "I," it is done without attaching to any self and without attaching to anything belonging to a self, so too it is with all buddhas, for when they refer to themselves as buddhas, this is done without any attachment to the existence of any self and without any attachment to anything belonging to a self.

Sons of the Devas, just as the sound that I emanate does not come from the east and does not come from the southerly, westerly, or northerly directions, the four midpoints, the zenith, or the nadir, so too it is with the karmic reward of realizing buddhahood, for it, too, does not come from any of the ten directions.

Sons of the Devas, this is just as when you previously dwelt in the hells, those hells as well as those bodies of yours did not come from any of the ten directions, but rather came from your own evil karmic deeds arising from inverted views and entangling bonds of delusion which caused rebirth into hell-realm bodies. These [hell-realm bodies] had no [other] originating basis and had no place from which they came.

Sons of the Devas, it is due to the power of Vairocana Bodhisattva's awesome virtue that he emanates great light even as this light does not come forth from any of the ten directions. Sons of the Devas, so too it is with the sound of my celestial drum. It does not come forth from any of the ten directions. It is only because of the power of roots of goodness associated with samādhi and because of the power of awesome virtue associated with the *prajñāpāramitā* that it emanates a pure sound such as this and manifests different sorts of sovereign powers such as these.

Sons of the Devas, this is just as in the case of the many different kinds of pleasing things within the supremely marvelous palace of the Trāyastriṃśa Heaven on Sumeru, king of the mountains. These pleasing things that are present there did not come there from any of the ten directions. So too it is with the sound of my celestial drum which is also not something that has come here from any of the ten directions.

Sons of the Devas, this is just as when, as I expound on the Dharma for beings as numerous as the atoms that would result from grinding to atoms a *koṭī* of *nayutas* of buddha *kṣetras*, speaking to them in accordance with what pleases them and thereby causing them to experience great joyous delight, doing so without growing weary, without shrinking from this, without becoming arrogant, and without becoming neglectful. So too it was, Sons of the Devas, with Vairocana Bodhisattva as he dwelt in the samādhi of stainless purity and, from a single subsidiary sign in his right palm, emanated a single ray of light that manifested countless sovereign spiritual powers which not even any *śrāvaka*-disciple or *pratyekabuddha* could ever know of, how much the less any other type of being.

Sons of the Devas, you should go to see that bodhisattva and draw near to him and make offerings to him. Do not indulge in any further desire-based attachment to any of the pleasurable objects of the five desires. Attachment to the pleasures of the five desires is an obstacle to the development of all roots of goodness. Sons of the Devas, just as the fires at the end of the kalpa burn up even Mount Sumeru, causing it to entirely disappear, leaving no residue that one can find, so too it is with the mind entangled in desire, for it prevents one from ever being able to bring forth any intention to abide in mindfulness of the Buddha.

Sons of the Devas, you should all know to recognize kindnesses and repay kindness. Sons of the Devas, wherever there are beings who do not know to repay kindnesses, they are more likely to meet an untimely death and be reborn in the hells. Sons of the Devas, you were all previously abiding in the hell realms, but then were able to encounter that light that illuminated your bodies, allowing you to relinquish that circumstance and take rebirth here. It would only be fitting if you were to now swiftly perform dedications to increase your roots of goodness.

Sons of the Devas, just as I, as a celestial drum, am neither male nor female, and yet I am able to bring forth countlessly and boundlessly many inconceivable phenomena, so too it is with you devas' sons and devas' daughters, for you are neither male nor female, and yet you are still able to enjoy the use of all sorts of different supremely marvelous palaces, parks, and groves. Just as my celestial drum is neither produced nor destroyed, so too it is with forms, feelings, perceptions, karmic formative factors, and consciousness, for they too are neither produced nor destroyed. If you are all able to awaken to and understand this, you should realize that you can then enter the samādhi with the seal of independence.

Having heard these sounds, those devas' sons attained what was unprecedented for them, whereupon they all transformationally created a myriad flower clouds, a myriad incense clouds, a myriad music clouds, a myriad banner clouds, a myriad canopy clouds, and a myriad clouds of singing praises, and, having transformationally created these, they all went together to the palace in which Vairocana Bodhisattva dwelt, and, having pressed their palms together respectfully, they stood off to one side wishing thus to be granted an audience with him. However they remained unable to see him. At that time, there was a devas' son who said, "Vairocana Bodhisattva has already disappeared from this place and descended to take rebirth among humans in the household of the Pure Rice King in which, residing within a sandalwood tower, he now abides in the womb of Lady Māyā."

At that time, those devas' sons used their heavenly eyes to see the body of that bodhisattva abiding in the human realm in the household of the Pure Rice King where he was being served and given offerings by the Brahma heaven devas and desire realm devas. That congregation of devas' sons then all had this thought, "So long as we have not gone to see the Bodhisattva and pay our respects, if we were to remain here and indulge so much as an instant of fond attachment for this heavenly palace, then that would be unacceptable."

At that time, every one of those devas' sons wished to descend to Jambudvīpa together with their retinues consisting of ten *nayutas* of retainers. The celestial drum then emanated a voice which told them:

> Sons of the Devas, it is not the case that this bodhisattva-mahāsattva reached the end of his life here and then took rebirth in that place. Rather, it is solely because of his spiritual superknowledges that, adapting to what is appropriate for the minds of beings, he has caused them to see this.
>
> Sons of the Devas, just as, even though I am now invisible, I am still able to emanate this voice, so too it is with the bodhisattva-mahāsattva who has entered the samādhi of stainless purity. Even though he is invisible, he is still able to manifest taking birth in place after place, having abandoned all discriminations, having done away with arrogance, and having become free of any defiled attachments.
>
> Sons of the Devas, you should all bring forth the resolve to attain *anuttara-samyak-saṃbodhi,* purify your minds, abide in the fine awesome deportment, repent of and rid yourselves of all karmic obstacles, all affliction obstacles, all retribution obstacles, and

all obstacles arising from views. Using bodies as numerous as all beings throughout the Dharma realm, using heads as numerous as all beings throughout the Dharma realm, using tongues as numerous as all beings throughout the Dharma realm, and using good physical actions, good verbal actions, and good mental actions as numerous as all beings throughout the Dharma realm, you should repent of and rid yourselves of all obstacles and faults.

At that time, having heard these words, all those devas' sons experienced what was unprecedented for them. With minds filled with great joyous delight, they then asked [the celestial drum], "How then is it that the bodhisattva-mahāsattva repents of and rids himself of all faults?"

At that time, relying on the power of the bodhisattva's samādhi and roots of goodness, that celestial drum emanated a voice with which he told them:

Sons of the Devas, the bodhisattva realizes that karma does not come from the east and does not come from the south, the west, the north, the four midpoints, the zenith, or the nadir, and yet it all joins in accumulating and remaining in the mind. It arises solely from the inverted views and it has no place in which it dwells. It is in this way that the bodhisattva has a definite and clear perception of this which is free of any doubts.

Sons of the Devas, just as I, as a celestial drum, speak of karmic deeds, speak of karmic retributions, speak of actions, speak of the moral precepts, speak of joyousness, speak of peace, and speak of the samādhis, in this same way, the buddhas and bodhisattvas speak of a self, speak of possessions of a self, speak of beings, and speak of greed, hatred, delusion, and the many different kinds of karmic deeds, doing so even as, in truth, there is no self nor are there any possessions of a self and all karmic deeds that are done as well as the karmic rewards and retributions in the six destinies of rebirth are all such that, even if one were to search for them throughout the ten directions, none of them would be apprehensible.

Sons of the Devas, just as my voice is neither produced nor destroyed, and yet those devas who have done evil deeds will still hear no other sounds, but rather will only hear this sound that awakens them to the prospect of the hells, so too it is with all karmic deeds, for, even though they are neither produced nor destroyed, they still correspond to whatever one has cultivated and accumulated and hence they then result in experiencing their corresponding retributions.

Sons of the Devas, sounds such as those emanating from my celestial drum, even in countless kalpas, can never come to an end and remain uninterrupted, even as, whether it be their coming or going, none of them are apprehensible at all. Sons of the Devas, if they were to have any coming or going, then that would involve either nihilism or eternalism. All buddhas never speak of the existence of any dharma of nihilism or eternalism except as an expedient to assist the ripening of beings.

Sons of the Devas, just as this sound of mine adapts to the minds of beings in countless worlds and enables them all, as fitting, to be able to hear it, so too it is with all buddhas who, adapting to the minds of beings, thereby enable them all to succeed in seeing them.

Sons of the Devas, it is as if there were a crystal mirror known as "able to illuminate" that, immaculately clean and possessed of penetrating clarity in its reflections, was precisely equal in size to ten worlds and was such that the reflections of all the countlessly and boundlessly many lands with all their mountains, rivers, and beings, and even their hells, animals, and hungry ghosts were all revealed there within it. Sons of the Devas, what do you think? Can one or can one not say of those reflected images that they come and enter the mirror and then depart from the mirror?

They replied, "No, one could not."

Sons of the Devas, so too it is with all karmic deeds. Although they are able to produce all kinds of karmic rewards and retributions, they have no place from whence they come and no place to which they go. Sons of the Devas, it is as if there were a master conjurer who used illusions to deceive people's vision. One should realize that all karmic deeds are just the same as this. If one knows them in this way, then this constitutes [the means of] genuine repentance by which all the evils of one's karmic offenses can be purified.

When he taught this Dharma, a number of Tuṣita Heaven devas' sons equal to the atoms in a hundred thousand *koṭīs* of *nayutas* of buddha *kṣetras* gained the unproduced-dharmas patience, incalculably and inconceivably many *asaṃkhyeyas* of Six Desire Heaven devas' sons resolved to attain *anuttara-samyak-saṃbodhi*, and all the female devas in the six desire heavens relinquished the female body and resolved to attain unsurpassed bodhi.

At that time, due to having reached the ten grounds by hearing the teaching of Samantabhadra's vast dedications, due to acquiring samādhis adorned with powers, and due to repenting and ridding themselves of all their heavy karmic obstacles by engaging in the three kinds of pure karmic actions as numerous as all beings, all those devas immediately saw seven-jeweled lotus flowers as numerous as the atoms in a hundred thousand *koṭīs* of *nayutas* of buddha *kṣetras*. Atop every one of those flowers, there was a bodhisattva seated in the lotus posture emanating a great light. Every one of the subsidiary signs of those bodhisattvas emanated light rays as numerous as all beings and, within those light rays, there were buddhas as numerous as all beings who were seated in the lotus posture, speaking the Dharma for beings in ways adapted to the minds of those beings, and yet they still had not yet manifested even a small amount of the powers of the samādhi of stainless purity.

At that time, issuing from every one of their hair pores, those devas' sons also transformationally created clouds of many different kinds of supremely fine flowers as numerous as beings which they then presented as offerings to Vairocana Tathāgata, doing so by taking them up and scattering them down over the Buddha, where all those flowers then remained suspended in the air above the Buddha's body. All their clouds of fragrance then everywhere rained down their fragrances across a number of worlds as numerous as the atoms in countless buddha *kṣetras*. Wherever any being's body received this fragrance, his body felt peace and happiness comparable to that of a bhikshu who, on entering the fourth *dhyāna*, then experiences the complete melting away of all of his karmic obstacles.

As for all those who heard this teaching, each of those beings possessed five hundred inwardly related afflictions and five hundred outwardly related afflictions related to their forms, sounds, smells, tastes and touchables. In the case of those more extensively coursing in desire, they had twenty-one thousand. In the case of those more extensively coursing in hatred, they had twenty-one thousand. In the case of those more extensively coursing in delusion, they had twenty-one thousand. In the case of those coursing equally in all of them, they also had twenty-one thousand. Whenever any of these beings smelled this fragrance, they completely realized the inherent unreality of all of these. Once they realized this in this way, they then created fragrance banner clouds and spontaneously radiant pure roots of goodness. Whenever any beings saw their canopy clouds, they thereby planted roots of goodness equal to those of pure gold net wheel-turning kings as numerous as the sands in the Ganges River.

Sons of the Buddha, when a bodhisattva dwells in the position of this wheel-turning king, he teaches being in worlds as numerous as the atoms in a hundred thousand *koṭīs* of *nayutas* of buddha *kṣetras*.

Sons of the Buddha, this circumstance is analogous to that of Lunar Wisdom Tathāgata in the Bright Mirror World who always has bhikshus, bhikshunis, *upāsakas, upāsikās,* and others from countless other worlds who transformationally manifest bodies in his presence, thereby coming to listen to his expounding on the Dharma, whereupon he then extensively discourses for their benefit on the events of his former lifetimes, never having so much as a single mind-moment in which his teaching is interrupted. In any instance where there is a being who so much as hears this buddha's name, he most certainly will then succeed in being reborn in that buddha's land.

So too it is in the case of a bodhisattva who comes to abide in the position of a pure gold net wheel-turning king. If one only briefly encounters a ray of his light, one thereby definitely becomes bound to attain the position of a bodhisattva on the tenth bodhisattva ground due to the power of having previously cultivated roots of goodness.

Sons of the Buddha, this is just as when one reaches the first *dhyāna,* even though one has not come to the end of this lifetime, he still sees all the palaces where the Brahma Heaven devas dwell and becomes able to enjoy the happiness of those who dwell in the Brahma World. When one reaches the other *dhyānas,* one's experiences are all of this same sort.

The bodhisattva-mahāsattva who abides in the position of a pure gold net wheel-turning king emanates pure light from his *maṇi* jewel topknot. If there are any beings who encounter this light, they all become bound to reach the station of the tenth bodhisattva ground, to completely develop the light of measureless wisdom, to acquire the ten kinds of pure eye faculty, and so forth, including their becoming bound to acquire the ten kinds of pure mind faculty, bound to completely fulfill countless extremely deep samādhis, and bound to perfect a pure fleshly eye of this same kind.

Sons of the Buddha, suppose that there was a person who ground into atoms a *koṭī* of *nayutas* of buddha *kṣetras* and then also ground to atoms yet another buddha *kṣetra* for each one of those resulting atoms and then took all of those atoms, placed them in his left hand, and then set out in an easterly direction, whereupon, only after passing beyond just such a number of worlds as all of those atoms would he then and only then set down a single one of those atoms, continuing to travel farther on to the east to the point where he finally used up all of these atoms, after which he then did this very same thing as he traveled off to the south, the west, the north, the four midpoints, the zenith, and the nadir. Suppose then that one formed together into one single buddha land all those worlds of the ten directions that he had thereby passed, whether or not they were worlds in which he had set down one of those atoms. Jewel Hand, what do you think? Would the measureless vastness of a buddha land such as this be conceivable, or not?

He replied, "No, it would not be. A buddha land such as this would be so measurelessly vast, rare, and especially extraordinary as to be completely inconceivable. If there were to be any being at all who might hear this analogy and be able to develop resolute faith it, one should realize that they themselves would be even more rare and especially extraordinary than this."

The Buddha then said to Jewel Hand:

So it is. So it is. It is precisely as you say. If there were any son or daughter of good family who, hearing this analogy, was then able to believe in it, I would transmit to them their prediction prophesying that they would definitely be bound to realize *anuttara-samyak-saṃbodhi* and they would definitely be bound to realize the unsurpassable wisdom of the Tathāgata.

Jewel Hand, suppose that there was a person who ground to atoms a number of such vast buddha lands as this which were as numerous as the atoms in a thousand *koṭīs* of buddha *kṣetras* and, in accordance with this previously described analogy, he then took these atoms and set every one of them down until they were all gone, and so forth until we come once again to his putting so very many worlds together to form a single buddha world which he then yet again ground to atoms, continuing on sequentially in this way until he had passed through eighty such repeating cycles in this manner. The bodhisattva with the pure fleshly eye acquired as a karmic reward is able in but a single mind-moment to clearly see all the atoms resulting from grinding up all these vast buddha lands. He is also able to see a number of buddhas equal to the atoms contained in a hundred *koṭīs* of such vast buddha *kṣetras*, seeing them just as clearly as when that crystal mirror with its immaculate radiance illuminates a number of worlds equal to the atoms contained in ten buddha *kṣetras*.

Jewel Hand, all circumstances such as these are brought to perfect development through the extremely deep samādhi, merit, and roots of goodness of a pure gold net wheel-turning king.

The End of Chapter Thirty-Five

Chapter 36
The Practices of Samantabhadra

At that time, Samantabhadra Bodhisattva-mahāsattva again addressed that immense congregation of bodhisattvas, saying:

Sons of the Buddha, as for the preceding proclamation, it represents only a general explanation of a small part of the Tathāgata's domain of objective experience that has been adapted as fitting to the faculties and capacities of beings. Why? All of the buddhas, the *bhagavats*, come forth into the world for the sake of beings, doing so because:

[Beings], having no wisdom, commit evil deeds;
They conceive the existence of a self and possessions of a self;
They are attached to the body;
They are affected by inverted views and skeptical doubt;
They engage in discriminations based on wrong views;
They constantly involve themselves with the fetters and the bonds;
They follow along with the flow of *saṃsāra*; and
They stray far away from the path of the Tathāgata.

Sons of the Buddha, I see no single dharma constituting a greater transgression than that of bodhisattvas who produce thoughts of hatred toward other bodhisattvas. And why is this? Sons of the Buddha, if bodhisattvas produce thoughts of hatred or anger toward other bodhisattvas, they immediately create a gateway to a million obstacles.

What sorts of circumstances constitute those million obstacles? They are as follows:

The obstacle of not perceiving bodhi;
The obstacle of not hearing right Dharma;
The obstacle of being reborn in an impure world;
The obstacle of being reborn in the wretched rebirth destinies;
The obstacle of being reborn into the [eight] difficult circumstances;[345]
The obstacle of being much beset by illnesses;
The obstacle of being extensively slandered by others;
The obstacle of being reborn in destinies where beings are unintelligent;[346]
The obstacle of diminished right mindfulness;

The obstacle of deficient wisdom;
Obstacles associated with the eyes;
Obstacles associated with the ears;
Obstacles associated with the nose;
Obstacles associated with the tongue;
Obstacles associated with the body;
Obstacles associated with the mind;
The obstacle of association with bad spiritual guides;
The obstacle of association with bad companions;
The obstacle of merely delighting in Small Vehicle practice;
The obstacle of delighting in proximity to what is common and coarse;
The obstacle of not having resolute faith[347] in those possessed of great awesome virtue;
The obstacle of delighting in dwelling with those who have abandoned right views;
The obstacle of being reborn into households of those adhering to non-Buddhist paths;
The obstacle of abiding in realms of objective experience influenced by *māras*;
The obstacle of being separated from the Buddha's right teachings;
The obstacle of never encountering a good spiritual guide;[348]
The obstacle of encountering restraining difficulties[349] in developing roots of goodness;
The obstacle of increasing unwholesome dharmas;
The obstacle of coming upon inferior circumstances;[350]
The obstacle of birth into outlying lands;
The obstacle of birth into the household of evil people;
The obstacle of being born among evil spirits;
The obstacle of being born among evil dragons, evil *yakṣas,* evil *gandharvas,* evil *asuras,* evil *garuḍas,* evil *kiṃnaras,* evil *mahoragas,* or evil *rākṣasas;*
The obstacle of not delighting in the Buddha's Dharma;
The obstacle of habitually immature behavior;
The obstacle of delighting in attachment to the Small Vehicle;
The obstacle of not delighting in the Great Vehicle;
The obstacle of being naturally excessively fearful;
The obstacle of having a mind always afflicted by worry;
The obstacle of being fondly attached to [life in] *saṃsara;*
The obstacle of not remaining focused on the Buddha's Dharma;
The obstacle of not delighting in seeing or hearing of the Buddha's mastery of the spiritual superknowledges;

The obstacle of not acquiring the faculties of a bodhisattva;
The obstacle of not practicing the bodhisattva's pure practices;
The obstacle of timidly retreating from the bodhisattva's deep resolve;[351]
The obstacle of not making the bodhisattva's great vows;
The obstacle of not resolving to acquire all-knowledge;
The obstacle of indolence in carrying out the bodhisattva practices;
The obstacle of being unable to purify all of one's karma;
The obstacle of being unable to gather an immense accumulation of merit;
The obstacle of being unable to develop clarity and acuity in the power of one's knowledge;
The obstacle of interrupting one's development of vast wisdom;
The obstacle of not preserving and sustaining all the bodhisattva practices;
The obstacle of delighting in slandering the words of those who are omniscient;
The obstacle of distancing oneself from the bodhi of the buddhas;
The obstacle of delighting in abiding in the spheres of experience of the many *māras;*
The obstacle of not focusing on cultivating the Buddha's sphere of action;
The obstacle of not decisively making the bodhisattva's vast vows;
The obstacle of not delighting in dwelling together with bodhisattvas;
The obstacle of not seeking to develop the bodhisattva's roots of goodness;
The obstacle of being naturally inclined to hold numerous views and have many doubts;
The obstacle of having a mind that is always dull and dim;
The obstacle of not relinquishing things that arises due to an inability to practice the bodhisattva's impartial giving;
The obstacle of creating broken moral precepts that arises due to an inability to uphold the Tathāgata's moral prohibitions;
The obstacle of stupidity, maliciousness, and hatred that arises due to an inability to enter the gateway of patience;
The obstacle of indolence-related defilements that arises due to an inability to practice the bodhisattva's great vigor;
The obstacle of being scattered and disordered that arises due to an inability to acquire any of the samādhis;

The obstacle of developing an evil intelligence that arises due to failing to cultivate the *prajñāpāramitā;*

The obstacle of not having skillfulness sufficient to deal with various possible and impossible situations;[352]

The obstacle of having no skillful means with which to liberate beings;

The obstacle of being unable to apply analytic contemplations to the wisdom of the bodhisattva;

The obstacle of being unable to completely understand the dharmas by which a bodhisattva achieves emancipation;

The obstacle of having eyes like those born blind due to not perfecting the bodhisattva's ten kinds of great eyes;[353]

The obstacle of having verbal abilities like those who are mute because one's ears have never heard the unimpeded Dharma;

The obstacle of having diminished olfactory faculties because one does not possess the major marks and subsidiary characteristics;

The obstacle of impaired verbal skills due to being unable to distinguish and completely understand beings' speech;

The obstacle of impaired physical faculties due to having slighted other beings;

The obstacle of impaired mental faculties due to having a crazed and disordered mind;

Physical karmic obstacles due to not upholding three categories of moral precepts;[354]

Verbal karmic obstacles developed due to constantly committing four types of transgressions;[355]

Mental karmic obstacles developed due to much production of covetousness, ill will, and wrong views;[356]

The obstacle of seeking the Dharma with the mind of a thief;

The obstacle of having cut oneself off from the bodhisattva's domain of objective experience;

The obstacle of having a mind that timidly retreats from the bodhisattva's heroically courageous dharmas;

The obstacle of having a mind that is indolent in its pursuit of the bodhisattva's path of emancipation;

The obstacle of having a mind that stops and rests at the gateway to the bodhisattva's light of wisdom;

The obstacle of having a mind that becomes inferior and weak in developing the bodhisattva's power of mindfulness;

The obstacle of being unable to maintain and preserve the Tathāgata's teaching dharmas;

The obstacle of being unable to draw near to the bodhisattva's path of transcending births in cyclic existence;
The obstacle of being unable to cultivate the uncorrupted path of the bodhisattva;
The obstacle of pursuing realization of the Two Vehicles' right and fixed position;[357] and
The obstacle of distancing oneself from the lineage of all buddhas and bodhisattvas of the three periods of time.

Sons of the Buddha, if a bodhisattva raises even a single thought of hatred for another bodhisattva, he then produces a million obstacles such as these. And why? Sons of the Buddha, I do not see any single dharma constituting such an immense transgression as that created by any bodhisattva who produces thoughts of hatred toward other bodhisattvas. Therefore, if a bodhisattva-mahāsattva wishes to swiftly fulfill all the bodhisattva practices, he should diligently cultivate ten kinds of dharmas. What then are those ten? They are as follows:

His mind never abandons any being;
He envisions all bodhisattvas as *tathāgatas;*
He never slanders any dharma of the Buddha;
He realizes that all lands are endless;
He feels deep faith and delight in the bodhisattva practices;
He never relinquishes a bodhi resolve that is commensurate with empty space and the Dharma realm;
He contemplates bodhi and enters the powers of the Tathāgata;
He is energetically diligent in cultivating unimpeded eloquence;
He is tireless in teaching beings; and
He abides in any world with a mind free of attachments.

These are the ten.

Sons of the Buddha, after the bodhisattva-mahāsattva comes to securely abide in these ten dharmas, he is then able to completely fulfill ten kinds of purity. What then are the ten? They are as follows:

Purity in the penetrating comprehension of extremely profound dharmas;
Purity in drawing close to good spiritual guides;
Purity in guarding and preserving all dharmas of the Buddha;
Purity in the complete penetration of the realm of empty space;
Purity in deeply entering the Dharma realm;
Purity in contemplation of the boundless mind;
Purity in roots of goodness identical to those of all bodhisattvas;

Purity in refraining from attachment to any kalpa;
Purity in contemplation of the three periods of time; and
Purity in cultivation of all buddhas' dharmas.

These are the ten.

Sons of the Buddha, after the bodhisattva-mahāsattva abides in these ten dharmas, he then completely fulfills ten kinds of vast knowledge. What then are those ten? They are as follows:

The knowledge that knows the actions of all beings' minds;
The knowledge that knows the consequences of all beings' karma;
The knowledge that knows all dharmas of the Buddha;
The knowledge that knows the deeply secret principles and purport of all dharmas of the Buddha;
The knowledge that knows all *dhāraṇī* gateways;
The knowledge that knows and possesses eloquence in all written languages;
The knowledge by which one knows all beings' languages and speech and is skillful in the unimpeded knowledge of eloquent phrasing;[358]
The knowledge by which one everywhere manifests bodies in all worlds;
The knowledge by which one everywhere manifests reflected images within all congregations; and
The knowledge by which one possesses all-knowledge wherever one is born.

These are the ten.

Sons of the Buddha, after the bodhisattva-mahāsattva comes to abide in these ten types of knowledge, he then succeeds in entering into ten kinds of universal penetration. What then are those ten? They are as follows:

All worlds enter into a single hair pore and a single hair pore enters all worlds;
All beings' bodies enter a single body and a single body enters all beings' bodies;
An ineffable[359] number of kalpas enter a single mind-moment and a single mind-moment enters an ineffable number of kalpas;
All dharmas of the Buddha enter a single dharma and a single dharma enters all dharmas of the Buddha;
An ineffable number of places enter a single place and a single place enters an ineffable number of places;
An ineffable number of faculties enter a single faculty and a single faculty enters an ineffable number of faculties;

All faculties enter what is not a faculty at all and what is not a faculty at all enters all faculties;
All thoughts enter a single thought and a single thought enters all thoughts;
All sounds of speech enter a single sound of speech and a single sound of speech enters into all sounds of speech; and
All three periods of time enter a single period of time and a single period of time enters all three periods of time.

These are the ten.

Sons of the Buddha, after the bodhisattva-mahāsattva has contemplated in this way, he then abides in ten kinds of supremely sublime mind. What then are those ten? They are as follows:

He abides in the supremely sublime mind that comprehends all worlds' language and non-language;
He abides in the supremely sublime mind that comprehends that the thoughts of all beings have nothing whatsoever on which they rely;
He abides in the supremely sublime mind that comprehends the realm of ultimate emptiness;
He abides in the supremely sublime mind that comprehends the boundless Dharma realm;
He abides in the supremely sublime mind that comprehends all the deeply secret dharmas of the Buddha;
He abides in the supremely sublime mind that comprehends the extremely profound Dharma as free of any differentiations;
He abides in the supremely sublime mind that extinguishes all doubt;[360]
He abides in the supremely sublime mind that comprehends all periods of time[361] as the same and as free of any differentiation;
He abides in the supremely sublime mind that comprehends the equality of all buddhas of the three periods of time; and
He abides in the supremely sublime mind that comprehends the immeasurable powers of all buddhas.

These are the ten.

Sons of the Buddha, after the bodhisattva-mahāsattva has come to abide in these ten kinds of supremely sublime mind, he then acquires ten kinds of skillful knowledge with regard to the Dharma of the Buddha. What then are these ten? They are as follows:

The skillful knowledge that completely comprehends the extremely profound Dharma of the Buddha;
The skillful knowledge that brings forth the vast Dharma of the Buddha;

The skillful knowledge that proclaims the many different kinds of dharmas of the Buddha;
The skillful knowledge that brings about realization of and entry into the equally accessible Dharma[362] of the Buddha;
The skillful knowledge that completely understands the different dharmas of the Buddha;
The skillful knowledge that awakens to and understands the absence of differences in the Dharma of the Buddha;
The skillful knowledge that deeply enters into the adornments of the Dharma of the Buddha;
The skillful knowledge that uses a single expedient means to penetrate the Dharma of the Buddha;
The skillful knowledge that uses countlessly many expedient means to penetrate the Dharma of the Buddha;
The skillful knowledge that knows the absence of differences in the boundlessly many dharmas of the Buddha;[363] and
The skillful knowledge by which, relying on one's own resolve and one's own powers, one does not retreat from any of the Buddha's dharmas.

These are the ten.[364]

Sons of the Buddha, once they have heard these dharmas, all bodhisattva-mahāsattvas should resolve to respectfully accept and uphold them. Why is this? By applying a small amount of effort, the bodhisattva-mahāsattvas who uphold these dharmas will be able to quickly reach *anuttara-samyak-saṃbodhi* and completely fulfill all dharmas of the Buddha which are equal to the dharmas of all buddhas of the three periods of time.

At that time, because of the Buddha's spiritual powers and because the Dharma is just this way, in worlds in each of the ten directions as numerous as the atoms in ten ineffable numbers of hundreds of thousands of *koṭīs* of *nayutas* of buddha *kṣetras*, there occurred the six kinds of shaking and moving along with the raining down of flower clouds superior even to those of the devas, incense clouds, powdered incense clouds, clouds of robes, canopies, banners, pennants, *maṇi* jewels, and other such things, as well as clouds of all manner of adornments.

There were clouds that rain the many kinds of music, clouds that rain bodhisattvas, clouds that rain an ineffable number of *tathāgatas'* physical signs, clouds that rain an ineffable number of praises of the Tathāgata, exclaiming "Good indeed!," clouds that rain *tathāgatas'* voices that fill the entire Dharma realm, clouds that rain an ineffable number of adorned worlds, clouds that rain an ineffable number of means to promote the realization of bodhi, clouds that rain an ineffable number of brightly shining lights, and clouds that rain an ineffable number of proclamations of Dharma through the use of spiritual powers.

And just as, in this world with its four continents, beneath the bodhi tree, in the *bodhimaṇḍa*, within the bodhisattva's palace, one could see the Tathāgata realize the universal and right enlightenment and then proclaim this Dharma, so too could one see this in all worlds throughout the ten directions.

At that time, because of the Buddha's spiritual powers and because the Dharma is just this way, from each of the ten directions, beyond a number of worlds as numerous as the atoms in ten ineffable numbers of large buddha *kṣetras*, bodhisattva-mahāsattvas as numerous as the atoms in ten buddha *kṣetras* came forth to this land to pay their respects and, filling up the ten directions, they spoke words such as these: "It is good indeed, good indeed, O Son of the Buddha, that you have now been able to speak of the profound dharmas of the greatest vows and the prediction of buddhahood of all buddhas, all *tathāgatas*.

"O Son of the Buddha, all of us have the same name, 'Samantabhadra.' We have each come to pay our respects in this land, coming here from the abode of Universal Banner of Mastery Tathāgata in the Universal Supremacy World. Through the Buddha's spiritual powers, all of us proclaim this Dharma everywhere just as it is set forth in the midst of this congregation, doing so in a way that everything is the same, free of any additions or omissions. Through having received the aid of the Buddha's awesome spiritual power, we have all come to this *bodhimaṇḍa* to serve as certifying witnesses for you. And just as we bodhisattvas as numerous as the atoms in ten buddha *kṣetras* have come to this *bodhimaṇḍa* to serve here as certifying witnesses, so too is this also so in all other worlds throughout the ten directions."

At that time, in reliance upon the Buddha's spiritual power and the power of his own roots of goodness, Samantabhadra Bodhisattva-mahāsattva surveyed the ten directions, including everywhere throughout the Dharma realm, and:

Wishing to provide instruction in the bodhisattva practices;
Wishing to proclaim his teaching on the Tathāgata's realm of bodhi;
Wishing to speak of the realm of great vows;
Wishing to explain all worlds' permutations of kalpas;

Wishing to clarify the manner in which the buddhas appear in accordance with the time;
Wishing to explain how the Tathāgata appears for the sake of beings with ripened faculties to enable them to make offerings;
Wishing to clarify that the efforts of the Tathāgata in appearing in the world are never wasted;
Wishing to clarify that roots of goodness that have been planted will definitely result in harvesting karmic rewards; and
Wishing also to clarify the manner in which the bodhisattva possessed of great awesome virtue manifests his forms for the sake of all beings, speaking Dharma for them in a manner that causes them to awaken—

He then spoke verses, saying:

You should all be filled with joyous delight,
abandon all of the hindrances,
and single-mindedly and respectfully listen
to the vows and practices of the bodhisattva.

Just as it has been with all bodhisattvas of the distant past
as well as with the supreme lions among men,[365]
in accordance with what they have cultivated,
so shall I now explain it in accordance with its sequence.

I shall also describe the numbers of all kalpas,
the world systems, and all karma,
as well as the peerless Bhagavat's
coming forth and appearing within them,

how these buddhas of the past,
due to great vows, came forth into the world,
how it was that, for beings' sakes,
they extinguished sufferings and afflictions,

and how it has been that all the lions of reasoned discourse[366]
have so continuously fulfilled what they have practiced
and have acquired the Buddha's equal Dharma
and their omniscient sphere of cognition.

Seeing that all the Lions Among Men
throughout the past
have emanated a great net of light
that everywhere illuminates the worlds of the ten directions,

they reflected on this and then made this vow:
"I shall become a lamp for the world
and perfect the meritorious qualities of the Buddha,
the ten powers, and all-knowledge.

The greed, hatred, and delusion
of all the many kinds of beings blazes intensely.
I shall rescue and liberate them all
and enable them to extinguish the wretched destinies' sufferings."

They have brought forth vows such as this
that are solid and irreversible
and, completely cultivating the bodhisattva practices,
they acquire the ten unimpeded powers.[367]

Having made vows such as this,
they then cultivate without ever retreating in fear
and whatever they do is never done in vain.
It is these who are known as "lions of reasoned discourse."

In this single age, "the worthy kalpa,"
a thousand buddhas come forth into the world.
All of those possessed of universally seeing eyes,
I shall proceed to describe here in an orderly fashion.

Just as this is the circumstance in this one "worthy kalpa,"
so too shall this be so in a measureless number of kalpas.
I shall now describe in a way that distinguishes them
the practices engaged in by those buddhas of the future.

Just as the circumstances exist in a single type of *kṣetra,*
so too do they also exist in a measureless number of *kṣetras.*
I shall now discuss all the practices
engaged in by those future *bhagavats* possessed of the ten powers.

Those buddhas sequentially appear in the world,
doing so in accordance with vows and their corresponding names,
in accordance with the predictions that they have received,
in accordance with the life spans they are destined to fulfill,

in accordance with the right Dharma they cultivate
and their focused quest to pursue the unimpeded path,
in accordance with those beings that they teach
and the right Dharma that abides in the world,

in accordance with the buddha *kṣetras* that they purify,
their beings, their turning of the wheel of Dharma,
and their expounding according to what is and is not the right time
as they pursue the orderly purification of the many types of beings,

and in accordance with all those beings' karmic deeds,
what they practice, what they resolutely believe in,
and how they differ due to superior, middling, and inferior capacities
as they teach them and influence them to pursue the cultivation.

[I shall describe as well] how they penetrate such types of knowledge,
cultivate their supreme types of practices,
and always perform the works of Samantabhadra,
and engage in the extensive liberation of beings,

doing so with physical actions that are never impeded,
with verbal actions that are entirely pure,
and with mental actions that are also of this same sort so that,
in all three periods of time, there are none that are not this way.

It is in this way that the bodhisattva practices
the ultimate path of Samantabhadra
and brings forth the rising of pure wisdom's sun
to everywhere illuminate the Dharma realm.

In all the kalpas of future time,
there are an ineffable number of lands.
In but a single mind-moment, they completely know them all
even as they make no discriminations regarding any of them.

The practitioner is able to progress into
such supreme grounds as these.
I shall now describe a minor portion
of these dharmas of the bodhisattva.

Their boundless wisdom penetratingly comprehends
the Buddha's spheres of cognition.
They skillfully enter them all
and never retreat from what they practice.

They become fully possessed of the wisdom of Samantabhadra,
completely fulfill the vows of Samantabhadra,
and enter into incomparable wisdom.
I shall describe their practices.

Within but a single atom,
they completely see all worlds.
If beings were to hear of this,
they would become so confused as to be driven insane.

Just as this is so with a single atom,
so too is this true of every atom.
The worlds all enter into them
in such an inconceivable manner as this.

In each and every atom there exist
the dharmas of the ten directions and three periods of time.
The rebirth destinies and *kṣetras* therein are countless,
yet they are able to distinguish and know them all.

In each and every atom there exist
countless types of buddha *kṣetras*.
Every one of those types is measurelessly numerous,
yet there is not even a single one they do not know.

All of the Dharma realm's
many different types of varying aspects,
the rebirth destinies, and types of beings, each of which are different—
They are able to distinguish and know them all.

They deeply enter into the most subtly refined knowledge,
with which they distinguish all worlds
and they are able to thoroughly understand and explain
the development and destruction of all kalpas.

They know the length[368] of all kalpas
and know the three periods of time as but a single mind-moment.
They are able to distinguish and know
of the many types of practices, all their identities and differences.

They deeply enter into all worlds,
whether they be vast or not vast,
manifesting a single body in countless *kṣetras,*
or countless bodies within a single *kṣetra.*

With regard to the different types of worlds
throughout the ten directions
and their vastness as well as their countless other characteristics,
they are able to completely know them all.

With regard to all the countlessly many lands
throughout the three periods of time,
completely possessed of such extremely deep knowledge,
they entirely know both their creation and ruination.

In all the worlds throughout the ten directions,
some are just being formed and some are being destroyed.
Those possessed of the worthy's[369] virtue deeply comprehend
all the ineffable number of phenomena such as these.

Some have all kinds of lands
possessed of many different types of adornments of their grounds.
So too it is with their rebirth destinies.
This all arises from the purity of karmic deeds.

In some cases there are all kinds of worlds
possessed of countless types of defilement.
These arise as circumstances elicited by beings
that are all accordant with their own actions.

They completely know the countless and boundless *kṣetras*
as identical with any single *kṣetra.*
In this way, they enter into all *kṣetras*
whose number is so great that it cannot be known.

All of those many worlds
entirely enter into but a single *kṣetra*
even as those worlds still do not become but one
and even as they still do not become mixed together or disordered.

Worlds may exist in either an upright or inverted position
and may be characterized by either lofty terrain or low-lying terrain.
In all cases, these circumstances reflect the thoughts of their beings.
They are able to distinguish and know all of these matters.

All of these vast worlds
are countlessly and boundlessly many.
They know the many different types to be but one
and know the one to be the many different types.

All of these Samantabhadras, these sons of the Buddha,
are able by using Samantabhadra's knowledge
to completely know the number of all these *kṣetras*
whose number is so boundlessly large.

They know the transformations of all worlds,
the transformations of the *kṣetras,* the transformations of beings,
the transformations of dharmas, and the transformations of buddhas,
and know them all to the most ultimate degree.

They know with regard to all worlds,
including the very small *kṣetras* as well as the vast *kṣetras,*
including, too, all of their many different kinds of adornments,
that all of these phenomena arise as a consequence of karmic actions.

Even if countless sons of the Buddha
who were well trained in entering the Dharma realm
and who were possessed of mastery in the spiritual powers
by which they could go everywhere throughout the ten directions

were to recite the names of all those worlds
for kalpas equal in number to that of all beings,
they would still be unable to come to the end of them all
unless this was disclosed to them by the Buddha.

Even if, in reciting all the many different names
of those worlds and their *tathāgatas,*
they continued to do so for a measureless number of kalpas,
they would still be unable to reach the end of their recitation.

How much the less, with their supreme knowledge, could they do so
with the dharmas set forth by all buddhas of the three periods of time
which, having come forth from the Dharma realm,
completely pervade the ground of the Tathāgatas.

With pure and unimpeded mindfulness
and unimpeded wisdom,
they made distinctions as they explained the Dharma realm
and achieved complete perfection[370] in doing so.

As for all the worlds throughout the past,
whether vast or whether minute,
which were then adorned by cultivation—
they are able to know them all in but a single mind-moment,[371]

knowing as well how, within them, the lions among men
cultivated the many different types of practices of a buddha
and then reached the universal and right enlightenment
and manifested all the sovereign masteries.[372]

In this same way, during the course of the future,
how all of those most revered among men
will sequentially appear in countless ensuing kalpas—
these bodhisattvas are also able to know all of these matters,

including the content of all their practices and vows
and all of their domains of objective experience
as, in this way, they shall proceed with their diligent cultivation
and then will achieve right enlightenment during those times.

They also know their future congregations,
the life spans they will have, and the way they will teach beings
as, using all of these gateways into the Dharma,
they will turn the wheel of Dharma for the sake of the multitude.

Bodhisattvas who are possessed of these kinds of knowing
dwell on the ground of Samantabhadra's practices.
This wisdom that completely understands all these matters
is what gives birth to all buddhas.

All of the buddha lands
that exist during this present period of time—
they also deeply enter into all of those *kṣetras*
and command a penetrating comprehension of the Dharma realm

and all buddhas of the present
within all those worlds,
those who have gained sovereign mastery of the Dharma
and who are unimpeded in their discourse.

They also know these buddhas' congregations,
their pure lands, and their powers to manifest in response to beings.
Throughout countless *koṭīs* of kalpas,
they always contemplate these matters.

All of the awesome spiritual powers
of these world-taming *bhagavats*
as well as their inexhaustible treasury of wisdom—
they are able to know them all.

They develop the unimpeded eye,
the unimpeded ear, nose, and body,
and the unimpeded vast and long tongue
with which they can inspire joyous delight in the many.

They develop supremely unimpeded minds
that are vast in their reach and thoroughly pure
and wisdom that is universally pervasive
with which they know all dharmas of the three periods of time.

They thoroughly train in all types of transformations,
including transformations of *kṣetras,* transformations among beings,
transformations of worlds, transformations in training beings,
and ultimately achieve perfection in the practice of transformations.[373]

That the world's many different kinds of distinctions
all arise and abide because of thought—
Through penetrating the Buddha's knowledge of skillful means,
they completely understand all of these matters.

They manifest bodies in each and every one
of an ineffable number of congregations,
enabling them all to see the Tathāgata,
and thereby liberating a boundless multitude of beings.

The extremely profound wisdom of all buddhas
is like the sun when it rises in the world.
Within all of the countries,
it keeps appearing everywhere incessantly.

They completely comprehend the entire world
as but artificial designations devoid of any reality,
while understanding both its beings and the world
as like dreams or like lights and shadows.

They do not produce any discriminations or views
regarding any of the world's dharmas.
They skillfully transcend "one who discriminates"
while also not even perceiving "that which is discriminated."

They understand a period of measureless and countless kalpas
to be identical to a single mind moment even as
they realize mind-moments themselves are devoid of mind-moments.
It is in this way that they perceive the world.

They step beyond a measureless number of lands
in but a single mind-moment
and pass through a measureless number of kalpas
without ever moving from their original place.

An ineffable number of kalpas
are identical to a single instant.
To never even perceive "long" as opposed to "short"
is the ultimate *kṣaṇa* dharma.[374]

The mind abides in the world
and the world abides in the mind.
With regard to these, they do not erroneously generate
any discriminations construing them to be either dual or non-dual.

Beings, worlds, and kalpas,
the buddhas, and the dharmas of the buddhas—
They are all comparable to conjurations or transformations
even as the Dharma realm itself is everywhere the same.

They manifest incalculably many bodies
everywhere throughout the *kṣetras* of the ten directions
even as they realize that the body arises from conditions
and that there is ultimately nothing to which one can be attached.

Relying on their non-dual wisdom,
they come forth and appear as the lions among men
even as they do not become attached to non-dual dharmas
and realize that there is nothing that is either dual or non-dual.

They completely realize that the entire world
is like flames, like lights and shadows,
like echoes, like dreams,
like conjurations, or like transformations.

It is in this way that they accord with and enter into
the stations of all buddhas' action,
perfect the wisdom of Samantabhadra,
and everywhere illuminate the deep Dharma realm.

The defiling attachments associated with beings and *kṣetras*—
they completely relinquish all of them
and then raise up their minds of great compassion
to everywhere purify the entire world.

The bodhisattvas always abide in right mindfulness
of the wondrous Dharma of the lions of reasoned discourse
and, with purity like that of empty space,
they then bring forth their great skillful means.

Seeing that the world always abides in confusion and inverted views,
they resolve to rescue and liberate everyone.
Whatever they practice is in all cases pure
as they go forth everywhere throughout the entire Dharma realm.

All buddhas as well as all bodhisattvas,
the Dharma of the Buddha, and the dharmas of the world—
If one perceives their reality,
one realizes they are all devoid of any differences.

The treasury of the Tathāgata's Dharma body
everywhere enters into the world.
Yet, although it abides within the world,
it has nothing in the world to which it is attached.

Just as it is true of a body of clear water
that the reflected images on it neither come into it nor leave it,
in the case of the Dharma body's pervasive presence in the world,
one should realize it is just the same as this.

In this same way, they transcend all defiling attachments,
both the body and the world are seen to be pure
and as quiescent as empty space,
and everything is realized as unproduced.

They realize that the body is endless,
that it is neither produced nor destroyed,
that it is neither permanent nor impermanent,
and that it manifests throughout the world.[375]

They extinguish all wrong views
and reveal right views.
They realize the nature of dharmas has no coming or going
and they are not attached to a self or anything belonging to a self.

It is just as in the case of a master conjurer
who manifests many different kinds of phenomena which,
when they appear, have no place from which they come,
and when they disappear, have no place to which they go.

The nature of those conjurations is not finite,
nor is it infinite.
Yet, in the midst of those large crowds,
he manifests both the finite and the infinite.

Using this mind of quiescent meditative absorption,
they cultivate all roots of goodness
and bring about the birth of all buddhas.
This is not inherently either finite or infinite.

The finite and the infinite
are in every case merely erroneous perceptions.
They completely comprehend all destinies of rebirth
and do not become attached to either the finite or the infinite.

The extremely profound Dharma of all buddhas
is that of vast and deep quiescence.
Their extremely profound and measureless wisdom
knows the extremely profound aspects of all the rebirth destinies.

The bodhisattvas abandon confusion and inverted views.
The purity of their minds is continuous
as they skillfully use the powers of their spiritual superknowledges
to liberate countless beings.

Those who have not yet reached peace, they enable to find peace.
To those who have already found peace, they reveal the *bodhimaṇḍa*.
In this way, as they go everywhere throughout the Dharma realm,
their minds having nothing at all to which they are attached.

They do not dwell in ultimate reality
and do not opt for entry into nirvāṇa.
In this way, they go everywhere throughout the world,
awakening the many kinds of beings.

They completely understand and yet are not attached to
all the categories of dharmas and the categories of beings.
They everywhere rain down the Dharma rain,
causing it to completely drench the entire world.

Everywhere in all worlds and in each successive mind-moment,
they are achieving right enlightenment
and are cultivating the bodhisattva practices
without ever retreating from them.

They completely understand
all of the world's many different kinds of bodies,
and, by understanding the Dharma as it pertains to those bodies,
they are then able to acquire the body of all buddhas.

They everywhere know all beings,
all kalpas, and all *kṣetras*
throughout the boundless realms of the ten directions,
and they have no part of the ocean of wisdom they do not enter.

The bodies of beings are incalculably many,
yet they manifest bodies for each of them.
Though the Buddha's bodies are boundlessly many,
the wise are able to contemplate and see them all.

What they know in a single mind-moment
about the manifestations of all *tathāgatas* is so much that,
were they to spend countless kalpas attempting to do so,
they still could never come to the end of their praises.

All buddhas are able to manifest bodies
that, in place after place, enter *parinirvāṇa,*
producing in but a single mind-moment countless
śarīra relics, each of them distinctly different from the others.

In this way, throughout the course of the future,
there will be those who seek the fruit of buddhahood
and there will be countless beings who resolve to attain bodhi.
With their definitive wisdom, they know all of these matters.

In this manner, they are all able to entirely know
all of the *tathāgatas*
throughout the three periods of time.
This is what is known as "dwelling in Samantabhadra's practices."

In this way, they distinguish and know
countless practices and grounds,
enter into the stations of wisdom,
and never retreat from their turning of the Dharma wheel.

Their sublime and vast wisdom
deeply penetrates the Tathāgata's domain of objective experience
and, once it has entered it, they attain irreversibility.
This is what is known as "Samantabhadra's wisdom."

All of these who become supremely revered ones
everywhere enter the Buddha's domain of objective experience,
cultivate the practices without ever retreating,
and attain unsurpassable bodhi.

The countlessly and boundlessly many minds—
each and every one of them has different karma
and it all accumulates due to thoughts.
They know all of them equally and completely.

Whether they be defiled or undefiled,
and whether they be minds still in training or minds beyond training,
in each successive mind-moment, they completely know
all of these ineffably numerous minds.

They completely realize that they are neither singular nor dual,
that they are neither defiled nor pure,
that they are also free of any mixing or disorder,
and that, in every case, they arise from one's own thoughts.

In this way, they completely and clearly see
with regard to all beings,
that their minds and thoughts are all different
and that this is what creates the many different kinds of worlds.

With skillful means such as these,
they cultivate all of the supreme practices,
become transformationally born from the Buddha's Dharma,
and come to be known as "Samantabhadra."[376]

Beings all erroneously generate
thoughts leading to the good and bad destinies.
Because of this, they may be reborn in the heavens
or else may fall into the hells.

The bodhisattvas contemplate the world
as produced by karmic actions based on erroneous thoughts.
Because erroneous thoughts are boundlessly numerous,
the worlds themselves are also measurelessly manifold.

All lands are manifestations
produced by networks of thoughts.
Due to skillful means addressing these networks of illusions,
they are able to enter them all in but a single mind-moment.

The eye, ear, nose, tongue, body,
and mind faculties are also like this,
for they each differ due to the thoughts of those in the world.
They are equally able to fathom all of them.

Each and every one of those realms of visual experience
as well as their countless eye faculties—they enter all of them.
So, too, in the case of the differences in all the various kinds of natures
which are measurelessly and ineffably numerous.

There are no differences in what each one sees,
nor is there any mixing up or disorder in this,
for each one, in accordance with his individual karma,
experiences his own resulting karmic consequences.

The powers of Samantabhadra are measureless.
They completely know all of those things.
Such great wisdom is able to completely penetrate
all of those realms of visual experience.

They are entirely able to distinguish and know
all such aspects of the world as these
even as they cultivate all of the practices
and still never retreat from practicing them.

The speech of the buddhas and the speech of beings
as well as the speech particular to various lands—
speech like this as it is spoken throughout the three periods of time—
they completely know it all in all its many different variations.

The future within the past,
the present within the future,
and all such mutual perceptions between the three periods of time—
they clearly know each and every one of them.

They use countlessly many different approaches such as these
to awaken everyone throughout the world.
Their all-knowledge and skillful means are so extensive
that their bounds could never be found.

The End of Chapter Thirty-Six

Chapter 37
The Manifestation of the Tathāgata

At that time, from the white hair mark between his brows, the Bhagavat emanated a great light known as "the manifestation of the Tathāgata" that had a retinue of countless hundreds of thousands of *koṭīs* of *nayutas* of *asaṃkhyeyas* of light rays. Its brilliance everywhere illuminated all worlds throughout the ten directions of space and the Dharma realm. It then circumambulated him ten times to his right, revealed the Tathāgata's measureless feats of sovereign spiritual powers, awakened a multitude of countless bodhisattvas, caused shaking and movement in all worlds of the ten directions, extinguished all the sufferings in the wretched destinies, obscured all the palaces of the *māras* with its brightness, revealed all the buddhas, the *tathāgatas*, seated on their bodhi seats, attaining the universal and right enlightenment, revealed too everyone within their *bodhimaṇdas'* congregations, and then, having accomplished all of this, it came and circumambulated to their right the congregation of bodhisattvas and then entered the top of the head of Sublime Qualities of the Manifestations of the Tathāgata's Nature Bodhisattva.

At that time, everyone in the great assembly at this site of enlightenment was delighted in body and mind and filled with happiness, whereupon they had this thought, "How very extraordinary this is that the Tathāgata has now emanated this immensely brilliant light. Surely he is about to proclaim an extremely profound and great dharma."

Then, from his place where he was seated on a lotus, Sublime Qualities of the Manifestations of the Tathāgata's Nature Bodhisattva then bared his right shoulder, knelt on his right knee, joined his palms, single-mindedly faced the Buddha, and then spoke these verses:

The Rightly Enlightened One's qualities arise from great wisdom
whose universal penetration of the objective sphere has been perfected
and equals that of all *tathāgatas* throughout the three periods of time.
Therefore I now bow down in reverence.

He has already ascended to the far shore of the realm of signlessness,
and yet he manifests his body adorned with the marvelous marks.
He emanates thousands of rays of immaculate radiance,
vanquishes Māra's army's hordes, and causes them all to disappear.

He is able to cause shaking and movement
in all worlds of the ten directions without exception,
doing so without frightening even a single being.
The Well Gone One's awesome spiritual powers are of this very sort.

Equal to empty space and the nature of the Dharma realm—
he has already become able to abide in this way.
He is able to cause all of the countless and measurelessly many beings
to extinguish evil and eliminate their many defilements.

Exerting diligent effort in austere practices for countless kalpas,
he achieved success in the path to supreme bodhi,
acquired unimpeded wisdom in all realms,
and became identical in nature with all buddhas.

The Master Guide emanated this great light
and caused shaking and movement in all worlds of the ten directions.
Having shown the measureless powers of spiritual superknowledges,
they have returned and entered my body.

Having been well able to train well in the definitive Dharma,
these countless bodhisattvas have all come and gathered here,
thereby causing me to raise the thought to ask about the Dharma.
Therefore I shall now pose a question to the Dharma King.

Now this congregation is entirely pure
and well able to liberate everyone in the world.
Their wisdom is boundless and free of defiling attachments.
Such supreme worthies have all come and assembled here.

The revered Master Guide who benefits the world
is possessed of wisdom and vigor that are both beyond measure.
Now he has illuminated the great assembly with this great radiance
and thus caused me to inquire about the most supreme Dharma.

Who is it that is able to truly and completely expound
on the Great Rishi's deep spheres of action?
Who is the Tathāgata's most senior Dharma son?
We pray the revered Guide of the World will reveal this to us.

At that time, the Tathāgata immediately emanated a great light from his mouth known as "unimpeded fearlessness" that had a retinue of hundreds of thousands of *koṭīs* of *asaṃkhyeyas* of light rays. It everywhere illuminated all worlds throughout the ten directions of space commensurate with the entire Dharma realm. It then circumambulated him ten times to his right, revealed the Tathāgata's many different feats of sovereign spiritual powers, awakened a multitude of countless bodhisattvas, caused shaking and movement in all worlds of the ten directions, extinguished all the sufferings in the wretched destinies, obscured all the palaces of the *māras* with its brightness, revealed all the buddhas, the *tathāgatas,* seated on their bodhi seats, attaining the universal and right enlightenment, revealed too everyone in their *bodhimaṇdas'* congregations, and then, having accomplished all of this, it came and circumambulated to their right the congregation of bodhisattvas and entered the mouth of Samantabhadra Bodhisattva-mahāsattva. After that light had entered there, the splendor of Samantabhadra Bodhisattva's body and lion throne came to surpass their original state by a hundredfold, surpassing too that of the bodies and lion thrones of all the other bodhisattvas, with the sole exception of the Tathāgata's lion throne.

At that time, Sublime Qualities of the Manifestations of the Tathāgata's Nature Bodhisattva asked Samantabhadra Bodhisattva-mahāsattva, "O Son of the Buddha, the vast spiritual transformations manifested by the Buddha have caused all of these bodhisattvas to be filled with such inconceivable joyous delight that no one in the world could imagine it. What sort of auspicious sign is this?"

Samantabhadra Bodhisattva-mahāsattva then replied, "O Son of the Buddha, in the distant past, I have seen the Tathāgatas, the Right and Universally Enlightened Ones, manifest such vast spiritual transformations as this, whereupon they straightaway explained the Dharma gateway of 'the manifestation of the Tathāgata.' According to my assessment, that he has now displayed these signs indicates that he is about to teach that very dharma." When he spoke these words, the entire great earth shook and moved and sent forth measurelessly many rays of light associated with the requesting of Dharma.

Then Sublime Qualities of the Manifestations of the Tathāgata's Nature Bodhisattva asked Samantabhadra Bodhisattva, "O Son of the Buddha, how should the bodhisattva-mahāsattva know the dharma of the manifestation of the buddhas, the right and universally enlightened ones? Please speak about this matter for our sakes.

"Son of the Buddha, those in this congregation of countless hundreds of thousands of *koṭīs* of *nayutas* of bodhisattvas have all already long cultivated pure karmic works, have already completely developed their mindfulness and wisdom, have perfected the great adornments, have become possessed of the awesome deportment associated with the practices of all buddhas, and have established themselves in unfailing right mindfulness of all buddhas. They contemplate all beings with great compassion, definitely and completely know the spheres of action of the great bodhisattvas' spiritual superknowledges, have already acquired the assistance of all buddhas' spiritual powers, are able to take on the sublime Dharma of all *tathāgatas*, and, having become possessed of all such countlessly many meritorious qualities as these, have already come and assembled here.

"O Son of the Buddha, you have already served and made offerings to measurelessly many hundreds of thousands of *koṭīs* of *nayutas* of buddhas, have perfected the bodhisattva's most supremely marvelous practices, have achieved sovereign mastery in all gateways to samādhi, have entered the secret stations of all buddhas, have known all dharmas of the Buddha, have severed all of the many doubts, and have been assisted by the spiritual powers of all *tathāgatas*. You know the faculties of beings, adapt to whatever they find pleasing, and explain for them the dharmas of genuine liberation. You accord with the knowledge of the Buddha and thus achieve perfection in expounding the Dharma of the Buddha. You possess countlessly many meritorious qualities such as these.

"This is good indeed. O Son of the Buddha, we only wish that you will please speak about the dharma of the manifestation of the Tathāgata, the One of Universal and Right Enlightenment, about his physical signs, his voice, his mind's spheres of action, the practices in which he engages, his realization of the path, his turning of the Dharma wheel, and so forth, including his manifestation of entry into *parinirvāṇa*, the roots of goodness arising from seeing him, hearing him, and drawing near to him, as well as other such matters. We wish that you will please explain all of these matters for us."

At that time, wishing to clarify this meaning once again, Sublime Qualities of the Manifestations of the Tathāgata's Nature Bodhisattva addressed Samantabhadra Bodhisattva with verses, saying:

It is good indeed, you who are possessed of unimpeded great wisdom
and who has well awakened to the boundless realm of equality.
Please speak about the countless practices of the buddha.
Having listened, the sons of the Buddha will all feel joyous delight.

How does the bodhisattva accord with and enter into
the Buddha's, the Tathāgata's, emergence into the world?
What are his physical, verbal, and mental spheres of action
as well as the stations in which he practices? Please speak of all of this.

How is it that all buddhas attain right enlightenment?
How is it that the Tathāgata turns the wheel of the Dharma?
And how is it that the Well Gone One enters *parinirvāṇa*?
Hearing this, the minds of those in the Great Assembly will be happy.

If there be anyone who sees the Buddha, the great king of the Dharma,
or draws near to him, he will increase his roots of goodness.
Please speak of the treasury of all his meritorious qualities
and of what results shall be reaped after beings have seen him.

If there be anyone who hears the Tathāgata's name,
whether in the present era or after his nirvāṇa,
and then develops deep faith in his treasury of merit,
what benefit will then accrue to him? Please expound on this matter.

All of these bodhisattvas have placed their palms together
and gaze up in admiration at the Tathāgata, you, and me.
The sphere of action of the Great Ocean of Meritorious Qualities
and his purification of beings—please explain these matters for them.

Please use causes and conditions as well as analogies
to expound on the meanings of the sublime Dharma.
Having heard this, beings will arouse the great resolve,
their doubts will end, and their wisdom will become as pure as space.

Just as it is set forth by the adorned bodies
manifested by all buddhas everywhere in all lands,
please use your sublime voice as well as causal factors and analogies
to reveal the bodhi of the Buddha just as they do.

Even in the hundreds of myriads of buddha lands in all ten directions
throughout *koṭīs* of *nayutas* of incalculably long kalpas,
an assembly of bodhisattvas such as has now assembled here,
in all those circumstances, could only rarely be encountered.

These bodhisattvas are all filled with reverential respect
and have aroused a longing admiration for the sublime meaning.
We all pray that, with your purified mind, you will fully expound
on the vast dharma of the manifestation of the Tathāgata.

At that time, Samantabhadra Bodhisattva-mahāsattva informed the great assembly of Sublime Qualities of the Manifestations of the Tathāgata's Nature Bodhisattva and all the other bodhisattvas:

Sons of the Buddha, this circumstance is inconceivable. That is to say, it is because of countless dharmas that the right and universal enlightenment of the Tathāgata, the Arhat, is able to manifest. How is this so? It is not because of but a single condition and not because of but a single matter that the manifestation of the Tathāgata is able to be accomplished. Rather it is because of ten measureless matters subsuming hundreds of thousands of *asaṃkhyeyas* of factors that it is able to be accomplished. What are those ten? They are as follows:

This is accomplished due to measureless past instances of the bodhi resolve in gathering in all beings;

This is accomplished due to measureless past instances of pure and especially supreme aspiration;
This is accomplished due to measureless past instances of great kindness and great compassion devoted to rescuing and protecting all beings;
This is accomplished due to measureless past instances of continuously implemented conduct and vows;
This is accomplished due to measureless past cultivation of merit and wisdom with insatiable resolve;
This is accomplished due to measureless past offerings to buddhas and teaching of beings;
This is accomplished due to measureless past uses of wisdom and skillful means on the path of purity;
This is accomplished due to measureless past accumulation of a treasury of pure meritorious qualities;
This is accomplished due to measureless past uses of path-adorning wisdom; and
This is accomplished due to measureless past penetrating comprehensions of Dharma's meanings.

Sons of the Buddha, it is through the complete fulfillment of measurelessly many *asaṃkhyeyas* of Dharma gateways such as these that one succeeds in becoming a *tathāgata*. Sons of the Buddha, this is just as the complete creation of the worlds of a great trichiliocosm is not accomplished solely due to a single condition or due to a single matter. Rather it is because of measurelessly many conditions and measurelessly many matters that it then and only then is created. For instance, there is the spreading forth of great clouds and the falling of the great drenching rains. There are the four kinds of spheres of wind upon which it continuously depends. What are those four? They are as follows:

The first is known as "able to retain" because of its ability to retain the waters;
The second is known as "able to dissipate" because of its ability to dissipate the great waters;
The third is known as "establishment" because it establishes all places; and
The fourth is known as "adornment" because the adornments and their distribution are all skillfully created.

All such phenomena as these arise due to beings' jointly created karma and also due to the bodhisattvas' roots of goodness which together allow all the beings therein to be able to obtain and use whatever is fitting for each of them.

Sons of the Buddha, it is because of countless causes and conditions such as these that there then occurs the creation of the worlds of a great trichiliocosm. The nature of dharmas is of this very sort. There is no one who produces them, no one who makes them, no one who knows them, and no one who creates them, and yet those worlds are still able to become completely established.

The manifestation of the Tathāgatas is also of this very sort. It is not due to but a single condition and not due to but a single matter that this circumstance is fully realized. Rather, it is due to countless causes and conditions and due to countless phenomenal characteristics that it is then able to become completely realized. In particular, in the presence of past buddhas, they have heard, absorbed, and retained the rains sent down by the great Dharma clouds. It is because of this that they were able to produce the four kinds of great wisdom wind spheres of a *tathāgata*. What are those four? They are as follows:

The first is "the remembering and never forgetting *dhāraṇī* great wisdom wind sphere" by which they are able to retain the rains from the great Dharma clouds of all *tathāgatas*;

The second is "the development of calming and contemplation great wisdom wind sphere" by which they are able to dissipate all afflictions;

The third is "the skillful dedications great wisdom wind sphere" by which they are able to completely develop all roots of goodness; and

The fourth is "the production of different immaculately pure adornments great wisdom wind sphere" by which they cause all beings they have taught in the past to acquire purified roots of goodness and then perfect the power of a *tathāgata*'s uncontaminated roots of goodness.

It is in this way that the Tathāgata brings about the realization of the universal and right enlightenment. It is in the very nature of Dharma that, in this way, even without any arising at all and without any creation at all, it is nonetheless brought to complete fulfillment.

Sons of the Buddha, this is the first of the marks of the manifestation of the Tathāgata, the Arhat, the One of Right and Universal Enlightenment. The bodhisattva-mahāsattva should know it in this way.

Moreover, Sons of the Buddha, this is just as when the great trichiliocosm is about to be created. Great clouds send down great rains known as "the vast torrential deluge" that no other place is able to absorb or able to retain aside from the great chiliocosms at such time as they are about to be created.

Sons of the Buddha, so too it is with the Tathāgata, the Arhat, the One of Right and Universal Enlightenment. He spreads forth the great Dharma clouds and rains down the great Dharma rain known as "establisher of the Tathāgata's manifestation," one that no practitioners of the two vehicles are able to absorb or retain. This is because of their narrow and inferior resolve. It is only the great bodhisattvas who are able to do so. This is because of the continuous power of their resolve.

Sons of the Buddha, this is the second of the marks of the manifestation of the Tathāgata, the Arhat, the One of Right and Universal Enlightenment. The bodhisattva-mahāsattva should know it in this way.

Moreover, Sons of the Buddha, this is just as when, due to the power of beings' karmic actions, the great clouds send down the rains, and yet, in coming, they have no place from which they come and, in going, they have no place to which they go.

So too it is with the Tathāgata, the Arhat, the One of Right and Universal Enlightenment. Due to the power of the bodhisattvas' roots of goodness, he spreads forth the great Dharma clouds and rains down the great Dharma rains even as they have no place from which they come and have no place to which they go.

Sons of the Buddha, this is the third of the marks of the manifestation of the Tathāgata, the Arhat, the One of Right and Universal Enlightenment. The bodhisattva-mahāsattva should know it in this way.

Moreover, Sons of the Buddha, this is just as when the great clouds send down the great drenching rains. There is no being anywhere in the great chiliocosm who would be able to know the number of those rain drops, and if they wished to count them, they would needlessly go insane. It is only Maheśvara, the lord of the great chiliocosm, who, because of the power of roots of goodness he cultivated in the past, is able to know this even to the extent that there would not be even a single drop about which he would not be completely clear.

Sons of the Buddha, so too it is with the Tathāgata, the Arhat, the One of Right and Universal Enlightenment. When he spreads forth the great Dharma clouds and rains down the great Dharma rain, there is no being, no *śrāvaka* disciple, and no *pratyekabuddha* who would be able to know the extent of this. Were they to even attempt to assess this through contemplation, their minds would certainly be bound to become crazed and confused. It is only the lords of all worlds, the bodhisattva-mahāsattvas, who, due to the power of their past cultivation of enlightened wisdom, could know this even to the extent that there would not be even a single passage or a single statement entering any being's mind about which they would not be completely clear.

Sons of the Buddha, this is the fourth of the marks of the manifestation of the Tathāgata, the Arhat, the One of Right and Universal Enlightenment. The bodhisattva-mahāsattva should know it in this way.

Moreover, Sons of the Buddha, this is just as when the great clouds send down their rains:

- There is a rain that falls from great clouds known as "able to extinguish" that is able to extinguish fire disasters;
- There is a rain that falls from great clouds known as "able to produce" that is able to produce great bodies of water;
- There is a rain that falls from great clouds known as "able to halt" that is able to halt great floods of water;
- There is a rain that falls from great clouds known as "able to create" that is able to create all kinds of *maṇi* jewels; and
- There is a rain that falls from great clouds known as "able to distinguish" that is able to distinguish all worlds of the great trichiliocosm.

Sons of the Buddha, so too it is with the manifestation of the Tathāgata in which he spreads forth the great Dharma clouds and rains down the great Dharma rains:

- There is a rain of great Dharma known as "able to extinguish" that is able to extinguish all beings' afflictions;
- There is a great Dharma rain known as "able to produce" that is able to produce roots of goodness in all beings;
- There is a rain of great Dharma known as "able to halt" that is able to halt all beings' view delusions;
- There is a rain of great Dharma known as "able to create" that is able to create the Dharma jewel of all-knowledge;
- And there is a rain of great Dharma known as "able to distinguish" that is able to distinguish whatever pleases the minds of all beings.

Sons of the Buddha, this is the fifth of the marks of the manifestation of the Tathāgata, the Arhat, the One of Right and Universal Enlightenment. The bodhisattva-mahāsattva should know it in this way.

Moreover, Sons of the Buddha, this is just as when a great cloud rains down rain of a single flavor and adapts to the countless differences in whatever it rains upon. So too it is with the manifestation of the Tathāgata when he rains down the waters of Dharma that have the singular flavor of great compassion with which he adapts to whatever is fitting in any given situation as he teaches the Dharma in accordance with countless differences.

Sons of the Buddha, this is the sixth of the marks of the manifestation of the Tathāgata, the Arhat, the One of Right and Universal Enlightenment. The bodhisattva-mahāsattva should know it in this way.

Moreover, Sons of the Buddha, this is just as when the great trichiliocosm is first being formed. First, the palaces of the form-realm devas are formed. Next, the palaces of the desire-realm devas are formed. And then all the dwelling places of humans and other beings are formed.

Sons of the Buddha, so too it is with the manifestation of the Tathāgata. First, he brings forth the wisdom associated with the bodhisattvas' practices. Next, he brings forth the wisdom associated with the *pratyekabuddhas'* practices. Next, he brings forth the wisdom associated with the *śrāvaka* disciples' roots of goodness and practices. And then he brings forth the wisdom associated with other beings' conditioned roots of goodness and practices.

Sons of the Buddha, this is just like when the great clouds rain down a single flavor of water and just like when, in accordance with differences in beings' roots of goodness, there are all kinds of differences in the palaces that are created. The single flavor of Dharma rain that comes forth from the Tathāgata's great compassion adapts to beings' capacities and thus possesses corresponding differences.

Sons of the Buddha, this is the seventh of the marks of the manifestation of the Tathāgata, the Arhat, the One of Right and Universal Enlightenment. The bodhisattva-mahāsattva should know it in this way.

Moreover, Sons of the Buddha, this is just as when the world is first about to be formed. A great flood arises everywhere filling the great trichiliocosm which then produces immense lotus blossoms known as "the jeweled adornments of the qualities of the Tathāgata's manifestation" which everywhere cover the surface of those waters and radiate light illuminating all worlds of the ten directions. Then, having seen these flowers, Maheśvara, the devas of the Pure Dwelling Heaven, and the others all immediately know with certitude that in this very kalpa there will be precisely just so very many buddhas that will come forth and appear in the world.[377]

Sons of the Buddha, at that time, in that very place:

There arises a sphere of wind known as "light of excellent purity" that is able to create the palaces of the form-realm devas;

There arises a sphere of wind known as "pure light adornment" that is able to create the palaces of the desire-realm devas;

There arises a sphere of wind known as "indestructibly solid and dense" that is able to create all of the greater and lesser mountain rings as well as the mountain of vajra;

There arises a sphere of wind known as "supremely lofty" that is able to create Sumeru, king of the mountains;

There arises a sphere of wind known as "immovable" that is able to create the ten great mountain kings. What are those ten? They are: Khadira Mountain, Rishi Mountain, Māra-Vanquishing Mountain, Great Māra-Vanquishing Mountain, Yugaṃdhara Mountain, Nemiṃdhara Mountain, Mucilinda Mountain, Mahāmucilinda Mountain, Incense Mountain, and Snow Mountain.

There arises a sphere of wind known as "stable abiding" that is able to create the great earth;

There arises a sphere of wind known as "adornment" that is able to create the palaces of the earthly devas, the palaces of the dragons, and the palaces of the *gandharvas*;

There arises a sphere of wind known as "endless treasury" that is able to create all the great oceans throughout the worlds of the great trichiliocosm;

There arises a sphere of wind known as "universal light treasury" that is able to create all the *maṇi* jewels throughout the worlds of the great trichiliocosm; and

There arises a sphere of wind known as "solid root" that is able to create all the wish-fulfilling trees.

Sons of the Buddha, the waters of a single flavor rained down from the great clouds has no distinctions. It is because of differences in beings' roots of goodness that the spheres of wind are different and it is because of differences in the spheres of wind that there are differences in the worlds.

Sons of the Buddha, so too it is with the manifestation of the Tathāgata. Perfectly replete in all meritorious qualities and roots of goodness, he emanates the light of unexcelled great wisdom known as "the inconceivable wisdom that prevents the severance of the lineage of the *tathāgatas*." It everywhere illuminates all worlds of the ten directions and bestows on all bodhisattvas the prediction that all *tathāgatas'* will give them their summit-anointing consecrations after which they will attain right enlightenment and appear in the world [as buddhas].

Sons of the Buddha, in association with the manifestation of the Tathāgata:

There is also a light of unexcelled great wisdom known as "immaculately pure" that is able to produce the Tathāgata's uncontaminated and inexhaustible wisdom;

There is also a light of unexcelled great wisdom known as "universal illumination" that is able to produce the Tathāgata's inconceivable wisdom which everywhere enters the Dharma realm;

There is also a light of unexcelled great wisdom known as "sustainer of the Buddha's lineage" that is able to produce the Tathāgata's power to remain unshaken;

There is also a light of unexcelled great wisdom known as "utterly transcendent indestructibility" that is able to produce the Tathāgata's fearless and indestructible wisdom;

There is also a light of unexcelled great wisdom known as "all spiritual superknowledges" that is able to produce the Tathāgata's exclusive dharmas and the wisdom of all-knowledge;

There is also a light of unexcelled great wisdom known as "generating transformations" that is able to produce the Tathāgata's wisdom which prevents the loss or destruction of beings' roots of goodness acquired by seeing him, hearing him, or drawing near to him;

There is also a light of unexcelled great wisdom known as "universal adaptation" that is able to produce the Tathāgata's body endowed with inexhaustible merit and wisdom which does whatever is beneficial for all beings;

There is also a light of unexcelled great wisdom known as "interminable" that is able to produce the Tathāgata's extremely profound and sublime wisdom which, through those who are enlightened by it, prevents the lineage of the Three Jewels from ever being cut off;

There is also a light of unexcelled great wisdom known as "various adornments" that is able to produce the Tathāgata's body adorned with the major marks and subsidiary signs which causes all beings encountering it to be filled with joyous delight; and

There is also a light of unexcelled great wisdom known as "indestructible" that is able to produce the Tathāgata's extraordinary and supreme life span which is as endlessly enduring as the Dharma realm and the realms of empty space.

Sons of the Buddha, the Tathāgata's waters with the single flavor of the great compassion are free of any discriminations. It is because beings' aspirations and predilections differ and because the nature of their faculties each differ that there then arise the various types of great wisdom wind spheres which cause the bodhisattvas to perfect the dharmas of the Tathāgata's manifestation.

Sons of the Buddha, the great wisdom sphere of all *tathāgatas'* identical essential nature produces all different kinds of wisdom light. Sons of the Buddha, you should all realize that, from the Tathāgata's single flavor of liberation, countlessly many different kinds of inconceivable meritorious qualities are produced. Beings think, "This is a something created by the Tathāgata's spiritual powers." However, Sons of the Buddha, this is not something created by the Tathāgata's spiritual powers.

Sons of the Buddha, it is utterly impossible that even a single bodhisattva might be able to acquire even a small amount of the Tathāgata's wisdom without having already planted roots of goodness in the presence of buddhas. It is only through the power of all buddhas' awesome virtue that any being is enabled to perfect any of the Buddha's meritorious qualities. And yet the Buddha, the Tathāgata, remains free of any discriminations. In this, there is no creation, no destruction, no agent of creative action, or any dharma of creation.

Sons of the Buddha, this is the eighth of the marks of the manifestation of the Tathāgata, the Arhat, the One of Right and Universal Enlightenment. The bodhisattva-mahāsattva should know it in this way.

Moreover, Sons of the Buddha, this is just as when, in reliance on empty space, there arise four wind spheres that are able to support the sphere of water. What are those four? The first is known as "stable abiding," the second is known as "forever abiding," the third is known as "ultimate," and the fourth is known as "solid."

These four spheres of wind are able to support the sphere of water and the sphere of water is able to support the great earth and prevent it from disintegrating. Therefore it is said that the sphere of earth depends on the sphere of water, the sphere of water depends on the spheres of wind, the spheres of wind depend on empty space, and empty space has nothing that it depends on. Although it has nothing upon which it depends, it enables the stable abiding of the entire great trichiliocosm.

Sons of the Buddha, so too it is with the manifestation of the Tathāgata, for it is in reliance on the light of unimpeded wisdom that the Buddha's four kinds of great wisdom wind spheres arise which are able to support all beings' roots of goodness. What are those four? They are:

The great wisdom wind sphere that everywhere attracts beings and causes them to be delighted;

The great wisdom wind sphere that establishes right Dharma and causes all beings to be pleased;

The great wisdom wind sphere that preserves and protects all beings' roots of goodness; and

The great wisdom wind sphere that possesses all skillful means and enables the penetrating comprehension of the realm that is free of the contaminants.

These are the four.

Sons of the Buddha, all of the buddhas, the *bhagavats*, use the great kindness in rescuing and protecting all beings and use the great compassion in liberating all beings. Their great kindness and great compassion bestow benefit on everyone everywhere. Even so, the great kindness and the great compassion rely on proficiency in the use of great skillful means. Proficiency in the use of great skillful means relies on the manifestation of the Tathāgata. The manifestation of the Tathāgata relies on the light of unimpeded wisdom. The light of unimpeded wisdom has nothing that it relies on.

Sons of the Buddha, this is the ninth of the marks of the manifestation of the Tathāgata, the Arhat, the One of Right and Universal Enlightenment. The bodhisattva-mahāsattva should know it in this way.

Moreover, Sons of the Buddha, this is just as when, after the great trichiliocosm has been completely formed, benefit is bestowed on the many different kinds of beings, for instance: water-coursing beings obtain the benefit of water; earth-coursing beings obtain the benefit of land; palace-dwelling beings obtain the benefit of palaces; and space-dwelling beings obtain the benefit of space.

So too it is with the manifestation of the Tathāgata which bestows many different kinds of benefit on countless beings, for instance:

Those who see the Buddha and experience joyous delight acquire that benefit of joyous delight;

Those who abide in the pure moral precepts acquire the benefit of the pure moral precepts;

Those who abide in the *dhyāna* absorptions or in the immeasurable minds acquire the benefit of the *āryas'* great world-transcending spiritual superknowledges;

Those who abide in the light of the Dharma gateways acquire the benefit of the indestructibility of cause and effect; and

Those who abide in the light of the nonexistence of anything at all acquire the benefit of the indestructibility of all dharmas.

Therefore it is said that the manifestation of the Tathāgata benefits all the countlessly many beings.

Sons of the Buddha, this is the tenth of the marks of the manifestation of the Tathāgata, the Arhat, the One of Right and Universal Enlightenment. The bodhisattva-mahāsattva should know it in this way.

Sons of the Buddha, as for the bodhisattva-mahāsattva:

If he knows the manifestation of the Tathāgatas, then he knows their measurelessness;

If he knows their perfection of the immeasurable practices, then he knows their vastness;

If he knows their universal presence throughout the ten directions, then he knows they have no coming or going;

If he knows their transcendence of birth, abiding, and destruction, then he knows the nonexistence of any practicing or anything that is practiced;

If he knows their transcendence of the mind, the intellect, and consciousness, then he knows they have no body;

If he knows their similarity to empty space, then he knows their uniform equality;

If he knows that all beings have no self, then he knows their endlessness;

If he knows their endless presence everywhere in all *kṣetras*, then he knows their irreversibility;

If he knows they are never cut off even to the end future time, then he knows their indestructibility;

If he knows the Tathāgatas' wisdom is free of any polar opposites, then he knows their non-duality; and

If he knows the uniformly equal contemplation of the conditioned and the unconditioned, then he knows that all beings acquire benefit because the Tathāgatas' dedication of their original vows to them is fulfilled with sovereign mastery.

At that time, wishing to restate the meaning of this, Samantabhadra Bodhisattva-mahāsattva then spoke these verses:

The great hero possessed of the ten powers is the most unsurpassable.
Comparable to space, he is the peer of even the peerless.
His sphere of action is measurelessly vast and
his meritorious qualities are foremost, surpassing any in the world.

The Ten-Powered One's qualities are boundless and measureless
and such that the mind's reflections cannot reach.
Even a single Dharma gateway of the Lion Among Men
is such that no being could ever understand it even in a *koṭī* of kalpas.

If the lands throughout the ten directions were all ground to dust,
perhaps one might still be able to calculate the number of dust motes.
Still, even in ten million *koṭīs* of kalpas, no one could describe
the number of qualities creating but a single hair of the Tathāgata.

Just as if someone took up a ruler attempting to measure empty space
while someone else followed along and recorded his calculations,
they would still never be able to find the boundaries of space,
so too would it be in trying to fathom the Tathāgata's sphere of action.

Perhaps there might be someone able in but a single *kṣaṇa*'s instant
to know the minds of all beings throughout the three periods of time.
Still, even if he spent kalpas as numerous as all beings,
he could still never know the nature of but one thought of the Buddha.

Just as the Dharma realm pervades all things,
even as it cannot be seen and seized upon as being all things,
so too it is with the sphere of action of one possessing the ten powers,
for, although it pervades all things, it is not the case that it is all things.

True suchness transcends the false, is constantly quiescent,
is neither produced nor destroyed, and is universally pervasive.
So too it is with all buddhas' sphere of action:
Their essential nature, uniformly equal, is not increased or decreased.

Just as ultimate reality's limits are no limits at all and it is everywhere
in the three times yet is not identical with those universal phenomena,
so too it is with the Master Guide's sphere of action
which is unimpeded in its pervasion of the three periods of times.

The nature of dharmas is free of any actions, unchanging,
and, like empty space, it is fundamentally pure.
All buddhas' nature is pure in this very same way:
Its basic nature, not a nature, transcends existence and nonexistence.

The nature of dharmas does not reside in verbal discourse.
It has no speech, transcends speech, and is constantly quiescent.
So too it is with the sphere of action of he who has the ten powers,
for no literary phrasing could ever describe it.

He has completely fathomed the quiescence of all dharmas' nature
and he is like a bird flying through the sky without leaving any tracks.
It is by the power of original vows that he manifests his form bodies,
allowing all to witness the Tathāgata's great spiritual transformations.

If one aspires to know the Buddha's sphere of action,
he should so purify his mind as to make it like empty space,
should abandon erroneous perceptions and all forms of grasping,
and thus allow the mind's pursuit of its aims to always be unimpeded.

Therefore, Sons of the Buddha, you should all listen well
as I use a few analogies to explain a buddha's sphere of action.
Although the qualities of the Ten-Powered One are measureless,
I shall now only briefly describe them in order to awaken beings.

I shall now describe all the roots of goodness associated with
all spheres of action manifested by the Master Guide
in physical actions, verbal actions, and mental actions,
from his turning the wheel of the sublime Dharma to his *parinirvāṇa.*

Just as it is with the initial establishment of the world
in which it is not by a single cause or condition that it can be formed,
but rather there are countless skillful means and causes and conditions
that bring about the establishment of this great trichiliocosm,

so too it is with the manifestation of the Tathāgata,
for it is only by countless meritorious qualities that it may then occur.
One may know the number of atoms in a *kṣetra* or of beings' thoughts,
but no one can fathom all the causes of the Ten-Powered One's birth.

Just as, at the beginning of a kalpa, clouds send down drenching rains
and then give rise to four kinds of great wind spheres which,
together with beings' roots of goodness and the bodhisattvas' powers,
all establish the secure abiding of the trichiliocosm,

so too it is with the Dharma clouds of the Ten-Powered One
that produce the wisdom wind spheres and the purified mind which,
together with past dedications made for the benefit of all beings,
all guide and cause the establishment of this unsurpassed fruition.

Just as when the great rains known as "the vast torrential deluge" fall,
there is no place able to take it in and contain it
with the sole exception of that time prior to the world's formation
when it purifies space together with the power of the great winds,

so too it is with the manifestation of the Tathāgata
who everywhere rains the Dharma rain that fills the Dharma realm.
Of all those of inferior mind, there are none who are able to retain it,
for it can only be retained by those with pure and vast minds.

Just as when great drenching rains fall from the sky,
they have no place from which they come, no place to which they go,
and those who create them and experience them are both nonexistent,
even as they naturally everywhere soak everything in this way,

so too it is with the Dharma rains of the Ten-Powered One
which have no going, no coming, and no one who creates them.
His original practices are the cause along with bodhisattvas' powers.
Hence all who have great minds then listen to and absorb them.

Just as, when the clouds in the sky pour down great rains,
there is no one able to count all its raindrops
with the sole exception of the trichiliocosm's sovereign king,[378] who,
by the power of his meritorious qualities, entirely knows all this,

so too it is with the Well Gone One's Dharma rain
which, even among all beings, there are none who can measure it
with the sole exception of those with sovereign mastery in the world
who clearly perceive all this as if looking at jewels in their own palms.

Just as clouds in the sky pouring down great rains can extinguish,
can generate, and can also put an end to things while also being able
to bring about the production of all kinds of precious jewels,
even as they are able to distinguish everything in the trichiliocosm,

so too it is with the Dharma rains of the Ten-Powered One
which extinguish delusions, produce goodness, put an end to views,
cause the creation of the jewels of all-knowledge,
and distinguish all the mental inclinations of beings.

Just as the rain falling from the sky is of but a single flavor
which then adapts to the differences in whatever it falls upon,
how could it be in the nature of that rain to have discriminations?
Still, in accordance with beings' differences, the Dharma is like this.

The Tathāgata's Dharma rain is neither the same nor different,
It is uniformly equal, quiescent, and free of discriminations.
Still, according with the many different distinctions in those taught,
it naturally manifests boundlessly many characteristics such as these.

Just as when the world is first being formed,
there is first the formation of the palaces of the form-realm devas,
then those of the desire-realm devas, then the human abodes,
and, finally, the *gandharvas'* palaces are the very last to be formed,

so too it is with the manifestation of the Tathāgata,
wherein first brought forth are the boundless bodhisattva practices,
then those used in teaching *pratyekabuddhas* delighting in stillness,
then those for the *śrāvaka* sangha, and, last, those for other beings.

On first seeing the auspicious sign of the lotus blossoms, the devas,
realizing the Buddha is about to appear, are filled with joyous delight.
The force of water interacting with wind gives rise to the world,[379]
whereupon its palaces, mountains, and rivers are all then established.

The great illumination from the Tathāgata's goodness in previous lives
skillfully distinguishes the bodhisattvas and gives them predictions.
The essential nature of all the wisdom spheres is pure
and they are each able to reveal the Dharma of all buddhas.

Just as the forests exist in reliance on the earth,
the earth achieves its indestructibility in reliance on water,
the spheres of water rely on the wind, the wind relies on space,
and the space between them has nothing on which it depends,

so, too, all of the Buddha's dharmas rely on kindness and compassion,
kindness and compassion in turn rely on establishing skillful means,
skillful means rely on knowledge, knowledge relies on wisdom,
and the body of unimpeded wisdom has nothing on which it relies.

Just as, once the world has already become established,
all beings then acquire their respective benefits
so that those dwelling on land or in water and the space dwellers,
bipeds, and quadrupeds all then receive benefits,

so too it is with the manifestation of the Dharma King
when all beings then acquire their respective benefits.
Whether there are those who see, hear, or draw near to him,
they are all enabled to extinguish all their delusions and afflictions.

The dharmas of the Tathāgata's manifestation are boundless,
such that none of the world's deluded beings could know them.
In order to awaken all sentient beings,
amidst matters with no analogies, I have here set forth their analogies.

Sons of the Buddha, how is it that all bodhisattva-mahāsattvas should see the body of the Tathāgata, the Arhat, the One of Right and Universal Enlightenment? Sons of the Buddha, all bodhisattva-mahāsattvas should see the Tathāgata's body in countless places. How is this so? All bodhisattva-mahāsattvas should not see the Tathāgata in but a single dharma, in but a single phenomenon, in but a single body, in but a single land, or in but a single being, but rather they should see the Tathāgata everywhere and in all places.

Sons of the Buddha, he is like empty space which reaches everywhere to all places with and without form, but which still does not either reach or fail to reach them. How is this so? This is because empty space is nonphysical. So too it is with the body of the Tathāgata which pervades all places, pervades all beings, pervades all dharmas, and pervades all lands, but which still does not either reach them or fail to reach them. And how is this so? This is because the body of the Tathāgata is nonphysical. He only manifests his body for the sake of beings.

Sons of the Buddha, this is the first of the marks of the Tathāgata's body. All bodhisattva-mahāsattvas should perceive it in this way.

Furthermore, Sons of the Buddha, just as empty space is vast and formless and yet is able to reveal all forms even as that empty space has no discriminations and also has no conceptual proliferation, so too it is with the Tathāgata's body. With the pervasively illuminating brightness of his wisdom light, he enables all beings to accomplish all the karmic works which establish their worldly and world-transcending roots of goodness, and yet the Tathāgata's body remains free of all discriminations and all conceptual proliferation. And how is this the case? This is because, from the very beginning to the present, he has forever severed all attachments and all forms of conceptual proliferation.

Sons of the Buddha, this is the second of the marks of the Tathāgata's body. All bodhisattva-mahāsattvas should perceive it in this way.

Furthermore, Sons of the Buddha, this is just as when the sun rises over the continent of Jambudvīpa, countless beings all acquire its benefits, namely:

It dispels darkness and creates brightness;
It transforms moisture and causes dryness;
It brings about the growth of the grasses and trees;
It ripens food grains;
Its illumination permeates empty space;
It causes the lotuses to bloom;
It allows travelers to see the road; and
It allows those who dwell there to do their work.

And why do these things occur? It is because the sun emanates measureless light which shines everywhere.

Sons of the Buddha, so too it is with the wisdom sun of the Tathāgata which, in countless matters, everywhere benefits beings, namely:

It extinguishes evil and produces goodness;
It demolishes stupidity and creates wisdom;
It rescues and protects beings with loving-kindness;
It liberates beings with great compassion;
It enables them to increase their development of the roots, powers, and limbs of enlightenment;[380]
It enables the development of deep faith and the abandonment of turbid thoughts;
It enables them to see and learn not to go against cause and effect;

It enables them to acquire the heavenly eye and see the places where they have died and been reborn;

It enables their minds to become unimpeded and hence to refrain from ruining their roots of goodness;

It enables them to become wise and cultivate the illumination by which the flower of enlightenment may bloom; and

It enables them to arouse the resolve by which they can perfect their original practices.

And why do these things occur? It is because the body of the Tathāgata's vast wisdom sun emanates measureless light that shines brightly everywhere.

Sons of the Buddha, this is the third of the marks of the Tathāgata's body. All bodhisattva-mahāsattvas should perceive it in this way.

Furthermore, Sons of the Buddha, this is just as when the sun rises over Jambudvīpa, it first illuminates all the kings of mountains such as Mount Sumeru, then illuminates the black mountains, then illuminates the high plains, and then later everywhere illuminates the entire great earth. The sun does not think, "I shall first illuminate this and I shall later illuminate that." It is only because the mountains and the earth have higher and lower terrain that this illumination occurs either earlier or later.

So too it is with the Tathāgata, the Arhat, the One of Right and Universal Enlightenment, for, having fully developed the sphere of boundless Dharma realm wisdom, he always emanates the light of unimpeded wisdom which:

First illuminates the bodhisattva-mahāsattvas who are like the great kings of mountains;

Next illuminates the *pratyekabuddhas*;

Next illuminates *śrāvaka* disciples;

Next illuminates the beings possessed of definite roots of goodness, revealing vast wisdom to them in accordance with their mental capacities; and

Later on everywhere illuminates all beings, including even those fixated on wrong actions[381] so that it everywhere reaches even all of them in order that they may create causes and conditions for future benefit through which they will be caused to become fully ripened.

In doing so, that light of the Tathāgata's great wisdom sun does not think: "I should first illuminate the bodhisattvas who cultivate the great practices, and then should illuminate the others until, at the very last, I should illuminate the beings fixated on wrong actions." Rather it simply emanates its light that then equally and universally illuminates in a way that is unimpeded, free of all obstacles, and free of any sort of discriminations.

Sons of the Buddha, just as the sun and moon appear in accordance with the time and everywhere illuminate the great mountains and deep valleys without any selfishness in doing so, so too it is with the Tathāgata's wisdom. Rather, it everywhere illuminates everyone without making any discriminations. As it accords with differences in beings' faculties and aspirations, the light of wisdom manifests all kinds of differences.

Sons of the Buddha, this is the fourth of the marks of the Tathāgata's body. All bodhisattva-mahāsattvas should perceive it in this way.

Furthermore, Sons of the Buddha, this is just as when the sun rises, beings who are born blind have never been able to see it because they have no visual faculty. Although they have never been able to see it, they are still benefited by the sunlight. How is this so? This is because, on account of it, they are able to recognize the day, the night, and the seasons and put to use all different kinds of clothing, drink, and food which cause their bodies to remain well adapted and free from the many kinds of illnesses.

So too it is with the Tathāgata's wisdom sun. Those who have no faith, who have no understanding, who violate moral precepts, who denigrate [right] views, or who live by wrong livelihoods—because they do not have the eye of faith, they are of the same sort as those who are born blind. Hence they do not see the buddhas' wisdom sun. But, although they fail to see the buddhas' wisdom sun, they are still benefited by their sun of wisdom. And how is this so? This is because of the Buddha's awesome power to enable the complete melting away of all those beings' physical sufferings, afflictions, and causes of future suffering.

Sons of the Buddha, the Tathāgata [has the following kinds of lights]:

He has a light known as "accumulation of all meritorious qualities";

He has a light known as "universal illumination of everything";

He has a light known as "pure and freely produced illumination";

He has a light known as "emanation of the great sublime sound";

He has a light known as "universal comprehension of all language dharmas by which he delights others";

He has a light known as "manifestation of freely invoked spheres of experience by which he forever severs all doubts";

He has a light known as "freely invoked universal illumination of the wisdom of non-abiding";
He has a light known as "freely invoked wisdom that forever cuts off all conceptual proliferation";
He has a light known as "sublime sounds emanated in accordance with whatever is fitting"; and
He has a light known as "emanation of pure and freely produced sounds which adorn lands and ripen beings."

Sons of the Buddha, every one of the Tathāgata's pores emanates a thousand light rays such as these of which five hundred light rays everywhere illuminate the regions below and five hundred light rays everywhere illuminate the various congregations of bodhisattvas in the many different abodes of the buddhas in the many different kinds of *kṣetras* in the regions above. When those bodhisattvas see these light rays, they all at once acquire the Tathāgata's spheres of experience in which they are possessed of ten heads, ten pairs of eyes, ten pairs of ears, ten noses, ten tongues, ten bodies, ten pairs of hands, ten pairs of feet, the ten grounds, and the ten types of knowledge, all of which are completely purified. All of those bodhisattvas are ones who had previously perfected all the stations and all the grounds. On seeing those light rays, they achieve even greater levels of purity, accomplish the complete ripening of all their roots of goodness, and progress toward the realization of all-knowledge.

Those who abide in the two vehicles extinguish all their defilements. Another category of beings, those born blind, their bodies having experienced feelings of happiness, their minds then also become purified, pliant, well-trained, and capable of cultivating mindfulness and wisdom.[382] All the beings in the destinies of the hell realms, the hungry ghost realms, and the animal realms become happy and liberated from their many kinds of sufferings. Then, at the end of their lives, they are all reborn among the devas or within the human realm.

Sons of the Buddha, all those beings remain unaware and do not know due to which causes and conditions or because of what kinds of spiritual powers they came to be reborn here. Those born blind think, "I am a Brahma Heaven deva," or "I am an emanation of Brahmā."

At this time, the Tathāgata, abiding in the samādhi of universal sovereign mastery, sends forth sixty varieties of sublime voices[383] by which he tells them: "You are not Brahma Heaven devas, are not emanations of Brahmā, and are also not the creations of either **Śakra** or the World-protecting Heavenly Kings. All of this has occurred because of the awesome spiritual powers of the Tathāgata."

Once those beings hear these statements, due to the Buddha's spiritual powers, they all acquire the knowledge of their previous lifetimes and then feel great joyous delight. Because their minds feel joyous delight, they then spontaneously emanate clouds of *udumbara* flowers, clouds of perfumes, clouds of music, clouds of robes, clouds of canopies, clouds of banners, clouds of pennants, clouds of powdered incense, clouds of jewels, clouds of lion banners and half-moon towers, clouds of praise songs, and clouds of many different types of adornments, all of which they offer up to the Tathāgata with reverential minds. Why do they do so? This is because these beings have acquired purified eyes. The Tathāgata then bestows on them predictions of their future attainment of *anuttara-samyak-saṃbodhi.*

Sons of the Buddha, it is in ways such as these that the Tathāgata's wisdom sun benefits beings born blind, thereby enabling them to acquire roots of goodness that then become fully ripened.

Sons of the Buddha, this is the fifth of the marks of the Tathāgata's body. All bodhisattva-mahāsattvas should perceive it in this way.

Furthermore, Sons of the Buddha, this is comparable to the moon's four extraordinarily special and unprecedented dharmas. What are those four? They are:

First, it outshines the light of all the other stars and constellations;
Second, it displays its waning and waxing in accordance with the time;
Third, there is no still and clear body of water on the continent of Jambudvīpa in which its reflection does not appear; and
Fourth, to all who see it, it appears directly before their own eyes, and yet the orb of the moon is free of any discriminations or conceptual proliferation.

Sons of the Buddha, so too it is with the moon of the Tathāgata's body, for it has four extraordinarily special and unprecedented dharmas. What are those four? They are:

It outshines all *śrāvaka* disciples, *pratyekabuddhas,* and others in the congregations of those still in training or beyond training;
In accordance with what is fitting, it manifests with life spans of varying duration even as, in this circumstance, the Tathāgata's body itself does not undergo any increase or decrease;
Of all the pure-minded beings in all worlds who have the capacity to realize bodhi, there are none to whom his reflected image does not appear; and

Of all beings who gaze with admiration upon it, they all feel that, "The Tathāgata is appearing only before me." Then, in accordance their mental dispositions, he speaks Dharma for them. In accordance with the particular ground on which they dwell, he enables them to achieve liberation. And, in accordance with those who should receive transformative teaching, he then causes them to see the body of a buddha. Yet the Tathāgata's body does not engage in any discriminations and does not engage in any conceptual proliferation as the benefits it bestows all achieve their ultimate ends.

Sons of the Buddha, this is the sixth of the marks of the Tathāgata's body. All bodhisattva-mahāsattvas should perceive it in this way.

Furthermore, Sons of the Buddha, this is just as when the great trichiliocosm's king of the Great Brahma Heaven uses a minor expedient to manifest his body everywhere throughout the worlds of a great chiliocosm. All of those beings then see the Brahma Heaven king manifesting directly before them, even as this Brahma Heaven king still does not divide his body and does not have many different bodies.

Sons of the Buddha, so too it is with the buddhas, the Tathāgatas. They do not engage in any discriminations, do not engage in any conceptual proliferation, do not divide their bodies, and do not have many different bodies. Even so, adapting to beings' mental dispositions, they manifest their bodies while still not thinking to create some particular number of bodies.

Sons of the Buddha, this is the seventh of the marks of the Tathāgata's body. All bodhisattva-mahāsattvas should perceive it in this way.

Furthermore, Sons of the Buddha, this is just as when some physician king who knows well the many kinds of medicines as well as the many kinds of mantras and treatises so that, of all the medicines on the continent of Jambudvīpa, there are none he does not extensively use.

Moreover, because of skillful means he has created through the power of roots of goodness from previous lives and the power of great bright mantras, among the beings who see him, there are none whose diseases are not cured.

When that great king of physicians realizes that his life is about to come to an end, he thinks, "After I die, all the beings will have no one on whom they can rely. It would be fitting if I were to manifest an expedient for them." Then that physician king mixes together a medicinal potion with which he smears his body and also uses the power of bright mantras to preserve it so that, after his death, his body does not disintegrate, does not atrophy, does not wither. Consequently his appearance and the experience of seeing him are no different than before and, whichever diseases come for treatment, they are all able to be cured.

Sons of the Buddha, so too it is with the Tathāgata, the Arhat, the One of Right and Universal Enlightenment, the unsurpassed king of physicians who for countless hundreds of thousands of *koṭīs* of *nayutas* of kalpas has formulated the medicines of Dharma, has fulfilled the cultivation and study of all skillful uses of expedient means, and has perfected the powers of the great bright mantras. He is well able to eliminate the diseases of all beings' afflictions and, moreover, he dwells for a life span that continues for countless kalpas during which his body remains pristine and there is no reflective deliberation and no functional activity even as he never ceases to carry forth all the buddha works in such a way that the affliction-based diseases of all beings who see him can all be melted away.

Sons of the Buddha, this is the eighth of the marks of the Tathāgata's body. All bodhisattva-mahāsattvas should perceive it in this way.

Furthermore, Sons of the Buddha, this is just as it is in the case of an immense *maṇi* jewel found in the great ocean known as "the *vairocana* treasury that collects all light." If any beings contact its light, they all turn that same color, if any beings see it, their eyes become purified, and wherever its light shines, it rains *maṇi* jewels known as "happiness" jewels which cause all beings there to be relieved of suffering and experience well-being.

Sons of the Buddha, so too it is with the bodies of the Tathāgatas, for they constitute a great accumulation of jewels and a treasury of all meritorious qualities and great wisdom. If any beings contact the wisdom light emanating from the jewel of the Buddha's body, they become the same color as the Buddha's body and, if they so much as see it, their Dharma eyes then become purified. Wherever his light shines, it causes all beings to leave the suffering of poverty and ultimately enables them to fully possess the bliss of the Buddha's bodhi.

Sons of the Buddha, the Tathāgata's Dharma body is free of discriminations and also free of conceptual proliferation and yet it is still everywhere able to perform the Buddha's great works for the sake of all beings.

Sons of the Buddha, this is the ninth of the marks of the Tathāgata's body. All bodhisattva-mahāsattvas should perceive it in this way.

Furthermore, Sons of the Buddha, this is just as it is in the case of an immense sovereign wish-fulfilling *maṇi* jewel found in the great ocean known as "treasury of the entire world's adornments" which embodies the complete perfection of a million meritorious qualities and, wherever it is located, it enables the elimination of all beings' disastrous calamities and the fulfillment of whatever they wish for. However, this sovereign wish-fulfilling *maṇi* jewel is not something that beings possessed of but a small amount of merit would ever be able to see.

So too it is with the sovereign wish-fulfilling jewel of the Tathāgata's body known as "able to gladden all beings." If any beings see his body, hear his name, or praise his qualities, they are all thereby enabled to forever leave behind the sorrows and calamities of *saṃsāra*. If all beings in all worlds simultaneously and single-mindedly wished to see the Tathāgata, he would allow them all to see him and would ensure that all their wishes were fulfilled.

Sons of the Buddha, the Buddha's body is not something that beings possessed of a small amount of merit would be able to see, the sole exception to this being those whom the Tathāgata should use his freely invoked spiritual powers to train. If there are any beings who, because of seeing the Buddha's body, could then plant roots of goodness and even bring them to full maturity, he would then enable them to see the body of the Tathāgata.

Sons of the Buddha, this is the tenth of the marks of the Tathāgata's body. All bodhisattva-mahāsattvas should perceive them in these ways, doing so for these reasons:

Because their minds are measureless and pervade the ten directions;
Because their practice is as unimpeded as empty space itself;
Because they everywhere enter the Dharma realm;
Because they abide in the very apex of reality;
Because they are beyond either production or destruction;
Because they dwell equally in all three periods of time;
Because they have forever abandoned all discriminations;
Because they abide in vows that extend to the very end of future time;
Because they purify all worlds; and
Because they adorn the bodies of every buddha.

At that time, wishing to again clarify the meaning of this, Samantabhadra Bodhisattva-mahāsattva then spoke these verses:

Just as empty space pervades the ten directions,
reaching all that has form, is formless, exists, or does not exist
including the three times, beings' bodies, and lands,
thus being everywhere present and boundless in this way,

so too it is with the true body of the Buddha
which, in all the Dharma realm, has no place it does not pervade.
Although it cannot be seen and cannot be grasped,
it still manifests forms for the sake of teaching beings.

Just as empty space cannot be seized upon
even as it everywhere allows beings to do the many kinds of actions
and does not, in so doing, think, "This is what I am now doing,
this is how I am doing it, and these are those for whom I am doing it,"

so too it is with the physical actions of all buddhas by which
they everywhere cause the many beings to cultivate good dharmas,
for the Tathāgata never engages in any discrimination such as:
"I am now doing various kinds of things for them."

Just as when the sun rises over Jambudvīpa
and its light dispels all darkness without exception
and the mountains, trees, ponds, lotuses, and the many earthly beings
of many different categories and types all thereby receive its benefits,

so too it is with the rising of the Buddha sun
which begets and grows the many good actions of humans and devas
and forever dispels delusion's darkness so they attain wisdom's light
and always receive every happiness bestowed by the Glorious One.

Just as when the light of the sun first appears,
it first illuminates the mountain kings, then the other mountains,
and only afterward illuminates the high plains and the great earth
even as, in all of this, the sun has never had any discriminations,

so too it is with the radiant light of the Well Gone One
which first illuminates bodhisattvas, then the *pratyekabuddhas*,
and only afterward illuminates the *śrāvaka* disciples and other beings
even as, from the start, the Buddha has had no movement of thought.

Just as those born blind never see the sun
yet the sunlight still serves their benefit,
causes them to know time and season, to receive food and drink, and
to forever abandon the many calamities and gain physical security,

so too it is when beings without faith do not see the Buddha,
yet the Buddha still provides for their benefit,
so that those who hear his name or are touched by his light,
because of this, eventually achieve the realization of bodhi.

Just as when the purely shining moon abiding up in space
is able to outshine the many stars and show its waxing and waning
as it appears reflected in all the many bodies of water
while all who gaze upon it see it as appearing directly before them,

So too, the brightly shining moon of the Tathāgata
is able to outshine other vehicles and appear for a long or short time
as he manifests in the waters of devas' and humans' pure minds
so that they all feel he is appearing directly before them.

Just as the Brahma Heaven King abiding in his palace
everywhere manifests in all the chiliocosm's abodes of Brahmā
so that all humans and devas are able to see him in all those places,
even as, in truth, he never divides his bodies or goes there,

so too it is with the Buddha's manifestation of his bodies
that have no place throughout the ten directions they do not pervade
as he displays so countlessly many bodies they cannot be described
even as he still does not divide his body or engage in discriminations.

Just as with the physician king skilled in the art of healing formulas
who, if anyone but saw him, their illnesses were all healed—
although his life had ended, having smeared his body with potions,
he was still able to continue performing all his works just as before—

so too it is with the supreme king of physicians
who is fully possessed of both skillful means and all-knowledge—
Because of his past marvelous practices, he manifests buddha bodies
which, if beings but see them, their afflictions are then extinguished.

Just as when there is a sovereign jewel in the ocean
which everywhere emanates countless rays of light
that, when beings are touched by them, they become the same color,
and, when they see them, their eyes are purified,

so too it is with the supreme king of all jewels who,
when beings are touched by his light, they all become the same color,
and when they see it, their five eyes all open so that it dispels
the darkness of sense objects and they dwell on the buddha ground.

Just as it is with a wish-fulfilling *maṇi* jewel
which completely fulfills all wishes for whatever is sought
even as beings of little merit are unable to even see it—
but it is not that the king of jewels discriminates against them.

So too it is with the Well Gone One, the King of Jewels,
who fulfills all wishes for whatever is sought
even as beings without faith are unable to even see the Buddha—
but it is not that the mind of the Well Gone One has forsaken them.

Sons of the Buddha, how is it that the bodhisattva-mahāsattva should know the voice of the Tathāgata, the Arhat, the One of Right and Universal Enlightenment? Sons of the Buddha, the bodhisattva-mahāsattva should know it in these ways:

He should know the Tathāgata's voice as reaching everywhere because it everywhere pervades all the countless other sounds;

He should know the Tathāgata's voice as enabling everyone to be delighted by conforming to their mental dispositions because his explanations of Dharma are clear and ultimate;

He should know the Tathāgata's voice as enabling everyone to be delighted by adapting to their resolute beliefs because their minds are then able to experience clarity and coolness;

He should know the Tathāgata's voice as teaching in a manner that never misses the right time because those who should listen to it are all able to hear it;

He should know the Tathāgata's voice as neither produced nor destroyed because it is like a resounding echo;

He should know the Tathāgata's voice as having no subjective agent of actions because it arises due to his having cultivated all the karmic works;

He should know the Tathāgata's voice as extremely profound because it is difficult to fathom;

He should know the Tathāgata's voice as free of any error or distortion because it arises from the Dharma realm itself;

He should know the Tathāgata's voice as never ending because it everywhere penetrates the Dharma realm; and

He should know the Tathāgata's voice as unchanging because it reaches the very ultimate.

Sons of the Buddha, the bodhisattva-mahāsattva should know the Tathāgata's voice as neither finite nor infinite, as neither possessed of nor devoid of any subjective agent, and as neither providing nor not providing instruction. And why is this? Sons of the Buddha, just as, when the world is about to be destroyed, even in the absence of any subjective agent and even in the absence of any deliberate action, there spontaneously arise four verbal declarations. What are those four?

The first of those voices says: "You should all come to know the happiness of the first *dhyāna* which leaves behind the bad aspects of the desires and surpasses the desire realm." Having heard this, beings are then naturally able to accomplish the attainment of the first *dhyāna* whereupon they relinquish their desire-realm bodies and take rebirth in the Brahma Heaven.

The second of those voices says: "You should all come to know the happiness of the second *dhyāna* which is free of initial ideation and free of mental discursiveness and which surpasses the Brahma Heaven." Having heard this, beings are then naturally able to accomplish the attainment of the second *dhyāna* whereupon they relinquish their Brahma Heaven bodies and take rebirth in the Light-and-Sound Heaven.

The third of those voices says: "You should all come to know the happiness of the third *dhyāna* which is free of faults and which surpasses the Light-and-Sound Heaven." Having heard this, beings are then naturally able to accomplish the attainment of the third *dhyāna* whereupon they relinquish their Light-and-Sound Heaven bodies and take rebirth in the Universal Purity Heaven.

The fourth of those voices says: "You should all come to know the quiescence of the fourth *dhyāna* which surpasses the Universal Purity Heaven. Having heard this, beings are then naturally able to accomplish the attainment of the fourth *dhyāna* whereupon they relinquish their Universal Purity Heaven bodies and take rebirth in the Vast Fruition Heaven.

These are the four. Sons of the Buddha, all of these voices arise without any subjective agent of action and without any deliberate effort. They arise solely by the power of beings' good karmic deeds.

Sons of the Buddha, so too it is with the voice of the Tathāgata. It arises without any subjective agent of actions, without any deliberate effort, without any making of discriminations, and neither enters nor leaves. It is solely through the power of the dharma of the Tathāgata's meritorious qualities that there arise four kinds of vast voices. What are those four?

The first of those voices says: "You should all realize that all actions[384] are freighted with sufferings, in particular: the sufferings of the hell realms, the sufferings of the animal realms, the sufferings of the hungry ghost realms, the sufferings of an absence of karmic merit, the sufferings of seizing upon the existence of a self and possessions of a self, and the sufferings associated with all bad actions. If one wishes to attain rebirth in the human or heavenly realms, one must plant roots of goodness adequate to achieve rebirth in the human or heavenly realms apart from places beset by the difficulties."[385] Having heard this, beings then abandon their inverted views, cultivate the good actions, leave the places beset by the difficulties, and then achieve rebirth in the human or heavenly realms.

The second of those voices says: "You should all realize that all actions are as ablaze with manifold sufferings as the burning hot iron pellets.[386] All actions are impermanent and are dharmas of destruction. The quiescence of nirvāṇa is the bliss of the unconditioned in which one leaves such burning heat far behind and eliminates all of the hot afflictions." Having heard this, beings then diligently cultivate good dharmas and acquire the "acquiescence in sounds" patience as it is found in the *śrāvaka*-disciple vehicle.[387]

The third of those voices says: "You should all realize that the *śrāvaka*-disciple vehicle's understanding developed by according with teachings from others produces narrow and inferior wisdom. There is also a superior vehicle known as the *pratyekabuddha* vehicle in which one becomes awakened without relying on a teacher. You should all train in it. Having heard this voice, those beings who delight in supreme paths relinquish the *śrāvaka*-disciple path and then cultivate the *pratyekabuddha* vehicle.

The fourth of those voices says: "You should all realize that, beyond the positions of the two vehicles, there is yet another superior path known as "the Great Vehicle" that is cultivated by the bodhisattvas who accord with the six *pāramitās,* never cease the bodhisattva practices, never relinquish the bodhi resolve, abide within it for countless births and deaths, and yet never weary of this. It surpasses the two vehicles and is known as "the Great Vehicle," "the foremost vehicle," "the supreme vehicle," "the most supreme vehicle," "the superior vehicle," "the unexcelled vehicle," and "the vehicle which benefits all beings." Wherever there are beings whose resolute faith is vast, whose faculties are especially sharp, who have planted roots of goodness in past lives, who are aided by the spiritual powers of the *tathāgatas,* who are possessed of supreme zeal, and who seek to acquire the fruit of buddhahood, once they have heard this voice, they then arouse the resolve to attain bodhi.

Sons of the Buddha, the Tathāgata's voice does not come forth from the body and does not come forth from the mind. Even so, it is able to benefit countless beings. Sons of the Buddha, this is the first of the marks of the Tathāgata's voice. All bodhisattva-mahāsattvas should perceive it in this way.

Furthermore, Sons of the Buddha, just as the echoes which occur due to the encounter between a mountain valley and voices have no form or appearance, cannot be seen, and have no discriminations even as they are still able to follow after everything that one says, so too it is with the Tathāgata's voice. It has no form or appearance, cannot be seen, and neither has a location nor does not have a location. It arises solely in accordance with conditions associated with beings' aspirations and understandings. Its nature is ultimately devoid of either words or instruction and is inexpressible. Sons of the Buddha, this is the second of the marks of the Tathāgata's voice. All bodhisattva-mahāsattvas should perceive it in this way.

Furthermore, Sons of the Buddha, this is just as it is with the devas who have a great Dharma drum known as "the awakener." Whenever any of the devas' sons indulge in neglectful behavior, it emanates a voice from space that calls out, saying: "You should all realize that all desire-based pleasures are impermanent, false, born of inverted views, destined to fade away in an instant, and only serve to deceive foolish common people and cause them to become affectionately attached. You must not become neglectful. If you become neglectful, you will fall into the wretched destinies, at which point, it will be too late to regret this."

Having heard this voice, those neglectful devas then become filled with worry and fearfulness and relinquish all their desire-based pleasures in their palaces, and then go to pay their respects to the heavenly king and request the Dharma for practicing the path.

Sons of the Buddha, the voices emanating from that heavenly drum have no subjective agent, no deliberate actions, no arising, and no cessation, and yet they are able to benefit countless beings.

One should realize that the Tathāgata is also just like this. Wishing to awaken neglectful beings, he emanates countless voices speaking the sounds of the sublime Dharma, namely: the voice speaking of nonattachment, the voice speaking of avoiding neglectfulness, the voice speaking of impermanence, the voice speaking of the sufferings, the voice speaking of non-self, the voice speaking of impurity, the voice speaking of quiescence, the voice speaking of nirvāṇa, the voice speaking of measureless spontaneously arising wisdom, the voice speaking of the indestructible bodhisattva practices, and the universally pervading voice speaking of the Tathāgata's ground of effortless wisdom.

He uses these voices which reach everywhere throughout the Dharma realm to then bring about their awakening. Having heard these voices, countless beings become filled with joyous delight and diligently cultivate good dharmas, whereupon each of them seeks to achieve transcendence by resort to their own vehicle. For instance, some of them cultivate the *śrāvaka*-disciple vehicle, some of them cultivate the *pratyekabuddha* vehicle, and some of them cultivate the bodhisattva's unexcelled great vehicle, and yet the voices of the Tathāgata do not abide in any particular place and do not have anything they say.

Sons of the Buddha, this is the third of the marks of the Tathāgata's voice. All bodhisattva-mahāsattvas should perceive it in this way.

Furthermore, Sons of the Buddha, this is just as it is with the Vaśavartin Heaven King's celestial palace maiden named Fine Mouth who is able to emanate a single voice from her mouth the sound of which resonates with a hundred thousand kinds of music of which each kind of music contains a hundred thousand different voices. Sons of the Buddha, as for that maiden Fine Mouth's emanation of so countlessly many voices from but a single voice—one should realize that the Tathāgata's voice is just like this, for from but a single sound, he emanates countless voices adapted to beings' different mental dispositions which then go everywhere and cause them all to understand.

Sons of the Buddha, this is the fourth of the marks of the Tathāgata's voice. All bodhisattva-mahāsattvas should perceive it in this way.

Furthermore, Sons of the Buddha, this is just as it is when the great Brahma Heaven King dwelling in the Brahma Heaven palace speaks with the voice of Brahmā and then no one in the assembly of Brahmā fails to hear this even as that voice does not go beyond that assembly and everyone in the assembly of Brahmā thinks, "The Brahma Heaven King is speaking solely to me."

So too it is with the sublime sound of the Tathāgata's voice. No one in the assembly at the site of enlightenment fails to hear it and yet it does not go beyond that congregation. Why is this so? This is because those whose faculties are not yet ripened should not hear it. Those who do hear his voice all think, "The Tathāgata, the Bhagavat, is speaking solely to me."

Sons of the Buddha, the Tathāgata's voice has no going forth or remaining and yet it is able to bring all kinds of karmic works to completion. This is the fifth of the marks of the Tathāgata's voice. All bodhisattva-mahāsattvas should perceive it in this way.

Furthermore, Sons of the Buddha, just as the many rivers' waters are all of the same flavor and yet, in accordance with different containers, those waters manifest differences without those waters thinking about this or making discriminations, so too it is with the voice of the Tathāgata which is of only a single flavor, namely the flavor of liberation. Because it adapts to differences in beings' mental capacities, it manifests countless differences and yet he does not think about this or make any discriminations in this regard.

Sons of the Buddha, this is the sixth of the marks of the Tathāgata's voice. All bodhisattva-mahāsattvas should perceive it in this way.

Furthermore, Sons of the Buddha, this is just as it is when the dragon king, Anavatapta, spreads forth dense clouds that cover the entire continent of Jambudvīpa, everywhere sending down the sweet seasonal rains which allow the seedlings of the hundred kinds of grains to grow and which also allow all the rivers, springs, and ponds to become full. The waters of these great rains do not come forth from the body or mind of this dragon king and yet they are still able to bring beings many different kinds of benefits.

Sons of the Buddha, so too it is with the Tathāgata, the Arhat, the One of Right and Universal Enlightenment. He spreads forth the clouds of great compassion which cover all realms throughout the ten directions and which everywhere rain down the unexcelled sweet-dew Dharma rains that cause all beings to be filled with joyous delight, increase their development of good dharmas, and fulfill all the vehicles [of Dharma practice].

Sons of the Buddha, the Tathāgata's voice does not come from without and does emerge from within, and yet it is able to benefit all beings. This is the seventh of the marks of the Tathāgata's voice. All bodhisattva-mahāsattvas should perceive it in this way.

Furthermore, Sons of the Buddha, this is just as it is when the dragon king, Manasvin, is about to send down the rains. Since it would not be suitable to just let them suddenly descend, he first produces immense clouds that completely cover the entire sky and remain there for seven days, waiting for all beings to complete their work. And why does he do this? Because that great dragon king has thoughts of kindness and compassion and hence does not wish to distress or disrupt beings, he waits until seven days have passed before he sends down a fine drizzling rain that everywhere moistens the great earth.

Sons of the Buddha, so too it is with the Tathāgata, the Arhat, the One of Right and Universal Enlightenment. When he is about to send down the Dharma rains, since it would not be suitable to just let them suddenly descend, he first spreads forth Dharma clouds which ripen beings. Because he wishes to prevent their minds from becoming frightened, he waits until they have become ripened, after which he then everywhere sends down the sweet-dew Dharma rain with which he proclaims and explains the extremely profound and sublime good Dharma and gradually allows them to gain satisfaction with the flavor of the Tathāgata's unexcelled Dharma of the wisdom of all-knowledge.

Sons of the Buddha, this is the eighth of the marks of the Tathāgata's voice. All bodhisattva-mahāsattvas should perceive it in this way.

Furthermore, Sons of the Buddha, this is just as it is with the dragon king in the ocean known as Vāsuki or "Great Adornment." When he sends down the rains out in the great ocean, he may send down ten kinds of adorning rains, a hundred kinds, a thousand kinds, or a hundred thousand kinds of adorning rains. Sons of the Buddha, the rainwater itself has no discrimination by which it accomplishes this. Rather it is solely due to the inconceivable powers of that dragon king that he causes his adornments to manifest even up to countless hundreds of thousands of differences.

So too it is with the Tathāgata, the Arhat, the One of Right and Universal Enlightenment. When he explains the Dharma for beings, he may use ten different kinds of voices, may use a hundred, a thousand, a hundred thousand, or eighty-four thousand different kinds of voices in explaining eighty-four thousand different kinds of practices, or he may even use up to countless hundreds of thousands of *koṭīs* of *nayutas* of voices with each of which he teaches the Dharma in different ways, thereby causing all who hear them to be filled with joyous delight.

Still, the Tathāgata's voice remains entirely free of any kinds of discriminations. Rather, it is solely due to all buddhas' perfect fulfillment of purity throughout the extremely deep Dharma realm that he is able to accord with whatever is fitting for beings' faculties as he sends forth these many different kinds of voices and causes everyone to feel joyous delight.

Sons of the Buddha, this is the ninth of the marks of the Tathāgata's voice. All bodhisattva-mahāsattvas should perceive it in this way.

Furthermore, Sons of the Buddha, this is just as it is with the dragon king, Sāgara, when, wishing to display a dragon king's immense powers of sovereign mastery to benefit and delight beings, he then spreads forth a great net of clouds that extends all around, covering everything from the four continents on up to the Paranirmita-vaśavartin Heaven. Those clouds have countless different colors and characteristics:

Some glow with the color of *jambūnada* gold;
Some glow with the color of *vaiḍūrya;*
Some glow with the color of white silver;
Some glow with the color of crystal;
Some glow with the color of *musaragalva;*
Some glow with the color of emerald;
Some glow with the color of excellent-treasury jewels;
Some glow with the color of red pearls;

Some glow with the color of infinity incense;
Some glow with the color of stainless robes;
Some glow with the color of pure waters; and
Some glow with the color of all different kinds of adornments.

A net of clouds like this spreads everywhere over everything and then, after it has spread forth, it flashes with lightning bolts of many different colors, for instance:

Clouds the color of *jambūnada* gold send forth lightning flashes the color of *vaiḍūrya;*
Clouds the color of *vaiḍūrya* send forth lightning flashes the color of gold;
Clouds the color of silver send forth lightning flashes the color of crystal;
Clouds the color of crystal send forth lightning flashes the color of silver;
Clouds the color of *musaragalva* send forth lightning flashes the color of emeralds;
Clouds the color of emeralds send forth lightning flashes the color of *musaragalva;*
Clouds the color of excellent treasury jewels send forth lightning flashes the color of red pearls;
Clouds the color of red pearls send forth lightning flashes the color of excellent treasury jewels;
Clouds the color of infinity incense send forth lightning flashes the color of immaculate robes;
Clouds the color of immaculate robes send forth lightning flashes the color of infinity incense;
Clouds the color of pure waters send forth lightning flashes the color of various adornments; and
Clouds the color of various adornments send forth lightning flashes the color of pure waters.

And so these examples continue on through to the point where clouds of many different colors send forth lightning flashes of a single color and clouds of a single color send forth many-colored lightning flashes.

Furthermore, from within all of those clouds, there come forth many different types of thunder which, adapting to beings' minds, cause them all to feel joyous delight. For instance:

Some sound like the singing of celestial maidens;
Some sound like the music of celestial musicians;
Some sound like the singing of dragon maidens;

Some sound like the singing of *gandharva* maidens;
Some sound like the singing of *kiṃnara* maidens;
Some sound like the great earth's quaking;
Some sound like the ocean waves' breaking surf;
Some sound like the king of beasts' roaring; and
Some sound like the pleasant singing of birds or like many other kinds of different sounds.

Following upon these manifestations of quaking thunder, there also arise cool breezes that cause beings' minds to be pleased, after which all different kinds of rain fall which bring benefit and happiness to countless beings from the Paranirmita-vaśavartin Heaven on down to the surface of the earth. In all these places, the rain that falls is different. For instance:

Out on the great ocean, there falls a rain of clear and cold waters known as "incessant."
In the Paranirmita-vaśavartin Heaven, there falls a rain sounding like the music of pipes and flutes known as "beautifully sublime."
In the Nirmāṇarati Heaven, there falls a rain of great *maṇi* jewels known as "great radiance emanation."
In the Tuṣita Heaven, there falls a rain of great adornments known as "hanging tresses."
In the Yama Heaven, there falls a rain of immense and marvelous flowers known as "all kinds of adornments."
In the Trāyastriṃśa Heaven, there falls a rain of many marvelous fragrances known as "pleasing the mind."
In the Heaven of the Four Heavenly Kings, there falls a rain of bejeweled celestial robes known as "covering."
In the palaces of the dragon kings, there falls a rain of red pearls known as "upwelling radiance."
In the palaces of the *asuras*, there falls a rain of weapons known as "conquering the enemy."
On this continent of Uttarakuru, there falls a rain of all kinds of different flowers known as "blooming" while, on the other three continents, all that transpires is also like this.

Thus, in accordance with each location, what falls as rain is different. Although the mind of that dragon king is impartial and free of any discriminations with regard to this one or that one, solely due to differences in beings' roots of goodness, the rain which falls has differences.

Sons of the Buddha, so too it is with the Tathāgata, the Arhat, the One of Right and Universal Enlightenment, the unsurpassed king of Dharma. When he is about to use right Dharma to teach beings, he first spreads forth clouds of bodies which cover the Dharma realm and appear for beings in different ways in accordance with their preferences. For instance:

For some beings, he manifests clouds of mortal bodies;
For some beings, he manifests clouds of emanation bodies;
For some beings, he manifests clouds of bodies sustained by his powers;
For some beings, he manifests clouds of form bodies;
For some beings, he manifests clouds of bodies with the major marks and subsidiary signs;
For some beings, he manifests clouds of merit bodies;
For some beings, he manifests clouds of wisdom bodies;
For some beings, he manifests clouds of bodies with indestructible powers;
For some beings, he manifests clouds of fearless bodies; and
For some beings, he manifests clouds of Dharma realm bodies.

Sons of the Buddha, the Tathāgata uses countless clouds of bodies such as these which spread everywhere across all worlds of the ten directions and adapt to the difference in beings' preferences by manifesting many different kinds of brilliant lightning. For instance:

He may manifest brilliant lightning known as "reaching everywhere";
He may manifest brilliant lightning known as "boundless radiance";
He may manifest brilliant lightning known as "penetrating buddhas' secret dharmas";
He may manifest brilliant lightning known as "reflected light";
He may manifest brilliant lightning known as "dazzling illumination";
He may manifest brilliant lightning known as "penetrating endless *dhāraṇī* gateways";
He may manifest brilliant lightning known as "undisturbed right mindfulness";
He may manifest brilliant lightning known as "ultimate indestructibility";
He may manifest brilliant lightning known as "adaptive entry into all rebirth destinies"; or
He may manifest brilliant lightning known as "causing joyous delight through fulfilling all wishes."

Sons of the Buddha, having displayed countless brilliant lightning flashes such as these, the Tathāgata, the Arhat, the One of Right and Universal Enlightenment then also adapts to what pleases beings' minds by manifesting countless kinds of samādhi-related thunder. For instance:

The thunder of the "thoroughly awakened wisdom" samādhi.
The thunder of the "brilliant immaculate ocean" samādhi.
The thunder of the "sovereign mastery of all dharmas" samādhi.
The thunder of the "vajra wheel" samādhi.
The thunder of the "Mount Sumeru banner" samādhi.
The thunder of the "oceanic imprint" samādhi.
The thunder of the "solar lamp" samādhi.
The thunder of the "endless treasury" samādhi.
And the thunder of the "indestructible power of liberation" samādhi.

Sons of the Buddha, having emanated countless different kinds of samādhi-related thunder such as these from within the clouds of *tathāgata* bodies, in preparation for letting fall the Dharma rain, the Buddha first manifests an auspicious sign to awaken beings, for instance: From his unimpeded mind of great kindness and compassion, he manifests the Tathāgata's great wisdom wind sphere known as "able to cause all beings to experience inconceivable delight and enjoyment." Having manifested this sign, the bodies and minds of all bodhisattvas and other beings become clear and cool.

After this, from the Tathāgata's great Dharma body clouds, great kindness and compassion clouds, and great inconceivability clouds, there comes forth the raining down of inconceivably vast rains of Dharma that cause the bodies and minds of all beings to become purified. For instance:

For bodhisattvas seated at the site enlightenment, he rains a great Dharma rain known as "the undifferentiated Dharma realm";

For bodhisattvas in their very last body, he rains a great Dharma rain known as "the bodhisattva's easeful mastery of the Tathāgata's secret teachings";

For bodhisattvas with but one more incarnation, he rains a great Dharma rain known as "pure universal light";

For bodhisattvas at the stage of the crown-anointing consecration, he rains a great Dharma rain known as "adornment with the Tathāgata's adornments";

For bodhisattvas who have achieved realization of the patience,[388] he rains a great Dharma rain known as "the bodhisattva's unceasing practice of the great compassion arising from the jewels of meritorious qualities and the blooming of the flowers of wisdom";

For bodhisattvas at the stages of the dwellings, the dedications, or the practices,[389] he rains a great Dharma rain known as "entry into the extremely profound gateway of directly manifested transformations while incessantly and tirelessly practicing the bodhisattva practices";

For bodhisattvas who have made the initial resolve, he rains a great Dharma rain known as "rescuing and protecting beings through producing the Tathāgata's great kindness and compassion";

For beings seeking to cultivate the *pratyekabuddha* vehicle, he rains a great Dharma rain known as "deep realization of the dharma of conditioned arising, abandoning the two extremes, and acquiring the fruit of indestructible liberation";

For beings seeking to cultivate the *śrāvaka*-disciple vehicle, he rains a great Dharma rain known as "using great wisdom's sword to cut off all the affliction adversaries"; and

For beings who have accumulated either definite or indefinite roots of goodness, he rains a great Dharma rain known as "able to perfect many different Dharma gateways and produce immense joyous delight."

Sons of the Buddha, adapting to beings' minds, all buddhas, the *tathāgatas*, rain vast Dharma rains such as these which fill all the boundlessly many worlds. Sons of the Buddha, the mind of the Tathāgata, the Arhat, the One of Right and Universal Enlightenment, is impartial and free of any miserliness with respect to the Dharma. It is solely due to differences in beings' faculties and predilections that the Dharma rain they rain down manifests as having differences.

This is the tenth of the marks of the Tathāgata's voice. All bodhisattva-mahāsattvas should perceive it in this way.

Furthermore, Sons of the Buddha, one should realize that the Tathāgata's voice has ten kinds of measurelessness. What are those ten? They are as follows:

Because it reaches all places, it is as measureless as the realm of empty space;

Because it has no place it does not pervade, it is as measureless as Dharma realm;

Because it delights everyone's mind, it is as measureless as the realm of beings;

Because it explains their resultant retributions, it is as measureless as all karmic actions;

Because it causes the complete extinguishing of all afflictions, it is as measureless as all afflictions;

Because it causes beings to hear in a manner adapted to their capacity to understand, it is as measureless as beings' speech;

Because it contemplates all beings and strives to rescue and liberate them, it is as measureless as all beings' individual aspirations and understandings;

Because it is boundless, it is as measureless as the three periods of time;

Because it distinguishes everything, it is as measureless as wisdom; and

Because it penetrates the realm of the Buddha's Dharma, it is as measureless as the Buddha's sphere of action.

Sons of the Buddha, the voice of the Tathāgata, the Arhat, the One of Right and Universal Enlightenment, has achieved *asaṃkhyeyas* of types of measurelessness such as these. All bodhisattva-mahāsattvas should know them in these ways.

At that time, wishing to once again clarify the meaning of this, Samantabhadra Bodhisattva-mahāsattva then spoke these verses:

When the trichiliocosm is about to be destroyed,
due to the power of beings' merit, a voice tells them:
"The quiescence of the four *dhyānas* is free of all forms of suffering,"
thus allowing all of them, having heard this, to abandon their desires.

So too it is with the Bhagavat possessed of the ten powers
who emanates a wondrous voice that pervades the Dharma realm and,
for beings' sakes, says, "All formations[390] are suffering and transient,"
thus allowing them to be forever liberated from the ocean of *saṃsāra*.

Just as when, in a great valley in the deep mountains,
whenever a voice calls out, there are always echoes which respond,
and, although they are able to follow upon the speech of others,
those echoes are still ultimately free of any discriminations—

so too it is in the case of the speech of the Ten-Powered One
which manifests for others in accordance with their faculties' ripeness,
thus enabling them to receive the training and feel joyous delight,
even as it never thinks, "I am now able to expound."

Just as, in the heavens, there is a drum called "able to awaken" that,
from the midst of space, always resounds with the sound of Dharma
and admonishes those sons of the devas who have become negligent,
thus enabling them, having heard this, to then abandon attachments—

so too it is with the Ten-Powered One's Dharma drum
that sends forth many different kinds of sublime voices
which awaken all the many kinds of beings,
thus enabling them all to attain the fruit of bodhi.

The king of the Paranirmita-vaśavartin Heaven has a precious maiden
from whose mouth comes the skillful singing of all kinds of music,
each sound of which is able to emanate a hundred thousand sounds,
every sound of which in turn makes a hundred thousand more.

So too it is with the voice of the Well Gone One
that, from a single sound, emanates all sounds
which adapt to the differences in others' natures and predilections,
thus allowing each being, having heard this, to cut off their afflictions.

Just as when the Brahma Heaven King utters but a single sound
able to cause delight in all his Brahma Heaven followers,
the sound reaches only Brahma devas and does not go beyond them
and every one of them claims he was the only one to hear it,

so too it is with the Brahma King of the Ten Powers,
who may utter a single sound that fills the Dharma realm
which only benefits those in the assembly and does not go farther, for,
because others have no faith, they would not yet be able to accept it.

Just as the many bodies of water have a single identical nature
in which the flavor of their eight qualities does not differ,
but, due to differences in lands of origin and vessels retaining them,
they are therefore caused to have many different kinds of distinctions,

so too it is with the voice of the Omniscient One—
The Dharma's nature is of a single flavor free of any discriminations,
but, because it adapts to the differences in beings' actions,
it is caused to acquire a variety of differences in what they hear.

Just as the dragon king Anavatapta
sends down rains everywhere moistening the lands of Jambudvīpa
which are able to cause all the grasses and trees to grow
even as those rains do not come forth from either his body or mind,

so too it is with the marvelous voices of all buddhas which let fall
rains throughout the Dharma realm, completely soaking everything.
They are able to cause growth of goodness and the cessation of evils
even as they do not come into existence either from within or without.

Just as the dragon king known as Manasvin
spreads forth rain clouds which stay for seven days before first raining
as he awaits beings' completion of their work
and only after that begins to let them fall and achieve their benefits,

so too it is with the Ten-Powered One's expounding of meanings
in which he first teaches beings, thus causing their ripening,
and only later expounds the extremely deep Dharma for them,
thereby preventing those listening to him from being frightened.

Just as, out on the seas, the dragon known as Vāsuki
pours down ten kinds of adornment-filled rains,
perhaps of a hundred, or a thousand, or a hundred thousand types,
in which, though the water is of but one taste, the adornments differ,

so too it is with he who possesses the most ultimate eloquence
as he expounds on ten or twenty Dharma gateways,
or a hundred, or a thousand, on up to incalculably many,
yet still does not produce thoughts possessed of discriminations.

Just as Sāgara, the supreme king of the dragons,
spreads forth clouds which everywhere cover over the four continents
and sends down rains everywhere which differ in each place
and yet that dragon's mind remains free of twofold considerations,

so too it is with all the buddhas, the Dharma kings, whose clouds
of bodies motivated by the great compassion fill all ten directions
and send down rains for all who cultivate, each of whom are different,
and yet they stay free of any discriminations regarding any of them.

Sons of the Buddha, how should the bodhisattva-mahāsattva know the mind of the Tathāgata, the Arhat, the One of Right and Universal Enlightenment? Sons of the Buddha, the Tathāgata's mind, intellect, and consciousness are all inapprehensible. It is only by the measurelessness of his wisdom that one should know the mind of the Tathāgata. Just as empty space is relied upon by all things but has nothing on which it relies, so too it is with the wisdom of the Tathāgata, for it is relied upon by all worldly and world-transcending wisdom and yet the Tathāgata's wisdom has nothing on which it relies.

Sons of the Buddha, this is the first of the marks of the Tathāgata's mind. All bodhisattva-mahāsattvas should know it in this way.

Furthermore, Sons of the Buddha, just as the Dharma realm always produces the liberations of all *śrāvaka* disciples, *pratyekabuddhas,* and bodhisattvas and yet the Dharma realm itself is neither increased nor decreased, so to it is with the Tathāgata's wisdom which constantly produces all the different kinds of worldly and world-transcending wisdom and yet the Tathāgata's wisdom is neither increased nor decreased.

Sons of the Buddha, this is the second of the marks of the Tathāgata's mind. All bodhisattva-mahāsattvas should know it in this way.

Furthermore, Sons of the Buddha, just as the waters of the great ocean flow beneath the earth of the four continents as well as the eighty *koṭīs* of small islands so that, whenever someone drills down into them, no one fails to find water, and yet that great ocean does not make discriminations such as, "I shall send forth water," so too it is with the waters of the Buddha's wisdom ocean which flow into the minds of all beings. If any being contemplates the objective realms and cultivates the Dharma gateways, then he will acquire wisdom that is pure and utterly clear, and yet the Tathāgata's wisdom is impartial, non-dual, and free of discrimination, for it is solely in accordance with the differences in beings' mental actions that the wisdom they acquire differs for each of them.

Sons of the Buddha, this is the third of the marks of the Tathāgata's mind. All bodhisattva-mahāsattvas should know it in this way.

Furthermore, Sons of the Buddha, by way of analogy, consider the following: The great ocean contains four precious pearls possessed of countless qualities that can produce all the precious jewels in the ocean. If the great ocean did not contain these precious pearls, one would never be able to find even a single jewel. What are these four? The first is known as "accumulator of jewels," the second is known as "endless treasury," the third is known as "far from flaming fire," and the fourth is known as "replete with adornments."

Sons of the Buddha, these four precious pearls cannot be seen by any common person, dragon, spirit, or other such being. And why is this so? Because these precious pearls are so magnificent and perfectly formed that the dragon king, Sāgara, keeps them in a very secret place in his palace.

Sons of the Buddha, so too it is with the great ocean of wisdom of the Tathāgata, the Arhat, the One of Right and Universal Enlightenment. Within it, there are four precious pearls of great wisdom that are possessed of the qualities of measureless merit and wisdom. It is from these that there can be produced the jewels of wisdom possessed by all beings, by *śrāvaka* disciples, by *pratyekabuddhas*, by those at the stages of learning and beyond learning, and by all bodhisattvas. What are these four? They are:

The great wisdom jewel of skillful means free of defiling attachments;

The great wisdom jewel of skillful discernment of conditioned and unconditioned dharmas;

The great wisdom jewel of differentiating discussion of countless dharmas without contradicting the nature of dharmas; and

The great wisdom jewel of never erring in knowing what is and is not the right time.

If the *tathāgatas'* ocean of great wisdom did not contain these four jewels, it would be forever impossible for even a single being to enter the Great Vehicle. These four wisdom jewels cannot be seen by beings possessed of only meager merit. And why is this so? This is because they have been placed within the Tathāgata's extremely secret treasury.

These four wisdom jewels are equally symmetrical, rightly and evenly formed, exquisite, pristine, and marvelously fine. They are everywhere able to benefit the entire congregation of bodhisattvas and enable them to completely acquire the light of wisdom.

Sons of the Buddha, this is the fourth of the marks of the Tathāgata's mind. All bodhisattva-mahāsattvas should know it in this way.

Furthermore, Sons of the Buddha, by way of analogy, consider the following: The great ocean contains four immense jewels which radiate flaming light that are spread out on the ocean floor. By nature, they possess the most ultimately ferocious heat with which they are forever able to drink in and withdraw the measurelessly great volume of water that pours into the ocean from the hundred rivers. As a consequence, the great ocean neither increases nor decreases in volume. What are these four? The first is known as "solar treasury," the second is known as "moisture remover," the third is known as "blazing fire light," and the fourth is known as "complete consumption."

Sons of the Buddha, if the great ocean did not contain these four jewels, then everything from the four continents on up to the summit of existence would become inundated and submerged.

Sons of the Buddha, when the illumination created by the light of this immense "solar treasury" jewel contacts the ocean's waters, it transforms them all into milk. When the illumination created by the light of the immense "moisture remover" jewel contacts that milk, it is all transformed into curds. When the illumination created by the light of the immense "blazing fire light" jewel contacts those curds, they are all transformed into butter. And when the illumination created by the light of the immense "complete consumption" jewel contacts that butter, it is all transformed into ghee which, as if by blazing fire, is then completely consumed.

Sons of the Buddha, so too it is with the great ocean of wisdom of the Tathāgata, the Arhat, the One of Right and Universal Enlightenment. It contains four kinds of great wisdom jewels which are fully possessed of the light of measureless awesome virtue.

When the light of these wisdom jewels touches the bodhisattvas, it causes them to ultimately attain the great wisdom of the Tathāgata. What are these four? They are:

The great wisdom jewel that stills all waves of scattered goodness;[391]
The great wisdom jewel that eliminates all affection for dharmas;
The great wisdom jewel that everywhere emanates wisdom light;
The jewel of boundless and effortless great wisdom equal to that of the Tathāgata;

Sons of the Buddha, when bodhisattvas cultivate all the path-assisting dharmas, they produce countless waves of scattered goodness which not even any of the world's devas, humans, or *asuras* can overcome. The Tathāgata sends forth light from "the great wisdom jewel that stills all waves of scattered goodness." When it touches those bodhisattvas, it causes them to leave behind all waves of scattered goodness, hold their minds on a single object, and dwell in samādhi.

He then also sends forth light from "the great wisdom jewel that eliminates all affection for dharmas." When it touches those bodhisattvas, it causes them to abandon any attachment to the delectable flavor of samādhi and produce vast spiritual superknowledges.

He then also sends forth light from "the great wisdom jewel that everywhere emanates wisdom light." When it touches those bodhisattvas, it causes them to relinquish the vast spiritual superknowledges they produced and abide in the practice of greatly radiant functional effort.

He then also sends forth light from "the jewel of boundless and effortless great wisdom equal to that of the Tathāgata." When it touches those bodhisattvas, it causes them to relinquish the practice of greatly radiant functional effort up until they reach the ground of equality with the Tathāgata where they put to rest all functional effort without exception.

Sons of the Buddha, if they had not been touched by the greatly radiant illumination cast by these four wisdom jewels of the Tathāgata, it would be utterly impossible for there to be even a single bodhisattva who could ever reach the ground of the Tathāgata.

Sons of the Buddha, this is the fifth of the marks of the Tathāgata's mind. All bodhisattva-mahāsattvas should know it in this way.

Furthermore, Sons of the Buddha, by way of analogy, consider the following: From the edge of [the sphere of] water[392] all the way up to the heaven of neither perception nor non-perception, of all the great chiliocosm's lands and of all the stations in which beings of the desire realm, form realm, and formless realms dwell, there are none that do not entirely rely upon empty space for their origination while also relying upon empty space for their abiding. And why is this? It is because empty space is universally pervasive. Although that empty space completely includes within itself everything within the three realms of existence, it is still entirely free of any discrimination [with respect to any of them].

Sons of the Buddha, so too it is with the wisdom of the Tathāgata, for, whether it be the wisdom of *śrāvaka* disciples, the wisdom of *pratyekabuddhas*, the wisdom of bodhisattvas, the wisdom of conditioned practice, or the wisdom of unconditioned practice, they all rely upon the Tathāgata's wisdom for their origination while also relying upon the Tathāgata's wisdom for their abiding. And why is this? It is because the Tathāgata's wisdom is universally pervasive. Although it also completely includes all the countless other kinds of wisdom, it is still entirely free of any discrimination [with respect to any of them].

Sons of the Buddha, this is the sixth of the marks of the Tathāgata's mind. All bodhisattva-mahāsattvas should know it in this way.

Furthermore, Sons of the Buddha, by way of analogy, consider the following: There is a medicine king tree which grows on the summit of the Himalaya Mountains which is known as "endless roots." The roots of that medicine tree grow forth from one hundred and sixty-eight thousand *yojanas* below at the junction of the vajra ground and the sphere of water. When the roots of that medicine king tree began to grow, it caused the growth of all of Jambudvīpa's tree roots. When its trunk began to grow, it caused the growth of all of Jambudvīpa's tree trunks. So too it was with its branches, leaves, blossoms, and fruit.

It is due to the ability of the roots of this medicine king tree to cause the growth of trunks and due to its trunk's ability to cause the growth of roots that its roots are therefore endless. Hence it is known as "endless roots."

Sons of the Buddha, that medicine king tree is able to bring about growth in all places with the sole exception of two places in which it is unable to produce the benefits of growth. Specifically, those are in the deep abyss of the hell realms and within the wheel of water. Even so, even from the very beginning, it has still never had any sort of aversion for those places.

Sons of the Buddha, so too it is with the great medicine king tree of the Tathāgata's wisdom. It takes as its roots vast and greatly compassionate past vows to perfect all wise and good dharmas, vows which, extending everywhere and extending to all realms of beings, are intent upon extinguishing all sufferings of the three wretched destinies. It grows forth from the lineage of all *tathāgatas'* genuine wisdom, takes solid and unshakable skillful means as its trunk, takes the wisdom which pervades the Dharma realm and the *pāramitās* as its branches, takes the *dhyāna* absorptions, the liberations, and the great samādhis as its leaves, takes the complete-retention *dhāraṇīs,* eloquence, and the dharmas of the factors of enlightenment as its blossoms, and takes all buddhas' ultimate and unchanging liberations as its fruits.

Sons of the Buddha, why is the great medicine king tree of the Tathāgata's wisdom known as "endless roots"? This is because it ultimately never rests and because it never allows the bodhisattva practices to be cut off. The bodhisattva practices are just the very nature of the Tathāgata. The nature of the Tathāgata is just the bodhisattva practices. It is for these reasons that it is known as "endless roots."

Sons of the Buddha, when the roots of the great medicine king tree of the Tathāgata's wisdom grow forth, they cause all bodhisattvas to produce the roots of the great kindness and compassion by which they never abandon beings.

When its trunk grows forth, it causes all bodhisattvas to increase the growth of the trunk of their solid vigor and deep resolve.

When its branches grow forth, they cause all bodhisattvas to increase the growth of the branches of all the *pāramitās.*

When its leaves grow forth, they cause all bodhisattvas to bring forth growth in the leaves of the pure precepts, the *dhūta* austerities, the meritorious qualities, and the ability to be easily satisfied with but few desires.

When its blossoms grow forth, they cause all bodhisattvas to acquire the blossoms consisting of the roots of goodness and the adornments of the major marks and subsidiary signs.

When its fruits grow forth, they cause all bodhisattvas to acquire the fruits of the unproduced-dharmas patience and so forth up to and including the patience associated with all buddhas' bestowal of the crown-anointing consecration.

Sons of the Buddha, the great medicine king tree of the Tathāgata's wisdom has only two places it is unable to provide the benefit of growth, namely the vast and deep abyss of the unconditioned into which the adherents of the two vehicles have fallen and also the immense river of wrong views and desires in which beings are drowning who have destroyed their roots of goodness and are not fit vessels to receive it. Even so, he has never had any aversion for beings in those places.

Sons of the Buddha, the Tathāgata's wisdom neither increases nor decreases for, because its roots are well established, it grows incessantly.

Sons of the Buddha, this is the seventh of the marks of the Tathāgata's mind. All bodhisattva-mahāsattvas should know it in this way.

Furthermore, Sons of the Buddha, by way of analogy, consider the following: In the worlds of the great trichiliocosm, when the fires arise at the end of the kalpa, they incinerate everything from the grasses, trees, and dense forests to the iron ring mountains and the great iron ring mountains, burning them all so completely with their blazing flames that nothing is left.

Sons of the Buddha, if someone clutched up dry grasses in his hands and then threw them into those fires, what do you think? Is it possible that they would not be burned, or not?

They replied: "No, it would not be possible."

Sons of the Buddha, even supposing that somehow the grass they threw into the fires might not be burned, still, the Tathāgata's wisdom distinguishes all beings, all lands, all kalpa enumerations, and all dharmas of the three periods of time, having none among them it does not know. Were one to claim there is something it does not know, that would be an utter impossibility. And why is this so? It is because his wisdom has an equally and completely clear comprehension of everything.

Sons of the Buddha, this is the eighth of the marks of the Tathāgata's mind. All bodhisattva-mahāsattvas should know it in this way.

Furthermore, Sons of the Buddha, by way of analogy, consider the following: When the wind disaster that destroys the world occurs, a great wind arises known as "scattering destruction" that is able to so completely destroy even the great trichiliocosm's iron ring mountains and other features that they are all reduced to dust. Then another great wind known as "able to block" encircles the great trichiliocosm and blocks that "scattering destruction" wind and prevents it from being able to reach the worlds in any other regions.

Sons of the Buddha, if one somehow caused this "able to block" wind to no longer exist, none of the worlds of the ten directions would not be completely destroyed.

So too it is with the Tathāgata, the Arhat, the One of Right and Universal Enlightenment, for he has a great wisdom wind known as "able to extinguish" which is able to extinguish the afflictions and habitual karmic propensities of all the great bodhisattvas. He also has a great wisdom wind known as "skillful sustenance" which skillfully sustains those bodhisattvas whose faculties have not yet become ripe by preventing the "able to extinguish" great wisdom whirlwind from cutting off all their afflictions and habitual karmic propensities.

Sons of the Buddha, if the Tathāgata's "skillful sustenance" wisdom wind did not exist, countless bodhisattvas would fall down to the grounds of *śrāvaka* disciples and *pratyekabuddhas*. It is due to this wisdom that all bodhisattvas are enabled to step beyond the grounds of the two vehicles practitioners and become securely established in the Tathāgata's ultimate position.

Sons of the Buddha, this is the ninth of the marks of the Tathāgata's mind. All bodhisattva-mahāsattvas should know it in this way.

Furthermore, Sons of the Buddha, the wisdom of the Tathāgata has no place it does not reach. And why is this so? This is because there is not a single being that does not possess the Tathāgata's wisdom. It is solely due to erroneous perceptions, inverted views, and attachments that they do not bring it to realization. If they were to abandon their erroneous thinking, then all-knowledge, spontaneous wisdom, and unimpeded wisdom would all manifest directly before them.

Sons of the Buddha, by way of analogy, consider the following: Suppose there was a great scriptural scroll equal in size to the great trichiliocosm in which there was exhaustively recorded everything in the great trichiliocosm, including for instance:

A written record of everything within the area encircled by the iron ring mountains which was equal in size to the great iron ring mountains themselves;

A written record of everything on the great earth which was equal in size to the great earth itself;

A written record of everything throughout a medium-sized chiliocosm which was equal in size to that medium-sized chiliocosm itself;

A written record of everything throughout a small chiliocosm which was equal in size to that small chiliocosm itself; and

In this same way, written records of everything on the four continents, the great ocean, Mount Sumeru, the palaces of the earthly

> devas, the palaces of the desire realm's space-dwelling devas, the palaces of the form realms, and the palaces of the formless realm devas, for every one of which these written records were equal in size to each of these phenomena.

Although these great scriptural scrolls might be equal in size to the great chiliocosm, they would all still be able to abide completely within a single atom. And just as this would be so with regard to a single atom, so too would this be so with regard to all atoms.

Suppose then that there was a single person possessed of clear and penetrating wisdom who, having completely purified the heavenly eye, saw this scriptural scroll within an atom and realized that it was not benefiting beings in the least, whereupon he thought, "I should use the power of vigor to break open this atom, draw forth this scriptural scroll, and then make it benefit all beings." Then, having thought in this way, suppose he immediately produced some skillful means to break open this atom, draw forth this immense scripture, and then use it to cause all beings to acquire its benefits. Then, just as he had done this with a single atom, one should realize he also did so with all atoms.

Sons of the Buddha, so too it is with the Tathāgata's wisdom. It is measureless, unimpeded, and universally able to benefit all beings. It is fully present in all beings.[393] It is solely because of all common people's erroneous perceptions and attachments that they do not know this, do not awaken to it, and thus fail to gain its benefits.

Then, the Tathāgata, using the unimpeded vision of his pure wisdom eye, everywhere contemplates all beings throughout the Dharma realm and speaks these words: "This is strange indeed, strange indeed! How could it be that all these beings completely possess the Tathāgata's wisdom, yet, because of foolishness and delusion, they do not realize this and do not perceive this? I should instruct them in the path of the *āryas* and enable them to forever abandon erroneous perceptions and attachments so that they can see in their own persons the vast wisdom of the Tathāgata which is no different than that of the Buddha himself."

He then instructs those beings in the cultivation of the path of the *āryas*, thereby enabling them to abandon their erroneous perceptions. Then, having abandoned their erroneous perceptions, they realize the measureless wisdom of the Tathāgata and bestow benefit and happiness on all beings.

Sons of the Buddha, this is the tenth of the marks of the Tathāgata's mind. All bodhisattva-mahāsattvas should know it in this way.

Sons of the Buddha, the bodhisattva-mahāsattva should know the mind of the Tathāgata, the Arhat, the One of Right and Universal Enlightenment on the basis of countless unimpeded and inconceivably vast marks such as these.

At that time, wishing to once again clarify the meaning of this, Samantabhadra Bodhisattva-mahāsattva then spoke these verses:

If one wishes to know the mind of all buddhas,
one should contemplate the Buddha's wisdom.
The Buddha's wisdom has no place on which it depends
just as empty space has nothing on which it depends.

Beings' many different ways of finding happiness
as well as all their knowledge of skillful methods
all rely on the wisdom of the Buddha,
yet Buddha's wisdom has nothing on which it depends.

The liberations gained by *śrāvaka* disciples,
pratyekabuddhas, and buddhas
all rely upon the Dharma realm,
yet the Dharma realm is neither increased nor decreased.

So too it is with the wisdom of the Buddha.
It produces all forms of wisdom,
yet it is neither increased nor decreased,
and it is neither produced nor exhausted.

Just as the water flowing beneath the earth
is such that, if one searches for it, no one fails to find it, and just as,
without thought and without ever being exhausted,
its functions and powers reach throughout the ten directions,

so too it is with the Buddha's wisdom
which, being universally present in all beings' minds,
is such that, if one diligently cultivates it,
one will swiftly acquire the light of wisdom.

Just as the dragon has four pearls
which themselves create all other jewels
and which he places in an extremely secret place
so that no common person could ever even see them,

So too it is with the Buddha's four types of wisdom
which produce all other kinds of wisdom
and which are such that no one could ever see them
with the sole exception of the great bodhisattvas.

Just as the ocean has four kinds of jewels
that are able to drink in the waters of all the rivers

and thus prevent the oceans from overflowing,
while also ensuring that they neither increase nor decrease,

so too it is with the Tathāgata's wisdom
which stills the waves and eliminates all affection for dharmas,
which is so vast as to be boundless,
and which is able to give birth to buddhas and bodhisattvas.

Just as from the regions below on up to the peak of existence
throughout the desire realm, form realm, and formless realm,
everything whatsoever relies upon empty space,
even as empty space itself does not discriminate among them,

so too, the many types of wisdom of *śrāvaka* disciples,
pratyekabuddhas, and bodhisattvas
all rely upon the Buddha's wisdom
even as the Buddha's wisdom does not discriminate among them.

Just as the Himalaya Mountains have a medicine king tree
known as "endless roots"
which is able to bring about growth in all other trees,
including their roots, trunks, leaves, blossoms, and fruit,

so too it is with the wisdom of the Buddha
which comes forth from the lineage of the Tathāgatas,
and, having already attained the realization of bodhi,
still continues to bring forth the bodhisattva practices.

Supposing someone were to take up dry grasses
and place them into the kalpa-ending fires
in which even vajra would be completely incinerated,
there would be no basis for supposing they would not be burned,

but even supposing it was possible those grasses might not be burned,
of the three times' kalpas and *kṣetras*
as well as all the beings within them,
the Buddha would still have none of these matters he does not know.

Just as there is a wind known as "scattering destruction"
which is able to destroy the entire great chiliocosm,
one that, were it not for another wind's stopping it,
its destruction would extend to all the countlessly many other worlds,

so too it is with the wind of great wisdom
which extinguishes all the bodhisattvas' delusions
and which is attended by another wind possessed of an excellent skill
to enable them to dwell on the ground of the Tathāgata.

Just as, supposing there was an immense scriptural scroll
equal in size to the great trichiliocosm

which resided within a single atom
and, in the same way, such scriptures resided in all other atoms—

and supposing, too, that there was a person of acute intelligence who,
with the purified eye, clearly saw them all
and then broke open those atoms, drew forth the scripture scrolls,
and used them to abundantly benefit beings everywhere—

So too it is with the wisdom of the Buddha
which is everywhere present within the minds of beings
in which it is bound up by their erroneous perceptions
so that they do not awaken to it or even know of it.

The buddhas then bring forth their great kindness and compassion
and enable them to rid themselves of such erroneous perceptions.
Thus, in this same way, they bring it forth and reveal it
so that it benefits all bodhisattvas.

Sons of the Buddha, how should the bodhisattva-mahāsattva know the objective realms of the Tathāgata, the Arhat, the One of Right and Universal Enlightenment? Sons of the Buddha, with unobstructed and unimpeded wisdom, the bodhisattva-mahāsattva knows the objective realms of all worlds as being the Tathāgata's objective realms, knows the objective realms of all three periods of time, the objective realms of all *kṣetras*, the objective realms of all dharmas, the objective realms of all beings, the undifferentiated objective realm of true suchness, the unimpeded objective realm of the Dharma realm, the limitless objective realm of the apex of reality, the undivided objective realm of empty space, and the objective realm of no objective realm at all—[he knows] these are the Tathāgata's objective realms.

Sons of the Buddha, just as the objective realms of all worlds are measureless, so too are the Tathāgata's objective realms also measureless. Just as the objective realms of all three periods of time are measureless, so too are the Tathāgata's objective realms also measureless, and so forth up to and including the fact that, just as the objective realm of no objective realm at all is measureless, so too is the Tathāgata's objective realm also measureless. And just as the objective realm of no objective realm at all does not exist anywhere, so too is this so of the Tathāgata's objective realm. It does not exist anywhere.

Sons of the Buddha, the bodhisattva-mahāsattva should know that the mind's objective realms are the Tathāgata's objective realms. Just as the mind's objective realms are measureless and boundless, neither bound up nor liberated, so too are the Tathāgata's objective realms also measureless and boundless and neither tied up nor liberated. And how is this so? This is because, it is due to just such kinds of thought and discrimination as these that there occur just such countless manifestations as these.

Sons of the Buddha, just as it is with the great dragon king for whom it is in accordance with his thoughts that he sends down the rain so that his rain then neither arises from within nor arises from without, so too it is with the Tathāgata's objective realms in which it is in accordance with just such thoughts and discriminations that there then occur just such countless manifestations throughout the ten directions, all of which have no place from which they come.

Sons of the Buddha, just as the waters of the great ocean all come forth from the power of the dragon king's mind, so too it is with the ocean of all-knowledge of all buddhas, the *tathāgatas,* which all arises from the Tathāgata's great vows made in the distant past.

Sons of the Buddha, the ocean of all-knowledge is measureless, boundless, inconceivable, and indescribable. Nonetheless, by way of analogy, I shall now present a general description. You should all listen closely.

Sons of the Buddha, this continent of Jambudvīpa has two thousand five hundred rivers that flow into the great ocean. The western continent of Aparagodānīya has five thousand rivers that flow into the great ocean. The eastern continent of Pūrvavideha has seven thousand five hundred rivers that flow into the great ocean. And the northern continent of Uttarakuru has ten thousand rivers that flow into the great ocean. Sons of the Buddha, in this way, these four continents have twenty-five thousand rivers that continuously and uninterruptedly flow into the great ocean. What do you think? Is this a great deal of water, or not?

They replied: "It is an extremely great amount."

Sons of the Buddha, in addition, there is the dragon king known as "Ten Light Rays" whose rains entering the great ocean amount to twice the volume of water described above. Moreover, the rains entering the great ocean sent down by the dragon king known as "Hundred Light Rays" amount to twice the previously mentioned volume of water.

In addition, the rains entering the great ocean sent down by Great Adornment Dragon King, Manasvin Dragon King, Rumbling Thunder Dragon King, Nanda Dragon King, Upananda Dragon King, Measureless Light Dragon King, Continuous Downpour Dragon King, Great Supremacy Dragon King, Great Bounding Speed

Dragon King, and eighty *koṭīs* of other great dragon kings such as these in each case amount to twice that of the one before. And the rains entering the great ocean sent down by "Jambu Banner," the dragon prince son of the Dragon King, Sāgara, amount to twice that of the one before.

Sons of the Buddha, the waters flowing into the great ocean from the palace of Ten Light Rays Dragon King are twice the previous amount. So too, the waters flowing into the great ocean from the palace of Hundred Light Rays Dragon King are twice the previous amount. So too, the amount of water pouring into the great ocean from the palaces of Great Adornment Dragon King, Manasvin Dragon King, Rumbling Thunder Dragon King, Nanda Dragon King, Upananda Dragon King, Measureless Light Dragon King, Continuous Downpour Dragon King, Great Supremacy Dragon King, Great Bounding Speed Dragon King, and the eighty *koṭīs* of other great dragon kings is different in each case so that the amount of water flowing from each of these palaces is in turn twice that of the previous amount. And the water that flows into the great ocean from the palace of Jambu Banner, the dragon prince son of Sāgara, the Dragon King, is again twice that of the previous amount.

Sons of the Buddha, the waters pouring into the great ocean from the continuous rains of Sāgara, the dragon king, are again twice the previous amount. The waters gushing forth into the ocean from the palace of Sāgara, the dragon king, are again twice those previously described [that he sends down as rain]. The waters it gushes forth are purple colored and their gushing forth is timed so that the great ocean's tides never lose their normal timing.

Sons of the Buddha, just as, in this way, the waters of the great ocean are immeasurable, so too, its many jewels are measurelessly many, its beings are measurelessly many, and the ground of the great earth upon which they all rest is also measurelessly vast. Sons of the Buddha, What the do you think? Is that great ocean measureless, or not?

They replied: "It truly is measureless, so measureless as to be indescribable even by resort to analogy."

Sons of the Buddha, compared to the measurelessness of the Tathāgata's ocean of wisdom, the measurelessness of this great ocean does not amount to even a hundredth part, does not amount to even a thousandth part, and so forth until we come to its not amounting to even a single part in an *upaniṣad* of parts. It is solely to adapt to beings' minds that one makes such analogies, for the objective realms of the Buddha cannot be described even by resort to analogies.

Sons of the Buddha, as for the bodhisattva-mahāsattva:

He should realize that the Tathāgata's ocean of wisdom is measureless because, from the time of his initial resolve, he has incessantly cultivated the bodhisattva practices;

He should realize that the aggregations of jewels within it are measureless because the dharmas constituting the limbs of bodhi and the lineage of the Three Jewels continue on incessantly;

He should realize that the beings in which it abides are measureless because it is taken in and put to use by those still in training or beyond training, including by all *śrāvaka*-disciple and *pratyekabuddha* practitioners; and

He should realize that the grounds on which they dwell are measureless because, from the first ground, the ground of joyfulness, on up to the most ultimate and unimpeded of all the grounds, those [grounds] are where all bodhisattvas reside.

Sons of the Buddha, in order to access measureless wisdom and benefit all beings, the bodhisattva-mahāsattva should know in these ways the objective realms of the Tathāgata, the Arhat, the One of Right and Universal Enlightenment.

At that time, wishing to once again clarify the meaning of this, Samantabhadra Bodhisattva-mahāsattva then spoke these verses:

Just as the mind's objective realms are measureless,
so too is this true of the Buddha's objective realms.
Just as the mind's objective realms arise from the mind,
so too should one contemplate the realms of the Buddha.

Just as, even without leaving their original place, the dragons
use their minds' awesome power to pour down the great rains
and those rains have no place whence they come or to which they go,
still, by according with the dragons' minds, they drench everything,

so too it is that the Muni of Ten Powers
who, though he has no place whence he comes or to which he goes,
if there are any with pure minds, he manifests his body there so that,
even being the size of the Dharma realm, he can enter a single pore.

Just as the extraordinary jewels in the oceans are measureless
just as are the number of beings and the size of the earth,
and just as its waters by nature are of a single undifferentiated flavor,
yet each being living within it receives its own benefit,

so too it is with the Tathāgata's ocean of wisdom
in which everything it contains is measureless
and those in training, beyond training, or dwelling on its grounds
all acquire their own benefit there within it.

Sons of the Buddha, how should the bodhisattva-mahāsattva know the actions of the Tathāgata, the Arhat, the One of Right and Universal Enlightenment? Sons of the Buddha, the bodhisattva-mahāsattva should know that it is unimpeded action that constitutes the actions of the Tathāgata and he should know that it is actions of true suchness that constitute the actions of the Tathāgata.

Sons of the Buddha, just as true suchness was not created in the past, does not move into the future, and does not arise in the present, so too it is with the Tathāgata's actions which are not created, do not move, and do not arise.

Sons of the Buddha, just as the Dharma realm is not finite nor infinite because it has no form, so too it is with the Tathāgata's actions, for they are neither finite nor infinite because they have no form.

Sons of the Buddha, by way of analogy, it is just as if a bird flew through space for a hundred years, the regions already passed by and the regions not yet passed by would both be measureless. And why is this so? This is because the realm of space is boundless.

So too it is with the Tathāgata's actions for, even if someone spent a hundred thousand *koṭīs* of *nayutas* of kalpas in differentiating and expounding on them, what he had already described and what he had not yet described would both be measureless. And why is this so? This is because the Tathāgata's actions are boundless.

Sons of the Buddha, as he abides in unimpeded actions, the Tathāgata, the Arhat, the One of Right and Universal Enlightenment has no place in which he abides and yet he is able to manifest actions everywhere for the sake of all beings. Then, after they have been allowed to see them, they are able to step beyond all paths beset with obstacles.

Sons of the Buddha, by way of analogy, it is just as when the golden-winged king of birds, flying through the sky, begins to circle without flying on, and then uses his clear-eyed vision to look into the dragon palaces down in the waters of the ocean. Then, energetically exerting his courageous and fierce strength to sweep his left and then his right wings, he sweeps aside the ocean's waters and causes them to part, whereupon, knowing of those sons and daughters of the dragons which ones' lives are about to come to an end, he then pounces on them and snatches them up.

So too it is with the Tathāgata, the Arhat, the One of Right and Universal Enlightenment, the king of golden-winged birds. Abiding as he does in unimpeded actions, he uses his pure Buddha eye to contemplate all beings in all the palaces throughout the Dharma realm and, wherever there are those who have planted roots of goodness that have now become ripened, summoning the courageous strength of the ten powers, he uses his two wings of calming and contemplation to sweep aside the waters of *saṃsāra*'s great ocean of desires, thereby causing them to part. He then pulls forth those beings, places them within the Dharma, enables them to cut off all their erroneous perceptions and conceptual proliferations, and then establishes them in the nondiscriminating unimpeded actions of the Tathāgata.

Sons of the Buddha, just as the sun and moon, each alone and with no companions, circle through space, benefiting beings, never thinking as they do so, "I have come from such and such a place and am going on to such and such a place," so too it is with the buddhas, the *tathāgatas*, whose nature is originally quiescent and free of discriminations. They manifest as roaming throughout the entire Dharma realm, wishing to benefit all beings, and never resting. They do not produce conceptual proliferations and discriminations such as this: "I have come from that place and am going to that place."

Sons of the Buddha, it is by such measureless skillful means and measureless nature and marks that the bodhisattva-mahāsattva should know the actions engaged in by the Tathāgata, the Arhat, the One of Right and Universal Enlightenment.

At that time, wishing to once again clarify the meaning of this, Samantabhadra Bodhisattva-mahāsattva then spoke these verses:

Just as true suchness is neither produced nor destroyed,
has no place in which it resides, and cannot be seen by anyone,
so too it is with the actions of the Greatly Beneficial One which,
having transcended the three periods of time, are immeasurable.

Just as the Dharma realm is neither a realm nor not a realm
and is neither finite nor infinite,
so too it is with the actions of the One of Great Meritorious Qualities
who is neither finite nor infinite because he has no body at all.

Just as when a bird has flown on for a thousand *koṭīs* of years,
the regions of space behind and ahead are the same and no different,
so too, if one expounded for many kalpas on the Tathāgata's actions,
the already told of and not yet told of would both be measureless.

As when the golden-winged bird in the sky looks at the great ocean,
parts the waters, pounces, and seizes the dragons' sons and daughters,
so too, the Ten-Powered One can pull forth those with good roots,
enable them to escape the ocean of existence, and be rid of their many delusions.

Just as the sun and moon roam through empty space
and their illumination reaches everyone without discrimination,
so too, the Bhagavat goes everywhere throughout the Dharma realm
and provides teaching to beings without ever moving a thought.

Sons of the Buddha, how should the bodhisattva-mahāsattva know the attainment of right enlightenment as achieved by the Tathāgata, the Arhat, the One of Right and Universal Enlightenment? Sons of the Buddha, the bodhisattva-mahāsattva should know the attainment of right enlightenment as achieved by the Tathāgata:

As not requiring any contemplation of any meaning;
As regarding all dharmas equally;
As free of doubt;
As non-dual and signless;
As neither going nor stopping;
As measureless and boundless;
As having abandoned the two extremes;
As abiding in the Middle Way;
As having gone beyond all language and speech; and
As knowing the actions of all beings' thoughts, the nature of their faculties, their aspirations, their afflictions, and their defiled habitual tendencies.

Or, to state it in terms of what is most essential, he should understand it as knowing in a single mind-moment all dharmas of the three periods of time.

Sons of the Buddha, just as the great ocean is known by all as "the great ocean" due to its ability to everywhere reflect the shapes and appearances of all beings on the four continents, so too it is with the bodhi of the Buddha which is known as "the Buddha's bodhi" due to its ability to everywhere manifesting all beings' thoughts, the nature of their faculties, and their aspirations, even without manifesting anything at all. Therefore it is known as "the bodhi of the Buddha."

Sons of the Buddha, the bodhi of all buddhas cannot be depicted by any literary passage, cannot be gotten at by any verbal description, and cannot be described in any language. It can only be explained by the use of skillful means adapted to what is most fitting.

Sons of the Buddha, when the Tathāgata, the Arhat, the One of Right and Universal Enlightenment, attains right enlightenment:

He acquires bodies as measureless as all beings;
He acquires bodies as measureless as all dharmas;
He acquires bodies as measureless as all *kṣetras*;
He acquires bodies as measureless as the three periods of time;
He acquires bodies as measureless as all buddhas;
He acquires bodies as measureless as all languages;
He acquires bodies as measureless as true suchness;
He acquires bodies as measureless as the Dharma realm;
He acquires bodies as measureless as the realms of empty space;
He acquires bodies as measureless as the unimpeded realms;
He acquires bodies as measureless as all vows;
He acquires bodies as measureless as all practices; and
He acquires bodies as measureless as the realm of quiescent nirvāṇa.

Sons of the Buddha, just as it is with the bodies he acquires, so too it is with his speech and mind in which he also acquires just such measureless and innumerable endowments of all three of these pure spheres.[394]

Sons of the Buddha, when the Tathāgata attains right enlightenment, within his body, he sees all beings attaining right enlightenment, and so forth, including even seeing all beings entering nirvāṇa and including seeing them all as of a single identical nature, namely the absence of any nature at all. What kinds of nature do they not have? This refers to:

No nature of signs;
No nature of exhaustibility;
No nature of production;
No nature of destruction;
No nature of self;
No nature of non-self;
No nature of being any being;
No nature of not being any being;
No nature of bodhi;
No nature of the Dharma realm;
No nature of empty space; and
No nature of the attainment of right enlightenment.

Because they realize all dharmas have no nature, they therefore attain all-knowledge and the continuous great compassion with which they rescue and liberate beings.

Sons of the Buddha, this is just as it is with empty space which, whether all worlds are created or destroyed, is never either increased or decreased. Why is this so? This is because empty space is unproduced. So too it is with the bodhi of all buddhas which, whether beings do or do not attain right enlightenment, is still neither increased nor decreased. And how is this so? This is because bodhi is neither possessed of signs nor signless and neither singular nor multifarious.

Sons of the Buddha, suppose that there was someone who was able to transformationally create a Ganges' sands number of minds who was then also able to transformationally create from every one of those minds a Ganges' sands number of buddhas, all of whom were formless, shapeless, and signless, and suppose he ceaselessly continued on in this same way to the exhaustion of a Ganges' sands number of kalpas. Sons of the Buddha, what do you think? How many transformationally created *tathāgatas* would that man have created from those transformationally created minds?

Then Sublime Qualities of the Manifestations of the Tathāgata's Nature Bodhisattva replied: "As I understand the meaning of what the Humane One has described, there would be no difference between transformationally created and not being transformationally created. Why then would one even pose the question as to how many there would be all together in such a circumstance?"

Samantabhadra Bodhisattva replied:

Good indeed! Good indeed! Son of the Buddha, it is just as you have declared. Even supposing that all beings attained right enlightenment in but a single mind-moment, this would be the same and no different from when they had not yet attained right enlightenment. And why is this so? This is because bodhi is signless. If it is signless, then it would be neither increased nor decreased.

Sons of the Buddha, the bodhisattva-mahāsattva should understand this in this way. Attainment of the universal and right enlightenment is identical to bodhi in that its singular sign is signlessness. When the Tathāgata attains right enlightenment, he uses the skillful means of this singular sign to enter the "thoroughly enlightened wisdom" samādhi. Having entered it, within the singular vast body in which he realizes right enlightenment, he manifests a number of bodies as numerous as all beings, all of which dwell within that body. Then, just as it is with that single vast body in which he attains right enlightenment, so too is this so with all the vast bodies in which right enlightenment is attained.

Sons of the Buddha, the Tathāgata has countless gateways such as these associated with the attainment of right enlightenment. One should therefore realize that the bodies manifested by the Tathāgata are measureless. Because they are measureless, it is said of the Tathāgata's bodies that they constitute a measureless realm equal in number to the realm of beings.

Sons of the Buddha, the bodhisattva-mahāsattva should realize that, in but a single pore of the Tathāgata's body, there are buddha bodies equal to the number of all beings' bodies. And how is this so? This is because, the body in which the Tathāgata attains right enlightenment is ultimately neither produced nor destroyed. Just as a single pore pervades the Dharma realm, so too is this true of all such pores. One should realize that there is not even the smallest empty place in which there is no buddha body. And how is this so? This is because, when the Tathāgata attains right enlightenment, there is no place he does not reach. In accordance with his abilities and in accordance with his powers, as he is seated on the lion throne at the site of enlightenment beneath the bodhi tree, he attains the universal and right enlightenment with many different types of bodies.

Sons of the Buddha, the bodhisattva-mahāsattva should realize that, within one's own mind, in each successive mind-moment, buddhas are always attaining right enlightenment. How is this so? This is because, it is not apart from this very mind that all buddhas, the *tathāgatas,* attain right enlightenment. And just as it is with one's own mind, so too it is with the minds of all beings. In all of them, there are *tathāgatas* attaining the universal and right enlightenment which, vast and universally pervasive, has no place in which it is not present. It is never abandoned, never cut off, and never ceases. So it is that one enters the gateway of inconceivable skillful means.

Sons of the Buddha, it is in these ways that the bodhisattva-mahāsattva should know the Tathāgata's attainment of right enlightenment.

At that time, wishing to once again clarify the meaning of this, Samantabhadra Bodhisattva-mahāsattva then spoke these verses:

The Rightly Enlightened One completely knows all dharmas
as non-dual, apart from duality, as all of a uniform equality,
as possessed of an essential nature of purity comparable to space,
and as not involving discriminations regarding "self" or "not-self."

Just as the ocean reflects the bodies of beings
and because of this is said to be "the great ocean,"

so too, bodhi everywhere reflects all thoughts and actions
and is therefore described as "right enlightenment."

Just as when the worlds undergo creation and destruction,
empty space is still not thereby either increased or decreased,
so too, when all buddhas appear in the world,
bodhi still has but a single sign, that of being forever signless.

If someone conjured minds and transformed them into buddhas—
conjured and not-conjured, the nature of the matter would not differ.
So too, even if all beings were to realize bodhi, both after realization
and before realization, it would neither increase nor decrease.

The Buddha has a samādhi called "thoroughly enlightened wisdom."
It is beneath the bodhi tree that he enters this meditative absorption,
emanates countless light rays as numerous as beings,
and then awakens the many beings as if causing lotuses to bloom.

It is because of the manifestation of bodies as numerous
as the thoughts, faculties, and inclinations of all beings
throughout all the kalpas and *kṣetras* of the three periods of time
that right enlightenment is therefore described as "measureless."

Sons of the Buddha, how should the bodhisattva-mahāsattva know the turning of the Dharma wheel as accomplished by the Tathāgata, the Arhat, the One of Right and Universal Enlightenment? Sons of the Buddha, the bodhisattva-mahāsattva should know it in these ways:

Through the sovereign power of the mind and without any arising and without any turning, the Tathāgata turns the wheel of Dharma, for he knows all dharmas as forever unarisen;

Through three kinds of turning by which one cuts off what should be cut off he turns the wheel of Dharma, for he knows all dharmas transcend the extreme views;

Through transcendence of both the extreme of desire and the extreme of its negation, he turns the wheel of Dharma, for he has penetrated to the utmost that all dharmas are like space;

Without resort to speech, he turns the wheel of Dharma, for he knows all dharmas as ineffable;

Through ultimate quiescence, he turns the wheel of Dharma, for he knows all dharmas as having the nature of nirvāṇa;

Through all languages and through all forms of speech, he turns the wheel of Dharma, for there is no place the voice of the Tathāgata does not reach;

Through knowing all sounds as like echoes, he turns the wheel of Dharma, for he completely understands the true nature of all dharmas;

Through sending forth all voices from within a single voice, he turns the wheel of Dharma, for there is ultimately no subjective agent;[395] and

Through doing so endlessly and without omission, he turns the wheel of Dharma, for he is free of any inward or outward attachment.

Sons of the Buddha, just as one could never finish describing all that is expressed through language and speech even if one attempted to do so until the very end of all future kalpas, so too it is with the Buddha's turning of the wheel of Dharma for, even if one used every kind of language and ceaselessly described all that he has thereby established and revealed, one would never come to the end of it.

Sons of the Buddha, the Tathāgata's turning of the Dharma wheel enters all speech and language and yet does not abide there. Just as the alphabet everywhere enters all affairs, all speech, all numerical calculations, and all worldly and world-transcending circumstances and yet does not abide there, so too it is with [what has been described by] the Tathāgata's voice, for it everywhere enters all places, all beings, all dharmas, all karmic actions, and all karmic retributions, and yet it still has no place in which it abides.

None of the many different kinds of language of all beings exist apart from [what has been taught through] the Tathāgata's turning of the Dharma wheel. And how is this so? It is because the true character of words and speech is identical to the wheel of Dharma. Sons of the Buddha, the bodhisattva-mahāsattva should know the Tathāgata's turning of the Dharma wheel in this way.

Moreover, Sons of the Buddha, the bodhisattva-mahāsattva who wishes to know the Dharma wheel as it is turned by the Tathāgata should know the place of origination of the Tathāgata's wheel of Dharma. What then is the place of origination of the Tathāgata's wheel of Dharma? Sons of the Buddha, it is in accordance with the incalculably many differences in all beings' mental actions and inclinations that he sends forth just so very many voices in his turning of the wheel of Dharma.

Sons of the Buddha, the Tathāgata, the Arhat, the One of Right and Universal Enlightenment, has a samādhi known as "ultimate unimpeded fearlessness." Having entered this samādhi, in his state of realization of right enlightenment, from every mouth of every one of his bodies, he emanates voices as numerous as all beings. Every one of those voices is itself possessed of many voices, each of which in turn is different in how it turns the wheel of Dharma and causes all beings to be filled with joyous delight.

One should realize that whoever is able to know the turning of the Dharma wheel in this way is one who accords with the Dharma of all buddhas. Whoever does not know it in this way is not one who accords with it.

Sons of the Buddha, all bodhisattva-mahāsattvas should know the Buddha's turning of the Dharma wheel in this way because it everywhere enters the countless realms of beings.

At that time, wishing to once again clarify the meaning of this, Samantabhadra Bodhisattva-mahāsattva then spoke these verses:

When the Tathāgata turns the Dharma wheel, nothing at all is turned,
In all three times, there is neither any arising nor any attainment.
Just as there will be no time when all written words are exhausted,
so too it is with the Dharma wheel as turned by the Ten-Powered One.

Just as words can enter all places and yet still never reach them,
so too it is with the Dharma wheel of the Rightly Enlightened One.
It enters all verbal expressions and yet has nothing at all it enters
even as it is still able to cause all beings to feel joyous delight.

The Buddha has a samādhi called "ultimate unimpeded fearlessness."
After he has entered this concentration, he then speaks the Dharma.
For all the countless beings, he everywhere speaks in their languages,
thereby causing them to awaken and thus then understand.

Every one of those voices in turn additionally expounds
in countlessly many languages, each of which are different,
with which he freely holds forth in the world without discrimination,
adapting to their individual dispositions, thus enabling all to hear.

Those words do not arise from within or from without,
are never lost, and are free of any accumulation,
yet he thereby turns the wheel of Dharma for the sake of beings
with just such sovereign mastery in his very extraordinary manner.

Sons of the Buddha, how should the bodhisattva-mahāsattva know the *parinirvāṇa* of the Tathāgata, the Arhat, the One of Right and Universal Enlightenment? Sons of the Buddha, the bodhisattva-mahāsattva who wishes to know the great nirvāṇa of the Tathāgata should and must completely know its fundamental and essential nature:

Just as it is with the nirvāṇa of true suchness, so too it is with the Tathāgata's nirvāṇa;
Just as it is with the nirvāṇa of the apex of reality, so too it is with the Tathāgata's nirvāṇa;

Just as it is with the nirvāṇa of the Dharma realm, so too it is with the Tathāgata's nirvāṇa;
Just as it is with the nirvāṇa of empty space, so too it is with the Tathāgata's nirvāṇa;
Just as it is with the nirvāṇa of the nature of dharmas, so too it is with the Tathāgata's nirvāṇa;
Just as it is with the nirvāṇa of the apex of dispassion, so too it is with the Tathāgata's nirvāṇa;
Just as it is with the nirvāṇa of the apex of signlessness, so too it is with the Tathāgata's nirvāṇa;
Just as it is with the nirvāṇa of the apex of the nature of a self, so too it is with the Tathāgata's nirvāṇa;
Just as it is with the nirvāṇa of the apex of the nature of all dharmas, so too it is with the Tathāgata's nirvāṇa; and
Just as it is with the nirvāṇa of the apex of true suchness, so too it is with the Tathāgata's nirvāṇa.

And how is this so? This is because nirvāṇa has no arising and no manifestation. If a dharma has no arising and no manifestation, then it has no cessation.

Sons of the Buddha, the Tathāgata does not speak about the *tathāgatas'* ultimate nirvāṇa for the bodhisattvas, nor does he show that matter to them. Why not? He prefers to enable them to see all *tathāgatas* always abiding directly before them so that, in but a single mind-moment, they also see all buddhas of the past and future with their perfectly fulfilled physical marks just as if they were here now, doing so without raising any dual or non-dual perceptions. And why? Because the bodhisattva-mahāsattvas have forever abandoned all attachments to perceptions.

Sons of the Buddha, it is in order to enable beings to find happiness that all buddhas, *tathāgatas,* appear in the world and it is out of a wish to cause beings to develop a fond admiration for it that they manifest the appearance of nirvāṇa. However, in truth, the Tathāgata has no emergence into the world nor does he have any nirvāṇa. How is this so? The Tathāgata forever dwells in the pure Dharma realm. It is as an adaptation to the minds of beings that he manifests the appearance of entering nirvāṇa.

Sons of the Buddha, by way of analogy, this is just as when the sun rises, it everywhere illuminates the world and, of all of its vessels containing pure water, there are none in which its reflection does not then appear. Its illumination reaches everywhere to all the many places even as it has neither any coming nor any going.

Sometimes one of these vessels breaks at which point it no longer shows the sun's reflection.

Sons of the Buddha, what do you think? When that reflection no longer appears, is that the fault of the sun, or not?

They replied: "No. It was only because the vessel was broken and not due to any fault on the part of the sun."

Sons of the Buddha, so too it is with the Tathāgata's wisdom sun. In its appearance everywhere throughout the Dharma realm, there is no before or after involved. Among all beings' vessels of the pure mind, there are none in which the Buddha does not appear. Wherever the vessel of the mind is forever pure, one always sees the body of the Buddha. If the mind becomes turbid and the vessel thereby breaks, then one is no longer able to see it.

Sons of the Buddha, wherever there is any being who should be able to achieve liberation through the appearance of nirvāṇa, the Tathāgata then manifests the appearance of nirvāṇa for him even though, in truth, the Tathāgata has no birth, has no death, and has no passage into nirvāṇa.

Sons of the Buddha, by way of analogy, fire as one of the great elements is able to create fires throughout the world, but sometimes in a particular time and place, its fire is extinguished. What do you think? Could it be that, as a result, all of the world's fires would be extinguished?

They replied: "No, that would not occur."

Sons of the Buddha, so too it is with the Tathāgata, the Arhat, the One of Right and Universal Enlightenment, who carries out the Buddha's works in all worlds. Sometimes, in a single world, when the works he has been able to accomplish have been concluded, he manifests the appearance of entry into nirvāṇa. How could it be then that, as a consequence, all buddhas, *tathāgatas,* in all worlds would then pass into nirvāṇa?

Sons of the Buddha, it is in this way that the bodhisattva-mahāsattva should know the great *parinirvāṇa* of the Tathāgata, the Arhat, the One of Right and Universal Enlightenment.

Moreover, Sons of the Buddha, it is as if there was a master magician who, understanding well the magical arts, used the powers of his magical conjuration to manifest the appearance of conjured bodies in all the cities and villages of all countries throughout the worlds of the great trichiliocosm and then used those magical powers to sustain their appearance throughout the entire kalpa. Then, in some other place where his magical performances had been finished, he allowed that conjured body to disappear.

Sons of the Buddha, what do you think? Could it be that, having allowed a single body in a single place to disappear, all of them everywhere would therefore disappear?

They replied: "No, that would not occur."

Sons of the Buddha, so too it is with the Tathāgata, the Arhat, the One of Right and Universal Enlightenment. Being thoroughly cognizant of the many different kinds of supernatural arts used in implementing countless types of wise skillful means, he manifests his bodies everywhere throughout the entire Dharma realm and sustains their appearance so that they are allowed to abide forever to the very exhaustion of future time. It may happen that, in a particular single place, the works he has done in accordance with those beings' minds come to an end, whereupon he manifests entry into nirvāṇa there. How could one consequently claim that, just because he manifested entry into nirvāṇa in that one place, he would therefore pass into nirvāṇa everywhere?

Sons of the Buddha, it is in this way that the bodhisattva-mahāsattva should know the great *parinirvāṇa* of the Tathāgata, the Arhat, the One of Right and Universal Enlightenment.

Moreover, Sons of the Buddha, when the Tathāgata, the Arhat, the One of Right and Universal Enlightenment, manifests entry into nirvāṇa, he enters the "unshakable" samādhi and, having entered this samādhi, every one of his bodies then emanates incalculably many hundreds of thousands of *koṭīs* of *nayutas* of great light rays. Each of those light rays then sends forth an *asaṃkhyeya* of lotus flowers. Each of those lotus flowers has ineffably many marvelously bejeweled flower stamens.

Each of those flower stamens has a lion throne on it and, on each of those thrones, there is a *tathāgata* seated there in the lotus posture. The number of all of those buddha bodies is precisely equivalent to that of all beings. All of them possess supremely marvelous qualities of adornment which originate from the power of original vows.

Wherever there are any beings with ripened roots of goodness who see one of these buddha bodies, they all receive instruction. In this way, those buddha bodies continue to abide until the ultimate end of all future time during which, adapting to whatever is fitting, they teach and liberate all beings, never missing the right time in doing so.

Sons of the Buddha, the body of the Tathāgata has no location and is neither real nor false. It is only due to the power of the original vows of all buddhas that, if there are beings capable of being liberated, they then appear. It is in this way that the bodhisattva-mahāsattva should know the great *parinirvāṇa* of the Tathāgata, the Arhat, the One of Right and Universal Enlightenment.

Sons of the Buddha, the Tathāgata abides in the measureless, unimpeded, and ultimate Dharma realm, the realm of empty space, the true suchness nature of dharmas, beyond production or destruction, in the apex of reality. Sustained by original vows, he then appears for beings in accordance with the appropriate time, doing so ceaselessly, never forsaking any being, any *kṣetra*, or any dharma.

Then, wishing to once again clarify the meaning of this, Samantabhadra Bodhisattva-mahāsattva then spoke these verses:

Just as when the sun shines its light, illuminating the Dharma realm,
when broken vessels' waters flow out, its reflections then disappear,
so too it is with the wisdom sun of the Supreme One
which beings without faith see as disappearing into nirvāṇa.

This is just as when the fire element creates fires in the world,
and then, in one town, perhaps the fires are temporarily extinguished,
so too, the most supreme of men is everywhere in the Dharma realm,
yet, when teaching works end somewhere, he manifests his final end.

It is just as if a master conjurer manifested bodies in all *kṣetras*,
then, when finishing his work in some place, he was able to disappear.
When the Tathāgata's teachings end somewhere, he too does the same,
but, even so, in other lands, one still always sees the Buddha.

The Buddha has a samādhi known as "unshakable."
On finishing teachings for particular beings, he enters this absorption.
In but a single mind-moment, his body emanates countless light rays.
Their light then manifests lotuses and those flowers all have buddhas.

Those countless buddhas' bodies equal to the Dharma realm's beings
are such that beings possessed of merit are able then to see them.
Each of those countless bodies such as these
are replete in both their life spans and their adornments.

Though he has the nature of nonproduction, the Buddha still appears.
Though he has the nature of nondestruction, Buddha enters nirvāṇa.
Such phenomena cut short all verbal descriptions and analogies.
Perfectly realizing every form of meaning, he is entirely without peer.

Sons of the Buddha, how should the bodhisattva-mahāsattva know the roots of goodness which are planted through seeing, hearing, or drawing near to the Tathāgata, the Arhat, the One of Right and Universal Enlightenment? Sons of the Buddha, the bodhisattva-mahāsattva should know that none of the roots of goodness planted in the presence of the Tathāgata through seeing him, hearing him, or drawing close to him are planted in vain. This is:

Because they produce the inexhaustible wisdom of enlightenment;
Because they allow one to leave behind the difficulties of all obstacles;
Because they ensure one will definitely reach the ultimate;
Because they are free of any false or deceptive aspects;
Because they enable one to fulfill all vows;
Because they lead one to never end one's practices in the realm of the conditioned;
Because they accord with unconditioned wisdom;
Because they produce the wisdom of all buddhas;
Because they continue on to the end of future time;
Because they lead to perfecting all the many kinds of supreme practices; and
Because they allow one to reach the ground of effortless wisdom.

Sons of the Buddha, by way of analogy, it is as if there were some great man who, having eaten a small piece of vajra, would then never finally be able to digest it, for it would pass through his body and be expelled to the outside. Why is this? This is because vajra cannot remain together with the various kinds of filth in the flesh body.

So too it is when one plants even a few roots of goodness in the presence of the Tathāgata. They will necessarily lead one to pass through and beyond all of the affliction-ridden body's practices in the realm of the conditioned and will finally lead one to reach the station of unconditioned ultimate wisdom. How is this so? It is because even these small roots of goodness will not remain together with the afflictions associated with conditioned practice.

Sons of the Buddha, even if one piled up a mass of dry grass the size of Mount Sumeru and then threw into it a flaming ember that was only the size of a mustard seed, it would still all definitely burn up. And why would this be so? This is because of fire's capacity to burn things. So too, even if one plants only small roots of goodness in the presence of the Tathāgata, one will still definitely be able to completely burn away all of one's afflictions and ultimately succeed in reaching the nirvāṇa without residue. And why is this? This is because of the ultimate nature of even these small roots of goodness.

Sons of the Buddha, by way of analogy, this is like the medicine king tree known as "Good to See" which grows in the Himalaya Mountains. When seen, the eyes become purified; when heard, the ears become purified; when smelled, the nose becomes purified; when tasted, the tongue becomes purified; and when touched, the body becomes purified. When any being so much as takes up some of its soil, that too can provide its healing benefits.

Sons of the Buddha, so too it is with the Tathāgata, the Arhat, the One of Right and Universal Enlightenment, the unexcelled physician king who is able to bestow every form of benefit on beings. If anyone is able to see the form body of the Tathāgata, his eyes will become purified; if anyone is able to hear the name of the Tathāgata, his ears will become purified; if anyone smells the fragrance of the Tathāgata's moral virtue, his nose will become purified; and if anyone is able to taste the flavor of the Tathāgata's Dharma, his tongue will become purified and he will possess the vast and long tongue and come to understand the dharma of languages. If anyone is able to be touched by the Tathāgata's light, his body will become purified and he will ultimately acquire the unexcelled Dharma body.

If anyone develops mindfulness of the Tathāgata, he will acquire the purification of the mindfulness-of-the-Buddha samādhi. If any being makes an offering to a spot of land the Tathāgata has passed through or makes an offering to one of his stupas or shrines, then he will acquire roots of goodness allowing him to extinguish all affliction-based troubles and he will also acquire the bliss of the worthies and the *āryas*.

Sons of the Buddha, I shall now tell you: Even if there is some being who sees or hears the Buddha, but then, due to being encumbered by karmic obstructions, fails to develop faith and feel happiness on this account, they still thereby plant roots of goodness which will not have been planted in vain, for even this will eventually culminate in his entering nirvāṇa.

Sons of the Buddha, it is in this way that the bodhisattva-mahāsattva should know the roots of goodness planted in the presence of the Tathāgata by seeing, hearing, or drawing near to him. This will in all cases lead to abandoning all bad dharmas and perfecting the good dharmas.

Sons of the Buddha, the Tathāgata uses all kinds of analogies to describe many different situations, yet he has no analogy adequate to describe this dharma. How is this so? This is because the road of intellectual knowledge ends here and because this matter is so inconceivable. All buddhas and bodhisattvas only use analogies when teaching in order to adapt to beings' minds and delight them. They are not ultimate.

Sons of the Buddha, this Dharma gateway:

Is known as the place which holds the Tathāgata's secrets;
Is known as that which no one in the world can know;
Is known as the entryway to the seal of the Tathāgata;
Is known as the gateway to developing great wisdom;
Is known as that which reveals the lineage of the Tathāgata;
Is known as that which perfects all bodhisattvas;
Is known as that which cannot be destroyed by anyone in the world;
Is known as that which continuously accords with the realm of the Tathāgata;
Is known as that which is able to purify all realms of beings; and
Is known as the inconceivable ultimate dharma which expounds the fundamental true nature of the Tathāgata.

Sons of the Buddha, this Dharma gateway is not spoken for the sake of any other beings: It is spoken only for bodhisattvas progressing in the Great Vehicle and is spoken only for bodhisattvas who have entered the inconceivable vehicle. This Dharma gateway is not to enter the hands of any other kinds of beings aside from those who are bodhisattva-mahāsattvas.

Sons of the Buddha, by way of analogy, this is like the seven treasures owned by a wheel-turning sage king on account of which he manifests as a wheel-turning king. These treasures of his do not pass into the hands of any other being aside from the prince born to his number one wife, the prince who is completely endowed with the marks of a sage king. If a wheel-turning king had no prince who was completely endowed with those many qualities, then, after the king's life came to an end, within seven days, all of those treasures and other such possessions would scatter and completely disappear.

Sons of the Buddha, the precious treasure of this sutra is also of this very sort. It is not to enter into the hands of any other beings with the exception of the true sons of the Tathāgata, the Dharma King, those sons born into the clan of the Tathāgata who have planted the roots of goodness which produce the marks of a *tathāgata*.

Sons of the Buddha, if there were no true sons of the Buddha such as these, Dharma gateways such as these would scatter and disappear before long. Why? All those who are adherents of the two vehicles do not even hear this sutra, how much the less could they accept it, preserve it, study it, recite it, write it out, and analytically explain it. It is only the bodhisattvas who are able to act in such ways. Therefore, the bodhisattva-mahāsattvas who hear this Dharma gateway should feel great happiness and then, with a reverential mind, they should accept it with the highest level of respect. And why? This is because, if a bodhisattva-mahāsattva has faith in and delights in this sutra, he will swiftly attain *anuttara-samyak-saṃbodhi.*

Sons of the Buddha, even if a bodhisattva practiced the six *pāramitās* and cultivated all the different aids to enlightenment, doing so for countless hundreds of thousands of *koṭīs* of *nayutas* of kalpas, still, if he had not yet heard this Dharma gateway of the Tathāgata's inconceivable and great awesome virtue, or if heard it at some point in time but failed to believe in it, failed to understand it, failed to accord with it, and failed to enter into it, then he does not qualify to be referred to as a genuine bodhisattva, for he has still been unable to achieve birth into the clan of the Tathāgata.

If one succeeds in hearing this Dharma gateway of the Tathāgata's incalculable, inconceivable, unobstructed, and unimpeded wisdom and then, having heard it, has faith in it, understands it, accords with it, awakens to it, and enters into it, one should know that this person:

- Is one who has been born into the clan of the Tathāgata;
- Is one who accords with the realm of all *tathāgatas;*
- Is one who completely fulfills all the bodhisattva dharmas;
- Is one who abides securely in the realm of the knowledge of all modes;
- Is one who has left all worldly dharmas far behind;
- Is one who has developed all of the Tathāgata's practices;
- Is one who has a penetrating comprehension of the nature of all bodhisattva dharmas;
- Is one whose mind is free of doubts about the Buddha's powers of transformation;
- Is one who abides in the independently realized Dharma; and
- Is one who has deeply entered the unimpeded realm of the Tathāgata.

Sons of the Buddha, after hearing this Dharma, the bodhisattva-mahāsattva:

- Is able to use the knowledge of equality to know the immeasurable dharmas;
- Is able to use the correct and straight mind to abandon all discriminations;

Is able through supreme aspiration to see all buddhas directly before him;

Is able through the power of mental engagement to enter a realm of uniform equality like empty space;[396]

Is able through sovereign mastery of mindfulness to travel throughout the boundless Dharma realm;

Is able to use the power of wisdom to possess all the meritorious qualities;

Is able to use spontaneously arising wisdom to abandon all of the world's defilements;

Is able to use the bodhi resolve to enter the web of all the ten directions;

Is able to use great contemplation to know all buddhas of the three periods of time as of the same single essential nature; and

Is able to use the wisdom that dedicates one's roots of goodness to everywhere enter dharmas such as these, not entering them and yet entering them, not seizing on even a single dharma even as he constantly contemplates all dharmas through but a single dharma.

Sons of the Buddha, the bodhisattva-mahāsattva perfects meritorious qualities such as these and, with the power of but a minor effort, acquires the spontaneously arising wisdom realized without the assistance of a teacher.

At that time, wishing to once again clarify the meaning of this, Samantabhadra Bodhisattva-mahāsattva then spoke these verses:

If one sees, hears, or makes offerings to the Tathāgatas,
the merit thus acquired is so measureless that
it could never be exhausted even during all of conditioned existence.
He will soon extinguish the afflictions and leave the many sufferings.

Just as, if a man swallowed a small piece of vajra,
it could never be digested and would necessarily be expelled,
so too, merit acquired from offerings to the One of Ten Powers
will extinguish the afflictions and definitely lead one to vajra wisdom.

Just as, if one gathered dry grass equal in size to Mount Sumeru and
threw only a mustard seed-sized ember into it, it would still all burn,
so too, the small amount of merit gained from offerings to buddhas
will definitely lead to cutting off the afflictions and arriving at nirvāṇa.

The Himalaya Mountains have a medicine called "Good to See" that,
when seen, heard, smelled, or touched, heals the many diseases.
So too, if one but sees or hears the One of Ten Powers,
one will gain supreme merit and then reach the Buddha's wisdom.

At that time, due to the Buddha's spiritual powers and also because Dharma is of this very sort, ten ineffable numbers of hundreds of thousands of *koṭīs* of *nayutas* of worlds in each of the ten directions all moved and shook in six ways, namely upward thrusting in the east together with sinking in the west, upward thrusting in the west together with sinking in the east, upward thrusting in the south together with sinking in the north, upward thrusting in the north together with sinking in the south, upward thrusting at the periphery together with sinking in the middle, and upward thrusting in the middle together with sinking at the periphery. Eighteen types of movement then occurred, namely movement, pervasive movement, universally pervasive movement, rising, pervasive rising, universally pervasive rising, upward thrusting, universal upward thrusting, universally pervasive upward thrusting, shaking, universal shaking, universally pervasive shaking, roaring, universal roaring, universally pervasive roaring, striking, universal striking, and universally pervasive striking.

Rains of adornments then fell which were superior even to those in all the heavens. They consisted of all kinds of flower blossom clouds, all kinds of canopy clouds, banner clouds, pennant clouds, fragrance clouds, garland clouds, perfume clouds, adornment clouds, clouds of immensely radiant *maṇi* jewels, clouds of all kinds of bodhisattva praises, clouds of an ineffable number of many different types of bodhisattva bodies, clouds raining displays of realizations of right enlightenment, clouds causing the purification of inconceivably many worlds, and clouds raining down sounds of the Tathāgata's sayings. They completely filled the boundless Dharma realm. Just as, within these four continents, due to the Tathāgata's spiritual powers, there were manifestations such as these which caused the bodhisattvas to all be filled with great joyous delight, so too did this occur everywhere throughout all worlds of the ten directions.

At that time, from beyond a number of worlds off in each of the ten directions as numerous as the atoms in eighty ineffable numbers of hundreds of thousands of *koṭīs* of *nayutas* of buddha *kṣetras*, there came *tathāgatas* as numerous as the atoms in eighty ineffable numbers of hundreds of thousands of *koṭīs* of *nayutas* of buddha *kṣetras*. They were all identically named "Samantabhadra." They all appeared directly before them and said:

> It is good indeed, good indeed, Son of the Buddha, that you have been able to receive the assistance of the Buddha's awesome powers

and, according with the nature of dharmas, expound upon the inconceivable Dharma of the manifestation of the Tathāgata. Son of the Buddha, all of us identically named buddhas from each of the ten directions, in each case as numerous as the atoms in eighty ineffable numbers of hundreds of thousands of *koṭīs* of *nayutas* of buddha *kṣetras*—we all speak this very Dharma. And just as it is what is spoken by us, so too is it also what is spoken by all buddhas of the ten directions.

O Son of the Buddha, now, within this congregation, there are bodhisattva-mahāsattvas as numerous as the atoms in ten myriads of buddha *kṣetras* who have acquired the spiritual superknowledges and samādhis of all bodhisattvas. We now bestow upon them their predictions of being bound to realize *anuttara-samyak-saṃbodhi* in but one more lifetime.

There are also beings here as numerous as the atoms in a buddha *kṣetra* who have resolved to attain *anuttara-samyak-saṃbodhi*. We also bestow predictions on them that, in a future age, after passing through kalpas as numerous as the atoms in an ineffable number of buddha *kṣetras*, they will all succeed in attaining buddhahood at which time they will all be identically named "Especially Supreme Realm of the Buddha." In order to enable future bodhisattvas to hear this Dharma, we shall all join in protecting and preserving it.

Just as it is so for the beings brought across to liberation here in these four continents, so too is this so for the beings brought across to liberation in the ten directions' countlessly and immeasurably many hundreds of thousands of *koṭīs* of *nayutas* of worlds even up to all the ineffable-ineffable number of worlds throughout the Dharma realm and the realm of empty space.

At that time:

Because of the awesome spiritual powers of all buddhas of the ten directions;

Because of the power of the original vows of Vairocana;

Because Dharma is of this very sort;

Because of the power of roots of goodness;

Because the arising of the Tathāgata's wisdom never skips even a single mind-moment;

Because the Tathāgata's responses to conditions never fail to occur at the right time;

Because they awaken all bodhisattvas in accordance with the right time;

Because whatever they have done in the distant past is never lost;

Because they enable the attainment of Samantabhadra's vast practices; and
Because they manifest the sovereign mastery of all-knowledge—

From beyond a number of worlds in each of the ten directions equal to the atoms in ten ineffable numbers of hundreds of thousands of *koṭīs* of *nayutas* of buddha *kṣetras*, there then came, intent on paying their respects, bodhisattvas from each of those directions as numerous as the atoms in ten ineffable numbers of hundreds of thousands of *koṭīs* of *nayutas* of buddha *kṣetras* who, completely filling up the entire Dharma realm's ten directions, then manifested the bodhisattva's vast adornments, emanated an immense net of light rays, caused quaking in all worlds of the ten directions, caused the destruction and scattering of all the palaces of the *māras*, melted away all the sufferings in all the wretched destinies, displayed the awesome virtue of all *tathāgatas*, sang the praises of the Tathāgata's incalculably many different meritorious dharmas, everywhere rained down all the many different kinds of rain, manifested countlessly many different kinds of bodies, and received the Dharma of incalculably many buddhas.

Then, aided by the Buddha's spiritual powers, they each proclaimed:

It is good indeed, Son of the Buddha, that you have been able to speak about this indestructible Dharma of the Tathāgata. Son of the Buddha, we are all identically named "Samantabhadra" and we have all come here from the presence of the *tathāgata* named "Universal Banner of Sovereign Mastery" in worlds known as "Universal Light." In all those places, they also teach this very Dharma with just such phrasings as these, just such principles as these, just such explanations as these, and just such certitude as this. They are all the same as found here, neither more nor less.

It is due to the aid of the Buddha's spiritual powers and due to having acquired the Dharma of the Tathāgata that we have come here to pay our respects and bear witness for you. And just as we have come here for this purpose, so too is this also occurring in just this same way in all of the four-continent worlds throughout the ten directions of empty space everywhere throughout the Dharma realm.

At that time, aided by the Buddha's spiritual powers, Samantabhadra Bodhisattva surveyed that entire great congregation of bodhisattvas, and, wishing to once again clarify:

The vast awesome virtue of the manifestation of the Tathāgata;
The indestructibility of the Tathāgata's right Dharma;

The non-futility of planting measureless roots of goodness;
The inevitability that, when all buddhas appear in the world, they will be completely possessed of all the most superior dharmas;
Their excellent ability to contemplate the minds of all beings;
Their adaptation to whatever is appropriate in speaking the Dharma without ever missing the right time;
Their production of all bodhisattvas' measureless light of Dharma;
The miraculous adornment of all buddhas;
All *tathāgatas'* sharing of a single body free of individual differences; and
Their arising from their great original practices—

He then spoke these verses:

All that is done by all the *tathāgatas* is so indescribable
that none of the worlds' analogies could even come close.
Still, to enable beings to awaken and understand,
in what is inaccessible to analogies, I make analogies to instruct.

Such subtle, secret, and extremely deep Dharma
could only rarely be heard in a hundred thousand myriads of kalpas.
It is only those who are vigorous, wise, and well trained
who are then able to hear these mysterious and abstruse meanings.

Whoever, on hearing this Dharma, is filled with rejoicing
is one who has already made offerings to incalculably many buddhas,
is one who is supported and drawn forth by the Buddha, and
is one to whom men and devas give praise and always make offerings.

This constitutes the foremost world-transcending wealth,
this is able to rescue and liberate all the many kinds of beings,
and this is able to bring forth the path of purity.
You should all uphold it and must never be neglectful in doing so.

The End of Chapter Thirty-Seven

Chapter 38
Transcending the World

At that time, the Bhagavat, dwelling in the state of Magadha, was residing at the site of enlightenment in accordance with the *araṇya* dharma of forest dwelling, seated on a lotus flower dais lion throne in the Hall of Universal Light where:

His marvelous awakening was in all respects completely fulfilled;
He had forever cut off the two kinds of action;[397]
He had acquired the penetrating comprehension of the dharma of signlessness;
He had come to dwell where buddhas dwell;[398]
He had attained the equality of the buddhas;[399]
He had reached the station free of obstacles;
He had attained the Dharma that cannot be overturned;[400]
He had become unimpeded in his actions;[401]
He had established what is inconceivable;[402] and
He had attained the universal vision of the three periods of time.

His body constantly and completely pervaded all lands, his wisdom constantly and clearly penetrated all dharmas, and he had completed all the practices.[403] He had put an end to all doubts, had acquired the body that no one is able to fathom, and had acquired the wisdom that all bodhisattvas equally seek to acquire. He had achieved the ultimate perfection in the non-duality of the Buddha, had completely fulfilled the liberations which are the same for all *tathāgatas*, and had realized the ground equally shared by all buddhas in which neither the middle nor the extremes exist and he is present throughout the entire Dharma realm and commensurate with the realm of empty space.

He dwelt together there with bodhisattva-mahāsattvas as numerous as the atoms in an ineffable number of hundreds of thousands of *koṭīs* of *nayutas* of buddha *kṣetras*, all of whom had reached the stage of having but one more lifetime before they would realize *anuttarasamyaksaṃbodhi*. They had all come and gathered there from many different countries in other regions and all of them possessed the bodhisattva's skillful means and wisdom. That is to say:

They were well able to contemplate all beings and use the power of skillful means to enable them to undergo the training and dwell in the bodhisattva dharmas;

They were well able to contemplate all worlds and use the power of skillful means to go forth everywhere to visit them all;

They were well able to contemplate the realm of nirvāṇa, reflect upon it, and assess it;

They forever abandoned all conceptual proliferation and discriminations and incessantly cultivated the marvelous practices;

They were well able to attract all beings and skillfully penetrated all the countless dharmas of skillful means;

They realized all beings are empty and nonexistent and yet they still did not deny the fruits of karmic actions;

They thoroughly knew all of the many kinds of differences in beings' minds, latent tendencies, faculties, spheres of cognition, and skillful means;

They were able to take on and uphold the dharmas of all buddhas of the three periods of time, to completely understand them by themselves, and to then also explain them for others;

They skillfully and securely dwelt in the countless worldly and world-transcending dharmas while also knowing them in accordance with reality;

They skillfully contemplated all conditioned and unconditioned dharmas and realized their non-dual character;

In but a single mind-moment, they were able to acquire all the wisdom of all buddhas of the three periods of time;

They were able in each successive mind-moment to manifest the realization of the right and perfect enlightenment and enable all beings to resolve to attain enlightenment;

In the objective conditions focused on by a single being, they thoroughly knew all beings' spheres of cognition;

Although they entered the Tathāgata's ground of all-knowledge, they still did not relinquish the bodhisattva practices;

They use wisdom and skillful means in all the works they do, and yet they have nothing at all that they do;

They dwelt for countless kalpas for the sake of every being, and yet they were difficult to encounter even in *asaṃkhyeyas* of kalpas;

They turned the wheel of right Dharma and trained beings, never doing so in vain;

They had already completely fulfilled the pure conduct and vows of all buddhas of the three periods of time; and

They had all perfected countless meritorious qualities such as these which were so extensive that, even if all *tathāgatas* tried to do so for boundlessly many kalpas, they could still never finish describing them.

Their names were: Universal Worthy [Samantabhadra][404] Bodhisattva, Universal Eye Bodhisattva, Universal Transformation Bodhisattva, Universal Wisdom Bodhisattva, Universal Vision Bodhisattva, Universal Radiance Bodhisattva, Universal Contemplation Bodhisattva, Universal Illumination Bodhisattva, Universal Banner Bodhisattva, and Universal Enlightenment Bodhisattva.

Bodhisattvas such as these were as numerous as the atoms in ten ineffables of hundreds of thousands of *koṭīs* of *nayutas* of buddha *kṣetras*. They had all already perfected the conduct and vows of Samantabhadra. They had already completely fulfilled all their deep-minded great vows. Wherever any buddha appeared in the world, they were all able to go forth there, pay their respects, and request the turning of the Dharma wheel. They were well able to take on and sustain the Dharma eye of all buddhas. They ensured that the lineage of all buddhas would never be cut off. They knew well the sequence of all buddhas' appearances in the world and their bestowing of predictions, their names, their lands, their realization of the right and perfect enlightenment, and their turning of the Dharma wheel. In worlds without buddhas, they manifested bodies realizing buddhahood. They were able to cause all beings possessed of defilements to become purified. They were able to extinguish the karmic obstacles of all bodhisattvas. And they entered the unimpeded pure Dharma realm.

At that time, Samantabhadra Bodhisattva-Mahāsattva entered a vast samādhi known as "the flower adornment of the Buddha." When he entered this samādhi, all worlds of the ten directions shook in six ways, moved in eighteen ways, and produced a loud sound that no one did not hear. After this, he arose from his samādhi.

Then Universal Wisdom Bodhisattva, knowing that the assembly had already gathered together there, proceeded to pose questions to Samantabhadra Bodhisattva, saying:

O Son of the Buddha, please expound on the following matters:

What does the bodhisattva-mahāsattva rely on?

What constitutes his extraordinary kinds of thought?

What constitutes his practices?

What serves as his good spiritual guide?

What constitutes his diligent vigor?
What constitutes his bases for attaining peace of mind?
What constitutes his ways to develop beings?
What constitutes his moral precepts?
What constitutes his bases for realizing he is bound to receive his prediction?
What constitutes his entry among the bodhisattvas?
What constitutes his entry among the *tathāgatas*?
What constitutes his penetration of beings' mental actions?
What constitutes his entry into worlds?
What constitutes his entry into kalpas?
What constitutes his ways of speaking of the three periods of time?
What constitutes his penetrating knowledge of the three periods of time?
What constitutes his bringing forth of the tireless mind?
What constitutes his knowledge of differences?
What constitutes his *dhāraṇīs*?
What constitutes his proclamations regarding buddhas?[405]
What constitutes his bringing forth of the universally worthy mind [of Samantabhadra]?[406]
What constitutes his dharmas of universally worthy practice [of Samantabhadra]?
What constitutes his reasons for generating the great compassion?
What constitutes the causes and conditions for his arousing the bodhi resolve?
What are the types of mind he uses in revering the good spiritual guide?
What constitutes his purity?
What constitutes his *pāramitās*?
What constitutes his knowledge pursuant to awakening?
What constitutes his knowing based on realizations?
What constitutes his powers?
What constitutes his equal regard?
What constitutes his statements on the true meaning of the dharmas of the Buddha?
What constitutes his speaking about dharmas?
What constitutes what he preserves?
What constitutes his eloquence?
What constitutes his sovereign masteries?
What is the nature of his nonattachment?

What constitutes his types of impartial mind?
What constitutes his ways of developing wisdom?
What constitutes his transformations?
What constitutes his means of empowerment?
What constitutes the bases for great happiness and satisfaction?
What constitutes his deep penetration of the Buddha's Dharma?
What constitutes those things on which he is based?
What constitutes his ways of arousing fearless resolve?
What constitutes his ways of arousing doubt-free resolve?
What constitutes his inconceivability?
What constitutes his skillful and esoteric speech?
What constitutes his skillfully distinguishing wisdom?
What constitutes his kinds of entry into samādhi?
What constitutes his kinds of pervasive penetration?
What constitutes his gateways to liberation?
What constitutes his spiritual superknowledges?
What constitutes his clarities?
What constitutes his liberations?
What constitutes his gardens and groves?
What constitutes his palaces?
What constitutes his bases of delight?
What constitutes his kinds of adornments?
What constitutes his manifestations of the unshakable mind?
What constitutes his kinds of never-relinquished profound and great resolve?
What constitutes his kinds of [wise] contemplations?[407]
What constitutes his explanations of dharmas?
What constitutes his [other] kinds of purity?[408]
What constitutes his seals?
What constitutes his illumination with the light of wisdom?
What constitutes his peerless dwelling?
What constitutes his types of flawless resolve?
What constitutes his types of especially superior mountain-like mind?
What constitutes his oceanic wisdom by which he enters unexcelled bodhi?
What constitutes his jewel-like abiding?
What constitutes his generation of the vajra-like Great Vehicle resolve?
What constitutes his great undertakings?
What constitutes his ultimate and great endeavors?

What constitutes his indestructible faith?
What constitutes his ways of receiving the prediction [of future buddhahood]?
What constitutes his ways of dedicating roots of goodness?
What constitutes his ways of attaining wisdom?
What constitutes his ways of arousing boundlessly vast resolve?
What constitutes his hidden treasures?
What constitutes his types of moral standards?
What constitutes his sovereign masteries?
What constitutes his unimpeded functions?
What constitutes his unimpeded functions in relation to beings?
What constitutes his unimpeded functions in relation to *kṣetras?*
What constitutes his unimpeded functions in relation to dharmas?
What constitutes his unimpeded functions in relation to bodies?
What constitutes his unimpeded functions in relation to vows?
What constitutes his unimpeded functions in relation to realms?
What constitutes his unimpeded functions in relation to knowledge?
What constitutes his unimpeded functions in relation to the spiritual superknowledges?
What constitutes his unimpeded functions in relation to the spiritual powers?
What constitutes his unimpeded functions in relation to the powers?
What constitutes his easeful mastery?[409]
What constitutes his spheres of action?[410]
What constitutes his [other kinds of] powers?[411]
What constitutes his kinds of fearlessness?
What constitutes his exclusive dharmas?
What constitutes his works?
What constitutes his bodies?
What constitutes his physical actions?
What constitutes his [other] bodies?[412]
What constitutes his speech?
What constitutes his ways of purifying speech?
What constitutes his sources of protection?
What constitutes his accomplishment of great endeavors?
What constitutes his types of mind?
What constitutes his resolutions?
What constitutes his types of all-pervasive mind?

What constitutes his faculties?
What constitutes his deep mind?
What constitutes his kinds of especially superior deep mind?
What constitutes his diligent cultivation?
What constitutes his definite understanding?
What constitutes his definite understanding in entering worlds?[413]
What constitutes his definite understanding in entering the realms of beings?[414]
What constitutes his habitual karmic propensities?
What constitutes his grasping?
What constitutes his cultivation?
What constitutes his fulfillment of the dharmas of the Buddha?
What constitutes the ways of retreating from the path of the Buddha's Dharma?[415]
What constitutes his paths for transcendence of rebirths?
What constitutes his definite dharmas?
What constitutes the paths by which he develops the dharmas of the Buddha?
What constitutes his names that are used for great men?
What constitutes his paths?
What constitutes his measureless paths?
What constitutes his provisions for enlightenment?[416]
What constitutes his cultivation of the path?[417]
What constitutes his adornments of the path?
What constitutes his feet?
What constitutes his hands?
What constitutes his stomach?
What constitutes his inner organs?
What constitutes his heart?
What constitutes his armor?
What constitutes his weapons?
What constitutes his head?
What constitutes his eyes?
What constitutes his ears?
What constitutes his nose?
What constitutes his tongue?
What constitutes his body?
What constitutes his mind?
What constitutes his practices?
What constitutes his abiding?
What constitutes his sitting?

What constitutes his recumbence?
What constitutes his abodes?
What constitutes his places of practice?
What constitutes his [other] contemplations?[418]
What constitutes his universal contemplations?
What constitutes his swiftness?
What constitutes his lion's roar?
What constitutes his pure giving?
What constitutes his pure moral precepts?
What constitutes his pure patience?
What constitutes his pure vigor?
What constitutes his pure meditative concentration?
What constitutes his pure wisdom?
What constitutes his pure kindness?
What constitutes his pure compassion?
What constitutes his pure sympathetic joy?
What constitutes his pure equanimity?
What constitutes his meanings?
What constitutes his dharmas?
What constitutes his merit-based provisions for the enlightenment?
What constitutes his wisdom-based provisions for enlightenment?
What constitutes his completely developed clarities?
What constitutes his ways of seeking the Dharma?
What constitutes his dharmas for attaining complete understanding?
What constitutes his cultivation dharmas?
What constitutes the *māras*?
What constitutes the works of the *māras*?
What constitutes the ways of abandoning the works of the *māras*?
What constitutes the ways of seeing the Buddha?
What constitutes the buddha works?
What constitutes the arrogant actions?
What constitutes the wise actions?
What constitutes the ways of being possessed by Māra?
What constitutes the ways of being possessed by the Buddha?
What constitutes the ways of being possessed by the Dharma?
What constitutes the works accomplished while dwelling in the Tuṣita Heaven?
Why does he pass away from his dwelling in the Tuṣita Heaven?

Why does he manifest as dwelling within the womb?
What then constitutes his manifestation of subtle endeavors?
Why does he manifest as having just taken birth?
Why does he manifest a subtle smile?
Why does he manifest the walking seven steps?
Why does he manifest on the ground of the pure youth?
Why does he manifest abiding within the inner palace?
Why does he manifest as leaving the household life?
Why does he manifest as practicing the austerities?
Why does he then go to the site of enlightenment?
Why does he then sit at the site of enlightenment?
What constitutes the extraordinary signs that occur when he sits at the site of enlightenment?
Why does he manifest as conquering the *māras*?
What constitutes his realization of the Tathāgata's powers?
Why does he turn the wheel of the Dharma?
How is it that, because of turning the wheel of the Dharma, he acquires the dharmas of purity?
Why does the Tathāgata, the Arhat, the One of Right and Perfect Enlightenment manifest *parinirvāṇa*?

It would be good indeed, O Son of the Buddha, if you would please expound on dharmas such as these for our benefit.

Samantabhadra Bodhisattva then told Universal Wisdom and the other bodhisattvas:

Sons of the Buddha, the bodhisattva-mahāsattva has ten kinds of things upon which he relies. What are those ten? They are as follows:

He relies on the resolve to attain bodhi, doing so through never forgetting or losing it;
He relies on the good spiritual guide, doing so by remaining as harmoniously united with him as if they were one;
He relies on roots of goodness, doing so through cultivating, accumulating, and increasing them;
He relies on the *pāramitās,* doing so through cultivating them to complete fulfillment;
He relies on all dharmas, doing so because they ultimately result in emancipation;
He relies on great vows, doing so because they cause the growth of bodhi;
He relies on all the practices, doing so by completely developing them all;

He relies on all the bodhisattvas, doing so because they share the same single [body of] wisdom;

He relies on offerings to all buddhas, doing so through maintaining purity in the mind of faith; and

He relies on all *tathāgatas* because, like a kindly father, they incessantly provide him with instruction.

These are the ten. If bodhisattvas abide in these dharmas, then they themselves will succeed in becoming abodes of the Tathāgata's unexcelled wisdom.

Sons of the Buddha, the bodhisattva-mahāsattva has ten kinds of extraordinary thought. What are those ten? They are as follows:

He thinks of all roots of goodness as his own roots of goodness;

He thinks of all roots of goodness as seeds of bodhi;

He thinks of all beings as vessels of bodhi;

He thinks of all vows as his own vows;

He thinks of all dharmas as [means of attaining] emancipation;

He thinks of all practices as his own practices;

He thinks of all dharmas as dharmas of the Buddha;

He thinks of all dharmas of speech as constituting the path of speech;

He thinks of all buddhas as kindly fathers; and

He thinks of all *tathāgatas* as non-dual.

These are the ten. If bodhisattvas abide in these dharmas, then they acquire thought which is unexcelled in its skillful means.

Sons of the Buddha, the bodhisattva-mahāsattva has ten kinds of practices. What are those ten? They are as follows:

Practices related to all beings, to enable them all to become ripened;

Practices related to all means of seeking Dharma, to cultivate and train in them all;

Practices related to all roots of goodness, to cause them all to grow;

Practices related to all samādhis, to bring about undistracted single-mindedness;

Practices related to all [aspects of] wisdom, to have none of them he does not completely understand;

[Practices related to all the spiritual superknowledges, to facilitate sovereign mastery in spiritual transformations];[419]

Practices related to all means of cultivation, to have none he is unable to cultivate;

Practices related to all buddha *kṣetras, to* adorn them all;

Practices related to all good spiritual guides, to respect and make offerings to them; and

Practices related to all *tathāgatas,* to revere and serve them.

These are the ten. If bodhisattvas abide in these dharmas, then they acquire practices related to the unexcelled great wisdom of the Tathāgata.

Sons of the Buddha, the bodhisattva-mahāsattva has ten kinds of good spiritual guides. What are those ten? They are as follows:

The good spiritual guide who enables one to abide in the bodhi resolve;

The good spiritual guide who enables one to produce roots of goodness;

The good spiritual guide who enables one to practice the *pāramitās;*

The good spiritual guide who enables one to explain all dharmas;

The good spiritual guide who enables one to ripen all beings;

The good spiritual guide who enables one to acquire decisive eloquence;

The good spiritual guide who enables one to not become attached to anything in the world;

The good spiritual guide who enables one to cultivate tirelessly throughout all kalpas;

The good spiritual guide who enables one to securely abide in the practices of Samantabhadra; and

The good spiritual guide who enables one to penetrate everything penetrated by the wisdom of all buddhas.

These are the ten.

Sons of the Buddha, the bodhisattva-mahāsattva has ten kinds of diligent vigor. What are those ten? They are as follows:

The diligent vigor with which he teaches all beings;

The diligent vigor with which he deeply penetrates all dharmas;

The diligent vigor with which he purifies all worlds;

The diligent vigor with which he cultivates everything in which all bodhisattvas train;

The diligent vigor with which he extinguishes the evil of all beings;

The diligent vigor with which he stops all the sufferings in the three wretched destinies;

The diligent vigor with which he vanquishes all the many *māras;*

The diligent vigor with which he wishes to serve all beings as their purified vision;

The diligent vigor with which he makes offerings to all buddhas; and

The diligent vigor with which he pleases all *tathāgatas.*

These are the ten. If bodhisattvas abide in these dharmas, then they are able to completely fulfill the Tathāgata's *pāramitā* of unexcelled vigor.

Sons of the Buddha, the bodhisattva-mahāsattva has ten bases for attaining peace of mind. What are those ten? They are as follows:

He attains peace of mind through personally dwelling in the resolve to attain bodhi while also feeling he should enable others to dwell in the resolve to attain bodhi;

He attains peace of mind through personally ultimately abandoning anger and disputation while also feeling he should enable others to abandon anger and disputation;

He attains peace of mind through personally abandoning the dharmas of the foolish common person while also enabling others to abandon the dharmas of the foolish common person;

He attains peace of mind through personally diligently cultivating roots of goodness while also enabling others to diligently cultivate roots of goodness;

He attains peace of mind through personally dwelling in the path of the *pāramitās* while also enabling others to dwell in the path of the *pāramitās;*

He attains peace of mind through personally being born into the family of the buddhas while also feeling he should enable others to be born into the family of the buddhas;

He attains peace of mind through personally deeply penetrating the genuine dharma of the nonexistence of any inherently existent nature while also enabling others to penetrate the genuine dharma of the nonexistence of any inherently existent nature;

He attains peace of mind through personally refraining from ever slandering the Dharma of all buddhas while also enabling others to refrain from ever slandering the Dharma of all buddhas;

He attains peace of mind through personally fulfilling the bodhi vow to attain all-knowledge while also enabling others to fulfill the bodhi vow to attain all-knowledge; and

He attains peace of mind through personally deeply entering all *tathāgatas'* treasury of inexhaustible wisdom while also enabling others to enter all *tathāgatas'* treasury of inexhaustible wisdom.

These are the ten. If bodhisattvas abide in these dharmas, then they attain the peace of mind of the Tathāgata's unexcelled great wisdom.

Sons of the Buddha, the bodhisattva-mahāsattva has ten ways of developing beings. What are these ten? They are as follows:

He develops beings through giving;
He develops beings through use of the form body;
He develops beings through speaking Dharma;
He develops beings through engaging in joint endeavors with them;
He develops beings through remaining free of defiling attachments;
He develops beings through providing instruction in the bodhisattva practices;
He develops beings through brightly revealing all worlds to them;
He develops beings through revealing the great awesome virtue of the Buddha's Dharma;
He develops beings through using the appearance of many different kinds of transformations produced by his spiritual superknowledges; and
He develops beings through using many different kinds of subtle and esoteric skillful means.

These are the ten. The bodhisattva uses these to develop those in the realms of beings.

Sons of the Buddha, the bodhisattva-mahāsattva has ten kinds of moral precepts. What are those ten? They are as follows:

The moral precept requiring that one never relinquish the bodhi resolve;
The moral precept requiring that one abandon the grounds of the two vehicles;
The moral precept requiring one to contemplate and benefit all beings;
The moral precept requiring one to enable all beings to abide in the Buddha's Dharma;
The moral precept requiring one to cultivate everything in which all bodhisattvas train;
The moral precept requiring one to realize that all dharmas are inapprehensible;[420]
The moral precept requiring one to dedicate all roots of goodness to the realization of bodhi;
The moral precept requiring one to remain unattached to any of the bodies of all *tathāgatas*;
The moral precept that requires one to reflect on all dharmas and abandon any attachment to them; and

The moral precept requiring that one observe the right regulation of all one's faculties.

These are the ten. If bodhisattvas abide in these dharmas, then then they acquire the Tathāgata's unexcelled and vast *pāramitā* of moral virtue.

Sons of the Buddha, the bodhisattva-mahāsattva has ten dharmas associated with receiving the prediction [of future buddhahood]. It is due to these that the bodhisattva knows he is bound to receive the prediction. What are those ten? They are as follows:

It is through especially superior will in generating the bodhi resolve that he knows he is bound to receive the prediction;
It is through never wearying of or abandoning any of the bodhisattva practices that he knows he is bound to receive the prediction;
It is through abiding throughout all kalpas in practicing the bodhisattva practices that he knows he is bound to receive the prediction;
It is through cultivating all dharmas of the Buddha that he knows he is bound to receive the prediction;
It is through always having deep faith in all teachings of the Buddha that he knows he is bound to receive the prediction;
It is through cultivating all roots of goodness and causing them all to become completely developed that he knows he is bound to receive the prediction;
It is through establishing all beings in the Buddha's bodhi that he knows he is bound to receive the prediction;
It is through joining together harmoniously with all good spiritual guides in a state of non-dual unity that he knows he is bound to receive the prediction;
It is through envisioning all good spiritual guides as *tathāgatas* that he knows he is bound to receive the prediction; and
It is through constantly diligent preservation of his original vow to realize bodhi that he knows he is bound to receive the prediction.

These are the ten.

Sons of the Buddha, the bodhisattva-mahāsattva has ten kinds of entry among the bodhisattvas. What are those ten? They are as follows:

Entry into their original vows;
Entry into their practices;
Entry into their accumulations;[421]
Entry into their *pāramitās*;

Entry into their successful achievements;
Entry into their various different vows;
Entry into their many different kinds of understandings;
Entry into their adornment of buddha lands;
Entry into their sovereign mastery of the spiritual powers; and
Entry into their manifesting the taking on of births.

These are the ten. The bodhisattva uses these to everywhere enter among all bodhisattvas of the three periods of time.

Sons of the Buddha, the bodhisattva-mahāsattva has ten kinds of entry among the Tathāgatas. What are those ten? They are as follows:

Entry into their boundless realization of right enlightenment;
Entry into their boundless turning of the Dharma wheel;
Entry into their boundless dharmas of skillful means;
Entry into their boundlessly many different voices;
Entry into their boundless training of beings;
Entry into their boundless sovereign mastery of the spiritual powers;
Entry into their boundlessly many different kinds of bodies;
Entry into their boundless samādhis;
Entry into their boundless powers and fearlessnesses; and
Entry into their boundless manifestations of nirvāṇa.

These are the ten. The bodhisattva uses these to everywhere enter among all *tathāgatas* of the three periods of time.

Sons of the Buddha, the bodhisattva-mahāsattva has ten kinds of penetration of beings' actions. What are those ten? They are as follows:

Penetration of all beings' past actions;
Penetration of all beings' future actions;
Penetration of all beings' present actions;
Penetration of all beings' good actions;
Penetration of all beings' bad actions;
Penetration of all beings' mental actions;
Penetration of all beings' actions arising from their faculties;
Penetration of all beings' actions arising from their understandings;
Penetration of all beings' actions arising from their affliction-based habitual karmic propensities; and
Penetration of all beings' actions in relation to their teaching and training and whether it was provided at the right time or the wrong time.

These are the ten. The bodhisattva uses these to everywhere penetrate the practices of all beings.

Sons of the Buddha, the bodhisattva-mahāsattva has ten kinds of entry into worlds. What are those ten? They are as follows:

Entry into defiled worlds;
Entry into pure worlds;
Entry into small worlds;
Entry into large worlds;
Entry into worlds within atoms;
Entry into minute worlds;
Entry into inverted worlds;
Entry into upward-facing worlds;
Entry into worlds in which buddhas are present; and
Entry into worlds without buddhas.

These are the ten. The bodhisattva uses these to everywhere enter all worlds of the ten directions.

Sons of the Buddha, the bodhisattva-mahāsattva has ten kinds of entry into kalpas. What are those ten? They are as follows:

Entry into past kalpas;
Entry into future kalpas;
Entry into present kalpas;
Entry into calculably many kalpas;
Entry into incalculably many kalpas;
Entry into calculably many kalpas that are just incalculably many kalpas;
Entry into incalculably many kalpas that are just calculably many kalpas;
Entry into all kalpas that are just non-kalpas;
Entry into non-kalpas that are just all kalpas; and
Entry into all kalpas that are just a single mind-moment.

These are the ten. The bodhisattva uses these to enter all kalpas.

Sons of the Buddha, the bodhisattva-mahāsattva has ten ways of speaking of the three periods of time. What are those ten? They are as follows:

Speaking of past periods of time in the past;
Speaking of future periods of time in the past;
Speaking of present periods of time in the past;
Speaking of past periods of time in the future;
Speaking of present periods of time in the future;
Speaking of the future as endless;

Speaking of the past in the present;
Speaking of the future in the present;
Speaking of their uniform equality in the present; and
Speaking in the present of the three periods of time being equal to but a single mind-moment.

These are the ten. The bodhisattva uses these to speak of all three periods of time.

Sons of the Buddha, the bodhisattva-mahāsattva has ten kinds of knowing of the three periods of time. What are those ten? They are as follows:

He knows all of their arrangements;
He knows all of their languages;
He knows all of their discussions;
He knows all of their rules and regulations;
He knows all of their declarations;
He knows all of their edicts;
He knows all of their false designations;
He knows their endlessness;
He knows their quiescence; and
He knows them all as entirely empty [of inherent existence].

These are the ten. The bodhisattva uses these to know all dharmas of the three periods of time.

Sons of the Buddha, the bodhisattva-mahāsattva brings forth ten kinds of tireless mind. What are those ten? They are as follows:

The mind that is tireless in making offerings to all buddhas;
The mind that is tireless in drawing near to all good spiritual guides;
The mind that is tireless in seeking all dharmas;
The mind that is tireless in listening to right Dharma;
The mind that is tireless in proclaiming and explaining right Dharma;
The mind that is tireless in teaching and training all beings;
The mind that is tireless in establishing all beings in the bodhi of the Buddha;
The mind that is tireless in passing through an ineffable-ineffable number of kalpas in each and every world as he practices the bodhisattva practices;
The mind that is tireless in traveling to all worlds; and
The mind that is tireless in contemplating and reflecting on all dharmas of the Buddha.

These are the ten. If bodhisattvas abide in these dharmas, then they acquire the Tathāgata's tireless and unexcelled great wisdom.

Sons of the Buddha, the bodhisattva-mahāsattva has ten kinds of knowledge of differences. What are those ten? They are as follows:

The knowledge that knows the differences in beings;
The knowledge that knows the differences in their faculties;
The knowledge that knows the differences in their karmic consequences;
The knowledge that knows the differences in their taking on of rebirths;
The knowledge that knows the differences in the worlds;
The knowledge that knows the differences in the Dharma realm;
The knowledge that knows the differences among all buddhas;
The knowledge that knows the differences in all dharmas;
The knowledge that knows the differences throughout the three periods of time; and
The knowledge that knows the differences in the paths of speech.

These are the ten. If bodhisattvas abide in these dharmas, then they acquire the Tathāgata's unexcelled and vast knowledge of differences.

Sons of the Buddha, the bodhisattva-mahāsattva has ten kinds of *dhāraṇīs*. What are those ten? They are as follows:

The "listening-and-retaining" *dhāraṇī,* so called because, through it, one retains all dharmas and never forgets them;
The "cultivation" *dhāraṇī,* so called because it facilitates the skillful contemplation of all dharmas in accordance with reality;
The "reflective contemplation" *dhāraṇī,* so called because it facilitates the complete knowing of the nature of all dharmas;
The "Dharma light" *dhāraṇī,* so called because it facilitates illumination of the inconceivable Dharma of all buddhas;
The "samādhi" *dhāraṇī,* so called because it facilitates remaining unconfused with regard to right Dharma as heard in the abodes of all buddhas of the present;
The "perfect sound" *dhāraṇī,* so called because it facilitates the complete understanding of inconceivably many voices and languages;
The "three periods of time" *dhāraṇī,* so called because it facilitates expounding on inconceivably many dharmas of all buddhas of the three periods of time;
The "various forms of eloquence" *dhāraṇī,* so called because it facilitates expounding the boundless Dharma of all buddhas;

The "producer of the unimpeded ear" *dhāraṇī*, so called because it facilitates the ability to hear all Dharma spoken by an ineffable number of buddhas; and

The "Dharma of all buddhas" *dhāraṇī*, so called because it facilitates abiding in the Tathāgata's powers and fearlessnesses.

These are the ten. If bodhisattvas wish to acquire these dharmas, then they should engage in diligent cultivation and training [in them].

Sons of the Buddha, the bodhisattva-mahāsattva speaks of ten kinds of buddhas. What are those ten? They are as follows:

The rightly enlightened buddha;

The buddha of vows;

The buddha of karmic rewards;

The abiding and sustaining buddha;

The nirvāṇa buddha;

The Dharma realm buddha;

The mind buddha;

The samādhi buddha;

The buddha of the fundamental nature; and

The buddha who adapts to the dispositions [of beings].

These are the ten.

Sons of the Buddha, the bodhisattva-mahāsattva brings forth ten kinds of universally worthy mind [of Samantabhadra]. What are those ten? They are as follows:

He brings forth the mind of great kindness to rescue and protect all beings;

He brings forth the mind of great compassion to substitute for all beings in undergoing sufferings;

He brings forth the mind that gives away everything to relinquish all that he owns;

He brings forth the mind that takes mindfulness of all-knowledge as what is foremost to happily seek all dharmas of the Buddha;

He brings forth the mind adorned with meritorious qualities to train in all the bodhisattva practices;

He brings forth the vajra-like mind to never forget any of the places he has taken rebirth;

He brings forth the ocean-like mind so that all the dharmas of purity will flow into it;

He brings forth the mind like the great king of mountains to patiently endure all harsh speech;

He brings forth the peaceful and secure mind to remain fearless in giving away everything to beings;

He brings forth the ultimate mind of the *prajñāpāramitā* to skillfully contemplate all dharmas as devoid of anything at all that exists.

These are the ten. If bodhisattvas abide in these types of minds, then they swiftly succeed in perfecting the universally worthy skillful wisdom [of Samantabhadra].

Sons of the Buddha, the bodhisattva-mahāsattva has ten kinds of universally worthy practice [of Samantabhadra]. What are those ten? They are as follows:

The universally worthy practice dharma of vowing to remain [in the world] for all kalpas of the future;

The universally worthy practice dharma of vowing to make offerings to and revere all buddhas of the future;

The universally worthy practice dharma of vowing to establish all beings in the practices of Samantabhadra;

The universally worthy practice dharma of vowing to accumulate all kinds of roots of goodness;

The universally worthy practice dharma of vowing to enter all the *pāramitās*;

The universally worthy practice dharma of vowing to completely fulfill all the bodhisattva practices;

The universally worthy practice dharma of vowing to adorn all worlds;

The universally worthy practice dharma of vowing to take on rebirths in all buddha *kṣetras*;

The universally worthy practice dharma of vowing to skillfully contemplate all dharmas; and

The universally worthy practice dharma of vowing to realize the unsurpassed bodhi in all buddha lands.

These are the ten. If bodhisattvas diligently cultivate these dharmas, then they swiftly succeed in completely fulfilling the universally worthy conduct and vows [of Samantabhadra].

Sons of the Buddha, the bodhisattva-mahāsattva arouses the great compassion by using ten kinds of contemplations of beings. What are those ten? They are as follows:

Arousing the great compassion by contemplating beings as having no one to depend upon or rely on;

Arousing the great compassion by contemplating beings as being, by their very nature, untrained and non-compliant;

Arousing the great compassion by contemplating beings as poverty-stricken through having no roots of goodness;

Arousing the great compassion by contemplating beings as sleeping throughout the long night [of ignorance];
Arousing the great compassion by contemplating beings as practicing unwholesome dharmas;
Arousing the great compassion by contemplating beings as tied up by the bonds of desire;
Arousing the great compassion by contemplating beings as sunken into the ocean of *saṃsāra*;
Arousing the great compassion by contemplating beings as forever entangled in the suffering of sickness;
Arousing the great compassion by contemplating beings as having no wish to practice wholesome dharmas; and
Arousing the great compassion by contemplating beings as having lost the Dharma of the buddhas.

These are the ten. The bodhisattva constantly uses these types of thoughts in contemplating beings.

Sons of the Buddha, the bodhisattva-mahāsattva has ten kinds of causes and conditions for arousing the bodhi resolve. What are those ten? They are as follows:

He arouses the bodhi resolve to teach and train all beings;
He arouses the bodhi resolve to do away with all beings' accumulations of sufferings;
He arouses the bodhi resolve to bestow complete happiness on all beings;
He arouses the bodhi resolve to cut off all beings' delusions;
He arouses the bodhi resolve to bestow the wisdom of the Buddha on all beings;
He arouses the bodhi resolve to revere and make offerings to all buddhas;
He arouses the bodhi resolve to accord with the Tathāgata's teachings and please the Buddha;
He arouses the bodhi resolve to see the major marks and secondary signs of all buddhas' form bodies;
He arouses the bodhi resolve to enter the vast wisdom of all buddhas; and
He arouses the bodhi resolve to reveal the powers and fearlessnesses of all buddhas.

These are the ten.

Sons of the Buddha, if the bodhisattva brings forth the unexcelled bodhi resolve in order to awaken to and enter the wisdom of all-knowledge, when drawing near to and making offerings to the good spiritual guide, he should arouse ten kinds of mind. What are those ten? They are as follows:

The mind intent on serving him;
The mind of joyous delight;
The mind that is free of any opposition;
The mind that is compliant;
The mind that has no differing motivations;
The mind that is single-mindedly focused;
The mind that shares the same roots of goodness;
The mind that shares the same vows;
The mind of the Tathāgata; and
The mind intent on fulfilling the same practices.

These are the ten.

Sons of the Buddha, if the bodhisattva-mahāsattva arouses types of mind such as these, then he acquires ten kinds of purity. What are those ten? They are as follows:

Purity of deep resolve which reaches all the way to its ultimate destination without ever deteriorating;
Purity of the physical body which manifests for others in accordance with what is appropriate;
Purity of voice to ensure comprehension of all speech;
Purity of eloquence to skillfully expound on the boundlessly many dharmas of all buddhas;
Purity of wisdom to leave behind all the darkness of delusion;
Purity in the taking on of births through complete fulfillment of the bodhisattva's sovereign powers;
Purity of retinue through developing all roots of goodness with other beings who have joined in the same practices in the past;
Purity of karmic rewards and consequences through extinguishing all karmic obstacles;
Purity of great vows through having a nature no different from that of all other bodhisattvas; and
Purity of practice through achieving emancipation in reliance on the universally worthy vehicle [of Samantabhadra].

These are the ten.

Sons of the Buddha, the bodhisattva-mahāsattva has ten kinds of *pāramitās*. What are those ten? They are as follows:

The *pāramitā* of giving based on the complete relinquishing of everything one possesses;
The *pāramitā* of moral virtue based on purity in the Buddha's moral precepts;

The *pāramitā* of patience based on abiding in the Buddha's patience;
The *pāramitā* of vigor based on irreversibility in all that one does;
The *pāramitā* of *dhyāna* based on mindfulness focused on a single object;
The *pāramitā* of *prajñā* based on contemplation of all dharmas in accordance with reality;
The *pāramitā* of knowledge based on entering the Buddha's powers;[422]
The *pāramitā* of vows based on complete fulfillment of all the great vows of Samantabhadra;
The *pāramitā* of spiritual superknowledges based on manifesting all the functions of sovereign spiritual powers; and
The *pāramitā* of Dharma based on penetrating all the dharmas of all buddhas.[423]

These are the ten. If bodhisattvas abide in these dharmas, then they achieve the complete fulfillment of the Tathāgata's unexcelled *pāramitā* of great wisdom.

Sons of the Buddha, the bodhisattva-mahāsattva has ten kinds of knowledge pursuant to awakening. What are those ten? They are as follows:

The knowledge pursuant to awakening that knows the countlessly many differences in all worlds;
The knowledge pursuant to awakening that knows the inconceivability of all realms of beings;
The knowledge pursuant to awakening that knows with regard to all dharmas how any single phenomenon enters into all the many different phenomena and how all the many different phenomena enter into any single phenomenon;
The knowledge pursuant to awakening that knows the vastness of the entire Dharma realm;
The knowledge pursuant to awakening that knows the ultimate nature of all realms of empty space;
The knowledge pursuant to awakening that knows all worlds as they entered the past;
The knowledge pursuant to awakening that knows all worlds as they enter the future;
The knowledge pursuant to awakening that knows all worlds as they enter the present; and
The knowledge pursuant to awakening that knows the countless practices and vows of all *tathāgatas* can all be fulfilled with a single [act of] cognition;

The knowledge pursuant to awakening that knows all buddhas of the three periods of time as all sharing a single practice to attain emancipation.

These are the ten. If bodhisattvas abide in these dharmas, then they acquire the radiance of sovereign mastery in all dharmas, all their vows become fulfilled, and, in but the instant of a single mind-moment, they all become able to completely comprehend all dharmas of the Buddha and realize the right and perfect enlightenment.

Sons of the Buddha, the bodhisattva-mahāsattva has ten kinds of knowing based on realizations. What are those ten? They are as follows:

He knows all dharmas have but a single sign;

He knows all dharmas have measurelessly many signs;

He knows all dharmas reside in but a single mind-moment;

He knows the unimpeded nature of all beings' mental actions;

He knows the faculties of all beings are the same;

He knows the actions arising from all beings' afflictions and habitual karmic propensities;

He knows the actions associated with the latent tendencies in the minds of all beings;[424]

He knows all beings' good and bad actions;

He knows all bodhisattvas' sovereign mastery of conduct and vows, their preservation [of the Dharma], and their spiritual transformations; and

He knows the *tathāgatas'* complete fulfillment of the ten powers as well as their realization of the right and perfect enlightenment.

These are the ten. If bodhisattvas abide in these dharmas, then they acquire skillful means in all dharmas.

Sons of the Buddha, the bodhisattva-mahāsattva has ten kinds of powers. What are those ten? They are as follows:

The power to comprehend the inherent nature of all dharmas;

The power to comprehend all dharmas as comparable to transformationally created phenomena;

The power to comprehend all dharmas as comparable to mere illusory conjurations;

The power to comprehend all dharmas as dharmas of the Buddha;

The power to remain free of any defiling attachment to any dharma;

The power to possess a very clear understanding of all dharmas;

The power to never abandon the reverential mind toward all good spiritual guides;

The power to enable all roots of goodness to lead to the unexcelled king of all types of wisdom;
The power to maintain deep faith in the Dharma of all buddhas and never slander it; and
The power to skillfully ensure that one will never retreat from one's resolve to attain all-knowledge.

These are the ten. If bodhisattvas abide in these dharmas, then they come to possess all of the unexcelled powers of the Tathāgata.

Sons of the Buddha, the bodhisattva-mahāsattva has ten kinds of equal regard. What are those ten? They are as follows:

Equal regard for all beings;
Equal regard for all dharmas;
Equal regard for all *kṣetras;*
Equal regard for all kinds of resolute intentions;
Equal regard for all roots of goodness;
Equal regard for all bodhisattvas;
Equal regard for all vows;
Equal regard for all *pāramitās;*
Equal regard for all the practices; and
Equal regard for all buddhas.

These are the ten. If bodhisattvas abide in these dharmas, then they acquire all buddhas' unexcelled dharma of equal regard for all.

Sons of the Buddha, the bodhisattva-mahāsattva has ten kinds of statements on true meaning according to the dharmas of the Buddha. What are those ten? They are as follows:

All of these dharmas only have names;
All of these dharmas are like mere conjurations;
All of these dharmas are like reflections;
All of these dharmas arise solely from conditions;
All actions based on these dharmas are pure;
All of these dharmas are merely creations of language;
All of these dharmas are synonymous with the apex of reality;
All of these dharmas are signless;
All of these dharmas are synonymous with the ultimate truth; and
All of these dharmas are synonymous with the Dharma realm.

These are the ten. If bodhisattvas abide in these dharmas, then they skillfully penetrate the unexcelled and genuine meaning of the wisdom of all-knowledge.

Sons of the Buddha, the bodhisattva-mahāsattva speaks of ten kinds of dharmas. What are those ten? They are as follows:

They speak of very profound dharmas;
They speak of vast dharmas;
They speak of all kinds of different dharmas;
They speak of the dharma of all-knowledge;
They speak of dharmas which accord with the *pāramitās;*
They speak of dharmas which produce the Tathāgata's powers;
They speak of dharmas related to the three periods of time;
They speak of dharmas which enable the bodhisattva's irreversibility;
They speak of dharmas of praise for the Buddha's meritorious qualities; and
They speak of dharmas corresponding to all bodhisattvas' training, the equality of all buddhas, and all *tathāgatas'* spheres of cognition and action.

These are the ten. If bodhisattvas abide in these dharmas, then they acquire the Tathāgata's unexcelled skill in speaking about the Dharma.

Sons of the Buddha, the bodhisattva-mahāsattva has ten kinds of things he preserves. What are those ten? They are as follows:

He preserves all the merit and roots of goodness he has accumulated;
He preserves all dharmas spoken by the Tathāgata;
He preserves all analogies;
He preserves all the gateways to the principles and purport of the Dharma;
He preserves all gateways to the production of *dhāraṇīs;*
He preserves all the dharmas for doing away with doubts;
He preserves all the dharmas used to bring about the complete development of all bodhisattvas;
He preserves all the gateways to the samādhis of equality taught by the Tathāgata;
He preserves all the gateways to the bright illumination of dharmas; and
He preserves all the powers of all buddhas' easeful mastery in the spiritual superknowledges.

These are the ten. If bodhisattvas abide in these dharmas, then they acquire the powers of preservation of the Tathāgata's unexcelled and great wisdom.

Sons of the Buddha, the bodhisattva-mahāsattva has ten kinds of eloquence. What are those ten? They are as follows:

The eloquence that remains free of discriminations in speaking of all dharmas;
The eloquence that remains effortless in speaking of all dharmas;
The eloquence that remains free of attachment in speaking of all dharmas;
The eloquence that completely comprehends emptiness in speaking of all dharmas;
The eloquence that remains free of doubts or dullness in speaking of all dharmas;
The eloquence that receives the assistance of the Buddha in speaking of all dharmas;
The eloquence that brings about self-awakening in speaking of all dharmas;
The eloquence that is skillful in explaining differences in textual passages in speaking of all dharmas;
The eloquence that accords with reality in speaking of all dharmas; and
The eloquence that gladdens all beings by adapting to their minds.

These are the ten. If all bodhisattvas abide in these dharmas, then they acquire the Tathāgata's unexcelled skillful and sublime eloquence.

Sons of the Buddha, the bodhisattva-mahāsattva has ten kinds of sovereign mastery. What are those ten? They are as follows:

Sovereign mastery in the teaching and training of all beings;
Sovereign mastery in the universal illumination of all dharmas;
Sovereign mastery in cultivating the practices producing all roots of goodness;
Sovereign mastery in vast wisdom;
Sovereign mastery in the moral virtue that has nothing at all that it relies on;
Sovereign mastery in dedicating all roots of goodness to the realization of bodhi;
Sovereign mastery in irreversible vigor;
Sovereign mastery in the wisdom that utterly vanquishes all the many kinds of *māras*;
Sovereign mastery in enabling beings to resolve to attain bodhi by adapting to their individual inclinations;
Sovereign mastery in manifesting the realization of right enlightenment in accordance with those who should be taught.

These are the ten. If bodhisattvas abide in these dharmas, then they acquire the sovereign mastery of the Tathāgata's unexcelled great wisdom.

Sons of the Buddha, the bodhisattva-mahāsattva has ten kinds of nonattachment. What are those ten? They are as follows:

Nonattachment to any world;
Nonattachment to any being;
Nonattachment to any dharma;
Nonattachment to anything he does;
Nonattachment to any roots of goodness;
Nonattachment to any place in which he takes on rebirth;
Nonattachment to any vows;
Nonattachment to any practices;
Nonattachment to any bodhisattva; and
Nonattachment to any buddha.

These are the ten. If bodhisattvas abide in these dharmas, then they are able to swiftly transform all the many kinds of thought into the attainment of unexcelled and pure wisdom.

Sons of the Buddha, the bodhisattva-mahāsattva has ten kinds of impartial mind. What are those ten? They are as follows:

The mind that impartially accumulates all meritorious qualities;
The mind that impartially makes all the different kinds of vows;
The mind that is impartial toward the bodies of all beings;
The mind that is impartial toward the karmic consequences of all beings;
The mind that is impartial toward all dharmas;
The mind that is impartial toward all lands no matter whether they are pure or defiled;
The mind that is impartial toward all beings no matter what their levels of understanding might be;
The mind that is impartial and nondiscriminating toward all practices;
The mind that is impartial toward all the powers and fearlessnesses of the buddhas; and
The mind that is impartial toward all the types of wisdom of the *tathāgatas*.

These are the ten. If bodhisattvas abide in these, then they acquire the Tathāgata's unexcelled great mind of impartial regard for all.

Sons of the Buddha, the bodhisattva-mahāsattva has ten ways of developing wisdom. What are those ten? They are as follows:

Developing wisdom through knowing all beings' levels of understanding;
Developing wisdom through knowing the many kinds of differences in all buddha *kṣetras*;

Developing wisdom through knowing the distinct details throughout the network of the ten directions;
Developing wisdom through knowing all the inverted worlds, upward-facing worlds, and other kinds of worlds;
Developing wisdom through knowing with respect to all dharmas their single nature, their many different types of natures, and their vast scale of abiding;
Developing wisdom through knowing all the different kinds of bodies;
Developing wisdom through knowing all the worlds' inverted views and false conceptions while having no attachment to any of them;
Developing wisdom through knowing all dharmas ultimately bring about emancipation through but a single path;
Developing wisdom through knowing the Tathāgata's spiritual powers are able to enter the entire Dharma realm; and
Developing wisdom through knowing that the seed of buddhahood in all beings of the three periods of time is never cut off.

These are the ten. If bodhisattvas abide in these dharmas, then they have no dharma that they do not completely comprehend.

Sons of the Buddha, the bodhisattva-mahāsattva has ten kinds of transformations that he performs. What are those ten? They are as follows:

Transformations of all kinds of beings;
Transformations of all kinds of bodies;
Transformations of all kinds of *kṣetras*;
Transformations of all kinds of offerings;
Transformations of all kinds of voices;
Transformations of all kinds of conduct and vows;
Transformations of all ways to teach and train beings;
Transformations of all ways of realizing right enlightenment;
Transformations in all ways of speaking the Dharma; and
Transformations of all means of empowerment.

These are the ten. If bodhisattvas abide in these dharmas, then they achieve complete fulfillment of all the unexcelled dharmas of transformation.

Sons of the Buddha, the bodhisattva-mahāsattva has ten kinds of empowerment. What are those ten? They are as follows:

Empowerment by the Buddha;
Empowerment by the Dharma;
Empowerment by beings;

Empowerment by karmic actions;
Empowerment by the practices;
Empowerment by vows;
Empowerment by spheres of cognition;
Empowerment by time;
Empowerment by goodness; and
Empowerment by knowledge.

These are the ten. If bodhisattvas abide in these dharmas, then, in all dharmas, they will attain unsurpassed mastery of empowerments.

Sons of the Buddha, the bodhisattva-mahāsattva has ten kinds of bases for feeling great happiness and satisfaction. What are those ten? They are as follows:

All bodhisattvas make a resolution such as this: "To the very end of future time, when buddhas appear in the world, I shall follow, serve, and please them all." When they think in this way, they experience great happiness and satisfaction;

They also think: "When those *tathāgatas* appear in the world, I shall reverently make offerings of unexcelled gifts to all of them." When they think in this way, they experience great happiness and satisfaction;

They also think: "When, in the presence of all those buddhas, I present offerings to them, those *tathāgatas* will certainly provide me with instruction in the Dharma. In all such instances, with deep resolve, I shall respectfully listen and cultivate in accordance with what they teach so that it must certainly be the case that I have attained birth on the bodhisattva grounds in the past, that I have been reborn there in the present, and that will continue to be reborn there in the future." When they think in this way, they experience great happiness and satisfaction;

They also think: "I shall practice the bodhisattva practices for an ineffable-ineffable number of future kalpas and shall always succeed in dwelling together with all buddhas and bodhisattvas." When they think in this way, they experience great happiness and satisfaction;

They also think: "In the past, before I resolved to attain the unexcelled great bodhi, I had all kinds of fears, namely: the fear of not surviving, the fear of a bad reputation, the fear of death, the fear of falling into the wretched destinies, and the fear of the awesome virtue of great assemblies.[425] However, once I made that resolve, I abandoned all those fears so that I am no longer alarmed, no longer full of trepidation, no longer fearful, no longer beset with terror, no longer timid, and no longer scared. I have become invulnerable to being destroyed by any of the many kinds of *māras* or any of the adherents of non-Buddhist paths." When they think in this way, they experience great happiness and satisfaction;

They also think: "I shall enable all beings to attain unexcelled bodhi and, once they have attained bodhi, I shall cultivate the bodhisattva practices in the presence of those buddhas where, to the very end of their lives, with a mind of great faith, I shall engage in extensively bestowing offerings of all kinds of gifts appropriate for presenting to buddhas, doing so all the way up to the time when they enter nirvāṇa, after which I shall raise up countless stupas commemorating each of them. I shall then make offerings to their *śarīra* and see to the preservation and protection of the Dharma they leave behind." When they think in this way, they experience great happiness and satisfaction;

They also think: "I shall use the most unexcelled adornments to adorn all worlds of the ten directions, thereby ensuring that they all are fully adorned with the many different kinds of extraordinarily marvelous adornments and are all then equally purified. Moreover, I shall then use many different kinds of great spiritual powers through which I cause them all to quake, move, and become everywhere illuminated with brilliant radiance." When they think in this way, they experience great happiness and satisfaction;

They also think: "I shall sever all beings' doubts, purify all beings' inclinations, open up of all beings' minds, extinguish all beings' afflictions, close all beings' gates to the wretched destinies, open all beings' gates to the good destinies, dispel all beings' darkness, shine light on all beings, enable all beings to depart from the works of the many kinds of *māras*, and influence all beings to reach the place of peace and security." When they think in this way, they experience great happiness and satisfaction;

The bodhisattva-mahāsattva also thinks: "The buddhas, the *tathāgatas*, are as rarely met as the blooming of the *udumbara* flower and are so rare that one may never see them even once in a measureless number of kalpas. May it be that, in the future, when I wish to see the Tathāgata, I will then succeed in seeing all the buddhas, the *tathāgatas*. May it then be that they will never abandon me, but rather will constantly dwell wherever I am, allowing me to see them, speaking Dharma for my sake, doing so ceaselessly so that, having heard that Dharma, my mind will become purified and I will abandon flattery and deviousness and become straightforward in character and entirely free of falseness, whereupon I may then always be able to see all buddhas in each successive mind-moment." When they think in this way, they experience great happiness and satisfaction; and

They also think: "May it be that, in the future, I will realize buddhahood and become able then to use a buddha's spiritual powers to individually manifest the realization of the right and perfect enlightenment for each one of all the beings, manifesting purity, fearlessness, and the great lion's roar, using great original vows to go everywhere throughout the entire Dharma realm, beating the great Dharma drum, raining down the great Dharma rain, and engaging in the great Dharma giving whereby, throughout countless kalpas, I constantly expound right Dharma, sustained in this by the great compassion so that I remain tireless in all associated physical, verbal, and mental karmic deeds." When they think in this way, they experience great happiness and satisfaction.

Sons of the Buddha, these are the bodhisattva-mahāsattva's ten kinds of bases for great happiness and satisfaction. If bodhisattvas abide in these dharmas, then they acquire the great happiness and satisfaction of the wisdom arising from the realization of the unexcelled right enlightenment.

Sons of the Buddha, the bodhisattva-mahāsattva has ten kinds of deep penetration of the Buddha's Dharma. What are those ten? They are as follows:

They enter all worlds of the past;

They enter all worlds of the future;

They enter the worlds of the present, including the numbers of those worlds, the practices of those worlds, the speech of those worlds, and the purity of those worlds;

They penetrate the many different kinds of natures of all worlds;

They penetrate the many different kinds of karmic consequences of all beings;

They penetrate the many different kinds of practices of all bodhisattvas;

They know the sequence of all buddhas of the past;

They know the sequence of all buddhas of the future;

They know with regard to all present-era buddhas throughout the Dharma realm and the ten directions of empty space their lands, their congregations, their speaking of Dharma, and their training of beings;

They know the dharmas of the world, the dharmas of *śrāvaka* disciples, the dharmas of *pratyekabuddhas*, the dharmas of bodhisattvas, and the dharmas of the Tathāgata and, although they know all these dharmas have no bases for discriminations, they still speak about the many different kinds of dharmas. They completely penetrate the Dharma realm, and because, in so doing, they have nothing whatsoever that they penetrate, in accordance with their Dharma discourse, they have nothing at all to which they become attached.

These are the ten. If bodhisattvas abide in these dharmas, then they succeed in entering the extremely profound nature of the great wisdom of *anuttarasamyaksaṃbodhi*.

Sons of the Buddha, the bodhisattva-mahāsattva has ten kinds of bases. The bodhisattva bases himself on these as he practices the bodhisattva practices. What are these ten? They are as follows:

He bases himself on making offerings to all buddhas as he practices the bodhisattva practices;

He bases himself on training all beings as he practices the bodhisattva practices;

He bases himself on drawing near to all good spiritual friends as he practices the bodhisattva practices;

He bases himself on accumulating all kinds of roots of goodness as he practices the bodhisattva practices;

He bases himself on purifying all buddha lands as he practices the bodhisattva practices;

He bases himself on never abandoning any being as he practices the bodhisattva practices;

He bases himself on deeply entering all the *pāramitās* as he practices the bodhisattva practices;

He bases himself on completely fulfilling all the bodhisattva vows as he practices the bodhisattva practices;

He bases himself on the measureless bodhi resolve as he practices the bodhisattva practices; and

He bases himself on the bodhi of all buddhas as he practices the bodhisattva practices.

These are the ten. The bodhisattva bases himself on these as he practices the bodhisattva practices.

Sons of the Buddha, the bodhisattva-mahāsattva has ten kinds of arousal of fearless resolve. What are those ten? They are as follows:

The arousal of fearless resolve by which he extinguishes all obstructive karma;

The arousal of fearless resolve by which he protects and preserves right Dharma after the Buddha enters nirvāṇa;

The arousal of fearless resolve by which he conquers all *māras;*

The arousal of fearless resolve by which he does not even spare his own body or life;

The arousal of fearless resolve by which he utterly vanquishes the deviant doctrines of all adherents of the non-Buddhist paths;

The arousal of fearless resolve by which he causes all beings to rejoice;

The arousal of fearless resolve by which he causes all congregations to rejoice;

The arousal of fearless resolve by which he trains all the devas, dragons, *yakṣas, gandharvas, asuras, garuḍas, kiṃnaras,* and *mahoragas;*

The arousal of fearless resolve by which he abandons the grounds of the two vehicles and enters the extremely profound Dharma; and

The arousal of fearless resolve by which he tirelessly practices the bodhisattva practices for an ineffable-ineffable number of kalpas.

These are the ten. If bodhisattvas abide in these dharmas, then they acquire the fearless resolve accompanying the Tathāgata's unexcelled great wisdom.

Sons of the Buddha, the bodhisattva-mahāsattva has ten ways of arousing doubt-free resolve by which his mind remains free of doubt regarding any of the Buddha's dharmas. What are those ten? They are as follows:

The bodhisattva-mahāsattva arouses resolve such as this: "I should use giving to gather in all beings and shall use moral virtue, patience, vigor, *dhyāna* concentration, wisdom, kindness, compassion, sympathetic joy, and equanimity to gather in all beings." When he arouses this resolve, he is resolutely decisive and free of all doubt. Hence there is no possibility that he might produce any thoughts of doubt. This is the first of his ways of arousing doubt-free resolve;

The bodhisattva-mahāsattva also arouses this resolve: "When all buddhas of the future come forth and appear in the world, I shall serve and make offerings to them all." When he arouses this resolve, he is resolutely decisive and free of all doubt. Hence there is no possibility that he might produce any thoughts of doubt. This is the second of his ways of arousing doubt-free resolve;

The bodhisattva-mahāsattva also arouses this resolve: "I shall use many different kinds of extraordinarily marvelous nets of light to everywhere adorn all worlds." When he arouses this resolve, he is resolutely decisive and free of all doubt. Hence there is no possibility that he might produce any thoughts of doubt. This is the third of his ways of arousing doubt-free resolve;

The bodhisattva-mahāsattva also arouses this resolve: "I shall cultivate the bodhisattva practices until the very end of all kalpas of the future during which time I shall use all the unexcelled teaching and training dharmas to ripen all beings to the very ends of the Dharma realm and the realm of empty space in which those beings are so countlessly many, measurelessly many, boundlessly many, incomparably many, innumerably many, inexpressibly many, inconceivably many, immeasurably many, ineffably many, and ineffably-ineffably many as to entirely surpass all means of numerical calculation." When he arouses this resolve, he is resolutely decisive and free of all doubt. Hence there is no possibility that he might produce any thoughts of doubt. This is the fourth of his ways of arousing doubt-free resolve;

The bodhisattva-mahāsattva also arouses this resolve: "I shall cultivate the bodhisattva practices, fulfill the great vows, become possessed of all-knowledge, and abide within it." When he arouses this resolve, he is resolutely decisive and free of all doubt. Hence there is no possibility that he might produce any thoughts of doubt. This is the fifth of his ways of arousing doubt-free resolve;

The bodhisattva-mahāsattva also arouses this resolve: "For the sake of everyone in all worlds, I shall everywhere practice the bodhisattva practices and become a pure light of all dharmas which clearly illuminates all dharmas of the Buddha." When he arouses this resolve, he is resolutely decisive and free of all doubt. Hence there is no possibility that he might produce any thoughts of doubt. This is the sixth of his ways of arousing doubt-free resolve;

The bodhisattva-mahāsattva also arouses this resolve: "I shall realize that all dharmas are dharmas of the Buddha and shall adapt to beings' minds as I expound on the Dharma for them to enable them all to awaken." When he arouses this resolve, he is resolutely decisive and free of all doubt. Hence there is no possibility that he might produce any thoughts of doubt. This is the seventh of his ways of arousing doubt-free resolve;

The bodhisattva-mahāsattva also arouses this resolve: "I shall acquire the unobstructed gateway to all dharmas through realizing all obstructions are inapprehensible." In this way his mind becomes free of doubts and he abides in the nature of reality all the way until he realizes *anuttarasamyaksaṃbodhi*. When he arouses this resolve, he is resolutely decisive and free of all doubt. Hence there is no possibility that he might produce any thoughts of doubt. This is the eighth of his ways of arousing doubt-free resolve;

The bodhisattva-mahāsattva also arouses this resolve: "I shall realize that there are no dharmas that are not world-transcending dharmas, shall abandon all false conceptions and inverted views, and shall use a single kind of adornment to accomplish the self-adornment in which there is no one at all who is adorned so that, in this way, I reach complete understanding myself and become awakened without relying on anyone else." When he arouses this resolve, he is resolutely decisive and free of all doubt. Hence there is no possibility that he might produce any thoughts of doubt. This is the ninth of his ways of arousing doubt-free resolve; and

The bodhisattva-mahāsattva also arouses this resolve: "I shall achieve the most supreme and right enlightenment with regard to all dharmas, accomplishing this through abandoning all false conceptions and inverted views, through acquiring the wisdom that responds in but a single mind-moment, through realizing that whether it be unity or difference, such things are all inapprehensible, through transcending all enumerations, through realizing the ultimate state of the unconditioned, through transcending all words and speech, and through abiding at the very apex of the ineffable sphere of cognition." When he arouses this resolve, he is resolutely decisive and free of all doubt. Hence there is no possibility that he might produce any thoughts of doubt. This is the tenth of his ways of arousing doubt-free resolve.

If bodhisattvas abide in these dharmas, then their minds remain free of any doubts regarding any of the Buddha's dharmas.

Sons of the Buddha, the bodhisattva-mahāsattva has ten kinds of inconceivability. What are those ten? They are as follows:

The inconceivability of all his roots of goodness;

The inconceivability of all his vows;

The inconceivability of his knowing that all dharmas are like mere conjurations;

The inconceivability of his arousal of the resolve to attain bodhi, his cultivation of the bodhisattva practices, his never losing his roots of goodness, and his remaining free of discriminations;

The inconceivability of the fact that, although he has already deeply penetrated all dharmas, he still does not choose to enter nirvāṇa because his vows have not yet all been fulfilled;

The inconceivability of his cultivating the bodhisattva path, manifesting the appearance of his spirit's descent [from the Tuṣita Heavens], entering the womb, being reborn, leaving the home life, engaging in the austerities, going to the site of enlightenment, conquering the many *māras,* realizing the supreme and right enlightenment, turning the wheel of right Dharma, entering *parinirvāṇa,* incessantly manifesting mastery of the spiritual transformations, never relinquishing his compassionate vows, and rescuing and protecting beings;

The inconceivability of the fact that, although he is able to manifest the Tathāgata's ten powers and mastery of the spiritual transformations, he still never relinquishes his resolve as vast as the Dharma realm to continue teaching beings;

The inconceivability of his knowing with regard to all dharmas that whatever is signless is possessed of signs, that whatever is possessed of signs is signless, that whatever is free of discriminations involves discriminations, that whatever involves discriminations is free of discriminations, that nonexistence is existence, that existence is nonexistence, that effortlessness is effortful, that what is effortful is effortless, that what is unspoken is spoken, and that what is spoken is unspoken;

The inconceivability of his knowing that the mind is the same as bodhi, bodhi is the same as the mind, and the mind, bodhi, and beings are the same, this even as he still avoids producing inverted thoughts, inverted conceptions, or inverted views; and

The inconceivability of his entering the complete cessation absorption in each successive mind-moment while putting an end to all the contaminants, this even as he still refrains from entering the realization of the apex of reality and still refrains from putting an end to his roots of goodness associated with the contaminants. Although he does know all dharmas are free of the contaminants, he does know the ending of the contaminants and also does know the extinguishing of the contaminants. Although he knows that the dharmas of the Buddha are just the dharmas of the world and does know that the dharmas of the world are just the dharmas of the Buddha, he still does not distinguish worldly dharmas within the dharmas of the Buddha and still does not distinguish the dharmas of the Buddha within the dharmas of the world, this because all dharmas enter the Dharma realm even as there is no entry that occurs at all, and also because he knows all dharmas are in all cases non-dual due to their being free of any transformation at all. This is the tenth of these kinds of inconceivability.

Sons of the Buddha, these are the bodhisattva-mahāsattva's ten kinds of inconceivability. If bodhisattvas abide in them, then they acquire all buddhas' unexcelled dharmas of inconceivability.

Sons of the Buddha, the bodhisattva-mahāsattva has ten kinds of skillful and esoteric speech. What are those ten? They are as follows:

Skillful and esoteric speech in all the Buddha's sutras;

Skillful and esoteric speech regarding all the stations of rebirth;

Skillful and esoteric speech regarding all bodhisattvas, their spiritual superknowledges, their transformations, and their realization of the right and perfect enlightenment;

Skillful and esoteric speech regarding all beings' karmic consequences;

Skillful and esoteric speech regarding the defilement and purity created by all beings;

Skillful and esoteric speech regarding the gateway by which there are ultimately no obstacles with regard to any dharmas;

Skillful and esoteric speech regarding the presence of worlds in each and every place throughout all realms of space that, whether they are being created or destroyed, have no empty places between them;

Skillful and esoteric speech regarding the existence of the *tathāgatas* in even the most minute locations in all places throughout the ten directions of the entire Dharma realm, including their manifestation of the appearance of first taking birth, and so forth up to and including their realization of buddhahood, their entry into *parinirvāṇa,* and their completely filling the entire Dharma realm in which they all may be distinctly seen;

Skillful and esoteric speech regarding perceiving all beings as equally abiding in nirvāṇa because they are completely unchanging, and yet he, [the bodhisattva-mahāsattva], still never relinquishes his great vow because he has not yet completely fulfilled his vow to attain all-knowledge and hence he persists in fulfilling it; and

Skillful and esoteric speech regarding his knowing that all dharmas do not depend on awakening induced by others even as he still never abandons his good spiritual guides, but rather ever increases his venerating esteem toward the Tathāgata and becomes so closely united with his good spiritual guides as to be as if no different in his cultivation, accumulation, and planting of all forms of roots of goodness, in his dedications, in his abiding, in his same endeavors, in his same essential nature, in his same emancipation, and in his same fulfillment.

These are the ten. If bodhisattvas abide in these, then they acquire the Tathāgata's unexcelled skillful and esoteric discourse.

Sons of the Buddha, the bodhisattva-mahāsattva has ten kinds of skillfully distinguishing wisdom. What are those ten? They are as follows:

Skillfully distinguishing wisdom that penetrates all *kṣetras;*

Skillfully distinguishing wisdom that penetrates every place that there are beings;

Skillfully distinguishing wisdom that penetrates all beings' mental actions;

Skillfully distinguishing wisdom that penetrates all beings' faculties;

Skillfully distinguishing wisdom that penetrates all beings' karmic consequences;

Skillfully distinguishing wisdom that penetrates all the *śrāvaka*-disciple practices;

Skillfully distinguishing wisdom that penetrates all the *pratyekabuddha* practices;

Skillfully distinguishing wisdom that penetrates all the bodhisattva practices;

Skillfully distinguishing wisdom that penetrates all worldly dharmas; and

Skillfully distinguishing wisdom that penetrates all dharmas of the Buddha.

These are the ten. If bodhisattvas abide in these, then they acquire all buddhas' unexcelled skillfully distinguishing wisdom with respect to all dharmas.

Sons of the Buddha, the bodhisattva-mahāsattva has ten kinds of entry into samādhi. What are those ten? They are as follows:

He may enter samādhis in all worlds;

He may enter samādhis in the bodies of all beings;

He may enter samādhis on all dharmas;

He may enter samādhis in which he sees all buddhas;

He may enter samādhis in which he abides in all kalpas;

He may enter samādhis in which, when he arises from samādhi, he manifests inconceivably many bodies;
He may enter samādhis focused on the bodies of all buddhas;
He may enter samādhis in which he awakens to the equality of all beings;
He may enter samādhis in which, in but a single mind-moment, he enters the samādhis and wisdom of all bodhisattvas; and
He may enter samādhis in which, in but a single mind-moment, he uses unimpeded wisdom to ceaselessly fulfill the practices and vows of all bodhisattvas.

These are the ten. If bodhisattvas abide in these, then they acquire all buddhas' unexcelled dharmas of skillful samādhi practice.

Sons of the Buddha, the bodhisattva-mahāsattva has ten kinds of pervasive penetration. What are those ten? They are as follows:

Pervasive penetration of beings;
Pervasive penetration of lands;
Pervasive penetration of the world's many different kinds of signs;
Pervasive penetration of fire disasters;
Pervasive penetration of flood disasters;
Pervasive penetration among buddhas;
Pervasive penetration of adornments;
Pervasive penetration of the Tathāgata's body possessed of boundless meritorious qualities;
Pervasive penetration of all of the many different ways of explaining the Dharma; and
Pervasive penetration of the many different kinds of offerings made to all buddhas.

These are the ten. If bodhisattvas abide in these dharmas, then they acquire the Tathāgata's unexcelled dharmas of pervasive penetration with great wisdom.

Sons of the Buddha, the bodhisattva-mahāsattva has ten kinds of gateways to liberation. What are those ten? They are as follows:

The gateway of liberation in which a single body everywhere pervades all worlds;
The gateway of liberation in which one manifests incalculably many different kinds of forms and appearances in all worlds;
The gateway of liberation in which one enables all worlds to enter but a single buddha *kṣetra*;
The gateway of liberation in which one provides supportive empowerment to all realms of beings;
The gateway of liberation in which the adorned bodies of all buddhas completely fill all worlds;

The gateway of liberation in which one sees all worlds within one's own body;

The gateway of liberation in which, in but a single mind-moment, one goes to all worlds;

The gateway of liberation in which one manifests all *tathāgatas* coming forth into the world within but a single world;

The gateway of liberation in which a single body completely fills the entire Dharma realm; and

The gateway of liberation in which, in but a single mind-moment, one manifests all buddhas' easeful mastery of the spiritual superknowledges.

These are the ten. If bodhisattvas abide in these, then they acquire the Tathāgata's unexcelled gateways to liberation.

Sons of the Buddha, the bodhisattva-mahāsattva has ten kinds of spiritual superknowledges. What are those ten? They are as follows:

The expedient superknowledge with which he remembers past lives;

The expedient superknowledge with which he possesses the unimpeded heavenly ear;

The expedient superknowledge with which he knows the inconceivable mental actions of other beings;

The expedient superknowledge with which his heavenly eye is unimpeded in what it observes;

The expedient superknowledge with which he adapts to the minds of beings in manifesting the inconceivably great power of the spiritual superknowledges;

The expedient superknowledge in which a single body appears everywhere in countless worlds;

The expedient superknowledge with which, in but a single mind-moment, he everywhere enters an ineffable-ineffable number of worlds;

The expedient superknowledge with which he produces countless adornments with which he adorns an inconceivable number of worlds;

The expedient superknowledge with which he manifests an ineffable number of transformation bodies; and

The expedient superknowledge with which he adapts to the minds of inconceivably many beings in an ineffable number of worlds for whom he manifests the realization of *anuttarasamyaksaṃbodhi*.

These are the ten. If bodhisattvas abide in these, then they acquire the Tathāgata's unexcelled great expedient superknowledges with which they bring forth many different kinds of manifestations for all beings in order to enable them to cultivate and pursue the training.

Sons of the Buddha, the bodhisattva-mahāsattva has ten kinds of clarities. What are those ten? They are as follows:

The skillful cognitive clarity with which he knows all beings' karmic consequences;

The skillful cognitive clarity with which he knows all beings' spheres of cognition as quiescent, pure, and free of all conceptual proliferation;

The skillful cognitive clarity with which he knows all beings' many different objective conditions have but a single sign, that of inapprehensibility, and with which he knows all dharmas are [as indestructible] as vajra;

The skillful cognitive clarity with which he is able to use countless extremely subtle sounds to be heard in all worlds throughout the ten directions;

The skillful cognitive clarity with which he destroys all of the mind's defiling attachments;

The skillful cognitive clarity with which he is able to use skillful means to manifest as either being reborn or as not being reborn;

The skillful cognitive clarity with which he abandons all objects of perception and feeling;

The skillful cognitive clarity with which he knows all dharmas as neither possessed of signs nor signless, with which he knows them to be of but a single nature, that of having no nature, with which he remains free of discriminations yet is still able to completely know all the many different kinds of dharmas throughout measureless kalpas, distinguishing them and expounding on them, and with which he abides in the Dharma realm, realizing *anuttarasamyaksaṃbodhi*;

The skillful cognitive clarity with which he knows all beings as born and yet as originally unborn because he completely understands that taking birth is inapprehensible, and with which he knows causes, knows conditions, knows phenomena, knows spheres of cognition, knows actions, knows production, knows cessation, knows words and speech, knows delusion, knows the transcendence of delusion, knows inverted views, knows the transcendence of inverted views, knows defilement, knows purity, knows *saṃsāra,* knows nirvāṇa, knows apprehensibility, knows inapprehensibility, knows attachment, knows the absence of attachment, knows abiding, knows movement, knows going, knows returning, knows arising, knows non-arising, knows destruction, knows emancipation, knows ripening, knows faculties, and knows training—and thus, by adapting to what is appropriate, he provides all different kinds of teaching and never forgets what the bodhisattva practices. And how is this the case? It is solely in order to benefit beings that the bodhisattva brings forth the resolve to attain *anuttarasamyaksaṃbodhi*. He has no other motivation aside from this. The bodhisattva therefore always pursues the teaching of beings without ever becoming weary and without opposing what those in the worlds do. This is known as the skillful cognitive clarity with respect to conditioned arising; and

The skillful cognitive clarity by which the bodhisattva-mahāsattva has no attachment to the buddha and does not produce any thoughts of attachment thereto, has no attachment to the Dharma and does not generate any thoughts of attachment thereto, has no attachment to *kṣetras* and does not generate any thoughts of attachment thereto, has no attachment to beings and does not generate any thoughts of attachment thereto, and does not perceive the existence of beings and yet still engages in teaching, training, and teaching Dharma for their benefit. Thus he still never abandons any of the bodhisattva practices including the great compassion, the great vows, the seeing of buddhas, the hearing of the Dharma, the cultivation in accordance with it, the reliance upon the Tathāgata, the planting of all kinds of roots of goodness, and the respectful making of offerings, all of which he incessantly continues to pursue. In this, he is able to use his spiritual powers to cause quaking and movement in the countless worlds of the ten directions, this because his mind is as vast as the Dharma realm. In this, he knows the many different ways of explaining the Dharma, knows how many beings there are, knows the differences among beings, knows the arising of suffering, knows the cessation of suffering, knows all actions as like reflected images, practices the bodhisattva practices, and forever severs the very root of all rebirths. It is only for the sake of rescuing and protecting all beings that he practices the bodhisattva practices, and yet he has nothing whatsoever that he practices. He accords with the lineage of all buddhas and brings forth a resolve [as unshakable as] the great king of mountains. He recognizes that even all falseness and inverted views are subsumed within the gateway of the knowledge of all modes. His wisdom is so vast that it cannot be the least bit shaken. He is one who is bound for realization of the right enlightenment who equally rescues all beings from the ocean of births and deaths.

These are the ten. If bodhisattvas abide in these, then they acquire the Tathāgata's unexcelled great skillful cognitive clarity.

Sons of the Buddha, the bodhisattva-mahāsattva has ten kinds of liberations. What are those ten? They are as follows:

The liberation from afflictions;

The liberation from wrong views;

The liberation from all grasping;

The liberation from the aggregates, sense realms, and sense bases;

The liberation that steps beyond the two vehicles;

The liberation of the unproduced-dharmas patience;

The liberation that abandons attachment to all worlds, all *kṣetras*, all beings, and all dharmas;

The liberation of boundless dwelling;

The liberation by which he begins all the bodhisattva practices and enters the Tathāgata's ground of nondiscrimination; and

The liberation by which, in but a single mind-moment, he is able to completely know all three periods of time.

These are the ten. If bodhisattvas abide in these dharmas, then they are able to carry out the unexcelled buddha works, teaching and ripening all beings.

Sons of the Buddha, the bodhisattva-mahāsattva has ten kinds of gardens and groves. What are those ten? They are as follows:

Saṃsāra is the bodhisattva's garden and grove because he does not loathe and abandon it;

Teaching beings is the bodhisattva's garden and grove because he never wearies of it;

Dwelling in all kalpas is the bodhisattva's garden and grove because he thereby accumulates all the great practices;

Pure worlds are the bodhisattva's garden and grove because this is where he dwells;

All the palaces of the *māras* are the bodhisattva's garden and grove because he conquers their hordes;

Meditative contemplation on the Dharma that he hears is the bodhisattva's garden and grove because he contemplates it in accordance with principle;

The six *pāramitās*, the four means of attraction,[426] and the thirty-seven aids to enlightenment are the bodhisattva's garden and grove because he thereby sustains the realm passed on by the kindly father;[427]

The ten powers, four fearlessnesses, eighteen dharmas exclusive to the buddhas, and so forth until we come to all dharmas of the buddhas are the bodhisattva's garden and grove because he does not devote mindfulness to any other kinds of dharmas;

The manifestation of all bodhisattvas' awesome powers and sovereign spiritual superknowledges are the bodhisattva's garden and grove because he uses those great spiritual powers to ceaselessly turn the wheel of right Dharma, thereby training beings; and

The manifestation of the realization of right enlightenment for all beings in every place in but a single mind-moment is the bodhisattva's garden and grove because the Dharma body everywhere pervades all worlds throughout empty space.

These are the ten. If bodhisattvas abide in these dharmas, then they acquire the Tathāgata's unexcelled, worry-free, and immensely blissful conduct.

Sons of the Buddha, the bodhisattva-mahāsattva has ten kinds of palaces. What are those ten? They are as follows:

The resolve to attain bodhi is the bodhisattva's palace because he never forgets it;

The ten courses of good karmic action, merit, and wisdom are the bodhisattva's palace because he uses them to teach the beings of the desire realm;

The *dhyāna* absorptions corresponding to the four abodes of Brahma[428] are the bodhisattva's palace because he uses them to teach the beings of the form realm;

Birth into the Pure Dwelling Heavens is the bodhisattva's palace because there he remains undefiled by any of the afflictions;

Birth into the formless realm is the bodhisattva's palace because he thereby enables beings to leave behind the stations beset by the difficulties;[429]

Birth into defiled worlds is the bodhisattva's palace because there he enables all beings to sever the afflictions;

Manifesting as dwelling in the inner palace with wife, children, and retinue is the bodhisattva's palace because there he thereby assists the development of those beings he has practiced with in the past;

Manifesting as dwelling in the position of a wheel-turning king, a world-protecting deva king, Śakra, or Brahma is the bodhisattva's palace because it is done in order to train beings with the mind of a sovereign;

Abiding in all the bodhisattva practices with easeful mastery of the spiritual superknowledges, in all cases attaining sovereign mastery of them—this is the bodhisattva's palace because he thereby skillfully acquires easeful mastery in all the *dhyānas*, liberations, samādhis, and wisdom; and

As received from all buddhas, the summit-anointing consecration and prediction of attaining unsurpassed sovereign mastery as a king of all-knowledge—this is the bodhisattva's palace because he thereby comes to abide in the adornment of the ten powers and thereby accomplishes the masterful works of all the Dharma kings.

These are the ten. If bodhisattvas abide in these, then they acquire the crown-anointing consecration of the Dharma and will attain sovereign mastery in the use of spiritual powers throughout all worlds.

Sons of the Buddha, the bodhisattva-mahāsattva has ten bases for delight. What are those ten? They are as follows:

He delights in right mindfulness because his mind is thereby neither scattered nor confused;

He delights in wisdom because he thereby distinguishes all dharmas;

He delights in visiting all buddhas because he is tireless in listening to the Dharma;

He delights in all buddhas because they fill the boundless realms of the ten directions;

He delights in bodhisattvas because of their sovereign mastery in using countless approaches to manifest bodies for the benefit of beings;

He delights in all the samādhi gateways because, through entering but a single samādhi gateway, he enters all samādhi gateways;

He delights in the *dhāraṇīs* because he thereby retains the Dharma, never forgets it, and then transmits it on to beings;

He delights in unimpeded eloquence because, by resort to it, he may endlessly distinguish and expound upon but a single passage or a single sentence for an ineffable number of kalpas;

He delights in the realization of right enlightenment because it entails using countless means to manifest bodies and realize right enlightenment for the benefit of beings; and

He delights in turning the wheel of the Dharma because he thereby utterly vanquishes the dharmas promoted by all non-Buddhist paths.

These are the ten. If bodhisattvas abide in these dharmas, then they acquire the unexcelled Dharma bliss of all buddhas, the *tathāgatas*.

Sons of the Buddha, the bodhisattva-mahāsattva has ten kinds of adornment. What are those ten? They are as follows:

- Adornment with the powers, because they are indestructible;
- Adornment with the fearlessnesses, because they are insurmountable;
- Adornment with meanings, because he endlessly expounds on ineffably many meanings;
- Adornment with Dharma, because he contemplates and expounds on the collection of eighty-four thousand dharmas, never forgetting any of them;
- Adornment with vows, because of the irreversibility of the vast vows made by all bodhisattvas;
- Adornment with practices, because he attains emancipation by cultivating Samantabhadra's practices;
- Adornment with *kṣetras*, because he makes a single *kṣetra* of all *kṣetras*;
- Adornment with the universally pervasive voice, because it everywhere pervades all buddha worlds, raining the Dharma rain;
- Adornment with empowerments, because he thereby incessantly practices innumerable practices throughout all kalpas; and
- Adornment with transformations, because he manifests bodies as numerous as all beings in the body of a single being, thus enabling all beings to acquire knowledge and vision and seek all-knowledge without ever retreating.

These are the ten. If bodhisattvas abide in these dharmas, then they acquire all of the Tathāgata's unexcelled Dharma adornments.

Sons of the Buddha, the bodhisattva-mahāsattva manifests ten kinds of unshakable mind. What are those ten? They are as follows:

- The unshakable mind that is able to relinquish all his possessions;
- The unshakable mind that reflects upon and contemplates all dharmas of the Buddha;
- The unshakable mind that recollects and makes offerings to all buddhas;
- The unshakable mind that vows to refrain from tormenting or injuring any being;
- The unshakable mind that gathers in all beings without distinguishing between adversaries and close relations;
- The unshakable mind that ceaselessly seeks all dharmas of the Buddha;

The unshakable mind that tirelessly and irreversibly practices the bodhisattva practices for an ineffable-ineffable number of kalpas as numerous as all beings;

The unshakable mind that develops deeply-rooted faith, faith free of turbidity, pure faith, ultimately pure faith, immaculate faith, faith with radiant clarity, faith associated with revering and making offerings to all buddhas, irreversible faith, endless faith, indestructible faith, and faith suffused with exultant joyfulness;

The unshakable mind that perfects the path of skillful means leading to the development of all-knowledge; and

The unshakable mind that, on hearing the Dharma of all the bodhisattva practices, believes in, accepts, and never disparages them.

These are the ten. If bodhisattvas abide in these dharmas, then they acquire the unexcelled unshakable mind of all-knowledge.

Sons of the Buddha, the bodhisattva-mahāsattva has ten kinds of never-relinquished profound and great resolve. What are those ten? They are as follows:

He never relinquishes the profound and great resolve to completely fulfill the bodhi of all buddhas;

He never relinquishes the profound and great resolve to teach and train all beings;

He never relinquishes the profound and great resolve to ensure that the lineage of all buddhas will never be cut off;

He never relinquishes the profound and great resolve to draw near to all good spiritual guides;

He never relinquishes the profound and great resolve to make offerings to all buddhas;

He never relinquishes the profound and great resolve to especially focus on seeking to acquire all dharmas possessed of the Great Vehicle's meritorious qualities;

He never relinquishes the profound and great resolve to practice *brahmacarya* and preserve the pure precepts in the presence of all buddhas;

He never relinquishes the profound and great resolve to draw near to all bodhisattvas;

He never relinquishes the profound and great resolve to seek the skillful means by which to protect and preserve all dharmas of the Buddha; and

He never relinquishes the profound and great resolve to fulfill the conduct and vows of all bodhisattvas and accumulate the dharmas of all buddhas.

These are the ten. If bodhisattvas abide in these, then they are able to never relinquish any of the dharmas of the Buddha.

Sons of the Buddha, the bodhisattva-mahāsattva has ten kinds of wise contemplations. What are those ten? They are as follows:

The wise contemplation by which he skillfully distinguishes and expounds on all dharmas;

The wise contemplation by which he completely knows all roots of goodness of the three periods of time;

The wise contemplation by which he completely knows all the practices of all bodhisattvas as well as their sovereign mastery of spiritual transformations;

The wise contemplation by which he completely knows all the gateways to the meaning of all dharmas;

The wise contemplation by which he completely knows the awesome powers of all buddhas;

The wise contemplation by which he completely knows all of the *dhāraṇī* gateways;

The wise contemplation by which he expounds on right Dharma everywhere in all worlds;

The wise contemplation by which he enters the entire Dharma realm;

The wise contemplation by which he knows the inconceivability everywhere throughout the ten directions; and

The wise contemplation by which he knows the unimpeded wisdom light of all dharmas of the Buddha.

These are the ten. If bodhisattvas abide in these, then they acquire the Tathāgata's unexcelled and greatly wise contemplations.

Sons of the Buddha, the bodhisattva-mahāsattva has ten kinds of explanations about dharmas. What are those ten? They are as follows:

He explains all dharmas as arising from conditions;

He explains all dharmas as like conjurations;

He explains all dharmas as free of any mutual contradiction;

He explains all dharmas as boundless;

He explains all dharmas as independent;

He explains all dharmas as like vajra;

He explains all dharmas as characterized by true suchness;

He explains all dharmas as quiescent;

He explains all dharmas as leading to emancipation; and

He explains all dharmas as in every case abiding in ultimate truth[430] and as perfect by virtue of their original nature.

These are the ten. If bodhisattvas abide in these, then they are able to skillfully explain all dharmas.

Sons of the Buddha, the bodhisattva-mahāsattva has ten [other] kinds of purity. What are those ten? They are as follows:

Purity of deep resolve;

Purity in severing doubts;

Purity in abandoning views;

Purity of spheres of cognition and action;

Purity in the quest for all-knowledge;

Purity in eloquence;

Purity in fearlessness;

Purity in abiding in the wisdom of all bodhisattvas;

Purity in taking on the moral code of all bodhisattvas; and

Purity in the complete perfection of unexcelled bodhi, the thirty-two marks of hundredfold merit, the dharmas of purity, and all roots of goodness.

These are the ten. If bodhisattvas abide in these, then they acquire all *tathāgatas'* dharmas of unexcelled purity.

Sons of the Buddha, the bodhisattva-mahāsattva has ten kinds of seals. What are those ten? They are as follows:

The bodhisattva-mahāsattva knows the suffering of suffering, the suffering of deterioration, and the suffering of the *saṃskāras'* karmic formative factors.[431] He especially focuses on the quest for the Buddha's Dharma. He never indulges the arising of any indolence in his tireless practice of the bodhisattva practices, is never alarmed, never fearful, never beset by trepidation, and is never struck with terror. He never relinquishes the great vows, he is solid and unretreating in his quest for all-knowledge, and thus he ultimately reaches *anuttarasamyaksaṃbodhi*. This is the first of his seals;

When the bodhisattva-mahāsattva observes that there are beings who are crazed and confused by stupidity who may use coarse and vile words in defaming and vilifying him, or who may use knives, staves, tiles, or stones to injure him, he still never allows these kinds of objective circumstances to cause him to relinquish the bodhisattva resolve. Rather, he simply endures such abuse and persists in the gentle, harmonious, and especially focused cultivation of the Buddha's Dharma, abides in the supreme path, and enters the positions [on the path] in which births are transcended. This is the second of his seals;

When the bodhisattva hears teachings related to all-knowledge from the extremely profound Dharma of the Buddha, relying on his own wisdom, he is able to recognize their validity with deep faith, completely comprehends them, and enters them. This is the third of his seals;

The bodhisattva-mahāsattva also thinks thus: "Just as I who have brought forth the deep resolve to seek all-knowledge am thereby bound to become a buddha and realize *anuttarasamyaksaṃbodhi,* so too, given that all beings, flowing along and turning about in the five destinies, are thus bound to undergo measureless suffering, I should also enable them to bring forth the bodhi resolve, to develop deep faith and joyous delight, to become diligent and vigorous in cultivation, and to become solidly irreversible in this." This is the fourth of his seals;

The bodhisattva-mahāsattva realizes that the Tathāgata's wisdom is so boundless that one could never fathom the Tathāgata's wisdom through the use of limited means. Because the bodhisattva has already heard the Tathāgata's boundless wisdom under countless buddhas, he is able to refrain from using such limited means to fathom it. He realizes that discussions using any of the world's languages are so limited that they would all be incapable of knowing the Tathāgata's wisdom. This is the fifth of his seals;

The bodhisattva-mahāsattva acquires for his quest to realize *anuttarasamyaksaṃbodhi* the most supreme zeal,[432] extremely profound zeal, vast zeal, great zeal, all different forms of zeal, indomitable zeal, unexcelled zeal, solid zeal, zeal indestructible by any of the many *māras,* non-Buddhists, or their retinues, and zeal that is irreversible in its quest for all-knowledge. Abiding in types of zeal such as these, the bodhisattva achieves ultimate irreversibility with respect to the attainment of unexcelled bodhi. This is the sixth of his seals;

In his practice of the bodhisattva practices, the bodhisattva-mahāsattva, being unconcerned with preserving his own body or life, cannot be hindered by anyone. Because he has generated the resolve to proceed toward all-knowledge, because the nature of all-knowledge always manifests directly before him, and because he has acquired the wisdom light of all buddhas, he never abandons the bodhi of the buddhas and never abandons his good spiritual guides. This is the seventh of his seals;

When the bodhisattva-mahāsattva observes a son or daughter of good family who is progressing in the Great Vehicle, he enables them to increase their resolve to seek the Buddha's Dharma, enables them to abide in all kinds of roots of goodness, enables them to consolidate their resolve for all-knowledge, and enables them to become irreversible in their quest for unexcelled bodhi. This is the eighth of his seals;

The bodhisattva-mahāsattva enables all beings to acquire the mind of equal regard for all and encourages them to diligently cultivate the path to all-knowledge. With the mind of great compassion, he explains the Dharma for them and enables them to become forever irreversible in their progress toward *anuttarasamyaksaṃbodhi*. This is the ninth of his seals; and

The bodhisattva-mahāsattva possesses roots of goodness that are one and the same with those of all buddhas of the three periods of time. He never allows the severance of the lineage of all buddhas and ultimately succeeds in acquiring the wisdom of all-knowledge. This is the tenth of his seals.

Sons of the Buddha, these are the ten kinds of seals of the bodhisattva-mahāsattva. Relying on these, the bodhisattva swiftly succeeds in realizing *anuttarasamyaksaṃbodhi* and in completely perfecting the seal of the Tathāgata's unexcelled wisdom in all dharmas.

Sons of the Buddha, the bodhisattva-mahāsattva has ten kinds of illumination with the light of wisdom. What are those ten? They are as follows:

The illumination with the light of wisdom by which he knows he will definitely attain *anuttarasamyaksaṃbodhi*;

The illumination with the light of wisdom by which he sees all buddhas;

The illumination with the light of wisdom by which he sees all beings dying in this place and being reborn in that place;

The illumination with the light of wisdom by which he understands all the Dharma gateways contained in the sutras;

The illumination with the light of wisdom by which he relies on the good spiritual guide, makes the bodhi resolve, and accumulates all roots of goodness;

The illumination with the light of wisdom by which all buddhas are revealed;

The illumination with the light of wisdom by which he teaches all beings and enables them all to abide on the ground of the Tathāgata;

The illumination with the light of wisdom by which he expounds on the inconceivable and vast gateways to the Dharma;

The illumination with the light of wisdom by which he skillfully and completely knows the spiritual superknowledges and awesome powers of all buddhas; and

The illumination with the light of wisdom by which he completely fulfills all the *pāramitās*.

These are the ten. If bodhisattvas abide in these dharmas, then they acquire all buddhas' unexcelled illumination with the light of wisdom.

Sons of the Buddha, the bodhisattva-mahāsattva has ten kinds of peerless dwelling which are unequaled by any being, any *śrāvaka* disciple, or any *pratyekabuddha*. What are those ten? They are as follows:

Although the bodhisattva-mahāsattva contemplates the apex of reality, he still does not choose to bring it to full realization because all his vows have not yet been completely fulfilled. This is the first of his peerless dwellings;

The bodhisattva-mahāsattva plants all roots of goodness equal in their expansiveness to the Dharma realm and yet he does not retain even the slightest attachment to any of them. This is the second of his peerless dwellings;

In his cultivation of the bodhisattva practices, the bodhisattva-mahāsattva realizes that they are like transformationally created phenomena because all dharmas are quiescent. Even so, he never develops any doubts regarding the Buddha's Dharma. This is the third of his peerless dwellings;

Although the bodhisattva-mahāsattva has abandoned all the world's false conceptions, he is still able to engage in mental actions devoted to practicing the bodhisattva practices for an ineffable number of kalpas, completely fulfilling the great vows and never having any thought of weariness in this. This is the fourth of his peerless dwellings;

The bodhisattva-mahāsattva has no attachment to any dharma, this because all dharmas are by nature quiescent. Still, he refrains from opting for the realization of nirvāṇa. Why? Because he has not yet completely fulfilled the path to the acquisition of all-knowledge. This is the fifth of his peerless dwellings;

The bodhisattva-mahāsattva knows all kalpas are just non-kalpas and yet he still truthfully speaks of all the types of kalpas.[433] This is the sixth of his peerless dwellings;

The bodhisattva-mahāsattva realizes that all dharmas have no actions at all that they perform and yet he still never relinquishes the actions in which he engages on the path in seeking the Dharma of all buddhas. This is the seventh of his peerless dwellings;

The bodhisattva-mahāsattva realizes that the three realms are only mind and that the three periods of time are only mind even as he completely realizes his mind is measureless and boundless. This is the eighth of his peerless dwellings;

For the sake of but a single being, the bodhisattva-mahāsattva may practice the bodhisattva practices for an ineffable number of kalpas, wishing thereby to enable that being to dwell on the ground of all-knowledge. And just as he may do so for but a single being, so too may he also do so for all beings in this very same way, and yet he still never grows weary of this. This is the ninth of his peerless dwellings; and

Although the bodhisattva-mahāsattva achieves the complete fulfillment of his cultivation, he still refrains from the complete realization of bodhi. And why is this? This is because the bodhisattva thinks: "Whatever I do is originally done for the sake of beings. Therefore I should remain for a long time in *saṃsāra,* using skillful means to benefit them and enable them all to dwell securely in the unexcelled path to buddhahood." This is the tenth of his peerless dwellings.

These are the ten peerless dwellings of the bodhisattva-mahāsattva. If bodhisattvas abide in them, then they acquire the peerless dwelling in the unexcelled great wisdom with regard to all dharmas of the Buddha.

Sons of the Buddha, the bodhisattva-mahāsattva makes ten kinds of flawless resolve.[434] What are those ten? Sons of the Buddha:

The bodhisattva-mahāsattva thinks thus: "I should subdue all the deva-*māras* along with all their retinues." This is the first of his kinds of flawless resolve;

He also thinks thus: "I should demolish all the non-Buddhist paths and their deviant dharmas." This is the second of his kinds of flawless resolve;

He also thinks thus: "I should present such skillfully worded explanations to all beings that they are all delighted." This is the third of his kinds of flawless resolve;

He also thinks thus: "I should fulfill the *pāramitā* practices everywhere throughout the Dharma realm." This is the fourth of his kinds of flawless resolve;

He also thinks thus: "I should accumulate a treasury of all kinds of merit." This is the fifth of his kinds of flawless resolve;

He also thinks thus: "Although the unexcelled bodhi is vast and difficult to fully realize, I should cultivate it and bring it to complete fulfillment." This is the sixth of his kinds of flawless resolve;

He also thinks thus: "I should use unexcelled teaching and unexcelled training to teach and train all beings." This is the seventh of his kinds of flawless resolve;

He also thinks thus: "All worlds have various kinds of differences. I should use countless bodies in accomplishing the realization of the right and perfect enlightenment." This is the eighth of his kinds of flawless resolve;

He also thinks thus: "If, when I am cultivating the bodhisattva practices, beings come and beg from me my hands, feet, ears, nose, blood, flesh, bones, marrow, wives, sons, elephants, horses, and so forth until we come to the position of kingship, I shall be able to relinquish all such things, doing so without even an instant of worried or regretful thought, doing so solely to benefit all beings, and doing so without seeking karmic rewards, taking the great compassion as what is foremost and the great kindness as what is ultimate." This is the ninth of his kinds of flawless resolve; and

He also thinks thus: "As for all that exists in the three periods of time, all buddhas, all dharmas of the Buddha, all beings, all lands, all worlds, all three periods of time, all realms of space, the entire Dharma realm, all realms established through words and speech, all realms of quiescent nirvāṇa—with wisdom that responds in but a single mind-moment, I should completely know, completely awaken to, completely perceive, completely realize, completely cultivate, and completely sever all the many different kinds of dharmas such as these. However, with regard to everything among them, I should remain free of discriminations and abandon discriminations, should remain free of [any conception of] the many kinds of differences, free of [any conception of] meritorious qualities or objective realms, and free of [any conception of] "neither existent nor nonexistent" or "neither singular nor dual," and:

I should use non-dual wisdom to know all dual phenomena;

I should use signless wisdom to know all signs;

I should use nondiscriminating wisdom to know all discriminations;

I should use nondifferentiating wisdom to know all differences;
I should use the wisdom that does not conceive of differences to know all distinctions;
I should use the wisdom that realizes the nonexistence of the world to know the entire world;
I should use the wisdom that realizes the nonexistence of the periods of time to know all periods of time;
I should use the wisdom that realizes the nonexistence of beings to know all beings;
I should use the wisdom free of attachments to know all attachments;
I should use non-abiding wisdom to know all abodes;
I should use undefiled wisdom to know all defilements;
I should use endless wisdom to know all endings;
I should use the wisdom that reaches throughout the Dharma realm to manifest bodies in all worlds;
I should use the wisdom that transcends words and voice to manifest ineffably many words and voices;
I should use the wisdom cognizing but a single inherent nature to penetrate the nonexistence of any inherent nature at all;
I should use the wisdom of the singular objective realm to manifest all kinds of different objective realms;
I should know all dharmas are ineffable and yet manifest great sovereign mastery in the use of words and speech;
I should realize entry into the ground of all-knowledge; and
For the sake of teaching and training all beings, I should manifest transformations in all worlds with the great spiritual superknowledges."

This is the tenth of his kinds of flawless resolve.

Sons of the Buddha, these are the ten kinds of flawless resolve made by the bodhisattva-mahāsattva. If bodhisattvas abide in these types of resolve, then they acquire all of the most supreme and flawless dharmas of the Buddha.

Sons of the Buddha, regarding *anuttarasamyaksaṃbodhi,* the bodhisattva-mahāsattva has ten kinds of especially superior mountain-like mind.[435] What are those ten? Sons of the Buddha:

The bodhisattva-mahāsattva is always determined to diligently cultivate the dharma of all-knowledge. This is the first of his types of especially superior mountain-like mind;

He constantly contemplates all dharmas as having the original nature characterized by emptiness [of inherent existence] and the absence of anything that is apprehensible. This is the second of his types of especially superior mountain-like mind;

He vows to practice the bodhisattva practices for incalculably many kalpas during which he cultivates all the dharmas of purity. Due to abiding in all those dharmas of purity, he comes to know and perceive the Tathāgata's measureless wisdom. This is the third of his types of especially superior mountain-like mind;

In order to seek out all dharmas of the Buddha, with a mind of equal regard for them all, he reverently serves all good spiritual guides, doing so without any other kinds of aspirations, and doing so without any intention to steal their Dharma. He only brings forth reverential esteem for them and never indulges any [other kinds of] intentions. In this, he is able to relinquish everything that he possesses. This is the fourth of his types of especially superior mountain-like mind;

If beings curse him, vilify him, disparage him, slander him, strike him with cudgels, butcher him, or otherwise inflict suffering on his physical body even to the point that they cut short his life, he is able to endure all such circumstances as these and never allows his mind to become either shaken or confused by this, nor does he raise even a single thought motivated by hatred or the intent to harm others. Nor does he then retreat from or abandon his greatly compassionate and vast vows. Rather, it causes them to incessantly grow ever stronger. And why is this? This is because, due to the complete development of his equanimity, the bodhisattva, according with reality, has become emancipated from [any attachment to] any dharma. It is also because he has realized the dharmas of all *tathāgatas* and because he has already developed sovereign mastery of gentle and harmonious patience. This is the fifth of his types of especially superior mountain-like mind;

The bodhisattva-mahāsattva perfects supreme great meritorious qualities, namely:

The supreme meritorious qualities of the devas;
The supreme meritorious qualities of humans;
The supreme meritorious qualities of his physical form;
The supreme meritorious qualities of his powers;
The supreme meritorious qualities of his retinue;
The supreme meritorious qualities of his aspirations;
The supreme meritorious qualities of a king;

The supreme meritorious qualities of his sovereign masteries;
The supreme meritorious qualities of his merit; and
The supreme meritorious qualities of his wisdom.

Although he develops meritorious qualities such as these, he never develops any kind of defiling attachment for any of these things. In particular, he is not attached to whatever is delectable, he is not attached to the desires, he is not attached to wealth, and he is not attached to any retinue. He only deeply delights in the Dharma and thus goes forth in accordance with the Dharma, abides in accordance with the Dharma, progresses along in accordance with the Dharma, reaches the most ultimate point in accordance with the Dharma, takes the Dharma as what he relies upon, take the Dharma as the source of his rescue, takes the Dharma as his refuge, takes the Dharma as his shelter, preserves and guards the Dharma, cherishes and delights in the Dharma, seeks the Dharma, and reflects on the Dharma.

Sons of the Buddha, although the bodhisattva-mahāsattva completely experiences all the many different kinds of Dharma bliss, he still always abandons the realms of the many kinds of *māras*. And why is this? This is because, in the past, the bodhisattva-mahāsattva brought forth this kind of resolve: "I shall enable all beings to forever abandon the many realms of the *māras* and shall instead enable them to abide in the realms of the Buddha." This is the sixth of his types of especially superior mountain-like mind;

For the sake of his quest to reach *anuttarasamyaksaṃbodhi,* the bodhisattva-mahāsattva has already cultivated the bodhisattva path for incalculably many *asaṃkhyeyas* of kalpas during which he has been intensely diligent and never indolent. Even so, he still thinks, "I have only now just brought forth my initial resolve to gain *anuttarasamyaksaṃbodhi.*" In his practice of the bodhisattva practices, he is neither terrified nor frightened nor beset with fearfulness. Although he is able in but a single mind-moment to immediately realize *anuttarasamyaksaṃbodhi,* for the sake of beings, he still incessantly practices the bodhisattva practices for incalculably many kalpas. This is the seventh of his types of especially superior mountain-like mind;

The bodhisattva-mahāsattva realizes that all beings by nature are not harmonious and good, that they are difficult to train and difficult to liberate, that they are unable to feel gratitude for kindnesses bestowed on them, and they are unable to repay kindnesses bestowed on them. As a consequence, he makes a great vow for their sakes in which he wishes to enable them all to attain sovereign mastery of the mind, to remain unimpeded in their actions, to abandon evil thoughts, and to refrain from generating afflicted emotions toward others. This is the eighth of his types of especially superior mountain-like mind;

The bodhisattva-mahāsattva also has this thought: "It is not the case that anyone else has caused me to bring forth the bodhi resolve, nor is it the case that I wait on others to assist me in cultivation. Rather it is I alone who make this resolve to accumulate all the Buddha dharmas and exhort myself to practice the bodhisattva path to the end of all future kalpas in order to realize *anuttarasamyaksaṃbodhi*. It is for this reason that I now cultivate the bodhisattva practices. I shall purify my own mind and shall also assist others in purifying their own minds. I should know my own sphere of cognition and should know the spheres of cognition of others as well. I should develop a sphere of cognition which is the same as that of all buddhas of the three periods of time." This is the ninth of his types of especially superior mountain-like mind; and

The bodhisattva-mahāsattva takes up a contemplation of this sort: "There is not so much as a single dharma by which one cultivates the bodhisattva practices, not so much as a single dharma by which one fulfills the bodhisattva practices, not so much as a single dharma by which one teaches and trains all beings, not so much as a single dharma by which one makes offerings to and reveres all buddhas, not so much as a single dharma by which *anuttarasamyaksaṃbodhi* has ever been realized, is now realized, or ever will be realized in the future, and there is not so much as a single dharma that has ever been spoken, is now spoken, or ever will be spoken in the future. The one who speaks as well as the dharmas that are spoken are both inapprehensible."

Even so, he still does not abandon his vow to attain *anuttarasamyaksaṃbodhi*. And why is this? Whenever the bodhisattva seeks to find any dharma at all, they are all inapprehensible. And so it is that he succeeds in bringing forth [the realization of] *anuttarasamyaksaṃbodhi*. Therefore, although nothing is apprehensible in any dharma, he still diligently cultivates the especially superior good works, the pure means of counteraction, and the complete fulfillment of wisdom, increasing these in each successive mind-moment to the point that he completely perfects them all. In this, his mind is never frightened or fearful, nor does he have this thought: "If it is the case that all dharmas are quiescent, what meaning could there be for me in continuing to seek the path to unexcelled bodhi?"

This is the tenth of his types of especially superior mountain-like mind.

Sons of the Buddha, these are the bodhisattva-mahāsattva's ten kinds of especially superior mountain-like mind in relation to *anuttarasamyaksaṃbodhi.* If bodhisattvas abide in these, then they acquire the especially superior mind associated with the Tathāgata's mountain king of unexcelled great wisdom.

Sons of the Buddha, the bodhisattva-mahāsattva has ten kinds of oceanic wisdom with which he enters *anuttarasamyaksaṃbodhi.* What are those ten? They are as follows:

That by which he enters all the realms of the incalculably many beings. This is the first of his types of oceanic wisdom;

That by which he enters all worlds and yet never generates any discriminations. This is the second of his types of oceanic wisdom;

That by which he knows all the measureless and unimpeded realms of empty space and everywhere enters the network of all the different worlds of the ten directions. This is the third of his types of oceanic wisdom;

The bodhisattva-mahāsattva skillfully enters the Dharma realm, namely through endless entry, noneternal entry, measureless entry, unproduced entry, undestroyed entry, and comprehensive entry, accomplishing this because he completely knows them all. This is the fourth of his types of oceanic wisdom;

With regard to all the roots of goodness collected in the past, collected in the present, and collected in the future by all past, future, and present buddhas, bodhisattvas, masters of the Dharma, *śrāvaka* disciples, *pratyekabuddhas,* and all common people, all the roots of goodness garnered by all buddhas of the three periods of time in their past, present, and future realizations of *anuttarasamyaksaṃbodhi,* and all the roots of goodness garnered by all buddhas of the three periods of time in their speaking of the Dharma and their training of all beings, whether speaking in the past, speaking in the present, or speaking in the future, the bodhisattva-mahāsattva completely knows them all, believes in them deeply, joyfully accords with them, and happily aspires to cultivate them while never growing weary of doing so. This is the fifth of his types of oceanic wisdom;

In each successive mind-moment, the bodhisattva-mahāsattva enters all the ineffably many kalpas of the past in which, within a single kalpa, there may have been a hundred *koṭīs* of buddhas who came forth into the world, or a thousand *koṭīs* of buddhas who came forth into the world, or a hundred thousand *koṭīs* of buddhas who came forth into the world, or a numberless number, or a measureless number, or a boundless number, or an incomparable number, or an innumerable number, or an inexpressible number, or an inconceivable number, or an incalculable number, or an ineffable number, or an ineffable-ineffable number, or a number of buddhas, *bhagavats,* who came forth into the world exceeding the capacity of calculation or enumeration during which kalpas he is able to completely and clearly see all buddhas such as these, their sites of enlightenment, congregations, *śrāvaka* disciples, and bodhisattvas, as well as the Dharma that they taught, their training of beings, the relative length or brevity of the life spans of those beings, the length of their Dharma's duration, and all other matters such as these.

And just as this is the case for a single kalpa, so too is it also the case that he completely knows this of all kalpas even as he also completely knows of those kalpas that have no buddhas all the roots of goodness planted by all their beings in relation to *anuttarasamyaksaṃbodhi.* In cases where there are beings within them whose roots of goodness have already become ripened to the point that they are thereby bound to succeed in seeing a buddha at some point in the future, he also completely knows all of those matters as well. It is in this way that he contemplates an ineffable-ineffable number of kalpas of the past, doing so without his mind ever growing weary of this. This is the sixth of his types of oceanic wisdom;

The bodhisattva-mahāsattva enters the future, contemplates and distinguishes all of its countlessly and boundlessly many kalpas, and knows which of those kalpas will have a buddha, which of those kalpas will have no buddha, which kalpas will have how many *tathāgatas* who will come forth into the world, and knows of each and every one of those *tathāgatas* what their names will be, which worlds they will abide in, what the names of those worlds will be, how many beings they will liberate, and how long their life spans will be. He endlessly and tirelessly engages in contemplations such as these which exhaust the bounds of the future. Thus he completely knows it all. This is the seventh of his types of oceanic wisdom;

The bodhisattva-mahāsattva enters the present, contemplating and reflecting upon it in such a way that, in each successive mind-moment, he everywhere sees the boundlessly many classes of beings throughout the ten directions in an ineffable number of worlds in all of which there are buddhas who have already realized, now realize, or shall realize the unexcelled bodhi, observing with regard to them all their going forth to their sites of enlightenment, their sitting on the auspicious grass seat beneath the bodhi tree, their conquering of the armies of Māra, their realization of *anuttarasamyaksaṃbodhi,* their entering the cities and villages after rising from where they sat, their ascendance to the celestial palaces, their proclamation of the sublime Dharma, their turning of the great wheel of the Dharma, their manifestation of spiritual superknowledges, their training of beings, and so forth on through to their passing on the dharma of *anuttarasamyaksaṃbodhi,* their relinquishing of this life span, their entry into *parinirvāṇa,* the gathering together of their Dharma treasury after they have entered nirvāṇa whereby it is enabled to remain in the world for a long time, the raising of adorned commemorative buddha stupas, and the offerings to them of the many different kinds of offerings.

They also see all the beings in those worlds encountering the Buddha, hearing the Dharma, accepting it, retaining it, reciting it, bearing it in mind, meditating on it, and thereby increasing their wise understanding of it. He extends meditations such as these to include all places everywhere throughout the ten directions and still never becomes mistaken in his understanding of the Dharma of the Buddha. And why is this? This is because the bodhisattva-mahāsattva completely understands all buddhas as like a dream and yet he is still able to travel to the abodes of all buddhas, revering them and making offerings to them. At this time, the bodhisattva is not attached to his own body, is not attached to the buddhas, is not attached to worlds, is not attached to those congregations, is not attached to the teaching of the Dharma, and is not attached to any of those types of kalpas. So it is that he sees the Buddha, hears the Dharma, contemplates the worlds, and enters all the different types of kalpas without ever growing weary of doing so. This is the eighth of his types of oceanic wisdom;

Throughout every kalpa among an ineffable-ineffable number of kalpas, the bodhisattva-mahāsattva makes offerings and pays reverence to an ineffable-ineffable number of measurelessly many buddhas as he manifests his own bodies there, dying in this place and then taking rebirth in that place, making offerings to them exceeding the sum total of all gifts throughout the three realms of existence even as he also makes offerings to bodhisattvas, to *śrāvaka* disciples, and to all beings. When each of those *tathāgatas* enters *parinirvāṇa*, he presents unexcelled gifts as offerings to their *śarīra* while also engaging in extensive kindly giving sufficient to satisfy those beings.

Sons of the Buddha, the bodhisattva-mahāsattva uses an inconceivable mind, a mind that does not seek any reward, an ultimate mind, and a beneficial mind to make offerings to all buddhas, to benefit beings, to protect and preserve right Dharma, and to explain it and expound upon it, doing so for an ineffable-ineffable number of kalpas for the sake of *anuttarasamyaksaṃbodhi*. This is the ninth of his types of oceanic wisdom; and

In the presence of all buddhas, all bodhisattvas, and all masters of the Dharma, the bodhisattva-mahāsattva continuously and single-mindedly seeks the Dharma proclaimed by the bodhisattva, the Dharma studied by the bodhisattva, the Dharma taught by the bodhisattva, the Dharma cultivated by the bodhisattva, the Dharma by which the bodhisattva becomes purified, the Dharma by which the bodhisattva becomes ripened, the Dharma in which the bodhisattva trains, the bodhisattva's dharmas of equanimity, the bodhisattva's dharmas of emancipation, and the bodhisattva's *dhāraṇī* dharmas for complete-retention [of the Dharma]. Having acquired dharmas such as these, he absorbs them, retains them, studies them, recites them, and analyzes and explains them, never tiring of this, thereby enabling countless beings to resolve to attain all-knowledge in reliance on Dharma of the Buddha, to penetrate the character of reality, and to become irreversible in progressing toward the realization of *anuttarasamyaksaṃbodhi*. The bodhisattva tirelessly continues on in this way for an ineffable-ineffable number of kalpas. This is the tenth of his types of oceanic wisdom.

Sons of the Buddha, these are the bodhisattva-mahāsattva's ten kinds of oceanic wisdom with which he enters *anuttarasamyaksaṃbodhi*. If bodhisattvas abide in these dharmas, then they acquire all buddhas' ocean of unexcelled great wisdom.

Sons of the Buddha, the bodhisattva-mahāsattva has ten kinds of jewel-like abiding with regard to [accomplishing the realization of][436] *anuttarasamyaksaṃbodhi*. What are those ten? They are as follows:

Sons of the Buddha, the bodhisattva-mahāsattva is able to go to visit all the countless worlds, paying his respects to the *tathāgatas*, gazing up at them in admiration, bowing down to them in reverence, serving them, and making offerings to them. This is the first of his types of jewel-like abiding;

He listens to right Dharma from an inconceivable number of *tathāgatas*, absorbs it, retains it, bears it in mind, does not allow it to be forgotten, analyzes it, reflects upon it, and thus increases his awakened wisdom. The activities of this sort that he engages in fill the ten directions. This the second of his types of jewel-like abiding;

When he dies in this *kṣetra* and then manifests rebirth in some other place, he still remains free of any delusion regarding the Buddha's Dharma. This is the third of his types of jewel-like abiding;

He realizes that all dharmas come forth from a single dharma and thus he is able to analyze and expound upon every one of them because all the many different meanings of all dharmas ultimately constitute but a single meaning. This is the fourth of his types of jewel-like abiding;

He knows the renunciation of the afflictions, knows the stopping and extinguishing of the afflictions, knows the guarding against the arising of afflictions, and knows the severance of the afflictions. In his cultivation of the bodhisattva practices, he refrains from realizing the apex of reality even as he achieves ultimate perfection in fathoming the apex of reality. With clever skillful means, he studies well what is to be studied and thus enables his past vows and conduct to all become completely fulfilled, doing so without ever becoming physically wearied by this. This is the fifth of his types of jewel-like abiding;

He knows that all things distinguished by the minds of all beings have no place where they abide even as he still speaks of the existence of many different kinds of places. Although he is free of discriminations and has nothing that he creates, because he wishes to train all beings, he still has that which he cultivates and that which he accomplishes. This is the sixth of his types of jewel-like abiding;

He realizes that all dharmas have the same single nature, namely the absence of any nature at all. They are devoid of any of the many different kinds of natures, are devoid of any measureless nature, are devoid of any calculable nature, are devoid of any measurable nature, and are formless and signless. Whether one or many, they are all inapprehensible. And yet he still definitely and completely knows:

"This one is a dharma of all buddhas."

"This one is a dharma of the bodhisattva."

"This one is a dharma of the *pratyekabuddha*."

"This one is a dharma of the *śrāvaka* disciple."

"This one is a dharma of the common person."
"This one is a good dharma whereas this other one is a bad dharma."
"This one is a worldly dharma whereas this other one is a world-transcending dharma."
"This one is a faulty dharma whereas this other one is a dharma free of faults."
"This is a contaminated dharma whereas this other one is a dharma free of all contaminants," and so forth, up to and including:
"This one is a conditioned dharma, whereas this other one is an unconditioned dharma."
This is the seventh of his types of jewel-like abiding;

In seeking to find any buddha, the bodhisattva-mahāsattva finds that no such thing can be found at all. In seeking to find any bodhisattva, he finds that no such thing can be found at all. In seeking to find any dharma, he finds that no such thing can be found at all. And in seeking to find any being, he finds that no such thing can be found at all. Even so, he never relinquishes his vow to train beings and enable them to attain right enlightenment with respect to all dharmas. And why is this? This is because the bodhisattva-mahāsattva skillfully contemplates and thereby knows the discriminations of all beings, knows all beings' spheres of cognition, and then uses skillful means to teach and guide them and enable them to reach *nirvāṇa*, doing so in order to completely fulfill his vow to teach beings and engage in brilliantly blazing cultivation of the bodhisattva practices. This is the eighth of his types of jewel-like abiding.

The bodhisattva-mahāsattva knows that using skillful means to teach the Dharma, manifesting entry into nirvāṇa, and all the skillful means used to liberate beings are all established on the basis of the mind and perceptions. They are not a function of inverted views and are not either false or deceptive. And how is this so? The bodhisattva fully realizes that all dharmas are the same throughout the three periods of time, are true suchness, are unmoving, are the apex of reality, and are non-abiding. He does not perceive the existence of even a single being who has ever undergone teaching, is now undergoing teaching, or ever will undergo teaching. He also fully realizes for himself that there is nothing that is cultivated, that there is not even the slightest dharma that is ever produced, that is ever destroyed, or that is at all apprehensible. Even so, relying on all dharmas, he enables whatever he has vowed to not have been in vain. This is the ninth of his types of jewel-like abiding.

In the abodes of every one of the buddhas among an inconceivable and measureless number of buddhas, the bodhisattva-mahāsattva hears an ineffable-ineffable number of instances of the dharma of bestowing predictions [of future buddhahood] in which the names [of the future buddhas] are each different and the number of kalpas [before attaining buddhahood] are not the same, varying from but a single kalpa all the way up to an ineffable-ineffable number of kalpas. He always hears them in this way and then, having heard them, he cultivates accordingly, is not frightened, is not fearful, is not confused, and is not deluded because he realizes that the wisdom of the Tathāgata is inconceivable, because he knows the words of the Tathāgata's bestowals of predictions are unequivocal, because of the especially superior power of his own practice and vows, and because, in accordance with those who should receive teaching, he enables their realization of *anuttarasamyaksaṃbodhi* and fulfills all his vows equal in their expansiveness to the Dharma realm. This is the tenth of his types of jewel-like abiding.

Sons of the Buddha, these are the bodhisattva-mahāsattva's ten kinds of jewel-like abiding in accomplishing the realization of *anuttarasamyaksaṃbodhi*. If bodhisattvas abide in these dharmas, then they acquire the jewel of all buddhas' unexcelled great wisdom.

Sons of the Buddha, the bodhisattva-mahāsattva arouses ten kinds of vajra-like Great Vehicle resolve. What are these ten? Sons of the Buddha:

The bodhisattva-mahāsattva has this thought: "All dharmas are so boundless as to be inexhaustible. I should use wisdom capable of exhaustively knowing the three periods of time to become completely awakened to all of them without exception." This is the first of his types of vajra-like Great Vehicle resolve;

The bodhisattva-mahāsattva also has this thought: "Even on the tip of but a single hair, there are incalculably and boundlessly many beings. How much the more is this so of the entire Dharma realm. I should enable them all to reach the liberation of cessation by resort to the unexcelled nirvāṇa." This is the second of his types of vajra-like Great Vehicle resolve;

The bodhisattva-mahāsattva also has this thought: "The worlds of the ten directions are so measureless, boundless, and unlimited as to be endless. I should use the most supreme adornments in the lands of all buddhas to adorn all worlds such as these so that all their adornments are genuine. This is the third of his types of vajra-like Great Vehicle resolve;

The bodhisattva-mahāsattva also has this thought: "All beings are so measureless, boundless, and unlimited as to be endless. I should dedicate all roots of goodness to them and use the light of unexcelled wisdom to illuminate them with brilliant light." This is the fourth of his types of vajra-like Great Vehicle resolve;

The bodhisattva-mahāsattva also has this thought: "All buddhas are so measureless, boundless, and unlimited as to be endless. I should dedicate all the roots of goodness I have planted to making offerings to them so that [those offerings] are present everywhere and there is no shortage of anything. Afterward, I should accomplish the realization of *anuttarasamyaksaṃbodhi*." This is the fifth of his types of vajra-like Great Vehicle resolve;

Sons of the Buddha, when the bodhisattva-mahāsattva sees all buddhas and hears the Dharma that they proclaim, he is filled with great joy. He is not attached to his own body, is not attached to the Buddha's body, and understands the Tathāgata's body is neither real nor false, is neither existent nor nonexistent, is neither possessed of any nature nor devoid of a nature, is neither possessed of form nor formless, is neither possessed of signs nor signless, is neither produced nor destroyed, and, in truth, is devoid of anything that exists even as this does not undermine its existence. And why is this? This is because he cannot take any nature or sign as the basis for forming attachments. This the sixth of his types of vajra-like Great Vehicle resolve;

Sons of the Buddha, if the bodhisattva-mahāsattva encounters any being who scolds or disparages him, who beats or flogs him, who cuts off his hands and feet, who cuts off his ears and nose, who plucks out his eyes, or who even decapitates him, he is able to patiently endure all of this and never reacts to this by becoming angry or wanting to harm his attacker. Throughout an ineffable-ineffable and endless number of kalpas, he cultivates the bodhisattva practices, attracts beings [into the Dharma], and never abandons them. And why is this? This is because, having already skillfully contemplated all dharmas and realized they are devoid of any such dual opposition, his mind is never shaken or thrown into confusion. Hence he is able to relinquish even his own body and endure its sufferings. This is the seventh of his types of vajra-like Great Vehicle resolve;

Sons of the Buddha, the bodhisattva-mahāsattva also has this thought: "The kalpas of the future are so measureless, boundless, and unlimited as to be endless. I should exhaust all of those kalpas in practicing the bodhisattva path and teaching all the beings in one of those worlds and, just as I should do this in this one world, so too should I also do so in all worlds throughout the entire Dharma realm and the realms of empty space." In so doing, his mind is not terrified, frightened, or fearful. And why is this? In practicing for the sake of the bodhisattva path, this is the way the Dharma should be, for it is to benefit all beings that one cultivates in this way. This is the eighth of his types of vajra-like Great Vehicle resolve;

Sons of the Buddha, the bodhisattva-mahāsattva also has this thought: "It is the mind itself that constitutes the very root of *anuttarasamyaksaṃbodhi*. If one's mind is pure, then one is able to completely develop all roots of goodness. Then one is certainly bound to attain such sovereign mastery with respect to the Buddha's bodhi that one only needs to wish to realize *anuttarasamyaksaṃbodhi,* whereupon, whenever one decides to do so, one will immediately gain that very realization. If I but wished to cut off all grasping at conditions and abide in the direct path, then I too could succeed in doing so. However, I do not cut it all off because I wish to reach all the way to the complete realization of the bodhi of the Buddha. Thus I do not elect to immediately realize the unexcelled bodhi. Why is this? This is to fulfill my original vow to practice the bodhisattva practices throughout all worlds in order to teach the beings within them." This is the ninth of his types of vajra-like Great Vehicle resolve;

Sons of the Buddha, the bodhisattva-mahāsattva realizes that the buddha is inapprehensible,[437] that bodhi is inapprehensible, that bodhisattvas are inapprehensible, that all dharmas are inapprehensible, that beings are inapprehensible, that the mind is inapprehensible, that the practices are inapprehensible, that the past is inapprehensible, that the future is inapprehensible, that the present is inapprehensible, that the entire world is inapprehensible, and that both the conditioned and the unconditioned are inapprehensible. In this way, the bodhisattva abides in stillness, abides in the extremely profound, abides in quiescence, abides in noncontentiousness, abides in wordlessness, abides in non-duality, abides in peerlessness, abides in the essential nature, abides in accordance with principle, abides in liberation, abides in nirvāṇa, and abides in the apex of reality, and yet he still never relinquishes any of his great vows, never relinquishes the resolve to attain all-knowledge, never relinquishes the bodhisattva practices, never relinquishes the teaching of beings, never relinquishes any of the *pāramitās*, never relinquishes the training of beings, never relinquishes his serving of all buddhas, never relinquishes his expounding on all dharmas, and never relinquishes his adornment of worlds. And why is this so? This is because the bodhisattva-mahāsattva has made the great vow.

Although he completely comprehends the signs of all dharmas, his mind of great kindness and compassion grows ever stronger and he perfects the cultivation of all the countless meritorious qualities to the point that his mind is unwilling to ever abandon any being. And why is this? Although all dharmas are nonexistent, common people, being deluded and confused, do not know this and remain unaware of this. [Hence he thinks], "I should enable them all to awaken to the nature of all dharmas so that it becomes clearly and completely illuminated for them. Why? All buddhas abide in quiescence, and yet, relying on the mind of great compassion, they still proclaim the Dharma and teach it in all worlds, never desisting from this. How then could I now relinquish the great compassion?

Moreover, in the past, I produced the resolve of the vast vow by which I resolved to definitely benefit all beings, resolved to accumulate all roots of goodness, resolved to abide in skillful dedications [of merit], resolved to develop extremely deep wisdom, resolved to include all beings, and resolved to remain impartial toward all beings. I am one who speaks what is true and does not speak what is false or deceptive. I vowed to bestow the unexcelled great Dharma on all beings. I vowed to ensure that the lineage of all buddhas is never cut off. Now, it is still the case that all beings have not yet gained liberation, have not yet attained right enlightenment, and do not yet possess the Dharma of the Buddha. With my great vows not yet fulfilled, how could I wish to abandon the great compassion? This is the tenth of his types of vajra-like Great Vehicle resolve.

Sons of the Buddha, these are the ten kinds of vajra-like Great Vehicle resolve produced by the bodhisattva-mahāsattva. If bodhisattvas abide in these dharmas, then they acquire the Tathāgata's vajra-natured unexcelled great spiritual superknowledges and wisdom.

Sons of the Buddha, the bodhisattva-mahāsattva has ten kinds of great undertakings. What are those ten? They are as follows:

The bodhisattva-mahāsattva thinks: "I should make offerings to and revere all buddhas." This is the first of his great undertakings;

He also thinks: "I should foster the growth of all bodhisattvas' roots of goodness." This is the second of his great undertakings;

He also thinks: "After the *parinirvāṇa* of all *tathāgatas,* I should adorn buddha stupas for them and make offerings to them of all kinds of flowers, all kinds of garlands, all kinds of incenses, all kinds of perfumes, all kinds of powdered incenses, all kinds of robes, all kinds of canopies, all kinds of banners, and all kinds of pennants while also absorbing, retaining, preserving, and protecting the right Dharma of those buddhas." This is the third of his great undertakings;

He also thinks: "I should teach and train all beings and enable them to attain *anuttarasamyaksaṃbodhi.*" This is the fourth of his great undertakings;

He also thinks: "I should adorn all worlds with the unexcelled adornments of all buddha lands." This is the fifth of his great undertakings;

He also thinks: "Bringing forth the mind of great compassion, for the sake of a single being, I should practice the bodhisattva practices in all worlds, doing so in each and every one of them to the end of all future kalpas. And just as I should do this for a single being, so too should I also do so for all beings so that I can thereby enable them all to succeed in acquiring the Buddha's unexcelled bodhi while never in all this time ever generating even a single thought of weariness." This is the sixth of his great undertakings;

He also thinks: "All those *tathāgatas* are countlessly and boundlessly many. In the presence of one of those *tathāgatas,* I should revere him and make offerings to him for an inconceivably great number of kalpas. And just as I do so for that one *tathāgata,* so also should I do so for all *tathāgatas* in this very same manner." This is the seventh of his great undertakings;

The bodhisattva-mahāsattva also thinks: "After those *tathāgatas* pass into nirvāṇa, for the *śarīra* of every one of those *tathāgatas,* I should raise bejeweled stupas of such lofty and vast dimensions that they are equal in scale to an ineffable number of worlds. I should also create images of those buddhas in just this same way, making offerings to them of all kinds of bejeweled banners, pennants, canopies, incense, flowers, and robes, doing so for an inconceivably great number of kalpas during which I never have even a single mind-moment's thought of weariness in this, doing so to enable the complete success of the Buddha's Dharma, doing so to make offerings to all buddhas, doing so to teach beings, and doing so to protect and preserve right Dharma by revealing it and expounding on it." This is the eighth of his great undertakings;

The bodhisattva-mahāsattva also thinks: "I should use these roots of goodness to gain unexcelled bodhi, to succeed in entering the ground of all *tathāgatas*, and to become of the same essential nature as all *tathāgatas*." This is the ninth of his great undertakings; and

The bodhisattva-mahāsattva also thinks: "After gaining right enlightenment, I should expound on right Dharma in all worlds for an ineffable number of kalpas, manifesting inconceivable sovereign mastery of the spiritual superknowledges, never becoming weary of this in body, speech, or mind, and never separating from right Dharma due to being sustained by the Buddha's powers, due to diligently implementing the great vows for the sake of all beings, due to taking the great kindness as foremost, due to taking the great compassion as what is most ultimate, due to comprehending the dharma of signlessness, due to abiding in truthful speech, due to gaining the realization that all dharmas are quiescent, due to realizing all beings are inapprehensible while still realizing this does not contradict the effects of karmic deeds, due to being of the same single essential nature as all buddhas of the three periods of time, due to pervading the Dharma realm and the realms of empty space, due to gaining a penetrating comprehension of the signlessness of all dharmas, due to completely realizing they are neither produced nor destroyed, due to completely fulfilling all dharmas of the Buddha, and due to relying on the power of great vows in incessantly training beings and accomplishing great buddha works." This is the tenth of his great undertakings.

Sons of the Buddha, these are the bodhisattva-mahāsattva's ten kinds of great undertakings. If bodhisattvas abide in these dharmas, then they incessantly continue in the bodhisattva practices and completely fulfill the Tathāgata's unexcelled great wisdom.

Sons of the Buddha, the bodhisattva-mahāsattva has ten kinds of ultimate and great endeavors. What are those ten? They are as follows:

The ultimate and great endeavor of revering and making offerings to all *tathāgatas*;

The ultimate and great endeavor of being able to rescue and protect whichever beings he brings to mind;

The ultimate and great endeavor of single-mindedly seeking all dharmas of the Buddha;

The ultimate and great endeavor of accumulating all roots of goodness;
The ultimate and great endeavor of the meditative contemplation of all dharmas of the Buddha;
The ultimate and great endeavor of completely fulfilling all vows;
The ultimate and great endeavor of accomplishing all the bodhisattva practices;
The ultimate and great endeavor of serving all good spiritual guides;
The ultimate and great endeavor of traveling to all worlds to pay respects to all *tathāgatas;* and
The ultimate and great endeavor of listening to and retaining the right Dharma of all buddhas.

These are the ten. If all bodhisattvas abide in these dharmas, then they accomplish the ultimate and great endeavor of acquiring the great wisdom of *anuttarasamyaksaṃbodhi.*

Sons of the Buddha, the bodhisattva-mahāsattva has ten kinds of indestructible faith. What are those ten? They are as follows:

Indestructible faith in all buddhas;
Indestructible faith in the Dharma of all buddhas;
Indestructible faith in all those in the *ārya* Sangha;
Indestructible faith in all bodhisattvas;
Indestructible faith in all good spiritual guides;
Indestructible faith in all beings;
Indestructible faith in all the great vows of the bodhisattvas;
Indestructible faith in all the practices of the bodhisattvas;
Indestructible faith in revering and making offerings to all buddhas; and
Indestructible faith in bodhisattvas' skillful and esoteric expedient means for teaching and training all beings.

These are the ten. If bodhisattvas abide in these dharmas, then they acquire indestructible faith in the unexcelled great wisdom of all buddhas.

Sons of the Buddha, the bodhisattva-mahāsattva has ten ways of receiving the prediction [of future buddhahood]. What are those ten? They are as follows:

Receiving the prediction through extremely profound inward understanding;
Receiving the prediction through the ability to accord with and produce the bodhisattva's roots of goodness;
Receiving the prediction through cultivating vast practices;

Receiving the prediction directly;
Receiving the prediction indirectly;
Receiving the prediction due to his own mind's realization of bodhi;
Receiving the prediction through the complete realization of patience;[438]
Receiving the prediction through teaching and training beings;
Receiving the prediction through continuing on even to the very end of all kalpas; and
Receiving the prediction through sovereign mastery of all of the bodhisattva practices.

These are the ten. If bodhisattvas abide in these dharmas, then they receive the prediction [of future buddhahood] from all buddhas.

Sons of the Buddha, the bodhisattva-mahāsattva has ten ways of dedicating roots of goodness. Because of these, the bodhisattva is able to dedicate all his roots of goodness. What are those ten? They are as follows:

May my roots of goodness be perfected in the same way and no differently from my good spiritual guide as regards our vows;
May my roots of goodness be perfected in the same way and no differently from my good spiritual guide as regards our minds;
May my roots of goodness be perfected in the same way and no differently from my good spiritual guide as regards our practices;
May my roots of goodness be perfected in the same way and no differently from my good spiritual guide as regards our roots of goodness;
May my roots of goodness be perfected in the same way and no differently from my good spiritual guide as regards our equanimity;
May my roots of goodness be perfected in the same way and no differently from my good spiritual guide as regards our mindfulness;
May my roots of goodness be perfected in the same way and no differently from my good spiritual guide as regards our purity;
May my roots of goodness be perfected in the same way and no differently from my good spiritual guide as regards where we dwell;
May my roots of goodness be perfected in the same way and no differently from my good spiritual guide as regards our fulfillment; and

May my roots of goodness be perfected in the same way and no differently from my good spiritual guide as regards our indestructibility.

These are the ten. If bodhisattvas abide in these dharmas, then they acquire the unexcelled practice of dedicating roots of goodness.

Sons of the Buddha, the bodhisattva-mahāsattvas has ten ways of attaining wisdom. What are those ten? They are as follows:

Attaining wisdom through sovereign mastery in giving;

Attaining wisdom through deep understanding of all dharmas of the Buddha;

Attaining wisdom through entering the Tathāgata's boundless knowledge;

Attaining wisdom through the ability to sever doubts in all responses to queries;

Attaining wisdom through penetration of the meanings of the wise;

Attaining wisdom through the deep understanding of all *tathāgatas'* skillfulness in discourse on all dharmas of the Buddha;

Attaining wisdom through the deep understanding that even the most minor roots of goodness planted in the presence of buddhas results in the certain ability to completely fulfill all dharmas of purity and acquire the Tathāgata's measureless wisdom;

Attaining wisdom through complete development of the bodhisattva's inconceivable abodes;

Attaining wisdom through the ability to travel to and visit an ineffable number of buddha *kṣetras* in but a single mind-moment; and

Attaining wisdom through awakening to the bodhi of all buddhas, entering the entire Dharma realm, hearing and retaining the Dharma proclaimed by all buddhas, and deeply penetrating the many different adorned statements of all *tathāgatas.*

These are the ten. If bodhisattvas abide in these Dharmas, then they attain the unexcelled directly realized wisdom of all buddhas.

Sons of the Buddha, the bodhisattva-mahāsattva has ten ways of generating measurelessly and boundlessly vast resolve. What are those ten? They are as follows:

The arousal of measurelessly and boundlessly vast resolve in the presence of all buddhas;

The arousal of measurelessly and boundlessly vast resolve through contemplating all realms of beings;

The arousal of measurelessly and boundlessly vast resolve throughout contemplating all *kṣetras*, all periods of time, and the entire Dharma realm;

The arousal of measurelessly and boundlessly vast resolve through contemplating all dharmas as like empty space;

The arousal of measurelessly and boundlessly vast resolve through contemplating the vast practices of all bodhisattvas;

The arousal of measurelessly and boundlessly vast resolve through right mindfulness of all buddhas of the three periods of time;

The arousal of measurelessly and boundlessly vast resolve through contemplating the inconceivable rewards and consequences of all karmic deeds;

The arousal of measurelessly and boundlessly vast resolve through the purification of all buddha *kṣetras*;

The arousal of measurelessly and boundlessly vast resolve through everywhere entering the congregations of all buddhas; and

The arousal of measurelessly and boundlessly vast resolve through contemplating the sublime voice of all *tathāgatas*.

These are the ten. If bodhisattvas abide in these types of resolve, then they acquire the measurelessly and boundlessly vast ocean of wisdom of the Dharma of all buddhas.

Sons of the Buddha, the bodhisattva-mahāsattva has ten kinds of hidden treasures. What are those ten? They are as follows:

His knowing of all dharmas constitutes the treasure of generating the practice of meritorious qualities;

His knowing of all dharmas constitutes the treasure of right thought;

His knowing of all dharmas constitutes the treasure of illuminating radiance produced by *dhāraṇīs*;

His knowing of all dharmas constitutes the treasure of eloquent expository discourse;

His knowing of all dharmas constitutes the treasure of an ineffable number of thorough awakenings to reality;

His knowing of all buddhas' sovereign mastery of spiritual superknowledges constitutes the treasure of contemplations of their manifestations;

His knowing of all dharmas constitutes the treasure of the skillful generation of equanimity;

His knowing of all dharmas constitutes the treasure of always seeing all buddhas;

His knowing of all the inconceivably many kalpas constitutes the treasure of skillfully understanding all of them as abiding like mere conjurations; and

His knowing of all buddhas and bodhisattvas constitutes the treasure of the arousal of joyous delight and pure faith.

These are the ten. If bodhisattvas abide in these dharmas, then they acquire the Dharma treasure of all buddha's unexcelled wisdom with which they are able to train all beings.

Sons of the Buddha, the bodhisattva-mahāsattva has ten kinds of moral standards. What are those ten? They are as follows:

The moral standard of never slandering any of the Buddha's dharmas;

The moral standard of maintaining an indestructible mind of resolute faith in all buddhas;

The moral standard of arousing reverential respect for all bodhisattvas;

The moral standard of never abandoning their mind of fond devotion for all good spiritual guides;

The moral standard of refraining from thoughts recalling [the paths of] *śrāvaka* disciples or *pratyekabuddhas*;

The moral standard of abandoning any inclination to retreat from the bodhisattva path;

The moral standard of never producing any malicious thoughts toward other beings;

The moral standard of cultivating all roots of goodness so that they all reach a state of ultimate development;

The moral standard of maintaining the ability to conquer all *māras*; and

The moral standard of enabling the complete fulfillment of all the *pāramitās*.

These are the ten. If bodhisattvas abide in these dharmas, then they acquire the moral standard of unexcelled great wisdom.

Sons of the Buddha, the bodhisattva-mahāsattva has ten kinds of sovereign mastery. What are those ten? They are as follows:

Sovereign mastery of life span based on the ability to abide for a life span of ineffably many kalpas;

Sovereign mastery of mind based on having wisdom capable of entering an *asaṃkhyeya* of samādhis;

Sovereign mastery of resources based on the ability to use countless adornments to adorn all worlds;

Sovereign mastery in karmic actions based on the ability to receive their associated karmic rewards whenever they choose;

Sovereign mastery in the taking on of births based on the ability to manifest birth in all worlds;

Sovereign mastery in understanding based on the ability to see buddhas filling all worlds;

Sovereign mastery in vows based on the ability to attain right enlightenment in all *kṣetras* however and whenever they wish;

Sovereign mastery in spiritual powers based on the ability to manifest every kind of great spiritual transformation;

Sovereign mastery in Dharma based on the ability to manifest all of the boundlessly many Dharma gateways; and

Sovereign mastery of cognition based on the ability to manifest in each successive mind-moment the Tathāgata's ten powers, fearlessnesses, and realization of right enlightenment.

These are the ten. If bodhisattvas abide in these dharmas, then they acquire the sovereign mastery of the complete fulfillment of all buddhas' *pāramitās*, wisdom, spiritual powers, and bodhi.

Sons of the Buddha, the bodhisattva-mahāsattva has ten kinds of unimpeded functions. What are those ten? They are as follows:

Unimpeded function in relation to beings;

Unimpeded function in relation to lands;

Unimpeded function in relation to dharmas;

Unimpeded function in relation to bodies;

Unimpeded function in relation to vows;

Unimpeded function in relation to realms;

Unimpeded function in relation to knowledge;

Unimpeded function in relation to spiritual superknowledges;

Unimpeded function in relation to spiritual powers; and

Unimpeded function in relation to the powers.

Sons of the Buddha, what then constitutes the bodhisattva-mahāsattva's unimpeded functions in relation to beings and so forth? Sons of the Buddha, the bodhisattva-mahāsattva has ten kinds of unimpeded functions in relation to beings. What are those ten? They are as follows:

The unimpeded function of knowing all beings as devoid of any beings;

The unimpeded function of knowing all beings are sustained solely through thought;

The unimpeded function of never missing the right time in speaking Dharma for beings;

The unimpeded function of everywhere manifesting all realms of beings;

The unimpeded function of placing all beings within but a single pore without their being crowded;
The unimpeded function of manifesting for all beings all the worlds of other regions, thereby enabling them all to see them;
The unimpeded function of manifesting for all beings the bodies of the devas Śakra, Brahma, and the World Protecting Kings;
The unimpeded function of manifesting for all beings the serene awesome deportment of *śrāvaka* disciples and *pratyekabuddhas;*
The unimpeded function of manifesting for all beings the bodhisattva practices; and
The unimpeded function of manifesting for all beings the major marks and secondary signs of the buddhas' bodies, their powers of all-knowledge, and their realization of the right and perfect enlightenment.

These are the ten.

The bodhisattva-mahāsattva has ten kinds of unimpeded functions in relation to lands. What are those ten? They are as follows:

The unimpeded function of making all *kṣetras* into a single *kṣetra;*
The unimpeded function of making all *kṣetras* enter a single pore;
The unimpeded function of knowing the endlessness of all *kṣetras;*
The unimpeded function of causing a single body sitting in the lotus posture to completely fill all *kṣetras;*
The unimpeded function of showing all *kṣetras* appearing within a single body;
The unimpeded function of causing all *kṣetras* to quake even while not causing the beings within them to become frightened;
The unimpeded function of adorning a single *kṣetra* with the adornments of all *kṣetras;*
The unimpeded function of adorning all *kṣetras* with the adornments of a single *kṣetra;*
The unimpeded function of revealing to beings a single *tathāgata* and his single congregation pervading all buddha *kṣetras;* and
The unimpeded function of everywhere showing all beings all the countless differences in *kṣetras* everywhere throughout their network which pervades all the directions, including the small *kṣetras,* mid-sized *kṣetras,* large *kṣetras,* vast *kṣetras,* deep *kṣetras,* upward-facing *kṣetras,* inverted *kṣetras,* laterally facing *kṣetras,* and upright *kṣetras.*

These are the ten.

Sons of the Buddha, the bodhisattva-mahāsattva has ten kinds of unimpeded functions in relation to dharmas. What are those ten? They are as follows:

The unimpeded function of knowing all dharmas enter a single dharma and a single dharma enters all dharmas, and yet [still being able to explain this in such a way that] it does not contravene beings' capacity to comprehend this;

The unimpeded function of bringing forth all dharmas from within the *prajñāpāramitā* and explaining them for others, thereby enabling them all to awaken;

The unimpeded function of knowing all dharmas transcend expression in words even as he still enables all beings to successfully awaken to and penetrate them;

The unimpeded function of knowing all dharmas enter but a single sign while still being able to expound on countless signs of dharmas;

The unimpeded function of knowing all dharmas transcend words and speech even as he is still able to explain boundlessly many Dharma gateways for others;

The unimpeded function of skillfully turning the universal gateway's syllabary wheel in relation to all dharmas;

The unimpeded function of enabling all dharmas to enter a single Dharma gateway without any mutual contradiction between them as he expounds on them for an ineffable number of kalpas without ever coming to the end of them;

The unimpeded function of enabling all dharmas to enter the Dharma of the Buddha, thereby enabling all beings to succeed in awakening and understanding;

The unimpeded function of knowing all dharmas have no boundaries; and

The unimpeded function of knowing all dharmas as devoid of obstructive boundaries and as like an illusory network possessed of countless differences which he explains for beings for countless kalpas without ever being able to come to the end of them all.

These are the ten.

Sons of the Buddha, the bodhisattva-mahāsattva has ten kinds of unimpeded functions in relation to bodies. What are these ten? They are as follows:

The unimpeded function of causing the bodies of all beings to enter his own body;

The unimpeded function of causing his own body to enter all beings' bodies;

The unimpeded function of causing all buddhas' bodies to enter a single buddha's body;

The unimpeded function of causing a single buddha's body to enter all buddhas' bodies;
The unimpeded function of causing all *kṣetras* to enter his own body;
The unimpeded function of showing beings a single body completely pervading all dharmas of the three periods of time;
The unimpeded function of showing boundlessly many bodies entering samādhi in a single body;
The unimpeded function of showing bodies as numerous as beings realizing right enlightenment within a single body;
The unimpeded function of revealing a single being's body in all beings' bodies and revealing all beings' bodies in a single being's body; and
The unimpeded function of revealing the Dharma body in all beings' bodies and revealing all beings' bodies in the Dharma body.

These are the ten.

Sons of the Buddha, the bodhisattva-mahāsattva has ten kinds of unimpeded functions in relation to vows. What are those ten? They are as follows:

The unimpeded function of making the vows of all bodhisattvas his own vows;
The unimpeded function of using the vow power by which all buddhas realized bodhi to manifest his own realization of right enlightenment;
The unimpeded function of realizing *anuttarasamyaksaṃbodhi* in a manner adapted to the beings he teaches;
The unimpeded function of having great vows that remain interminable even throughout the course of all boundless kalpas;
The unimpeded function of leaving the conscious body far behind and not attaching to the wisdom body while using masterful vows to manifest all kinds of bodies;
The unimpeded function of sacrificing his own body to bring about the complete fulfillment of others' vows;
The unimpeded function of everywhere teaching all beings while still never abandoning his great vows;
The unimpeded function of practicing the bodhisattva practices in all kalpas while still never cutting short his great vows;
The unimpeded function of manifesting the realization of the right enlightenment in a single pore while, through the power of vows, everywhere filling all buddha lands, manifesting in this way for the sake of every one of those beings residing in an ineffable-ineffable number of worlds; and

The unimpeded function of uttering a single sentence of Dharma that pervades the entire Dharma realm, brings forth a cloud of great right Dharma, sets loose the dazzling light of the lightning of liberation, creates the quaking thunder of the true Dharma, rains down the rain with the flavor of the elixir of immortality, and uses the power of great vows to drench all realms of beings.

These are the ten.

Sons of the Buddha, the bodhisattva-mahāsattva has ten kinds of unimpeded functions in relation to realms. What are those ten? They are as follows:

The unimpeded function of abiding in the realm of the Dharma realm even while still not abandoning the realms of beings;

The unimpeded function of abiding in the realm of the Buddha even while still not abandoning the realm of the *māras;*

The unimpeded function of abiding in the realm of nirvāṇa even while still not abandoning the realm of *saṃsāra;*

The unimpeded function of entering the realm of all-knowledge even while still never severing the realm of the bodhisattva's lineage;

The unimpeded function of abiding in the realm of quiescence even while never relinquishing the realms that conduce to distraction;

The unimpeded function of abiding in the realm that has no going and no coming, no conceptual proliferation, no appearances, no essential nature, no words and speech, and that is like empty space even while still not abandoning the realm of all beings' conceptual proliferation;

The unimpeded function of abiding in the realm of the powers and the liberations even while still not abandoning the realm that extends throughout all directions and places;

The unimpeded function of entering the realms without any beings even while still not abandoning the teaching of all beings;

The unimpeded function of abiding in the quiescent realms of the *dhyāna* absorptions, liberations, spiritual superknowledges, and clear knowledges even while still manifesting the taking on of birth in all worlds; and

The unimpeded function of abiding in the realm of all the Tathāgata's practices and adornments and his realization of right enlightenment even while still manifesting all the quiescence and awesome deportment of *śrāvaka* disciples and *pratyekabuddhas.*

These are the ten.

Sons of the Buddha, the bodhisattva-mahāsattva has ten kinds of unimpeded functions in relation to knowledge. What are those ten? They are as follows:

The unimpeded function of inexhaustible eloquence;

The unimpeded function of all the complete-retention *dhāraṇī* formulae by which he never forgets anything;

The unimpeded function of being able to definitely know and definitely explain all beings' faculties;

The unimpeded function of using unimpeded knowledge in knowing in but a single mind-moment the mental actions of all beings;

The unimpeded function of knowing the illnesses associated with all beings' dispositions, latent tendencies, habitual karmic propensities, and afflictions and then bestowing the appropriate medicine in accordance with what is fitting;

The unimpeded function of being able in but a single mind-moment to enter the Tathāgata's ten powers;

The unimpeded function of using unimpeded knowledge in knowing all kalpas of the three periods of time as well as the beings within them;

The unimpeded function of, in each successive mind-moment, endlessly revealing for beings the realization of right enlightenment;

The unimpeded function of knowing through the thoughts of but a single being the karmic actions of all beings; and

The unimpeded function of understanding through the voice of a single being the speech of all beings.

These are the ten.

Sons of the Buddha, the bodhisattva-mahāsattva has ten kinds of unimpeded functions in relation to the spiritual superknowledges. What are those ten? They are as follows:

The unimpeded function of revealing the bodies of all worlds in but a single body;

The unimpeded function of hearing in the congregation of a single buddha the Dharma spoken in the congregations of all buddhas;

The unimpeded function of using the thoughts in the mind of a single being to accomplish an ineffable number of realizations of unexcelled bodhi through which he awakens to the minds of all beings;

The unimpeded function of using but a single voice to manifest all the different voices in all worlds, thereby enabling all beings to completely understand him;

The unimpeded function of revealing in but a single mind-moment all the many different karmic effects as they unfolded in all kalpas of the past, thereby enabling all beings to know and see them;

The unimpeded function of manifesting within a single atom the measureless adornments of a vast buddha *kṣetra*;[439]

The unimpeded function of causing all worlds to become completely adorned;

The unimpeded function of everywhere entering all three periods of time;

The unimpeded function of emanating great Dharma light which reveals the bodhi of all buddhas as well as the conduct and vows of all beings; and

The unimpeded function of skillfully protecting all devas, dragons, *yakṣas, gandharvas, asuras, garuḍas, kiṃnaras, mahoragas,* Śakra, Brahma, the World Protecting Heavenly Kings, *śrāvaka* disciples, *pratyekabuddhas,* bodhisattvas, the ten powers of all *tathāgatas,* and the bodhisattvas' roots of goodness.

These are the ten. If bodhisattvas acquire these unimpeded functions, then they are able to everywhere penetrate all dharmas of the Buddha.

Sons of the Buddha, the bodhisattva-mahāsattva has ten kinds of unimpeded functions in relation to the spiritual powers. What are those ten? They are as follows:

The unimpeded function of placing an ineffable number of worlds into but a single atom;

The unimpeded function of revealing in but a single atom all buddha *kṣetras* equal in number to all those contained in the entire Dharma realm;

The unimpeded function of placing the waters of all the great oceans into but a single pore and then traveling everywhere, going forth and returning from all worlds of the ten directions, yet doing so in a manner that involves no contact with or disturbance of any of those beings within them;

The unimpeded function of placing an ineffable number of worlds into his own body while revealing all the deeds accomplished with the spiritual superknowledges;

The unimpeded function of using a single strand of hair to string together an innumerable number of vajra ring mountains and then carry them along as he roams to all worlds, doing so without ever causing any of the beings there to have any fearful thoughts;

The unimpeded function of making a single kalpa from an ineffable number of kalpas and making an ineffable number of kalpas from a single kalpa even while revealing the different phases of creation and destruction within them without ever frightening any beings;

The unimpeded function of revealing in all worlds the many different kinds of destructive changes produced by water, fire, and wind disasters while still not troubling any of their beings;

The unimpeded function of being able to protect all the life-sustaining possessions of all beings when the three kinds of disasters cause destruction in all worlds, thereby preventing them from becoming damaged or diminished;

The unimpeded function of being able to pick up in one hand an ineffable number of worlds and then pitch them beyond an ineffable number of worlds, all while not causing any of their beings to become terrified by this; and

The unimpeded function of enabling all beings to attain awakened understanding by speaking of all *kṣetras* as identical to empty space.

These are the ten.

Sons of the Buddha, the bodhisattva-mahāsattva has ten kinds of unimpeded functions in relation to the powers. What are those ten? They are as follows:

The unimpeded function of powers in relation to beings with which he teaches and trains them and never abandons them;

The unimpeded function of powers in relation to *kṣetras* with which he manifests an ineffable number of adornments and then adorns them;

The unimpeded function of powers in relation to the Dharma with which he causes all bodies to enter what is not a body at all;

The unimpeded function of powers in relation to kalpas with which he cultivates incessantly;

The unimpeded function of powers in relation to buddhahood with which he awakens beings from their slumber;

The unimpeded function of powers in relation to the practices with which he consolidates all the bodhisattva practices;

The unimpeded function of powers in relation to the Tathāgata with which he liberates all beings;

The unimpeded function of powers in relation to the absence of a teacher with which he becomes independently awakened to all dharmas;

The unimpeded function of powers in relation to all-knowledge with which he attains right enlightenment through all-knowledge; and

The unimpeded function of powers in relation to the great compassion with which he never abandons any being.

These are the ten.

Sons of the Buddha, factors such as these constitute what is meant by the bodhisattva-mahāsattva's ten kinds of unimpeded functions. Wherever there is anyone who acquires these ten kinds of unimpeded functions, he becomes one who, whether or not he wishes to gain *anuttarasamyaksaṃbodhi,* is but a matter of his own inclinations in which he would meet no opposition in either case. Although he could gain right enlightenment, he would still never cut off his practice of the bodhisattva practices. And why is this? This is because the bodhisattva-mahāsattva makes the great vow to enter boundlessly many gateways of unimpeded functions and uses skillful means to manifest them.

Sons of the Buddha, the bodhisattva-mahāsattva has ten kinds of easeful mastery. What are those ten? They are as follows:

Using the body of a being, he creates the body of a *kṣetra* and yet still does not damage the body of that being. This is an instance of the bodhisattva's easeful mastery;

Using the body of a *kṣetra,* he creates the body of a being and yet still does not damage the body of that *kṣetra.* This is an instance of the bodhisattva's easeful mastery;

He manifests the bodies of *śrāvaka* disciples and *pratyekabuddhas* in the body of a buddha and yet still does not thereby diminish the body of that *tathāgata.* This is an instance of the bodhisattva's easeful mastery;

He manifests the body of a *tathāgata* in the bodies of *śrāvaka* disciples and *pratyekabuddhas* and yet still does not thereby bring about any increase in the bodies of those *śrāvaka* disciples and *pratyekabuddhas.* This is an instance of the bodhisattva's easeful mastery;

He manifests a body gaining right enlightenment in a body which practices the bodhisattva practices and yet still does not thereby cut short the actions of that body practicing the bodhisattva practices. This is an instance of the bodhisattva's easeful mastery;

He manifests a body cultivating the bodhisattva practices in the body that realizes the right enlightenment and yet still does not thereby diminish that body that realizes bodhi. This is an instance of the bodhisattva's easeful mastery;

He manifests a *saṃsāra* body in the realm of nirvāṇa and yet does not become attached to *saṃsāra*. This is an instance of the bodhisattva's easeful mastery;

He manifests nirvāṇa in the realm of *saṃsāra* and yet still does not then achieve the ultimate entry into nirvāṇa. This is an instance of the bodhisattva's easeful mastery;

He enters samādhi and then manifests all of the actions of walking, standing, sitting, and lying down, and yet he still does not relinquish the right meditative absorption of samādhi. This is an instance of the bodhisattva's easeful mastery; and

He resides with an unmoving body in the presence of a single buddha, listening to the Dharma, absorbing it, and retaining it even as, through the power of samādhi, he manifests bodies in the congregations of every one of an ineffable number of buddhas. Yet he still does not create any division bodies and still does not arise from meditative concentration as he continuously and ceaselessly listens to those expositions of Dharma, absorbing and retaining them. In this manner, in each successive mind-moment, he sends forth from each and every one of those samādhi-dwelling bodies an ineffable-ineffable number of additional samādhi-dwelling bodies. Though all the kalpas through which he sequentially passes in this way might still come to an end, those bodhisattva samādhi-dwelling bodies still could never come to an end. This is an instance of the bodhisattva's easeful mastery.

These are the ten. If bodhisattvas abide in these dharmas, then they acquire the easeful mastery of the Tathāgata's unexcelled great wisdom.

Sons of the Buddha, the bodhisattva-mahāsattva has ten kinds of spheres of action. What are those ten? They are as follows:

Revealing boundlessly many gateways to the Dharma realm and enabling beings to enter them is a sphere of action of the bodhisattva;

Revealing the countless marvelous adornments of all worlds and enabling beings to enter them is a sphere of action of the bodhisattva;

Creating transformations that travel to the realms of all beings and use skillful means to awaken them all is a sphere of action of the bodhisattva;

To emanate bodhisattva bodies from a *tathāgata*'s body and emanate *tathāgata* bodies from a bodhisattva body is a sphere of action of the bodhisattva;

To manifest worlds in the realm of empty space and manifest realms of empty space among worlds is a sphere of action of the bodhisattva;

To manifest the realm of nirvāṇa in the realm of *saṃsāra* and manifest the realm of *saṃsāra* in the realm of *nirvāṇa* is a sphere of action of the bodhisattva;

To produce the language of the Dharma of all buddhas from the language of a single being is a sphere of action of the bodhisattva;

To use boundlessly many bodies to manifest the creation of a single body and to manifest the creation of all different kinds of bodies from a single body is a sphere of action of the bodhisattva;

To use a single body to completely fill the entire Dharma realm is a sphere of action of the bodhisattva; and

To enable all beings in but a single mind-moment to resolve to attain bodhi whereupon each of them manifests countless bodies realizing the right and perfect enlightenment is a sphere of action of the bodhisattva.

These are the ten. If bodhisattvas abide in these dharmas, then they gain the sphere of action of the Tathāgata's unexcelled great wisdom.

Sons of the Buddha, the bodhisattva-mahāsattva has ten [other] kinds of powers. What are those ten? They are as follows:

The power of the deep mind by which he does not mix in any worldly sentiments;

The power of the predominant deep mind by which he never abandons any of the dharmas of the Buddha;

The power of skillful means by which whatever he does is ultimate;

The power of knowledge by which he completely knows all mental actions;

The power of vows by which he enables the fulfillment of whatever he strives to accomplish;

The power of the practices by which he continues on to the very end of future time;

The power of the vehicles by which he is able to manifest all the vehicles while still never abandoning the Great Vehicle;

The power of spiritual transformations by which, in every pore, he reveals all the pure worlds and all the *tathāgatas* appearing in the world;

The power of bodhi by which he incessantly enables all beings to resolve to become buddhas; and

The power of turning the Dharma wheel by which, in explaining but a single sentence of Dharma, he matches the faculties, natures, and aspirations of all beings.

These are the ten. If bodhisattvas abide in these dharmas, then they acquire all buddhas' unexcelled all-knowledge and ten powers.

Sons of the Buddha, the bodhisattva-mahāsattva has ten kinds of fearlessness. What are those ten? They are as follows:

Sons of the Buddha, the bodhisattva-mahāsattva is so well able to hear and retain all speech that he hears that he reflects in this way: "Even if countlessly and boundlessly many beings were to come here from all the ten directions and then use a hundred thousand great dharmas to pose questions to me, I would not see in any of their questions even the slightest aspect worthy of considering their questions difficult to answer." Due to seeing no difficulty in this, his mind becomes fearless and he reaches the ultimate perfection of great fearlessness. No matter what they might ask, he is able to reply in a manner that severs the questioner's doubts without feeling any sort of timidity. This is the first of the bodhisattva's kinds of fearlessness;

Sons of the Buddha, the bodhisattva-mahāsattva acquires the Tathāgata's crown-anointing consecration and the unimpeded eloquence with which he achieves ultimate perfection in explaining the esoteric meaning of all writing and speech. He reflects in this way: "Even if countlessly and boundlessly many beings were to come here from all the ten directions and then used countless dharmas to question me, I would not see in any of their questions even the slightest aspect worthy of considering their questions difficult to answer." Due to seeing no difficulty in this, his mind becomes fearless and he reaches the ultimate perfection of great fearlessness. No matter what they might ask, he is able to reply in a manner that severs the questioner's doubts without feeling any sort of fearful trepidation. This is the second of the bodhisattva's kinds of fearlessness;

Sons of the Buddha, the bodhisattva-mahāsattva realizes that all dharmas are empty, are devoid of a self, are devoid of anything belonging to a self, are devoid of anything done, are devoid of any agent of actions, are devoid of any knower, are devoid of any entity possessed of a life span, are devoid of any soul,[440] are devoid of any *pudgala,* and are apart from any of the aggregates, sense realms, or sense bases. He has forever transcended all views and his mind is like empty space. He reflects in this way: "I do not see even the slightest sign that there might be any being able to injure or trouble me through any physical, verbal, or mental action." And why is this so? This is because the bodhisattva has abandoned the self and all possessions of a self. He does not perceive the existence of any dharma at all that is possessed of even the slightest nature or characteristic. Because he sees no such thing, his mind becomes fearless and he reaches the ultimate perfection of great fearlessness. He is so steadfast and courageous that he cannot be obstructed. This is the third of the bodhisattva's kinds of fearlessness;

Sons of the Buddha, the bodhisattva-mahāsattva is protected by the Buddha's power, is sustained by the Buddha's power, and abides in the Buddha's awesome deportment. Whatever he practices is genuine and unchanging. He reflects in this way: "I do not perceive even the slightest aspect of this awesome deportment that might give any being cause to criticize it." On account of seeing no such thing, his mind gains that fearlessness by which, in the midst of the Great Assembly, he remains peaceful and secure in his expositions of the Dharma. This is the fourth of the bodhisattva's kinds of fearlessness;

Sons of the Buddha, the bodhisattva-mahāsattva's physical, verbal, and mental karmic actions are all pure, immaculate, gentle, and free of the many kinds of evil. He reflects in this way: "I do not perceive in any of my physical, verbal, or mental actions even the slightest aspect worthy of criticism." Due to seeing no such thing, his mind achieves that fearlessness by which he is able to cause beings to dwell in the Buddha's Dharma. This is the fifth of the bodhisattva's kinds of fearlessness;

Sons of the Buddha, the bodhisattva-mahāsattva is always followed and protected by vajra stalwarts, devas, dragons, *yakṣas, gandharvas, asuras,* Śakra, the Brahma Heaven King, the Four Heavenly Kings, and others. He is held in protective mindfulness by all *tathāgatas* and is never abandoned by them. The bodhisattva-mahāsattva reflects in this way: "I do not see even the slightest sign that any among the many *māras,* the adherents of the non-Buddhist traditions, or beings holding the view that existence is real might be able to come and obstruct my practice of the Bodhisattva path." Due to seeing no such thing, his mind becomes fearless and he reaches the ultimate perfection of great fearlessness. He brings forth a mind of joyous delight in his practice of the bodhisattva practices. This is the sixth of the bodhisattva's kinds of fearlessness;

Sons of the Buddha, the bodhisattva-mahāsattva has already perfected the foremost faculty of mindfulness. His mind has become free of forgetfulness and is approved of by the Buddha. He reflects in this way: "In the Dharma of the scriptures and statements of the path to bodhi as proclaimed by the Tathāgata, I do not see even the slightest sign that I might have forgotten any of it." Due to seeing no such sign, his mind becomes fearless in absorbing and sustaining the right Dharma of all Tathāgatas and in practicing the bodhisattva practices. This is the seventh of the bodhisattva's kinds of fearlessness;

Sons of the Buddha, the bodhisattva-mahāsattva has already gained a penetrating comprehension of wisdom and skillful means and he has already reached the ultimate development of all the powers of the bodhisattva. He always diligently teaches all beings and he constantly relies on the resolve of his vows to keep him connected to the bodhi of the Buddha. Even so, because of his compassionate pity for beings and because he is devoted to ripening beings, he manifests the appearance of taking birth in worlds beset by the turbidity of the afflictions, being born into a venerable and noble clan with a full retinue in circumstances where whatever he desires appears at will and he is able to delight in the pleasures and dwell in happiness. Still, he reflects in this way: "Although I have gathered together here with this retinue, I do not see even the slightest sign of anything worthy of any desire-based attachment which would lead to the deterioration of my cultivation of the dharmas of the bodhisattva path, including the *dhyāna* absorptions, the liberations, the samādhis, the complete-retention *dhāraṇīs,* and eloquence."

And why is this so? This is because the bodhisattva-mahāsattva has already achieved perfection in the sovereign mastery of all dharmas. He has vowed to never discontinue his cultivation of the bodhisattva practices and he does not see anywhere in the world even a single sphere of experience which could delude or confuse one who is on the bodhisattva path. Due to seeing no such thing, his mind becomes fearless and he reaches the ultimate perfection of great fearlessness. Hence, relying on the power of his great vows, he manifests the taking on of births in all worlds. This is the eighth of the bodhisattva's kinds of fearlessness;

Sons of the Buddha, the bodhisattva-mahāsattva never forgets his resolve to gain all-knowledge. Riding in the Great Vehicle, he practices the bodhisattva practices. Using the strength of his great resolve to gain all-knowledge, he manifests the serene awesome deportment of the *śrāvaka* disciple and *pratyekabuddha* practitioners. He reflects in this way: "I do not perceive in myself even the slightest sign of any inclination to seize on emancipation in reliance on the two vehicles." Due to seeing no such thing, his mind becomes fearless and he reaches the perfection of unexcelled great fearlessness. He is everywhere able to manifest the paths of all vehicles even as he achieves the ultimate fulfillment of the impartial Great Vehicle. This is the ninth of the bodhisattva's kinds of fearlessness; and

Sons of the Buddha, the bodhisattva-mahāsattva perfects all the dharmas of purity, completely fulfills the roots of goodness, perfectly fulfills the spiritual superknowledges, and ultimately comes to abide in the Buddha's bodhi. He completely fulfills all the bodhisattva practices and receives from all buddhas the crown-anointing prediction of all-knowledge even as he always continues to teach beings and practice the bodhisattva path. He reflects in this way: "I do not perceive any sign of even a single being appropriate for ripening for whom I would not be able to manifest all buddhas' sovereign mastery in bringing about their ripening." Due to seeing no such thing, his mind becomes fearless and he reaches the ultimate perfection of great fearlessness. He never ceases the bodhisattva practices, never abandons the bodhisattva vows, and reveals the realms of the Buddha for whichever beings should be taught and thereby teaches and liberates them. This is the tenth of the bodhisattva's kinds of fearlessness.

Sons of the Buddha, these are the bodhisattva-mahāsattva's ten kinds of fearlessness. If bodhisattvas abide in these dharmas, then they acquire the unexcelled fearlessness of the Buddha and yet still do not relinquish the fearlessness of the bodhisattva.

Sons of the Buddha, the bodhisattva-mahāsattva has ten kinds of exclusive dharmas. What are those ten? They are as follows:

Sons of the Buddha, even without depending on teachings provided by others, the bodhisattva-mahāsattva naturally cultivates the six *pāramitās*. Thus he always delights in great giving and does not become miserly. He constantly upholds the pure moral precepts and remains free of transgressions against them. He completely fulfills the practice of patience by which his mind is never shaken. He possesses great vigor by which he never retreats. He skillfully enters the *dhyānas* and never becomes scattered. And he skillfully cultivates wisdom and rids himself of all wrong views. This is the first of his exclusive dharmas, that by which, without depending on teachings provided by others, he follows the path of the *pāramitās* and thus cultivates the six perfections;

Sons of the Buddha, the bodhisattva-mahāsattva is everywhere able to attract and gather in all beings, in particular doing so: by practicing kindly giving of material wealth or the Dharma; by manifesting right mindfulness and a harmonious countenance as he uses pleasing words in such a way that others are delighted; by revealing to them meanings in accordance with reality, thereby causing them to awaken to and understand the bodhi of all buddhas; and by remaining free of dislike or disapproval as he benefits others equally. This is the second of his exclusive dharmas, that by which, without depending on teachings provided by others, he accords with the path of the four means of attraction as he diligently attracts and gathers in beings;

Sons of the Buddha, the bodhisattva-mahāsattva is skillful in making dedications, namely: dedications in which he does not seek any resulting rewards; dedications which accord with the Buddha's bodhi; dedications in which he is not attached to any worldly *dhyāna* absorptions or samādhis; dedications for the benefit of beings; and dedications to prevent the severance of the wisdom of the Tathāgata. This is the third of his exclusive dharmas, that by which, without depending on teachings provided by others, for the benefit of others, he produces roots of goodness and seeks the wisdom of the Buddha;

Sons of the Buddha, the bodhisattva-mahāsattva achieves ultimate perfection in skillful means. His mind is constantly concerned with caring for all beings. Thus he does not detest the mind states of the world's foolish common people, does not delight in the path of emancipation of adherents of the two vehicles, and does not become attached to his own pleasures. Rather he only devotes himself to diligently teaching and liberating them.

He is well able to enter and emerge from the *dhyāna* samādhis and liberations. He gains sovereign mastery of all the samādhis and goes forth and returns in *saṃsāra* as if wandering about in gardens and terraces, never even briefly wearying of this. He sometimes dwells in the palace of the *māras*, sometimes becomes Śakra Deva, sometimes becomes the Brahma Heaven King, and sometimes becomes a ruler in the world. Of all the places of rebirth, there are none in which he does not manifest his bodies.

He may become a monastic within the communities of non-Buddhist traditions, but always stays far away from all their erroneous views. He may manifest the skills associated with all of the world's literary abilities, mantra formulae, calligraphy, seal carving, mathematics, and so forth, including even the methods of entertainments, singing, and dancing, having none of these in which his skills are not especially refined.

He may manifest in the form of a beautiful woman possessed of such wisdom and talent that it is foremost in the entire world, as one who has acquired the most ultimate ability to pose questions on, discuss, answer questions, and sever doubts about both worldly and world-transcending dharmas, as one who has achieved perfection in the penetrating comprehension of all worldly and world transcending matters, as one whom all beings constantly come to and look up to with admiration.

Although he manifests the awesome deportment of *śrāvaka* disciples and *pratyekabuddhas,* he still never loses his resolve to abide in the Great Vehicle. Although he manifests the realization of right enlightenment in each successive mind-moment, he still never quits practicing the bodhisattva practices. This is the fourth of his exclusive dharmas, that by which, without depending on teachings provided by others, he reaches the ultimate perfection of skillful means;

Sons of the Buddha, the bodhisattva-mahāsattva knows well the path of joint practice of both the provisional and the true and has reached the ultimate degree of the sovereign mastery of wisdom. That is to say:

He abides in nirvāṇa and yet manifests in *saṃsāra;*

He realizes that no beings exist and yet he diligently practices teaching them;

He has reached ultimate quiescence and yet may manifest the arising of afflictions;

He abides in the one Dharma body of solid wisdom and yet may everywhere manifest countless bodies of beings;

He is always immersed in deep *dhyāna* absorptions and yet may manifest as one who enjoys the pleasures of the desires;

He has forever left the three realms of existence and yet never abandons beings;

He always delights in Dharma bliss and yet may appear as attended by talented ladies who sing and provide joyous entertainments;

Although his body is adorned with the many major marks and secondary signs, he may still manifest in the form of one who is ugly, poor, or of low social class;

He always accumulates the many types of goodness, remains free of all faults, and yet may manifest as one born into the hell realms, the animal realms, or the hungry ghost realms; and

Although he has already reached perfection in the buddha's wisdom, he still never relinquishes the bodhisattva's wisdom body.

The bodhisattva-mahāsattva perfects such measureless wisdom as this which cannot even be known of by *śrāvaka* disciples or *pratyekabuddhas,* how much the less by any of the ignorant common beings. This is the fifth of his exclusive dharmas, that by which, without depending on teachings provided by others, he implements the joint practice of both the provisional and the true;

Sons of the Buddha, the physical, verbal, and mental actions of the bodhisattva-mahāsattva are enacted in accordance with the wisdom and are all pure. That is to say, he is fully possessed of great kindness, forever abandons the motivation to kill, is fully possessed of right understanding, and is free of wrong views. This is the sixth of his exclusive dharmas, that by which, without depending on teachings provided by others, his physical, verbal, and mental actions are enacted in accordance with wisdom;

Sons of the Buddha, the bodhisattva-mahāsattva is fully possessed of the great compassion, never abandons beings, and substitutes for all beings in undergoing sufferings, in particular, the sufferings of the hells, the sufferings of the animals, and the sufferings of the hungry ghosts, doing so in order to benefit beings and never growing weary of this. He wishes only to liberate all beings and never indulges in any of the defiled spheres of experience related to the five types of desire. He is always intensely diligent in extinguishing the many kinds of sufferings. This is the seventh of his exclusive dharmas, that by which, without depending on teachings provided by others, he always arouses the great compassion;

Sons of the Buddha, the bodhisattva-mahāsattva is one whom beings always delight in seeing. The Brahma Heaven King, Śakra, the Four Heavenly Kings, and the other devas as well as all beings never weary of seeing him. And why is this? From the long distant past on forward to the present, the bodhisattva-mahāsattva has practiced deeds which are pure and free of all faults. It is for this reason that beings who see him never grow weary of this. This is the eighth of his exclusive dharmas, that by which, without depending on teachings provided by others, he becomes one whom all beings delight in seeing;

Sons of the Buddha, the bodhisattva-mahāsattva's [quest to attain] all-knowledge is adorned with the great vow and characterized by solidly enduring zeal. Although he resides in the dangerous and difficult abodes of common people, *śrāvaka* disciples, and *pratyekabuddhas*, he never retreats from or loses the bright, pure, and marvelous jewel of his resolve to attain all-knowledge;

Sons of the Buddha, just as there is a precious jewel known as "pure adornment" which, when placed in muddy water, its radiance and color remain unchanged and it retains the capacity to clarify and purify those turbid waters, so too it is with the bodhisattva-mahāsattva. Although he resides in the foolish common person's places so characterized by the various kinds of turbidity and such, he still never loses his resolve to seek the pure jewel of all-knowledge, and yet he is still able to cause those beings ensconced in all kinds of evil to depart far from the filth and turbidity of their wrong views and afflictions and then become able themselves to seek the pure mind jewel of all-knowledge. This is the ninth of his exclusive dharmas, that by which, without depending on teachings provided by others and even when residing in the many kinds of difficult circumstances, he never loses the jewel of his resolve to attain all-knowledge; and

Sons of the Buddha, the bodhisattva-mahāsattva completely develops the knowledge of his self-enlightened sphere of cognition and reaches perfection in gaining ultimate sovereign mastery in his self-awakening attained without a teacher. He uses the headband of immaculately pure Dharma to crown his head, never abandons his close relationship with his good spiritual guide, and always delights in revering all the *tathāgatas*. This is the tenth of his exclusive dharmas, that by which, without depending on teachings provided by others, he acquires the most supreme Dharma, never parts from his good spiritual guide, and never abandons his veneration of the Buddha.

Sons of the Buddha, these are the bodhisattva-mahāsattva's ten kinds of exclusive dharmas. If bodhisattvas abide in these, then they acquire the Tathāgata's unexcelled and vast exclusive dharmas.

Sons of the Buddha, the bodhisattva-mahāsattva has ten kinds of works. What are those ten? They are as follows:

Works related to all worlds, based on his ability to purify them all;
Works related to all buddhas, based on his ability to make offerings to them all;
Works related to all bodhisattvas, based on his ability to plant roots of goodness the same as theirs;
Works related to all beings, based on his ability to teach them all;
Works related to all of future time, based on his continuing to attract and gather them in until the very end of future time;
Works related to all the spiritual powers, based on his never leaving one world even as he travels everywhere to all worlds;
Works related to all light, based on his emanation of rays of light of boundlessly many colors, every ray of which has a lotus flower throne on each of which he manifests a bodhisattva sitting there in the lotus posture;
Works related to preventing the lineages of all Three Jewels from ever being cut off, based on his continuing to preserve, protect, and sustain the Dharma of all buddhas after the buddhas have passed into *parinirvāṇa*;
Works related to all spiritual transformations, based on his proclaiming the Dharma and teaching beings in all worlds; and
Works related to all his empowerments, based on his adaptation in but a single mind-moment to whatever beings' minds wish for by manifesting for them all and enabling all their wishes to be completely fulfilled.

These are the ten. If bodhisattvas abide in these dharmas, then they acquire the Tathāgata's unexcelled vast works.

Sons of the Buddha, the bodhisattva-mahāsattva has ten kinds of bodies. What are those ten? They are as follows:

The body that does not come forth, so called because it does not take on births in any world;
The body that does not go forth, so called because it is inapprehensible in any world;
The unreal body, so called because, in all worlds, it is [only] as if truly acquired;[441]
The non-false body, so called because, it is by resort to reality-accordant noumenal principle[442] that it appears in the world;
The unending body, so called because it continues on to the very end of the future without being cut off;
The solid body, so called because none of all the many kinds of *māras* are able to destroy it;
The unmoving body, so called because it cannot be moved by any of the many kinds of *māras* or adherents of non-Buddhist paths;

The body possessed of the signs, so called because it manifests the pure signs arising from the hundredfold merits;

The signless body, so called because the marks of dharmas are all devoid of any signs at all; and

The body that reaches everywhere, so called because all buddhas of the three periods of time share this same single body.

These are the ten. If bodhisattvas abide in these dharmas, then they acquire the Tathāgata's unexcelled and endless body.

Sons of the Buddha, the bodhisattva-mahāsattva has ten kinds of physical actions. What are those ten? They are as follows:

The physical actions by which a single body completely fills all worlds;

The physical actions by which he is able to manifest directly before all beings;

The physical actions by which he is able to take on births in all the destinies of rebirth;

The physical actions by which he travels throughout all worlds;

The physical actions by which he visits all buddhas and their congregations;

The physical actions by which he is able to cover all worlds with one hand;

The physical actions by which he is able with one hand to rub all worlds' vajra ring mountains and thus reduce them to atom-like particles;

The physical actions by which he reveals within his own body the creation and destruction of all buddha *kṣetras* and shows this to beings;

The physical actions by which he includes all realms of beings within a single body; and

The physical actions by which he reveals within his own body all the pure buddha *kṣetras* in which all beings are attaining complete enlightenment.[443]

These are the ten. If bodhisattvas abide in these dharmas, then they acquire the Tathāgata's unexcelled actions of buddhas by which they are all able to awaken all beings.

Sons of the Buddha, the bodhisattva-mahāsattva has ten [other] kinds of bodies.[444] What are those ten? They are as follows:

The body of the *pāramitās*, so called because of his correct cultivation of them all;

The body of the four means of attraction, so called because he never abandons any being;

The body of great compassion, so called because he tirelessly substitutes for all beings in enduring measureless suffering;

The body of great kindness, so called because he rescues all beings;

The body of merit, so called because he benefits all beings;

The body of wisdom, so called because it is of the same single nature as the bodies of all buddhas;

The body of the Dharma, so called because he forever transcends taking rebirth in any of the rebirth destinies;

The body of skillful means, so called because he appears in all places;

The body of spiritual powers, so called because he manifests all the spiritual transformations; and

The body of bodhi, so called because he gains right enlightenment however he pleases and whenever he chooses.

These are the ten. If bodhisattvas abide in these dharmas, then they acquire the Tathāgata's unexcelled great wisdom body.

Sons of the Buddha, the bodhisattva-mahāsattva has ten kinds of speech. What are those ten? They are as follows:

Gentle speech, so called because it enables all beings to feel safe;

Speech like the elixir of immortality, so called because it enables all beings to feel clear and cool;

Nondeceptive speech, so called because everything he says accords with reality;

Truthful speech, so called because, even in dreams, he is free of false speech;

Vast speech, so called because it is universally respected even by all devas such as Śakra, Brahma, the Four Heavenly Kings, and others;

Extremely profound speech, so called because it reveals the nature of dharmas;

Solid speech, so called because it endlessly speaks about the Dharma;

Direct speech, so called because it is easy to understand whatever he says;

Multifarious speech, so called because it manifests in accordance with the particular time; and

Speech that awakens all beings, so called because it accords with their inclinations and thereby enables them to fully understand.

These are the ten. If bodhisattvas abide in these dharmas, then they acquire the Tathāgata's unexcelled sublime speech.

Sons of the Buddha, the bodhisattva-mahāsattva has ten ways of purifying speech. What are those ten? They are as follows:

Purifying speech by delighting in listening to the voice of the Tathāgata;
Purifying speech by delighting in listening to discussions of the bodhisattva's meritorious qualities;
Purifying speech by not saying what beings do not wish to hear;
Purifying speech by truly abandoning the four speech faults;[445]
Purifying speech by feeling exultant joy in praising all *tathāgatas;*
Purifying speech by loudly praising the Buddha's true meritorious qualities at stupas commemorating the Tathāgata;
Purifying speech by using a deeply pure mind in bestowing Dharma on beings;
Purifying speech by praising the Tathāgata with music and songs;
Purifying speech by not even sparing his own body or life for the sake of hearing right Dharma taught by the buddhas; and
Purifying speech by being willing to sacrificing his own life to receive the sublime Dharma through serving all bodhisattvas and teachers of the Dharma.

These are the ten.

Sons of the Buddha, if bodhisattva-mahāsattvas use these ten means to purify their speech, they acquire ten kinds of protection. What are those ten? They are as follows:

Protection provided by all the congregations of devas headed by the Heavenly Kings;
Protection provided by all the congregations of dragons headed by the dragon kings themselves;
Protection provided by the *yakṣa* kings and their followers;
Protection provided by the *gandharva* kings and their followers;
Protection provided by the *asura* kings and their followers;
Protection provided by the *garuḍa* kings and their followers;
Protection provided by the *kiṃnara* kings and their followers;
Protection provided by the *mahoraga* kings and their followers;
Protection provided by the Brahma Heaven Kings and their followers so that in every case, he is protected by these kings and their followers; and
Protection provided by all the masters of the Dharma headed by the *tathāgatas,* the Dharma kings.

These are the ten.

Sons of the Buddha, having acquired protection such as this, the bodhisattva-mahāsattva is then able to accomplish ten kinds of great endeavors. What are those ten? They are as follows:

They enable all beings to be happy;

They are able to travel and visit all worlds;
They are able to completely know all the faculties of others;
They purify all their resolute beliefs;
They eliminate all afflictions;
They relinquish all habitual karmic propensities;
They cause all their mental dispositions to be bright and immaculately pure;
They increase all kinds of profound mind;
They become pervasively present throughout the entire Dharma realm; and
They enable all instances of entering nirvāṇa to be clearly seen.

These are the ten.

Sons of the Buddha, the bodhisattva-mahāsattva has ten kinds of mind. What are those ten? They are as follows:

The mind that is like the great earth in its ability to support and promote the growth of all beings' roots of goodness;
The mind that is like the great ocean because all the Dharma waters of all buddhas' measureless and boundless great wisdom flow into it;
The mind that is like Sumeru, the king of mountains, in its ability to place all beings in the very highest place [for the growth] of the most superior roots of world-transcending goodness;
The mind that is like a sovereign *maṇi* jewel in the purity of its aspirations and in its absence of defilements;
The mind that is like vajra by virtue of its decisive and deep penetration of all dharmas;
The mind that is like the vajra ring mountains in its ability to remain unshaken by any of the *māras* or the followers of non-Buddhist traditions;
The mind that is like a lotus flower because it cannot be defiled by any of the worldly dharmas;
The mind that is like the *udumbara* flower because it is only rarely encountered in any kalpa;
The mind that is like the clearly shining sun because it dispels the obstacle of darkness; and
The mind that is like empty space because it is immeasurable.

These are the ten. If bodhisattvas abide in these, then they acquire the Tathāgata's unexcelled great and pure mind.

Sons of the Buddha, the bodhisattva-mahāsattva makes ten kinds of resolutions. What are those ten? They are as follows:

They resolve: "I shall liberate all beings";

They resolve: "I shall enable all beings to cut off their afflictions";
They resolve: "I shall enable all beings to melt away their habitual karmic propensities";
They resolve: "I shall cut off all doubts";
They resolve: "I shall extinguish all beings' anguishing afflictions";
They resolve: "I shall do away with the wretched destinies and the difficulties";[446]
They resolve: "I shall respectfully follow all *tathāgatas*";
They resolve: "I shall thoroughly train in whatever all bodhisattvas train in";
They resolve: "I shall reveal all buddhas' realization of right enlightenment on the tip of every hair in all worlds"; and
They resolve: "I shall beat the drum of the unexcelled Dharma in all worlds and enable all beings to gain awakened understanding in a manner adapted to their faculties and inclinations."

These are the ten. If bodhisattvas abide in these, then they acquire the Tathāgata's unexcelled and great resolve to do what they are able to do.

Sons of the Buddha, the bodhisattva has ten kinds of all-pervasive mind. What are those ten? They are as follows:

The mind that pervades all of empty space due to the vastness of its resolve;
The mind that pervades the entire Dharma realm due to its infinitely deep penetration;
The mind that pervades all three periods of time due to knowing them all in but a single mind-moment;
The mind that is pervasively present wherever all buddhas appear due to its complete knowledge of whenever they enter the womb, take birth, leave the home life, attain complete enlightenment, turn the Dharma wheel, and enter *parinirvāṇa*;
The mind that pervades all [realms of] beings due to its knowing all their faculties, inclinations, and habitual karmic propensities;
The mind that is pervasively [cognizant] of all types of wisdom due to its accordance with and complete knowing of the Dharma realm;
The mind that pervades all that is boundless due to its knowing all the different aspects of the web of illusory phenomena;
The mind that pervades the unproduced due to not apprehending any inherently existent nature in any dharma;

The mind that is unimpeded in pervading all things due to not dwelling in either his own mind or the minds of others; and
The mind that has sovereign mastery in pervading everything due to manifesting the realization of buddhahood everywhere in but a single mind-moment.

These are the ten. If bodhisattvas abide in these, then they acquire the pervasive adornment of the countless unexcelled dharmas of the Buddha.

Sons of the Buddha, the bodhisattva-mahāsattva has ten kinds of faculties. What are those ten? They are as follows:

The faculty of joyfulness by which he sees all buddhas and has indestructible faith;
The faculty of zeal by which he awakens to and understands all the Dharma of the Buddha that he hears;
The faculty of irreversibility by which he completes everything he does;
The faculty of secure abiding by which he never ceases practicing any of the bodhisattva practices;
The faculty of subtlety by which he penetrates the sublime principles of the *prajñāpāramitā*;
The faculty of never resting by which he completes all endeavors he does for the benefit of beings;
The faculty of being like vajra by which he realizes the nature of all dharmas;
The faculty of flaming vajra radiance by which he everywhere illuminates the sphere of action of all buddhas;
The faculty of nondifferentiation by which [he realizes] all *tathāgatas* share the same single body; and
The faculty of unimpeded boundlessness by which he deeply penetrates the Tathāgata's ten kinds of powers.

These are the ten. If bodhisattvas abide in these, then they acquire the faculty of the Tathāgata's unexcelled and perfectly fulfilled great wisdom.

Sons of the Buddha, the bodhisattva-mahāsattva has ten kinds of deep mind. What are those ten? They are as follows:

The deep mind that remains undefiled by any worldly dharma;
The deep mind that does not mix in any of the paths of the two vehicles;
The deep mind that completely comprehends the bodhi of all buddhas;
The deep mind that accords with the path to the wisdom of all-knowledge;

The deep mind that remains unmoved by any of the many *māras* or followers of non-Buddhist paths;
The deep mind that purely cultivates the perfectly fulfilled wisdom of all *tathāgatas;*
The deep mind that absorbs and retains all Dharma that is heard;
The deep mind that remains unattached to any of the stations of rebirth;
The deep mind that is equipped with all forms of subtle wisdom; and
The deep mind that cultivates all dharmas of all buddhas.

These are the ten. If bodhisattvas abide in these, then they acquire the deep mind possessed of the unexcelled purity of the All-Knowing One.

Sons of the Buddha, the bodhisattva-mahāsattva has ten kinds of especially superior deep mind. What are those ten? They are as follows:

The especially superior deep mind of irreversibility, so called because he accumulates all roots of goodness;
The especially superior deep mind free of all doubts, so called because he understands the esoteric speech of all *tathāgatas;*
The especially superior deep mind of rightly maintaining [his cultivation], so called because of what flows from his great vows and great practices;
The especially superior deep mind of supremacy, so called because he deeply penetrates all dharmas of the Buddha;
The especially superior deep mind of mastery, so called because he has attained sovereign mastery in all dharmas of the Buddha;
The especially superior deep mind of vast penetration, so called because he everywhere penetrates the many different kinds of gateways into the Dharma;
The especially superior deep mind of supreme leadership, so-called because he completely accomplishes everything he does;
The especially superior deep mind of sovereign mastery, so called because he is adorned with all the samādhis, spiritual superknowledges, and transformations;
The especially superior deep mind of secure abiding, so called because he embraces his original vows; and
The especially superior deep mind of incessant effort, so called because he fully ripens all beings.

These are the ten. If bodhisattvas abide in these dharmas, then they acquire all buddhas' especially superior mind of unexcelled purity.

Sons of the Buddha, the bodhisattva-mahāsattva has ten kinds of diligent cultivation. What are those ten? They are as follows:

The diligent cultivation of giving in which he gives away everything and seeks no reward;

The diligent cultivation of upholding the moral precepts in which he is free of any deception in practicing the *dhūta* austerities and in being easily satisfied with but few wishes;

The diligent cultivation of patience in which he abandons concepts of "self" and "other," endures all kinds of evil treatment, and never arouses any thoughts of anger or malice;

The diligent cultivation of vigor in which he never becomes distracted in actions of body, speech, or mind, never retreats from any endeavors, and completes them all;

The diligent cultivation of *dhyāna* absorption in which he cultivates the liberations and samādhis and manifests the spiritual superknowledges while abandoning all desires, afflictions, contentiousness, and their associated manifestations;

The diligent cultivation of wisdom in which he tirelessly cultivates the accumulation of all the meritorious qualities;

The diligent cultivation of great kindness in which he realizes that all beings have no inherently existent nature;

The diligent cultivation of great compassion in which he realizes the emptiness of all dharmas and everywhere substitutes for all beings in tirelessly taking on their sufferings;

The diligent cultivation of awakening to the Tathāgata's ten powers in which he gains an unimpeded and complete comprehension of them and reveals them to beings; and

The diligent cultivation of turning the irreversible wheel of the Dharma so that it reaches the minds of all beings.

These are the ten. If bodhisattvas abide in these dharmas, then they acquire the diligent cultivation of the Tathāgata's unexcelled great wisdom.

Sons of the Buddha, the bodhisattva-mahāsattva has ten kinds of definite understanding. What are those ten? They are as follows:

The definite understanding of supremacy, so called because he plants roots of goodness of veneration;

The definite understanding of adornment, so called because he produces many different kinds of adornments;

The definite understanding of vastness, so called because his mind has never been inclined toward narrowness or inferiority;

The definite understanding of quiescence, so called because he is able to penetrate the extremely deep nature of dharmas;
The definite understanding of universal pervasiveness, so called because his generation of the resolve has no place it does not reach;
The definite understanding of capacities, so called because he is able to receive the support of the Buddha's powers;
The definite understanding of solidity, so called because he demolishes all the works of the *māras;*
The definite understanding of clear judgment, so called because he completely knows the karmic results of all actions;
The definite understanding of direct manifestation, so called because he is able to manifest the spiritual superknowledges at will;
The definite understanding of continuing the legacy of the lineage, so called because he acquires predictions from all buddhas; and
The definite understanding of the sovereign masteries, so called because he can reach buddhahood whenever he pleases.

These are the ten. If bodhisattvas abide in these dharmas, then they acquire the Tathāgata's unexcelled definite understanding.

Sons of the Buddha, the bodhisattva-mahāsattva has ten kinds of definite understanding in knowing all worlds. What are those ten? They are as follows:

He knows all worlds enter a single world;
He knows all worlds enter all worlds;
He knows all worlds are everywhere pervaded by a single body of the Tathāgata and his single lotus flower throne;
He knows all worlds are like empty space;
He knows all worlds possess the adornment of the Buddha;
He knows all worlds as filled with bodhisattvas;
He knows all worlds enter a single pore;
He knows all worlds enter a single being's body;
He knows all worlds are everywhere pervaded by a single buddha's bodhi tree and a single buddha's site of enlightenment; and
He knows all worlds are everywhere pervaded by a single voice that enables all beings to each understand differently and thus be delighted.

These are the ten. If bodhisattvas abide in these dharmas, then they acquire the Tathāgata's unexcelled vast and definite understanding of the buddha *kṣetras.*

Sons of the Buddha, the bodhisattva-mahāsattva has ten kinds of definite understanding in knowing the realms of beings. What are those ten? They are as follows:

He knows all realms of beings have a fundamental nature of unreality;

He knows all realms of beings enter a single being's body;

He knows all realms of beings enter the bodhisattva's body;

He knows all realms of beings enter the matrix of the Tathāgata;[447]

He knows a single being's body everywhere enters all realms of beings;

He knows those in all realms of beings are capable of becoming vessels containing the Dharma of all buddhas;

He knows all realms of beings and accords with whatever they wish for by manifesting for them in the body of Śakra, Brahma, or a world-protecting heavenly king;

He knows all realms of beings and accords with whatever they wish for by manifesting for them the serene awesome deportment of a *śrāvaka* disciple or a *pratyekabuddha;*

He knows all realms of beings and manifests for them in the body of a bodhisattva adorned with the meritorious qualities; and

He knows all realms of beings and, to awaken beings, manifests for them a *tathāgata*'s major marks, secondary signs, and serene awesome deportment.

These are the ten. If bodhisattvas abide in these dharmas, then they acquire the definite understanding of the Tathāgata's unexcelled great awesome powers.

Sons of the Buddha, the bodhisattva-mahāsattva has ten kinds of habitual karmic propensities. What are those ten? They are as follows:

Habitual karmic propensities related to the resolve to attain bodhi;

Habitual karmic propensities related to roots of goodness;

Habitual karmic propensities related to teaching beings;

Habitual karmic propensities related to seeing buddhas;

Habitual karmic propensities related to being born in pure worlds;

Habitual karmic propensities related to practices;

Habitual karmic propensities related to vows;

Habitual karmic propensities related to the *pāramitās;*

Habitual karmic propensities related to contemplative meditation on the dharma of impartiality; and

Habitual karmic propensities related to the many different kinds of spheres of experience.

These are the ten. If bodhisattvas abide in these dharmas, then they forever leave behind all habitual karmic propensities related to the afflictions and acquire habitual karmic propensities related to the Tathāgata's great wisdom, that wisdom which is not itself a function of habitual karmic propensities.

Sons of the Buddha, the bodhisattva-mahāsattva has ten kinds of grasping. It is because of these that he never discontinues any of the bodhisattva practices. What are those ten? They are as follows:

He grasps all realms of beings to ultimately teach them all;

He grasps all worlds to ultimately purify them all;

He grasps the *tathāgatas* to cultivate the bodhisattva practices as an offering to them;

He grasps roots of goodness to accumulate the meritorious qualities that produce all buddhas' major marks and secondary signs;

He grasps great compassion to extinguish the sufferings of all beings;

He grasps great kindness to bestow the happiness of all-knowledge on all beings;

He grasps the *pāramitās* to accumulate the bodhisattva's adornments;

He grasps the skillful means to appear in all places;

He grasps bodhi to acquire unimpeded wisdom; and

To state it briefly, he grasps all dharmas in all places to use radiant wisdom to completely reveal them all.

These are the ten. If bodhisattvas abide in these types of grasping, then they become able to never discontinue the bodhisattva practices and able to acquire all *tathāgatas'* unexcelled dharma of having nothing at all that they grasp.

Sons of the Buddha, the bodhisattva-mahāsattva has ten kinds of cultivation. What are those ten? They are as follows:

Cultivation of all of the *pāramitās*;

Cultivation of the trainings;

Cultivation of wisdom;

Cultivation of meaning;

Cultivation of Dharma;

Cultivation of emancipation;

Cultivation of manifestations;

Cultivation of incessantly diligent practice;

Cultivation of the realization of the right and perfect enlightenment; and

Cultivation of turning the wheel of right Dharma.

These are the ten. If bodhisattvas abide in these, then they attain unexcelled cultivation in their cultivation of all dharmas.

Sons of the Buddha, the bodhisattva has ten ways of fulfilling the dharmas of the Buddha. What are those ten? They are as follows:

Fulfillment of the Buddha's dharma of never abandoning the good spiritual guide;

Fulfillment of the Buddha's dharma of deep faith in the Buddha's words;

Fulfillment of the Buddha's dharma of never speaking ill of right Dharma;

Fulfillment of the Buddha's dharma of dedicating measureless and endless roots of goodness;

Fulfillment of the Buddha's dharma of resolute faith in the boundlessness of the Tathāgata's sphere of action;

Fulfillment of the Buddha's dharma of knowing all worlds' spheres of experience;

Fulfillment of the Buddha's dharma of never abandoning the Dharma realm as one's sphere of experience;

Fulfillment of the Buddha's dharma of abandoning the realms of the *māras;*

Fulfillment of the Buddha's dharma of right mindfulness of the sphere of action of all buddhas; and

Fulfillment of the Buddha's dharma of delighting in seeking to acquire the sphere of action of the Tathāgata's ten powers.

These are the ten. If bodhisattvas abide in these dharmas, then they succeed in fully developing the Tathāgata's unexcelled great wisdom.

Sons of the Buddha, the bodhisattava-mahāsattva has ten ways of retreating from the Buddha's Dharma that he should abandon. What are those ten? They are as follows:

Retreating from the Buddha's Dharma through slighting good spiritual guides;

Retreating from the Buddha's Dharma through becoming fearful of the sufferings of *saṃsāra;*

Retreating from the Buddha's Dharma through growing weary of cultivating the bodhisattva practices;

Retreating from the Buddha's Dharma through unhappiness in abiding in the world;

Retreating from the Buddha's Dharma through indulgent attachment to samādhis;

Retreating from the Buddha's Dharma through becoming attached to roots of goodness;

Retreating from the Buddha's Dharma through disparaging right Dharma;

Retreating from the Buddha's Dharma through ceasing to practice the bodhisattva practices;

Retreating from the Buddha's Dharma through delighting in the paths of the two vehicles; and

Retreating from the Buddha's Dharma through hating bodhisattvas.

These are the ten. If bodhisattvas abandon these dharmas, then they enter the paths by which the bodhisattva gains emancipation from rebirths.

Sons of the Buddha, the bodhisattva-mahāsattva has ten kinds of paths for transcendence of rebirths. What are those ten? They are as follows:

He develops the *prajñāpāramitā,* and yet constantly contemplates all beings. This is the first;

He avoids all views, and yet liberates all view-bound beings. This is the second;

He does not bear any signs in mind, and yet he never abandons any of the beings who are so attached to signs. This is the third;

He steps beyond the three realms of existence, and yet he always resides in all worlds. This is the fourth;

He forever abandons the afflictions, and yet he resides together in the company of all beings. This is the fifth;

He acquires the dharmas used to abandon the desires, and yet, because of the great compassion, he feels deep sympathy for all beings who are so attached to the desires. This is the sixth;

He always delights in quiescence, and yet he constantly manifests with all kinds of retinues. This is the seventh;

He transcends birth in the world, and yet, having died here, he is reborn there and then takes up the bodhisattva practices. This is the eighth;

He remains unstained by any worldly dharmas, and yet he never ceases his endeavors in all worlds. This is the ninth; and

The bodhi of all buddhas has already manifested directly before him, and yet he still never abandons any of the bodhisattva's practices or vows. This is the tenth.

Sons of the Buddha, these are the bodhisattva-mahāsattva's ten paths by which he transcends rebirths and gains emancipation from the world. These are not held in common with those who abide in the world and they are they admixed with the practices of the two vehicles, either. If bodhisattvas abide in these dharmas, then they acquire the bodhisattva's definite dharmas.

Sons of the Buddha, the bodhisattva-mahāsattva has ten kinds of definite dharmas. What are those ten? They are as follows:

He definitely takes birth within the clan of the *tathāgatas*;
He definitely dwells in the realms of the buddhas;
He definitely completely knows the works done by the bodhisattva;
He definitely abides in the *pāramitās*;
He definitely joins the Tathāgata's congregations;
He is definitely able to manifest in the lineage of the Tathāgata;
He definitely abides in the Tathāgata's powers;
He definitely deeply enters the bodhi of the Buddha;
He definitely shares the same single body as all *tathāgatas*; and
The place in which he abides is definitely not other than where all *tathāgatas* abide.

These are the ten.

Sons of the Buddha, the bodhisattva-mahāsattva has ten kinds of paths by which he develops the dharmas of the Buddha. What are those ten? They are as follows:

Following along in accordance with the good spiritual guide is a path by which he develops the dharmas of the Buddha because he thereby plants the same roots of goodness;
Deep-minded resolute faith is a path by which he develops the dharmas of the Buddha because he thereby comes to know the sovereign masteries of the Buddha;
Making the great vows is a path by which he develops the dharmas of the Buddha because his mind thereby becomes vast;
Having patience in his own development of roots of goodness is a path by which he develops the dharmas of the Buddha because he thereby realizes that karmic actions are never lost;
Insatiable cultivation throughout all kalpas is a path by which he develops the dharmas of the Buddha because he thereby continues on to the very end of future time;
Manifesting in all the *asaṃkhyeyas* of worlds is a path by which he develops the dharmas of the Buddha because he thereby brings about the ripening of beings;

Never ceasing the bodhisattva practices is a path by which he develops the dharmas of the Buddha because he thereby brings about the growth of the great compassion;

The immeasurable minds[448] constitute a path by which he develops the dharmas of the Buddha because, in but a single mind-moment, he pervades all realms of space;

Especially superior practice is a path by which he develops the dharmas of the Buddha because whatever he originally cultivated is never destroyed; and

The lineage of the Tathāgata is a path by which he develops the dharmas of the Buddha because it enables all beings to delight in making the bodhi resolve and because it is sustained by all good dharmas.

These are the ten. If bodhisattvas abide in these dharmas, then they acquire the names given to great men.

Sons of the Buddha, the bodhisattva-mahāsattva has ten names that are used for great men. What are those ten? They are as follows:

He is known as a "bodhisattva" because he is born from the wisdom of bodhi;

He is known as a "mahāsattva" because he abides in the Great Vehicle;

He is known as a "foremost *sattva*"[449] because he realizes the foremost Dharma;

He is known as a "supreme *sattva*" because he awakens to the supreme Dharma;

He is known as a "most supreme *sattva*" because his wisdom is the most supreme;

He is known as a "superior *sattva*" because he brings forth superior vigor;

He is known as an "unexcelled *sattva*" because he explains the unexcelled Dharma;

He is known as a "powerful *sattva*" because he possesses the vast knowledge of the ten powers;

He is known as a "peerless *sattva*" because he has no match anywhere in the entire world; and

He is known as an "inconceivable *sattva*" because he attains buddhahood in but a single mind-moment.

These are the ten. If the bodhisattva acquires these names, then he is one who completely fulfills the bodhisattva path.

Sons of the Buddha, the bodhisattva-mahāsattva has ten kinds of paths. What are those ten? They are as follows:

A single path is the bodhisattva path because he never abandons the one bodhi resolve.

A twofold path is the bodhisattva path because it involves the development of wisdom and skillful means.

A threefold path serves as the bodhisattva path because, by practicing emptiness, signlessness, and wishlessness, he refrains from attachment to the three realms of existence.

A fourfold practice serves as the bodhisattva path based on incessantly eliminating karmic obstacles through repentance, rejoicing in others' meritorious deeds, respectfully venerating and entreating the Tathāgata [to teach the Dharma], and skillfully dedicating merit.

The five roots serve as the bodhisattva path based on:

Abiding in pure faith that is solid and unshakable;

Generating great vigor by which all that is done is completed;

Abiding in continuous right mindfulness by which one does not seize on extraneous objective conditions;

Skillfully knowing the means for entering and emerging from the samādhis; and

Being well able to distinguish wise spheres of experience.

The six spiritual superknowledges serve as the bodhisattva path based on the following:

With the heavenly eye, he sees the many forms in all worlds and knows of all beings that they died here and then were reborn there;

With the heavenly ear, he hears all the Dharma spoken by all buddhas, absorbs and upholds it, remembers it, and extensively expounds on it for beings in ways that are adapted to their faculties;

With the knowledge of others' thoughts, he possesses unimpeded sovereign mastery in knowing the thoughts of others;

Through the recall of previous lifetimes, he recalls and knows the growth of roots of goodness as it has occurred across the course of all past kalpas;

Through the superknowledge of psychic powers, he brings forth all kinds of different manifestations adapted to those beings he should teach, thereby causing them to delight in the Dharma; and

Through the knowledge of the complete cessation of all contaminants, he manifests the realization of the apex of reality, and ceaselessly develops the bodhisattva practices.

The seven types of mindfulness serve as the bodhisattva path based on the following:

Mindfulness of the Buddha through seeing in but a single pore countless buddhas awakening the minds of all beings;

Mindfulness of the Dharma through never leaving the congregation of a single *tathāgata* even as he personally receives the sublime Dharma in the congregations of all *tathāgatas,* adapts to the nature of beings' faculties and inclinations, and then expounds on the Dharma for their sakes to enable them to awaken to it and enter it;

Mindfulness of the Sangha through constantly, continuously, and ceaselessly seeing bodhisattvas in all worlds;

Mindfulness of relinquishing through fully knowing all bodhisattvas' practice of relinquishing, thereby increasing the vastness of his mind of giving;

Mindfulness of the moral precepts through never abandoning the bodhi resolve while dedicating all roots of goodness to beings;

Mindfulness of the heavens through always bearing in mind the bodhisattva abiding in the Tuṣita Heaven palace who has but one more birth prior to buddhahood; and

Mindfulness of beings through the uninterrupted use of wisdom and skillful means in reaching all of them everywhere with his teaching and training.

The *āryas'* eightfold path to the realization of bodhi is the bodhisattva path based on the following:

Practicing the path of right views through abandoning all wrong views;

Bringing forth right thought through abandoning erroneous discriminations and causing the mind to always accord with [the path to] all-knowledge;

Always practicing right speech through abandoning the four speech faults and according with the words of the *āryas;*

Constantly cultivating right action through teaching beings and enabling them to take on the training;

Abiding in right livelihood through practicing the *dhūta* austerities, being easily satisfied, practicing the awesome deportment, reflecting critically on what is right, according with bodhi, practicing the four lineage bases of the *ārya,*[450] and forever abandoning all faults;

Arousing right vigor through diligently cultivating all the bodhisattva austerities and being unimpeded in entering the ten powers of the Buddha;

Always having the mind abide in right mindfulness through being able to remember all that is spoken while also extinguishing scattered worldly thoughts; and

Always having the mind abide in right meditative concentration through skillfully entering the bodhisattva's inconceivable gates of liberation and through bringing forth all samādhis from within a single samādhi.

The nine sequential meditative absorptions[451] constitute the bodhisattva path based on the following:

Abandoning the harm arising from desire and hatred even as he uses all forms of verbal actions in unimpeded discourse on the Dharma;

Extinguishing both ideation and discursion even as he uses ideation and discursion arising from all-knowledge to teach beings;

Relinquishing joy even as he feels great joy at the sight of all buddhas;

Abandoning worldly bliss even as he accords with the world-transcending bliss of the bodhisattva path;

Through remaining unshakable in this, he enters the formless meditative absorptions even as he does not abandon the taking on of births in both the desire realm and the formless realm; and

Although he abides in the meditative absorption in which all perception and feeling are extinguished, he still never ceases the bodhisattva practices.

Training in the ten powers of the Buddha is the bodhisattva path, based on the following:

The knowledge that well knows what can and cannot be;

The knowledge that well knows all beings' karmic consequences, causes, and effects of the past, the future, and the present;

The knowledge that well knows the differences in all beings superior, middling, and inferior faculties and accords with what is fitting in teaching them the Dharma;

The knowledge that well knows the countless different natures of all beings;

The knowledge that well knows the skillful means by which all beings of different weak, middling, or superior understanding may be enabled to enter the Dharma;

The knowledge by which he pervades all worlds, all *kṣetras*, all three periods of time, and all kalpas, everywhere manifesting the Tathāgata's form, signs, and awesome deportment even while still never abandoning the bodhisattva practices;

The knowledge that well knows with regard to all the *dhyānas*, liberations, and samādhis what is defiled and what is pure as well as what is timely and what is untimely while using skillful means to bring forth the bodhisattvas' gates to liberation;[452]

The knowledge that knows with regard to all beings in all the destinies of rebirth the differences in their dying in this place and being reborn in that place;

The knowledge that knows in but a single mind-moment all kalpas of the three periods of time; and

The knowledge that well knows the complete cessation of all the desires, latent tendencies, delusions, and habitual karmic propensities to which all beings are subject, yet never abandons any of the bodhisattva practices.

These are the ten. If beings abide in these dharmas, then they acquire all *tathāgatas'* unexcelled path of skillful means.

Sons of the Buddha, the bodhisattva-mahāsattva has measureless paths, measureless provisions for enlightenment, measureless ways of cultivating the path, and measureless adornments of the path.

Sons of the Buddha, the bodhisattva-mahāsattva has ten kinds of measureless path. What are those ten? They are as follows:

Because empty space is measureless, so too is the bodhisattva's path also measureless;

Because the Dharma realm is boundless, so too is the bodhisattva's path also measureless;

Because the realms of beings are endless, so too is the bodhisattva's path also measureless;

Because the worlds are boundless, so too is the bodhisattva's path also measureless;

Because the number of kalpas is endless, so too is the bodhisattva's path also measureless;

Because the dharmas associated with all beings' languages are measureless, so too is the bodhisattva's path also measureless;

Because the Tathāgata's body is measureless, so too is the bodhisattva's path also measureless;

Because the Buddha's voice is measureless, so too is the bodhisattva's path also measureless;

Because the Tathāgata's powers are measureless, so too is the bodhisattva's path also measureless; and

Because the wisdom of all-knowledge is measureless, so too is the bodhisattva's path also measureless.

These are the ten.

Sons of the Buddha, the bodhisattva-mahāsattva has ten kinds of measurelessness of his provisions for enlightenment. They are as follows:

Just as the realms of empty space are measureless, so too are the provisions for enlightenment accumulated by the bodhisattva also measureless;

Just as the Dharma realm is boundless, so too are the provisions for enlightenment accumulated by the bodhisattva also boundless;

Just as the realms of beings are endless, so too are the provisions for enlightenment accumulated by the bodhisattva also endless;

Just as the worlds are boundless, so too are the provisions for enlightenment accumulated by the bodhisattva also boundless;

Just as the number of kalpas is inexhaustible through verbal description, so too are the provisions for enlightenment accumulated by the bodhisattva also inexhaustible through the verbal descriptions uttered by anyone in any world;

Just as the dharmas of all beings' languages are measureless, so too are the provisions for enlightenment measureless that are accumulated by the bodhisattva in producing the wisdom that knows all language dharmas;

Just as the Tathāgata's bodies are measureless, so too are the provisions for enlightenment measureless that are accumulated by the bodhisattva in pervading all [realms of] beings, all *kṣetras*, all worlds, and all kalpas;

Just as the Buddha's voices are measureless, so too are the provisions for enlightenment measureless that are accumulated by the bodhisattva in his utterance of but a single voice that reaches everywhere throughout the Dharma realm to all beings of whom none fail to hear and understand it;

Just as the Tathāgata's powers are measureless, so too are the provisions for enlightenment measureless that are accumulated by the bodhisattva through taking on the powers of the Tathāgata; and

Just as the wisdom of all-knowledge is measureless, so too are the provisions for enlightenment measureless that are accumulated by the bodhisattva.

These are the ten. If bodhisattvas abide in these dharmas, then they acquire the Tathāgata's measureless wisdom.

Sons of the Buddha, the bodhisattva-mahāsattva has ten kinds of measureless cultivation of the path. What are those ten? They are as follows:

Cultivation in which he neither comes nor goes, this due to his remaining entirely motionlessness even in physical, verbal, and mental actions;

Cultivation in which there is neither any increase nor any decrease, this due to its accordance with the fundamental nature;

Cultivation that is neither existent nor nonexistent, this due to its absence of any inherently existent nature;

Cultivation that is like a conjuration, like a dream, like a shadow, like an echo, like an image reflected in a mirror, like the flames of a mirage in the hot-season, and like the moon reflected in the water, this due to having abandoned all attachments;

Cultivation characterized by emptiness, signlessness, wishlessness, and effortlessness, this due to his clear perception of the three realms of existence even as he ceaselessly accumulates merit;

Cultivation that is ineffable, wordless, and transcendent of words and speech, this due to having abandoned the creation or establishment of dharmas;

Cultivation that is not contradictory to the Dharma realm, this due to his wisdom's direct knowing of all dharmas;

Cultivation that does not contradict true suchness or the apex of reality, this due to his everywhere entering the realms of true suchness, the apex of reality, and empty space;

Cultivation imbued with vast wisdom, this due to his endless powers in whatever he does; and

Cultivation that equally abides in the Tathāgata's ten powers, four fearlessnesses, and wisdom of all-knowledge, this due to his freedom from doubt in the direct perception of all dharmas.

These are the ten. If bodhisattvas abide in these dharmas, then they acquire the Tathāgata's cultivation possessed of the unexcelled skillful means of all-knowledge.

Sons of the Buddha, the bodhisattva-mahāsattva has ten kinds of adornments of the path. What are those ten? They are as follows:

Sons of the Buddha, without leaving the desire realm, the bodhisattva-mahāsattva enters the *dhyāna* absorptions, liberations, and samādhis of the form and formless realms, and yet he still does not take rebirths there because of this. This is the first of his adornments of the path;

His wisdom directly manifests so that he could enter the path of the *śrāvaka* disciples, yet he still does not use this path to gain emancipation. This is the second of his adornments of the path;

His wisdom directly manifests so that he could enter the path of the *pratyekabuddhas*, yet he ceaselessly arouses the great compassion. This is the third of his adornments of the path;

Although he may be surrounded by a retinue of humans and devas and be attended by a hundred thousand female retainers who sing, dance, serve, and follow him, he still never for even a moment withdraws from his *dhyāna* absorptions, liberations, or samādhis. This is the fourth of his adornments of the path;

He may enjoy all kinds of pleasures and mutual amusements together with all other beings, yet he still never for even a single mind-moment withdraws from the bodhisattva's samādhi of equanimity. This is the fifth of his adornments of the path;

He has already achieved perfection in everything related to the world and is free of any attachments to worldly dharmas, yet he still never relinquishes his practice of liberating beings. This is the sixth of his adornments of the path;

He abides in right path, right knowledge, and right views, yet he is still able to manifest the appearance of entry into erroneous paths in which he does not seize on them as real and does not seize on them as pure, doing so to enable other beings to abandon erroneous dharmas. This is the seventh of his adornments of the path;

He always skillfully guards and upholds the Tathāgata's pure moral precepts so that he is free of all faults in his physical, verbal, and mental actions. Still, wishing to teach beings who transgress against the moral precepts, he may manifest the appearance of practicing all the actions of a foolish common person. Although he is fully equipped with pure merit and thus already dwells in the destinies of a bodhisattva, he still manifests the appearance of being reborn into the hell realms, the animal realms, and the hungry ghost realms as well as into all kinds of dangerous, difficult, and poverty-stricken circumstances, doing so in order to enable all the other beings there to gain liberation. Even so, in truth, the bodhisattva is never actually reborn in those rebirth destinies. This is the eighth of his adornments of the path;

Even without depending on instruction provided by others, he acquires unimpeded eloquence and the light of wisdom with which he is able to everywhere completely illuminate all dharmas of the Buddha. He is supported by the spiritual powers of all *tathāgatas*, shares the same single Dharma body as that of all buddhas, perfects the radiant and pure esoteric dharmas of all the steadfast great men, and securely dwells in all the uniformly equal vehicles. The spheres of action of all buddhas manifest directly before him. He becomes fully endowed with the light of all worldly knowledge, illuminates and sees all realms of beings, and is able to serve all beings as a knowledgeable master of the Dharma even as he manifests as never resting in his search for right Dharma. Although, in truth, he is one who serves beings as an unexcelled teacher, he still manifests the practice of venerating the *acāryas* and *upādhyāyas*. And why is this so? This is because the bodhisattva-mahāsattva uses skillful means as he abides in the bodhisattva path, thereby manifesting for everyone in accordance with what is fitting. This is the ninth of his adornments of the path; and

Having become perfectly complete in his roots of goodness and having achieved the ultimate consummation of all of the practices, he becomes one who receives the simultaneous joint crown-anointing consecration from all *tathāgatas*. He reaches the far shore of perfection in the sovereign mastery of all dharmas and uses the headband of unimpeded Dharma to crown his head. His body everywhere reaches all worlds and everywhere manifests the Tathāgata's unimpeded body. He achieves the most supreme and ultimate sovereign mastery of the Dharma and turns the wheel of the unimpeded pure Dharma.

Having already achieved the complete development of all the bodhisattva's dharmas of sovereign mastery, for the sake of beings, he manifests as taking rebirths in all lands. He shares the same spheres of action as all buddhas of the three periods of time, yet still never neglects the bodhisattva practices, never relinquishes the bodhisattva's dharmas, never diminishes his accomplishment of the bodhisattva's works, never abandons the bodhisattva path, never relaxes his observance of the bodhisattva's demeanor, never ceases his grasp of whatever the bodhisattva grasps, never rests in implementing the bodhisattva's skillful means, never cuts off his accomplishment of the bodhisattva's endeavors, never wearies of the bodhisattva's initiation and achievement of whatever is useful, and never ceases providing the bodhisattva's supportive sustaining power. And why is this so? This is because, wishing to swiftly attain *anuttarasamyaksaṃbodhi*, the bodhisattva contemplates the gateway of all-knowledge and ceaselessly cultivates the bodhisattva practices. This is the tenth of his adornments of the path.

If bodhisattvas abide in these dharmas, then they acquire the Tathāgata's unexcelled and great adornments of the path even as they never abandon the bodhisattva path.

Sons of the Buddha, the bodhisattva-mahāsattva has ten kinds of feet. What are those ten? They are as follows:

The feet of upholding the moral precepts with which he completely fulfills all of his extraordinarily superior great vows;
The feet of vigor with which he irreversibly accumulates all the dharmas leading to bodhi;
The feet of the spiritual superknowledges with which he gladdens beings by adapting to whatever they wish for;
The feet of the spiritual powers with which he never leaves a single buddha *kṣetra* even as he goes to all buddha *kṣetras;*
The feet of the deep resolve with which he vows to seek all the most especially superior dharmas;
The feet of solid vows with which he completes everything he does;
The feet of accordant compliance with which he never opposes the teachings of all the venerable ones;
The feet of delight in the Dharma with which he never wearies of hearing and retaining all dharmas spoken by the Buddha;
The feet of the Dharma rain with which he fearlessly expounds the Dharma for beings; and
The feet of cultivation with which he abandons all forms of evil.

These are the ten. If bodhisattvas abide in these dharmas, then they acquire the Tathāgata's unexcelled and supreme feet with which, through the lifting of his foot to take but a single footstep, he is able to go everywhere throughout all worlds.

Sons of the Buddha, the bodhisattva-mahāsattva has ten kinds of hands. What are those ten? They are as follows:

The hands of deep faith with which he continuously adopts and ultimately absorbs and upholds whatever the Buddha has taught;
The hands of giving with which he completely fulfills the requests for whatever any supplicant desires;
The hands that are the first to offer pressed-palms greetings followed by the extended right hand with which he welcomes and leads others;
The hands that make offerings to all buddhas with which he tirelessly accumulates the many kinds of merit;
The hands of skill in abundant learning with which he severs the doubts of all beings;

The hands that enable transcendence of the three realms of existence which he extends to beings to pull them out of the mire of desire;

The hands that place beings on the far shore with which he rescues beings drowning in the four floods;[453]

The hands that are never miserly with right Dharma with which he explains all the sublime Dharma that he possesses;

The hands that skillfully use the many kinds of doctrines with which he uses the medicine of wisdom to extinguish all physical and mental disorders; and

The hands that constantly hold the jewels of wisdom with which he shines the light of Dharma to dispel the darkness of afflictions.

These are the ten. If bodhisattvas abide in these dharmas, then they acquire the Tathāgata's unexcelled hands which cover all worlds of the ten directions.

Sons of the Buddha, the bodhisattva-mahāsattva has ten kinds of belly. What are those ten? They are as follows:

The belly that abandons flattering deviousness, because his mind is pure;

The belly that abandons deceptive artifice, because he has a straightforward character;

The belly that is never false, because he is free of dishonesty;

The belly that is free of any inclination to engage in bullying or forceful confiscation, because he has nothing that he covets;

The belly that cuts off the afflictions, because he is wise;

The belly with a pure mind, because he abandons all evils;

The belly that subjects food and drink to analytic contemplation, because his mindfulness accords with the true Dharma;

The belly that contemplates the uncreated, because he awakens to conditioned arising;

The belly that awakens to all paths of emancipation, because he thoroughly ripens his deep resolve; and

The belly that abandons the defilement of all extreme views, because he enables all beings to succeed in entering the belly of the Buddha.

These are the ten. If bodhisattvas abide in these dharmas, then they acquire the Tathāgata's unexcelled and vast belly that is able to take in and hold all beings.

Sons of the Buddha, the bodhisattva-mahāsattva has ten kinds of inner organs. What are those ten? They are as follows:

Never severing the lineage of the Buddha is a bodhisattva organ with which he explains the measureless awesome qualities of the Buddha's Dharma;

Extending the lineage of the Dharma is a bodhisattva organ with which he brings forth the vast light of wisdom;

Sustaining the lineage of the Sangha is a bodhisattva organ with which he enables others to succeed in gaining access to the irreversible wheel of the Dharma;

Awakening beings fixed in what is right[454] is a bodhisattva organ with which he skillfully accords with the right time for them, not missing it by even a single mind-moment;

Achieving the ultimate ripening of beings who are not fixed in [either what is right or what is wrong] is a bodhisattva organ with which he enables them to establish uninterrupted continuity of associated causes;

Bringing forth the great compassion for beings who are fixed in what is wrong is a bodhisattva organ with which he ensures that their future causes will all lead to their ripening;

Fulfillment of the indestructible causes for attaining the Buddha's ten powers is a bodhisattva organ with which he fully develops the roots of goodness by which he is unopposable in conquering the armies of Māra;

The lion's roar of supreme fearlessness is a bodhisattva organ with which he causes all beings to feel joyful;

Acquisition of the Buddha's eighteen dharmas exclusive to the buddhas is a bodhisattva organ with which his wisdom reaches everywhere; and

Universally and completely understanding all beings, all *kṣetras*, all dharmas, and all buddhas is a bodhisattva organ with which, in but a single mind-moment, he clearly sees them all.

These are the ten. If bodhisattvas abide in these dharmas, then they acquire the Tathāgata's unexcelled organ of roots of goodness and indestructible great wisdom.

Sons of the Buddha, the bodhisattva-mahāsattva has ten kinds of heart. What are those ten? They are as follows:

The heart that is energetically diligent by which he completes everything he does;

The heart that is never indolent by which he accumulates the merit-generating practices producing the major marks and secondary signs;

The heart that is immensely brave and strong by which he utterly vanquishes all the armies of Māra;

The heart that accords with principle in its actions by which he gets rid of all afflictions;

The heart that is irreversible by which he never rests until he achieves the realization of bodhi;

The heart that is pure in nature by which his knowing mind is unshakable because it is free of attachments;

The heart that knows beings by which he adapts to their understandings and desires and thereby enables them to gain emancipation;

The heart of the great *brāhma-vihāras, [or four immeasurable minds],*[455] which enable entry into the Dharma of the Buddha by which he knows all beings' various understandings and desires and rescues them without resorting to any other vehicle;

The heart of emptiness, signlessness, wishlessness, and effortlessness by which he perceives the signs of the three realms of existence without ever seizing on any of them; and

The heart that, adorned with the sign of the *svastika,* serves as a supreme treasury of vajra solidity by which, even if *māras* as numerous as all beings were to come and assail him, they would be unable to shake even a single hair on his body.

These are the ten. If bodhisattvas abide in these dharmas, then they acquire the Tathāgata's heart that is a treasury of the light of his unexcelled great wisdom.

Sons of the Buddha, the bodhisattva-mahāsattva has ten kinds of armor. What are those ten? They are as follows:

He dons the armor of great kindness with which he rescues and protects all beings;

He dons the armor of great compassion with which he is able to endure all sufferings;

He dons the armor of great vows with which he completes everything he does;

He dons the armor of dedications with which he establishes all the adornments of the buddhas;

He dons the armor of merit with which he benefits all beings;

He dons the armor of the *pāramitās* with which he liberates all sentient beings;

He dons the armor of wisdom with which he dispels the darkness of all beings' afflictions;

He dons the armor of skillful means with which he develops the roots of goodness of the universal gateways;

He dons the armor of the solid and undistracted resolve to attain all-knowledge by which he does not delight in any of the other vehicles; and

He dons the armor of single-minded certainty with which he abandons doubts about any of the Dharma teachings.

These are the ten. If bodhisattvas abide in these dharmas, then they don the Tathāgata's unexcelled armor with which they are able to vanquish all the armies of Māra.

Sons of the Buddha, the bodhisattva-mahāsattva has ten kinds of weapons. What are those ten? They are as follows:

Giving is the bodhisattva's weapon with which he vanquishes all miserliness;

Upholding moral precepts is the bodhisattva's weapon with which he casts out all forms of transgressions;

Impartiality is the bodhisattva's weapon with which he cuts off all discriminations;

Wisdom is the bodhisattva's weapon with which he eliminates all afflictions;

Right livelihood is the bodhisattva's weapon with which he abandons all forms of wrong livelihood;

The use of skillful means is the bodhisattva's weapon with which he manifests in all places;

Briefly stated, greed, hatred, delusion, and all the other kinds of afflictions are the bodhisattva's weapons for it is through the gateway of the afflictions that he is able to liberate beings;

Saṃsāra is the bodhisattva's weapon by which he never ceases the bodhisattva practice of teaching beings;

The proclamation of Dharma in accordance with reality is the bodhisattva's weapon by which he is able to demolish all attachments; and

All-knowledge is the bodhisattva's weapon by which he never abandons the bodhisattva's gateways of practice.

These are the ten. If bodhisattvas abide in these dharmas, then they are able to rid all beings of the fetters and afflictions they have accumulated throughout the long night [of *saṃsāra*].

Sons of the Buddha, the bodhisattva-mahāsattva has ten kinds of head. What are those ten? They are as follows:

The head of nirvāṇa, the summit of which no one can see;

The venerated head, revered by all humans and devas;

The head of vast and supreme understanding, supreme of all in the trichiliocosm;

The head of foremost roots of goodness, to which beings of the three realms of existence all make offerings;

The head that supports beings, it has developed the fleshy prominence on the crown of the head;

The head that does not slight or look down on others, it is revered as supreme in all places;

The *prajñāpāramitā* head, it promotes the growth of all dharmas of the meritorious qualities;

The head that is compatible with the knowledge of skillful means, it everywhere manifests bodies the same as those of others;

The head that teaches all beings, it takes all beings as disciples; and

The head that preserves and protects the Dharma eye of all buddhas, it is able to prevent the lineage of the Three Jewels from being cut off.

These are the ten. If bodhisattvas abide in these dharmas, then they acquire the Tathāgata's head possessed of unexcelled great wisdom.

Sons of the Buddha, the bodhisattva-mahāsattva has ten kinds of eyes, namely:

The fleshly eye, so called because it sees all forms;

The heavenly eye, so called because it sees all beings' minds;

The wisdom eye, so called because it sees all beings' faculties and spheres of cognition;

The Dharma eye, so called because it sees all dharmas in a manner consistent with their true character;

The Buddha eye, so called because it sees the Tathāgata's ten powers;

The eye of knowledge, so called because it knows and sees all dharmas;

The light eye, so called because it sees the Buddha's light;

The eye that transcends *saṃsāra*, so called because it sees nirvāṇa;

The unimpeded eye, so called because it has unimpeded vision of everything it sees; and

The eye of all-knowledge, so called because it sees the Dharma realm of the universal gateway.

These are the ten. If bodhisattvas abide in these dharmas, then they acquire the Tathāgata's eye of unexcelled great wisdom.

Sons of the Buddha, the bodhisattva-mahāsattva has ten kinds of ears. What are those ten? They are as follows:

The ear that, hearing the sounds of praise, severs all covetousness;

The ear that, hearing the sounds of disparagement, severs all hatred;

The ear that, on hearing of the two vehicles, is not attached to them and does not seek them;

The ear that, hearing of the bodhisattva path, is filled with joyous exultation;

The ear that, on hearing of the hells and the other places beset by every sort of suffering and difficulty, arouses the mind of great compassion and makes the vast vow;

The ear that, hearing of the supremely marvelous phenomena within the realms of humans and devas, realizes they are all impermanent dharmas;

The ear that, hearing the praises of all buddhas' meritorious qualities, becomes diligently vigorous in causing them all to become quickly and completely fulfilled;

The ear that, hearing of the dharmas of the six perfections, the four means of attraction, and other such dharmas, resolves to cultivate them and vows to perfect them;

The ear that, hearing all the sounds of the worlds of the ten directions, knows them all as like mere echoes and then penetrates their ineffable and extremely profound and sublime meanings; and

The ear that, from the time the bodhisattva-mahāsattva makes the initial resolve until he reaches the site of enlightenment, always listens to right Dharma, never ceasing for even a moment, and yet never relinquishes the work of teaching beings.

These are the ten. If bodhisattvas perfect these dharmas, then they acquire the Tathāgata's unexcelled ear of great wisdom.

Sons of the Buddha, the bodhisattva-mahāsattva has ten kinds of nose. What are those ten? They are as follows:

The nose that, on smelling all kinds of things that are foul smelling, does not take them to be foul smelling;

The nose that, on smelling all kinds of things that are pleasantly fragrant, does not take them to be pleasantly fragrant;

The nose that, on smelling things that are both pleasantly fragrant and foul smelling remains even-minded;

The nose that, on smelling that which is neither pleasantly fragrant nor foul smelling, abides in equanimity;

The nose that, whenever it smells all the smells of the fragrances and foul smells of beings' clothes, bedding, or bodies is thereby able to know the character of their practice as associated with either greed, hatred, or delusion, or a relatively equal portion of all of these;

The nose that, whenever it smells the fragrances of grasses, trees, and other such things at the site of hidden treasures is able to clearly distinguish them as if they were directly present before his very eyes;

The nose that, whenever it smells any smell from anywhere at all, whether it be from as far down as the Avīci Hells or from as high as the peak of existence, he then knows the actions those beings practiced in the past;
The nose that, whenever it smells the fragrance of *śrāvaka* disciples' giving, moral-precept observance, or wisdom based on abundant learning, he still continues to abide in the resolve to gain all-knowledge and is not caused to become distracted by it;
The nose that, on smelling the fragrance associated with all the bodhisattva practices, uses equanimous wisdom to enter the ground of the Tathāgata; and
The nose that, even on smelling the fragrance of all buddhas' spheres of cognition, still refrains from abandoning the bodhisattva practices.

These are the ten. If bodhisattvas perfect these dharmas, then they acquire the Tathāgata's nose possessed of measureless and boundless purity.

Sons of the Buddha, the bodhisattva-mahāsattva has ten kinds of tongue. What are those ten? They are as follows:

The tongue that reveals and expounds upon the actions of infinitely many beings;
The tongue that reveals and expounds upon infinitely many Dharma gateways;
The tongue that praises all buddhas' endless meritorious qualities;
The tongue that preaches with endless eloquence;
The tongue that explains the Great Vehicle's provisions for enlightenment;
The tongue that everywhere covers the ten directions of space;
The tongue that everywhere illuminates all buddha *kṣetras;*
The tongue that everywhere enables beings to awaken and understand;
The tongue that elicits the praise and happiness of all buddhas; and
The tongue that conquers all *māras* and followers of non-Buddhist paths, extinguishes all of *saṃsāra*'s afflictions, and enables beings to reach nirvāṇa.

These are the ten. If bodhisattvas perfect these dharmas, then they acquire the Tathāgata's unexcelled tongue that everywhere covers all buddha lands.

Sons of the Buddha, the bodhisattva-mahāsattva has ten kinds of bodies. What are those ten? They are as follows:

The human body, in order to teach all people;
The nonhuman body, in order to teach the hell-dwellers, the animals, and the hungry ghosts;
The deva body, in order to teach those beings in the desire realm, form realm, and formless realm;
The body of those still in training, in order to reveal the grounds of training;
The body of those beyond training, in order to reveal the grounds of the arhats;
The body of the *pratyekabuddha,* in order to teach beings and enable them to enter the grounds of the *pratyekabuddha;*
The body of the bodhisattva, in order to enable beings to achieve success in the Great Vehicle;
The body of a *tathāgata,* in order to enable crown-anointing consecrations with the waters of wisdom;
The mind-generated body, in order to use skillful means to manifest birth; and
The Dharma body free of contaminants, in order to effortlessly appear in the bodies of every kind of being.

These are the ten. If bodhisattvas perfect these dharmas, then they acquire the Tathāgata's unexcelled body.

Sons of the Buddha, the bodhisattva-mahāsattva has ten kinds of mind. What are those ten? They are as follows:

The supreme leader mind with which he produces all kinds of roots of goodness;
The securely abiding mind with which he maintains deep and unshakably solid faith;
The deeply penetrating mind with which he accords with the Buddha's Dharma and thus understands it;
The inwardly understanding mind with which he understands the mental dispositions of beings;
The undisturbed mind with which he is not contaminated by any of the afflictions;
The clear and pure mind with which he is invulnerable to being stained by the adventitious defilements;
The mind that skillfully contemplates beings with which he never misses the right time by even a single mind-moment;
The mind that skillfully chooses what is to be done with which he never has even a single circumstance in which he commits a transgression;
The mind that skillfully guards all the sense faculties with which he trains them and does not allow them to become scattered; and

The mind that skillfully enters samādhi with which he deeply enters the Buddha's samādhi free of a self or any possessions of a self.

These are the ten. If bodhisattvas abide in these dharmas, then they acquire the unexcelled mind of all buddhas.

Sons of the Buddha, the bodhisattva-mahāsattva has ten kinds of practices. What are those ten? They are as follows:

The practice of listening to the Dharma by which he enjoys the Dharma;

The practice of speaking the Dharma by which he benefits beings;

The practice of abandoning desire, hatred, delusion, and fear by which he trains his own mind;

Desire realm practice by which he teaches desire-realm beings;

Form and formless realm samādhi practice by which he causes those beings to quickly return;

Practice that pursues the meaning of Dharma by which he swiftly acquires wisdom;

Practice in all the stations of rebirth by which he exercises sovereign mastery in teaching beings;

Practice in all buddha *kṣetras* by which he reveres and makes offerings to all buddhas;

Nirvāṇa practice by which he never ceases his continuous presence in *saṃsāra;* and

Practice that achieves complete fulfillment of all the dharmas of the Buddha by which he never abandons his practice of the dharmas of the bodhisattva.

These are the ten. If bodhisattvas abide in these dharmas, then they acquire the Tathāgata's practice which is free of either coming or going.

Sons of the Buddha, the bodhisattva-mahāsattva has ten kinds of abiding. What are those ten? They are as follows:

Abiding in the resolve to attain bodhi, never forgetting it;

Abiding in the *pāramitās,* never wearying of the provisions for enlightenment;

Abiding in speaking the Dharma, increasing his wisdom;

Abiding in an *araṇya,* [a forest dwelling], realizing the great *dhyāna* absorptions;

Abiding in compliance with all-knowledge, the *dhūta* austerities, being easily satisfied, and the four lineage-bases of the *āryas,* having but few desires and few concerns;

Abiding in deep faith, supporting right Dharma;

Abiding in drawing near to the Tathāgata, training in the Buddha's awesome deportment;

Abiding in developing the spiritual superknowledges, achieving the complete fulfillment of great wisdom;

Abiding in the realization of patience,[456] achieving the complete fulfillment of his prediction [of future buddhahood]; and

Abiding at the site of enlightenment, reaching the complete fulfillment of the powers, the fearlessnesses, and all the other dharmas of the Buddha.

These are the ten. If bodhisattvas abide in these Dharmas, then they acquire the unexcelled abiding in all-knowledge.

Sons of the Buddha, the bodhisattva-mahāsattva has ten kinds of sitting. What are those ten? They are as follows:

Sitting on the seat of the wheel-turning king from which he promotes the ten courses of good karmic action;

Sitting on the seat of the Four Heavenly Kings from which he freely establishes the Buddha's Dharma in all worlds;

Sitting on the seat of Lord Śakra from which he serves as the supreme lord of all beings;

Sitting on the seat of the Brahma Heaven King from which he gains sovereignty over his own mind and others' minds;

Sitting on the lion's seat from which he is able to teach the Dharma;

Sitting on the seat of right Dharma from which he uses the power of complete-retention *dhāraṇīs* and eloquence to reveal and explain it;

Sitting on the seat of solidity from which his vows are completely fulfilled;

Sitting on the seat of the great kindness from which he gladdens even evil beings;

Sitting on the seat of the great compassion from which he tirelessly endures all kinds of sufferings; and

Sitting on the vajra seat from which he subdues the many *māras* and followers of non-Buddhist paths.

These are the ten. If bodhisattvas abide in these dharmas, then they are able to sit on the Tathāgata's unexcelled throne of right enlightenment.

Sons of the Buddha, the bodhisattva-mahāsattva has ten kinds of recumbence. What are those ten? They are as follows:

Quiescent recumbence, with peacefulness in both body and mind;

Recumbence in *dhyāna* absorption, cultivating in accordance with principle;

Recumbence in samādhi, with pliancy in both body and mind;
Brahma Heaven recumbence, refraining from any disturbance of either self or others;
Recumbence in the good karmic deeds, not having regrets later on;
Recumbence in right faith, which cannot be shaken even slightly;
Recumbence in the right path, as awakened by the good spiritual guide;
Recumbence in marvelous vows, with skillful dedications;
Recumbence in the completion of all his endeavors, having done what is to be done; and
Recumbence in effortlessness, everything having become a matter of course.

These are the ten. If bodhisattvas abide in these dharmas, then they acquire the Tathāgata's recumbence in the unexcelled great Dharma in which they are all able to awaken all beings.

Sons of the Buddha, the bodhisattva-mahāsattva has ten kinds of places in which he abides. What are those ten? They are as follows:

He takes the great kindness as his abode, for his mind regards all beings equally;
He takes the great compassion as his abode, for he never slights those who have not yet received the training;
He takes the great sympathetic joy as his abode, for he has abandoned all worry and affliction;
He takes the great equanimity as his abode, for he regards the conditioned and the unconditioned equally;
He takes all the *pāramitās* as his abode, for he takes the resolve to attain bodhi as foremost;
He takes the emptiness of everything as his abode, for he is skillful in his contemplations;
He takes signlessness as his abode, for he never abandons the right and fixed position;[457]
He takes wishlessness as his abode, for he contemplates rebirth;
He takes mindfulness and wisdom as his abode, for his patience with dharmas has become completely fulfilled; and
He takes the uniform equality of all dharmas as his abode, for he has received his prediction [of future buddhahood].

These are the ten. If bodhisattvas abide in these dharmas, then they acquire the Tathāgata's unexcelled and unimpeded abode.

Sons of the Buddha, the bodhisattva-mahāsattva has ten kinds of bases of practice. What are those ten? They are as follows:

He takes right mindfulness as his place of practice to completely fulfill [the practice of] the stations of mindfulness;
He takes all of the rebirth destinies as his place of practice for he is rightly enlightened to the aims of the Dharma;
He takes wisdom as his place of practice to be able to please the Buddha;
He takes the *pāramitās* as his place of practice to completely fulfill the wisdom of all-knowledge;
He takes the four means of attraction as his place of practice to teach beings;
He takes *saṃsāra* as his place of practice to accumulate roots of goodness;
He takes various sorts of talking and light-hearted interaction with beings as his place of practice to adapt to what is fitting in teaching them and enabling them to gain eternal emancipation;
He takes the spiritual superknowledges as his place of practice to know all beings' faculties and spheres of experience;
He takes skillful means as his place of practice in order to accord with the *prajñāpāramitā*; and
He takes the site of enlightenment as his place of practice to succeed in attaining all-knowledge while still never ceasing the bodhisattva practices.

These are the ten. If bodhisattvas abide in these dharmas, then they acquire the Tathāgata's unexcelled place of practicing great wisdom.

Sons of the buddha, the bodhisattva-mahāsattva has ten [other][458] kinds of contemplations. What are those ten? They are as follows:

The contemplation that knows all actions through perceiving all their subtleties;
The contemplation that knows all the rebirth destinies through not seizing on [the existence of] beings;
The contemplation that knows all faculties through completely comprehending the nonexistence of faculties;
The contemplation that knows all dharmas as not incompatible with the Dharma realm;
The contemplation that sees the Buddha's Dharma through diligently cultivating the Buddha eye;
The contemplation leading to the attainment of wisdom through explaining the Dharma in accordance with its principles;
The contemplation leading to the unproduced-dharmas patience through a definite and complete comprehension of the Buddha's Dharma;

The contemplation leading to the ground of irreversibility through extinguishing all afflictions and stepping beyond the three realms of existence and the grounds of the two vehicles;
The contemplation leading to the ground of the crown-anointing consecration through gaining unshakable sovereign mastery of all dharmas of the Buddha; and
The contemplation leading to the samādhi of well awakened wisdom through doing the Buddha's works throughout the ten directions.

These are the ten. If bodhisattvas abide in these dharmas, then they acquire the Tathāgata's unexcelled great contemplative wisdom.

Sons of the Buddha, the bodhisattva-mahāsattva has ten kinds of universal contemplation. What are those ten? They are as follows:

Universal contemplation of all who come as supplicants with which, free of any thoughts of opposition, he fulfills their wishes;
Universal contemplation of all beings who transgress against the moral precepts with which he establishes them in the Tathāgata's pure moral precepts;
Universal contemplation of all beings with harmful intentions with which he establishes them in the Tathāgata's power of patience;
Universal contemplation of all indolent beings with which he encourages them and enables them to become energetically diligent in never give up bearing the Great Vehicle's burden;
Universal contemplation of all beings with muddled minds with which he enables them to abide free of distraction on the Tathāgata's ground of all-knowledge;
Universal contemplation of all evil-minded beings with which he enables them to become rid of doubts and dispels their existence-reifying views;
Universal contemplation of all impartial good spiritual guides with which he complies with their instructions and abides in the Buddha's Dharma;
Universal contemplation of all Dharma teachings he has heard with which he swiftly acquires realized perception of the ultimate meaning;
Universal contemplation of all of the boundlessly many beings with which he never abandons the power of great compassion; and
Universal contemplation of the Dharma of all buddhas with which he swiftly succeeds in fully realizing all-knowledge.

These are the ten. If bodhisattvas abide in these dharmas, then they acquire the Tathāgata's unexcelled universal contemplation with great wisdom.

Sons of the Buddha, the bodhisattva-mahāsattva has ten kinds of swiftness. What are those ten? They are as follows:

The swiftness like that of the king of bulls with which he outshines that of everyone in all the great congregations of devas, dragons, *yakṣas*, *gandharvas*, and others;

The swiftness like that of the king of elephants with which his mind is well-regulated and pliant as it bears the burden of all beings;

The swiftness like that of the king of dragons with which he spreads forth the dense clouds of the great Dharma, shines the dazzling light of liberation's lightning flashes, causes the quaking thunder of reality-accordant meaning, and pours down the elixir of immortality of all the roots, powers, enlightenment factors, *dhyāna* absorptions, liberations, and samādhis;

The swiftness like that of the king of the great golden-winged *garuḍa* birds with which he is able to dry up the waters of desire, break the shell of delusion, pounce on and seize the poisonous dragons of afflictions' evils, and enables liberation from *saṃsāra*'s great ocean of suffering;

The swiftness like that of the great king of lions with which he abides in fearlessness, impartiality, and great wisdom and, using them as his weapons, he vanquishes the many *māras* and the followers of non-Buddhist paths;

The swiftness like that of the valiant stalwarts with which he is able to vanquish all the adversarial afflictions on the great battlefield of *saṃsāra*;

The swiftness like that of the great wisdom with which he knows the aggregates, the sense realms, the sense bases, and all aspects of conditioned arising and thus explains all dharmas with sovereign mastery;

The swiftness like that of the *dhāraṇīs* with which, using the power of mindfulness and wisdom, he retains dharmas, never forgets them, and, adapting to beings' faculties, expounds on them for their benefit;

The swiftness of eloquence with which, with unimpeded speed, he swiftly analyzes everything and then benefits and gladdens everyone; and

The swiftness like that of the Tathāgata with which he fulfills the wisdom of all-knowledge and all the dharmas of the provisions for enlightenment and, using the wisdom which is responsive in but a single mind-moment, he sees to it that whatever should be realized is all realized, that whatever should be awakened to is all awakened to, and then, sitting on the lion throne, he conquers the *māra* adversaries and gains *anuttarasamyaksaṃbodhi.*

These are the ten. If bodhisattvas abide in these dharmas, then they acquire all buddhas' unexcelled and masterful swiftness in all dharmas.

Sons of the Buddha, the bodhisattva-mahāsattva has ten kinds of lion's roar. What are those ten? As follows, they are those in which he proclaims:

"I will certainly attain the right and perfect enlightenment." This is the great lion's roar of the bodhi resolve;

"I shall liberate all unliberated beings, emancipate all unemancipated beings, bring peace to all unpeaceful beings, and lead to nirvāṇa all beings who have not yet reached nirvāṇa." This is the great lion's roar of the great compassion;

"I shall prevent the lineage of the Buddha, Dharma, and Sangha from ever being cut off." This is the great lion's roar of repaying the Tathāgata's kindness;

"I shall purify all buddha *kṣetras*." This is the great lion's roar of ultimately solid of vows;

"I shall extinguish all the wretched destinies and the difficulties.[459]" This is the great lion's roar of personally upholding the pure moral precepts;

"I shall completely fulfill all the Buddha's physical, verbal, and mental adornments of the major marks and secondary signs." This is the great lion's roar of the tireless pursuit of merit;

"I shall completely fulfill the wisdom of all buddhas." This is the great lion's roar of the tireless pursuit of wisdom;

"I shall destroy all the many *māra*s as well as all the works of the *māras*." This is the great lion's roar of the cultivation of right practice in severing all afflictions;

"I shall completely realize all dharmas as devoid of self, as devoid of any being, as devoid of any life span, as devoid of any *pudgala*, as empty, signless, and wishless, and as pure as space." This is the great lion's roar of the unproduced-dharmas patience; and

The bodhisattva who has reached his last birth causes quaking in all buddha *kṣetras* and purifies them all. At this time, Śakra, Brahma, and all the Four Heavenly Kings come to him, utter praises, and make the request: "We only pray that the Bodhisattva, by resort to the dharma of the birthless, will manifest the taking on of birth." Then, using the eye of unimpeded wisdom, the Bodhisattva everywhere contemplates all beings in the world, realizes, "There are none among them like me," and then straightaway manifests birth into the palace of the King. Of his own accord, he strides seven steps and roars the great lion's roar, declaring: "I am the most supreme of all who abide in the world. I shall forever put an end to the boundaries imposed by *saṃsāra*." This is the great lion's roar of doing just as one has said.

These are the ten. If bodhisattvas abide in these dharmas, then they acquire the Tathāgata's unexcelled lion's roar.

Sons of the Buddha, the bodhisattva-mahāsattva has ten kinds of pure giving. What are those ten? They are as follows:

Equal giving, by which he does not discriminate among beings;

Giving that accords with others' wishes, by which he provides whatever they wish;

Undistracted giving, by which he causes others to benefit from it;

Giving which accords with whatever is fitting, by which he recognizes what is superior, middling, or inferior;

Non-abiding giving, by which he does not seek any reward;

Freely relinquishing giving, by which his mind does not retain any fond attachment;

The giving of everything, by which he attains ultimate purity;

Giving dedicated to the realization of bodhi, by which he abandons both the conditioned and the unconditioned;

Giving in the course of teaching beings, which he never relinquishes even on reaching the site of enlightenment; and

Giving in which the three spheres [involved in giving] have all been purified, by which, with right mindfulness, he contemplates the benefactor, the recipient, and the gift as like empty space.

These are the ten. If bodhisattvas abide in these, then they acquire the Tathāgata's unexcelled, pure, and vast giving.

Sons of the Buddha, the bodhisattva-mahāsattva has ten kinds of pure moral precepts. What are those ten? They are as follows:

The pure moral precepts of the body, by which he guards against the three evils of the body;[460]

The pure moral precepts of speech, by which he abandons the four transgressions in speech;[461]

The pure moral precepts of the mind, by which he forever abandons covetousness, ill will, and wrong views;[462]

The pure moral precept of refraining from transgressing against any of the aspects of the training, by which he becomes a venerated leader of all humans and devas;

The pure moral precept of preserving and protecting the resolve to attain bodhi, by which he does not delight in the small vehicle;

The pure moral precept of preserving and protecting whatever has been decreed by the Tathāgata, by which he remains immensely fearful of ever committing even the most subtle transgression;

The pure moral precept of guarding and upholding them even in secret, by which he skillfully rescues beings who transgress against the precepts;

The pure moral precept of not committing any kind of evil deed, by which he vows to cultivate all good dharmas;

The pure moral precept of abandoning all existence-reifying views, by which he remains free of attachment to the precepts themselves;[463] and

The pure moral precept of protecting all beings, by which he arouses the great compassion.

These are the ten. If bodhisattvas abide in these dharmas, then they acquire the Tathāgata's unexcelled flawless pure moral precepts.

Sons of the Buddha, the bodhisattva-mahāsattva has ten kinds of pure patience. What are those ten? They are as follows:

The pure patience that peacefully endures disparaging insults, by which he protects beings;

The pure patience that peacefully endures even attacks with knives and staves, by which he well protects both himself and others;

The pure patience that does not become angry or malicious, by which he maintains an unshakable mind;

The pure patience that refrains from censuring inferiors, by which he is able to be tolerant when serving as a superior;

The pure patience that rescues all who take refuge in him, by which he is willing to sacrifice even his own body and life;

The pure patience that abandons pride in self, by which he never slights those who are not yet well trained;

The pure patience that does not become angry even when subjected to cruelty or slander, by which he contemplates this as like a mere illusion;

The pure patience that does not seek to pay back offenses committed by others, by which he does not perceive the existence of either self or others;

The pure patience that does not follow the afflictions, by which he transcends all spheres of experience; and

The pure patience that accords with the bodhisattva's genuine wisdom and knows all dharmas as unarisen, by which he enters the sphere of cognition of all-knowledge even without depending on instruction from others.

These are the ten. If bodhisattvas abide in these, then they acquire all buddhas' unexcelled dharma patience to which they awaken without the assistance of others.

Sons of the Buddha, the bodhisattva-mahāsattva has ten kinds of pure vigor. What are those ten? They are as follows:

The pure vigor of the body, with which he is irreversibly persistent in serving and making offerings to the buddhas and bodhisattvas as well as his teachers, elders, and other fields of merit;

The pure vigor in speech, with which he extensively teaches others whatever Dharma he has heard while also tirelessly praising the meritorious qualities of the Buddha;

The pure vigor of mind, with which he is well able to ceaselessly enter and emerge from meditations on kindness, compassion, sympathetic joy, and equanimity, the *dhyāna* absorptions, the liberations, and the samādhis;

The pure vigor of the correct and straight mind, with which he remains free of deception, flattery, deviousness, and falseness as he irreversibly persists in all his diligent cultivation;

The pure vigor of the increasingly superior resolve, with which he resolutely and constantly pursues the most supreme wisdom while vowing to possess all the dharmas of purity;

The pure vigor not pursued in vain, with which, until he attains bodhi, he never rests in the midst of his accumulation of proficiency in giving, moral virtue, patience, and extensive learning;

The pure vigor in vanquishing all *māras,* with which he is able to utterly extinguish all desire, hatred, delusion, and wrong views as well as all afflictions and all the entangling hindrances;

The pure vigor in fully developing the light of wisdom, with which, in everything he does, he skillfully contemplates and ensures they are all completed so as to have no regrets and so as to acquire all buddhas' exclusive dharmas;

The pure vigor without coming or going, with which he acquires reality-accordant wisdom, enters the gateway to the Dharma realm, realizes the equality of body, speech, and mind, understands signs as non-signs, and becomes free of attachments; and

The pure vigor that perfects the light of Dharma, with which he steps beyond all the grounds, acquires the Buddha's crown-anointing consecration, and uses the body free of contaminants to manifest dying and being born, leaving the home life, becoming enlightened, proclaiming the Dharma, and crossing into nirvāṇa, thus completely fulfilling the works of Samantabhadra such as these.

These are the ten. If bodhisattvas abide in these dharmas, then they acquire the Tathāgata's unexcelled great pure vigor.

Sons of the Buddha, the bodhisattva-mahāsattva has ten kinds of pure *dhyāna*. What are those ten? They are as follows:

The pure *dhyāna* in which he always delights in leaving the home life, by which he relinquishes all that he possesses;

The pure *dhyāna* in which he finds the true good spiritual guide, by which he is shown and taught the right path;

The pure *dhyāna* in which he dwells in the *araṇya*, the forest dwelling, enduring wind, rain, and other such things, by which he abandons self and possessions of a self;

The pure *dhyāna* in which he abandons the troublesome disturbances of beings, by which he always delights in quiescence;

The pure *dhyāna* in which his mental actions are pliant, by which he guards all his faculties;

The pure *dhyāna* in which the mind and its cognition are quiescent, by which no sounds or other thorns of *dhyāna* absorption can disturb him;

The pure *dhyāna* of the skillful means for awakening to the path, by which, in contemplating all things, they all lead to direct realization;

The pure *dhyāna* in which he abandons all attachment to delectable experiences, by which he still does not abandon the desire realm;

The pure *dhyāna* in which he brings forth the superknowledges, by which he knows the faculties and natures of all beings; and

The pure *dhyāna* of sovereign and easeful mastery, by which he enters the Buddha's samādhi and realizes the nonexistence of self.

These are the ten. If bodhisattvas abide in these, then they acquire the Tathāgata's unexcelled great pure *dhyānas*.

Sons of the Buddha, the bodhisattva-mahāsattva has ten kinds of pure wisdom. What are those ten? They are as follows:

The pure wisdom that knows all causes, by which he does not negate their effects;

The pure wisdom that knows all conditions, by which he does not oppose how they come together;

The pure wisdom that knows both annihilationism and eternalism are untrue, by which he always comprehends conditioned arising in accordance with reality;

The pure wisdom that removes all views, by which he neither seizes upon nor rejects any of the characteristics of beings;

The pure wisdom that contemplates the mental actions of all beings, by which he fully realizes they are like mere conjurations;

The pure wisdom that is possessed of vast eloquence, by which he has unimpeded skill in questions and responses revealing the distinctions in all dharmas;

The pure wisdom that no *māra*, no follower of non-Buddhist paths, no *śrāvaka* disciple, and no *pratyekabuddha* could ever know, by which he deeply penetrates the wisdom of all *tathāgatas*;

The pure wisdom that perceives the sublime Dharma body of all buddhas, that perceives the fundamentally pure nature of all beings, that perceives the complete quiescence of all dharmas, and that perceives all *kṣetras'* identity with empty space, by which he has an unimpeded knowledge of all signs;

The pure wisdom that knows all the complete-retention *dhāraṇīs,* all the kinds of eloquence, all the skillful means, and all the *pāramitās,* by which he is enabled to acquire all the most supreme forms of wisdom; and

The pure wisdom in which, in but a single mind-moment of vajra wisdom, he knows the equality of all dharmas, by which he acquires the most supreme knowledge of all dharmas.

These are the ten. If bodhisattvas abide in these, then they acquire the Tathāgata's unimpeded great wisdom.

Sons of the Buddha, the bodhisattva-mahāsattva has ten kinds of pure kindness. What are those ten? They are as follows:

The pure kindness of the impartial mind, by which he everywhere attracts all beings without any selective discriminations;

The pure kindness that benefits others, by which he causes them all to be delighted with whatever he does;

The pure kindness that, in attracting beings, takes them to be the same as himself, by which he ultimately enables them all to escape from *saṃsāra;*

The pure kindness that never abandons those in the world, by which he always bears them in mind as he accumulates roots of goodness;

The pure kindness that is able to reach liberation, by which he everywhere enables beings to extinguish all their afflictions;
The pure kindness that brings forth bodhi, by which he everywhere enables beings to generate the resolve to seek all-knowledge;
The pure kindness that is unimpeded in the world, by which he emanates great light that illuminates everyone equally;
The pure kindness that completely fills all of empty space, by which there is no place it does not reach as he strives to rescue beings;
The pure kindness that focuses on dharmas, by which he realizes the genuine dharma of true suchness; and
The pure kindness that is free of conditions, by which he enters the bodhisattva's rebirth-transcending nature.

These are the ten. If bodhisattvas abide in these dharmas, then they acquire the Tathāgata's unexcelled and vast pure kindness.

Sons of the Buddha, the bodhisattva-mahāsattva has ten kinds of pure compassion. What are those ten? They are as follows:

The pure compassion even in the absence of companions, with which it is he alone who arouses his resolve;
The pure compassion that remains free of weariness, with which he does not even find it toilsome to substitute for all beings in taking on their sufferings;
The pure compassion that takes on births even among the difficulties,[464] doing so in order to liberate beings;
The pure compassion that takes on births in the good rebirth destinies, with which he reveals impermanence;
The pure compassion manifested for the sake of beings fixed in what is wrong, with which he will even pass through kalpas without ever abandoning his vast vows;
The pure compassion in which one is not attached to his own bliss, with which he everywhere bestows happiness on other beings;
The pure compassion in which one does not seek any reward for one's kindness, with which he cultivates the purification of his own mind;
The pure compassion that is able to do away with the inverted views, with which he teaches Dharma in accordance with reality;
The bodhisattva-mahāsattva knows that the fundamental nature of all dharmas is pure, free of defiling attachments, and free of feverish afflictions while knowing too that it is because of adventitious afflictions that one experiences the many kinds

of suffering. Having come to know such things, he arouses a great compassion for all beings known as "[the compassion of] the pure fundamental nature," with which he teaches the undefiled, pure, and radiant Dharma for their benefit; and

The bodhisattva-mahāsattva knows that all dharmas are like the tracks of birds flying across the sky and knows that beings, having their vision obscured by the cataracts of their delusions, are unable to completely illuminate them. Contemplating beings, he arouses the mind of great compassion known as "[the compassion of] genuine wisdom" with which he reveals the dharma of nirvāṇa for their sakes.

These are the ten. If bodhisattvas abide in these dharmas, then they acquire the Tathāgata's unexcelled and vast pure compassion.

Sons of the Buddha, the bodhisattva-mahāsattva has ten kinds of pure sympathetic joy. What are those ten? They are as follows:

The pure sympathetic joy with which he resolves to attain bodhi;

The pure sympathetic joy with which he relinquishes everything he possesses;

The pure sympathetic joy with which he does not blame and reject beings who have broken the moral precepts, but rather teaches and ripens them;

The pure sympathetic joy with which he is able to tolerate beings who do evil deeds and vows to rescue and liberate them;

The pure sympathetic joy with which he is even willing to sacrifice his own body in seeking the Dharma and still not raise any thoughts of regret;

The pure sympathetic joy with which he relinquishes his own sensual bliss and always delights in Dharma bliss;

The pure sympathetic joy with which he enables all beings to relinquish the bliss arising from material possessions and then always delight in Dharma bliss;

The pure sympathetic joy of impartiality throughout the Dharma realm with which he is insatiable in going to see all buddhas to revere and make offerings to them;

The pure sympathetic joy with which he enables all beings to cherish and delight in easeful mastery in entering and arising from the *dhyāna* absorptions, liberations, and samādhis; and

The pure sympathetic joy with which he delights in according with the bodhisattva path while completely practicing all the austere practices and realizing the Muni's unshakably quiescent and unexcelled meditative absorptions and wisdom.

These are the ten. If bodhisattvas abide in these dharmas, then they acquire the Tathāgata's unexcelled and vast pure sympathetic joy.

Sons of the Buddha, the bodhisattva-mahāsattva has ten kinds of pure equanimity. What are those ten? They are as follows:

The pure equanimity with which he refrains from becoming fondly attached when all beings revere and make offerings to him and the pure equanimity with which he refrains from becoming angry when all beings slight and disparage him;[465]

The pure equanimity with which he always remains in the world and yet is never defiled by the eight worldly dharmas;[466]

The pure equanimity with which he awaits the right time to teach beings who are vessels of the Dharma and does not dislike those who are not vessels of the Dharma;

The pure equanimity with which he does not seek the dharmas of the practitioners of the two vehicles who are either still in training or beyond training;

The pure equanimity with which his mind always abandons all dharmas related to the desire-based pleasures which lead to the afflictions;

The pure equanimity with which he refrains from praising the renunciation of *saṃsāra* as practiced by the practitioners of the two vehicles;

The pure equanimity with which he abandons all worldly discourse, all discourse not associated with nirvāṇa, all discourse not abandoning the desires, all discourse that does not accord with principle, all discourse that torments or disturbs others, all discourse of *śrāvaka* disciples or *pratyekabuddhas*, and, in general, all other such discourse up to and including that which obstructs the bodhisattva path, all of which he leaves far behind;

The pure equanimity with which, when there is some being whose faculties have already ripened to the point where they have developed mindfulness and wisdom but they have still not yet become able to know the most supreme Dharma, he awaits the right time and only then instructs them in it;

The pure equanimity with which, when some being taught by the bodhisattva in the past must await his reaching the ground of buddhahood before he can successfully train him, he even then awaits the appropriate time; and

The pure equanimity with which the bodhisattva-mahāsattva remains free of any conception of any of those two persons as either superior or inferior or as worthy of selection or rejection.

In this, he abandons all the many different kinds of discrimination, constantly abides in right meditative absorption, and then penetrates reality-accordant Dharma, whereupon his mind achieves the realization of patience.[467]

These are the ten. If bodhisattvas abide in these, then they acquire the Tathāgata's unexcelled and vast pure equanimity.

Sons of the Buddha, the bodhisattva-mahāsattva has ten kinds of meaning. What are those ten? They are as follows:

The meaning in extensive learning, by which he is steadfast in cultivation;

The meaning in Dharma, by which he uses skillful means in contemplating and discerning [how to proceed];

The meaning in emptiness, by which [he realizes] the supreme meaning;

The meaning in quiescence, by which he separates from the noise and confusion of beings;

The meaning in ineffability, by which he does not become attached to any speech or words;

The meaning in according with reality, by which he fully comprehends the identity of the three periods of time;

The meaning in the Dharma realm, by which [he realizes] all dharmas are of a single flavor;

The meaning in true suchness, by which all *tathāgatas* accord with and enter it;

The meaning in the apex of reality, by which he completely realizes the ultimate in accordance with reality; and

The meaning in the great *parinirvāṇa*, by which he extinguishes all suffering and yet still cultivates all bodhisattva practices.

These are the ten. If bodhisattvas abide in these dharmas, then they acquire the unexcelled meaning of all-knowledge.

Sons of the Buddha, the bodhisattva-mahāsattva has ten kinds of dharmas. What are those ten? They are as follows:

The dharma of reality, by which he cultivates in accordance with what has been taught;

The dharma of abandoning grasping, by which he transcends both the agent of grasping and the object of grasping;

The dharma of noncontentiousness, by which he is free of all deluded contentiousness;

The dharma of quiescence, by which he extinguishes all the feverish afflictions;

The dharma of dispassion, by which he cuts off all desire;

The dharma of nondiscrimination, by which he forever puts to rest all discriminations involved in manipulating objective conditions;

The dharma of the unproduced, by which he is as immovable as empty space;

The dharma of the unconditioned, by which he transcends all the signs of arising, abiding, and destruction;

The dharma of the original nature, by which the inherent nature is undefiled purity; and

The dharma of abandoning all forms of mere *upādhi*, [or semblance] nirvāṇa dharmas,[468] by which he is able to bring forth all the bodhisattva practices and cultivate them incessantly.

These are the ten. If bodhisattvas abide in these, then they acquire the Tathāgata's unexcelled vast Dharma.

Sons of the Buddha, the bodhisattva-mahāsattva has ten kinds of merit-based provisions for enlightenment.[469] What are those ten? They are as follows:

Encouraging beings to arouse the resolve to attain bodhi is a bodhisattva's merit-based provision for enlightenment, this because he thereby ensures that the lineage of the Three Jewels will never be cut off;

Following along in accordance with the ten kinds of dedication is a bodhisattva's merit-based provision for enlightenment, this because he thereby cuts off all bad dharmas and accumulates all good dharmas;

Using wisdom to guide and instruct is a bodhisattva's merit-based provision for enlightenment, this because he thereby steps entirely beyond all merit within the three realms of existence;

Tireless resolve is a bodhisattva's merit-based provision for enlightenment, this because he thereby ultimately liberates all beings;

Relinquishing all of one's inward and outward possessions is a bodhisattva's merit-based provision for enlightenment, this because he is thereby free of attachment to anything at all;

Irreversible vigor for the sake of the complete fulfillment of the major marks and secondary signs is a bodhisattva's merit-based provision for enlightenment, this because he thereby opens the gateway to limitless great giving;

Dedicating all three categories of superior, middling, and lesser roots of goodness to the realization of unexcelled bodhi, having none that one's mind looks on but lightly—this is a bodhisattva's merit-based provision for enlightenment, this because he thereby accords with skillful means;

Arousing the great compassion even for all beings who are fixed in what is wrong, inferior, or unwholesome while not cherishing any slighting or disdainful attitude toward them—this is a bodhisattva's merit-based provision for enlightenment, this because he thereby always arouses the great man's mind of vast vows;

Reverently making offerings to all *tathāgatas,* conceiving of all bodhisattvas as *tathāgatas,* and gladdening all beings—this is a bodhisattva's merit-based provision for enlightenment, this because he thereby preserves his original vows with ultimate solidity and durability; and

For *asaṃkhyeyas* of kalpas, the bodhisattva-mahāsattva accumulates roots of goodness wishing himself to take up the realization of unexcelled bodhi, thus bringing it to the point that it is as if resting in the palm of his hand, yet he relinquishes it all and bestows it on all beings with a mind entirely free of distress or affliction and also free of regrets, doing so with his mind as vast as the realm of empty space—this is a bodhisattva's merit-based provision for enlightenment, this because he thereby brings forth great wisdom and realizes the great Dharma.

These are the ten. If bodhisattvas abide in these, then they completely fulfill the Tathāgata's unexcelled and vast accumulation of merit.

Sons of the Buddha, the bodhisattva-mahāsattva has ten kinds of wisdom-based provisions for enlightenment. What are those ten? They are as follows:

He draws near to a genuine good spiritual guide possessed of abundant learning, respectfully makes offerings to him, deeply esteems him, bows down in reverence to him, and follows along in accordance with him in many different ways while never opposing his teachings. This is what constitutes the first of them. It is based on being correct and straightforward in all things and on remaining free of any deception;

He forever abandons arrogance and pride, always practices humility and respectfulness, maintains physical, verbal, and mental deeds entirely free of coarse and uncivilized actions, remains gentle, harmonious, and accordant with goodness, refrains from deceptiveness, and abstains from deviousness. This is what constitutes the second of them. It is based on his being personally capable of becoming a vessel for the Buddha's Dharma;

He possesses mindfulness and wisdom that accord with awakening, never becomes scattered and confused, and maintains a sense of shame, dread of blame, and gentle harmoniousness in which his mind is peaceful and imperturbable, in which he always bears in mind the six kinds of mindfulness,[470] in which he always practices the six kinds of [harmony and] respect,[471] and in which he always follows along in accordance with and abides in the six dharmas of solidity.[472] This is what constitutes the third of them. It is based on its serving as a skillful means for development of the ten kinds of knowledge;[473]

He delights in the Dharma, delights in meaning, and takes the Dharma as what is blissful. He always delights in listening to it and, in this, he is insatiable. He abandons worldly treatises and worldly discourse and especially focuses his mind on listening to world-transcending discourse while leaving the small vehicle far behind and entering the wisdom of the Great Vehicle. This is what constitutes the fourth of them. It is based on his being single-minded in his recollection and free of any scattered movement;

His mind is focused on taking up the burden of the six *pāramitās*. His practice of the four abodes of Brahma[474] has already become completely ripened. He accords with the dharmas of the clarities and skillfully cultivates them all.[475] He is diligent in posing questions to persons who are intelligent, quick-witted, and wise, abandons the wretched destinies, and takes refuge in the courses of good karmic action. His mind always cherishes and delights in right mindfulness and contemplation, he subdues his own emotions, and he guards the minds of others. This is what constitutes the fifth of them. It is based on solidly enduring cultivation of the genuine practices;

He always delights in emancipation from the three realms of existence and is not attached to them. He maintains constant awakened awareness of his own mind, is ever free of evil thoughts, and has already cut off the three types of ideation.[476] His three kinds of actions[477] are all good and he possesses a decisively resolute and complete knowledge of the mind's inherent nature. This is what constitutes the sixth of them. It is based on the ability to enable purity to arise in the minds of both himself and others;

He contemplates the five aggregates as in every case like illusory phenomena, the sense realms as comparable to poisonous snakes, the sense fields as like an empty village, and all dharmas as like conjurations, like mirages, like the moon reflected in water, like dreams, like shadows, like echoes, like reflected images, like images drawn in space, like the wheel shape created by a whirling firebrand, like the hues of rainbow, like the light of the sun or moon, as signless, as formless, as neither permanent nor annihilated, as neither coming nor going, and as having no place in which they abide. Contemplating them in this way, he knows that all dharmas are neither produced nor destroyed. This is what constitutes the seventh of them. It is based on realization that the nature of all dharmas is empty and quiescent;

When the bodhisattva-mahāsattva hears that all dharmas are devoid of self, devoid of any being, devoid of any life span, devoid of any *pudgala,* devoid of any mind, devoid of any objective realm, devoid of greed, hatred, or delusion, devoid of any body, devoid of any thing, devoid of any primary entity, devoid of any secondary entity, devoid of any attachment, devoid of any action, that all of these are in every case entirely nonexistent, and that they all trace back to quiescence—having heard this, he deeply believes it, does not doubt it, and does not repudiate it. This is what constitutes the eighth of them. It is based on the ability to develop perfectly fulfilled understanding;

The bodhisattva-mahāsattva skillfully trains all his faculties, cultivates in accordance with principle, and constantly dwells in the practice of calming and insight contemplation in which his mind is quiescent. None of the movements of thought arise at all. Thus there is no self, no other, no endeavors, no actions, no thought conceiving of a self, and no actions based on conceiving of a self. Thus he has no wounds, has no scars, and also does not even retain any of the patience he has acquired here.[478] In his actions of body, speech, and mind, he has neither any coming nor any going, has no vigor, and does not retain any valiant bravery, either.[479] In his contemplation of all beings and all dharmas, he observes them all impartially even as he has no place in which he abides, abiding thus neither on this shore nor on the far shore, for he has transcended any nature of either "this" or "that." He has no place from which he comes and no place to which he goes. He always uses wisdom in carrying out contemplations such as these. This is what constitutes the ninth of them. It is based on having reached the "far shore" of perfection in distinguishing signs; and

Because the bodhisattva-mahāsattva perceives the dharma of conditioned origination, he perceives dharmas as pure. Because he perceives dharmas as pure, he perceives lands as pure. Because he sees lands as pure, he perceives empty space as pure. Because he perceives empty space as pure, he perceives the Dharma realm as pure. Because he perceives the Dharma realm as pure, he sees wisdom as pure. This is what constitutes the tenth of them. It is based on the cultivation and accumulation of all-knowledge.

Sons of the Buddha, these are what constitute the bodhisattva-mahāsattva's ten kinds of wisdom-based provisions for enlightenment. If bodhisattvas abide in these dharmas, then they acquire the Tathāgata's accumulation of unimpeded and pure sublime wisdom with respect to all dharmas.

Sons of the Buddha, the bodhisattva-mahāsattva has ten kinds of completely developed clarities. What are those ten? They are as follows:

The completely developed clarity of skill in distinguishing all dharmas;

The completely developed clarity of not seizing on or attaching to any dharma;

The completely developed clarity of abandoning the inverted views;

The completely developed clarity of illuminating all faculties with the light of wisdom;

The completely developed clarity of skillfully arousing right vigor;

The completely developed clarity of the ability to deeply penetrate the knowledge of the truths;[480]

The completely developed clarity of extinguishing affliction-based karma and completely developing the knowledge of cessation and the knowledge of the unproduced;

The completely developed clarity of universal contemplation with the cognition of the heavenly eye;

The pure and completely developed clarity of recollective awareness of previous-life existences throughout the past; and

The completely developed clarity of the spiritual superknowledge of the cessation of the contaminants with which he cuts off the contaminants of beings.

These are the ten. If bodhisattvas abide in these dharmas, then they acquire the Tathāgata's unexcelled great illumination of all dharmas of the Buddha.

Sons of the Buddha, the bodhisattva-mahāsattva has ten ways of seeking the Dharma. What are those ten? They are as follows:

He seeks the Dharma with a straightforward mind, this because he is free of any flattery or deviousness;

He seeks the Dharma with vigor, this because he has abandoned indolence;

He seeks the Dharma wholeheartedly, this because he does not even begrudge his body or life to acquire it;

He seeks the Dharma to sever the afflictions of all beings, this because he is not motivated by the desire for fame, personal benefit, or reverence;

He seeks the Dharma to benefit self, others, and all beings, this because he does not seek to benefit only himself;

He seeks the Dharma to penetrate its wisdom, this because he does not merely delight in its language;

He seeks the Dharma to escape *saṃsāra,* this because he does not covet worldly happiness;

He seeks the Dharma to liberate beings, this because he has brought forth the resolve to attain bodhi;

He seeks the Dharma to sever the doubts of all beings, this because he wishes to enable them to be free of any hesitation; and

He seeks the Dharma for the sake of completely fulfilling the dharma of buddhahood, this because he does not delight in any of the other vehicles.

These are the ten. If bodhisattvas abide in these dharmas, then they acquire the great wisdom of the Dharma of all buddhas that does not rely on instruction from others.

Sons of the Buddha, the bodhisattva-mahāsattva has ten kinds of dharmas for attaining complete understanding. What are those ten? They are as follows:

According with mundane worldly conventions in producing and developing roots of goodness is a dharma for attaining complete understanding for common persons at beginning levels of practice;

Acquiring unimpeded and indestructible faith and awakening to the inherent nature of dharmas is a dharma for attaining complete understanding for those whose practice accords with faith;

Diligently cultivating and practicing the Dharma and dwelling in accordance with the Dharma is a dharma for attaining complete understanding for those whose practice accords with the Dharma;

Abandoning the eightfold wrong path and following the eightfold right path is a dharma for attaining complete understanding for those at the level of the eighth person;[481]

Extinguishing the many fetters, severing the contaminants associated with *saṃsāra,* and seeing the truths is a dharma for attaining complete understanding for who have reached the stage of a *srota-āpanna;*[482]

Regarding delectable meditation states as disastrous[483] and realizing there is neither any going nor any coming is a dharma for attaining complete understanding for a *sakṛd-āgāmin;*[484]

Not delighting in the three realms of existence, seeking to put an end to the contaminants, and not arousing so much as a single mind-moment of cherishing attachment for the dharmas of rebirth is a dharma for attaining complete understanding for an *anāgāmin;*[485]

Gaining the six spiritual superknowledges and acquiring the eight liberations, the nine meditative absorptions, and the four types of eloquence, completely developing them all—this is a dharma for attaining complete understanding for an arhat;

By nature delighting in contemplating single-flavored conditioned origination, having a mind that is always quiescent, being satisfied with but few things, reaching the understanding of causality himself, gaining awakening not reliant on others, and perfecting the many different kinds of spiritual superknowledges and wisdom—this is a dharma for attaining complete understanding for a *pratyekabuddha;* and

Acquiring vast wisdom and brilliantly sharp faculties, always delighting in liberating all beings, diligently cultivating the merit-based and wisdom-based dharmas of the provisions for enlightenment, and achieving the perfectly complete fulfillment of all of the Tathāgata's ten powers, fearlessnesses, and meritorious qualities is a dharma for attaining complete understanding for a bodhisattva.

These are the ten. If bodhisattvas abide in these dharmas, then they acquire the Tathāgata's dharma of complete understanding consisting of unexcelled great wisdom.

Sons of the Buddha, the bodhisattva-mahāsattva has ten kinds of cultivation dharmas. What are those ten? They are as follows:

The cultivation dharma of revering and honoring all good spiritual guides;

The cultivation dharma of always being awakened by the devas;

The cultivation dharma of always embracing a sense of shame and a dread of blame before the buddhas;

The cultivation dharma of deeply pitying beings and thus never leaving *saṃsāra;*

The cultivation dharma of certainly completely finishing all endeavors while maintaining an unchanging and unshakable resolve;

The cultivation dharma of single-minded energetic diligence in cultivating and training after the manner of the congregation of bodhisattvas who have aroused their resolve in the Great Vehicle;

The cultivation dharma of abandoning wrong views and diligently pursuing the path of what is right;

The cultivation dharma of vanquishing the many *māras* as well as all affliction-based actions;

The cultivation dharma of knowing the relative superiority or inferiority of all beings' faculties and natures and then explaining the Dharma for them so as to enable them to dwell on the ground of buddhahood; and

The cultivation dharma of abiding in the boundlessly vast Dharma realm, extinguishing afflictions, and enabling the purification of the person.

These are the ten. If bodhisattvas abide in these, then they acquire the Tathāgata's unexcelled cultivation dharmas.

Sons of the Buddha, the bodhisattva-mahāsattva has ten kinds of *māras*. What are those ten? They are as follows:

The *māras* of the aggregates, so called because they induce grasping;

The *māras* of the afflictions, so called because they constantly produce defilement;

The *māras* of karma, so called because they are able to create obstacles;

The *māras* of the mind, so called because they arouse arrogance;

The *māras* of death, so called because they cause him to leave the place in which he lives;

Heavenly *māras*, so called because they instigate arrogance and recklessness;

The *māras* of roots of goodness, so called because they cause constant attachment;

The *māras* of samādhi, so called because they cause him to develop an enduring obsession with delectable meditation states;

The *māras* of good spiritual guides, so called because they cause him to arouse thoughts of attachment; and

The *māras* of knowledge related to the dharma of bodhi, so called because they cause him to become unwilling to relinquish it.

These are the ten. Bodhisattva-mahāsattvas should create skillful means by which they swiftly seek to abandon them.

Sons of the Buddha, the bodhisattva-mahāsattva has ten kinds of *māra*-related actions. What are those ten? They are as follows:

Forgetting the bodhi resolve as he cultivates roots of goodness is a work of the *māras;*

Giving with an evil mind, upholding the moral precepts with a mind of hatred, abandoning evil-natured people, distancing himself from those who are indolent, slighting those with slow and confused minds, and maintaining ridiculing disdain for those who are evil-minded—these are works of the *māras;*

Becoming miserly with extremely profound Dharma so that, even when there are those capable of being taught, he does not explain it for them, and, although someone else is not Dharma vessel, if he has the prospect of receiving material benefits, reverence, or offerings for doing so, he insists on teaching it to him—these are works of the *māras;*

If he does not delight in hearing teachings on the *pāramitās,* if he hears them explained but does not cultivate them, if he does cultivate them but for the most part becomes indolent, or if, because of such indolence, his resolve becomes so feeble and inferior that he does not seek the Dharma of the unexcelled great bodhi—these are works of the *māras;*

If he distances himself from good spiritual guides, if he draws near to bad spiritual guides, or if he delights in pursuing the two vehicles in which one does not delight in taking on births and resolves to pursue nirvāṇa, transcendence of desires, and quiescence—these are works of the *māras;*

If he arouses thoughts of anger toward bodhisattvas, glowers at them with a loathing gaze, seeks out their transgressions and errors, or discusses their transgressions and faults so as to cut off all their material benefits and offerings—these are works of the *māras;*

If he slanders right Dharma, if he does not delight in hearing it, if he succeeds in hearing it but then disparages it, if he sees someone speak Dharma but does not revere it, or if he claims that when he speaks it, it is right, but when others speak it, it is wrong—these are works of the *māras;*

If he delights in studying worldly treatises, arts, or literary writings, if he presents explanations of the two vehicles while concealing the profound Dharma, if perhaps he does teach the marvelous meaning, but does so to those unfit to receive it, or if he abandons bodhi and then dwells in erroneous paths—these are works of the *māras;*

If he always delights in drawing near to and making offerings to those who have already gained liberation and who have already attained peace and security but cannot bring himself to draw near to or teach those who have not yet gained liberation and who have not yet attained peace and security—these are works of the *māras*; and

If his pride in self increases, if he has no respect for others, if he often torments or injures beings, if he does not seek right Dharma and genuine wisdom, or if his mind becomes so inferior and evil that he is difficult to awaken—these are works of the *māras*.

These are the ten. the bodhisattva-mahāsattva should swiftly abandon them and diligently seek the works of the Buddha.

Sons of the Buddha, the bodhisattva-mahāsattva has ten ways of abandoning the works of the *māras*. What are those ten? They are as follows:

He abandons the works of the *māras* by drawing near to good spiritual guides, revering them, and making offerings to them;

He abandons the works of the *māras* by refraining from honoring and elevating himself and by refraining from praising himself;

He abandons the works of the *māras* by having resolute faith in and not disparaging the profound Dharma of the Buddha;

He abandons the works of the *māras* by never forgetting his resolve to attain all-knowledge;

He abandons the works of the *māras* by diligently cultivating the sublime practices and never becoming neglectful in this;

He abandons the works of the *māras* by always seeking the Dharma of the canon of all bodhisattvas;

He abandons the works of the *māras* by constantly and tirelessly expounding on the Dharma;

He abandons the works of the *māras* by taking refuge in all buddhas of the ten directions and bringing forth the motivation to rescue and protect others;

He abandons the works of the *māras* by faith, acceptance, and recollection of all buddhas' use of spiritual powers in providing supportive assistance; and

He abandons the works of the *māras* by joining with all bodhisattvas in planting roots of goodness that are the same and no different from theirs.

These are the ten. If bodhisattvas abide in these dharmas, then they are able to escape from all the paths of the *māras*.

Sons of the Buddha, the bodhisattva-mahāsattva has ten ways of seeing the Buddha. What are those ten? They are as follows:

Seeing the buddha abiding in the world, achieving the right enlightenment, due to nonattachment;

Seeing the vow buddha, due to coming forth and taking birth;
Seeing the karmic rewards buddha, due to deep faith;
Seeing the abiding and sustaining buddha, due to adaptations;
Seeing the nirvāṇa buddha, due to deep penetration;
Seeing the Dharma realm buddha, due to universal reach;
Seeing the mind buddha, due to secure abiding;
Seeing the samādhi buddha, due to measureless independence;
Seeing the original nature buddha, due to clear comprehension; and
Seeing the buddha adapting to whatever delights others, due to universal acceptance.

These are the ten. If bodhisattvas abide in these dharmas, then they always succeed in seeing the unexcelled Tathāgata.

Sons of the Buddha, the bodhisattva-mahāsattva has ten kinds of buddha works. What are those ten? They are as follows:

Providing guidance in accordance with the right time is a buddha work done to enable right cultivation;
Causing beings to have visions in their dreams is a buddha work done to awaken them to roots of goodness from the past;
Expounding for beings sutras they have not yet heard is a buddha work done to enable them to develop wisdom and cut off doubts;
Teaching dharmas of emancipation for those bound up by the bonds of regretfulness is a buddha work done to enable separation from doubt-ridden thoughts;
Where there are beings who produce miserly thoughts and so forth, including evil-minded thoughts, thoughts of the two vehicles, thoughts of injuring others, doubt-ridden thoughts, scattered thoughts, or arrogant thoughts, manifesting for their sakes the Tathāgata's body adorned with the many signs is a buddha work done to enable the growth of past roots of goodness;
Extensively teaching the Dharma for others at a time when right Dharma has become difficult to encounter so that, having enabled them to hear it, they acquire the knowledge of the *dhāraṇīs* and the knowledge of the spiritual superknowledges—being able to everywhere benefit countless beings in this way is a buddha work done to enable them to acquire decisive understanding that is pure;
When works of *māra*s are arising, being able to use skillful means to manifest a voice equal in its range to all of space that, in order to counter these endeavors, speaks Dharma encouraging

refraining from injurious torment of others, thus enabling their awakening so that, once the many *māras* have heard this, their awesomely strong radiance recedes and disappears—this is a buddha work done to engender especially superior aspirations and vast awesome virtue;

To always guard his uninterrupted resolve by not allowing himself to gain realized entry into the right and fixed position of the two vehicles, and also, wherever there are beings whose faculties and natures are not yet ripened, to never teach them that sphere of liberation—this is a buddha work done to accord with his original vows;

To abandon all of *saṃsāra*'s fetters and contaminants, to continuously and uninterruptedly cultivate the bodhisattva practices, and to use the mind of great compassion to attract beings and enable them to begin the practices and ultimately reach liberation—this is a buddha work done to ceaselessly cultivate the bodhisattva practices; and

When the bodhisattva-mahāsattva fully comprehends that his own body as well as those of beings, from their very origin onward, are quiescent, he is neither startled or frightened, but rather proceeds then to insatiably pursue the diligent cultivation of merit and wisdom. In this:

Although he realizes all dharmas are uncreated, he still does not abandon dharmas' individual characteristics.

Although he has forever abandoned desire for any of the sense realms, he still always delights in looking up to and serving the buddhas manifesting in their form bodies.

Although he realizes that awakening and entering the Dharma does not depend on others, he still uses many different kinds of skillful means in his quest to reach all-knowledge.

Although he realizes all lands are like empty space, he still always delights in adorning all buddha *kṣetras*.

Although he constantly contemplates the nonexistence of others and the nonexistence of self, he still tirelessly teaches beings.

Although he is as originally unmoving as the Dharma realm itself, he still uses the power of his knowledge of the spiritual superknowledges to manifest a multitude of spiritual transformations.

Although he has already fully developed the wisdom of all-knowledge, he still incessantly cultivates the bodhisattva practices.

Although he realizes all dharmas are indescribable, he still turns the wheel of the pure Dharma, thereby enabling beings' minds to rejoice in it.

Although he is able to manifest the spiritual powers of all buddhas, he still does not disdain or relinquish the body of a bodhisattva.

Although he manifests the appearance of entering the great *parinirvāṇa,* he still manifests as taking rebirth everywhere.

The ability to carry out dharmas of simultaneous conventional and ultimate reality practice such as these is a buddha work.

These are the ten. If bodhisattvas abide in them, then they acquire the unexcelled and vast teacherless works not reliant on teaching provided by others.

Sons of the Buddha, the bodhisattva-mahāsattva has ten kinds of arrogant actions. What are those ten? They are as follows:

If he fails to respect teachers, members of the Sangha, parents, *śramaṇas,* brahmans, those who abide in the right path, those on the threshold of the right path, or other venerable fields of merit, this is an arrogant action;

If there is a master of the Dharma who has acquired the supreme Dharma, who has ascended to the Great Vehicle, who knows the path to emancipation, who has acquired the *dhāraṇīs,* and who ceaselessly expounds on the vast dharmas of the sutras, yet he generates thoughts of arrogance toward him or does not respect the Dharma that he teaches, this is an arrogant action;

If he hears the proclamation of the sublime Dharma in the midst of a congregation but cannot bring himself to praise its excellence and thereby cause others to believe and accept it, this is an arrogant action;

If he delights in thoughts of elevating arrogance[486] in which he elevates himself, assails others, fails to see his own faults, and fails to realize his own shortcomings, this is an arrogant action;

If he delights in thoughts of over-reaching arrogance[487] by which, on seeing a virtuous person, he does not praise him even though he should praise him and is not pleased when he sees him being praised by others, this is an arrogant action;

If he sees that there is a master of the Dharma teaching the Dharma for others and he realizes that this is indeed the Dharma, the moral code, the truth, and the words of the Buddha, yet, because he dislikes that person, he criticizes the Dharma as he teaches it and deliberately slanders him and causes others to slander him, this is an arrogant action;

If he seeks the high seat, calls himself a master of the Dharma worthy of offerings and support, claims he therefore should not have to do his usual work, and fails to greet and welcome senior and long-tenured cultivators while also being unwilling to serve them, this is an arrogant action;

If he sees that there is a virtuous person, but he knits his brows, acts displeased, and narrates his faults in coarse and fiercely rude terms, this is an arrogant action;

If he sees that there is an intelligent and wise person who knows the Dharma, yet he cannot bring himself to draw near to that person to pay his respects and present offerings and cannot bring himself to inquire as to what is good, what is not good, what he should do, what he should not do, and what actions there are that, pursued throughout the long night [of *saṃsāra*], would bring about all kinds of benefit and happiness, being so beset by delusion and dullness that he is swallowed up by self-imputing arrogance[488] and can never see the path to emancipation, this is an arrogant action;

And further, if there is a being whose mind is so covered over by arrogance that, even when buddhas come forth into the world, he is unable to draw near to them, revere them, or make offerings to them—one in whom new acts of goodness do not arise and old acts of goodness have passed away, one who says what should not be said and disputes what should not be disputed—in the future, he will certainly fall into a deep pit of hazards and difficulties and, even in a hundred thousand kalpas, he will never encounter a buddha, how much the less hear the Dharma. It is only due to having once already resolved to attain bodhi that he might finally eventually awaken on his own. This is an arrogant action.

These are the ten. If bodhisattvas abandon these arrogant actions, then they acquire the ten kinds of wise actions. What are those ten? They are as follows:

Maintaining resolute faith in karmic consequences that does not contradict cause and effect is a wise action;

Never relinquishing the resolve to attain bodhi and always remaining mindful of all buddhas—these are wise actions;

Drawing near to a good spiritual guide, respectfully making offerings to him with a reverential mind, and never wearying of this—these are wise actions;

Insatiably delighting in the Dharma and delighting in meaning while abandoning wrong mindfulness and diligently cultivating right mindfulness—these are wise actions;

Abandoning self-imputing arrogance in relating to other beings, conceiving of all bodhisattvas as *tathāgatas*, cherishing and revering right Dharma as he would his own person, honoring and serving the Tathāgata just as he would protect his own life, and conceiving of all cultivators as buddhas—these are wise actions;

Keeping his physical, verbal, and mental actions free of all that is not good, praising the worthies and the *āryas*, and compliantly pursuing bodhi—these are wise actions;

Refraining from acting in contradiction to conditioned origination, abandoning all wrong views, dispelling darkness and acquiring brilliance, and illuminating all dharmas—these are wise actions;

According with and cultivating the ten kinds of dedications, thinking of the *pāramitās* as he would a kindly mother, thinking of excellent skillful means as he would a kindly father, and using the deep and pure mind to enter the abode of bodhi—these are wise actions;

Always diligently accumulating giving, moral precepts, abundant learning, calming and contemplation, merit, and wisdom, all such provisions for enlightenment as these, doing so insatiably and tirelessly—these are wise actions; and

If there is one action that is praised by the Buddha, that is able to demolish the afflictions and disputation associated with the *māras*, that is able to cause one to abandon all obstructing hindrances and entangling bonds, that is able to bring about the teaching and training of all beings, that is able to accord with wisdom and accumulate right Dharma, that is able to purify the buddha *kṣetras*, and that is able to produce the superknowledges and clarities—where one always diligently cultivates it and never withdraws in retreat—this is a wise action.

These are the ten. If bodhisattvas abide in them, then they acquire all of the Tathāgata's skillful means and unexcelled wise actions.

Sons of the Buddha, the bodhisattva-mahāsattva has ten ways of being possessed by Māra. What are those ten? They are as follows:

To have an indolent mind is to be possessed by Māra;

To have narrow and inferior aspirations is to be possessed by Māra;

To be satisfied with but a minor level of practice is to be possessed by Māra;

Accepting but a single approach while regarding all others as wrong is to be possessed by Māra;

To fail to make great vows is to be possessed by Māra;

To delight [only] in abiding in quiescence and cutting off afflictions is to be possessed by Māra;

To forever cut off *saṃsāra* is to be possessed by Māra;

To abandon the bodhisattva practices is to be possessed by Māra;

To refrain from teaching beings is to be possessed by Māra; and

To doubt and slander right Dharma is to be possessed by Māra.

These are the ten. If bodhisattvas are able to cast off these ways of being possessed by Māra, then they acquire ten ways of being possessed by the Buddha. What are those ten? They are as follows:

With the initial instance of being able to resolve to attain bodhi, they are possessed by the Buddha;

When in life after life they maintain the resolve to attain bodhi and are not allowed to forget it, they are possessed by the Buddha;

When they are aware of all the works of the *māras* and are able to avoid them all, they are possessed by the Buddha;

When they hear the teaching of the *pāramitās* and then cultivate them as they were taught, they are possessed by the Buddha;

When they know the sufferings of *saṃsāra,* yet do not detest and abhor it, they are possessed by the Buddha;

When they contemplate the extremely profound Dharma and attain its measureless fruits, they are possessed by the Buddha;

When they explain the dharmas of the two vehicles for beings, yet do not opt for the realization of those vehicles' liberations, they are possessed by the Buddha;

When they delight in contemplating unconditioned dharmas, yet do not abide in them and do not form a dualistic conception of the conditioned and the unconditioned, they are possessed by the Buddha;

When they reach the station of the unproduced[489] and yet still manifest the appearance of taking on births, they are possessed by the Buddha; and

When, although they have realized the attainment of all-knowledge, they still bring forth the bodhisattva practices and do not cut off the lineage of the bodhisattvas, they are possessed by the Buddha.

These are the ten. If bodhisattvas abide in them, then they acquire the unexcelled power of being possessed by all buddhas.

Sons of the Buddha, the bodhisattva-mahāsattva has ten ways in which he is possessed by the Dharma. What are those ten? They are as follows:

When he realizes that all karmic formative factors are characterized by impermanence, he is possessed by the Dharma;
When he realizes that all karmic formative factors are characterized by suffering, he is possessed by the Dharma;
When he realizes that all karmic formative factors are characterized by the absence of any "self," he is possessed by the Dharma;
When he realizes that all dharmas are characterized by quiescence and nirvāṇa, he is possessed by the Dharma;
When he realizes that dharmas arise from conditions and that, in the absence of conditions, they do not arise at all, he is possessed by the Dharma;
When he realizes that: it is due to wrong thought that ignorance arises; that due to the arising of ignorance, the other links in the causal chain up to and including aging-and-death arise; that it is due to the extinguishing of wrong thought that ignorance is extinguished; and that due to the extinguishing of ignorance, the other links of the causal chain up to and including aging and death are extinguished, then he is possessed by the Dharma;
When he realizes that the three gates to liberation[490] are the basis for the arising of the *śrāvaka*-disciple vehicle and that realization of the dharma of non-contentiousness is the basis for the arising of the *pratyekabuddha* vehicle, he is possessed by the Dharma;
When he realizes that the six *pāramitās* and the dharmas constituting the four means of attraction are the bases for the arising of the Great Vehicle, he is possessed by the Dharma;
When he realizes that all *kṣetras*, all dharmas, all beings, and all worlds are realms of the Buddha's knowledge, he is possessed by the Dharma; and
When he realizes that cutting off all thought, relinquishing all grasping, and transcending the past and future are in accordance with nirvāṇa, he is possessed by the Dharma.

These are the ten. If bodhisattvas abide in them, then they acquire all buddhas' unexcelled possession by the Dharma.

Sons of the Buddha, the bodhisattva-mahāsattva who dwells in the Tuṣita Heaven has ten kinds of works he accomplishes. What are those ten? They are as follows:

For the sake of the young devas of the desire realm, he teaches the dharma of renunciation and tells them that all their sovereign powers are impermanent and that all their types of happiness are bound to wither and fade. He then exhorts all those devas to resolve to attain bodhi. This is the first of the works he accomplishes;

For the sake of the devas of the form realm, he teaches entry into and emergence from all the *dhyāna* absorptions, liberations, and samādhis. For those who develop cravings-based attachments to them, or then, because of such craving, also develop the body-centered identity view, other wrong views, ignorance, and so forth, he then teaches them with reality-accordant wisdom. For those who develop inverted conceptions imputing purity to all form and formless dharmas, he teaches them that they are impure and that they are all impermanent, whereupon he exhorts them and causes them to resolve to attain bodhi. This is the second of the works he accomplishes;

When the bodhisattva-mahāsattva dwells in the Tuṣita Heaven, he enters a samādhi known as "radiant adornment" in which his body emanates light that everywhere illuminates the worlds of the great trichiliocosm. Adapting to beings' minds, he uses all different kinds of voices with which he teaches the Dharma for their sakes. After those beings hear this, their minds of faith are purified. When their lives come to an end, they are then reborn in the Tuṣita Heaven where he exhorts them in ways that enable them to resolve to attain bodhi. This is the third of the works he accomplishes;

When the bodhisattva-mahāsattva is in the Tuṣita Heaven, with his unimpeded eye, he everywhere sees all the bodhisattvas in the Tuṣita heavens throughout the ten directions. All those other bodhisattvas also see this place. After they have all seen each other, they then discuss the sublime Dharma and speak of spiritually descending into the womb of their mother, taking birth, leaving the home life, and going to the site of enlightenment possessed of magnificent adornments. They then also manifest the appearances of the practices they have pursued from the past on forward to the present by which, because of those practices, they have perfected this great wisdom and all their meritorious qualities. Even without ever leaving their original place, they are able to reveal phenomena such as these. This is the fourth of the works he accomplishes;

When the bodhisattva-mahāsattva is dwelling in the Tuṣita Heaven, all those in the congregations of bodhisattvas in all the Tuṣita heaven palaces throughout the ten directions then come and respectfully gather around him. At that time, wishing to enable all those other bodhisattvas to fulfill their vows and be filled with joyous delight, the bodhisattva-mahāsattva adapts to whichever grounds those bodhisattvas should dwell on, to whatever they practice, to whatever they have already cut off, to whatever they have cultivated, and to whatever they have already realized and then expounds on Dharma gateways for their sakes. After those bodhisattvas have heard his teachings on the Dharma, they are all filled with great joyous delight and experience what they have never before experienced, whereupon they each return to the palaces where they dwell in the lands from which they came. This is the fifth of the works he accomplishes;

When the bodhisattva-mahāsattva dwells in the Tuṣita Heaven, wishing to damage and throw into disorder the bodhisattva's works, the lord of the desire realm, Pāpīyān, the *māra* of the heavens, surrounded by his retinue, goes to where the bodhisattva dwells. Then, to vanquish the armies of *māras*, dwelling in the *prajñāpāramitā*'s gateway of the vajra path's skillful means and expedient wisdom, the bodhisattva uses both gentle and harsh statements as he speaks the Dharma for their sakes. So it is that he prevents that *māra*, Pāpīyān, from having his way. When those *māras* see the awesome powers of the bodhisattva's sovereign masteries, they all resolve to attain *anuttarasamyaksaṃbodhi*. This is the sixth of the works he accomplishes;

When the bodhisattva-mahāsattva dwells in the Tuṣita Heaven, he realizes that the young devas of the desire realm do not delight in hearing the Dharma. At that time, the bodhisattva emanates a loud voice with which he everywhere announces to them: "Today, the bodhisattva shall manifest rare phenomena in his palace. If anyone wishes to see this, it would be fitting for them to quickly go there." Having heard these words, the young devas who number in measurelessly many hundreds of thousands of *koṭīs* of *nayutas* all come and gather together there. At that time, having observed that the congregation of devas has all come and assembled there, the bodhisattva then manifests for them all kinds of rare phenomena within his palace. Then, having been able to see what they had never before seen or heard, those young devas are all so moved to feelings of great joy that their minds are as if inebriated.

He then also emanates from the midst of musical sounds a voice that tells them, "O Worthy Ones, you should realize that all karmic formative factors are impermanent, all karmic formative factors are suffering, and all dharmas are devoid of any self and are characterized by the quiescence of nirvāṇa." He also informs them, "All of you should cultivate the bodhisattva practices and gain the complete fulfillment of the wisdom of all-knowledge." On hearing these sounds of the Dharma, those young devas are all moved to worried sighing and mutual exclamations of lamentation, whereupon they develop thoughts of renunciation. Then there are none among them who fail to resolve to attain bodhi. This is the seventh of the works he accomplishes;

Without ever leaving his original place, the bodhisattva-mahāsattva dwelling in the Tuṣita Heaven palace is able to go to the abodes of all the countless buddhas of the ten directions to see all *tathāgatas*, draw near to them, bow down in reverence to them, and respectfully listen to the Dharma. At that time, because the buddhas wish to enable the bodhisattva to acquire the dharma of the most supreme crown-anointing consecration, they speak for his sake on the bodhisattva ground known as "all superknowledges" through which, with but a single mind-moment of corresponding wisdom, he completely perfects all of the most supreme meritorious qualities and enters the station of the wisdom of all-knowledge. This is the eighth of the works he accomplishes;

Wishing to make offerings to all *tathāgatas*, the bodhisattva-mahāsattva dwelling in the Tuṣita Heaven palace uses great spiritual powers to offer up many different kinds of offering gifts known as "especially superior and delightful" which, as offerings to all buddhas, pervade all the worlds of the Dharma realm and the realms of space. On seeing these offerings, the countless beings in those worlds all resolve to attain *anuttarasamyaksaṃbodhi*. This is the ninth of the works he accomplishes; and

The bodhisattva-mahāsattva dwelling in the Tuṣita Heaven brings forth countlessly and boundlessly many Dharma gateways like illusions and like reflections which pervade all worlds of the ten directions, displaying all different kinds of colors, all different kinds of signs, all different kinds of bodies, all different kinds of awesome deportment, all different kinds of endeavors, all different kinds of skillful means, all different kinds of analogies, and all different kinds of expositions which, adapting to the minds of beings, cause them all to be filled with joyous delight. This is the tenth of the works he accomplishes.

Sons of the Buddha, these are the ten kinds of works accomplished by the bodhisattva-mahāsattva dwelling in the Tuṣita Heaven. If bodhisattvas perfect these dharmas, later on they are able to descend to take rebirth among humans.

Sons of the Buddha, when the bodhisattva-mahāsattva dwelling in the Tuṣita Heaven is about to descend to take birth, he manifests ten kinds of phenomena. What are those ten? [They are as follows]:

Sons of the Buddha, when the bodhisattva-mahāsattva dwelling in the Tuṣita Heaven is about to descend to take birth, he emanates from beneath his feet a great light known as "adornment with happiness" that everywhere illuminates all the wretched destinies in the worlds of the great trichiliocosm. When the beings beset with difficulties there are touched by this light, there are none among them who are not then able to abandon their sufferings and become happy. Having attained happiness, they all then realize that there is about to be some especially great man who is about to appear in the world. This is the first of the phenomena that he manifests;

Sons of the Buddha, when the bodhisattva-mahāsattva dwelling in the Tuṣita Heaven is about to descend to take birth, from the white hair mark between his brows, he emanates a great light known as "awakening" that everywhere illuminates the worlds of the trichiliocosm and illuminates the bodies of all the bodhisattvas with whom he has practiced together in previous lifetimes. When those bodhisattvas are illuminated by this light, they all realize that the bodhisattva is about to descend to take birth, whereupon each one of them then brings forth countless offering gifts which they take to the bodhisattva to present to him as offerings. This is the second of the phenomena that he manifests;

Sons of the Buddha, when the bodhisattva-mahāsattva dwelling in the Tuṣita Heaven is about to descend to take birth, he emanates a great light from his right palm known as "pure realms" that is able to purify all the worlds of the great trichiliocosm. If there are any *pratyekabuddhas* within them who have already succeeded in becoming free of the contaminants, on becoming aware this light, they immediately relinquish this lifetime. If they do not become aware of it, due to the power of this light, they then move away to some other world in some other region. If any *māras*, adherents of non-Buddhist paths, or beings clinging to existence-reifying views, they too then all also move off to some other world in some other region, leaving only those beings who should be taught who are supported by the spiritual powers of the buddhas. This is the third of the phenomena that he manifests;

Sons of the Buddha, when the bodhisattva-mahāsattva dwelling in the Tuṣita Heaven is about to descend to take birth, he emanates a great light from his two knees known as "pure adornment" that everywhere illuminates all heavenly palaces down to those of the World-Protecting devas and up to those of the Pure Dwelling devas, having none that it does not thoroughly pervade. All those devas, realizing that the bodhisattva is about to descend to take birth, are then filled with feelings of fond admiration, are moved to sighing with sadness and sorrow. They then each take up all different kinds of floral garlands, robes, perfumes, powdered incenses, banners, canopies, and music and then go to where the bodhisattva dwells where they respectfully present these gifts as offerings, and then follow him as he descends to take birth, continuing to accompany him all along until he enters nirvāṇa. This is the fourth of the phenomena that he manifests;

Sons of the Buddha, when the bodhisattva-mahāsattva dwelling in the Tuṣita Heaven is about to descend to take birth, from his heart adorned with the vajra *svastika* emblem he emanates a great light known as "invincible banner" that then everywhere illuminates the vajra stalwarts in all worlds of the ten directions at which time a hundred *koṭīs* of vajra stalwarts all come and assemble there, following and serving him then as guardians, doing so beginning with his descent to take birth and continuing on in this manner all the way until he reaches nirvāṇa. This is the fifth of the phenomena that he manifests;

Sons of the Buddha, when the bodhisattva-mahāsattva dwelling in the Tuṣita Heaven is about to descend to take birth, from all the pores of his body, he emanates a great light known as "distinguishing beings" that then everywhere illuminates all the worlds of the great chiliocosm and everywhere falls on the bodies of all bodhisattvas while also falling on all the devas and all the humans in the world. All the bodhisattvas and the others then think: "I should remain here, make offerings to the Tathāgata, and provide teachings to beings." This is the sixth of the phenomena that he manifests;

Sons of the Buddha, when the bodhisattva-mahāsattva dwelling in the Tuṣita Heaven is about to descend to take birth, from within the great Maṇi Jewel Treasury Palace, he emanates a great light known as "skillfully abiding contemplation" that illuminates the place where this bodhisattva is about to take birth and the royal palace wherein he is about to dwell. After his light illuminates them, all the other bodhisattvas then follow along together with him in descending to the continent of Jambudvīpa, taking rebirth there either within his clan, within his village, or within his city and its outlying precincts, doing so for the purpose of teaching all beings. This is the seventh of the phenomena that he manifests;

Sons of the Buddha, when the bodhisattva-mahāsattva dwelling in the Tuṣita Heaven is about to descend to take birth, from the adornments of his heavenly palace and its great towers, he emanates a great light known as "pure adornments of all palaces" that illuminates the belly of the mother to whom he is to be born. After this light has cast its illumination, it causes the bodhisattva's mother to feel safe, secure, and happy and fully possessed of all meritorious qualities. Then, within his mother's belly, there spontaneously manifests a vast tower adorned with immense *maṇi* jewels in order to provide a peaceful dwelling place for the bodhisattva's body. This is the eighth of the phenomena that he manifests;

Sons of the Buddha, when the bodhisattva-mahāsattva dwelling in the Tuṣita Heaven is about to descend to take birth, from beneath his two feet he emanates a great light known as "excellent dwelling." If any of the young devas or Brahma Heaven devas reaching the imminent end of their lives receive this light's illumination, they all succeed in continuing to abide in this lifetime to make offerings to the bodhisattva from the time when he takes birth all the way until he reaches his nirvāṇa. This is the ninth of the phenomena that he manifests;

Sons of the Buddha, when the bodhisattva-mahāsattva dwelling in the Tuṣita Heaven is about to descend to take birth, from his secondary signs he emanates a great light known as "adornment for the eyes" that manifests the appearances of all the many different kinds of deeds the bodhisattva has done. At that time, all the humans and devas may see the bodhisattva dwelling in the Tuṣita Heaven, or may see him entering the womb, or may see him when he is first born, or may see him when he leaves the home life, or may see him when he attains enlightenment, or may see him when he vanquishes the *māras*, or may see him when he turns the wheel of the Dharma, or may see him when he enters nirvāṇa. This is the tenth of the phenomena that he manifests.

Sons of the Buddha, the bodhisattva-mahāsattva emanates hundreds of myriads of *asaṃkhyeyas* of light rays such as these from his body, from his throne, from his palace, and from his towers, all of which display the many different kinds of bodhisattva works. Having revealed these works, due to having completely fulfilled all dharmas of the meritorious qualities, he then descends from the Tuṣita heaven and takes birth among humans.

Sons of the Buddha, there are ten phenomena associated with the bodhisattva-mahāsattva's manifesting as dwelling in the womb. What are those ten? They are as follows:

Sons of the Buddha, wishing to ripen beings with petty minds and inferior understanding, the bodhisattva-mahāsattva wishes to prevent them from generating such thoughts as this: "This bodhisattva has now been spontaneously transformationally born. Hence his wisdom and roots of goodness have not been acquired through cultivation." Therefore the bodhisattva manifests the appearance of abiding in the womb. This is the first of these phenomena;

In order to ripen the roots of goodness of his parents, family, and beings with whom he has practiced together in past lives, the bodhisattva-mahāsattva manifests as abiding in the womb. Why is this? They should all be able to ripen all their roots of goodness by seeing him dwelling in the womb. This is the second of these phenomena;

When the bodhisattva-mahāsattva enters his mother's womb, he maintains right mindfulness and right knowing free of confusion. Once he has come to abide in his mother's womb, his mind constantly remains in a state of right mindfulness in which he is free of either error or confusion. This is the third of these phenomena;

When the bodhisattva-mahāsattva is abiding in his mother's womb, he is always expounding on the Dharma. All the great bodhisattvas, Śakra, Brahma, and the four heavenly kings throughout the worlds of the ten directions all come and gather together there where he enables them all to acquire measureless spiritual powers and boundless wisdom. Even as the bodhisattva is abiding in the womb, he is implementing supreme functions of eloquence such as these. This is the fourth of these phenomena;

When the bodhisattva-mahāsattva is abiding in his mother's womb, he assembles a great congregation and, through the power of his original vows, teaches all the congregations of bodhisattvas. This is the fifth of these phenomena;

When the bodhisattva-mahāsattva appears among humans to realize buddhahood, it is only fitting that he have the best of human births. It is for this reason that he manifests as dwelling in his mother's womb. This is the sixth of these phenomena;

When the bodhisattva-mahāsattva abides in his mother's womb, the beings in the worlds of the great trichiliocosm all see the bodhisattva as clearly as if they were looking at their own faces in a brightly polished mirror. At that time, all of those possessed of great minds among the devas, dragons, *yakṣas, gandharvas, asuras, garuḍas, kiṃnaras, mahoragas,* humans, and nonhumans—they all come there to meet the bodhisattva and reverently present offerings. This is the seventh of these phenomena;

When the bodhisattva-mahāsattva is abiding in his mother's womb, all the bodhisattvas from the worlds of other regions who have reached their very last birth and are abiding in their mothers' wombs—they all come and gather together there whereupon he teaches a Dharma gateway of great accumulation known as "vast wisdom treasury." This is the eighth of these phenomena;

When the bodhisattva-mahāsattva is abiding in his mother's womb, he enters the immaculate treasury samādhi and, with the power of that samādhi, he manifests an immense palace in his mother's womb that has all kinds of different adornments, all of which are so wondrously fine that not even the Tuṣita Heaven Palace could compare with it. In doing so, he ensures that his mother's body is safe and free of any troubles. This is the ninth of these phenomena; and

When the bodhisattva-mahāsattva abides in his mother's womb, he uses his great awe-inspiring power to bring forth a collection of offering gifts known as "the opening of the immaculate treasury of great merit." He then makes offerings to all buddhas, the *tathāgatas,* everywhere throughout all worlds of the ten directions. All those *tathāgatas* then expound for him teachings on the boundless bodhisattva dwelling place, the treasury of the Dharma realm. This is the tenth of these phenomena.

Sons of the Buddha, these are the ten phenomena associated with the bodhisattva-mahāsattva's manifesting as dwelling in the womb. If bodhisattvas completely comprehend these dharmas, then they become able to manifest subtle endeavors.

Sons of the Buddha, the bodhisattva-mahāsattva has ten kinds of subtle endeavors. What are those ten? They are as follows:

While in his mother's womb, he manifests the initial resolve to attain bodhi and so forth up to and including the ground of the crown-anointing consecration;

While in his mother's womb, he manifests dwelling in the Tuṣita Heaven;

While in his mother's womb, he manifests first taking on birth;

While in his mother's womb, he manifests abiding on the ground of the pure youth;

While in his mother's womb, he manifests dwelling in the royal palace;

While in his mother's womb, he manifests leaving the household life;

While in his mother's womb, he manifests engaging in the austerities, going to the site of enlightenment, and realizing the right and perfect enlightenment;

While in his mother's womb, he manifests turning the wheel of the Dharma;

While in his mother's womb, he manifests *parinirvāṇa*; and

While in his mother's womb, he manifests the appearance of great subtle endeavors, namely the countless different gateways of all bodhisattvas' practices and all *tathāgatas'* sovereign spiritual powers.

Sons of the Buddha, these are the bodhisattva-mahāsattva's ten subtle endeavors while abiding in his mother's womb. If bodhisattvas abide in these dharmas, then they acquire the subtle endeavor of the Tathāgata's unexcelled great wisdom.

Sons of the Buddha, the bodhisattva-mahāsattva has ten kinds of birth. What are those ten? They are as follows:

The birth of abandoning delusion while abiding in right mindfulness and right knowing;

The birth of emanating a great net of light rays which everywhere illuminate the worlds of the great trichiliocosm;

The birth of abiding in his last existence after which he never receives another body;

The birth with no production and no arising;

The birth in which he realizes that the three realms of existence are like an illusion;

The birth in which he manifests bodies everywhere throughout the worlds of the ten directions;

The birth of the body in which he realizes the wisdom of all-knowledge;

The birth of the body in which he emanates the light of all buddhas which everywhere awakens all beings;

The birth of the body in which he enters the great wisdom contemplation samādhi; and

Sons of the Buddha, when the bodhisattva takes birth, he causes the shaking of all buddha *kṣetras,* liberates all beings, extinguishes all the wretched destinies, outshines all *māras*, and causes countless bodhisattvas to all come and gather together.

Sons of the Buddha, these are the bodhisattva-mahāsattva's ten kinds of birth. They are manifested in these ways in order to train beings.

Sons of the Buddha, it is due to ten kinds of circumstances that the bodhisattva-mahāsattva manifests a subtle smile and spontaneously makes a vow. What are those ten? They are as follows:

The bodhisattva-mahāsattva thinks, "Everyone in the world has sunken into the mud of the desires. With the exception of myself, this one person, there is no one able to rescue them." Having realized this, he subtly smiles and makes a vow to himself;

He also thinks, "Everyone in the world is blinded by the afflictions. There is only myself who now has developed completely fulfilled wisdom." Having realized this, he subtly smiles and makes a vow to himself;

He additionally thinks, "Because of this conventionally designated body, I shall now succeed in acquiring the Tathāgata's unexcelled Dharma body that completely fills up all three periods of time. Having realized this, he subtly smiles and makes a vow to himself;

At this time, the bodhisattva uses his unimpeded eye to everywhere contemplate throughout the ten directions all the Brahma Heaven devas and so forth on up to all the devas of the Great Maheśvara Heaven and thinks, "All of these beings are of the opinion that they possess the power of great wisdom." Having realized this, he subtly smiles and makes a vow to himself;

At this time, the bodhisattva contemplates all beings and observes that, having planted roots of goodness in the past, they now all regress. Having realized this, he subtly smiles and makes a vow to himself;

The bodhisattva contemplates and observes that, although seeds planted in the world may be but few, the fruits that are thereby reaped may be extremely abundant. Having realized this, he subtly smiles and makes a vow to himself;

The bodhisattva contemplates and observes that, when beings receive the Buddha's teachings, they become certain to realize benefits from this. Having realized this, he subtly smiles and makes a vow to himself;

The bodhisattva contemplates and observes that bodhisattvas with whom he cultivated together in past lives have developed defiling attachments to other things and thus have failed to acquire the vastly meritorious qualities associated with the Buddha's Dharma. Having realized this, he subtly smiles and makes a vow to himself;

The bodhisattva contemplates and observes that the devas, humans, and others with whom he gathered together in past lives—they even now still abide on the ground of the common person where they remain unable to abandon it and have not yet even grown weary of it. Having realized this, he subtly smiles and makes a vow to himself; and

At this time, the bodhisattva, touched by the light of all the *tathāgatas*, experiences doubly increased delight and happiness. He then subtly smiles and makes a vow to himself.

These are the ten. Sons of the Buddha, it is for the purpose of training beings that the bodhisattva appears in ways such as these.

Sons of the Buddha, it is for ten reasons that the bodhisattva-mahāsattva manifests the act of walking seven steps. What are those ten? They are as follows:

It is to reveal the power of the bodhisattva that he manifests the act of walking seven steps;

It is to reveal his bestowing of the seven kinds of wealth[491] that he manifests the act of walking seven steps;

It is to fulfill the wishes of the earth spirits that he manifests the act of walking seven steps;

It is to reveal the signs of stepping beyond the three realms that he manifests the act of walking seven steps;

It is to reveal the bodhisattva's supreme walk surpassing the walk of the king of elephants, the king of bulls, and the king of lions that he manifests the act of walking seven steps;

It is to reveal the signs of the vajra ground that he manifests the act of walking seven steps;

It is to reveal his wish to bestow on beings the power of courage that he manifests the act of walking seven steps;

It is to reveal the cultivation of the jewels of the seven enlightenment factors that he manifests the act of walking seven steps;

It is to reveal that the Dharma he has acquired did not arise from the teachings of others that he manifests the act of walking seven steps; and

It is to reveal that, of all who abide in the world, he is incomparably supreme that he manifests the act of walking seven steps.

These are the ten. Sons of the Buddha, it is for the purpose of training beings that the bodhisattva appears in ways such as these.

Sons of the Buddha, it is for ten reasons that the bodhisattva-mahāsattva manifests as abiding on the ground of the pure youth. What are those ten? They are as follows:

He manifests as abiding on the ground of the pure youth to demonstrate the complete comprehension of all the world's languages, mathematics, painting, calligraphy, seal-carving, and all the many other kinds of skills;

He manifests as abiding on the ground of the pure youth to demonstrate the complete comprehension of all the many different kinds of worldly skills such as riding elephants and horses, driving carriages and other vehicles, and wielding bows and arrows, swords, and halberds;

He manifests as abiding on the ground of the pure youth to demonstrate the complete comprehension of all the many different kinds of worldly arts such as literary composition, discussion, games, and entertainments;

He manifests as abiding on the ground of the pure youth to demonstrate the renunciation of all the faults in physical, verbal, and mental deeds;

He manifests as abiding on the ground of the pure youth for the sake of demonstrating entry into meditative absorption and abiding in the gateway of nirvāṇa throughout the countless worlds of the ten directions;

He manifests as abiding on the ground of the pure youth to demonstrate his powers surpassing those of all the devas, dragons, *yakṣas, gandharvas, asuras, garuḍas, kiṃnaras, mahoragas,* Śakra, Brahma, the world-protecting devas, humans, nonhumans, and others;

He manifests as abiding on the ground of the pure youth to reveal the bodhisattva's physical marks and awe-inspiring radiance surpassing those of all of the devas such as Śakra, Brahma, or the world-protecting devas;

He manifests as abiding on the ground of the pure youth to enable beings obsessively attached to the pleasures of the desires to find happiness and delight in the Dharma;

He manifests as abiding on the ground of the pure youth to revere right Dharma and diligently make offerings to the buddhas everywhere throughout all worlds of the ten directions; and

He manifests as abiding on the ground of the pure youth to show his empowerment by the Buddha and his illumination by the light of the Dharma.

These are the ten. Sons of the Buddha, after the bodhisattva-mahāsattva has manifested as abiding on the ground of the pure youth, he manifests as abiding in the royal palace for ten reasons. What are those ten? They are as follows:

He manifests as abiding in the royal palace to ripen the roots of goodness of those beings with whom he practiced together in previous lives;

He manifests as abiding in the royal palace to reveal the power of the bodhisattva's roots of goodness;

He manifests as abiding in the royal palace to reveal to devas and humans obsessively attached to sources of bliss the bodhisattva's greatly awe-inspiring sources of bliss;

He manifests as abiding in the royal palace to accord with the minds of beings abiding in the world of the five turbidities;[492]

He manifests as abiding in the royal palace to reveal the bodhisattva's great awe-inspiring powers and his ability to enter samādhi even in the depths of the palace;

He manifests as abiding in the royal palace to enable the fulfillment of the aspirations of those beings with whom he shared the same vows in previous lives;

He manifests as abiding in the royal palace to enable his parents, relatives, and retinue to fulfill their vows;

He manifests as abiding in the royal palace to use music to send forth the sounds of the sublime Dharma as offerings to all *tathāgatas;*

He manifests as abiding in the royal palace wishing within the inner palace to abide in the sublime samādhi which reveals everything beginning from his realization of buddhahood to his entry into nirvāṇa; and

He manifests as abiding in the royal palace to accord with and preserve the Dharma of all buddhas.

These are the ten. After the bodhisattva in his very last body manifests his abiding within the royal palace in these ways, he then leaves the householder's life.

Sons of the Buddha, it is for ten reasons that the bodhisattva-mahāsattva manifests as leaving the household life. What are those ten? They are as follows:

He manifests as leaving the household life to renounce dwelling in the household;

He manifests as leaving the household life to enable beings attached to the household to abandon it;

He manifests as leaving the household life to accord with his resolute faith in in the path of the *āryas;*

He manifests as leaving the household life to proclaim and praise the meritorious qualities of leaving the householder's life;

He manifests as leaving the household life to demonstrate detaching forever from the two extreme views;[493]

He manifests as leaving the household life to enable beings to leave behind delight in the desires and delight in the self;

He manifests as leaving the household life to be the first to show the appearance of transcending the three realms of existence;

He manifests as leaving the household life to demonstrate sovereign mastery not dependent on anyone else;

He manifests as leaving the household life to show that he is bound to gain the dharmas of the Tathāgata's ten powers and fearlessnesses; and

He manifests as leaving the household life because the dharma of the bodhisattva in his very last body should be of this very sort.

These are the ten. The bodhisattva uses these to train beings.

Sons of the Buddha, it is for ten reasons that the bodhisattva-mahāsattva manifests as practicing the austerities. What are those ten? They are as follows:

He manifests as practicing the austerities to enable the development of beings with inferior levels of understanding;

He manifests as practicing the austerities to remove the wrong views of beings with wrong views;

He manifests as practicing the austerities to enable beings who do not believe in karmic consequences to perceive the consequences arising from karmic actions;

He manifests as practicing the austerities because it is only fitting to do so when adapting to the dharmas of a defiled world;

He manifests as practicing the austerities to demonstrate the ability to endure even such strenuous exertion in diligent cultivation of the path;

He manifests as practicing the austerities to enable beings to delight in seeking the Dharma;

He manifests as practicing the austerities for the sake of beings attached to delighting in the desires and delighting in the self;

He manifests as practicing the austerities to show that the bodhisattva begins with especially supreme practice and continues on with it to the very last birth, even then still never relinquishing his diligence and vigor;

He manifests as practicing the austerities to enable beings to delight in the dharma of quiescence and increase their roots of goodness;[494] and

He manifests as practicing the austerities for the sake of devas and humans in the world whose faculties have not yet become ripened, thus awaiting the right time for their ripening.

These are the ten. The bodhisattva uses these skillful means to train all beings.

Sons of the Buddha, there are ten phenomena that occur when the bodhisattva-mahāsattva goes to the site of enlightenment. What are those ten? They are as follows.

When he goes to the site of enlightenment, he illuminates all worlds with shining light;

When he goes to the site of enlightenment, he causes shaking and movement in all worlds;

When he goes to the site of enlightenment, he manifests his body in all worlds;

When he goes to the site of enlightenment, he awakens all bodhisattvas as well as all those beings with whom he practiced together in previous lifetimes;

When he goes to the site of enlightenment, he reveals all the adornments of the site of enlightenment;

When he goes to the site of enlightenment, adapting to the aspirations in beings' minds, he manifests bodies for them which are possessed of all the many different types of awesome deportment and also manifests all the adornments of the bodhi tree;

When he goes to the site of enlightenment, he manifests the seeing of all *tathāgatas* of the ten directions;

When he goes to the site of enlightenment, even with every time he lifts his foot or sets down his foot, he is always immersed in samādhi and in each successive mind-moment, without interruption, he is realizing buddhahood;

When he goes to the site of enlightenment, all the devas, dragons, *yakṣas, gandharvas, asuras, garuḍas, kiṃnaras, mahoragas,* Śakra, Brahma, the world-protecting devas, and all kings, each unaware of the others, bring forth many different kinds of different supremely sublime offerings; and

When he goes to the site of enlightenment, using his unimpeded wisdom, he everywhere contemplates the cultivation of the bodhisattva practices and the realization of right enlightenment as carried out in all worlds by all buddhas, the *tathāgatas.*

These are the ten. The bodhisattva uses these to teach beings.

Sons of the Buddha, there are ten phenomena that occur when the bodhisattva-mahāsattva sits at the site of enlightenment. What are those ten? They are as follows:

When he sits at the site of enlightenment, he creates the many different kinds of shaking and movement in all worlds;
When he sits at the site of enlightenment, he equally illuminates all worlds;
When he sits at the site of enlightenment, he extinguishes all the sufferings of the wretched destinies;
When he sits at the site of enlightenment, he causes all worlds to be composed of vajra;
When he sits at the site of enlightenment, he everywhere contemplates the lion thrones of all buddhas, the *tathāgatas;*
When he sits at the site of enlightenment, his mind is like empty space, free of any discriminations;
When he sits at the site of enlightenment, he manifests bodies and types of awesome deportment in accordance with whatever is appropriate;
When he sits at the site of enlightenment, he accords with and securely abides in the vajra samādhi;
When he sits at the site of enlightenment, he receives the pure and sublime place supported by the spiritual powers of all *tathāgatas;* and
When he sits at the site of enlightenment, the power of his own roots of goodness is able to assist all beings.

These are the ten.

Sons of the Buddha, when the bodhisattva-mahāsattva sits at the site of enlightenment, ten kinds of extraordinary and unprecedented phenomena occur. What are those ten? They are as follows:

Sons of the Buddha, when the bodhisattva-mahāsattva sits at the site of enlightenment, all *tathāgatas* throughout the worlds of the ten directions appear directly before him, raise their right hands, and praise him, saying, "This is good indeed, good indeed, O Unexcelled Guide." This is the first of these unprecedented phenomena;
Sons of the Buddha, when the bodhisattva-mahāsattva sits at the site of enlightenment, all *tathāgatas* are protectively mindful of him and bestow on him their awesome powers. This is the second of these unprecedented phenomena;
Sons of the Buddha, when the bodhisattva-mahāsattva sits at the site of enlightenment, the congregation of all bodhisattvas with whom he cultivated together in the past surrounds him and reverently makes offerings to him of all different kinds of adornments. This is the third of these unprecedented phenomena;

Sons of the Buddha, when the bodhisattva-mahāsattva sits at the site of enlightenment, the grasses, trees, forests, and insentient things all bow their bodies and bend down their shadows in the direction of the site of enlightenment. This is the fourth of these unprecedented phenomena;

Sons of the Buddha, when the bodhisattva-mahāsattva sits at the site of enlightenment, he enters a samādhi known as "contemplation of the Dharma realm." The power of this samādhi is able to cause all the bodhisattva's practices to become completely fulfilled. This is the fifth of these unprecedented phenomena;

Sons of the Buddha, when the bodhisattva-mahāsattva sits at the site of enlightenment, he acquires a *dhāraṇī* known as "oceanic treasury of the most supremely pure and sublime light" with which he is able to take in all the Dharma rain falling from the great Dharma clouds of all buddhas, the *tathāgatas*. This is the sixth of these unprecedented phenomena;

Sons of the Buddha, when the bodhisattva-mahāsattva sits at the site of enlightenment, by the power of his awesome virtue, he raises up supremely marvelous gifts which everywhere pervade all worlds as offerings to all buddhas. This is the seventh of these unprecedented phenomena;

Sons of the Buddha, when the bodhisattva-mahāsattva sits at the site of enlightenment, he abides in the most supreme wisdom through which he manifests the complete knowing of the faculties, minds, and actions of all beings. This is the eighth of these unprecedented phenomena;

Sons of the Buddha, when the bodhisattva-mahāsattva sits at the site of enlightenment, he enters a samādhi known as "well awakened." By the power of this samādhi, he is able to cause his body to completely fill all worlds in all of space throughout the three periods of time. This is the ninth of these unprecedented phenomena; and

Sons of the Buddha, when the bodhisattva-mahāsattva sits at the site of enlightenment, he acquires the unimpeded great wisdom of immaculate radiance by which his physical actions everywhere enter all three periods of time. This is the tenth of these unprecedented phenomena.

Sons of the Buddha, these are the ten kinds of extraordinary and unprecedented phenomena that occur when the bodhisattva-mahāsattva sits at the site of enlightenment.

Sons of the Buddha, when the bodhisattva-mahāsattva sits at the site of enlightenment, it is due to contemplating ten meaningful considerations that he manifests the subduing of the *māras*. What are those ten? They are as follows:

Wishing to demonstrate the power of the bodhisattva's awesome virtue for beings in the world of the turbidities who are fond of fighting, he therefore manifests the subduing of the *māras*;

To cut off the doubts of devas and people of the world who cherish doubts, he therefore manifests the subduing of the *māras*;

To teach and subdue the armies of Māra, he therefore manifests the subduing of the *māras*;

Wishing to cause the subduing of the minds of devas and people of the world who so delight in the ranks of the army that they all come, congregate, and observe them, he therefore manifests the subduing of the *māras*;

To reveal all the awesome powers of the bodhisattva which no one in the world can oppose, he therefore manifests the subduing of the *māras*;

Wishing to bring forth the courageous power of all beings, he therefore manifests the subduing of the *māras*;

Out of deep sympathetic pity for all beings of the Dharma-ending age, he therefore manifests the subduing of the *māras*;

Wishing to reveal that, even when he reaches the site of enlightenment, Māra's armies still come to create disturbances and only after that does he go beyond the sphere of interference by the *māras*, he therefore manifests the subduing of the *māras*;

To reveal that the karmic functions of the afflictions are but thin and weak whereas the power of the roots of goodness of great kindness are strong and flourishing, he therefore manifests the subduing of the *māras*; and

Wishing to accord with the dharmas practiced in the evil world of the turbidities, he therefore manifests the subduing of the *māras*.

These are the ten.

Sons of the Buddha, the bodhisattva-mahāsattva has ten ways in which he perfects the Tathāgata's powers. What are those ten? They are as follows:

He perfects the Tathāgata's powers by stepping beyond the affliction-based actions of all the many *māras*;

He perfects the Tathāgata's powers by completely fulfilling all the bodhisattva practices and achieving easeful mastery in all the samādhi gateways of the bodhisattva;

He perfects the Tathāgata's powers by perfecting all the vast *dhyāna* absorptions of the bodhisattva;

He perfects the Tathāgata's powers by completely fulfilling all the pure dharmas among the provisions for enlightenment;

He perfects the Tathāgata's powers by acquiring the light of wisdom with respect to all dharmas through skillful meditative analysis;

He perfects the Tathāgata's powers through his body's[495] pervasive presence everywhere in all worlds;

He perfects the Tathāgata's powers through making his voice match the minds of all beings;

He perfects the Tathāgata's powers through his ability to use spiritual powers to assist and support everyone;

He perfects the Tathāgata's powers through actions of body, speech, and mind that are equal to and no different from those of all buddhas of the three periods of time and through completely understanding the dharmas of the three periods of time in but a single mind-moment; and

He perfects the Tathāgata's ten powers through acquiring the samādhi of well awakened knowledge. In particular, these refer to the wisdom power by which he knows what can be as what can be and what cannot be as what cannot be, and so forth, on through to the wisdom power that knows the complete cessation of all the contaminants.

These are the ten. If bodhisattvas perfect these ten powers, then they are known as "Tathāgata," "Arhat," and "The One of Right and Perfect Enlightenment."

Sons of the Buddha, when the Tathāgata, the Arhat, the One of Right and Universal Enlightenment turns the wheel of the great Dharma, this is attended by ten kinds of phenomena. What are those ten? They are as follows:

First, he is perfectly fulfilled in the purification of the knowledge of the four types of fearlessness;

Second, he produces statements corresponding to the four types of unimpeded knowledge;

Third, he is well able to explain the aspects of the four truths;

Fourth, he accords with the unimpeded liberation of all buddhas;

Fifth, he is able to enable all beings' minds to acquire purified faith;

Sixth, nothing that he utters is spoken in vain, for it is able to extricate from beings the arrows smeared with the poison of suffering;

Seventh, he is aided in this by the power of greatly compassionate vows;

Eighth, whatever utterances he produces pervade all worlds throughout the ten directions;

Ninth, he ceaselessly proclaims the Dharma for *asaṃkhyeyas* of kalpas; and

Tenth, whatever dharmas he teaches are all able to produce the roots, the powers, the factors of enlightenment, the components of the path, the *dhyāna* concentrations, the liberations, the samādhis, and other such dharmas.

Sons of the Buddha, when the Buddha, the Tathāgata, turns the wheel of the Dharma, this is attended by countless other such phenomena as these.

Sons of the Buddha, when the Tathāgata, the Arhat, the One of Right and Perfect Enlightenment, turns the wheel of the Dharma, it is due to ten things that he plants the dharmas of purity in beings' minds and does not do so in vain. What are those ten? They are as follows:

It is due to the power of past vows;

It is due to being sustained by the great compassion;

It is due to never abandoning beings;

It is due to speaking Dharma for them with wisdom and sovereign mastery adapted to whatever they delight in;

It is due to definitely according with and never missing the right time;

It is due to adapting to what is fitting without speaking wrongly;

It is due to knowing the wisdom of the three periods of time, knowing it thoroughly and completely;

It is due to having a body which is most excellent and without peer;

It is due to his mastery of verbal expression which no one can completely fathom; and

It is due to his sovereign mastery of wisdom with which, whatever he says, it awakens everyone.

These are the ten.

Sons of the Buddha, after the Tathāgata, the Arhat, the One of Right and Perfect Enlightenment finishes accomplishing his buddha works, it is due to contemplating ten meaningful considerations that he then manifests entry into *parinirvāṇa*. What are those ten? They are as follows:

To demonstrate that all actions are truly impermanent;

To demonstrate that all conditioned phenomena are unstable;

To demonstrate that the great nirvāṇa is the station of peace and security free of anything to fear;

Because all humans and devas take pleasure in and are attached to the physical body, he does this to demonstrate that the physical body is an impermanent dharma and to induce them to wish to abide in the pure Dharma body;

To demonstrate that the power of impermanence cannot be turned aside;

To demonstrate that all conditioned phenomena do not exist in accordance with one's intentions and have no inherent existence of their own;

To demonstrate that all things in the three realms of existence are like magical conjurations which are not durable;

To demonstrate that the nature of nirvāṇa is ultimately solid and indestructible;

To demonstrate that all dharmas are unproduced and non-arising and yet they present the appearance of coming together and being destroyed; and

Sons of the Buddha, once the buddhas, the *bhagavats,* have finished their buddha works, have fulfilled whatever they have vowed to do, have turned the wheel of the Dharma, have taught and liberated those whom they should rightly teach and liberate, and have bestowed predictions on those bodhisattvas deserving of receiving their venerable titles, as a matter of what the Dharma should rightly entail, they then enter the changeless great *parinirvāṇa.*

Sons of the Buddha, these are what constitute the ten meaningful considerations of the Tathāgata, the Arhat, the One of Right and Perfect Enlightenment on account of which he manifests entry into *parinirvāṇa.*

Sons of the Buddha, this gateway into the Dharma is known as "the bodhisattva's vast pure practice" which countless buddhas all join in proclaiming. It enables the wise to completely comprehend countless meanings and become filled with joyous delight. It enables the great vows and great practices of all bodhisattvas to be continuously sustained.

Sons of the Buddha, if there are any beings who are able to hear this Dharma and, having heard it, then believe and understand it, and having understood it, then cultivate it—they will definitely be able to swiftly realize *anuttarasamyaksaṃbodhi.* And why is this? This is due to their having cultivated it in accordance with what has been taught.

Sons of the Buddha, if bodhisattvas do not practice in accordance with what has been taught, one should realize these people will forever remain apart from the bodhi of the Buddha. Therefore the bodhisattva should practice in accordance with what has been taught.

Sons of the Buddha, this "Transcending the World" chapter is the basis for the practice of all bodhisattvas' meritorious qualities and is the flower of the definitive meaning which everywhere enters all dharmas, which everywhere produces all-knowledge, which steps beyond all worlds, which abandons the paths of the two vehicles, which is not held in common with any other class of being, which is able to completely illuminate all Dharma gateways, and which increases beings' world-transcending roots of goodness. One should revere it, listen to it, recite it, remember it, reflect on it, admire and delight in it, and cultivate it. If one is able to proceed in this manner, one should realize that such a person will swiftly gain *anuttarasamyaksaṃbodhi.*

When the proclamation of this chapter concluded, due to the Buddha's spiritual powers and also because the Dharma of this Dharma gateway is of this very sort, the countlessly and boundlessly many *asaṃkhyeyas* of worlds throughout the ten directions all quaked and shook and bright light illuminated them all.

At that time, the buddhas of the ten directions all appeared directly before Samantabhadra Bodhisattva and praised him, saying:

It is good indeed, good indeed, O Son of the Buddha, that you have now been able to proclaim this "Transcending the World" chapter, the basis for the practice of the meritorious qualities of all bodhisattva-mahāsattvas and the flower of the definitive meaning which everywhere enters all dharmas of the Buddha.

O Son of the Buddha, you have already well trained in this Dharma and well proclaimed this Dharma. With your awesome powers, you guard and preserve this Dharma. We buddhas all rejoice in accord with this and, just as we buddhas all rejoice in accord with what you do, so too is this true of all other buddhas as well.

O Son of the Buddha, we buddhas are all of the same mind in protecting and preserving this sutra to enable it to be heard by all present and future bodhisattva congregations who have not yet heard it.

At that time, aided by the Buddha's spiritual powers, Samantabhadra Bodhisattva-mahāsattva surveyed all the great assemblies throughout the ten directions of the Dharma realm and then spoke these verses:

Having cultivated austere practices for countless kalpas,
he is born from the right Dharma of countless buddhas.
He enables countless beings to abide in bodhi.
Listen as I speak of his unexcelled practice.

His offerings to countless buddhas, his forsaking of attachments,
his extensive liberation of beings while not even conceiving of them,
his quest for a buddha's qualities with a mind depending on nothing,
and his supremely marvelous practices—I shall now speak of them.

He abandons the *māras* of the three realms and affliction-based karma,
perfects the *āryas'* meritorious qualities and most supreme practices,
and extinguishes all delusions with a quiescent mind.
I shall now describe the path that he travels.

He forever abandons all the world's deceptive illusions,
emanates many different transformations to teach beings.
The minds' arising, abiding, and ceasing—he manifests many things.
I shall describe his abilities to gladden the multitude.

His seeing of all beings' birth, aging, death, and
entanglement and oppression by afflictions' worries and calamities,
and his wish to liberate them and teach them to make the resolve—
You should listen as I describe his meritorious practices.

Giving, moral virtue, patience, vigor, dhyāna, wisdom, skillful means,
kindness, compassion, sympathetic joy, equanimity, and such—
always cultivating these for a hundred thousand myriads of kalpas—
You Worthy Ones should hear of that man's meritorious qualities.

Seeking bodhi for thousands of myriads of *koṭīs* of kalpas,
never being sparing of any of his bodies or lives,
wishing to benefit the many beings, not doing so for himself—
I shall now describe his kindly and sympathetic practices.

Even if one expounded on his qualities for countless *koṭīs* of kalpas,
it would be like but one drop in an ocean, not even a minor part of it.
His qualities are incomparable and indescribable even by analogy.
Aided by Buddha's awesome powers, I will now briefly tell of them.

His mind is free of any conception of anyone being either high or low
and, in seeking the path, he never grows weary.
He everywhere enables all beings
to abide in goodness and in the dharmas of increasing purity.

His wisdom everywhere benefits others
like a tree, like a river, like a spring,
and also like the great earth itself
which serves as the place upon which all things depend.

The bodhisattva is like a lotus flower
with roots of kindness, a stem of peace and security,
with wisdom forming its many stamens,
and moral virtue forming its fragrance and purity.

The Buddha emanates the light of the Dharma,
which enables him to bloom
and remain unattached to the waters of conditioned existence.
All who see him are delighted.

The bodhisattva's tree of the sublime Dharma
grows on the ground of the straight mind.
His faith forms its seed, kindness and compassion forms its roots,
and wisdom forms its trunk.

Skillful means form its boughs.
Five perfections form their dense growth.
Concentration forms its leaves, the superknowledges form its flowers,
and all-knowledge forms the fruit.
The most supreme powers are the birds.[496]
It lets fall its shade to shelter those in three realms of existence.

The bodhisattva lion king
takes the dharmas of pristine purity as his body,
the four truths as his feet,
and right mindfulness as his neck.

Kindness forms his eyes and wisdom his head.
The crown of his head is tied with the silk headband of the liberations.
In the valley of the emptiness of the supreme meaning,
he roars the Dharma and frightens the many *māra*s.

The bodhisattva acts as a caravan leader
who everywhere sees the many kinds of beings
residing in the wasteland wilderness of *saṃsāra*
in hazardous and evil places beset by the afflictions.

Having been lured there by Māra's bandits
and having been blinded by delusion, they have lost the right path.
He shows them the right and straight road
and enables them to enter the city of fearlessness.

The bodhisattva sees beings
sickened by the afflictions of the three poisons,
and tormented and persecuted through the long night [of *saṃsāra*]
by the many different kinds of misery and distress.

Having aroused the greatly compassionate mind for their sakes,
he extensively explains the means of counteractive treatment,

that, in their eighty-four thousand different varieties,
extinguish the illnesses of the many types of suffering.

The bodhisattva serves as a king of the Dharma
who uses the path of what is right to teach beings,
enabling them to distance themselves from evil, cultivate goodness,
and single-mindedly seek the Buddha's meritorious qualities.

In the abodes of all buddhas, he receives
the crown-anointing consecration and the *bhagavats'* predictions
and extensively gives to others the many kinds of wealth of the *aryas*
and the precious jewels of the enlightenment factors.

The bodhisattva turns the wheel of the Dharma
just like that which is turned by the Buddha.
Moral virtue forms its hubs and samādhi forms its rims.
Wisdom's strong intelligence serves as his sword.

Having destroyed the insurgents of the afflictions,
he then also puts an end to the many *māra* adversaries.
Of all those who follow non-Buddhist paths,
there are none who do not scatter when they see him.

The bodhisattva's ocean of wisdom
is deep, vast, and unbounded.
It is suffused with the flavor of right Dharma
and is filled with the jewels of the enlightenment factors.

His great mind has no bounding shore.
All-knowledge forms its tides.
Among beings, there are none able to fathom it.
Any attempt to describe it could never come to the end.

The bodhisattva's Sumeru Mountain
rises up beyond the world.
The spiritual superknowledges and samādhi are its peaks
and it is made stable and unshakable by his great resolve.

If anyone draws near to it,
they take on its same color of wisdom
which goes far beyond the many other spheres of cognition
and is such that no one does not see it.

The bodhisattva is like vajra
in his resolve to seek all-knowledge
His mind of faith and practice of the austerities
are steadfast and unshakable.

His mind has nothing that it fears
as he strives to benefit the many kinds of beings.

As for the many *māra*s as well as the afflictions,
he has completely vanquished them all.

The bodhisattva's great kindness and compassion
are like clouds that are layered and dense
from which the three clarities[497] send down their lightning flashes
and the quaking thunder of the spiritual powers resounds.

He everywhere uses the four types of eloquence[498]
to rain down the waters of the eight qualities
which moisten and soak everything
and cause the heat of the afflictions to be dispelled.

In the bodhisattva's city of right Dharma,
it is *prajñā* that forms its walls,
his sense of shame and dread of blame that form its deep moats,
and wisdom that forms its enemy-repelling battlements.

He opens wide the gates to liberation and
relies on right mindfulness for constant protection and preservation,
the four truths to level the King's path,
and the six superknowledges to assemble his troops and armaments.

In addition, he raises the great Dharma banners
that are arrayed all around below him
so that, of all the hordes of *māras* of the three realms of existence,
there are none at all who are able to enter there.

For the bodhisattva, like a *garuḍa,*
it is his foundations of psychic power[499] that serve as his solid footing,
his skillful means that serve as the wings of his courage,
and kindness and compassion that serve him as bright and clear eyes.

Dwelling in the tree of all-knowledge
he surveys the great ocean of the three realms of existence,
pounces upon and clutches up the celestial and human dragons,
and sets them then on the shore of nirvāṇa.

The bodhisattva's sun of right Dharma
rises and appears in the world.
The moral precepts form its round and full orb
and the spiritual power of psychic travel propels its swift transit.

Its illumination with the light of wisdom
grows the medicinal herbs of the roots and the powers,
extinguishes the darkness of the afflictions,
and dries up the ocean of desire.

The bodhisattva's moon of wisdom light
takes the Dharma realm as its orbit

as it travels through the emptiness of the ultimate truth.
Of those who abide in the world, there are none who do not see it.

In the minds of the conscious beings within the three realms
it waxes and wanes in accordance with the time.
Among all the stars and constellations of the two vehicles,
there are none who are capable of comparing to it.

The body adorned with the meritorious qualities
possessed by the bodhisattva, the great king of the Dharma,
is complete in all the major marks and secondary signs
to which all humans and devas gaze up in admiration.

With the pure eyes of skillful means
and the vajra scepter of wisdom,
he attains sovereign mastery in the Dharma
and uses the path to teach the many kinds of beings.

The bodhisattva, like a great Brahma Heaven king,
with sovereign mastery, steps beyond the three realms of existence,
cuts off all the karma and afflictions, and, of kindness,[500] [compassion,
sympathetic joy], and equanimity, there are none he does not possess.

He manifests his body in every place
and, using the sound of the Dharma, instigates awakening,
and, in all those three realms of existence,
he extricates the very roots of all the wrong views.

The bodhisattva, like a *parinirmita-vaśavartin* deva,
steps beyond the grounds of *saṃsāra,*
has spheres of cognition that are always pure,
and possesses wisdom that has become irreversible.

He cuts off the paths of those lower vehicles,
receives the dharmas of the crown-anointing consecration,
becomes completely equipped with merit and wisdom,
and achieves such fame that no one does not hear of him.

The bodhisattva's mind of wisdom
is as pure as empty space.
It has no inherently existent nature, has nothing it depends upon,
and, for it, there is nothing at all that is apprehensible.

He is possessed of the power of the great sovereign masteries
by which he is able to accomplish works in the world.
Possessed of pure practice himself,
he enables beings to also do the same.

The bodhisattva's earth of skillful means
bestows benefit on all beings.

The bodhisattva's water of kindness and compassion
washes away all the afflictions.

The bodhisattva's fire of wisdom
burns up the tinder of all afflictions and habitual karmic propensities.
The bodhisattva's wind of non-abiding
roams through the emptiness of the three realms of existence.[501]

The bodhisattva is like a precious jewel
that is able to rescue beings from poverty and hardship.
The bodhisattva is like vajra
that is able to smash the inverted views.

The bodhisattva is like a pearl necklace
adorning the body of the three realms of existence.
The bodhisattva is like a [wish-fulfilling] *maṇi* jewel[502]
that is able to produce growth in all the practices.

The bodhisattva's qualities are like flowers
that always bloom with the enlightenment factors.[503]
The bodhisattva's vows are like garlands
that constantly tie [the topknots atop] the heads of beings.

The bodhisattva's fragrance of purity in the moral precepts
stems from solidly observing them without deficiency or infraction.
The bodhisattva's perfume of wisdom
everywhere imbues the three realms of existence with its scent.

The bodhisattva's powers are like screens
that are able to block the dust of the afflictions.
The bodhisattva's wisdom is like a banner
that is able to vanquish the enemy of pride.

His sublime practices are like silk pennants
serving as adornments for his wisdom.
A sense of shame and dread of blame serve as robes
everywhere covering the many kinds of beings.

The bodhisattva's unimpeded vehicle,
when mounted, allows him to escape from the three realms.
The bodhisattva's elephant of his great powers
is possessed of the mind that is well trained.

The bodhisattva's horse of travel by spiritual powers
leaps up and steps beyond all realms of existence.
The bodhisattvas Dharma-proclaiming dragon
everywhere rains Dharma into the minds of beings.

The bodhisattva, like the *udumbara* flower,
is only rarely ever encountered in the world.

The bodhisattva, like the greatly courageous general,
conquers all the many *māras*.

The bodhisattva's turning of the wheel of the Dharma
is like that turned by the Buddha.
The bodhisattva's lamp dispels the darkness
so that beings then see the right path.

The bodhisattva's river of meritorious qualities
constantly follows the flow of the right path.
The bodhisattva's bridge of vigor
extensively takes across to liberation all the many kinds of beings.

His great wisdom and vast vows
together create a solid and durable ship
into which he welcomes all beings
before he then places them securely on the shore of bodhi.

In the bodhisattva's gardens of easeful mastery,
he provides beings with genuine bliss.
The bodhisattva's flowers of liberation
adorn his temple of wisdom.

The bodhisattva is like a marvelous herbal medicine
that utterly extinguishes the illness of the afflictions.
The bodhisattva is like a snowy mountain
on which there grows the herbal medicine of wisdom.

The bodhisattva is the same as the Buddha
in his awakening of the many kinds of beings.
How could there be anything else in the mind of the Buddha
other than right enlightenment and the enlightenment of the world?

Just as the Buddha has come forth,
so too does the bodhisattva come forth.
So too, like the Omniscient One,
he uses wisdom to enter the universal gateway.

The bodhisattva skillfully guides
all the many kinds of beings.
The bodhisattva naturally awakens
to the sphere of cognition of all-knowledge.

The bodhisattva's measureless powers
are such that no one in the world can destroy them.
With his fearlessnesses and wisdom, the bodhisattva
knows beings as well as dharmas.

All of the worlds,
the differences in their forms and characteristics,

their languages, and also their names—
He is able to distinguish and know them all.

Although he has transcended both name and form,
he still manifests the many different kinds of appearances.
Of all the beings there are,
there are none who are able to fathom his path.

All such meritorious qualities as these—
the bodhisattva perfects them all.
He understands all natures as having no [inherently existent] nature
and has no attachment to either existence or nonexistence.

In this way, all-knowledge
is endless and free of anything on which it depends.
I shall now expound on this
to enable beings to rejoice.

Although he knows all the characteristic marks of dharmas
as like mere conjured illusions that are all empty and quiescent,
he still uses the resolve of his compassionate vows
as well as the Buddha's awesome spiritual powers,

manifesting transformations with his spiritual superknowledges
by which he brings forth countless phenomena of all different sorts.
You should all listen
as I speak of meritorious qualities such as these.

With a single body, he is able to manifest
countless different bodies as,
without mind or object,
he everywhere responds to all beings.

With but a single sound, he completely expounds
in all different kinds of voices
with the methods of beings' speech,
so that, as befits their type, he is able to interact with them all.

He forever transcends the body affected by the afflictions
and instead manifests bodies possessed of sovereign mastery.
Though he realizes that dharmas are beyond explanation,
he still engages in all kinds of different explanations.

His mind is always quiescent,
pure, and like empty space,
and yet he everywhere adorns *kṣetras*
and appears in all congregations.

He has no attachment to the body,
and yet he is able to manifest bodies.

Within all the worlds,
he takes on births according to whatever is fitting.

Although he takes birth in all places,
he still does not abide in taking on births,
for he realizes the body is like empty space
as, according with beings' minds, he appears in various ways.

The body of the bodhisattva is boundless
and everywhere appears in all places.
He always reveres and makes offerings
to the most revered ones of all who stand on two feet.[504]

Whether it be incense, flowers, the many kinds of music,
banners, pennants or bejeweled canopies,
he constantly uses a deep and pure mind
in presenting offerings to all buddhas.

He never leaves the assembly of any single buddha,
and yet he is everywhere in the presence of all buddhas
where, in the midst of their great assemblies,
he inquires on difficult points and listens to the Dharma.

He listens to the Dharma and enters samādhi
through every one of its countless gateways.
So too it is when he arises from these meditative absorptions,
manifesting endless appearances.

With his wisdom and skillful means,
he completely understands the world as like a mere illusion
and yet is still able to manifest in the world
boundlessly many illusory dharmas.

He manifests in many different forms
while also manifesting thoughts and words.
He enters into the web of conceptions,
and yet remains forever free of attachments.

Sometimes he manifests as one making the initial resolve
or as one who benefits those in the world.
Sometimes he manifests as one who has long cultivated
practices that are boundlessly vast

of giving, moral virtue, patience, vigor,
dhyāna concentration, wisdom,
the four *brāhma-vihāras*, the four means of attraction, and the others
among all those most supreme of dharmas.

Sometimes he manifests as one whose practice has become fulfilled
and has attained the patience free of discriminations.

Sometimes he manifests as one tied to but one more birth
upon whom all buddhas bestow the crown-anointing consecration.

Sometimes he manifests as bearing the marks of a *śrāvaka* disciple,
or instead manifests as a *pratyekabuddha,*
or as, in place after place, entering *parinirvāṇa,*
even as he still never relinquishes the bodhi practices.

Sometimes he manifests as Lord Śakra,
sometimes manifests as a Brahma Heaven king,
sometimes as surrounded by celestial maidens,
and sometimes as alone in silent meditation.

Sometimes he manifests as a *bhikṣu,*
abiding in quiescence, training his own mind.
Sometimes he manifests as a Paranirmita Vaśavartin Heaven king
who governs over the laws of the world.

Sometimes he manifests as a woman skilled in the arts,
sometimes manifests as one who cultivates austere practices,
sometimes manifests as indulging the five types of desire,
and sometimes manifests as entering the *dhyāna* absorptions.

Sometimes he manifests as one but newly born,
sometimes as a youth, or sometimes as one who is old or dying.
Were someone to try to contemplate and conceive of these matters,
his mind might become so plagued by doubts as to be driven mad.

Sometimes he manifests as abiding in a celestial palace,
sometimes manifests as having just spiritually descended from there,
sometimes as entering and sometimes as abiding in the womb, and
sometimes as attaining buddhahood and turning the Dharma wheel.

Sometimes it is as being born, sometimes as entering nirvāṇa,
and sometimes he manifests as entering the halls of study.
Sometimes it is as abiding in the midst of courtesans and
sometimes it is as leaving a common man's life to cultivate *dhyāna.*

Sometimes it is as sitting beneath the bodhi tree,
and then naturally gaining right enlightenment.
Sometimes he manifests as turning the wheel of the Dharma
and sometimes he manifests as having just begun to seek the path.

Sometimes he manifests in the body of a buddha,
calmly sitting in meditation in countless *kṣetras.*
Sometimes it is as cultivating irreversibility in the path,
accumulating the provisions essential to realizing bodhi,

or as deeply entering innumerable kalpas in which,
in every case, he reaches the far shore of perfection,

making countless kalpas become but a single mind-moment,
and making a single mind-moment include countless kalpas,

realizing all kalpas as but non-kalpas even as,
for the sake of the world, he manifests kalpas, and even as,
though he has no coming forth and has no such accumulation,
he accomplishes all his works in all those kalpas.

In but a single atom,
he everywhere sees all buddhas
and sees that, throughout the ten directions, and in all places,
there is no place where they do not exist.

He perceives in a sequentially orderly fashion
all dharmas associated with the lands and their beings
and their passing through a measureless number of kalpas,
the bounds of which, one could ultimately never exhaust.

The bodhisattva's knowing of beings
is so vast as to be boundless.
Even but a single one of those beings' bodies
arises due to countless causes and conditions.

Just as he knows these countless factors for any single one of them,
so too is this true of all others as well.
As befits whatever his penetrating comprehension has understood,
he proceeds then to teach all those who have not yet been trained.

He knows the faculties of all beings,
the differences in those who are superior, middling, and inferior,
and also knows how such faculties transform and develop,
and whether they should or should not then be taught.

Whether it be but a single faculty or all faculties,
or how they evolve through the power of causes and conditions,
he distinguishes the different subtleties involved in these
in a sequentially precise way free of error or disorder.

He also knows their desires and understandings,
all their afflictions and habitual karmic propensities,
and also knows with respect to their past, future, and present,
the course of all their thoughts and actions.

He completely comprehends all their actions
and that they neither come nor go.
Having thus known their actions,
he then explains for them the unexcelled Dharma.
As for their defiled actions and their pure actions,
he completely knows them all in all their many different varieties.

In but a single mind-moment, he attains bodhi
and achieves the perfection of all-knowledge.
He abides in the Buddha's inconceivable
mind of ultimate wisdom in which,
in but a single mind-moment, he is able to know
all the actions in which beings engage.

The bodhisattva's spiritual superknowledges, wisdom, and
power of skill in these has already attained such sovereign mastery
that he is able in but a single mind-moment
to travel and visit boundlessly many *kṣetras*.

He goes forth with such swiftness as this
throughout countless kalpas
in which there is no place he has not thus been everywhere present
even as, in all of this, he never moves even as far as the tip of a hair.

Just as in a case where a master conjurer
manifests all kinds of different forms,
if one searches in the midst of those illusions,
there would be nothing there that either has form or is formless,

so too it is with the bodhisattva when,
using the conjurations of skillful means and wisdom,
he produces all different kinds of manifestations
which completely fill the world.

Just as when the clearly shining sun and moon
beaming brightly in the midst of space
are reflected in the many bodies of water
and yet never become mixed with those waters,

one should realize that this is also just so
in the case of the bodhisattva's sphere of pure Dharma
when it appears in the waters of worldlings' minds
and yet never becomes mixed up with the world.

Just as, in a sleeping person's dream,
he may accomplish many different endeavors in which,
though he seems to have passed through thousands of *koṭīs* of years,
he has not yet even reached the end of that one single night,

so too, the bodhisattva, abiding in the nature of dharmas,
manifests all kinds of phenomena
that could stretch to the end of countless kalpas
even as his single mind-moment of wisdom is endless.

Just as in a mountain valley
or within a palace

many different sounds are all echoed
when, in truth, they do not distinguish among them,

so too, the bodhisattva abiding in the nature of dharmas
is able with masterful wisdom
to extensively emanate sounds according to each person's type
even as he is still free of any discriminations about them.

Just as, if one sees a mirage,
he may imagine it to be water
and race off after it, only to never find anything to drink,
so that, as a consequence, he becomes ever more thirsty,

so too it is with beings' affliction-ridden minds.
One should realize they are also just like this.
The bodhisattva arouses kindness and sympathy
to rescue them and enable them to make their escape.

He contemplates "form" as like a mass of sea foam,
"feelings" as like bubbles floating atop the water,
"perceptions" as like heat-wave mirages in the hot season,
"karmic formative factors" as like the stalk of the plantain,[505]

and the mind's "consciousnesses" as like conjured illusions
manifesting the many different kinds of phenomena.
Just so does he know the aggregates
for which the wise one has no attachment.

All the sense bases[506] are empty, quiescent, and
like a mechanism as they move and turn about.
All the sense realms[507] are forever free of any nature
even as they present a false appearance in the world.

The bodhisattva abides in the genuine
quiescence of the ultimate truth,
extensively and freely proclaiming it in many different ways,
and yet his mind remains free of anything upon which it depends.

He has neither any coming nor any going
and also has no abiding either.
The causes of suffering in the karma of the afflictions
constantly flow on and transform in three different ways.[508]

Conditioned origination is neither existent nor nonexistent,
and neither real nor insubstantial.
It is in this way that he enters the middle way.
In explaining it, he remains free of any attachment at all.

He is able in but a single mind-moment
to everywhere manifest the mind of the three periods of time

in all the many different kinds of phenomena
within the desire realm, the form realm, and the formless realm.

He accords with the three types of moral deportment,[509]
expounds on the three gates to liberation,[510]
establishes the paths of the Three Vehicles,[511]
and achieves the complete realization of all-knowledge.

He attains the complete comprehension of what is and is not possible,
of all karmic actions, of all faculties,
of the realms, understandings, and dhyāna concentrations,
of the points to which all paths lead,

of past life recall, of the heavenly eye,
and of the complete extinguishing of all delusions.
He knows the Buddha's ten powers,
but is not yet able to bring them to complete fulfillment.

He completely comprehends the emptiness of all dharmas,
and yet he always seeks the sublime Dharma.
He does not become involved with the afflictions,
and yet he still does not completely put an end to the contaminants.

He possesses a vast knowledge of the paths to emancipation,
and yet he uses them to liberate beings.
In this, he has attained the fearlessnesses
and still never relinquishes his cultivation of all the practices.

He remains free of error and free of any contradiction of the path,
and still never loses right mindfulness.
His vigor, zeal, and samādhi
as well as his wisdom arising from contemplation never diminish.[512]

He remains pure in all three accumulations of moral virtue,[513]
has a clear comprehension of all three periods of time,
treats beings with great kindness and sympathetic pity,
and, in all that he does, remains free of all obstacles.

It is due to having entered these gateways into the Dharma
that he has succeeded in perfecting practices such as these.
I describe here but a minor measure
of the meaning of his adornments with such meritorious qualities.

Even if one exhausted countless kalpas in trying to do so,
one could still never finish describing all his practices.
I now only describe but a small portion of them
comparable to a single mote of dust as contrasted with the great earth.

Abiding in reliance upon the Buddha's wisdom,
he brings forth extraordinary thought,

cultivates the most supreme practices,
and achieves complete fulfillment of great kindness and compassion.

Intensely diligent, yet personally abiding in tranquility,
he carries on the teaching of all sentient beings.
Having established himself in the pure precepts of moral virtue,
he fulfills all the practices leading to the bestowal of the prediction.[514]

He is able to penetrate the meritorious qualities of the Buddha,
the practices related to beings, and the *kṣetras*.
He also knows all the kalpas and periods of time,[515]
and yet never has any thoughts of weariness.

With differentiating wisdom and the complete-retention *dhāraṇīs*,
he reaches a penetrating comprehension of the true meaning.
He contemplates and expounds upon the incomparable,
and quiescently proceeds toward the right and perfect enlightenment.

He has brought forth the resolve of Samantabhadra
and also cultivates his conduct and vows.
By the power of kindness and compassion's causes and conditions,
he proceeds along the path with purity of mind.

He cultivates the *pāramitās*
and perfects the wisdom arising pursuant to awakening.
He achieves the realization of the powers and the sovereign masteries
and then attains the unexcelled bodhi.

He perfects the wisdom cognizing uniform equality
and expounds the most supreme Dharma.
He is able to preserve it and possesses sublime eloquence
and then arrives at the position of the king of the Dharma.

He abandons all attachments
and expounds on impartiality of mind.
Bringing forth his wisdom,
he transformationally manifests the realization of bodhi.

He preserves [the Dharma] in all kalpas
in ways that please and comfort the wise.
He deeply penetrates it, relies on it,
and becomes fearless and free of doubts.

He completely comprehends the inconceivable,
ably distinguishes the expedient and esoteric,
skillfully enters all the samādhis,
and everywhere perceives the spheres of wisdom.

He completely attains all the liberations,
achieves easeful mastery in the superknowledges,

forever abandons all of the entangling bonds,
and, in this, is as if roaming at will, abiding in parks and groves.

The dharmas of purity serve as his palace
and he finds all the practices to be delightful.
He manifests measureless adornments
and abides in the world with an unmoving mind.

With the deep mind, he skillfully contemplates,
and with marvelous eloquence, he is able to expound the Dharma.
He acquires the seal of pure bodhi
and illuminates everything with the light of wisdom.

The place where he dwells is one that no one can equal.
His mind does not involve itself with anything inferior.
He establishes resolve as [solid as] a great mountain
and the meritorious qualities he possesses are like a deep ocean.

He abides in the Dharma like a jewel,
dons the armor of the resolve of his vows,
and initiates all the great works
which can never be ruined by anyone.

He acquires the prediction of his realization of bodhi
and securely dwells in his vast resolve.
His treasury of esoteric knowledge is inexhaustible
and he becomes awakened in all the dharmas.

He attains sovereign mastery of all worldly knowledge
and is unimpeded in the sublime uses to which he applies it,
whether it be among beings, in all the *kṣetras,*
or in the sphere of the many different dharmas.

Through his bodies, vows, spheres of action,
wisdom, spiritual superknowledges, and such,
he brings forth manifestations within the world
numbering in countless hundreds of thousands of *koṭīs.*

Whether in his easeful mastery or in his spheres of action,
he possesses sovereign mastery which none can constrain.
All of his karmic actions are adorned
with the powers, the fearlessnesses, and the exclusive dharmas.[516]

In all his bodies and physical actions
and in his speaking as well as in his purified speech,
through having become one who is protected,
he succeeds in accomplishing ten kinds of things.[517]

In the bodhisattva's initial generation of the resolve
as well as in his mind's universally pervasive presence,

all of his faculties become undistracted
and he thus acquires the most supreme faculties.

Abiding in the deep mind and the especially superior mind,
he abandons all flattery and deception
and, through all different kinds of decisive understanding,
he everywhere enters the worlds.

He relinquishes his afflictions and habitual karmic propensities,
takes up this most supreme of paths,
skillfully cultivates it and brings it to complete fulfillment,
and then arrives at the realization of all-knowledge.

He goes beyond reversibility, enters the right and fixed position,[518]
achieves the definite realization of quiescence,
brings forth the path of the Buddha's Dharma, and
perfects the bases for the names of those with meritorious qualities.[519]

The path, the path of the immeasurable,
and so forth, on through to the path of adornment—
He successively becomes well established in each of them,
yet remains free of attachment to any of them.

His hands, feet, belly, and organs,
his heart made of vajra—
He cloaks them in the armor of kindness and deep sympathy
and thus becomes completely protected with the many weapons.

Wisdom serves as his head, clear comprehension as his eyes,
the bodhi practices as his ears,
and purity in the moral precepts as his nose.
Thus he dispels the darkness and remains free of obstacles.

He takes the types of eloquence as his tongue,
his ability to have no place he does not go as his body,
and the most supreme wisdom as his mind.
Walking and standing, he cultivates his actions.
He sits on the lion throne at the site of enlightenment,
lies down as in the Brahma heavens, and stands in emptiness.

In whatever he practices and contemplates,
he everywhere illuminates the Tathāgata's sphere of action.
He everywhere contemplates the actions of beings,
enters the lion-stretch [samādhi], and roars the lion's roar.

He abandons covetousness, practices pure giving,
relinquishes arrogance, and upholds purity in the moral precepts.
He does not become angry, always abides in patience,
does not become indolent, and is constantly vigorous.

He attains sovereign mastery in the *dhyāna* absorptions,
and, in his exercise of wisdom, has nothing at all that he practices.
With kindness he rescues beings and in compassion he is tireless.
He rejoices in the Dharma and with equanimity abandons afflictions.

In all spheres of experience,
he knows the meaning and he knows the Dharma.
His stock of merit has been brought to complete fulfillment
and his wisdom has become like sharp sword.

He everywhere casts his illumination, delights in extensive learning,
and progresses in the Dharma with complete understanding.
He is aware of the *māras* and the paths of the *māras*
and vows to leave them all behind.

He observes the Buddha as well as the works of the Buddha
and resolves to accumulate them all.
He abandons pride, cultivates wisdom,
and does not become possessed by the power of Māra.

He is drawn forth and supported by the Buddha
and is also supported by the Dharma.
He manifests as dwelling in the Tuṣita Heaven,
and then also appears to reach the end of his life there.

He then manifests as dwelling in his mother's womb
even as he also manifests subtle endeavors.
He manifests taking birth as well as the subtle smile,
and also appears as walking seven steps.

He manifests the cultivation of the many skills and arts
and also manifests as dwelling deep within the palace,
leaving the home life, cultivating the austerities,
and then going to the site of enlightenment.

There he sits up straight, emanating light,
and awakens the many kinds of beings.
He subdues the *māras*, gains right enlightenment,
turns the wheel of the unexcelled Dharma,
and then when his manifestations have come to an end,
he then enters the great nirvāṇa.

As for all of those bodhisattva practices
which he cultivates for countless kalpas,
they are so boundlessly expansive,
that I now describe only a small fraction of them.

Although he enables countless beings
to become established in the Buddha's meritorious qualities,

of those beings and those dharmas,
there is ultimately nothing on which he seizes.

He completely fulfills practices such as these,
gains such easeful mastery of all the spiritual superknowledges
that he can place the many *kṣetras* on the tip of a single hair
and pass through thousands of *koṭīs* of kalpas.

Holding countless *kṣetras* in his palm,
he travels everywhere, never feeling any physical weariness,
and then returns to place them in their original location,
as the beings in them remain unaware.

The bodhisattva may take all
the many different kinds of adorned *kṣetras*
and place them in a single pore
so that everyone can see them as they truly are.

He may also take all the oceans
and place them in but a single pore
without those great oceans either increasing or diminishing
and without those beings being either disturbed or harmed.

Suppose he took countless iron ring mountains,
grasped them in his hand, ground them to particles,
then set down but one of those particles in each *kṣetra,*
doing so until all those particles were used up.

Suppose too that he took all those *kṣetras* as many as those particles
and again ground them all into particles.
Though one might calculate the number of all those particles,
he would still find it difficult to measure this bodhisattva's wisdom.

He may emanate so countlessly many light rays
from within but a single pore
that the light of the sun, moon, stars, and constellations,
the blazing light of the *maṇi* jewels,

and the light of all the devas
are all completely outshone by that light
which extinguishes all the sufferings in the wretched destinies
as he then proclaims for them the unexcelled Dharma.

The many different kinds of voices
within all worlds—
with but a single voice, the bodhisattva
is able to speak them all.

He decisively distinguishes and explains
all dharmas of all buddhas,

everywhere enabling the many kinds of beings
to feel immense joy upon hearing them explained.

He is able to take all kalpas of the past
and place them into the future and the present
and is able to take the kalpas of the future and present
and place them far back into the past.

He shows countless *kṣetras*
burning, forming, and abiding,
and shows all worlds
entirely contained in a single pore.

Of all the buddhas throughout the ten directions
of the future as well as of the present,
there are none of them that are not clearly revealed
within his very own body.

Deeply knowing the methods of transformation,
he skillfully responds to the minds of beings
by manifesting all kinds of different bodies,
and even so, he retains no attachment to any of them.

He may appear within the six destinies of rebirth
in the bodies of all kinds of beings,
appearing in the body of Brahma, Śakra, or a world-protecting deva,
in the body of a deva or human,

in the body of a *śrāvaka* disciple or *pratyekabuddha,*
in the body of buddhas, the *tathāgatas,*
or he may appear in the body of a bodhisattva
who is cultivating the path to all-knowledge.

He skillfully enters into the web of thought
of beings possessed of weak, middling, and superior capacities,
manifesting the realization of bodhi
as well as all the buddha *kṣetras.*

He completely knows the web of all thought,
attains sovereign mastery in such thought,
and then reveals the cultivation of the bodhisattva practices
and all the works in which he uses skillful means.

He manifests all such as these
of his vast spiritual transformations.
All his spheres of action such as these
are such that no one in the entire world could ever know.

Although he manifests them, he has no manifestations at all,
for ultimately they are transmutations of what is most supreme

which are thus adapted to the minds of beings
to enable them to practice the genuine path.
His body, speech, and mind
are all equally comparable to empty space.

His purity in the moral precepts is his perfume
and his many practices are his robes.
His silken headband of Dharma adorns his topknot of purity
which is crested by the *maṇi* jewel of all-knowledge.

Of all the meritorious qualities, there are none that are not complete.
By the crown-anointing consecration, he ascends to the royal throne.
Taking the *pāramitās* as his wheel,
all the spiritual superknowledges as his elephant,

the spiritual power of psychic travel as his horse,
wisdom as his shining jewel,
the sublime practices as his maiden retainers,
the four means of attraction as his minister overseeing the treasury,

and the skillful means as the lord's armies,
the bodhisattva thus appears like a wheel-turning king.
His samādhis serve as his city's surrounding walls,
and emptiness and quiescence serve as his palace and royal hall.[520]

Kindness is his armor and wisdom his sword,
whereas mindfulness is his bow and sharp faculties[521] are his arrows.
He raises high the canopy of his spiritual powers,
erects the banners of his wisdom,

remains unshaken due to the power of patience,
and straightaway demolishes the armies of the king of the *māras*.
His complete-retention *dhāraṇīs* serve him as level ground,
his manifold practices are his rivers and streams,

his pure wisdom serves as gushing springs,
and his sublime wisdom serves as his forest groves.
Emptiness serves as his limpid pristine ponds
and the enlightenment factors serve as his lotus flowers.

He adorns himself with the spiritual powers,
and always delights in samādhi.
He takes meditative contemplations as his maiden retainers,
takes the elixir of immortality as his delectable sustenance,
and takes the flavors of liberation as his broth
as he roams with easeful mastery in the Three Vehicles.

As for all of these bodhisattva practices,
their sublimity becomes ever more supreme.

He cultivates them for measurelessly many kalpas
during which his resolve remains ever tireless.

He makes offerings to all buddhas
and purifies all the *kṣetras*
as he everywhere enables all beings
to become securely established in all-knowledge.

Though one might be able to know the number
of all the atoms in all *kṣetras,*
though one might measure all the realms of empty space
using but a single sand grain [as his ruler],

and though one might be able to count all beings' thoughts
in every successive mind-moment—
one could still never reach the end of any description
of all the meritorious qualities possessed by this Buddha's son.

If one wishes to possess these meritorious qualities
as well as all of these superior and sublime dharmas—
If one wishes too to cause all beings
to abandon suffering and always abide in happiness—

And if one wishes to enable his own body, speech, and mind
to become the same as those of all the buddhas,
then one should arouse the vajra-like resolve
and train in these meritorious qualities and practices.

The End of Chapter Thirty-Eight

Volume Two Endnotes

1. "Clear knowledges" refers here to the "three knowledges" (*trividyā*): 1) The remembrance of previous lives (*pūrvavanivāsānusmṛti*); 2) Knowledge of beings' rebirth destinies (*cyutyupapattijñāna*); and 3) Knowledge of the destruction of the contaminants or "taints" (*āsravakṣaya*).
2. A *bodhimaṇḍa* is the "site of enlightenment" wherein enlightenment is cultivated and fully realized. It may be used as a general reference to Buddhist temples, though it often refers specifically to the site beneath the bodhi tree where a buddha gains complete realization of the utmost, right, and perfect enlightenment.
3. The "wheel of Dharma" or "Dharma wheel" (*dharmacakra*) refers to the eight-spoked wheel emblematic of the Buddha's teaching of the eightfold path of the *āryas* or "noble ones" consisting of right views, right thought or intention, right speech, right physical action, right livelihood, right effort, right mindfulness, and right meditative absorption (*samādhi*).
4. As a Buddhist technical term, "Dharma realm" or "dharma realm," *dharma-dhātu,* has at least several levels of meaning, of which this refers to the second of the three listed below:
   1) At the most granular level, "dharma realm" refers to the objective contents of one of the eighteen sense realms, dharmas as "objects of mind" (*dharma-āyatana*);
   2) In the most cosmically and metaphysically vast sense, "Dharma realm" refers in aggregate to all conventionally existent phenomena and the universally pervasive noumenal "true suchness" (*tathatā*) that is the nature of all of those phenomena. In this sense, it is identical with the "Dharma body" (*dharma-kāya*);
   3) As a classifying term, "dharma realm" is used to distinguish realms of existence (as in "the ten dharma realms" that consist of the realms of buddhas, bodhisattvas, *śrāvaka* disciples, *pratyekabuddhas,* devas, *asuras,* humans, animals, hungry ghosts, and hell-dwellers) or metaphysical modes of existence (as in the "four dharma realms" of the Huayan hermeneutic tradition that speaks of: a] the dharma realm of the "noumenal" [synonymous with emptiness or *śūnyatā*]; b] the dharma realm of the "phenomenal"; c] the dharma realm of the unimpeded interpenetration of the phenomenal and the noumenal; and d] the dharma realm of the unimpeded interpenetration of all phenomena with all other phenomena in a manner that resonates somewhat with quantum entanglement and non-locality).

5. An "ineffable"(*anabhilāpya*) is a specific nearly unimaginably large number that is the 120th of 123 numbers described in Chapter Thirty of the Flower Adornment Sutra wherein each of those numbers is defined as being the square of the immediately previous number the first of which is a *lakṣa* (100,000).
6. Per DSBC, the Sanskrit names of these bodhisattva-mahāsattvas, (37 in BB and KB, 38 in BR, 39 in SA, SD and the Sanskrit) are:

   Vajragarbha, Ratnagarbha, Padmagarbha, Śrīgarbha, Padmaśrīgarbha, Ādityagarbha, Sūryagarbha, Kṣitigarbha, Śaśivimalagarbha, Sarvavyūhālaṃkārapratibhāsasaṃdarśanagar bha, Jñānavairocanagarbha, Ruciraśrīgarbha, Candanaśrīgarbha, Puṣpaśrīgarbha, Kusumaśrīgarbha, Utpalaśrīgarbha, Devaśrīgarbha, Puṇyaśrīgarbha, Anāvaraṇajñānaviśuddhigarbha, Guṇaśrīgarbha, Nārāyaṇaśrīgarbha, Amalagarbha, Vimalagarbha, Vicitrapratibhānālaṃkāragarbha, Mahāraśmijālāvabhāsagarbha, Vimalaprabhāsaśrītejorājagarbha, Sarvalakṣaṇapratimaṇ ḍitaviśuddhiśrīgarbha, Vajrārciḥśrīvatsālaṃkāragarbha, Jyotirjvalanārciḥśrīgarbha, Nakṣatrarājaprabhāvabhāsagarbha, Gaganakośānāvaraṇajñānagarbha, Anāvaraṇasvaramaṇḍalamadhur anirghoṣagarbha, Dhāraṇīmukhasarvajagatpraṇidhisaṃdhāraṇagar bha, Sāgaravyūhagarbha, Meruśrīgarbha, Sarvaguṇaviśuddhigarbha, Tathāgataśrīgarbha, Buddhaśrīgarbha, and Vimukticandra.
7. Jñānavairocanagarbha.
8. Anāvaraṇajñānaviśuddhigarbha.
9. Gaganakośānāvaraṇajñānagarbha.
10. A mahāsattva is a "great bodhisattva," one who has practiced the bodhisattva path for countless kalpas.
11. Most of these numerical descriptors: "countless" (perhaps equals an "innumerable" [*agaṇeya* = 112th level]), "measureless" (*aparimāṇa* = 106th level), "boundless" (*aparyanta* = 108th level), "unequalable" (*asamanta* = 110th level), "innumerable" (*agaṇeya* = 112th level), "indescribable" (*atulya* = 114th level), "inconceivable" (*acintya* = 116th level) "immeasurable" (*ameya* = 118th level), and "ineffable" (*anabhilāpya* = 120th level) represent a specific nearly unimaginably large number described in Chapter Thirty, "Asaṃkhyeyas," of the Flower Adornment Sutra wherein each of those numbers is defined as being the square of the immediately previous number the first of which is a *lakṣa* (100,000).
12. Although the Sanskrit refers here to this samādhi as "the bodhisattva samādhi known as 'the light of the Great Vehicle' (*mahāyānaprabhāsaṃ nāma bodhisattvasamādhiṃ*)," this may be a later textual modification of the text, for both SA and KB refer to it as "the great wisdom light samādhi."

13. A *koṭi* is a number that is defined in the Flower Adornment Sutra Chapter 30 as the product of multiplying a *lakṣa* (100,000) by a *lakṣa*. Hence it equals 10,000,000, i.e. ten million.

14. The text refers here to the first three of the ten standard names for a buddha.

15. "Contaminants" here translates the slightly ambiguous pre-Buddhist Jain term *āsrava*, translated into Chinese as "flows" (漏). The allusion is to the defiling influence (read "influents") of either three or four factors, as follows: 1) sensual desire (*kāma*); 2) [craving for] becoming (*bhāva*), i.e. the craving for continued existence; 3) ignorance (*avidyā*), i.e. delusion; 4) views (*dṛṣṭi*) This fourth type is not included in some listings. Often-encountered alternate translations include "taints," "outflows," "influxes," and "fluxes."

16. The Sanskrit references "*mahāprajñā*" here.

17. "*suviniścitamatikauśalyatāṃ*."

18. "*tathāgatavaiśāradyānavalīnatāṃ*."

19. The DSBC Sanskrit (*pratisaṃvid*) makes it clear that "knowledges" is intended to refer to the four types of unimpeded knowledge discussed at great length later in the text in the explanation of the ninth ground which SA renders as "Ground of Excellent Intelligence" (*sādhumatī-bhūmi*). Briefly, they are unimpeded knowledge of Dharma, meaning, language, and eloquence.

20. DSBC specifies: "*supariśodhitādhyāśayatayā ca*," i.e. "has well purified his *higher* resolute intentions (or 'higher aspirations')."

21. "*svavadātajñānamaṇḍalatayā* ca."

22. "*susaṃbhṛtasaṃbhāratayā ca*."

23. "*apramāṇasmṛtibhājanatayā*."

24. "Resolute faith" (*adhimukti*) is a term that generally refers to confidently held, rationally based inclinations toward wholesome objective conditions or path-associated endeavors. That said, this term is *also* used to refer to sentient beings' strongly held habitual interests or predilections toward the whole range of wholesome, unwholesome, or karmically neutral objective conditions or endeavors, hence it is incumbent on the teaching bodhisattva to be comprehensively cognizant of all of these different types of "resolute dispositions" along with the most skillful teaching stratagems to adopt in teaching the beings who possess them.

25. *Zongchi* (總持), "comprehensive retention," is the Chinese translation of the Sanskrit *dhāraṇī*. I sometimes redundantly translate the term as "comprehensive-retention *dhāraṇī*" to clarify what the Chinese text means by "comprehensive retention," especially when the term

is not simply referring to mantras. "*Dhāraṇīs*" refers primarily to formulae that constitute a kind of pronunciation-dependent Sanskrit code language consisting of Sanskrit syllables which may or may not have a translatable meaning but which can never be translated into another language without destroying their primary functions which are of primarily two types: a) to facilitate the remembrance of teachings and their meanings even for many lifetimes; and b) when more-or-less equivalent to mantras, to protect the practitioner or other vulnerable beings from danger, the manifestation of karmic obstacles, or demonic influences.

Dhāraṇīs may also facilitate the bodhisattva's unproduced-dharmas patience through which he can remain in *saṃsāra* for countless kalpas as he continues to work for the spiritual liberation of all other beings. They also may be used to invoke the manifestation of beneficial supernormal powers either in conjunction with or independent of *mudras* (hand postures) and/or visualizations.

26. "*dharmadhātujñānamudrāsumudritatayā ca.*"

27. Per DSBC, the names of the *bhūmis* are: *pramuditā; vimalā; prabhākarī; arciṣmatī; sudurjayā; abhimukhī; dūraṃgamā; acalā; sādhumatī; dharmameghā.*

28. SA, SD, and Prajñā all translate the name of this *bhūmi* as "the Ground of Blazing Intelligence" (焰慧地). This appears to be the result of an error arising from misinterpreting the Sanskrit name (*arciṣmatī*) by mistaking a suffix indicating possession (*-mat* modified to agree with the feminine noun *bhūmi* to become *-matī*) for a completely unrelated word that means "intelligence," "intellect," "mind" (*mati*). (BB, BR, KB, and the Tibetan all recognize *–matī* as a possessive suffix and hence accord with the Sanskrit meaning.) I have chosen to "bridge" the problem by translating the name of this ground as "the Ground of Blazing Brilliance" in order to allow both meanings the be reflected in the word "blazing" and thus more or less accurately translate both the (seemingly erroneous) SA translation and the correct meaning of the Sanskrit.

29. There seem to be two distinctly different understandings of the meaning of this ground:

    1) DR, SA, BB, BR, SD, and Prajñā all translate the name of this *bhūmi* as "the Ground of Excellent Intelligence" (善慧地). DR translates that same meaning slightly differently: (善哉意). The Tibetan translation also corresponds to this with "the Ground of Excellent Insight" (*legs pa'i blo gros*). Strictly speaking, one could infer that these renderings all appear to be the result of an error arising from misinterpreting the Sanskrit name (*sādhumatī*) by mistaking a suffix indicating possession (*-mat* modified to agree with the feminine noun *bhūmi* to become *-matī*) for a completely unrelated word that means "intelligence," "intellect," or "mind" (*mati*).

2) Of all of the Chinese and Tibetan translators, it appears that the Kumārajīva-Buddhayaśas translation team may have been the only one to render the name of this *bhūmi* more or less in accordance with the above-referenced "strictly correct" interpretation of the Sanskrit term as "the Ground of Sublime Goodness" (妙善地). The KB edition only employs the possibly erroneous Chinese and Tibetan default rendering once (in its initial listing of the ten bodhisattva grounds), but otherwise accords with the strictly grammatically correct interpretation of the term throughout its detailed discussion of the ninth *bhūmi* itself.

30. For the most part, throughout the text, in the introductory and reiterative verses for each of the chapters, SA's Chinese translation uses six or eight verse lines to translate the ideas contained in each four-line Sanskrit gatha when he is producing five-character Chinese verse lines. However, when he produces seven-character verse lines, he seems to more often follow the Sanskrit on a line-by-line basis. Even so, it is still not always possible to precisely map the Chinese onto the much later and somewhat "evolved" gathas found in the extant Sanskrit editions. Although the ideas are mostly all present in both editions, the exact content and sequencing often differ somewhat. To aid correlation with the Sanskrit edition, I have appended the verse number of the DSBC Sanskrit edition (in reduced font bold curly braces) to the last line of each equivalent SA verse.

31. Although the Chinese specifies "wisdom" here (*zhihui* / 智慧)," DSBC records the word more commonly rendered as "knowledge" (*jñāna*): "*guṇajñānasamanvitā.*"

32. "Resolute intentions" translates the Chinese *shenxin* (深心), one of SA's translations of the Sanskrit *āśaya*.

33. The "provisions for the realization of the Path" (*bodhisaṃbhāra*) are the requisites for realization of buddhahood. These are often explained as consisting of karmic merit on the one hand (*puṇya*) and "knowledge" (*jñāna*) or "wisdom" on the other.

34. "*mātṛkā.*"

35. An *asaṃkhyeya* is an exceedingly large number the definition for which varies so widely in Buddhist texts that I have seen definitions ranging between 10 to the fifty-first power and 10 to a power the exponent for which is transcribed with 35 placeholders (i.e. exponent = 74,436,000,000,000,000,000,000,000,000,000,000).

36. Vasubandhu explains the comparison of the Buddha to empty space thus: "Again, as for 'like empty space,' [just as empty space cannot be stained by anything at all, so too, the Buddha] cannot be stained by worldly dharmas, this because all habitual karmic propensities

associated with ignorance and afflictions have been extinguished." (復如虛空世間法不能染。無明煩惱習氣滅故。[131c05-06])

37. Because the Chinese text as passed down to us only titled the sections of this text with section numbers ("Chapter 26: The Ten Grounds: Part One," "...Part Two," etc., I have elected to provide more specific titling for each part of the text as in "The Joyfulness Ground," "The Stainlessness Ground," etc.

38. This is another reference to the provisions required for the realization of bodhi (*bodhisaṃbhāra*) usually explained as consistinig primarily of merit and knowledge or wisdom. "*susaṃbhṛtasaṃbhārāṇāṃ*."

39. DSBC: "*svayaṃbhūjñānānukūlaṃ*."

40. "*pramuditāyāṃ bodhisattvabhūmau sthito bodhisattvaḥ prāmodyabahulo bhavati prasādabahulaḥ prītibahula utplāvanābahula udagrībahula utsībahula utsāhabahulo 'saṃrambhabahulo 'vihiṃsābahulo 'krodhabahulo bhavati*."

41. Although the Chinese references "wisdom" here (*zhihui* / 智慧)," DSBC references the word more commonly rendered as "knowledge" (*jñāna*): "*jñānabhūmeḥ*."

42. Bhikkhu Bodhi points out that this same list appears in the Pali (albeit in slightly different order and with mild differences in the interpretation of two of the five points). See his translation of *Numerical Discourses* 9:5, p. 1255. The most exhaustive of all treatments of this list appears to be Nāgārjuna's discussion of it in his Ten Grounds Sutra commentary, for which see my complete translation of that entire text under separate cover.

43. "*prasādabahulatayā*." BHSD lists "faith" as the primary definition, although MW doesn't mention it at all and prefers definitions along the lines of "purity" and "tranquility" reflected here, hence the apparent discrepancy between KB and SA translations. BB follows KB precisely here, while SD similarly prefers "abundant realization of purity" (多證淨) and Bodhiruci falls somewhat farther afield with "abundant reverence" (多恭敬).

44. "*adhimuktiviśuddhyā*."

45. DSBC: "*ratnopamacittotpādātṛptābhinirhāratayā*."

46. In his Treatise on the Ten Grounds Sutra, (*Daśabhūmika-vibhāṣā* / 十住毘婆沙論 [T no. 1521]), Nāgārjuna devotes all of Chapter Five (T26n1521_p30b10-35a21) to an extensive explanation of the following ten vows. For an English translation of this, see my translation of this entire treatise.

47. DSBC = "*sarvajñajñānapratiṣṭhāpanāya*."

48. I opt for the first of Qingliang's two interpretations for the reading of this extremely ambiguous line not found at all in Bodhiruci, Śīladharma,

Buddhabhadra, or the Sanskrit and only obliquely alluded to in Kumarajiva. (QL's other approved interpretation of "若入若行若去" refers to these worlds subsuming or being subsumed by each other in an interpenetrating fashion wherein this bodhisattva freely travels to and returns from these many different sorts of worlds.)

49. DSBC doesn't specify "'wise' beings" so much as "beings possessed of knowledge": "*apramāṇajñānākarasattva.*"
50. DSBC doesn't specify "wisdom," but rather "knowledge": "*tathāgataprabhāvajñānānugamāya.*"
51. DSBC does not specify "wisdom," but rather "knowledge": "*sahaghoṣodāhārajñānānugamāya.*"
52. Again, DSBC specifies "knowledge" rather than "wisdom": "*mahābuddhaviṣayaprabhāva**jñānā**nugamāya.*"
53. Again, DSBC specifies "knowledge" rather than "wisdom": "*mahājñānabhūmi.*"
54. The following list of ten mental qualities is present with minor variations in BB, SA, and KB, but is missing seven of these mental qualities in SD and eight of these mental qualities in BR and the (very late) surviving Sanskrit editions of the Ten Grounds Sutra.
55. DSBC lists these expressions of faith as follows: "*tathāgatānām arhatāṃ samyaksaṃbuddhānāṃ pūrvāntacaryābhinirhārapraveśaṃ pāramitāsamudāgamaṃ bhūmipariniṣpattiṃ vaiśeṣikatāṃ balapariniṣpattiṃ vaiśāradyaparipūriṃ āveṇikabuddhadharmāsaṃhāryatām acintyāṃ buddhadharmatām anantamadhyaṃ tathāgataviṣayābhinirhāram aparimāṇajñānānugataṃ tathāgatagocarānupraveśaṃ phalapariniṣpattiṃ abhiśraddadhāti.*"
56. One could insert in brackets a tenth member of this list as "[and such insurmountability]" following both BB and KB (如是難壞), that is also found with mild permutations in most other editions. Bodhiruci (如是上。此諸佛法如是難得。) follows very closely the extant DSBC Sanskrit: "*evamudārāḥ evaṃ durāsadāśceme buddhadharmāḥ,*" i.e. "Such loftiness and so hard to approach."
57. This is a reference to the four inverted views (*viparyāsa*):
    1) Viewing as pleasurable what is in fact conducive to suffering;
    2) Viewing as permanent what is in fact impermanent;
    3) Viewing as lovely what is in fact unlovely by virtue of its impurity; and
    4) Viewing as "self" what is in fact devoid of anything constituting an inherently and enduringly existent self.
58. These are collectively referred to as "the four floods" (*ogha*).

59. "Name-and-form" is a reference to the five aggregates of mentality and physicality that are generally falsely construed by unenlightened beings to constitute an inherently existent "self."

60. "The six sense bases" is a reference to the six sense faculties: eye, ear, nose, tongue, body, and intellectual mind faculty. They are commonly metaphorically referred to as a village wherein beings falsely impute the existence of an inherently existent self.

61. DSBC specifies "knowledge" (*jñāna*) rather than "wisdom."

62. For "Diligently cultivates irreversible renunciaton" (勤修出離。不退不轉。), the DSBC Sanskrit has *"naiṣkramyacārī avivartya"* for which BHSD foregrounds as definitions for *"naiṣkramya"*: "departure from the world, renunciation of worldly things," and "renunciation as regards desires (lusts)" while Conze's MDPL has: "leaving home."

63. DSBC gives this entire list as: *"tadyathā - śraddhā karuṇā maitrī tyāgaḥ khedasahiṣṇutā śāstrajñatā lokajñatā hryapatrāpyaṃ dhṛtibalādhānaṃ tathāgatapūjopasthānamiti."*

64. Although the phrasing of the Chinese text might lead one to think these are two separate dharmas, I follow QLSC in combining these two subcomponents as a single grounds-purifying dharma. The surviving Sanskrit for this tenth member of the list (per DSBC) is: *"tathāgatapūjopasthānamiti."*

65. "The remaining two means of attraction" are "beneficial actions" and "joint endeavors."

66. *"yathābalaṃ yathābhajamānam."*

67. DSBC specifies "knowledge" (*jñāna*) rather than "wisdom."

68. DSBC specifies "knowledge" (*jñāna*) rather than "wisdom."

69. DSBC specifies "knowledge" (*jñāna*) rather than "wisdom."

70. DSBC specifies "knowledge" (*jñāna*) rather than "wisdom."

71. DSBC specifies "knowledge" (*jñāna*) rather than "wisdom."

72. For "… should bring forth ten types of resolute intentions," DSBC has: *"tasya daśa cittāśayāḥ pravartante."*

73. For these ten "resolute intentions" (*cittāśaya*), DSBC has: *ṛjvāśaya* (= *ārjava*?), *mṛdvāśaya, karmaṇyāśaya, damāśaya, śamāśaya, kalyāṇāśaya, asaṃsṛṣṭāśaya, anapekṣāśaya, udārāśaya, māhātmyāśaya.*

74. For these ten kinds of minds, DSBC gives: *"…hitacittatām utpādayati / sukhacittatāṃ maitracittatāṃ kṛpācittatāṃ dayācittatām anugrahacittatām ārakṣācittatāṃ samacittatām acāryacittatāṃ śāstṛcittatām utpādayati."*

75. "The view imputing the existence of a true self in association with one's body" corresponds to the Sanskrit *satkāya-dṛṣṭi.*

76. The SA Chinese gives "礬石," the modern translation of which is "aluminite." This does not correspond to the DSBC Sanskrit which specifies "*kāsīsa*," a type of iron oxide. Hence I am compelled to prefer the Sanskrit antecedent term.

77. One may notice the seeming absence in this verse of two of the ten resolute intentions: "the unmixed resolute intention" (*asaṃsṛṣṭāśaya*) and "the unattached resolute intention" (*anapekṣāśaya*). It would appear then that they have somehow been replaced here by the phrase: "the swift exits from *saṃsāra*." (The BB and SD verses specify all ten mental dispositions and do not refer to anything corresponding to this phrase.) That neither BB, SD, DR, nor the Sanskrit say anything at all about "*saṃsāra*" here suggests that perhaps this verse line was corrupted in the SA edition by a scribal error or translator misreading that ended up producing a substitution of "*saṃsāra*" for "*saṃsarga*," for the corresponding part of same line in the extant Sanskrit edition, per DSBC reads: "*saṃsargapekṣavigatāśca*," which clearly refers to the two missing list elements and does not refer to "swift exits from *saṃsāra*" at all.

78. As with the previous *bhūmi*, DSBC shows "*cittāśaya*" ("mental intentions") as the Sanskrit antecedent for "resolute intentions" (深心).

79. For these ten "resolute intentions" (*cittāśaya*), DSBC gives: *śuddha-cittāśaya, sthira-cittāśaya, nirvic-cittāśaya, avirāga-cittāśaya, avinivarta-cittāśaya, dṛḍha-cittāśaya, uttapta-cittāśaya, atṛpta-cittāśaya, udāra-cittāśaya*, and *māhātmya-cittāśaya*. (The last two correspond precisely to the last two listed for the second *bhūmi*.)

80. DSBC gives this tenfold list as: *acintya, atulya, aprameya, durāsada, asaṃspṛṣṭa, nirupadrava, nirupāyāsa, abhayapuragamanīya, apunarāvṛtti, bahujanaparitrāṇa*.

81. Again, DSBC has "*cittāśaya*" for these ten.

82. DSBC lists these as:

    anāthātrāṇāpratiśaraṇacittāśaya;
    nityadaridrapratiśaraṇacittāśaya;
    rāgadveṣamohāgnisaṃpradīptapratiśaraṇacittāśaya;
    bhavacārakāvaruddhapratiśaraṇacittāśaya;
    satatasamitaklaśagahenāvṛtaprasuptapratiśaraṇacittāśaya;
    vilokanasamarthapratiśaraṇacittāśaya;
    kuśaladharmacchandarahitapratiśaraṇacittāśaya;
    buddhadharmapramuṣitapratiśaraṇacittāśaya;
    saṃsārasrotonuvāhipratiśaraṇacittāśaya;
    mokṣopāyapraṇaṣṭapratiśaraṇacittāśaya.

83. DSBC seems to leave out part of this list, but it is complete in Rahder (herein bracketed): "...*paritrātavyāḥ parimocayitavyāḥ* [*pariśodhayitavyā*

uttārayitavyā niveśayitavyāḥ pratiṣṭhāpayitavyāḥ] paritoṣayitavyāḥ saṃropayitavyā vinetavyāḥ parinirvāpayitavyā...."

84. Both the BB and KB editions appear to dispense with "non-production" here. (It is retained in SA, BR, SD, and the Sanskrit.) DSBC: "*sa ca sarvadharmayathāvadavabodho nānyatra apracārānutpādacāriṇyāḥ prajñāyāḥ.*"

85. DSBC lists these ten as: "*...dharmārāmo dharmarato dharmapratiśaraṇo dharmanimno dharmapravaṇo dharmaprāgbhāro dharmaparāyaṇo dharmalayano dharmatrāṇo dharmānudharmacārī.*"

86. The DSBC Sanskrit text clarifies that *xin* (心), otherwise legitimately translated as "minds," in fact refers more specifically to "dispositions," "mental intentions," or "inclinations" (*āśaya*).

87. The DSBC Sanskrit, SA, BR, and SD all speak here of only one means of attraction (beneficial action) and only one *pāramitā* (patience). However, BB and KB both speak here of two means of attraction (pleasing words and beneficial actions) and two *pāramitās* (patience and vigor).

88. The "nonharming mind" in this verse section corresponds to and is at variance with the initial prose section's "nonretreating mind."

89. This is a reference to the four immeasurable minds (*apramāṇa-citta*), all of which require identifying with all beings everywhere as equally deserving of kindness, compassion, sympathetic joy, and equanimity.

90. "*dharmālokapraveśa.*"

91. Just as he did in the previous ground's introductory section, SA used *xin* (心) here in these last two members of this list as an abbreviation for *shenxin* (深心), his usually rather standard rendering of "resolute intentions" (*āśaya*). DSBC = "*udāra-āśaya-adhimukti-dhātu-vicaraṇāloka-praveśena.*")

92. "*māhātmya-āśaya-adhimukti-dhātu-vicaraṇāloka-praveśena.*"

93. "*jñānaparipācakairdharma.*"

94. "*tadātmakadharma.*"

95. "*saṃprajāna.*"

96. These contemplations are anchored to the four stations of mindfulness focusing on the body, feelings, thought / mind, and dharmas (*catuḥ-smṛty-upasthāna*).

97. This is a summation of the bodhisattva's exercise of the four right efforts (*samyak-pradhāna*).

98. "*vivekaniśritaṃ virāganiśritaṃ nirodhaniśritaṃ vyavasargapariṇataṃ.*"

99. This is a summation of the bodhisattva's practice of the four foundations of psychic power.

100. This is a summation of the bodhisattva's practice of the five root faculties.
101. This is a summation of the bodhisattva's practice of the five powers.
102. This is a summation of the bodhisattva's practice of the seven limbs of enlightenment.
103. This is a summation of the bodhisattva's practice of the eightfold right path, hereby concluding the narration of the bodhisattva's practice of the thirty-seven enlightenment factors.
104. "In order to further his quest to acquire the most especially supreme path" (*uttarottara-vaiśeṣika-dharma-parimārgaṇatayā*) is found here in SA as well as in BR, SD, and the DSBC Sanskrit, but it is not found in the three earliest extant editions of this scripture: DR, KB, and BB.
105. This short section of the text regarding aligning practice with whatsoever the Tathāgata censures or praises is not found in KB and BB. The corresponding DSBC text is: *"sa yānīmāni karmāṇyakaraṇīyāni samyaksaṃbuddhavivarṇitāni saṃkleśopasaṃhitāni, tāni sarveṇa sarvaṃ prajahāti / yāni cemāni karmāṇi karaṇīyāni samyaksaṃbuddhapraśastāni bodhimārgasaṃbhārānukūlāni, tāni samādāya vartate /."*
106. *"bodhimārgasaṃbhāra."*
107. In this tenfold list, SA, BR, SD, and the Sanskrit are very close, whereas KB and BB's lists are ninefold and slightly variant. DSBC's tenfold list gives us: *"snigdhacittaśca bhavati, maducittaśca karmaṇyacittaśca hitasukhāvahacittaśca aparikliṣṭacittaśca uttarottaraviśeṣaparimārga ṇacittaśca jñānaviśeṣaṇābhilāṣacittaśca sarvajagatparitrāṇacittaśca gurugauravānukūlacittaśca yathāśrutadharmapratipatticittaśca."*
108. SA, BR, SD, and the Sanskrit are all quite mutually consistent as reflected here in DSBC's tenfold list: "... *sa kṛtajñaśca bhavati, kṛtavedī ca sūrataśca sukhasaṃvāsaśca ṛjuśca mṛduśca agahanacārī ca nirmāyanirmāṇaśca suvacāśca pradakṣiṇagrāhī ca."* KB and BB include "implementation of the practice of right concentration."
109. The lists of ten types of vigor are generally quite consistent in all six extant editions with the sole exception of BB's noninclusion of the final member of all other lists: "The vigor that distinguishes what is and is not the Path." DSBC gives us: *"aprasrabdhavīryaśca bhavati aparikliṣṭaḥ / apratyudāvartyavīryaśca vipulavīryaśca anantavīryaśca uttaptavīryaśca asamavīryaśca asaṃhāryavīryaśca sarvasattvaparipācanavīryaśca nayānayavibhaktavīryaśca bhavati."*
110. It is clear from comparing all the editions and the Sanskrit that the first three elements referenced here, although differing somewhat in order from the Sanskrit, are higher aspirations (*adhyāśaya*), resolute intentions (*āśaya*), and resolute convictions (*adhimukti*).

111. *"apramāṇacittāśayatā ca samudāgacchāti."*

112. *"āśayādhyāśayādhimuktisamatā viśudhyati"* Most of the other editions (BB, KB, SD, DSBC) have not only SA's "resolute intentions" (*āśaya)* and "resolute faith" (*adhimukti*) but also include "higher aspirations" (*adhyāśaya*) and "impartiality" (*samatā*), thus producing a list of four elements. BR is slightly ambiguous and appears to include all but "higher aspirations."

113. DSBC: *"satkāyadṛṣṭi."*

114. This first quatrain condenses the first tenfold list ("the ten gateways to Dharma illumination") that opens the initial discussion of this ground.

115. This quatrain along with the quatrain immediately preceding it are a condensation of the second tenfold list set forth earlier in the discussion of this *bhūmi*, "the ten kinds of knowledge-maturing dharmas."

116. This quatrain together with the one immediately preceding it summarize the earlier discussion of the bodhisattva's cultivation of the thirty-seven enlightenment factors.

117. This quatrain together with the immediately preceding quatrain summarize the ten aims behind cultivation of the thirty-seven enlightenment factors that were brought up earlier in the discussion of this fourth ground.

118. Beginning here, these introductory verses to the fifth ground do not track well with the Sanskrit which itself is missing the ninth verse (which does survive in the Tibetan or the other Chinese editions). It appears from the Sanskrit that SA is missing the first line ("After such a long time, the Great Muni is now met.") and the fourth line ("The Great Śrāmaṇa, worthy of reverence, is revered.") of the sixth verse, which according to DSBC is:

    sucireṇa saṃgamu mahāmuninā
    saṃprāpta sarvagūṇapāramitaḥ |
    mada māna darpa prajahitva tamaṃ
    pūjārhu pūjima mahāśramaṇam || 6 ||

    What's more, SA seems to present verses seven and eight in reverse order.

119. *"āśayaviśuddhisamatā."*

120. HH explains this equally regarding pure mental disposition "toward the mind" as primarily meaning "toward the minds of beings."

121. Although DSBC gives us *"adhyāśaya"* here ("higher aspirations"), this is not supported by any other of the Chinese editions except the very latest one done by Śīladharma in 790 CE who renders this as "especially supreme dispositions / aspirations" (增上意樂). BB, KB, BR, and SA are

all clearly translating simply *"āśaya,"* ("resolute intentions" or "intentions").

122. *"saṃvṛtisatya."*
123. *"paramārthasatya."*
124. *"lakṣaṇasatya."*
125. *"vibhāgasatya."*
126. *"nistīraṇasatya."*
127. *vastusatya.*
128. *prabhavasatya.*
129. *kṣayānutpādasatya.*
130. *mārgajñānāvatārasatya.*
131. *sarvabodhisattvabhūmikramānusaṃdhiniṣpādanatayā yāvat tathāgatajñānasamudayasatya.*
132. *"sa parasattvānāṃ yathāśayasaṃtoṣaṇātsaṃvṛtisatyaṃ prajānāti."*
133. *"ekanayasamavasaraṇātparamārthasatyaṃ prajānāti."*
134. *"svasāmanyalakṣaṇānubodhāllakṣaṇasatyaṃ prajānāti."*
135. *"dharmavibhāgavyavasthānānubodhādvibhāgasatyaṃ prajānāti."*
136. *"skandhadhātvāyatanavyavasthānānubodhānnistīraṇasatyaṃ prajānāti."*
137. *"cittaśarīraprapīḍanopanipātitatvādvastusatyam."*
138. *"gatisaṃdhisaṃbandhanatvātprabhavasatyam."*
139. *"sarvajvaraparidāhātyantopaśamātkṣayānutpādasatyam."*
140. For this passage, DSBC gives us the following: *"advayānutpādasatyam, advayābhinirhāranmārgajñānāvatārasatyam."*
141. DSBC: *"sarvākārābhisaṃbodhitsarvabodhisattvabhūmikramānusaṃdhiniṣp ādanatayā yāvattathāgatajñānasamudayasatyaṃ prajānāti."*
142. *"adhimukti."*
143. *"mārāśayagahana."*
144. Although the extant Sanskrit refers here only to *akuśalavitarka* ("bad initial ideation"), the Chinese text of most editions (BB, KB, SA, and SD) uses the translation for both *vitarka* and *vicāra* ("ideation and mental discursion").
145. Most editions seem to vary somewhat, but only slightly. DSBC has: *tatsarvasattvaparitrāṇāyārabhate, sarvasattvahitāya, sarvasattvasukhāya, sarvasattvānukampāyai, sarvasattvānupadravāya, sarvasattvaparimocanāya, sarvasattvānukarṣāya, sarvasattvaprasādanāya, sarvasattvavinayāya, sarvasattvaparinirvāṇāyārabhate.*
146. *"buddhi."*

147. *"jñāna."*

148. *"prajñā."*

149. *"puṇyasaṃbhāra."*

150. *"jñānasaṃbhāra."*

151. *"mahāmaitrīkṛpāsaṃbhāra."*

152. MW defines *musāragalva* as "a kind of coral." Other definitions state that it is a kind of shell or mother-of-pearl.

153. As is often the case with these radically and tersely condensed verse lines, this one can only be made fully sensible by referring back to information solely available in the main text of this *bhūmi*. For comparison here, we have the following:

DSBC and KB are equally terse, both literally translated more or less as: "... on up to the truth associated with what is unimpeded," (*yāvantanāvaraṇasatya samosaranti* [Rahder footnotes a variant ending the line as *"samāsaranti"*]).

SD: "... on up to truth associated with the unimpeded knowledge of the Buddha," (乃至無礙佛智諦). SD is the only truly clear edition here, for only it can stand on its own without reference to information found in the main fifth ground text.

BB is a complete outlier barely relating in these verse lines to most of the other editions. And of course BR has no verses at all, only the main text of the Sutra itself.

154. As in the main text, the Sanskrit verse refers again to *"musāragalva."*

155. "Knowing *dharmas as by nature transcendent*" (知法性離) corresponds to DSBC's *"sarvadharmāviviktāḥ"* which infers that all dharmas "are beyond distinctions or discriminations," hence my translation of the Chinese as "transcendent."

156. *"dharmasamatā."*

157. Most extant editions are quite similar but slightly variant in a few list components. The DSBC Sanskrit gives us: *animitta; alakṣaṇa; anutpāda; ajāta; vivikta; adiviśuddhi; niṣprapañca; anāvyūhānirvyūha; māyāsvapnapratibhāsapratiśrutkodakacandrapratibimbanirmāṇa; bhāvābhāvādvaya.*

158. Nāgārjuna provides an extensive discussion of these similes in his Mppu (T25.1509.101c6-105c18 [fasc. 6]).

159. DSBC: *"tīkṣṇayā ānulomikyā kṣāntyā."* (In MDPL, Conze suggests "adaptable patience" for *ānulomikī kṣānti.*)

160. In the following discussion of origination through causes and conditions (*pratitya-samutpāda*), each of the characteristic features associated with the twelve links is italicized to enhance the reader's ease of understanding.

161. DSBC: *"puṇyāpuṇyāneñjyānabhisaṃskāra."* Regarding the third of these three types of actions, QL interprets "actions leading to imperturbable states" as referring to the pure karma of the eight levels of *dhyāna* (which, of course would refer not only to abiding in those levels of meditative absorption, but also would refer to taking rebirth in the corresponding heavens). He also notes that this "pure karma of the eight *dhyānas* also qualifies as being a function of delusion," the rationale for that statement being that, rarified as these modes of existence are, as an end in themselves, they still do not constitute or conduce to liberation from cyclic existence and hence function as erroneous karmic paths.

162. The SA Chinese is mildly ambiguous here. Compare Buddhabhadra, Kumārajīva, and Bodhiruci, as below:

BB: "Because of prior and subsequent continuity, these three paths are not severed. These three paths occur apart from a self or possessions of a self, and yet production and extinction [continue to] occur." (No mention in BB of the "reeds" analogy.)

KB: "On account of past and future continuity, these three paths are not cut off. These three paths exist apart from any self or possessions of a self and yet there exists this production and extinction. This is analogous to [the mutual dependence occurring in] two stalks of bamboo that, through leaning on each other, are thus able to stand up. Although they are not solidly established, it still appears as if they are solidly established."

BR: "On account of the ceaseless continuity of past and future, these three paths are not cut off. These three paths exist apart from any self or possessions of a self. Because they only occur as a process of production and extinction, their existence is analogous to a bundle of bamboo stalks."

163. *Shulu* (束蘆) here translates the Sanskrit *naḍa-kalāpa,* standing sheaves of reeds (as, for instance, *Phragmites karka india*), wherein, whether as they grow in naturally occurring stands, or as they may be deliberately bundled together in the construction of shelters and such in order to remain upright, each reed serves to support the others while simultaneously relying entirely upon the support of the others to keep from collapsing. Hence we have in this phenomenon an analogy for the utter codependence of these three subsets of "links" comprising the twelvefold chain of serially unfolding conditioned coproduction. This is of course equally true of the mutually supporting and sustaining nature of all twelve of the links *individually* as well.

Bhikkhu Bodhi points out a scriptural citation for the "sheaves of reeds" causality analogy as *Saṃyutta Nikāya* 12-67: "The Sheaves of Reeds."

164. "Suffering associated with the karmic formative factors" = *xingku* (行苦) = *saṃskāraduḥkhatā.*

165. *Suffering of suffering* = *kuku* (苦苦) = *duḥkhaduḥkhatā.*

166. *Suffering associated with deterioration* = *huaiku* (壞苦) = *pariṇāmaduḥkhatā.*

167. *"sa evaṃ dvādaśākāraṃ pratītyasamutpādaṃ pratyavekṣate 'nulomapratilomaṃ."*

168. All editions are fairly consistent throughout this list of ten contemplations with the exception of a possible textual corruption in the second contemplation in the KB edition wherein "body" is included as a fundamental basis for the twelve causal links.

DSBC gives the list as follows:

bhavāṅgānusaṃdhitaśca;
ekacittasamavasaraṇataśca;
svakarmāsaṃbhedataśca;
avinirbhāgataśca;
trivartmānuvartanataśca;
pūrvāntapratyutpannāparāntāvekṣaṇataśca;
triduḥkhatāsamudayataśca;
hetupratyayaprabhavataśca;
utpādavyayavinibandhanataśca;
abhāvākṣayatāpratyavekṣaṇataśca.

169. HH identifies these as the three paths discussed earlier in this passage on conditioned origination: the path of afflictions, the path of karmic actions, and the path of suffering.

170. *"śūnyatāvimokṣamukha."*

171. *"ānimittavimokṣamukha."*

172. *"apraṇihitavimokṣamukha."*

173. These ten emptiness samādhis, per DSBC: *avatāraśūnyatā; svabhāvaśūnyatā; paramārthaśūnyatā; paramaśūnyatā; mahāśūnyatā; saṃprayogaśūnyatā; abhinirhāraśūnyatā; yathāvadavikalpaśūnyatā; sāpekṣaśūnyatā; vinirbhāgāvinirbhāgaśūnyatā.*

174. These ten types of resolute intentions per DSBC: *abhedyāśaya; niyatāśaya; kalyāṇāśaya; gambhīrāśaya; apratyudāvartyāśaya; apratiprasrabdhāśaya; vimalāśaya; anantāśaya; jñānābhilāṣāśaya; upāyaprajñāsaṃprayogāśaya.*

175. Context often requires a somewhat adaptive translation of *āśaya* that otherwise may mean "mental intention," "mental disposition,"

"intent," "resolution," or "mentality." Here I prefer Conze's (MDPL) "resolute intention."

176. "Acquiescent patience" = *ānulomikī kṣānti*. In his XHYJL, LTX points out that this "acquiescent patience" is the third of "the five types of patience" and the second of "the ten types of patience" and that in both cases, it is the level of patience acquired just before realizing "the unproduced-dharmas patience" (*anutpattika-dharma-kṣānti*). (T36n1739_p0899b7-12)

177. "King of the Fine Transformations Heaven" (善化天王) = *sunirmita-deva-rāja*. Bodhiruci translates this as "King of the Delight in Transformations Heaven" (化樂天王). This is a clear reference to the Nirmāṇa-rati Heaven, the heaven just above the Tuṣita Heaven within the six desire-realm heavens.

178. None of the Chinese editions (DR, BB, BR, KB, SA, SD) agree with the Sanskrit's inclusion of three instead of two factors here: skillful means, wisdom, and knowledge (*upāyaprajñājñāna*).

179. All other editions (BB, KB, BR, SD, and the Sanskrit) refer instead to the penetrating comprehension of dharmas' differences. DSBC: "*apramāṇaṃ ca dharmanānātvamavatarati.*"

180. "*apramāṇaṃ ca buddhānāṃ bhagavatāṃ jñānābhisaṃbodhimavatarati.*"

181. SA, BR, and SD all specify "name-and-form bodies," whereas BB, KB, and the Sanskrit all refer only to "form bodies" (*rūpakāya*).

182. The four types of retention: dharmas, meanings, mantras, and patience.

183. "*bodhyaṅga.*"

184. All other editions specify entry into both knowledge / wisdom and spiritual superknowledges (*jñānābhijñānacaryākramaṇī*).

185. All editions are fairly consistent here with the exception that BB and KB list eleven samādhis here, whereas most of the other editions collapse the final two list members in BB and KB into a single samādhi. DSBC provides the following list: *suvicitavicayaṃ; suvicintitārthaṃ; viśeṣamatiṃ; prabhedārthakośaṃ; sarvārthavicayaṃ; supratiṣṭhitadṛḍhamūlaṃ; jñānābhijñāmukhaṃ; dharmadhātu(pari) karmaṃ; tathāgatānuśaṃsaṃ; vicitrārthakośasaṃsāranirvāṇamukhaṃ.*

186. "*prajñājñānavicāraṇābhūmeḥ*" ("The ground of contemplating wisdom and knowledge.")

187. DSBC: "*na punaḥ svabuddhivicāreṇa.*"

188. The Sanskrit text makes it clear that SA's "ultimate reality" (實際) apparently refers here not to its usual Sanskrit antecedent (*bhūtakoṭi*), but rather to *nirodha*, i.e. to a state of quiescent cessation synonymous with nirvāṇa.

189. DSBC: *"buddhajñānaviṣayakośa."*

190. There are four types of *māras* (*catur-māra*) that are often translated elsewhere as "demons" when not directly referencing the celestial *māras*. Those four types of *māras* are: affliction *māras* (*kleśa-māra*), the *māras* of the aggregates (*skandha-māra*), the *māras* of death (*mṛtya-māra*), celestial *māras* (*deva-putra-māra*).

191. HH clarifies that these "adorning phenomena" refer to the bodhisattva's cultivation and accumulation of many different sorts of roots of goodness and meritorious qualities with which he, figuratively speaking, "adorns" buddha lands: "菩薩以他修積的種種善 根功德，莊嚴佛的國土，無不超過天、龍，及八部神祇、帝釋、梵王、 四大天王等所有的莊嚴之事。"

192. Although *huo* (惑) is often legitimately translated as "delusion" in these sorts of texts, it is also very often a translation of "afflictions" (*kleśa*), for which the Chinese translation is more ordinarily *fannao* (煩惱). The preceding text (at the end of Section F) and the DSBC Sanskrit both make it clear that SA is actually translating *kleśa* ("afflictions") here even though he switches to the more standard Chinese translation (煩惱) in the very next verse line. One obvious reason has to do with the need for economy in composing seven-character verse lines in sino-Buddhist Classical Chinese.

193. Vasubandhu correlates this with the bodhisattva's first ground practice.

194. Vasubandhu correlates this with the bodhisattva's second ground practice.

195. Vasubandhu correlates this with the bodhisattva's third ground practice.

196. Vasubandhu correlates this with the bodhisattva's fourth ground practice.

197. Vasubandhu correlates this with the bodhisattva's fifth ground practice. DSBC: *"supariśodhitādhyāśayasaṃkalpa."*

198. Vasubandhu correlates this with the bodhisattva's sixth ground practice.

199. Vasubandhu correlates this with the bodhisattva's seventh ground practice and also mentions that it is on account of his encounters with measurelessly many realms of beings that the bodhisattva "enters the path of measureless knowledge."

200. All editions' lists vary somewhat. DSBC has: *ajātatāṃ ca; alakṣaṇatāṃ ca; asaṃbhūtatāṃ ca; avināśitāṃ ca; aniṣṭhitatāṃ ca; apravṛttitāṃ ca; anabhinivṛttitāṃ ca; abhāvasvabhāvatāṃ ca; ādimadhyaparyavasānasamatāṃ ca; tathatāvikalpasarvajñajñānapraveśatāṃ ca.*

201. Vasubandhu notes that this refers to "skillful abiding in the *ālayavijñāna*'s dharma of true suchness" (善住阿梨耶識真如法中).

202. *The four floods* (四流) refer to beings' submersion in the floods of: views (見流), desire (欲流), becoming (有流), ignorance (無明流).

203. "*sarvadharmāṇāṃ dharmatā.*"

204. BB (圓光), BR (光輪), KB (圓光), SD (光輪), and the Sanskrit (*prabhāmaṇḍala*) all specify "aura."

205. "*dharmāloka.*"

206. "*sarvadharmanirvikalpālokaḥ.*"

207. It is apparent from the Sanskrit (*adhimukti*) as well as from DR, BB, KB, SD, and QLSC that SA's *jie* (解) is abbreviating *xinjie* (信解), "resolute faith."

208. "*āśayabala.*"

209. "*kumārabhūmi.*"

210. At this point in the text BB (566a10), KB (522b28), Bodhiruci (184c28), SD (561c08), and the Sanskrit all state that "He is able to receive measurelessly many predictions."

211. Neither the preceding prose text nor the Sanskrit support "meritorious qualities" here, but rather "merit and knowledge" (*punyajñāna*). Perhaps "meritorious qualities" here was the result of a scribal or SA translation error.

212. "*āśaya.*"

213. KB and BB (both have: 能得於十種 / 妙大自在智) as well as the Sanskrit (*vaśitā daśo vimala-jñāna-vicāra-prāptā*) clarify that this "ten *ārya* knowledges" refers to the ten types of "sovereign mastery" (*vaśitā*) listed earlier in the description of this eighth ground (sovereign mastery with regard to life span, mind, wealth, karmic deeds, rebirths, vows, understanding, utilization of psychic power, knowledge, and the Dharma).

214. "*praśamita.*"

215. Although, due to the need for economy in composing 7-character lines, the Chinese does not specify "vehicle," the Sanskrit does specify "*yāna*": "*yatra sattva tīkṣṇacitta pratyayānaniratā.*"

216. "Effects of practicing" (lit. "actions") = Skt. *abhisaṃskāra*. (BHSD foregrounds "performance," "accomplishment," and "accumulation.") The intended reference here is to this bodhisattva's knowing in accordance with reality the karmic effects of implementing the various categories of dharmas arrayed in this list.

217. "Entangling thicket" = Skt. *gahana*. SA, BR, and SD all translate this as *choulin* (稠林) which means "thicket," whereas KB and BB translate it as "difficulty" (難).

218. Each of these "entangling thickets" (*gahana*) is explored in greater detail below in the subsections corresponding to the Sanskrit text's sections "E" through "K."

219. It is apparent from the Sanskrit (*adhimukti*) that SA's *jie* (解) is abbreviating *xinjie* (信解), "resolute beliefs."

220. "Sense realms" = Skt. *dhātu*. This refers to the eighteen sense realms: the six sense faculties, the six sense objects, and the six sense consciousnesses.

221. "Resolute intentions" = "*āśaya*."

222. "Latent tendencies" = "*anuśaya*."

223. "*upapatti*."

224. "*vāsana-anusaṃdhi*."

225. These "three groups" (三聚) refer to: 1) those fixed in their adherence to what is wrong; 2) those fixed in their adherence to what is right; 3) those who are "unfixed" as to their adherence to either what is wrong or what is right.

226. "Devoid of physical form" = Rahder Skt. *aśarīratāṁ*. (There is an error in DSBC which has *śarīratāṁ*.)

227. Bhikkhu Bodhi points out that this is a reference to the Buddha's statements on the boundlessness of consciousness found in DN 11 and MN 49 wherein "consciousness" there may be equated with "mind" as intended here. See *Long Discourses*, Walshe, p. 179 and *The Middle Length Discourses*, Bhikkhus Ñāṇamoli & Bodhi, p. 428.

228. Bhikkhu Bodhi points out that this is an allusion to a fourfold classification of karma at AN 4:232-233 for which see *The Numerical Discourses of the Buddha*, Bhikkhu Bodhi, p.601. KB, Bodhiruci, BB, and SD all break these out as four clearly stated items, for instance KB, as follows:

> "Their characteristic of rewarding black actions with black retributions; their characteristic of rewarding white actions with white retributions; their characteristic of rewarding a combination of black and white actions with a combination of black and white retributions; their characteristic of being amenable to ending through actions that are neither black nor white…."

229. SA is very close to the Sanskit (*karmakṣetrāpramāṇatāṃ ca*).

    DR has "[The characteristic of having] farm fields of karmic offense and merit that are measureless" (罪福田地，則無有量).

Both KB and BB have: "He knows karmic actions' characteristic of involving countless causes and conditions in their arising" (知無量因緣起業相).

BR has "karmic actions' characteristic of involving measureless causes" (業因無量相).

SD has: "the field of karmic actions' nature of measurelessness" (業田無量性).

Hence we see that four editions (including the Sanskrit) involve a metaphor, whereas KB, BB, and BR all skip the metaphor entirely, preferring a brief explanation of the concept. For instance BR (very similar to KB and BB whose translations here are identical) has: "karmic actions' characteristic of involving measureless causes" (業因無量相).

230. "resolute beliefs" = "*adhimukti*."

231. "Sense realms" = "*dhātu*."

232. "Resolute intentions" = "*āśaya*."

233. "Latent tendencies" = "*anuśaya*

234. It is apparent from the Sanskrit that SA switched here to a different Chinese rendering for *āśaya* (深心 [*shenxin*]), a binome that literally means "resolute intentions."

235. "Habitual karmic propensities" = "*vāsanā*."

236. Again, this listing refers to the "three groups" of beings mentioned above as the last of the "entangling thickets" in Sanskrit section C above.

237. "Five heinous karmic offenses" refers to patricide, matricide, killing an arhat, spilling the blood of a buddha, and causing a sectarian schism in the monastic community.

238. As in the last of the "entangling thickets" in Sanskrit section C and as in the immediately preceding discussion that refers back to that particular "entangling thicket," "groups" here most likely refers to: 1) those fixed in their adherence to what is wrong; 2) those fixed in their adherence to what is right; 3) those who are "unfixed" as to their adherence to either what is wrong or what is right.

239. "*adhimukti*."

240. "Expounder" = "*dharmabhāṇaka*."

241. "Four unimpeded knowledges" = "*catuḥpratisaṃvid*." These are: *dharma-pratisaṃvid*, *artha-pratisaṃvid*, *nirukti-pratisaṃvid*, and pratibhāna-pratisaṃvid.

242. "*sarvadharmaprajñaptyacchedanadharmaṁ deśayati*." DSBC, BB, Bodhiruci, KB, and SD *all* specify what I insert in brackets here and

hereafter: "conventional designations" (*prajñapti*). (SA only implies it obliquely.)

243. "*pratibhānapratisaṃvidā ekaikaṃ yānamaparyantadharmābhāsena deśayati.*" BB, Bodhiruci, KB, and SD also corroborate this bracketed insertion of "light."
244. "*āśaya.*"
245. "*adhimukti.*"
246. "*adhimukti.*"
247. "*āśaya.*"
248. "The realm in which the Buddha courses" = Skt. *buddhagocara.*
249. "Mental dispositions" = "*āśaya*"
250. These three categorical types (三聚) refer to: 1) those fixed in their adherence to what is wrong; 2) those fixed in their adherence to what is right; 3) those who are "unfixed" as to their adherence to either what is wrong or what is right.
251. Neither BB nor KB include this first list component found in SA, BR, SD, and the Sanskrit (*suvicitavicayaḥ*).
252. This is clearly a reference to the ten types of "entangling thickets" (*gahana*) discussed at some length in relation to the ninth ground in a section beginning with their listing at 202a23–26.
253. Both BB and KB make the acquisition of the "stainless samādhi" a preliminary step before entering the ten samādhis listed immediately thereafter.
254. The Sanskrit samādhi designation per the DSBC text: "*sarvajñajñānaviś eṣābhiṣekavatannāma bodhisattvasamādhirāmukhībhavati.*"
255. In this case, "the beings residing in them" refers to the hungry ghosts (*pretas*).
256. I emend the reading of the Taisho text at 206a18 to correct a graphic-similarity scribal error that erroneously recorded *ge* (各) instead of *ming* (名). The emendation is supported by BB, QLSC, KB, BR, SD, the Sanskrit, one other edition of the SA text, and the requirements of sensibility.
257. Although the entire ensuing section of the Chinese text employs the Chinese character most commonly associated in Buddhist doctrinal discussions with the second of the four truths, i.e. "accumulation" or "origination" of suffering (集 [*ji*] = Skt. *samudaya*), as context demonstrates and the Sanskrit text corroborates, that is *not* the concept intended here. In this instance, the Sanskrit antecedent term is not *samudaya* but rather *samudāgama* which refers instead to "attainment." (MW = "Full or complete knowledge." BHSD = "*approach* [*to*], *arrival*

[*of*], *attainment* [*of*], a religious goal, esp. enlightenment, which is to be understood when no goal is specifically named.") This being the case, I translate this character in this context as "attainment."

258. "Sustaining Bases" (持) = *adhiṣṭhāna*. Although this technical term is often translated as "empowerment," that would not be an appropriate rendering here as many of the members of this list may or may not be sustained through empowerments as they are for the most part causally sustained by past karmic actions.
259. Bhikkhu Bodhi points out that one example of this may be the bodhisattva's power to consciously pass away in the Tuṣita Heaven before taking his last birth in the human realm.
260. "Penetrating knowledge" = "*avatārajñāna*."
261. "Ordinary common people," on the face of it, might appear to be a mistranslation of the Chinese term recorded here as 毛道, i.e. "hair path." But, as it turns out, this in fact *is* Śikṣānanda's very literal translation of the Sanskrit *vāla-patha*, lit. "hair path," apparently a traditional Sanskrit corruption of *bāla* that is in turn an abbreviation for *bāla-pṛthagjana*, literally "foolish common person."
262. "*buddhakṣetrakāyābhisaṃbodhyavatārajñānaṃ*."
263. "*mahāvijayo bhikṣu*."
264. "*vajrapadmottarasya tathāgata*."
265. An "ineffable" (*anabhilāpya*) is the name of one of a long series of extremely large numbers described in this scripture's "Asaṃkhyeya" chapter.
266. This samādhi per DSBC: "*sarvabuddhakṣetrakāyasvabhāvasaṃdarśanaṃ nāma bodhisattvasamādhiṃ*."
267. "*sarvābhijñāmatirājaṃ nāma tathāgataṃ*."
268. "*vaśavartino devarāja*."
269. "*maheśvarasya devarājasya*."
270. Bhikkhu Bodhi points out that eight of these comparisons are found in Anguttara Nikāya 8:19 (The Simile of the Ocean).
271. From this point on, the verses in the very late Sanskrit edition diverge entirely from those found in any of the Chinese texts. Because their composition must be of relatively recent origin, there appears to be no clear way to correlate these Sanskrit verses with those of any of the Chinese texts, whether it be DR, BB, SA, KB, or SD, all of which date from a millennium or more earlier than the surviving Sanskrit edition.
272. The Chinese name of this bodhisattva is identical to that of the thirty-ninth bodhisattva in this list. To differentiate it, I translate the name here as "King of Resolve Bodhisattva."

273. "*Namo*" is an expression of homage, obeisance, reverential salutation, or adoration, from the Sanskrit *namas*, which, per MW, p. 528, means: "*namas n. bow, obeisance, reverential salutation, adoration (by gesture or word*… ."

274. Both QL and HH indicate that, although the list statements are elevenfold, the actual number of topics is tenfold.

275. Although the Chinese translators in nearly all cases chose to translate the name of this contemplation as "the contemplation of impurity" (不淨觀), the Sanskrit *aśubha-bhāvanā* to which it is referring is instead more like "the contemplation of the *unloveliness*" of the body.

276. A "*pudgala*" is a supposedly permanent personal soul.

277. The Chinese *yisheng* (意生), otherwise literally "mind-made," is here a Chinese translation of the Sanskrit *manuja* which just means "born of Manu" (the Hindu progenitor of mankind), "man" or "human."

278. Here, this "*māṇava*" or "*mānava*" (摩納婆) which may mean "a brahman youth" or "a brahman adult," just means "a human" or "a man."

279. Although I suppose the sense of this passage would somehow seem more "profound" if I were to translate *xukong* (虛空) in these five clustered instances as "emptiness" instead of as "empty space" (as Cleary so weirdly and mistakenly did). But this simply would not do because the sino-translation generally distinguishes these two things so carefully that it should be impossible to make this mistake. There is no way that an experienced translator of Sino-Buddhist Classical Chinese could mistake the word for "empty space" (虛空 / *akāśa*) as referring to the Buddhist metaphysical concept of "emptiness" or "emptiness of inherent existence" (*śunyatā*).

280. I take the *shu* (數) of "the analytical knowledge of the world's illusory nature" (世幻數) to be translating *pratisaṃkhyā*, which, per BHSD (p. 371, Column 2) means "… *careful (point by point) consideration, thorough knowledge*." Although this may seem to be a rather unintuitive sino-translation of *pratisaṃkhyā*, there is precedent for it elsewhere.

281. "Signs" here is really more like "events" because it is referring to the various events in the life of a buddha such as descending from the Tuṣita Heaven, taking birth, walking seven steps, leaving the homelife, turning the wheel of the Dharma, etc.

282. In Buddhist texts, these three "factors" (lit. "wheels" or "spheres") generally refer to the three components of any action: a) the subjective agent (as, for instance, in any particular instance of giving, a "benefactor"), b) the particular action at issue (as, for instance "the action of giving" and the actual "gift"), and c) the objective recipient of the action (as, for instance the "recipient" who is given the gift). Here, QL

correlates the purification of these three factors in this circumstance with the nonexistence of any intrinsically existing: a) agent of knowing, b) any object of knowing, or c) any action of right knowing, i.e. with the emptiness of these three factors associated with the act of knowing. Specifically, he says: "There is no one able to know, there is nothing that is known, and there is no right knowing that is taking place." (無能知所知及正知. / L130n1557_p. 546b01)

283. A *kalala* is the first stage in the growth of an embryo.

284. What I translate here as "purity" is more literally "the white portion" (白分) which translates the Sanskrit *śukla-pakṣa* which means "the bright" (or "light" or "white") portion. This originally referred to the portion of the month when the moon was brightest, but came to be associated with purity, goodness, righteousness, etc.

285. Both HH and QL note that, although there are twelve statements here, the topics to which they refer are in fact tenfold.

286. What I translate here and below as "fruitfulness" is more literally "not-done-in-vain" or "non-futility" (不空), both of which are too clumsy for use here.

287. According to MW, p. 322, a *krośa* is "a cry, yell, shriek, shout, the range of the voice in calling or hallooing, a measure of distance (an Indian league)."

288. As HH points out in considerable detail (HYQS), the circumstance alluded to here is that of the post-death intermediary-body consciousness when it is wandering about in search of those with whom it has the karmic affinities to be born to them as their child. The intermediary body's consciousness eventually observes the yin light emanating from his future parents' act of coition, forms a thought of desire for one of them and a thought of jealousy toward the other and is right then conceived into the womb of the next-life mother where it is then immediately gendered according to which of the two of them he has deemed to be attractive and desirable: If that be the copulating woman, then he is conceived as a male fetus. If, on the other hand, that object of his desire is the woman's sexual partner, the man, then the intermediary body is right then conceived as a female fetus. The Chinese that I am herein rendering as "pure" (清淨) is probably a translation of the Sanskrit *śubha* ("beautiful," "lovely," "splendid," "agreeable," "pure," etc.) and not *viśuddhi* (the more typical Sanskrit antecedent for *qingjing* [清淨] when it is truly intended to refer to "purity").

289. "Two types of actions" (二行) refers to: a) those dominated by "views," among which the view that conceives the inherent existence of a self is the emblematic deluded view, and b) those dominated by "craving"

and the other delusion-generated afflictions among which craving is the emblematic affliction.

290. HH clarifies that this is referring to the Dharma body of all buddhas. (HYQS)

291. "Joining the red and the white" (赤白和合) is a traditional metaphoric reference to sexual intercourse alluding to the meeting of sperm and egg.

292. HH clarifies the meaning of this rather obscure statement by noting that these references to the "nonexistent" (無) and the "existent" (有) are referring to "true emptiness" (眞空) on the one hand and "sublime existence" (妙有) on the other. (HYQS)

293. "Right and fixed position" (正位 or 正定位, Skt. *samyaktva niyāma*) refers here to irreversibility in one's progression along the bodhisattva's path to buddhahood.

294. Here, "four types of eloquence" (四辯才) is a reference to the four unimpeded knowledges (*pratisaṃvid*).

295. Here, "eloquence with respect to meanings" (義辯才) is a reference to the second of the four unimpeded knowledges (*artha-pratisaṃvid*).

296. Here, "eloquence with respect to dharmas" (法辯才) is a reference to the first of the four unimpeded knowledges (*dharma-pratisaṃvid*).

297. Here, "eloquence with respect to the language of teachings" (訓辭辯) is a reference to the third of the four unimpeded knowledges (*nirukti-pratisaṃvid*).

298. Here, "endless eloquence" (無盡辯) is a reference to the fourth of the four unimpeded knowledges (*pratibhāna pratisaṃvid*).

299. In this context "three wheels" (三輪, *tri-maṇḍala*) refers to physical, verbal, and mental actions.

300. When it says here that dharmas "have no turning" (無轉), this is to say that they "undergo no transformation," about which HH says: "Although the bodhisattva knows that all dharmas are quiescent and that therefore there are no dharmas that can be 'turned' (i.e. made to undergo transformation), but he still must always turn the great Dharma wheel in order to teach beings." (菩薩雖然知道一切諸法是寂滅的，沒有法可轉，可是還要常轉大法輪，來教化眾生。 / HYQS)

301. HH explains the somewhat obscure "all dharmas have no emancipation" (諸法無有出離) with a quote from the Heart Sutra as follows: "Although the bodhisattva knows 'all dharmas have no emancipation' because the fundamental substance of all dharmas 'is unproduced and undestroyed, neither defiled nor pure, and neither increased nor increased,' the bodhisattva still explains how to cultivate the pure

gateways to the practices by which one gains emancipation from the three realms of existence." (菩薩雖然知道一切諸法，沒有出離。因為諸法的本體，是不生不滅、不垢不淨、不增不減的緣故，可是菩薩還要說怎樣修行清淨出離三界的行門。 / HYQS)

302. A *nārāyaṇa* is a vajra-bearing Dharma protector spirit or deva.

303. Because "universally worthy" is the English translation of Samantabhadra Bodhisattva's name, this would appear to in essence be saying: "... then he is a bodhisattva in the mold of Samantabhadra."

304. "The realm of King Yama" (閻魔王處) is a reference to King Yama's role as the king of the purgatorial hell realms who passes judgment on the dead.

305. "The difficulties" (諸難處) is another way of referring to the eight difficulties (八難 / *aṣṭa akṣaṇāḥ*) consisting of eight kinds of inopportune or unfortunate rebirths in which it is nearly impossible to encounter either a buddha or the Dharma.

306. HH interprets this as referring to "whether they will definitely be able to gain emancipation from the three realms of existence or whether they will not definitely gain emancipation from the three realms of existence." (或者能出離三界，或者不能出離三界。/ HYQS). In this case, "whether their liberation is certain or whether their liberation is uncertain" (若決定，若不決定) would be referring to whether or not they have reached what Nāgārjuna refers to in his Bodhisaṃbhara Śastra as "the right and fixed position" (正定位, *samyaktva-niyata*). This refers to reaching the stage of irreversibility on the path to one's chosen goal, whether that be arhatship (in which case it is synonymous with becoming a streamwinner or *śrota-āpanna*) or whether it be buddhahood.

307. There follows here a long list consisting of one hundred and three kinds of forms which, for ease of reading and absorbing (and breathing if reading aloud), I've broken into eleven clauses with all but the last clause having ten forms per clause. Even so, as with the Chinese text, the entire list can still be read as a single page-and-a-half-long sentence.

308. HH interprets this as referring to the thirty-two marks and the eighty subsidiary signs.

309. The Sanskrit for "illusion" (幻) is *māyā*. This is one of the ten rather standard similes for emptiness.

310. Without any context, one would have to translate this *bu* (步) which is a verb, not a noun, as "walking," "marching," etc. However, looking at the BB translation, we see that these first four list items were translated there as different categories of military units ("elephant

soldiers," "horse soldiers," "chariot soldiers," "marching soldiers"). Hence my decision to translate this as "soldiers."

311. I emend the text here to remedy an obvious graphic-similarity scribal error, restoring the *zheng wei* (正位) shown in four other editions to correct Taisho's clearly erroneous *zhengzhu* (正住). This "right and fixed position" (*samyaktva-niyāma*) is a milestone on the path corresponding to the stage of irreversibility and certain eventual success in one's chosen path, whether that be the individual-liberation path of the *śrāvaka* disciple or the universal-liberation path of the bodhisattva.

312. The Sanskrit for "transformations" (化) is *nirmāṇa*. This too is one of the standard similes for emptiness.

313. For the last two lines of this quatrain, the BB translation has: "He complies with their true suchness and thus acquires their genuine dharma." (隨順於真如，得彼真實法。/ T09n0278_p0583b17)

314. The three inverted mental factors are erroneous perceptions, views, and thoughts.

315. An *asaṃkhyeya* (which means "incalculable") is a huge number commonly used in Buddhist texts to describe the four phases of creation, abiding, destruction, and nonexistence associated with the longest of all world cycles, i.e., *kalpas*. It is also the 104th of the following 122 numerical designations (each of which is the square of the immediately previous number). As calculated by Upāsaka Ling Feng, an *asaṃkhyeya* equals 10^7.09884336127809E+031.

316. The Sanskrit names for the following 123 levels of Sanskrit numbers (each of which is the square of the immediately previous number) were for the most part drawn from the Mahāvyutpatti, nos. 7697-7820.

317. Beginning here, the numerical values for each of these numbers (as calculated by Upāsaka Ling Feng) are as follows:

asaṃkhyeya (阿僧祇) 10^7.09884336127809E+031
asaṃkhyeya-parivarta (阿僧祇轉) 10^1.41976867225562E+032
aparimāṇa (無量) 10^2.83953734451123E+032
aparimāṇa-parivarta (無量轉) 10^5.67907468902247E+032
aparyanta (無邊) 10^1.13581493780449E+033
aparyanta-parivarta (無邊轉) 10^2.27162987560899E+033
asamanta (無等) 10^4.54325975121797E+033
asamanta-parivarta (無等轉) 10^9.08651950243595E+033
agaṇeya (不可數) 10^1.81730390048719E+034
agaṇeya-parivarta (不可數轉) 10^3.63460780097438E+034
atulya (不可稱) 10^7.26921560194876E+034
atulya-parivarta (不可稱轉) 10^1.45384312038975E+035
acintya (不可思) 10^2.9076862407795E+035

acintya-parivarta (不可思轉) 10^5.81537248155901E+035
ameya (不可量) 10^1.1630744963118E+036
ameya-parivarta (不可量轉) 10^2.3261489926236E+036
anabhilāpya (不可說) 10^4.65229798524721E+036
anabhilāpya-parivarta (不可說轉) 10^9.30459597049441E+036
anabhilāpyānabhilāpya (不可說不可說) 10^1.86091919409888E+037
anabhilāpyānabhilāpya-parivarta (不可說不可說轉) = 10^3.72183838819776E+037

318. This second largest denomination of these Sanskrit numbers, "an *anabhilāpyānabhilāpa*," or "an ineffable-ineffable," is used throughout most of the following verses as a means of conveying the inconceivability of the concepts and circumstances associated with bodhisattvas, buddhas, and the path. As calculated by Upāsaka Ling Feng, its numerical value is 10^1.86091919409888E+037.

319. QL says: "The following one hundred and twenty verses consist of two major parts: The first six verses explain that Samantabhadra's meritorious qualities are so vast that one could never finish describing them. The remaining verses explain that the qualities of the Buddha are deep and vast and Samantabhadra exhaustively fathoms them all. Those first [six verses] are divided into two parts, of which the first four and a half verses clarify that the bases by which one is able to count them are numerous, whereas the last one and a half verses reveal that what is to be counted is vast." (百二十偈大分為二前六明普賢德廣說不可盡餘偈明佛德深廣普賢窮究前中分二前四偈半明能數多後一偈半顯所數廣 / L130n1557_0687b06)

QL next mentions that there are ten levels to the description of the phenomena which constitute the bases for enumerating the innumerable meritorious qualities of Samantabhadra. Obviously, this entire description is rooted in the Avataṃsaka Sutra's trademark principle of "the interpenetration of all phenomena (large and small) with all other phenomena" which is one of the most outstanding and pervasive ideas in this entire sutra.

320. "True character" (實相) is usually an abbreviation of "true character of dharmas" (諸法實相 / *dharmatā*).

321. "Right and fixed position" corresponds to the Sanskrit *samyaktva niyāma*. In this context, this is a reference to the stage of irreversibility on the bodhisattva path to buddhahood.

322. "Guide of the world" (世間導師) is a Chinese translation of the Sanskrit *lokanātha*, "protector, lord, or refuge for the world" which, per BHSD (p. 464, Column 1), is "frequent as an epithet of the historic Buddha or an epithet of a Buddha; it is not clear that Śākyamuni is meant, tho he may be."

323. HH points out in his HYQS: "This chapter compares the length of the life spans of those buddha *kṣetras*. Hence it is referred to as the 'Life Spans' chapter." (這一品，是比較那個佛刹的壽量長，故名壽量品。)

324. Per the surviving Sanskrit text of this chapter found in "Bhikṣuṇī Vinītā, A Unique Collection of Twenty Sūtras in Sanskrit Manuscript from the Potala," Volume I, 2, the Sanskrit for this Buddha's name is Vajra-sāra.

325. Although the above-mentioned Sanskrit text has the name of this buddha as Suniścita-padma-phullita-gātra, the anonymous BDK in-house manuscript reviewer is of the opinion that it should instead be *Suniścarita-prabhā-phullita-gātra.

326. Per the same Sanskrit text, the Sanskrit for the buddha *kṣetra* known as "Voice of the Irreversible Wheel" (不退轉音聲輪) is *avaivartika-cakra-nirghoṣā*.

327. "Dharma Banner" Buddha (法幢佛) = *dharma-dhvaja*.

328. "Lion" Buddha (師子佛) = Siṃha.

329. "Lunar Intelligence Buddha" (月智佛) = Candra-buddhi.

330. As is clear from referencing the extant Sanskrit of Chapter 39, *zizai* (自在) is often used in SA's translation to translate not only the usual *vaśī* or *vaśitā*, "mastery" or "sovereign masteries" but also *adhipateya*, "dominance," or, as is likely in this case, *vikurvita*, "magic" or "feats of spiritual power." My support for this is the BB translation's rendering of this line as "the buddhas' sovereign mastery of the spiritual powers is inconceivable." (諸佛神力自在不可思議. / T09n0278_p0590b18)

331. Both QL and HH interpret these "three kinds of sovereign mastery" (三種自在) as referring to sovereign mastery in the three types of karmic actions (physical, verbal, mental).

332. HH says this refers to "in a single mind-moment, manifesting the Dharma body of all buddhas of the past, the present, and the future." (在一念中，現出過去、現在、未來三世諸佛的法身。/ HYQS)

333. HH notes that "Dharma position" corresponds to realization of the unproduced-dharmas patience (*anutpattika-dharma-kṣānti*).

334. Number six in this list was left out in this SA translation. It is however included in the BB translation: "一切諸佛。常度一切眾生。" (BB = T09n0278_p0592b10). Hence its inclusion in brackets here as a suggested emendation.

335. What I translate here as "syllables" (味身), per BCSD, p. 250, is *vyañjana-kāya*. Perhaps this is referring to esoteric issues related to either mantras or *sandhi*.

336. "Right and fixed position" corresponds to the Sanskrit *samyktva-niyāma*. It is synonymous with irreversibility on the path.

337. Although with the first glance at the Chinese text it would be natural to suppose that the deeply abstruse concept of "non-duality" is somehow being referenced here, it is definitely not a topic anywhere in this entire passage. What I translate ten times in this paragraph as "it could definitely not be otherwise" is literally "definitely, without a second [outcome]" (決定無二). Per DDB, this *wu'er* (無二) can also mean: "The lack of a second (thing) (Skt. *advitīya*) [Charles Muller]."

338. "Three spheres of action" refers to a buddha's physical, verbal, and mental actions.

339. Again, "right and fixed position" corresponds to the Sanskrit *samyaktva-niyāma*. It is synonymous with irreversibility on the path.

340. Again, "three spheres of action" refers to a buddha's physical, verbal, and mental actions.

341. As should become evident soon to most readers, the descriptions of the physical adornments of the Tathāgatha described in this chapter and following chapter would be those associated with the Buddha's reward body or *saṃbhogakāya* as seen in a pure land setting.

342. QL interprets this as referring to the list also found in the *Yogācārabhūmi-śāstra* (T1579.30.565c16): the *pāramitās;* the practice of the enlightenment factors, the practice of the superknowledges; and the practice of maturing beings (當知略有四菩薩行。何等爲四。一者波羅蜜多行。二者菩提分法行。三者神通行。四者成熟有情行。). HH explains this as referring to the four bodhisattva vows or the four means of attraction.

343. According to Soothill (digital edition), this *ganpu* (紺蒲) is a transliteration of "*kamboja*," "described as a round, reddish fruit, the Buddha having something resembling it on his neck, one of his characteristic marks." HH points out that this is referring to the three horizontal creases in the flesh of the Buddha's soft and smooth neck (HYQS). Translator's note: One also sees these three creases in the neck flesh on the majority of bodhisattva images as well. Further investigation suggests that this is referring to the deep creases in the outer shape of *Garcinia gummi-gutta* or one of its subspecies, these being according to Wikipedia (as of 12/15/2021) "tropical species of *Garcinia* native to South Asia and Southeast Asia. Common names include *Garcinia cambogia* (a former scientific name), as well as brindle berry, and Malabar tamarind. The fruit looks like a small pumpkin and is green to pale yellow in color." As referenced in the text, one could probably rightly visualize it as like a small yellow pumpkin with very deep

creases in its outer flesh. As of this writing, images are available in abundance on the internet.

344. "Jewel King" (寶王 / *rāja-ratna*) is one of the titles of the Buddha. Although all three jewels of "the Three Jewels" are finally equally important, in this "Jewel King" or "King of Jewels" name, the inference appears to be that the buddhas are the most supreme of the Three Jewels (Buddha, Dharma, Sangha), for without them there would not be their teaching of the Dharma or their community of enlightened Sangha members.

345. As unequivocally specified in the BB translation (T09n0278_p0607a17: "生八難處障," or "The obstacle of being born in to the eight difficult circumstances."), "difficult circumstances" here refers to "birth into the eight difficult circumstances (*aṣṭa kṣaṇa*) consisting of inopportune rebirths: in the hells; among hungry ghosts; as an animal; in the long-life heavens; in a border region (where the Dharma does not exist); as deaf, blind, or mute; as one possessed of oratorical skill tethered to merely worldly knowledge; or at a time before or after a buddha appears in the world.

346. What I translate here as "unintelligent" is more literally "stupid" (頑鈍). Typically this is referring to rebirth among animals, among the hungry ghosts, or in the hells where the beings lives are so dominated by the three poisons and basic instincts that they remain unable to understand karma, unable to reliably distinguish right from wrong, and unable to understand the path of liberation from karma-bound suffering in *saṃsāra*.

347. *Xinle* (信樂), which would seem to mean "having faith in and being pleased by" is actually a Chinese translation of the Sanskrit *adhimukti* which, at least in this context, simply means "resolute faith."

348. The BB translation makes it clear that this refers directly to a *kalyāṇamitra* (T09n0278_p0607a22: "不見善知識障") and not merely to the SA translation's slightly ambiguous "good friends" (善友), hence my more specific translation: "good spiritual guide," what in common parlance one might refer to as "the good guru."

349. "Restraining difficulties" (*liunan* / 留難) often implies interference wrought by demonic influences which lead to the slowing or halting of a cultivator's attempts to advance on the path.

350. HH: "Although reborn as a human—but one's six sense faculties are incomplete, one's five sense organs are not normal—this is also an obstacle." (雖生為人，但六根不全，五官不正，這也是障。)

BB translated this as: "the obstacle of being born among evil people" (生惡人中障, T09n0278_p0607a23).

351. Comparison with the Sanskrit of the Ten Grounds Sutra shows that *shenxin* (深心) is one of Śikṣānanda's translations of āśaya ("resolution," "resolute intention," "intention," "inclination," etc.).

352. For the skill the absence of which is said to be an obstacle here "skill in dealing with various possible and impossible situations" (處非處善巧), BCSD (p. 1033), gives the Sanskrit as *sthāna-asthāna-kauśalya*. BHSD (p. 85, column 1) translates essentially the same phrase (*sthānāsthānakuśalāḥ*) as: "*clever in regard to various sound and unsound conclusions* (or, *possibilities and impossibilities*)."

The BB translation is perhaps a little clearer: "The obstacle of not knowing the skillful means [appropriate for dealing with various] possible or impossible situations." (不知是處非處方便障。 / T09n0278_p0607b10–11.)

353. Regarding the "ten eyes," in Chapter 38, "Transcending the World," we have:

> Sons of the Buddha, the bodhisattva-*mahāsattva* has ten kinds of eyes, namely:
>
> The fleshly eye, this associated with the seeing of all forms.
> The heavenly eye, this associated with the seeing of all beings' minds.
> The wisdom eye, this associated with the seeing of all beings' faculties and objective states.
> The Dharma eye, this associated with the seeing of all dharmas in a manner consistent with their real character.
> The Buddha eye, this associated with the perception of the Tathāgata's ten powers.
> The eye of knowledge, this associated with the knowing perception of all dharmas.
> The radiance eye, this associated with the seeing of the Buddha's light.
> The eye that transcends the realm of births and deaths, this associated with the perception of nirvāṇa.
> The unimpeded eye, this associated with its being unobstructed in all that it sees.
> The eye of all-knowledge, this associated with the seeing of the Dharma realm's universal gateways.
>
> These are the ten. If bodhisattvas abide in these dharmas, then they acquire the Tathāgata's eye of unexcelled great wisdom. (T10n0279_p302c17–25).

354. This is a reference to the three moral failings in physical conduct as listed in the ten courses of unwholesome karmic action, namely killing, stealing, and sexual misconduct.

355. This is a reference to the four moral failings in verbal conduct as listed in the ten courses of unwholesome karmic action, namely false speech, abusive speech, divisive speech, and frivolous or lewd speech.

356. This is a reference to the three moral failings in mental conduct as listed in the ten courses of unwholesome karmic action, namely covetousness, ill-will, and wrong views.

357. "Right and fixed position" corresponds here to the Sanskrit technical term, *samyaktva-niyāma,* which in the context of Two Vehicles practice refers to reaching a state of irreversibility on the path to arhatship. It is characterized as an obstacle here for anyone otherwise pursuing the bodhisattva path because to enter on such a state amounts to an immediate and permanent termination of the ability to ever complete the path to buddhahood. Nāgarjuna is emphatically clear in warning the aspiring bodhisattva against pursuing realization of this "right and fixed position."

358. Per BCSD, p. 1140, the Sanskrit antecedent for the Chinese (辭辯) which I translate as "unimpeded knowledge of eloquent phrasing" is *nirukti pratisaṃvid,* an unambiguous reference to the fourth of the Buddha's four unimpeded knowledges.

359. An "ineffable" (*anabhilāpya*) is an inexpressibly large number, the 121st highest level of 123 levels of Sanskrit denominational numbers described in the Āsaṃkhyeya chapter of the Avataṃsaka Sutra. In this numbering schema, each level of denomination is the square of the immediately previous denominational number. (The first and lowest of those 123 levels is a *lakṣa* [100,000].)

360. Although *yihuo* (疑惑) here would appear to mean "doubts and delusions," it usually translates the Sanskrit *vicikitsā* which is simply "skeptical doubt" or "doubt," the fifth of the five hindrances.

361. Although the SA text is slightly ambiguous as to whether this *yiqie shi* (一切世) is meant to refer to "all worlds" or "all periods of time," because the BB translation instead refers to *san shi* (三世) which *always* refers to "periods of time," I translate this as referring to "time" in accordance with the BB translation's corroborating evidence.

362. *Pingdeng fa* (平等法), translated here and subsequently as "equally accessible Dharma," although slightly opaque at the first glance as simply "equal Dharma," generally refers directly and specifically to the fact that the Dharma of the Buddha and eventual highest enlightenment are equally accessible to all beings.

363. Through comparison with the BB translation, it appears that this list component is an accidentally included redundancy repeating the essential meaning of number six. It has no correlate at this point in the BB translation's tenfold list.

364. As the reader may readily observe, there are eleven items in this supposedly tenfold list. This appears to be the result of the accidental inclusion as item number ten of a repetition of the meaning found in item number six. I believe this "tenth" of eleven list items may be a textual corruption because it has no correlate at this point in the tenfold list preserved in the BB translation.

365. "Lion Among Men" is an often-encountered reference to a buddha. In his exegesis on the *Mahāprajñāpāramitā* Sūtra, Nāgārjuna says, "Just as the lion walks alone among the four-legged animals without fear because he is able to subdue them all, so too it is with the Buddha. Because he is fearless in subduing the proponents of all of the ninety-six types of spiritual paths, he is referred to as 'the Lion Among Men.'" (T25n1509_p0111b06–08)

366. "Lion of reasoned discourse" is an epithet that refers to the Buddha's and great bodhisattvas' fearlessness in debating any and all challengers.

367. This is a reference to the ten powers of a buddha.

368. "Length" here translates a standard idiomatic expression for this concept, *xiuduan* (修短), lit. "length and brevity."

369. "Worthy" here can refer either to: a) anyone on any of the preparatory levels on the bodhisattva path prior to becoming an *ārya;* or b) via a play on words, to Samantabhadra Bodhisattva whose name in Chinese is usually rendered as "Universally Worthy."

370. "Achieved complete perfection" here is literally "succeeded in reaching the far shore" (得至於彼岸). "To reach the far shore" is just a Chinese translation of the Sanskrit term for "perfection" (*pāramitā*).

371. Both BB translation and HH clarify that it is these bodhisattvas that are the ones who are able to know these matters.

372. This is probably a reference to the ten types of sovereign mastery (*vaśitā*) listed in the discussion of the eighth bodhisattva ground in the Ten Grounds chapter of the Avataṃsaka Sutra and also in the same section of the Ten Grounds Sutra itself: sovereign mastery of the life span (*āyur-vaśitā*); sovereign mastery of the mind (*cittavaśitā*); sovereign mastery of equipage (*pariṣkāra-vaśitā*); sovereign mastery of karmic actions (*karma-vaśitā*); sovereign mastery of rebirths (*upapatti-vaśitā*); sovereign mastery of vows (*praṇidhāna-vaśitā*), sovereign mastery of resolute faith (*adhimukti-vaśitā*); sovereign mastery of spiritual powers (*ṛddhivaśitā*); sovereign mastery of the knowledges (*jñāna-vaśitā*); and sovereign mastery of Dharma (*dharma-vaśitā*).

373. Again, what would otherwise appear here to mean "[reaching] the far shore" (彼岸) is just a reference to the quaint etymology of the Sanskrit word for "perfection" (*pāramitā*).

374. A *kṣaṇa* is the shortest possible span of time. To say here that, "To never even perceive 'long' as opposed to 'short' is the ultimate *kṣaṇa* dharma" appears to mean that not making such discriminations is the ultimately correct relationship to the concept of time. In his oral commentary on this quatrain, HH mentioned the extreme relativity of time as it occurs when a meditator enters the *dhyānas* and then emerges in what seemed to him to be only a short while when in fact three weeks may have passed. He also mentioned the extreme relativity of the experience of time as demonstrated by fifty years among humans being equivalent to only a day and a night in the Heaven of the Four Heavenly Kings (HYQS).

375. Given that the "body" here is described as possessed of so many ultimately transcendent qualities, it would be reasonable to conclude that this verse is referring to the Dharma body.

376. Here, "Samantabhadra" is not just a reference to the name of that great bodhisattva, but also a play on words intended to refer to the qualities of these particular bodhisattvas, this because "Samantabhadra" means "universally worthy" (or "universally good," "universally excellent," etc.).

377. QLSC cites scriptural bases for understanding these lotuses to be many, not just one as rendered by Cheng Chien Bhikshu and BTTS (in its preliminary digital manuscript as of 06/28/20): "Ānanda, why is this known as 'the Worthy (*bhadra*) Kalpa?' Ānanda, when this great trichiliocosm is about to be established, everything is a single body of water. The devas of the Pure Abode Heavens use their heavenly eyes to see that, on this world's singular body of water, *there are a thousand marvelous lotus flowers*, seeing too that every one of these lotus flowers has a thousand petals that are especially lovely. Due to seeing these flowers, the minds of those Pure Abode Heaven devas are filled with measureless delight and exultation whereupon they utter praises, saying, 'How very strange and rare! How very strange and rare it is that in a kalpa such as this there will be a thousand buddhas who appear in the world!' It is for this reason that this kalpa came to be named 'the Worthy Kalpa.' After my entry into nirvāṇa, there will be another nine hundred and ninety-six buddhas." (經云阿難何故名為賢劫阿難此三千大千世界劫欲成時盡為一水淨居天子以天眼觀見此世界唯一大水見有千枝諸妙蓮華一一蓮華各有千葉甚可愛樂彼淨居天子因見此華心生歡喜踊躍無量而皆讚言奇哉希有奇哉希有如此劫中當有千佛出興於世以是因緣遂名此劫號之為賢 / L130n1557_836b04-837a01)

Additionally, this passage in the BB translation reads, "Then, after Maheśvara and the other devas of the Pure Abode Heavens have seen these lotus flowers, they immediately know with certainty that, *in accordance with the number of lotus flowers, the buddhas will appear in the world.*" (時摩醯首羅淨居天等。見蓮華已。即決定知如蓮華數諸佛興世。 / T09n0278_p0613b21–23)

378. The earlier part of this chapter (at 263c10–11) and the BB translation both specify this ruler as "Maheśvara" (摩醯首羅).

379. The BB translation says, "Because the rains are able to give rise to the winds, the winds are able to give rise to the world" (因雨能起風, 風能起世界. / T09n0278_p0615c22).

380. These are references to the five roots, the five powers, and the seven limbs of enlightenment, a.k.a. "the seven enlightenment factors."

381. Of the two relatively standard Sanskrit antecedents for 邪定, lit. "erroneous fixation," namely *mithyātva-niyata* ("fixated on what is erroneous or wrong") and *mithyā-samādhi* ("wrong meditative absorption,"), a review of the uses of this binome in the SA translation makes it clear that "fixated on what is wrong" is intended here and generally throughout all of its other occurrences in this scripture. In fact, the term is fairly nicely defined in fascicle thirty-eight as referring to beings who are fixated on wrong views, who are fixated on the five evil deeds leading to rebirth in the unremitting hells, who are fixated on the eight transgressions against the eightfold path of right practice, or who are deeply attached to wrong dharmas.

382. The BB translation refers here not to "capable of cultivating mindfulness and wisdom" (堪修念智) but rather to "complete perfection of the dharmas of the four stations of mindfulness." (具足成就四念處法. / T09_n278_616c28–29)

383. The BB translation refers only to "emanating eight kinds of sublime voices of the Tathāgata." (演出八種如來妙音. / T09_n278_617a04–05)

384. Here, "all actions" (一切諸行) clearly refers to "karmic formative factors" or "volitional factors" (*saṃskāras*), as a component of the five aggregates (*skandhas*) and the twelve links of conditioned co-production.

385. "Difficulties" here is a clear reference to the standard list of eight difficulties. Indeed, the BB translation refers at this point twice to "the eight difficulties." (T09_n278_619a15–16)

386. This is an allusion to various punishments found in the hot hells such as the one in which one is forced to swallow pellets so hot that they burn all the way through the body and then drop to the ground below.

387. This is listed as the first of the ten kinds of patience (十忍). See Foguang Dictionary, p. 438.

388. Per HH's HYQS (digital version), "Patience" here refers to the unproduced-dharmas patience (無生法忍, *anutpattika-dharma-kṣānti*).

389. "Bodhisattvas at the stages of the dwellings, the dedications, or the practices" (住向行菩薩) is a reference to the ten dwellings, the ten dedications, and the ten practices.

390. "All formations" here translates *zhu heng* (諸行) which in turn usually translates *sarva-saṃskāra,* otherwise rendered as "karmic formative factors," "fabrications," etc.

391. "Scattered goodness" (散善) usually refers to goodness done with a scattered mind as opposed to goodness done with a mind abiding in samādhi (定善).

392. Here the BB translation says, "From the edge of the sphere of water...." Just below SA himself refers to "the edge of the sphere of water" (水輪際). Based on this evidence, I interpolate here "sphere of" which SA leaves out at this point, probably due to a rather standard stylistic preference for four-character phrases.

393. Although both the BB and SA translations seem to literally refer to the Tathāgata's wisdom as "fully present in the bodies of beings" (具足在於眾生身中), because this is only a manner of speaking, I have instead translated it as "fully present in beings," as "present in the persons of all beings," etc. because, in classical Chinese, *shen* (身) does not just refer to the physical body, but rather also to what we think of as the "person." (Of course "person" in this context is itself a mere conventional way of speaking and a merely imputed concept devoid of any inherent existence of its own, hence it is not an ultimately real entity.) What this passage is really referring to is the fact that all beings fully possess *the potential* to awaken to the wisdom of the Tathāgata. It is only because of their erroneous perceptions, etc. that they have as yet remained unable to do so.

394. "Three spheres" (三輪), usually from the Sanskrit *trimaṇḍala,* refers to the body, speech, and mind of a buddha.

395. This rather opaquely phrased list item is probably intending to refer to the well-known ability of the Buddha to speak with a single voice and have all beings hear him as if he was speaking directly to them, addressing their particular individual concerns. The BB translation isn't much clearer: "He knows and sees all voices as constituting a single voice. It is by means of this that the Tathāgata turns the wheel of Dharma, for there is no subjective agent." (知見一切音聲皆是一聲。如來以此而轉法輪。佛轉法輪無有主故。T09n0278_p627c12-14) Of course the most impenetrable phrase is SA's "for there is ultimately no subjective agent" rendered by BB as "for there is no subjective agent." This seems to be referring to there being no "self" involved and hence perhaps no single subjective point from which the Buddha's voice emanates.

396. The BB translation indicates that this refers to cultivating a state of uniformly equal purity that is like empty space.

397. HH explains "two kinds of actions" (二行) here as referring to "views-based actions" (見行) and "cravings-based actions" (愛行), whereas QL obliquely refers to another of the several standard lists for "two kinds of actions" consisting of actions reflective of the two kinds of obstacles consisting of "affliction-associated obstacles" (煩惱障) and the "cognition-associated obstacles" (所知障).

398. In explaining this, QL quotes Vasubandhu: "As for 'dwelling where the buddhas dwell,' it is the place where one does not dwell anywhere." (L130n1557_p0076a06 / 世親云謂住佛所住無所住處.)

399. QL says: "This refers to all buddhas having three matters in which they are no different, namely: 1) The knowledge on which they rely is the same; 2) Their aspiration to benefit beings is the same; and 3) The actions which their reward bodies and transformation bodies perform are the same." (謂諸佛有三事無差。一所依智同。二益生意樂同。三報化作業同。 / L130n1557_p0076a06)

400. Per QL, "The Dharma that cannot be overturned" refers to that with which one "vanquishes all non-Buddhists." (不可轉法即降伏一切外道 / L130n1557_p0076a06)

401. Per QL, "He was unimpeded in his actions" refers to "being born in the world, but not being impeded by worldly dharmas." (所行無礙即生在世間不為世法所礙. / L130n1557_p0076a06)

402. Per QL: "'He had established what is inconceivable' is just the establishment of right Dharma." (立不思議即安立正法 / L130n1557_p0076a06)

403. HH: "As for his having completed all the practices, he had already reached the realm in which there is no [further] cultivation and no [further] realization." (了一切行：已到無修無證的境界。 / HYQS

404. "Universal Worthy" is the sino-translation of the Sanskrit name for "Samantabhadra" which is otherwise used throughout this text. I go ahead and translate it into English here to show the parallelism in the naming of these ten bodhisattvas.

405. The slightly different corresponding discussion later in the text begins with "The bodhisattva-mahāsattva speaks of ten kinds of buddhas." (菩薩摩訶薩。說十種佛。)

406. The Sanskrit for the famous bodhisattva's name "Samantabhadra" translates as "Universally Worthy." Its adjectival connotations in this and many of the following passages are twofold: a) as indicating a direct connection with Samantabhadra Bodhisattva; and b) as having the character of being, in the spiritual cultivation sense, "universally

worthy." The contexts in which the binome occurs lean somewhat in the direction of the latter, but also equally clearly reference the former, hence I have chosen to selectively include both of these meanings by including "Samantabhadra" in brackets to reflect the full range of implications intended by the text.

407. I enclose "wise" in brackets to accord with the ten kinds of "wise contemplation" (智慧觀察) listed later on in the chapter as the answer to this question. I also do this to distinguish this question from the otherwise identical question number one hundred and fifty-two (at 280a15).

408. I add "other kinds of" purity in brackets to help distinguish from the exact same question above as question number twenty-six (279c01). BB escapes this accidental duplication of questions by translating this not as "purity," but rather as "absence of defilement" (無垢).

409. What I translate here and later on as "easeful mastery" (遊戲) might ordinarily be more literally rendered as something like "roaming and sporting," however, scanning the extant Sanskrit texts for Chapter Thirty-Nine makes it clear that this is SA's translation of the Sanskrit *vikrīḍita* which, per BHSD (p. 482, Column 1), definition number two is "oftener, fig., something like *easy mastery*..." This "easeful mastery" seems to be a much better fit in most instances in SA's translation of this text than definition number one's "sporting."

410. The BB translation renders these as "supreme practices" (勝行).

411. I add "other kinds of" in brackets to help distinguish from the exact same question above as question number thirty.

412. This is another tenfold list of bodies, in this case bodies associated with important bodhisattva path factors such as the *pāramitās*, the four means of attraction, great compassion, and so forth. I include "other" in brackets to distinguish this question from the identical question two questions earlier.

413. In the subsequent discussion later in the chapter this is instead referred to as "ten kinds of definite understanding in knowing all worlds." (十種決定解知諸世界。/ 299a13–21)

414. In the subsequent discussion later in the chapter this is instead referred to as "ten kinds of definite understanding in knowing the realms of beings." (十種決定解知眾生界。/ 299a23–b03)

415. In the subsequent discussion later in the chapter this is instead referred to as "ten ways of retreating from the Buddha's Dharma." (十種退失佛法。 / 299c12–c18)

416. Here and elsewhere in this chapter, this "provisions for enlightenment" (助道), literally "path-assisting [dharmas]" is most likely intended to be a reference not to "the thirty-seven aids to enlightenment" or

"thirty-seven enlightenment factors" (*saptatriṃśat bodhipakṣika dharma*) which were often also translated into Chinese by this same term, but rather to "the provisions for enlightenment" (*bodhi-saṃbhāra*) consisting primarily of the merit-based and wisdom-based provisions for enlightenment which are each given their own separate questions and corresponding tenfold lists later on in this chapter.

417. This is later referred to instead as his "measureless cultivation of the path." (無量修道 / 301a22)

418. I insert the bracketed "other" both here and later in the chapter to distinguish this question and its later explanation from the otherwise identical question posed earlier as question number sixty-two.

419. The Ming edition (and now Cbeta as well) include this "Practices related to all the spiritual superknowledges, to facilitate sovereign mastery in spiritual transformations." (一切神通行。變化自在故。/ T10n0279_p0280b27) which I place here in brackets. It is missing in Taisho and in nearly all other received editions, hence there are otherwise only nine. HH follows QL in including this practice as a tenth list item (unlike the Ming and Cbeta editions which place it as sixth in this list). It is not found at all in the BB translation.

420. As for the "inapprehensibility" (不可得 / *anupalabdha*) of all dharmas, this is just a reference to the absence of any inherent existence in any and all phenomena, this because they are mere names, mere false conceptions, and mere conjunctions of subsidiary conditions and sequences of conditional causality which are in every case entirely devoid of any ultimate reality of their own.

421. This is most likely intended to refer to what Vasubandhu referred to in his Abhidharma works as the five "pure" accumulations (skandha) of: precepts, samādhi, *prajñā*, liberation, and the knowledge and vision of liberation.

422. QL identifies this "knowledge" *pāramitā* with the "skillful means" *pāramitā* of the standard list of ten *pāramitās*.

423. QL identifies this "Dharma" *pāramitā* with the "knowledges" *pāramitā* of the standard list of ten *pāramitās*.

424. Per HH's HYQS, "latent tendencies" (使) here refers to the ten latent tendencies (十使, *daśa-anuśaya*). These are usually said to consist of five views affecting even those of sharp faculties (personality view, extreme view, wrong view, views attaching to views, and the view attaching to moral prohibitions as constituting the path) and another five especially affecting those of duller faculties (desire, hatred, delusion, pride or conceit, and skeptical doubt).

425. "Fear of the awesome virtue of great assemblies" (大眾威德畏) refers to being fearful of speaking before a large audience of advanced practitioners of the path.

426. The "four means of attraction" consist of: giving, pleasing words, beneficial actions, and joint endeavors.

427. "Kindly father" here is a reference to the Buddha.

428. The "four abodes of Brahma" or "four pure abodes" (四梵住 / *catvāro brahma-vihārāḥ*) are identical to the four immeasurable minds (四無量心 / *catvāri-apramāna-citta*): loving-kindness, compassion, sympathetic joy, and equanimity. The "*dhyāna* absorption" alluded to here correspond to the first *dhyāna* heavens of the form realm.

429. "Stations beset by the difficulties" is almost certainly a reference to the eight difficulties.

430. Here, "ultimate truth" (*paramārtha*) is literally "the primary meaning" (一義).

431. These three, together, are known as "the three sufferings." My rendering of the third of them (*saṃskāra-duḥkhatā*), "the suffering of the saṃskāras' karmic formative factors" is simply a conjunction of the Sanskrit (*saṃskāra*) and the English for the fourth of the five aggregates that is here referenced as having inherent suffering as a cardinal quality.

432. "Zeal" here (欲), otherwise translatable as "desire," doubtless refers to *chanda*, the undefiled aspiration to achieve a wholesome objective which Nāgārjuna teaches is an indispensable component of vigor (*vīrya*), one of the six perfections.

433. By "types of kalpas," literally "kalpa numbers" or "kalpa denominations" (劫數) I am assuming the text is referring to the various designations based on kalpa size such as, "small kalpa," "large kalpa," "*asaṃkhyeya* kalpa," etc.

434. What I translate here as "flawless resolve" is literally "resolve that is free of inferior aspects" (無下劣心). The BB translation refers to these as "resolve free of indolence" (無懈怠心).

435. With regard to the rationale for these kinds of especially superior mind being referred to as "mountain-like," QL mentions that this has to do with: a) their being so lofty, one only gazes up to their heights with difficulty; and b) their being, (like a mountain), utterly unshakable in their progression toward bodhi. (L130n1557_0139b13)

436. Here I follow the sense of the BB translation to fill in (in brackets) what SA leaves out, namely the nature of the relationship between this jewel-like abiding and *anuttarasamyaksaṃbodhi*: "The bodhisattva-mahāsattva has ten kinds of jewel-like abiding in realizing *anuttarasamyaksaṃbodhi*."

(菩薩摩訶薩。有十種寶住成阿耨多羅三藐三菩提。/ T09n0278_p0644b19–20)

437. "Inapprehensibility" (不可得 / *anupalabdha*) here and throughout this text is just a reference to the absence of any inherent existence in any and all phenomena, this because they are mere names, mere false conceptions, and mere conjunctions of subsidiary conditions which are devoid of any ultimate reality of their own.

438. BB makes it clear that this refers specifically to "the unproduced dharmas patience" (*anutpattika-dharma-kṣānti*). (得法忍菩薩授記。 – T09n0278_p0646c11).

439. In their extant editions, both BB and SA have only nine unimpeded functions related to the spiritual superknowledges. However, one alternative edition of SA (the Ming edition) contains this unimpeded function as the sixth of a complete list of ten. I insert it here to accord with Cbeta's judgment that it should be adopted into the definitive edition of the canon. (一微塵出現廣大佛刹無量莊嚴無礙用 - T10n0279_p0294c18).

440. The Sanskrit for what I translate here as "devoid of any soul" (無養育者), per BCSD, p. 786 is *niṣpoṣa* or "no *poṣa*" which, per BHSD, p. 355, Column 1 would mean "[no] person, [no] individuality, [no] soul, [no] spirit," this apparently due to *poṣa* somehow being derived from *puruṣa*, "person." (Conze's MDPPL, p. 235 also defines *niṣpoṣa* as "no individuality.") Although the very unintuitive Chinese looks like it should be "no one who is raised up (or nourished)," this almost always occurs in statements about the emptiness of inherent existence of any "self," and, in particular, in a string of similar "no-self" similes, nearly always right before, as in this case, "no *pudgala*," so, no matter how seemingly odd SA's choice for a Chinese translation, there really can be no mistaking its intended meaning as synonymous with "no self." Incidentally, BB's translation is just as unintuitive and along the very same lines (無長養者無福伽羅), meaning, again, "no one who is raised up (or "nourished"), no *pudgala*," etc. The unintuitive translations of *niṣpoṣa* in both BB and SA reveal this to be as a result of their mixing it up with a different definition of the same Sanskrit word which does indeed mean "not being nourished" but which is instead derived from the root *puṣ*- which in nearly all cases *does* refer to "nourishment," etc.

441. In his HYQS, HH points out here how, because the body is reducible to the four codependent great elements (earth, water, fire, and wind), it is unreal and hence false.

442. In his HYQS, HH points out that this "[noumenal] principle" (理) is a reference to true suchness (真如 / *tathatā*). "Noumenal principle" (理),

otherwise perhaps translatable as just "noumenon," is not and never was really a Buddhist term at all. Rather it was used by sino-hermeneutic traditions such as the Huayan School as a terminological stand-in for "emptiness" and "true suchness." It may have occurred here due to the influence of Fazang (法藏) who was both a member of SA's translation team and the third patriarch of the Huayan School whose own writings and the writings of his predecessors relied very heavily on the use of this very term in explaining this very sutra, especially as it occurs in its tenfold schema (理事無礙十門) which treats in ten ways the unimpeded interrelationship of "noumenon" (理) and "phenomena" (事), sino-Buddhist philosophical substitutes for "the unconditioned" versus "the conditioned" and "emptiness" versus "conventional existence," etc.

443. What I translate as "gaining complete enlightenment" would appear in the somewhat euphemistic semi-Taoist Chinese rendering to be "realizing the path" (成道). However, the Sanskrit for this translation into Chinese shows that it is instead referring rather precisely to the attainment of "complete enlightenment" (*abhisaṃbodhi*, BCSD, p. 0517).

444. Again, this is another tenfold list of bodies, in this case bodies associated with important bodhisattva path factors such as the *pāramitās*, the four means of attraction, great compassion, and so forth. I include "other" in brackets to distinguish this question from the identical question and its associated list two questions earlier.

445. Here, what is referred to as "the four speech faults" (語四過失) is explained by HH to be lying, frivolous or lewd speech, harsh speech, and divisive speech. These are the four verbal transgressions against the ten courses of good karmic action.

446. "Difficulties" (諸難) here is primarily a reference to the eight difficulties.

447. This is most likely referring to the *tathāgata-garbha*.

448. "Immeasurable minds" (無量心) is a reference to the four immeasurable minds (四無量心 / *apramāṇa-citta*), namely: loving kindness; compassion; sympathetic joy; and equanimity.

449. "*Sattva*," here and in the following names means "being."

450. The four lineage bases of the *ārya* (四聖種 / *catur-ārya-vaṃśa*) refers to being pleased with mere sufficiency in robes, food and drink, and bedding, while delighting in severance and cultivation.

451. This refers to the four *dhyānas*, the four formless absorptions, and the meditative concentration in which the functioning of both the feeling and the perception aggregates is extinguished.

452. "Gates to liberation" in this context usually refers to the three gates to liberation (三解脫門) consisting of emptiness (*śūnyatā*), signlessness (*animitta*), and wishlessness (*apraṇihita*).

453. The four floods (四暴流 / *catur-ogha*) refer to: desire, existence, ignorance, and [wrong] views.

454. This list item and next two list items together refer to what is known in slightly varying order in nearly all Buddhist traditions as the "three groups [of beings]" (三聚, *tri-skandha*): 1) those who are fixed in what is right; 2) those who are not fixed [in either what is right or what is wrong], i.e. those who are as yet "unfixed" with regard to their inclinations toward doing what is right or what is wrong; and 3) those who are fixed in what is wrong.

455. This "*brāhma-vihāra*," otherwise known as "the four abodes of Brahma," or "the four immeasurable minds" refers to loving-kindness, compassion, sympathetic joy, and equanimity (慈, 悲, 喜, 捨).

456. The BB translation specifies what the SA translation only implies: "Abiding in the unproduced-dharmas patience." (無生忍住.)

457. "Right and fixed position" (usually *samyaktva-niyāma as defined in Conze's MDPPL, p. 415 as "certainty to have got safely out of this world."*) is generally associated with realization of the unproduced-dharmas patience (*anutpattika-dharma-kṣānti*) and the achievement of irreversibility in one's chosen path of liberation.

458. Again, I include the bracketed "other" here and earlier in the list of corresponding questions to distinguish this question and discussion from the otherwise identical question number sixty-two and its corresponding discussion.

459. Again, "difficulties" here is a reference to the eight difficulties.

460. The "three evils of the body" (身三惡) are killing, stealing, and sexual misconduct. These are the three physical transgressions against the ten courses of good karmic action.

461. The "four transgressions in speech" (語四過) are lying, harsh speech, divisive speech, and frivolous or lewd speech. These are the four verbal transgressions against the ten courses of good karmic action.

462. Covetousness, ill will, and wrong views are the three mental transgressions against the ten courses of good karmic action.

463. Lest one misinterpret the intent of this line, it is not that one should not be attached to according with the moral precepts, for, indeed, adherence to the moral precepts absolutely *does* constitute an indispensable prerequisite to gaining liberation. Rather it is that one should not see adherence to the precepts alone as constituting, in and of itself, the entire path to liberation. That is a function of *all three* of the three trainings: a) moral virtue; b) samādhi; and c) wisdom.

464. "Difficulties" here is a reference to the eight difficulties involving rebirth in inauspicious circumstances.

465. I string together these first two kinds of pure equanimity because, otherwise, the SA translation creates eleven rather than ten kinds of pure equanimity by breaking into two kinds of pure equanimity what the BB translation preserves as the first of ten kinds of pure equanimity as follows: "The pure equanimity with which he refrains from becoming fondly attached when all beings revere and make offerings to him and with which he refrains from becoming angry when all beings slight and disparage him." (一切眾生恭敬供養不生愛著，一切眾生輕慢毀辱，不生瞋恚淨捨. T09n0278_p0661b10–12)

466. The eight worldly dharmas (*aṣṭa-loka-dharma*) are: gain and loss, fame and disrepute, praise and blame, pleasure and pain.

467. HH points out that "patience" here refers to the unproduced-dharmas patience (*anutpattika-dharma-kṣānti*). Also, QL notes here that the BB edition does indeed have but ten of these pure patiences, this through its preserving as a single patience what has been broken into numbers one and two in the SA translation, thereby implying that the presence of eleven here in the SA edition is simply the result of a minor textual corruption.

468. Per MW (p. 213, Column 2), *upādhi* is "that which is put in the place of another thing, a substitute, substitution R.; anything which may be taken for or has the mere name or appearance of another thing, appearance, phantom, disguise.... " Hence the term "*upādhi* nirvāṇa" refers to all forms of mere semblance nirvāṇa clung to by non-Buddhist traditions that do not really constitute any form of genuine nirvāṇa as understood by Buddhists.

469. "Provisions for enlightenment" refers to the "provisions for the realization of bodhi" (*bodhi-saṃbhāra*) of which there are primarily two main categories: merit and wisdom. This list of ten represents the former. The ensuing list of ten constitutes the latter.

470. The six kinds of mindfulness are: mindfulness of the Buddha, mindfulness of the Dharma, mindfulness of the Sangha, mindfulness of the precepts, mindfulness of giving, and mindfulness of the heavens.

471. The six kinds of harmony and respect are six ways in which monastics live in harmony which refer to harmony in body, mouth, mind, precepts, views, and benefits.

472. The six dharmas of solidity (六堅固法) refer to solidity in faith, Dharma, cultivation, virtue, supremacy, and awakening.

473. There are many different lists of ten knowledges. In his HYQS, HH lists the ten kinds of knowledge (十種智) as: dharma knowledge, relative

knowledge, knowledge of others' thoughts, worldly knowledge, knowledge of the truth of suffering, knowledge of the truth of origination, knowledge of the truth of cessation, knowledge of the truth of the path, knowledge of cessation, and knowledge of the unproduced.

474. The "four abodes of Brahma" or "four pure abodes" (四梵住 / *catvāro brahma-vihārāḥ*) are identical to the four immeasurable minds (四無量心 / *catvāri-apramāna-citta*): loving-kindness, compassion, sympathetic joy, and equanimity.

475. "Clarities" is a general reference to all of the spiritual powers, but more specifically to the "three clarities" (*tri-vidya*), namely: clarity with regard to past lives of self and others, clarity with regard to the power of the heavenly eye, and clarity with regard to the cessation of all the contaminants.

476. QL identifies the three types of ideation as desire, hatred, and maliciousness (欲恚害).

477. "Three kinds of actions" (三業) refers to physical, verbal, and mental actions.

478. QL indicates that conceptions of a "self" and "karmic actions" performed by some supposed "self" in effect "wound" the Dharma body and that karmic transgressions not yet extinguished constitute its "scars." (L130n1557_p0224a05)

HH specifically points to delusive ignorance and afflictions as constituting "wounds" and karmic transgressions as constituting "scars." (HYQS, v. 18, p. 185)

479. Both QL and HH note that this entire passage down to the references to the absence of any conceptions of "vigor" or "valiant bravery" are related to the "calming" of "calming and contemplation" (*śamatha-vipaśyanā*), whereas the rest of the ensuing passage specifically correlates to the "contemplation" of "calming and contemplation." "Patience" here likely refers to his realization of "the unproduced-dharmas patience" (*anutpattika-dharma-kṣānti*).

480. The phrasing of the term for "truths" in the text (真諦) makes it clear that it is referring specifically and exclusively to the four truths of the *āryas*.

481. "Those at the level of the eighth person" refers specifically to those who are at the third of the ten stages common to *śrāvaka* disciples, *pratyekabuddhas*, and bodhisattvas who have reached the threshold stage immediately prior to realizing the "stream entry" of the *srota-āpanna*. This threshold stage is that of the *srota-āpatti-pratipannaka*.

482. A *srota-āpanna* or "stream enterer" has gained the first fruit on the path to arhatship.

483. Because delectable meditation states are more ecstatically pleasurable than any other experiences in the world, the meditator is prone to become attached to them and proceed no farther on the path. Worse yet, he may be then be led astray by *māras* so that he falls off the path completely.

484. A *sakṛd-āgāmin* or "once returner" has gained the second fruit on the path to arhatship.

485. An *anāgāmin* or "never returner" has gained the third fruit on the path to arhatship.

486. Per the fifth chapter ("Right Practice for Monastics") of Nāgārjuna's *Ratnāvalī* (in which he concisely and precisely defines the seven types of arrogance), "elevating arrogance" corresponds to the Sanskrit *atimāna*. Nāgārjuna says there that "It stems from elevating oneself to equality with superior persons." (See pages 159-61 of my Kalavinka Press translation: *A Strand of Dharma Jewels, A Bodhisattva's Profound Teachings on Happiness, Liberation, and the Path*.)

487. Again, per the *Ratnāvalī*, "over-reaching arrogance" corresponds to the Sanskrit *māna atimāna*. Nāgārjuna says there that "It is compared to developing a pustule on top of an abscess."

488. Again, per the *Ratnāvalī*, "Self-imputing arrogance" corresponds to the Sanskrit *asmi-māna*. Referring to the five aggregates, Nāgarjuna says there that "When, because of delusion, one imputes existence of a 'self' therein, this is known as 'self-imputing arrogance.'"

489. HH equates this "reaches the station of the unproduced" with the realization of the unproduced dharmas patience: "The bodhisattva gains the realization of the unproduced dharmas patience and thus puts an end to births and deaths." (菩薩證得無生法忍，而了生死…. / HYQS)

490. The three gates to liberation (三解脫門) consist of emptiness (*śūnyatā*), signlessness (*animitta*), and wishlessness (*apraṇihita*).

491. Lists of "the seven kinds of wealth" (七財) vary slightly, depending on the source. In his Treatise on the Ten Bodhisattva Grounds, Nāgārjuna lists: faith, moral virtue, a sense of shame, a dread of blame, relinquishing (i.e. "giving"), learning, and wisdom (信戒慚愧捨聞慧 / SZPPS_T26n1521_p0091c01–02.)

492. The "five turbidities" (五濁) are five kinds of deterioration occurring as each kalpa progresses past the point when beings' life spans begin to decrease. This refers then to deterioration in the quality of the kalpa, views, afflictions, beings, and life spans.

493. The "two extreme views" (二邊見) refers to views such as eternalism versus annihilationism, existence versus nonexistence, etc.

494. Here I follow the Ming Edition and more recent editions of Cbeta in restoring this ninth list item missing in all other editions: "He manifests as practicing the austerities to enable beings to delight in the dharma of quiescence and increase their roots of goodness." (為令眾生樂寂靜法增長善根故。示行苦行。 / T10n0279_p0312b10)

495. HH explains that this refers to the pervasive presence of the Buddha's Dharma body throughout all worlds. (HYQS)

496. Although Cbeta now incorporates "mistletoe" (蔦) into the text instead of Taisho's "birds" (鳥), prior to Cbeta's emendation, "mistletoe" only ever appeared in the Ming edition of the sutra. HH explains it as "birds." QL also has "birds." (最上力為鳥。 / T36n1736_p0135a25) Moreover, all the editions of the BB translation have "birds" (鳥) and none of them have the mistletoe character. Since mistletoe is a parasitic plant, it seems odd that Cbeta would think it wise to make this emendation.

497. The "three clarities" (三明) or *trividya* are the heavenly eye, cognition of past lives, and cessation of the contaminants.

498. "Four types of eloquence" (四辯) is actually a reference to the "four unimpeded knowledges" (四無礙智) with regard to dharmas, meanings, phrasing, and delight in speaking.

499. Although the SA translation is vague as to whether this refers to psychic powers in general or specifically to the four bases of psychic power. The BB translation makes it quite clear that it is the latter: "The four bases of psychic power are its feet." (四如意為足 / T09n0278_p0670c11). The four bases of psychic power (四如意足, *catvāra ṛddhi-pādāḥ*) consist of zeal (*chanda*), vigor (*vīrya*), concentration (*citta*), and investigation (*mīmāṃsa*).

500. By specifying all four members of the list, the BB translation makes it clear that it is all four of "the four immeasurable minds" of kindness, compassion, sympathetic joy, and equanimity that are being referred to in this verse, not merely the "kindness and equanimity" of the SA translation which was forced to leave out the middle two (compassion and sympathetic joy) only because of the constraints of the five-character line length. Hence I include in brackets here "compassion, sympathetic joy" to fill in the contraction which, for a Chinese Buddhist reader, would have been obviously implicitly included, whereas, for a reader of this English translation, this implicitly intended inclusion might not have been at all obvious.

Also, since this list is otherwise known as "the four abodes of Brahma" (四梵住 / *catvāro brahma-vihārāḥ*), the fact that this quatrain compares the bodhisattva to "a Brahma Heaven King" should make all of this doubly obvious to an experienced reader.

501. The BB translation makes it very clear that this *huo* character (惑) in the second line of this verse, otherwise very commonly and rightly translatable as "delusions" (*moha*), is here translating the Sanskrit for afflictions (*kleśa*): "...burns up the afflictions and habitual karmic propensities." (燒盡煩惱習 / T09n0278_p0671a12)

502. I add "wish-fulfilling" in brackets both because it is implicit in the meaning of the verse and also because magical wish-fulfillment is a connotation built in to the Sanskrit word *maṇi*. In short, all by itself, the word "*maṇi*" can mean "wish-fulfilling jewel."

503. "Enlightenment factors" (菩提分) is more specifically translated as "the seven enlightenment factors" (七覺) in the BB translation's: "...enable the seven enlightenment factors to bloom." (七覺令開敷 / T09n0278_p0671a18)

504. "The most revered ones of all who stand on two feet" is a reference to the buddhas that is interpreted in either a literal or metaphoric manner. In the former case, they are the most supreme among humans and devas as two-legged beings. In the latter case, they are the most supreme in the complete development of the two foundations of buddhahood: merit and wisdom.

505. The comparison for this fourth of the five aggregates is aimed at demonstrating that karmic formative factors have no true substantiality, for they are just like the plantain stalk which consists solely of layers which, when peeled away, leave nothing whatsoever.

506. This is a reference to the twelve sense bases consisting of the six sense faculties and their six respective sense objects.

507. This is a reference to the eighteen sense realms consisting of the six sense faculties, the six corresponding sense objects, and the six associated sense consciousnesses.

508. HH interprets these as the three obstacles: karmic obstacles, retribution obstacles, and affliction obstacles, though one might just as easily interpret them in accordance with the BB edition's "three sufferings" (三苦), usually explained as: the suffering of physical and mental pain (*duḥkha-duḥkha*), the suffering inherent in change (*vipariṇāma-duḥkha*), and the suffering inherent in the karmic formative factors (*saṃskāra-duḥka*).

509. The three types of moral precepts (三律儀) per HH are the moral precepts of individual liberation (別解脫律儀), the moral precepts produced by *dhyāna* (靜慮律儀), and the moral precepts of the cessation of the contaminants (無漏律儀). (HYQS)

510. Again, the "three gates to liberation" (三解脫門) consist of emptiness (*śūnyatā*), signlessness (*animitta*), and wishlessness (*apraṇihita*).

511. "Three Vehicles" refers to the vehicles of the *śrāvaka* disciples, the *pratyekabuddhas*, and the bodhisattvas.

512. Although one might otherwise translate these last two lines of this verse as "He remains vigorous in his zeal to abide in samādhi / and his wisdom arising from contemplation never diminishes," the language used in both the SA and BB translations makes it clear that this verse is instead referring to "the eighteen dharmas exclusive to the buddhas" (十八不共法) of which "right mindfulness," "vigor," "zeal," "samādhi," and "wisdom" are here serving as emblematic elements implying the presence of all the others as well.

513. The three types of accumulation of moral virtue (三聚戒) refer to: 1) the aggregation of the particular categories of moral precept obligation such as the five precepts, the eight precepts, or the ten precepts; 2) the aggregation of all good dharmas; and 3) the drawing forth of all beings through benefiting them with Dharma.

514. "Bestowal of the prediction" refers to receiving the Buddha's prediction of one's future buddhahood.

515. Although the SA translation is ambiguous, the BB translation makes it clear that the *shi* character (世) here is referring to "periods of time" and not to "worlds" as one might otherwise expect.

516. This line is alluding specifically to the Buddha's ten powers, four fearlessnesses, and eighteen dharmas exclusive to the Buddha.

517. HH explains these "ten kinds of things" according to the ten courses of good karmic action. (HYQS)

518. "Right and fixed position" refers to *samyaktva-niyāma* which corresponds to the stage of irreversibility on one's chosen path.

519. HH interprets this line as referring to the ten names of the Buddha. (HYQS, V. 18, p. 308)

520. Dividing into "palace" and "hall" the compound which in Chinese ordinarily means "palace" (宫殿), HH explains "palace" (宫) as referring to the place where the ruler takes his rest and "royal hall" (殿) as referring to the place where he conducts the business of the king's court. (HYQS)

521. Although ambiguous in the SA translation, the BB translation makes it clear that *mingli* (明利), ordinarily "sharp," is referring to "sharp faculties" (明利根 / T09n0278_p0674c18).

www.ingramcontent.com/pod-product-compliance
Lightning Source LLC
Chambersburg PA
CBHW031128160426
43193CB00008B/66
9781935413363